THE MEDIEVAL LITERATURE

OF WESTERN EUROPE

A Review of Research

THE

MEDIEVAL LITERATURE

OF WESTERN EUROPE

A Review of Research, Mainly 1930-1960

GENERAL EDITOR

John H. Fisher

New York University

Published for

THE MODERN LANGUAGE ASSOCIATION OF AMERICA
by The New York University Press

London · University of London Press Limited

REVOLVING FUND SERIES NUMBER 22

Second Printing, 1968

© 1966
The Modern Language Association of America
Library of Congress Catalog Card Number: 66–22346

FOREWORD

KNOWLEDGE, not personal experience, should guide the judge, Plato
observes in *The Republic*. The tendency to carry over into medieval
studies the analytical method and personal reaction appropriate to
the discussion of contemporary writing is gratifying evidence of the
continuity of human experience. We have come far since 1930 in
recognizing the subtlety and effectiveness of pieces once regarded as
naïve or grotesque. But interest in criticism cannot obscure the im-
placable need for knowledge in interpreting medieval literature—
knowledge of languages, of history, of texts, and of the tools of
scholarship.

This volume is intended as a guide through a small part of this
vast body of knowledge. The pervasiveness of the Latin Christian
culture makes the study of medieval literature to a considerable extent the study of variation from a norm. Philosophical concepts and
the themes of lyrics, romances, and dramas cannot be understood in
one vernacular without reference to the others. The need to know
both the primary works and the scholarship of Latin, French, Italian,
Spanish, German, English, and Celtic places a heavy burden on the
medievalist. The fundamental purpose of this collection has been to
lighten this burden by bringing together between the covers of a
single volume authoritative surveys of scholarship on the major
Western European medieval literatures.

This design imposed its own limitations of space upon the contributors. When the plans for the collection were presented to the
Medieval Interdepartmental Section of the Modern Language Association at the meeting in Madison, Wisconsin, in September 1957,
it was announced that each review would put into the hands of advanced graduate students and younger scholars working in medieval
studies, but not specializing in the area concerned, dependable evaluations of the research in medieval literature produced since 1930.
The reviews are not to be mistaken for literary histories. They do
not discuss the primary works and all the scholarship in each language. The chapters are confined to discussion of the tools for research and the most important research produced between about

1930 and 1960. Even here the exigencies of space have prevailed. The authors have been under constant pressure from the general editor to stay within bounds. Nevertheless the coverage of the volume is remarkable. Nowhere else can one find such comprehensive, integrated surveys of the scholarship on seven major literatures.

A word about the terminal dates is in order: 1930 appeared to be an appropriate *terminus ab quem* partly because the 1930s witnessed new approaches to medieval scholarship in several countries, but also because the 1930s marked the end of an era in American education. Until that time it had been customary for most serious American scholars to study for a period in British or European universities. After the 1930s, first the great depression and then the war brought study in Europe nearly to an end, with a consequent diminution of the firsthand familiarity with European scholars and scholarship that had characterized the first third of the century. Only in the last few years has this communication been actively resumed. In 1957, when this volume was planned, December 1960 was agreed upon as the date for submission of printer's copy. Some of the chapters actually were submitted by that date. But a collaborative work must wait upon its last chapter. Authors grew ill or were translated to deanships and had to be replaced. Others continued to work ahead, but slowly. It was September 1964 before all of the chapters were finally in hand. The terminal date for the research covered therefore runs between 1960 and 1964, depending upon when each author closed his books.

The chapters by Albert Friend and George K. Anderson were read in preliminary versions at the 1957 and 1958 meetings of the MLA Medieval Section. The early drafts of these and several of the other chapters were duplicated and circulated to all of the authors for their comments. We are grateful to Dean John W. Ashton and the Indiana University Graduate School for assistance that made this photo duplication possible. Dean George Winchester Stone, Jr., of New York University, then Executive Secretary of the Modern Language Association, encouraged us in this project between 1957 and 1962, and in the summer of 1963 circulated the nearly complete manuscript to members of the MLA Book Publications Committee for their approval. Otis Green of the University of Pennsylvania and Theodore Silverstein of the University of Chicago have read the entire manuscript for the Book Publications Committee. John G. Kunstmann of the University of North Carolina and Albert H. Marckwardt of Princeton University have read most of the chapters for the MLA Medieval Interdepartmental Section. In addition, Jules Piccus of the University of Rhode Island, and Morton Bloomfield and

Charles Dunn of Harvard University have read various chapters. All of these sections are the better for their comments and criticisms. Robert Raymo of New York University undertook the strenuous task of verifying and regularizing all of the many citations and abbreviations and has read proof on the entire volume. Jane Law Fisher retyped the verified and edited manuscript for the printer, read proof, and made the index. To each of these and to all of the authors I express my personal gratitude.

John H. Fisher

Upper Montclair, New Jersey
14 June 1965

CONTENTS

TABLE OF ABBREVIATIONS

AALIAM	Arcadia, accademia letteraria italiana. Atti e memorie
AAPont	Atti della Accademia Pontaniana
AASF	Annales Academiae Scientiarum Fennicae
AdTb	Altdeutsche Textbibliothek
AF	Anglistische Forschungen
AFP	Archivum Fratrum Praedicatorum. Roma.
AHMA	Archives d'histoire doctrinale et littéraire du moyen âge
AION-SG	Annali Istituto universitario orientale. Napoli. Sezione germanica
AIV	Atti del R. Istituto veneto di scienze, lettere ed arti. Venezia. Classe di scienze morali e lettere
AKG	Archiv für Kulturgeschichte
ALat	Archivum latinitatis medii aevi (Bulletin DuCange)
AnBol	Analecta Bollandiana
ANF	Arkiv för nordisk Filologi
ANTS	Anglo-Norman Text Society
APS	Acta Philologica Scandinavica
Archiv	Archiv für das Studium der neueren Sprachen und Literaturen
ARDS	Annual Report of the Dante Society
ArL	Archivum Linguisticum
ASAW	Abhandlungen der Sächsischen Akademie der Wissenschaften zu Leipzig. Philol.-hist. Klasse
ASI	Archivio storico italiano
ASNSP	Annali della scuola normale superiore di Pisa
AUC	Anales de la Universidad de Chile
BAGB	Bulletin de l'Association Guillaume Budé
BAWS	Bayerische Akademie der Wissenschaften. Phil.-hist. Klasse, Sitzungsberichte
BBMP	Boletín de la Biblioteca Menéndez Pelayo

BBSIA	Bulletin bibliographique de la Société Internationale Arthurienne
BdF	Boletim de filologia
BEP	Beiträge zur englischen Philologie
BEPIF	Bulletin des études portugaises et de l'Institut Français au Portugal
BFC	Boletín del Instituto de Filología de la Universidad de Chile
BGDSL	Beiträge zur Geschichte der deutschen Sprache und Literatur (Tübingen)
BGDSL (Halle)	Ibid. (Halle)
BH	Bulletin hispanique
BHR	Bibliothèque d'humanisme et Renaissance
BHS	Bulletin of Hispanic Studies
Biblio	Bibliofilia
BJRL	Bulletin of the John Rylands Library
BRAE	Boletín de la Real Academia Española
CCM	Cahiers de civilisation médiévales (X°–XII° siècles) (Univ. de Poitiers)
CE	College English
CFMA	Classiques français du moyen âge
CL	Comparative Literature
CN	Cultura Neolatina (Modena)
CP	Classical Philology
CS	Cahiers du Sud
DDJ	Deutsches Dante Jahrbuch
DTM	Deutsche Texte des Mittelalters
DU	Der Deutschunterricht
DVLG	Deutsche Vierteljahrsschrift für Literaturwissenschaft und Geistesgeschichte
EA	Etudes anglaises
E&S	Essays and Studies by Members of the English Association
EC	Etudes celtiques
EETS	Early English Text Society
EG	Etudes germaniques
EHR	English Historical Review
EIC	Essays in Criticism (Oxford)

EIE	English Institute Essays
EIP	Estudos italianos em Portugal
ELH	Journal of English Literary History
EM	English Miscellany
ES	English Studies
FiR	Filologia Romanza
FranS	Franciscan Studies
FSUS	Florida State University Studies
FuF	Forschungen und Fortschritte
GD	Giornale Dantesco
GIF	Giornale italiano di filologia
GL&L	German Life and Letters
GR	Germanic Review
GRM	Germanisch-romanische Monatsschrift, Neue Folge
GS	Germanistische Studien
GSLI	Giornale storico della letteratura italiana
HGS	Harvard Germanic Studies
HR	Hispanic Review
HumB	Humanitas (Brescia)
HZ	Historische Zeitschrift
ICS	L'Italia che scrive
ID	Italia dialettale
IMU	Italia medioevale e umanistica
IS	Italian Studies
JAF	Journal of American Folklore
JEGP	Journal of English and Germanic Philology
JNES	Journal of Near Eastern Studies (Chicago)
JWCI	Journal of the Warburg and Courtauld Institute
Lang	Language
LB	Leuvense Bijdragen
LI	Lettere italiane
LM	Letterature moderne
LR	Les lettres romanes
LSE	Lund Studies in English
LT	Levende Talen
LUÅ	Lunds Universitets Årsskrift
MA	Le moyen âge
Mae	Medium Aevum
M&H	Medievalia et Humanistica (Univ. of Colorado)

MHRA	Modern Humanities Research Association
MLA	Modern Language Association of America
MLN	Modern Language Notes
MLQ	Modern Language Quarterly
MLR	Modern Language Review
MM	Maal og Minne
MP	Modern Philology
MS	Mediaeval Studies (Toronto)
NA	Nuova antologia
N&Q	Notes and Queries
NAWG	Nachrichten von der Akademie der Wissenschaften zu Göttingen. Philol.-hist. Klasse
NdM	Niederdeutsche Mitteilungen (Lund)
Neophil	Neophilologus (Groningen)
NJ	Niederdeutsches Jahrbuch
NLWJ	National Library of Wales Journal
NM	Neuphilologische Mitteilungen
NRFH	Nueva revista de filología hispánica (Mexico)
NRS	Nuova rivista storica (Roma)
NT	Nordisk Tidskrift
PAPS	Proceedings of the American Philosophical Society
PBA	Proceedings of the British Academy
PBB	See *BGDSL*
PBB (Halle)	See *BGDSL* (Halle)
PLPLS-LHS	Proceedings of the Leeds Philosophical and Literary Society, Literary and Historical Section
PMASAL	Papers of the Michigan Academy of Science, Arts, and Letters
PMLA	Publications of the Modern Language Association of America
PQ	Philological Quarterly (Iowa City)
PTRSC	Proceedings & Transactions Royal Society of Canada
RABM	Revista de archivos, bibliotecas y museos
RBPH	Revue belge de philologie et d'histoire
RC	Ruperto-Carola: Mitteilungen der Vereinigung der Freunde der Studentenschaft der Universität Heidelberg
RDM	Revue des deux mondes
RES	Review of English Studies
RF	Romanische Forschungen
RFE	Revista de filología española

RIE	Revista de ideas estéticas
Rin	Rinascimento
RJ	Romanistisches Jahrbuch
RL	Revista de literatura
RLI	Rassegna della letteratura italiana
RPh	Romance Philology
RR	Romantic Review
RSH	Revue des sciences humaines
SacE	Sacris Erudiri
Scan	Scandinavica
SAQ	South Atlantic Quarterly (Durham, N. C.)
SATF	Société des anciens textes français
Scrip	Scriptorium
SD	Studi danteschi
SDAWB	Sitzungsberichte der deutschen Akad. der Wissenschaften zu Berlin. Sprachen, Lit. und Kunst
SFI	Studi di filologia italiana
SFr	Studi francesi
SG	Studium Generale
SMed	Studi Medievali (Roma)
SN	Studia neophilologica
SÖAW	Sitzungsberichte der österreichischen Akademie der Wissenschaften in Wien, Phil.-hist. Klasse
SoS	Syn og Segn
SP	Studies in Philology
SPetr	Studi Petrarcheschi
SRo	Studi romanzi
SS	Scandinavian Studies
SSLL	Stanford Studies in Language and Literature
SUS	Studi urbinati di storia, filosofia e letteratura
TA	Theater Annual
THSC	Transactions of the Honourable Society of Cymmrodorion
TLS	(London) Times Literary Supplement
TPS	Transactions of the Philological Society (London)
TR	La Table ronde
UCPES	University of California Publications, English Studies
UCPMP	University of California Publications in Modern Philology
UMCMP	University of Michigan Contributions in Modern Philology
UNCSGLL	University of North Carolina Studies in Germanic Languages and Literatures

UNCSRLL	University of North Carolina Studies in the Romance Languages and Literatures
UTQ	University of Toronto Quarterly
VL	Vetenskaps-societeten i Lund
VUSH	Vanderbilt University Studies in the Humanities
WW	Wirkendes Wort
YCGL	Yearbook of Comparative and General Literature
YWMLS	Year's Work in Modern Language Studies
ZCP	Zeitschrift für celtische Philologie (Tübingen)
ZDA	Zeitschrift für deutsches Altertum und deutsche Literatur
ZDP	Zeitschrift für deutsche Philologie (Berlin-Bielefeld-München)
ZFSL	Zeitschrift für französische Sprache und Literatur
ZMF	Zeitschrift für Mundartforschung
ZRP	Zeitschrift für romanische Philologie (Halle)

1

Medieval Latin Literature

By Albert C. Friend
CITY COLLEGE OF THE CITY
UNIVERSITY OF NEW YORK

I. BIBLIOGRAPHIES

AN IMPORTANT GUIDE to the student interested in the field is the latest revised edition of K. Strecker, *Introduction to Medieval Latin* (Berlin, 1929; rev. French ed. 1933) as it appears in an English translation by R. Palmer published in Berlin in 1957. This includes references to books on prose style—both rhymed prose and also the variations known as the *cursus*. Strecker lists histories of literature and collections of important texts, such as the *Monumenta Germaniae Historica*, which includes volumes devoted to the poets of the Carolingian age. Palmer's additions are important, especially his sections on photostats and microfilms, which help the student find original manuscript material. There are also useful comments on the development of medieval libraries. Another good introduction is G. Cremaschi's *Guida allo studio del latino medievale* (1959), reviewing material on language and important collections of texts, and K. Langosch, *Lateinisches Mittelalter, Einleitung in Sprache und Literatur* (1963).

One of the most widely used bibliographies of medieval Latin is the 1931 version of L. J. Paetow, *A Guide to the Study of Medieval History*, prepared under the auspices of the Mediaeval Academy of America and reprinted in 1959. The subjects cover many fields, including some of the best introductory books on paleography, philosophy, poetry, and the Latin sermon, and collections of *exempla*. The *Guide* includes V. Chevalier, *Répertoire des sources historiques du moyen âge: bio-bibliographie* (2 vols., 1877–86; 2nd ed. 1905–7), listing medieval authors, then dates and principal works. Another important subject in the *Guide* is a list of books on Latin grammar and its place in the changing structure of medieval Latin.

F. J. E. Raby's section on "Writings in Latin" in *The Cambridge Bibliography of English Literature*, Vol. I (1940), and the supplement, Vol. V (1957), should not be overlooked. He deals with the Latin writers of English and Irish origin to the year 1500, analyzing such great collections as the Rolls Series, the work of the

3

French librarian B. Hauréau on manuscripts, and other lists of manuscripts and published sources. New and helpful material can also be found in J. C. Russell, *Dictionary of Writers of Thirteenth-Century England* (1936).

One of the greatest contributions to the history of medieval literature is M. Manitius' *Geschichte der Lateinischen Literatur des Mittelalters* (3 vols., 1911–31). Volume I (rptd. 1959) begins with the work of Boethius and Cassiodorus, and the subsequent volumes go on through the twelfth century. Another valuable guide is J. E. Sandys, *A History of Classical Scholarship from the Sixth Century B.C. to the End of the Middle Ages* (3 vols., 1903; rev. 1906 and 1920; rptd. 1958). The section on the Middle Ages gives a brief and clear survey of the major authors, including such grammarians as Donatus. More recent is R. R. Bolgar, *The Classical Heritage and its Beneficiaries, 700–1700* (1954), an introductory volume, concise, easy to read, with, however, little annotation. H. O. Taylor's *The Classical Heritage of the Middle Ages* (1901) has been republished, with a helpful, up-to-date bibliography by K. M. Setton, under a new title, *The Emergence of Christian Culture in the West* (1958). Taylor discusses the growth of both poetry and prose and shows how such facets of medieval life as ethics, law, and religion are related to one another. There is also J. de Ghellinck's *Littérature latine au moyen âge* (2 vols., 1939) with a continuation, *L'essor de la littérature latine au XIIe siècle* (2 vols., 1946) containing valuable notes. An extremely useful catalogue of the lives and works of the great Paris scholars of the thirteenth century is P. Glorieux, *Répertoire des maîtres en théologie de Paris au XIIIe siècle* (2 vols., 1933–34). Two recent valuable books should be noted: F. Stegmüller, *Repertorium Biblicum Medii Aevi* (7 vols., 1950–61), especially Vols. II to V consisting of a long list of authors of commentaries on the Bible, and M. C. Díaz y Díaz, *Index Scriptorum Latinorum Medii Aevi Hispanorum* (2 vols., 1958–59), covering writings from 500 to 1350 A.D. The latest work concerning Latin literature written in Germany, especially from the ninth to the eleventh centuries, is included in W. Stammler, *Deutsche Philologie im Aufriss* (3 vols., 1952–57; rev. ed. 1957–63); in Vol. II of the new edition (1960), cols. 2555 ff, there is a helpful discussion of medieval Latin material by K. Hauck. A most useful directory, which gives the lives of prominent English writers, is A. B. Emden's *A Bibliographical Register of the University of Oxford to A.D. 1500* (3 vols., 1957–59).

For recent work in England and Europe including the U. S. S. R., there appeared in 1960 the *Répertoire des médiévistes europ-*

éens, edited by Marie Thérèse d'Alverny and E. R. Labande. A more complete compilation, including the work of American and Canadian scholars, was scheduled to be published at Poitiers in 1965: *Répertoire internationale des médiévistes*.

Current scholarship in medieval Latin language and literature is recorded in such periodicals as *PMLA*, *The Year's Work in Modern Language Studies*, and *L'année philologique*. Although largely concerned with classical studies, this last has many valuable entries for the field of medieval Latin. Critical reviews appear in such periodicals as *Speculum*, *Bibliothèque de l'École des Chartes*, and *Cahiers de civilisation médiévale, X^e–XIIe siècles*. Useful, too, is the mimeographed *Quarterly Check-List of Medievalia*, American Bibliographic Service. Books and articles on theology are reviewed in the *Bulletin de théologie ancienne et médiévale*.

To anyone interested in literature, E. H. Gilson, *The History of Christian Philosophy in the Middle Ages* (1955), is important. Its many bibliographical notes deal with the introduction of Arabic and Hebrew learning, the rise of the universities, and the translations of Aristotle and their place in the thirteenth century. Another book contributing to our understanding of medieval literature in its relation to ancient philosophy is Dom D. Knowles, *The Evolution of Medieval Thought* (1962). For those interested in esthetics there is E. de Bruyne, *Etudes d'esthétique médievale* (3 vols., 1946), which discusses, among many other subjects, the development of allegory and symbolism from Boethius through Thomas Aquinas and John Duns Scotus. A useful collection of articles, with extensive bibliographies, on medieval theology appears in the *Dictionnaire de théologie catholique*, ed. A. Vacant and E. Mangenot (1909–50; indexes still in the process of being completed). Two helpful guides to philosophy and theology are A. Pelzer, "Répertoires d'incipit pour la littérature latine philosophique et théologique du moyen âge," *Revue d'histoire ecclésiastique* (1948; separate rev. eds. 1951, 1958), and A. G. Little, *Initia Operum Latinorum* (1904; rptd. 1958), dealing with work from the thirteenth to the end of the fifteenth centuries.

P. O. Kristeller has compiled a list of pre-1600 catalogues of Latin manuscripts. In *Traditio* he published "a bibliography of the printed catalogues of extant collections" (1948) and "a tentative list of unpublished inventories of imperfectly catalogued extant collections" (1953), which have been republished together in revised form as *Latin Manuscript Books before 1600* (1960).

The appearance of the new bibliographies goes hand in hand with the increasing availability of microfilm. Most important is the collection at Saint Louis University of microfilms of the manuscripts and hand-written catalogues of the Vatican library. There is a guide to the collection in the periodical *Manuscripta* (begun in 1957 by the Saint Louis University Library) with a check list of available manuscripts listed by numbers. Another collection of microfilms has been catalogued by L. K. Born, *British Manuscript Project: A Checklist of the Microfilms Prepared in England and Wales for the American Council of Learned Societies, 1941–1945* (1955). According-ing to A. Kessin, "Microfilming of Manuscript Collections," *Libri* (1956), the University of Leyden in Holland has a microfilm library of more than five hundred Western manuscripts, and copies of available negatives may be borrowed.

II. TEXTS

STUDENTS OF LITERATURE will appreciate the work of P. Glorieux, *Pour revaloriser Migne: tables rectificatives*, which appeared in *Mélanges de science religieux, cahier supplémentaire* (1952). This is a new index, which clarifies and corrects certain dates and names in J. P. Migne's *Patrologia Latina*, published between 1844 and 1868 and still the indispensable repository of medieval texts. A new series entitled *Corpus Christianorum*, which is intended to replace Migne, began publication in 1954 under the aegis of St. Peter's Abbey in Steenbrugge, Belgium. Several volumes have ap-peared to date, notably a useful edition of Bede (2 vols., 1960). A prospectus for the series was published in *SacE* (1951) under the title, "Clavis Patrum Latinorum," and in a separate, revised edition by E. Dekkers and A. Gaar (1961). Another collection of carefully edited Latin texts is the *Corpus Scriptorum Ecclesiasticorum Latinorum* (Vienna), continuous from the nineteenth century to the present day. It also affords the scholar more critical texts with which to evaluate the material in Migne. A new edition of the works of Saint Bernard is being prepared by C. H. Talbot, J. Leclerq, and H. Rochais, of which Vol. I appeared in 1957.

Translated selections from the early writers of the church have been published in the *Library of Christian Classics* (26 vols.,

1953–57), ed. J. Baille, J. J. McNeill, and H. P. Van Dusen. The first fourteen volumes deal with the Middle Ages. Another series of translations, begun in 1948 and still in progress, is *The Fathers of the Church*, under the editorship of L. Schopp. Current work is recorded in the annual *Bibliographia Patristica*, ed. W. Schneemelcher, begun in 1959.

Outside of the field of patristic studies, several important new series of publications have been undertaken in recent years. Among these is a new edition of medieval and later Latin writers, the *Thesaurus Mundi*, begun in 1950. Of interest to students of English literature is its authoritative text of Cardinal L. Signini, later Pope Innocent III, *De miseria humane conditionis*, ed. M. Maccarrone (1955). The Nelson series, *Medieval Texts*, under the general editorship of R. A. B. Mynors, C. N. L. Brooke, and H. V. Galbraith, presents Latin texts with English translations. One of the significant volumes of the series is *The Letters of John of Salisbury*, Vol. I (1955), ed. W. J. Millor, H. E. Butler, and C. N. L. Brooke. Among the publications of Notre Dame University is the excellent series, *Texts and Studies in Mediaeval Education*, ed. A. L. Gabriel, which includes his own study, *The Educational Ideas of Vincent of Beauvais* (1956). A new collection of material by Irish writers is the *Scriptores Latini Hiberniae*, the first volume by A. Gwynn, *The Writings of Bishop Patrick, 1074–1085* (1955), and the second by G. S. M. Walker, *Opera Sancti Columbani* (1957).

III. DICTIONARIES, LANGUAGE

THE MOST COMPLETE dictionary of medieval Latin is still C. Du Cange, *Glossarium Mediae et Infimae Latinitatis*, first printed in 1678, enlarged in the Paris editions of 1882 and 1887, and reprinted by photo-offset in 1954. Useful supplementary works are A. Blaise, *Dictionnaire latin-français des auteurs chrétiens* (1954); A. Souter, *Glossary of Later Latin to the year 600* (1949); E. Habel and F. Gröbel, *Mittellateinisches Glossar* (1931; rptd. 1959); and A. Castro, *Glosarios latino-españoles de la edad media* (1936). It is generally agreed that a new dictionary of medieval Latin is a prime desideratum. At present such a project is being worked out by the

International Union of Academies. There are committees in various countries, and the work is reported from time to time in *The Bulletin Du Cange* (*ALat*). One of the first projects was *Mediaeval Latin Word-List from British and Irish Sources* (1934; rptd. 1947) by J. H. Baxter, C. Johnson, and P. Abraham. There are other dictionaries in process of being published in sections but not yet completed. F. Blatt is editing the *Novum Glossarium Mediae Latinitatis ab Anno DCCC usque ad Annum MCC* (Aarhuus, Denmark), begun in 1957, issued in parts including an *Index Scriptorum*, with the 1959 fascicule comprising the letters "Ma." O. Prinz is editing the *Mittellateinisches Wörterbuch* (Munich), begun in 1959, issued in parts; the 1963 fascicule ends with "armarium." M. Plezia is at present working on the *Lexicon Mediae et Infimae Latinitatis Polonorum* (1000 to 1506; Polish Academy, Warsaw), issued in parts beginning in 1953; Vol. III ends with "królewski." F. Arnaldi (1939), M. Turriani (1951), and P. Smiraglia (1958) have completed more than half of a dictionary from Italian sources. There is also R. Hakamies, *Glossarium Latinitatis Medii Aevi Finlandicae* (Helsinki), completed in 1958, and M. Bassols de Climent, *Glossarium Mediae Latinitatis Cataloniae*, begun in 1960, drawn from Catalan sources from the ninth to the twelfth centuries. An independent venture by F. J. Niermeyer is the *Mediae Latinitatis Lexicon Minus* (Leyden, 1954), issued in parts, the 1963 fascicule ending with "sequipeda." Based on texts of charters, laws, and chronicles, this dictionary surveys the entire field of western Europe, with quotations from material between A.D. 550 to 1150.

Strecker and Paetow list books tracing the changes in the Latin language during the Middle Ages. More recently there is the splendid work of Christine Mohrman, *Etudes sur le latin des Chrétiens* (1958), pointing out the variations in medieval Latin according to time and place and the tug of war in both religious and secular fields between writers of the classical school and writers who were trying to adapt the use of Latin to the changing times. Also helpful is R. A. Browne, *British Latin Selections* (1954), with an introduction and notes both linguistic and literary. Other introductory volumes are C. H. Grandgent, *Introduction to Vulgar Latin* (1907; rptd. 1962), and K. Vossler, *Einführung ins Vulgarlatein* (1914; rev. 1925; augmented ed. by H. Schmeck, 1954). A. Blaise in his *Manuel du latin chrétien* (1955) deals with the language of the first Christian centuries and shows the influence of Greek and the development of figurative and symbolic language. J. Bastardas Parera, *Particularidades sintácticas del latín medieval, cartularios españoles de los siglos VIII al XI* (1953), explores the use of language in charters rather than in literary works, because he believes that we can gain a better understanding of spoken Latin from diplomatic sources. The success of Y. Malkiel's *Studies in the Reconstruction of Hispano-Latin Word Families* (1954) indicates the need for further investigation into the connection between medieval Latin and the Romance languages.

IV. SPECIAL TOPICS

A REVIEW of scholarship dealing with paleography up to 1940 is to be found in P. Lehmann's *Erforschung des Mittelalters* (5 vols., 1959–62). He calls attention to the progress of studies in paleography and points out the need for further study of *scriptoria* where the writing was actually done rather than a study of individual manuscripts. A good introduction to this subject is J. W. Thompson, *The Medieval Library* (ed. 1939; rptd. 1957), a survey from the early Middle Ages to the close of the Renaissance. The 1939 edition is valuable because of the supplementary essay by Blanche B. Boyer suggesting topics not covered by Thompson. A brief introductory history of the changes in handwriting from the first through the fifteenth centuries is G. Battelli, *Lezioni di paleografia* (1936; 3rd ed. 1949). It gives useful pointers to the student who is learning how to distinguish and date scripts. Also helpful are E. M. Thompson's *An Introduction to Greek and Latin Paleography* (1912; rptd. 1964) and the careful history of Latin paleography by E. Strubbe, illustrated by clear texts, *Grondbegrippen van de paleografie der Middeleeuwen* (2 vols., 1961). An indispensable aid for anyone wishing to examine manuscripts is A. Cappelli, *Lexicon abbreviaturarum, dizionario di abbreviature latine ed italiane* (6th ed., rev. and rptd., 1961), an alphabetical list of abbreviations found in medieval Latin manuscripts throughout the West. Particularly significant is E. A. Lowe's *Codices Latini Antiquiores, A Paleographical Guide to Latin Manuscripts prior to the Ninth Century*, nearing completion. The work will comprise eleven sections. Section x (Austria, Belgium, Czechoslovakia, Denmark, Egypt, and Holland) appeared in 1963. A more detailed account of the progress of this project is to be found in the review by L. W. Jones in *Speculum* (1960). Jones

assisted in compiling the material and reports the contributions of
B. Bischoff to the work. N. Denholm-Young, *Handwriting in
England and Wales* (1954), is very useful and has clear plates.
Especially designed for students is the volume by J. Kirchner,
Scriptura Latina libraria (1955), made up of reproductions of the
"book hand" used in literary works rather than the script used for
legal documents. This compilation enables the student to observe in a
single volume changes that took place in handwriting from the
fourth to the fifteenth century.

Drama played a very important part in the Middle Ages. Its
beginning in the early liturgy of the church is best treated by K.
Young, *The Drama of the Medieval Church* (2 vols., 1933), which
includes many texts. Supplementing this study is R. B. Donovan,
The Liturgical Drama in Medieval Spain (1958). C. J. Stratman,
Bibliography of Medieval Drama (1954), is useful, but Mary H.
Marshall (*Speculum*, 1959) has pointed out deficiencies. Additional
bibliography is to be found in H. Kindermann's *Theatergeschichte
Europas*, Vol. I, *Das Theater der Antike und des Mittelalters*
(1957).

Students of medieval literature cannot overlook the history of
science. For anyone attempting to familiarize himself with this
subject, the following are important: P. Duhem, *Le système du
monde; histoire des doctrinès cosmologiques de Platon à Copernic*
(10 vols., 1913–59); L. Thorndike, *A History of Magic and
Experimental Science* (3 vols., 1923–58); L. Thorndike and Pearl
Kibre, *A Catalogue of Incipits of Mediaeval Scientific Writings in
Latin* (rev. ed. 1962); G. Sarton, *Introduction to the History of
Science* (3v in 5, 1927–48), with critical bibliography; A. C.
Crombie, *Augustine to Galileo, A.D. 400–1650* (1952), and under the
title *Medieval and Early Modern Science* (2 vols., rev. paperback ed.
1959); and M. Clagett, *The Science of Mechanics in the Middle
Ages* (1959). An annual bibliography appears in the periodical
Isis.

The *Bibliography of English Translations from Medieval
Sources* (1946), by C. P. Farrar and A. P. Evans, is of prime
importance to students whose language is English. It includes brief
but valuable summaries of works in foreign languages including
Latin. C. W. Jones, *Medieval Literature in Translation* (1950),
makes available in English some of the more important works of
Latin prose and poetry.

V. LITERARY HISTORY

TURNING FROM bibliography to literary history and criticism, one may well begin with books that deal with the transition from classical to medieval Latin, such as E. K. Rand, *Founders of the Middle Ages* (1928; rptd., paperback, 1957) and F. Lot, *The End of the Ancient World and the Beginnings of the Middle Ages*, introd. G. Downey (1961: a trans. of the French ed. of 1917). Another stimulating book is Eleanor S. Duckett's *Latin Writers of the Fifth Century* (1930), and its sequel, *The Gateway to the Middle Ages* (1938; paperback 1963). An important text of the fifth century that had a profound effect on the middle ages was Macrobius' *Commentary on the Dream of Scipio*, trans. W. H. Stahl (1952). This commentary on the last section of Cicero's *Republic* introduced a readily understandable discussion of the geography of the world and the nature of the universe. Making use of Plato and his Greek followers like Porphyry, Macrobius passed on to the Latin reader a point of view about the immortality of man's soul and its close relationship to God. He also made a contribution to literature with his view of the significance of fiction and of dreams. One of the greatest scholars and writers of the sixth century was Cassiodorus, whose *Institutions* was edited by R. A. B. Mynors (1937). A selective bibliography of Cassiodorus has been compiled by A. Momigliano (*PBA*, 1955) and his influence on medieval culture discussed by L. W. Jones (*Speculum*, 1945 and 1947). Under the direction of Cassiodorus, the work entitled *The Antiquities*, by the great historian Josephus, was translated from Greek into Latin. Using Greek sources, Josephus traced the history of the Jews from their earliest times to 67 A.D., the date of their rebellion against Rome. Books I–V of the Latin translation have been well edited by F. Blatt (1958), and the remainder of the work is forthcoming. The Latin version was a favorite handbook of the Middle Ages.

Ireland's great part in disseminating the Latin literature of the early Middle Ages is reviewed by L. Bieler, *Irland, Wegbereiter des Mittelalters* (1961; rev. English trans. 1963), with splendid plates.

11

He points out the importance of Irish art and Irish writings in Latin from the time of Saint Patrick in the fifth century to Sedulius Scotus in the ninth century. The influence of the Irish traveling monks and scholars, especially in the seventh century, is treated in a helpful article by B. Bischoff, "Wendepunkte in der Geschichte der lateinischen Exegese im Frühmittelalter" (*SacE*, 1954). The eighth century is treated by W. Levison, *England and the Continent in the Eighth Century* (1946), and a summary of recent scholarship may be found in L. Wallach, *Alcuin and Charlemagne* (1959). A chapter on the Latin work of Aldhelm, Bede, and Alcuin appears in G. K. Anderson, *The Literature of the Anglo-Saxons* (1949). The culture of the first centuries of the Middle Ages has been discussed in a general way by M. L. W. Laistner, *Thought and Letters of Western Europe*, A.D. *500 to 900* (1931; rev. ed. 1957). Among the changes in the second edition is a more complete study of the profound effect of Saint Augustine's *De Doctrina Christiana* on the style of writing in the first centuries, particularly his strong influence on the use of allegory, one of the distinguishing features of medieval literature.

The studies that have most influenced our present understanding of the background of allegory are E. Auerbach's *Mimesis* (published in German 1946, rev. 1959; English trans. 1953, paperback ed. 1957) and his illuminating essay, "Figura," translated in his *Scenes from the Drama of European Literature* (paperback 1959), as well as C. S. Lewis' *The Allegory of Love* (1936; rptd., paperback, 1958). In the opening chapter of *Mimesis* Auerbach traces important developments in literature from classical times through the Latin of the early Middle Ages. He points out how significant "differences in style between the writings of antiquity and early Christianity are conditioned by the fact that they were composed from a different point of view and for different people." Auerbach's method is to take significant passages from the authors under discussion and analyze the changes in style and in attitude toward their times. He traces the change from the Homeric epic to the complex style of late classical Latin prose (continued by Saint Augustine) and the turn to the uncomplicated style of the Latin Bible. Auerbach clearly points out the link with philosophy and its connections with the less rhetorical Latin style; he shows the difference between the worldly attitude of the late classical writers in their search for subtle causal connections between events in this world and the outlook of early Christian writers like Saint Augustine, who sought for a divine plan that would interpret events more clearly and more definitely as a pattern in history.

In "Figura," Auerbach traces the development of the use of the word "figura" by classical authors to indicate form, semblance, or type. This concept came to influence the thinking of the early Fathers of the church. Auerbach shows how Saint Augustine developed a fresh approach to interpreting history through "figurative or typological allegory"—using the personages and structure of events of the Old Testament as "figures" prophetic of the events of the New Testament.

In *The Allegory of Love*, Lewis discusses the development of allegory by late classical poets like Claudian and Statius, who personified such aspects of human experience as war and fear. Lewis shows how personification of abstract traits was developed into an important device by the fourth-century Christian poet Prudentius, whose *Psychomachia*, or battle of vices and virtues, initiated a theme much used by later medieval poets. A new edition of the poems of Prudentius with an English translation by H. J. Thomson was published in the *Loeb Classical Library* (2 vols., 1949–53). This kind of allegory was made fashionable by Martianus Capella, a contemporary of Saint Augustine, in a lengthy poem, *De Nuptiis Philologiae et Mercurii*. This allegorical wedding between Learning and Eloquence was celebrated in the presence of seven bridesmaids, the Seven Liberal Arts. The profound effect of these seven wedding guests on education up to the sixteenth century and the way in which they helped to form the curriculum of the schools is illustrated in an article by Mlle. Marie Thérèse d'Alverny, "La sagesse et ses sept filles," *Mélanges dédiés à la mémoire de Félix Grat*, Vol. I (1946).

Martianus' poem was the subject of lectures in the schools, as we know from the commentaries of those who taught. Fortunately, one such commentary containing some lectures of John the Scot in the ninth century has been edited by Cora E. Lutz, *Iohannis Scotti Annotationes in Marcianum* (1939). Her more recent work includes Remi of Auxerre's commentary, *Remigi Autissiodorensis Commentum in Marcianum Capellum* (1962). Another important school text dating from the early Middle Ages is Boethius' *Consolation of Philosophy* translated by Alfred the Great and Chaucer, among others, and most recently by R. H. Green (1962). The latest critical edition is that by L. Bieler in the *Corpus Christianorum* (1957). The influence of this work has been studied by H. R. Patch in *The Tradition of Boethius: A Study of His Importance in Medieval Culture* (1935). The modern scholar's increasing realization of the importance of the commentaries on Boethius ranging up to the fifteenth century is the subject of P. Courcelle, "Etude critique sur les commentaries de la Consolation de Boèce" (*AHMA*, 1939). An anonymous ninth-century commentary on Boethius has been edited by E. T. Silk (1935).

In the great rebirth of culture that marked the twelfth century we find new allegorical poets who, following the lead of Boethius and of Plato's *Timaeus* (known in a Latin translation), leaned heavily on the liberal arts as a medium for expressing their views. One of these poets was Bernard Sylvester of Tours whose *De Mundi Universitate* has been translated by W. Rath under the title, *Über die allumfassende Einheit der Welt* (1953). R. P. McKeon sheds light on the problems of Bernard and other twelfth-century writers in his distinguished article, "Poetry and Philosophy in the Twelfth Century: The Renaissance of Rhetoric" (*MP*, 1946). He shows how in a great poem like Bernard's "poetry and philosophy may deal in almost wholly pagan terms with a Christian theme such as the creation of the universe and man." Following McKeon's observations, T. Silverstein in "The Fabulous Cosmogony of Bernardus Silvestris" (*MP*, 1948) gives a more detailed interpretation of *De Mundi Universitate* as an allegory of a celestial journey, a combination of prose passages and verse of great beauty. Silverstein goes on to show that there are other influences, such as translations from Arabic, Biblical commentary, and "Hermetic texts," that greatly influenced this religious poem, and he shows how Bernard reflected the thinking of his time. The allegorical poetry of Alan of Lille has been given recognition with a new edition of the *Anticlaudianus* (1955) by R. Bossuat and by an enlightening review of the allegory of *De planctu naturae* by R. H. Green (*Speculum*, 1956). The dates of Alan's work and its significance are discussed by G. Raynaud de Lage, *Alain de Lille, poète du XIIe siècle* (1951).

In "Locus of Action in Medieval Narrative" (*RPh*, 1963) C. Muscatine shows how the background or setting of allegory developed from the work of Prudentius in the fourth century to the works of Dante and of Chaucer and other writers in the fourteenth century. We find the celestial battleground of the *Psychomachia* of Prudentius and the celestial journey of Alan of Lille and Bernard Silvester changing about the year 1200 to an earthly journey or pilgrimage that was the setting for many later poems.

Of course the correct interpretation of allegory in medieval poetry is itself a controversial subject. One view is presented by D. W. Robertson, Jr., in "Some Medieval Literary Terminology" (*SP*, 1951). He begins by quoting Alan of Lille's definition of poetry as allegory in *De planctu naturae*: "On the outside the fables of poets are false, but the reader should discover beneath the outer skin a kernel of truth." Robertson goes so far as to say that all serious poetry written in the Middle Ages must, as he puts it, "conduce to charity in the sense that Scripture does." If a poem appears clear on the surface but does not conduce to charity, then "it is necessary to determine the *sententia* (or higher meaning) by seeking a significance beyond the historical or literal plane." From this observation it would appear that Robertson is extending to all poetry a method advocated by Saint Augustine for interpreting the Bible. The best guide to the four senses of scripture is H. de Lubac, *Exégèse médiévale* (2 vols., 1959). Differing from Robertson, M. W. Bloomfield in "Symbolism in Medieval Literature" (*MP*, 1958) points out that there must be a difference in interpreting literature and in interpreting the Bible. To understand literature we must, first of all, attempt to see it in its historical context. Applying a method that employs a three- or fourfold level of meaning to a secular work can lead only to confusion. Bloomfield supports this argument by pointing out that Beryl Smalley in *The Study of the Bible in the Middle Ages* (rev. ed. 1952; paperback 1964) shows that, beginning in the twelfth century, commentators stressed the importance of historical criticism of the Bible rather than the complex multilevel interpretations of an earlier day. Bloomfield concludes that for literature, especially after the twelfth century, the attempt to apply a complex symbolic interpretation can be misleading unless the reader has a firm historical background. How far one can apply to poetry the methods of Biblical criticism has also been discussed in some of the 1958–59 English Institute papers collected in *Critical Approaches to Medieval Literature* (1960), ed. Dorothy Bethurum.

There are some good studies of individual allegorical figures. From classical times through the Middle Ages the conception of Lady Fortune played an important part in the history of allegory. For example, H. R. Patch in *The Goddess Fortuna in Medieval Literature* (1927) traced the theme of Dame Fortune and her wheel, famous or infamous, depending on how lucky one was. Another such study that deserves mention is the article by A. Hench on the allegory of Conscience and Reason as good councilors on the side of man, which he traced from Latin to *Piers Plowman* (*University of Virginia Studies*, 1951). M. W. Bloomfield's *The Seven Deadly Sins* (1952) shows, step by step, from pre-Christian through medieval literature, different versions of the sins as they reappear in changing guise.

Allegory, of course, does not always follow a consistent pattern. For example, a lion or a serpent may sometimes represent good qualities and sometimes bad, as Auerbach observed in *Typologische Motive in der mittelalterlichen Literatur* (Petrarca Institut, Cologne, Schriften 2, 1953). Where there is more than one valid interpretation of a figure, we can have what Saint Augustine called a *contraria significatio* as found in the bestiary.

A bestiary describes animals, birds, and stones, real or legendary, and sets forth the properties ascribed to them. An early form of the bestiary was studied by M. Wellman, "Der Physiologus" (*Philogogus*, 1930). He points out the early use of the *physiologus* by the church Fathers. A manuscript of the Latin version current in England in the twelfth century was reproduced by M. R. James, *The Bestiary* (1928). James's splendid introduction traces the development of the expanded text from the thirty-nine chapters of the earlier version, amplified by materials from such writers as Pliny and Isidore of Seville; but he concludes that "the ultimate sources lie in literature and folklore still to be explored." Using the same Latin manuscript, T. H. White made a delightful English adaptation, *The Book of Beasts* (1954; paperback 1960). The best over-all study of the Latin bestiary is that of Florence McCulloch, *Mediaeval Latin and French Bestiaries* (1960). Although the bestiary as a collection has been studied, there is still much work to be done tracing the role played by individual figures, such as O. Shepard's *The Lore of the Unicorn* (1930), H. W. Janson's *Apes and Apelore in the Middle Ages and Renaissance* (1952), and E. Faral's "La queue de poisson des sirènes" (*Romania*, 1953).

Alongside serious allegory there developed a humorous or satirical mode in which human beings appeared in the form of animals easily recognized by their characteristics. Members of society in the twelfth century are the real targets for the barbs of a long narrative poem dealing with the misadventures of Daun Burnel the Ass, under the title *Speculum Stultorum*, by Nigel de Longchamps (Wireker), which has been carefully edited with a good introduction by J. H. Mozley and R. R. Raymo (1960), and translated by J. H. Mozley, *A Mirror for Fools* (1961; paperback 1963). Nigel's 3900-line narrative poem is a satire based on the education, formal and informal, of Daun Burnel as he travels from Salerno to Paris in a vain effort to improve his lot. In his preface Nigel made clear that the hero is in reality a monk who has left his cloister in order to become a master rather than a mule, or, in other words, an abbot rather than a monk. Chaucer's reference in the *Nonnes Preestes Tale*, "I have wel rad in 'Daun Burnel the Asse,' " indicates that the satire was familiar in the fourteenth century. The progress of the central narrative is interrupted by other short tales, including a debate of birds.

A good example of an earlier narrative using animals for the purpose of satire is the poem *Ecbasis Captivi*, edited and translated into English by E. H. Zeydel (1964). This tenth-century allegorical narrative of a prisoner was written by a German monk who fled his monastery in Toul in northern France but was captured and held in confinement. Representing his own experience, the penitent monk pictures himself as a calf who has strayed from home, been captured by a wolf (possibly the devil), and finally rescued. As a story within a story, the wolf explains why the fox is his enemy by relating the fable of the healing of the sick lion by the fox, who recommends that he wrap himself in the wolf's skin. This is one of the basic plots in the later beast epics, such as the story of Reynard. In the *Ecbasis* we have the first of the long satirical poems of western Europe based upon animals. A more comprehensive discussion of this poem and also of the powerful twelfth-century *Ysengrimus*, in which the animals are given proper names, is to be found in W. T. H. Jackson, *The Literature of the Middle Ages* (1960). There is a German translation of the *Ysengrimus* by A. Schönfelder (1955).

The twelfth century saw the development of new forms of Latin verse marked by strong rhythm and internal rhyme, and in the short Latin poems can be found the background for the lyric forms of French and English. The long history of accentual verse, from the quantitative verse of classical times to verse with the accent marked by stress and the development of rhyme, has been traced by W. Beare, *Latin Verse and European Song: A Study in Accent and Rhythm* (1957). He calls attention to the influence of music and popular song, as does D. Norberg, *Introduction à l'étude de la versification latine médiévale* (1958).

On Latin religious verse the work of F. J. E. Raby is still unrivaled. In *A History of Christian-Latin Poetry from the Beginnings to the Close of the Middle Ages* (1927; 2nd ed. 1953), he shows the development of the "sequence" from the prolongation of the final *a* of the *Alleluia* in the liturgy. He discusses the innovations of the work of Notker at the monastery of Saint Gall in Switzerland in the tenth century. Raby's is likewise one of the best treatments of another of the greatest poets of the Middle Ages, Hildebert of Lavardin, early twelfth-century bishop of Le Mans, who had an extraordinary gift for writing works in the classical style resembling Ovid's. Hildebert was also adept at utilizing both the new accentual verse and rhyme. His contemporary, Marbod of Rennes,

was also skillful in the classical and the accentual styles. Most
popular was his *Liber Lapidum,* dealing with the symbolic meaning
of jewels, which was soon translated into French. L. R. Lind has
edited the work of another contemporary poet, *The Vita sancti
Malchi of Reginald of Canterbury* (1942). In the twelfth century
short religious poems reached a point of near perfection in the
sequences of Adam of St. Victor, in which we find the rhythm based
primarily on word accent. His technical achievement was never
equaled in other medieval Latin verse. In the same century another
outstanding poem was the *Dies Irae. Dies irae, dies illa,* carefully
controlled and deeply moving, deals with the terror of the last day,
when we must stand in judgment before God. At the time it appeared,
fear of the end of the world was widespread, as is evidenced by the
writings of Joachim of Flora, which will be discussed later in this
chapter.

A manuscript containing religious poems may also contain
secular lyrics. An example of such a collection is the *Cambridge
Songs* in a unique manuscript of the eleventh century in Cambridge
University Library. Some of the secular poems in this group are
lyric and some are short narratives. Since there are occasional
German words, it appears that the manuscript was written in
Germany. There is an edition by K. Strecker, *Die Cambridge Lieder*
(1926), and a later edition by W. Bulst (1950). Many of the lyrics
were written by scholars who wandered about Europe, and the themes
of their songs are the themes of their lives: love as they found it, and
the pleasure of wine, the coming of spring, and of course the poverty
that was always hovering nearby. Much of this verse came to be
known as Goliardic because the *clerici vagantes* identified themselves
with the image of Golias, a phantom figure of a rascally lover of
pleasure who appears in so many poems that one might almost
believe that he existed. J. H. Hanford, "The Progenitors of Golias"
(*Speculum,* 1926), brings together the traditions concerning this
figure. We must remember that for the most part the goliards were
clerici, a term not limited to priests but applied also to students of
all ages and to all who were considered literate.

In the twelfth century the secular lyric reached its highest
development. Some of the best examples, many with a satirical turn,
are to be found in the poems of Walter of Châtillon, who was for a
time employed in the chancery of the English King Henry II, but
lost favor at court and exiled himself to France and Italy (some of
his satire is directed at the papal court). Two editions of the shorter
poems by Walter have been edited by K. Strecker, *Die Gedichte
Walters von Châtillon* (1925) and *Moralisch-satirische Gedichte*

Walters von Châtillon (1929). Among the best poems of the wandering scholars are those ascribed to one known only as the Archpoet. All that we know of him is what he tells us in his poems: that for a time, as late as 1162, he was attached to the court of Rainald of Dassau, the archchancellor of Frederick Barbarossa. As a follower of Rainald, the poet journeyed to Italy, where he wrote the famous poem, "Confession of Golias," and, like so many wandering scholars before him, he died in poverty. The authoritative edition of his work is by H. Watenphul and H. Krefeld, *Die Gedichte des Archipoeta* (1958). Perhaps the best known collection of Goliardic poems is the *Carmina Burana*. This manuscript, of much later date than the *Cambridge Songs*, was compiled at the Benedictine house of Benediktbeuern in Bavaria in the thirteenth century. It includes prose selections, religious drama, and verse, as well as German songs, but the most interesting parts of the compilation are the Goliardic songs, some by Walter of Châtillon and the Archpoet, and many others anonymous. A good edition was started by A. Hilka and O. Schumann, *Carmina Burana*. Volume I, parts 1 and 2, with a critical introduction, and Volume II, part 1, appeared between 1931 and 1941. Unfortunately no further volumes of this edition have appeared.

A comprehensive study of the whole field is the authoritative work of F. J. E. Raby, *A History of Secular Latin Poetry* (2 vols., 1934; 2nd ed., enlarged, 1957), with extensive bibliographies. A most useful work of reference is H. Walther, *Initia carminum ac versuum medii aevi posterioris Latinorum* (1959), an alphabetic index of the first lines of Latin verse from 1100 to 1500. Walther includes over 22,000 references with cross indices. He refers to manuscripts and, when possible, to printed versions. Although he deals for the most part with secular verse, he includes material from the *Patrologia Latina*. P. Dronke's review in *Göttingische Gelehrte Anzeigen* (1962) adds material.

One of the best anthologies of Latin lyrics is F. J. E. Raby, *The Oxford Book of Medieval Latin Verse* (1959). There is also a limited but very interesting group of selections of Latin lyrics translated into English: for example, Helen Waddell, *The Wandering Scholars* (1927; rptd. 1957 and 1961), and her *Mediaeval Latin Lyrics* (1929; rptd. 1948; paperback 1963), a continuation of the first book including earlier poems and concluding with selections from the *Carmina Burana*. There are also J. Lindsay, *Medieval Latin Poets* (1934), and G. F. Whicher, *The Goliard Poets* (1949). German translations are in K. Langosch, *Hymnen und Vagantenlieder: Lateinische Lyrik des Mittelalters* (1954), containing the poems of the Archpoet, as well as those of another wandering scholar, Hugh of Orleans, fourteen songs of the Cambridge collection, and a selection of hymns and sequences. There is also E. Brost, *Carmina Burana; Lieder der Vaganten, Lateinisch und Deutsch nach Ludwig Laistner* (1954). A good collection of poems other than the *Carmina Burana* is F. Brittain's *Penguin Book of Latin Verse* (1962), containing the Latin with English translations, including religious and secular verse. Since an important facet in the education of the student was the disputation, it is not surprising to find many poems in the form of debates. The best general study of the subject is still H. Walther, *Das Streitgedicht in der lateinischen Literatur des Mittelalters* (1920), which includes several poems elsewhere unpublished. Among other topics, he discusses the medieval debate of vices and virtues (the theme of the *Psychomachia* of Prudentius) and the long-continuing debate between summer and winter that has for centuries been widespread in both folk and cultivated literature. The most popular of all topics is the debate between body and soul, to medieval man the most fundamental of all problems. By far the best known poem on this theme is the *Visio Philiberti*, a thirteenth-century version of an earlier poem.

In the twelfth century there appear several poems dealing with the perennially fascinating story of Troy. The versions that have come down to us from the Middle Ages may well contain aspects of classical tradition otherwise lost. The subject has been treated by A. Boutemy in "Le poème *Pergama flere volo* et ses imitateurs de XIIe siècle" (*Latomus*, 1946). Boutemy discusses five short poems, three of which can be traced to their authors, and the other two anonymous. One of these latter, erroneously ascribed to Hildebert, is a lament beginning "Pergama flere volo," considered by many to be one of the great poems concerning the fall of Troy. Boutemy also published one of the Troy poems by Simon Aurea Capra, or Chèvre d'Or, the *Ilias*, in *Scrip* (1946–47). Following closely the rules of medieval rhetoric, this version is remarkably similar to Chaucer's version of the adventures of Aeneas in *The House of Fame*, as pointed out by A. C. Friend, "Chaucer's Version of the Aeneid" (*Speculum*, 1953). A longer poem certainly known to Chaucer, Joseph of Exeter's famous epic in six books, *De Bello Troiano*, is being prepared for the press by G. B. Riddehough of the University of British Columbia. He has given a detailed description of this version, which is based on the account of Dares, in "A Forgotten Poet: Joseph of Exeter" (*JEGP*, 1947).

The three Latin prose works in which the medieval Troy material finds its origin are discussed by A. M. Young, *Troy and Her*

Legend (1948). One is Dares the Phrygian's *De Excidio Troiae*, believed in the Middle Ages to be based on an eyewitness account of the war, although the extant version is now thought to have been written as late as the fifth century A.D. Another is the Latin work ascribed to Dictes of Crete, supposedly another first-person account that has survived in a Latin text of the fourth century A.D. A critical edition with variant readings has been published by W. Eisenhut, *Dictys Cretensis, ephemeridos belli Troiani libri* (1958). The third is a Latin text that traces the history of the war and its consequences to the reign of Augustus Caesar, the *Excidium Troiae* (1944), ed. E. B. Atwood and V. K. Whitaker. This version, dating from sometime between the fourth and sixth centuries, is probably based on a Latin handbook of classical times, independent of either Dares or Dictes.

We may ask ourselves why there was such a change and development in so many different fields, including literature, in the twelfth century. An answer has been attempted by C. H. Haskins in *The Renaissance of the Twelfth Century* (1927; rptd., paperback, 1955). He shows that the new influence that made itself felt was science coming from the East, predominantly from the Arabs, who had independently developed on classical foundations a body of knowledge unknown to the Western world. This new learning was brought back by scholars who traveled through centers of study in Spain, southern Italy, and Sicily. With this new phase of learning came developments in mathematics, medicine, and classical knowledge. A review of the whole subject is to be found in important chapters in A. L. Poole, *Domesday Book to Magna Carta, 1087–1216* (1951; rev. ed. 1955).

The twelfth century also saw the beginning of a systematic study of canon law, which was very important in England as we know from statements by John of Salisbury. In 1955 the Institute of Research and Study in Medieval Canon Law was founded in Washington, D. C. A concise report of the project was published by S. Kuttner (*Traditio*, 1955), listing outstanding manuscripts of decretals gathered from various countries. This material is at present being studied.

For an illuminating study of the writings of Englishmen and their important contributions in many fields, one may turn to R. W. Hunt, "English Learning in the Late Twelfth Century" (*Transactions of the Royal Historical Society*, 1936). He includes among others important figures like Alexander Nequam and Clement, prior of Lanthony, who compiled a Gospel harmony and wrote a lengthy commentary on it that was still in use in Chaucer's time. Clement's *Harmony* became the standard work of reference for England.

One of the most perceptive accounts of the twelfth century has been given by R. W. Southern in *The Making of the Middle Ages* (1953; paperback 1961). He makes clear, among other things, the changes in the structure of society that took the individual out of his own back yard and gave him a keener insight into the world around him. This growing individualism showed itself in the theory of courtly love. At a time when marriages were made largely for economic reasons, Andreas Capellanus wrote a treatise, *De Amore*, that sets forth a new concept of love between man and woman. A new edition gives the Latin text with two Italian translations of the fourteenth century, *Trattato d'amore*, ed. S. Battaglia (1947). The major part of Andreas' book consists of a series of dialogues between lovers of different social levels and establishes a code of etiquette that governs the conduct of a love affair with the full understanding that the outcome will be love for love's sake and not marriage. The twelfth century sees woman gaining status and escaping from the drudgery of married life through the chivalrous attitude of her lover toward her. Perhaps because Andreas was a chaplain, the last section of the book is a retraction of the doctrine he so fully set forth in the earlier sections. W. T. H. Jackson, "The *De Amore* of Andreas Capellanus and the Practice of Love at Court" (*RR*, 1958), takes the view that the whole work was written in a farcical and tongue-in-cheek tone. D. W. Robertson, Jr., "The Subject of *De Amore* of Andreas Capellanus" (*MP*, 1953), likewise feels that Andreas makes fun of illicit love. An opposite view was taken by J. J. Parry in the introduction to his excellent translation of Andreas, *The Art of Courtly Love* (1941). J. F. Benton gives a helpful bibliography on the subject of courtly love in "The Court of Champagne as a Literary Center" (*Speculum*, 1961).

One of the most popular and influential books of the twelfth century was written about 1138–39 by a canon of Oxford named Geoffrey of Monmouth. Under the title *Historia Regum Britanniae* he presented colorful accounts of the early history of Britain derived in part from Latin sources like Bede, but in larger part from a composite of various Celtic sources. Perhaps Geoffrey's greatest contribution is the story of King Arthur, including his many adventures and conquests and the knights and people surrounding him. These are presented amid twelfth-century pageantry including tournaments and festive court life. Geoffrey describes vividly Arthur's last battle and passes quickly over his subsequent journey to the island of Avalon. The last authoritative edition of Geoffrey's history was published in 1951 by the late J. Hammer. The best review of all the Latin material concerning Arthur appears in R. S.

Loomis, *Arthurian Literature in the Middle Ages: A Collaborative History* (1959), in which the text of Hammer's edition, at first not fully appreciated, has been shown through the research of Robert Caldwell to be very close to the original version rather than a variant redaction, as Hammer believed it to be. An English translation of Geoffrey based on a text other than the one used by Hammer was made by S. Evans, *The History of the Kings of Britain* (1903; rptd. 1912), recently revised by C. W. Dunn (paperback 1958).

Another writer important for his influence on later literature is Walter Map, who held office in the household of King Henry II. His charming collection of stories was translated by F. Tupper and M. B. Ogle, *Master Walter Map's Book, De Nugis Curialium* (*Courtiers' Trifles* [1924]), and discussed by A. Boutemy, *Gautier Map, conteur anglais* (1945).

The thirteenth century was a period of great consolidation of knowledge, in which many encyclopedic works were compiled. It was the age in which the newly translated Aristotelian learning began to take root in the universities, where in time it was to overshadow the reading of the literary classics. A milestone in the study of the translations of Aristotle has been the study of the Latin manuscripts initiated by G. Lacombe with the assistance of A. Birkenmajer, M. Dulong, and E. Franceschini, *Aristotiles Latinus, Pars I* (1939; *Pars posterior* 1955). A good basic study is F. Van Steenberghen, *Aristote en Occident* (1946; Eng. trans., *Aristotle in the West: The Origins of Latin Aristotelianism*, 1955). D. A. Callus provided a clear characterization of the change from the twelfth to the thirteenth century in his fine article, "The Introduction of Aristotelian Learning to Oxford" (*PBA*, 1943). This points out that the masters in arts rather than the theologians first introduced the new Aristotle and made ready the way for Saint Edmund of Canterbury, who taught theology at Oxford and Paris. His *Speculum Ecclesie: A Mirror of Holy Church*, manuscripts in Latin, English, and French, appears in MLA Photographic Facsimiles No. 98 (1929). Perhaps the most influential English Schoolman was Robert Grosseteste, who encouraged translation from the Greek and commented on Aristotle. An authoritative study is S. H. Thomson, *The Writings of Robert Grosseteste, Bishop of Lincoln, 1235–1253* (1940). More recent works are A. C. Crombie, *Robert Grosseteste and the Origins of Experimental Science, 1100–1700* (1953), and a collection of essays by various scholars edited by D. A. Callus, *Robert Grosseteste, Scholar and Bishop* (1955). Although scholars like Grosseteste made a few texts available, it was not until the middle of the century that Albert the Great, among others, undertook the project of making available the whole of Aristotle in a Latin that could be clearly understood. The full development of Aristotle's influence that we associate with the commentaries of Thomas Aquinas was the end result of a long period of growth. The way in which Plato and the Neoplatonists strengthened the chain of medieval philosophy has been pointed out by R. Klibansky, *The Continuity of the Platonic Tradition during the Middle Ages* (1939; rptd. 1951). Klibansky is at present editing the Latin versions of Plato as known in the Middle Ages: *Plato Latinus* (3 vols., 1950–62). Plato, of course, did not displace Aristotle in the universities, where after the thirteenth century Aristotelian studies were dominant.

From the thirteenth century on, Latin classics were read with a new purpose. They were now recognized as sources of information as well as models of literature. One of the new uses of the classics was as a source of valuable material for collections of *exempla*, or illustrative stories for sermons. The most comprehensive survey of these collections was made by J. T. Welter, *L'exemplum dans la littérature religieuse et didactique du moyen âge* (1927). A well-known collection of *exempla* of the thirteenth century, *Die Wundergeschichten des Caesarius von Heisterbach*, has been edited by A. Hilka (3 vols., 1933–37, and another work of Caesar of Heisterbach, *The Dialogue on Miracles*, has been translated by H. von E. Scott and C. C. S. Bland (2 vols., 1929). F. M. Powicke in his bibliography in *The Thirteenth Century, 1216–1307*, in *The Oxford History of England*, Vol. IV (1953; 2nd ed. 1962), refers to other collections of *exempla* published before 1925 and to the work of H. Caplan, *Medieval artes praedicandi: A Handlist* (*Cornell Studies in Classical Philology*, 1934 and 1936) and T. M. Charland, *Artes praedicandi* (1936). Apart from the classics, one of the earliest sources for stories from sermons was the collection entitled *Disciplina Clericalis* by Petrus Alphonsi (Alfonsi) of the early twelfth century, who introduced Eastern tales. A new edition by A. G. Palencia, *Pedro Alfonso, Disciplina Clericalis* (1948), gives the Latin text with a Spanish translation. One of the most important articles tracing the sources is H. Schwarzbaum, "International Folklore Motifs in Petrus Alphonsi's 'Disciplina Clericalis' " (*Sefarad*, 1961–63), and the related study by W. F. Bolton, "Parable, Allegory and Romance in the Legend of Barlaam and Josaphat" (*Traditio*, 1958). Stories of Eastern origin were often provided with fictitious Roman characters and settings; examples can be found in the fourteenth-century *Gesta Romanorum*, as has been pointed out by Beryl Smalley, *English Friars and Antiquity in the Early Fourteenth Century* (1961).

The extent to which classical literature continued to be the subject of the arts curriculum was made evident in the important article by E. K. Rand, "The Classics in the Thirteenth Century" (*Speculum*, 1929), showing the continuing importance of grammar and the number of classical authors studied. At the same time, however, logic and law attracted students as being more practical courses to follow. The way in which these studies tended to overshadow the classics in the curriculum of the universities is made evident by the protest of John of Garland, an Englishman who was teaching in France when he wrote his *Morale Scolarium* advocating a return to the humanism of the twelfth century. L. J. Paetow edited this text, with a good introduction: *Two Medieval Satires on the University of Paris: La Bataille des VII Arts of Henri d'Ande'i and the Morale Scolarium of John of Garland* (1927). To kindle an interest in poetry, John devised an allegorical reading of Ovid, which he set forth in the *Integumenta Ovidii*, edited by F. Ghisalberti (1933). W. G. Waite in "Johannes de Garlandia, Poet and Musician" (*Speculum*, 1960) shows that John's program included all the liberal arts. Of still another type is John's poem exalting the miracles of the Virgin, the *Stella Maris*, ed. E. F. Wilson (1946). In her introduction, Miss Wilson has traced the growing popularity of the many miracles attributed to the Virgin, and C. G. Loomis has discussed the flurry of miracles recorded in the twelfth and thirteenth centuries ascribed to various minor saints. Many of these legends are recorded in Loomis' *White Magic, An Introduction to the Folklore of Christian Legend* (1948). R. Aigrain has given us an enlightening book on the problems of hagiography, *L'hagiographie, ses sources, ses méthodes, son histoire* (1953).

A figure whose teaching was very influential in the thirteenth century was the Italian Joachim, abbot of Flora, whose belief it was that the end of the world was near and whose writing was known to Dante. A review of Joachim was made by M. W. Bloomfield, "Joachim of Flora: A Critical Survey of His Canon, Teachings, Sources, Biography and Influence" (*Traditio*, 1957). There are two recent editions of Joachim's *Liber Figurarum*, the first edited by L. Tondelli in 1940 and the second based on a newly discovered manuscript edited by Tondelli, M. Reeves, and B. Hirsch-Reich (2 vols., 1953). Joachim's significance is fully reviewed by N. R. C. Cohn in *The Pursuit of the Millennium* (1957; paperback 1961), a book indicating how persistent from ancient times has been the belief in a millenium and the expectation of a period preceding the end of the world when men, hoping for a happier hereafter, will lead good lives.

Writers of the thirteenth century were concerned with establishing set rules of versification. An increasing number of schoolbooks appeared that showed how to develop a poem by using classical rhetoric as a model. The best collection of these rhetorical texts was edited by E. Faral, *Les arts poétiques du XIIᵉ et XIIIᵉ siècle* (1924; rptd. 1958). It includes what came to be the standard textbook on the art of poetry, the *Poetria Nova* of Geoffrey of Vinsauf, to whom Chaucer alluded by name in *The Nonnes Preestes Tale*. There is a close connection between these manuals of rules and the continuous use down through the ages of the *topos*. *Topos* simply means a theme or a treatment of a theme that has its roots partly in pagan, partly in Christian antiquity. The importance of *topoi* throughout Western literature is clearly illustrated by E. R. Curtius in his challenging book, *European Literature and the Latin Middle Ages* (1948; English trans. by W. R. Trask, 1953). In J. W. H. Atkins, *English Literary Criticism: The Medieval Phase* (1943), there is a helpful outline of the contributions of John of Salisbury, Geoffrey of Vinsauf, and John of Garland to medieval critical ideas.

One of the great compilers of encyclopedic work in the thirteenth century was Vincent of Beauvais, about whom much has been written. Pauline Aiken has shown in "Arcite's Illness and Vincent of Beauvais" (*PMLA*, 1936) that Chaucer was dependent to some extent on medical information in Vincent's *Speculum Maius* for the accurate description of Arcite's injury and the subsequent treatment in the *Knyghtes Tale;* and in "Vincent of Beauvais and Dame Pertelote's Knowledge of Medicine" (*Speculum*, 1935) she points out that Chaucer was also dependent on the dream lore from the *Speculum Maius* in the *Nonnes Preestes Tale*. Worthy of special mention is an article by B. L. Ullman, showing that in preparing his *Speculum Maius* Vincent made use of a *florilegium*, or selection, of the poems of Tibullus and other classical poets (*CP*, 1928). *Florilegia* collected from prose as well as verse were extremely popular in the Middle Ages as sources of literary and philosophical material. Moreover, the *florilegia* sometimes contain better readings from lost manuscripts of classical authors, as indicated by Ullman in a series of articles in *CP* (1928–32). A valuable study comparing authoritative printed texts of classics with the readings of a *florilegium* has been published by A. Gagnér, *Florilegium Gallicum: Untersuchungen und Texte zur Geschichte der Mittellateinischen Florilegienliteratur* (1936).

Another aspect of the thirteenth century appears in the devotional poems written by John of Howden, or Hoveden, who is distinguished by his deep feeling of compassion and tenderness for the suffering of Jesus and His Mother. A good edition of John's Latin work has been published by F. J. E. Raby, *Poems of John of Hoveden* (1939). In his introduction the editor shows how Hoveden links devotional literature in England with the mystical work of a later writer like Richard Rolle of the fourteenth century.

Among recent editions and commentaries upon the work of Rolle, there is an edition by G. M. Liegey of the *Canticum Amoris* (*Traditio*, 1956), with a helpful introduction pointing out how influential was the work of this writer. Another facet of Rolle's writing is the *Melos Amoris*, a prose work edited by E. J. F. Arnould (1957). This is a lengthy outpouring of Rolle's inner feelings in which he expresses his mystical experience, which he calls *melos*, a foretaste of heavenly joy. Essentially it is this personal elevation that he tries to convey to us. Another Latin work has been printed by G. M. Liegey, "*Carmen Prosaicum:* Edition and Commentary" (*MS*, 1957). It is Liegey's opinion that the alliterative Latin passages are arranged in a pattern fashioned after English alliterative verse. Rolle was a well-known, individualistic figure in a century that produced mystics in many lands.

The literature of mystical experience dates back to antiquity. One of the earliest records in Christian history is the vision ascribed to Saint Paul in Greek texts dating from the third century and Latin texts from the ninth. T. Silverstein in his authoritative study, *The Visio Sancti Pauli* (1935), and in his article, "The Vision of St. Paul: New Links and Patterns in the Western Tradition" (*AHMA*, 1959) has traced the different versions and their sources. The text was one of the chief formative elements in the development of later visions of purgatory and paradise, such as the *Divine Comedy*. Another important work dealing with a voyage to the other world is the *Navigatio Sancti Brendani Abbatis*, ed. C. Selmer (1959). The earliest manuscripts dating from the tenth century follow closely material that appears in the vision of Saint Paul, adding material from Irish legends of voyages to the other world and even, perhaps, material from Arabic sources. At once popular, the Latin text was soon translated into vernacular literatures. The pattern of the search for another world is continued in *Saint Patrick's Purgatory*, of the twelfth century. This is the account of the experience of an Irish knight, Owen, as recorded by a monk, Henry of Saltrey. The best edition is by K. Warnke, *Das Buch vom Espurgatoire S. Patrice der Marie de France und seine Quelle* (1938), which prints two versions of the Latin account of the monk of Saltrey with the French text of Marie, which Warnke finds very close to the lost original. It is the story of the visit of Owen to a purgatory in County Donegal, a single night in which he passed across a bridge from purgatory into the earthly paradise, characterized by blooming trees and sweet odors. A French translation has been made by J. H. Marchand, *L'autre monde au moyen âge: voyages et visions: La navigation de Saint Brendan, le purgatoire de Saint Patrice, la vision d'Albéric* (1946). *The Literature of the Other World, According to descriptions in medieval literature* (1950), by H. R. Patch, summarizes these and other expeditions to the other world.

The mystical approach to religion remained a very strong influence in the fourteenth-century writings in England and on the Continent. At the same time, however, science continued to develop. One of the paradoxes of the century can be seen in the attitude of William of Ockham, a devout Franciscan advocate of the mystical approach, who believed that God and his attributes were not always meant to be understood, certainly not by mere human reason, and that man should therefore turn his energies to exploring the world around him. This attitude was in direct contradiction to the teachings of Thomas Aquinas, which endeavored to bring reason and faith together into a single logical system. In her chapter, "Learning, Lollardy, and Literature" in *The Oxford History of England*, v (1959), May McKisack points out that Ockham's challenge did not go unanswered. Thomas Bradwardine, arguing from the Augustinian concept of grace, made an effective reply in *De Causa Dei contra Pelagianos*, which was extremely influential in the fourteenth century. G. Leff has provided us with a stimulating book, *Bradwardine and the Pelagians: A Study of His De Causa Dei and Its Opponents* (1957). Another major figure drawn into the controversy was John Wyclif, who likewise disagreed with Ockham, although for different reasons. In his lectures at Oxford, Wyclif taught that God's ways were not beyond man's ability to understand. He went on to say that corrupt men had no right to authority nor any power to judge others except by strict adherence to the teachings of the Bible. His followers, the Lollards, spread his teachings even though they had never known him. Two useful books on the man and his influence are H. B. Workman, *John Wyclif* (2 vols., 1926), and K. B. McFarlane, *John Wycliffe and the Beginnings of English Nonconformity* (1953). A general summary of the religious controversies of the time appears in W. A. Pantin, *The English Church in the Fourteenth Century* (1955; paperback 1963). He shows how later Latin literature touches on such Middle English texts as, for example, John Mirk's *Manuale Sacerdotum* and its English translation, the *Instructions for Parish Priests*, as well as Latin and English versions of *The Prick of Conscience,* whose texts are found in the MLA collection of Photographic Facsimiles, No. 182 (1931).

The rapid advances in scientific thought in the fourteenth century are discussed by F. M. Powicke, *The Medieval Books of Merton College* (1931). This furnishes not only a catalogue of the library of Merton, the medieval English seat of mathematics and physics, but also a valuable picture of a fourteenth-century library and a comprehensive study of fourteenth-century scientific writers and their works.

The subject of science leads us to the important topic of medieval education. What were the schools, what were the books read, and what do we know of them? On the one hand, we have the books that were used primarily by those training for a monastic vocation. A splendid study of the teaching in the monasteries, dating back to Saint Benedict and Cassiodorus and concluding with the period of Saint Bernard of Clairvaux in the twelfth century, is Dom J. Leclercq's *L'amour des lettres et le désir de Dieu: initiation aux auteurs monastiques du moyen âge* (1957; trans. by Catherine Misrahi under the title *The Love of Learning and the Desire for God,* paperback 1961). Leclercq's survey is intended primarily for students. He points out how the study of the liberal arts, trans-mitted from classical schools, became the basis of medieval education ; and the important part Cassiodorus played in establishing the *trivium* consisting of the basic literary studies, and the *quadrivium* leading to scientific studies. The author discusses the importance of the classics in monastic culture that produced such great historians as Otto of Freising and Ralph of Coggeshall. There was at the same time a keen interest on the part of the monks in the development of hagiography. High significance was given to one of the greatest contributions of the Middle Ages, the writing of books in the *scriptoria* for the use of the religious orders. Dom Leclercq presents the view that between the eighth and the twelfth centuries it is possible to distinguish two medieval cultures, one being what he calls monastic culture, based largely on the study and teaching of the early church Fathers, and the other being what he calls scholastic education, in the largest sense of the word, for those who did not wish to follow the monastic vocation.

Perhaps the best summary of this second facet of medieval teaching is G. Paré, A. Brunet, P. Tremblay, *La renaissance du XIIᵉ siècle. Les écoles et l'enseignement* (1933). At the conclusion of each section there is a helpful bibliography. The authors give a history of various methods of teaching, especially of the seven liberal arts. The emphasis is on the early years of the twelfth century, when so many changes were taking place. Among the subjects treated are the roles of the episcopal, or bishop's schools, the famous school of the canons regular of Saint Victor in Paris, and the great monastic schools. Much information concerning the curriculum can be derived from Abelard's autobiography, the *Historia Calamitatum*, of which a new edition has recently appeared, by J. Monfrin (1959). The book by Paré, Brunet, and Tremblay goes on to describe briefly the *scriptoria*, which produced texts for the schools, and the *stationarii*, which produced them for the universities. The books in use were of course primarily the *auctores*, but the texts often contained the comments of the teachers, entitled the *lectiones*, from which developed another form of text, the *questiones*, arguments for and against a given solution of a question; and finally from the *questiones* there developed the *disputatio*, which took many forms. Paré concludes with discussion of the work of Abelard and Peter Lombard on the methods of Biblical study. On the important subject of the growth of the schools and the consequent formation of the universities the best study is H. Rashdall, *The Universities of Europe*, ed. F. M. Powicke (3 vols., 1936; rev. ed., A. B. Emden, 1956). A series of detailed essays on the classical heritage of studies from the early Middle Ages through the thirteenth century has been compiled by J. Koch, *Artes Liberales von der antiken Bildung zur Wissenschaft des Mittelalters* (1959). These essays range from the *quadrivium* in the early Middle Ages, by H. M. Klenkenberg, to a study of *grammatica et ethica* in the twelfth century, by P. Delhaye, which is continued on into the thirteenth century by H. Roos. Included is an article on the study of history, by H. Wolter, pointing out the contribution of the *Didascalion* of Hugh of St. Victor, which is discussed below.

One of the oldest and most frequently used texts for beginners up to the close of the Middle Ages was the *Distichs* of Cato, probably composed about the third century A.D. The popularity of this text was recently discussed by R. Hazelton, "The Christianization of 'Cato': The *Disticha Catonis* in the Light of Late Mediaeval Commentaries," (*MS*, 1957). A definitive edition of the text was prepared by M. Boas and H. J. Botschauyver (1952). It is very likely that one method for teaching Latin was to translate proverbs into rhyming Latin verse. This was the method of Serlo of Wilton, who taught at schools in Paris and Oxford between 1150–70 and compiled a collection of proverbs in three languages, Anglo-Norman French, English, and Latin. In his rhyming verse he also made use of classical material. A study of his method of teaching and the text of his work has been published by A. C. Friend, "The Proverbs of Serlo of Wilton" (*MS*, 1954). A comprehensive collection of other proverbs has been compiled by S. Singer, *Sprichwörter des Mittelalters* (3 vols., 1944–47). Only the first volume, however, contains Latin proverbs: *Salamon and Marcolf* and the *Fecunda ratis* of Egbert of Liège of the eleventh century. A bibliography of proverbs is to be found in O. E. Moll, *Sprichwörterbibliographie* (1958), including a short section on Latin. Another vehicle used in the schools to teach reading was the moralized story, or *parabola*, following the model of the Aesopic fable. Many versions in both Greek and Latin, up to and including the thirteenth century, have been edited by B. E. Perry, *Aesopica*, Vol. I (1952).

Proverbs and fables were part of the curriculum of the seven liberal arts, which were the foundation of education in the medieval school. However, Hugh of St. Victor felt the need for expanding the curriculum itself. He rose from a teacher in the monastic school to head of the house of St. Victor in Paris in 1133, and died in 1141. His desire to enlarge the plan of studies is expressed in his book, the *Didascalion*, ed. C. H. Buttimer (1939), a critical text, with more variants than are to be found in Migne. There is a translation (1961) by Jerome Taylor, with an excellent introduction showing that Hugh was making a step forward by assigning to philosophy a place after the liberal arts as the next step to a higher education on the road to the study of theology. The methods of teaching an art or a science by exposition of a text of an ancient author, as advocated by the *Didascalion*, are discussed by R. W. Hunt, "The Introductions to the 'Artes' in the Twelfth Century" (*Studia Mediaevalia in honorem R. J. Martin*, 1948). To make available a larger selection of classical authors and to enrich the literature of the seven liberal arts by quotation from important but lesser known writers, such as Terence, Lucan, and Sallust, there were collections like *Moralium Dogma Philosophorum*, newly edited by J. Holmberg (1929), who ascribes the work to Guillaume de Conches of the School of Chartres (d. 1154). In 1957 J. R. Williams, "The Quest for the Author of *Moralium Dogma Philosophorum, 1931–1956*" (*Speculum*, 1957), revived the doubt as to whether Walter of Châtillon was not perhaps the author. The *Dogma* became very popular, and its influence appeared in Chaucer, as pointed out by R. Hazleton, "Chaucer's *Parson's Tale* and the *Moralium Dogma Philosophorum*" (*Traditio*, 1960). William of Conches was certainly one of the most influential teachers of the liberal arts in the twelfth century. There is a comprehensive study of his contribution by T. Gregory, *Anima mundi; la filosofia di Guglielmo di Conches e le scuola di Chartres* (1955). William established a program for teaching grammar that included both syntax and the study of classical authors, with emphasis on allegorical interpretations, as discussed by E. Jeauneau, "L'usage de la notion d'*Integumentum* à travers les gloses de Guillaume de Conches" (*AHMA*, 1957). The most detailed account of the techniques used in teaching Latin in the schools has been given by R. Hunt in two parts of an article, "Studies on Priscian in the Eleventh and Twelfth Centuries" and "Studies on Priscian in the Twelfth Century—II: The School of Ralph of Beauvais" (*Mediaeval and Renaissance Studies*, the Warburg Institute, 1943 and 1950). From the manuscripts of the grammarian Priscian, containing marginal notations as to arguments and questions, Hunt has reconstructed the changing methods of teaching grammar. Following the program of William of Conches, the first teacher to put in order the theories established by his predecessors was Petrus Helias, who taught between 1142 and 1166. He was followed by Ralph of Beauvais, the outstanding authority on grammar and literature from the late 1160s to 1185.

John of Salisbury, generally considered the foremost classical scholar of his time, has left the *Metalogicon*, showing the basic educational methods of his day as practiced on all levels. Completed in 1159, the book expanded the accepted study of the seven liberal arts; like Augustine and Jerome before him, John made available a larger selection of classical material for Christian education, which broadened the curriculum. The *Metalogicon* was edited by C. C. I. Webb (1929) and translated by D. D. McGarry (1955). H. Liebeschütz, *Mediaeval Humanism in the Life and Writings of John of Salisbury* (1950), pointed out how John instituted a plan for the study of the whole of Aristotle's logic and at the same time supported the study of classical poetry.

In the twelfth century, too, Conrad of Hirsau set down detailed biographies of the authors used in the schools and an account of their principal works. This record, set forth as a dialogue between a student and a teacher, shows us just what books were used. It has been edited by R. B. C. Huygens, *Conrad de Hirsau: dialogus super auctores* (1954). The same method was carried on by Hugh of Trimberg during the latter part of the thirteenth century. Like Conrad, he discussed the authors read in the schools. Although he restricted himself to verse (omitting therefore Cicero and Sallust), his list of authors is four times longer than Conrad's because he added many later writers, as seen in the edition of K. Langosch, *Das Registrum Multorum Auctorum des Hugo von Trimberg* (1942). In the next century, by 1345, when Richard de Bury wrote his *Philobiblon*, interest in books had become so great that he felt the need to inspire a love for them in the clergy and to set up rules for the establishment of a library and the proper care for its volumes. The edition of A. Altamura, *Ricardo da Bury, Philobiblon* (1954), replaces earlier editions. There is a translation by A. F. West with an introduction by A. Taylor (1948).

Another indication of the scope of medieval acquaintance with classical literature and literature of other countries is the early fifteenth-century *Cathologus de libris autenticis et apocrifis* of the monk, Boston of Bury. He intended to make an alphabetical list of all earlier authors with their dates and the titles of their works. Although never completed, the list gives us the books found in English libraries in the fourteenth century. The only extant copy of Boston's work is in a manuscript in Cambridge University Library published by T. Tanner in the eighteenth century, *Bibliotheca britannico-hibernica* (1748; rptd. 1964). For a careful study of the catalogue, see R. A. B. Mynors, "The Latin Classics Known to Boston of Bury" in *Fritz Saxl, A Volume of Memorial Essays*, ed. D. J. Gordon (1957). Mynors compares Boston's entries with references to printed catalogues of medieval libraries, especially the significant study of N. R. Ker, *Medieval Libraries of Great Britain* (1941). A summary of the development and growth of the history of medieval literature can be found in P. Lehmann, "Literaturgeschichte im Mittelalter" in his collected essays, *Erforschung des Mittelalters*, Vol. I (1959). Lehmann gives a survey of the biographical and literary collections beginning with Saint Jerome's *Liber de viris illustribus*, leading through the centuries to the great compilation of Vincent of Beauvais, especially his *Speculum Historiale*, considered as a compilation of anecdotes and biographies of authors. After Vincent we have the work of Boston of Bury (in 1410), leading to the literary history of John Trithemius of 1494, and later the great histories of the orders of friars of the seventeenth century. Lehmann's work provides a picture of the development of literary history through the Middle Ages.

2

Old English Literature

By George K. Anderson
BROWN UNIVERSITY

I N ONE OF HER many valuable contributions, *Changing Currents in Anglo-Saxon Studies* (1958), Dorothy Whitelock points out that the study of English literature before the Norman Conquest is drawing more and more upon allied fields—history, archaeology, fine arts, theology, law—to delineate in detail the civilization of the age. In short, Old English studies are building a *Kulturgeschichte* in which literature occupies the longest but by no means the only chapter. Moreover, the scholars themselves, while obligated to the work of the great German philologists of the later nineteenth century, have broken away from their domination and turned with profit to appropriate discussion of the surviving representatives of Old English literature, not only as social and historical documents but also as works of art.

Since 1925 well over three thousand studies of the civilization of England before the Norman Conquest (under which phrase is included, among other matters, the language and literature of Anglo-Saxon England) have been published here and abroad. They take the form of articles, extended notes, monographs, lectures, bibliographies, and full-length books. Reviews are not included in this number unless of major importance; their inclusion would bring the total close to four thousand. Most of these works have been written by British or American scholars, but German, Dutch, and Scandinavian writers have also made contributions of great merit. Here and there one will encounter a useful French or Italian study. The American studies are more numerous than the British—a fact for which the Second World War is mainly responsible; but it is interesting to note that the American contribution comprises many more studies of minutiae than the total of similar studies from across the Atlantic.

I. BIBLIOGRAPHY

A FEW BIBLIOGRAPHIES of the field have been published during the past generation, all of them helpful and all of them now somewhat dated. A. H. Heusinkveld and E. Bashe, *A Bibliographical Guide to Old English* (1931), was of great value when it first appeared, but that was more than thirty years ago. W. L. Renwick and H. Orton, *The Beginnings of English Literature to Skelton, 1509* (1939), was revised in 1952 and is therefore more useful. Similarly, a supplement to the *Cambridge Bibliography of English Literature* (1941) was published in 1957. There is also the fine two-volume work by W. Bonser, *Anglo-Saxon and Celtic Bibliography* (1957), ending with 1953, of value chiefly for the study of background material. Other works tread a borderline between outright bibliography and the collection of material, the net effect of which is primarily bibliographical. Among the former is N. R. Ker's *Catalogue of Manuscripts Containing Anglo-Saxon* (1957), which lists all known manuscripts containing writing in Old English. The latter include *English Historical Documents*, Vol. I, c. 500–1042 (1955), ed. Dorothy Whitelock, and *English Historical Documents*, Vol. II, 1042–1189 (1953), ed. D. C. Douglas and G. W. Greenaway, which print many items not otherwise available, or at least difficult of access; the second is noteworthy also for its discussion of the history of the late Anglo-Saxon and early Middle English periods. It also provides a facsimile of the Bayeux tapestry.

All of the preceding works are indispensable as grand contributions, but there are a few others of more limited importance, subject always to the restrictions laid upon them by time. So with J. B. Baxter, C. Johnson, and J. F. Willard, *An Index of British and Irish Latin Writers*, A.D. 400–1520 (*ALat*, 1932); "The Sutton-Hoo Ship-Burial: A Chronological Bibliography" in *Speculum*, by F. P. Magoun, Jr., in 1954, and by J. B. Bessinger in 1958. As a first resort we have the annual bibliographies of the *Modern Humanities Research Association* and the *Modern Language Association*. The MLA bibliography did not have international coverage until 1956 and still pays too little attention to material ancillary to the study of literature or language. *The Year's Work in English Studies* has managed to keep pretty well up to date, but it is too selective and too subjective in its commentary. Nor is it necessary to do more than cite *Progress of Medieval and Renaissance Studies in the United States and Canada*, published since 1923 (biennially since 1933), because it deals primarily with potential scholarship rather than with achieved publications. The quarterly bibliographies in *Speculum* are generally absorbed in the annual bibliographies already mentioned.

II. HISTORICAL AND CULTURAL BACKGROUNDS

THE TASK of the historian is to discover what can be discovered about the past. So far as literature is concerned, we are not likely to find many more primary texts in Old English. Our knowledge of what was written in Anglo-Saxon England will always be incomplete, as was demonstrated by R. W. Chambers in "The Lost Literature of Medieval England" (*Library*, 1925), and in more detail by R. M. Wilson in *The Lost Literature of Medieval England* (1952). But the historian is not dismayed. Special commendation is due those who during the past thirty years have been studying the historical, social, and archaeological backgrounds of the Old English period.

Three staple works on the Anglo-Saxon Conquest must be mentioned. R. H. Hodgkin, *The History of the Anglo-Saxons* (2 vols., 1935), massive and somewhat pedestrian, but important, brings us only to the death of Alfred the Great about 900. Its third edition (1953) contains in an appendix an excellent general account by R. L. S. Bruce-Mitford of the most important archaeological discovery of the generation in England, the ship burial at Sutton Hoo, Suffolk. A *sine qua non* is F. M. Stenton, *Anglo-Saxon England* (2nd rev. ed. 1947), the finest one-volume treatment of the period. Slighter in scope, but indispensable, is P. H. Blair, *An Introduction to Anglo-Saxon England* (1956; paperback 1962). This, however, is only a beginning. Studies of special aspects of the civilization of the Anglo-Saxons include over ten per cent of all the scholarship devoted to the period. To select the most distinguished is difficult. We may call attention to N. Aaberg, *The Anglo-Saxons in England During the Early Centuries After the Invasion* (1926). There has always been a tendency to slight the Celtic side of the story, but a good corrective to this, a work that set the standard for much subsequent investigation, is R. E. Zachrisson, *Romans, Kelts, and Saxons in Ancient Britain* (1927). Mrs. D. E. Martin-Clarke's *Culture in Early Anglo-Saxon England* (1947) is more popular in tone and is now overshadowed by Dorothy Whitelock's *The Beginnings of English Society* (1952).

The ancient religion of the Germanic peoples has been rather neglected in the present-day stampede to find a Christian behind every Anglo-Saxon tree. The two most important studies of the past generation remain C. Clemen, *Altgermanische Religionsgeschichte* (1934), and E. A. Philippson, *Germanisches Heidentum bei den Angelsachsen* (1929). The first, of course, is more general in scope, but the second is essential, though too often unfamiliar to students of Anglo-Saxon civilization. A very thoughtful and important study for its thesis that Christianity, when it came to the Anglo-Saxons, merely substituted one form of monotheism for another (Wyrd), is J. H. W. Rosteutscher, "Germanische Schicksalsglaube und angelsächsische Elegiendichtung" (*Englische Studien*, 1938). The persistence of heathendom is pointed up in G. Storms, *Anglo-Saxon Magic* (1948), and in F. Grendon, *The Anglo-Saxon Charms* (*JAF*, 1909; rptd. separately, 1930). The ability of a good folklorist to throw doubt upon the historical writings of the times is illustrated in A. H. Krappé, "Les dieux jumeaux dans la réligion germanique" (*APS*, 1931), in which Hengest and Horsa represent not human conquerors of Vortigern but rather the Dioscuri. This article may be considered in conjunction with G. Ward, *Hengest* (1949).

Krappé, or some one like him, should have written a comprehensive study of British folklore. There has been more than one attempt at such a work, but even the two that are probably best—Christina Hole, *English Folklore* (1940), and H. Bett, *English Myths and Traditions* (1952)—leave much to be desired. A better beginning, at least, is R. Bernheimer, *Wild Men in the Middle Ages: A Study in Art, Sentiment, and Demonology* (1952).

No less than four admirable biographies have come from the pen of Eleanor S. Duckett: *Anglo-Saxon Saints and Scholars* (1947), *Alcuin, Friend of Charlemagne* (1951), *Saint Dunstan of Canterbury* (1955), and *Alfred the Great* (1956). The best of three biographies of William the Conqueror, that by P. Russell (1933), seems mediocre by comparison with them; and the other two— Marjorie Coryn, *The Acquirer, 1027–1078* (1934), and G. Slo-

combe, *William the Conqueror* (1959) —are little more than romances.

To some the study of place names is a matter of linguistic
interest only; to others its attraction lies in its archaeological
orientation. The English Place-Name Society, however, takes a more
comprehensive view of such study, and the systematic efforts of E.
Ekwall, R. E. Zachrisson, F. Stenton, A. Mawer, and others have
resulted in a corpus of material comparable in its way to the
Victoria County histories. The starting point for a general study
was first established in E. Ekwall's edition of *The Concise Oxford
Dictionary of English Place-Names* (1936; 4th ed. 1960), but some
of his preliminary studies, such as "Englische Ortsnamenforschung"
(*Palaestra*, 1925), *English River-Names* (1928), and particularly
Studies on English Place- and Personal-Names (1931), are most
important. *The Concise Dictionary* has been supplemented from time
to time in various ways by various people. A good example is R.
Forsberg, *A Contribution to a Dictionary of Old English Place-
Names* (1950). *A Dictionary of British Surnames*, ed. P. H. Reaney,
appeared in 1958. The significance of all this for the history and
literature of the period is cogently explained by A. H. Smith in the
Gollancz Memorial Lecture of 1956, *Place-Names and the Anglo-
Saxon Settlement* (1957), and the broadest application of this
approach to the *Kulturgeschichte* of the age is the series of four fine
studies by F. M. Stenton: "The Historical Bearing of Place-Name
Studies: Anglo-Saxon Heathenism"; "The Historical Bearing of
Place-Name Studies: The English Occupation of Southern Britain";
"The Historical Bearing of Place-Name Studies: The Danish Settle-
ment of Eastern England"; and "The Historical Bearing of Place-
Name Studies: The Place of Women in Anglo-Saxon History" —all
printed in *Transactions of the Royal Historical Society* (1941,
1942, 1943).

III. THE STUDY OF OLD ENGLISH

A NUMBER of studies have been devoted to pioneer students of
Anglo-Saxon, old and respected names of early scholars about
whom there is little superfluous knowledge. These include Rosamond
Tuve's article on seventeenth-century scholars, "Ancients, Moderns,

and Saxons" (*ELH*, 1939), which is actually a good statement of the whole motivation of early study from the Tudor period onward; Margaret Ashdown, "Elizabeth Elstob, the Learned Saxonist" (*MLR*, 1925); F. Cooley, "William Taylor of Norwich and *Beowulf*" (*MLN*, 1940); and especially B. Dickins, "John Mitchell Kemble and Old English Scholarship" (*PBA*, 1939). R. Flower's Gollancz Memorial Lecture of 1934, *Lawrence Nowell and the Discovery of England in Tudor Times* (1936), is something of a landmark. There are also brief articles by B. Dickins, "William l'Isle the Saxonist and Three Eighteenth-Century Remainder-Issues" (*English and Germanic Studies*, 1947–48), and W. B. Gardner, "George Hickes and His *Thesaurus*" (*N&Q*, N.S., 1955). S. Kliger, "The Neo-Classical View of Old English Poetry" (*JEGP*, 1950), treats a subject hitherto virtually ignored. D. J. Savage, "Grundtvig: A Stimulus to Old English Scholarship" (*Philologica, the Malone Anniversary Studies*, 1949), and K. Malone, "Grundtvig as Beowulf Critic" (*RES*, 1941), are well-deserved tributes to a great nineteenth-century scholar. The most challenging comments on the study of Anglo-Saxon in the present generation have been made by H. M. Chadwick, *The Study of Anglo-Saxon* (1941; 2nd ed., rev. and enlarged by N. K. Chadwick, 1955). For the study in America, there is C. R. Thompson, "The Study of Anglo-Saxon in America" (*ES*, 1936).

IV. GENERAL STUDIES OF OLD ENGLISH LITERATURE

SINCE 1925 there have been two full-length books on the literature of the period—Edith E. Wardale, *Chapters on Old English Literature* (1935), and G. K. Anderson, *The Literature of the Anglo-Saxons* (1949). In view of the continuous output in the field, averaging about seventy-five miscellaneous items each year, the writing of a historical and descriptive survey of Old English literature becomes at once a difficult and thankless task and yet one that should be undertaken periodically. Both of these books have merit; both are readable and serve well their objectives of acquainting the reader with the literature *in extenso*. In addition there are briefer treat-

ments. First in time is E. Legouis's chapter on Old English literature
in E. Legouis and L. Cazamian, *Histoire de la littérature anglaise*
(1924; English trans. by Helen Irvine, 1926). This is a notably
unsympathetic treatment; Legouis is temperamentally unsuited to a
fair appreciation of Anglo-Saxon poetry. Next comes K. Malone,
"The Old English Period (to 1100)" in *A Literary History of
England* (1948), ed. A. C. Baugh. Finally, there is G. K. Anderson's
"Old and Middle English Literature," in the one-volume *Oxford
History of English Literature* (1950; rev. paperback 1962), ed. H.
Craig. A successful consideration of both Old and Middle English
literature is the older work of P. G. Thomas, *English Literature
before Chaucer* (1924), which unfortunately is lacking in biblio-
graphical equipment. Even more effective is Margaret Schlauch,
English Medieval Literature and Its Social Foundations (1956).

Certain portions of the literature of the Anglo-Saxons have
been studied separately—the poetry as distinct from the prose, for
example. Two of the most attractive works of this kind are C. W.
Kennedy, *The Earliest English Poetry* (1943) and *Early English
Christian Poetry* (1952), which are critical surveys of the poetry
written before the Norman Conquest, with illustrative translations,
for which Kennedy has shown great talent. These works must be
mentioned again later. K. Sisam, *Studies in the History of Old
English Literature* (1953), is a fine assemblage of many of the
author's previously published works on various topics—Cynewulf,
the Beowulf MS., the Vercelli MS., and others—and is not meant to
be a comprehensive history. Occasionally a certain genre or type of
literary expression has received particular study. B. J. Whiting,
"The Origin of the Proverb" (*Harvard Studies and Notes in
Philology and Literature*, 1931), is a good example.

If there is a tendency toward fragmentation in some of these
investigations, it is salutary to read F. P. Magoun, Jr., "A Note on
Old West Germanic Poetic Unity" (*MP*, 1945). Much praise is due
C. L. Wrenn, "On the Continuity of English Poetry" (*Anglia*,
1958), and R. W. Chambers, *On the Continuity of English Prose
from Alfred to More and His School* (1932; rptd. 1957), for their
insistence on the fact that English poetry and prose of the Anglo-
Saxon period are neither decadent nor primitive, but are essential
parts of an organic whole. The best effort to date to synthesize this
literature with other medieval literatures is W. T. H. Jackson, *The
Literature of the Middle Ages* (1960), although, because of its
scope, English gets rather short shrift.

The attempts to establish the chronology of Old English
literature, as the nineteenth-century German scholars often tried to

do, have not met with much success, although individual works have sometimes been dated satisfactorily. The fallacies inherent in the old-fashioned tests, such as the irregular use of the weak adjective and the appearance of weakened inflectional endings, are pointed out by A. Ricci in "The Chronology of Anglo-Saxon Poetry" (*RES*, 1929). Even Dorothy Whitelock, in *Anglo-Saxon Poetry and the Historian* (*Transactions of the Royal Historical Society*, 1949), admits that chronological criteria are doubtful and concludes rather lamely that *Beowulf* and the Caedmonian poems probably came before Cynewulf. We had heard that before 1925.

It would appear that scholarship has now decided to turn its efforts to more demonstrable matters—for instance, to the relation of the literature to the Continent, as in C. Albertson, "Anglo-Saxon Literature and Western Culture" (*Thought*, 1958), or the development of Germanic strains in England itself. C. E. Wright, *The Cultivation of Saga in Anglo-Saxon England* (1939), maintains that the Danes of the Danelagh circulated sagas for centuries in oral tradition and that these sagas were the English counterpart of the French *chansons de geste*. The perennial question of the blending of heathen and Christian in the literature, which we see being worried and harried in many studies of individual pieces, has been recognized by all students of Old English literature from the beginning. A heightened interest in it, however, is evident from about the time of B. J. Timmer, "Heathen and Christian Elements in Old English Poetry" (*Neophil*, 1944), which, if not the trigger to set off the present vogue, was at least symptomatic. There has been an undoubted renewal of interest in Latin sources, analogues, and general influence—for example, E. B. Irving, Jr., "Latin Prose Sources for Old English Verse" (*JEGP*, 1957). B. F. Huppé, *Doctrine and Poetry: Augustine's Influence on Old English Poetry* (1959), suggests that we should study Old English poetry with an eye always on the Christian Latin tradition of Biblical exegesis and commentary, particularly Augustine's. For the study of the indigenous sources of the literature there is the impressive work of H. M. and Nora K. Chadwick, *The Growth of Literature* (3 vols., 1932–40).

F. Klaeber in the introduction to his first edition of *Beowulf* (1922) gives more than two pages of fine print to the conventional nature of the style of West Germanic poetry in general and of *Beowulf* in particular, speaking of "a large stock of formulas, set combinations of words, phrases of transition, and similar stereotyped elements" as if they were to be taken for granted. And so they were for thirty years and more. Then F. P. Magoun, Jr., "Oral-

Formulaic Character of Anglo-Saxon Narrative Poetry" (*Speculum*, 1953), stimulated new discussion by envisaging a large storehouse of poetic formulas from which the *scop* drew for his oral composition. A good application of this theory to a short passage from *Beowulf* is made by R. P. Creed, "The Making of an Anglo-Saxon Poem" (*ELH*, 1959), in which he demonstrates how, out of a large number of possible choices of formulaic expression, the Beowulf poet selected what Creed thinks to be the most poetically satisfactory. Other scholars, however, have reservations about accepting Magoun's theory whole. C. Schaar, "On a New Theory of Old English Poetic Diction" (*Neophil*, 1956), would certainly not wish to restrict the use of formulas to oral composition alone, but would extend them to written composition also. A. Bonjour, "Poésie héroique du moyen âge et critique littéraire" (*Romania*, 1957), while not rejecting Magoun's theory, is nevertheless convinced that *Beowulf* and the Caedmonian poems were not composed orally. A. Brodeur, *The Art of Beowulf* (1959), to be mentioned again, observes that the style of *Beowulf* does not indicate a hardening into mere formula coming from the days of oral tradition. And S. B. Greenfield, "The Formulaic Expression of the Theme of 'Exile' in Anglo-Saxon Poetry" (*Speculum*, 1955), pointing out various common formulas to describe an exile, tries to draw the line between the formula and the original use of the formula.

Some of the critics of the oral-formulaic theory have not noticed that Magoun's article confined itself to Anglo-Saxon narrative poetry and avoided consideration of the elegiac or lyric except insofar as narrative elements may be present. Others have seen the formulaic theory as forcing the Anglo-Saxon poet into a state half-original and half-unoriginal at best, or wholly unoriginal at worst. If this be accepted, then we have only further confirmation of the old judgment, variously stated, that the Anglo-Saxon poetic style was as rigid and exacting as that of any major period of English poetry, not excluding the well-known requirements of the neoclassical age. How far the oral-formulaic theory can be carried—whether, for example, it is applicable to Norse poetry—remains to be seen.

If we postpone for a moment consideration of the individual poems, then the discussion of particular themes, motifs, moods, and doctrines in Anglo-Saxon poetry becomes most important. Here it is convenient to refer to a few subheads. We may begin by returning for a moment to the treatment of Wyrd. Bertha S. Philpotts, "Wyrd and Providence in Anglo-Saxon Thought" (*E&S*, 1928), has great value. A later important treatment is by B. J. Timmer, "Wyrd in Anglo-Saxon Prose and Poetry" (*Neophil*, 1940, 1941), in which, through a close semantic analysis of the word *wyrd,* it is made clear that the pagan conception of fate is modified after the Christianization of the Anglo-Saxons into something close to "divine decree," and so the word continued to be used in an altered sense. This modification, which Dame Bertha had recognized and attributed to a compromise not unlike the Victorian compromise, Timmer refers to as a tension between pagan and Christian. This tension would then underlie the whole elegiac tradition in Anglo-Saxon literature. The ensuing conflict Timmer treats in "The Elegiac Mood in Old English Poetry" (*ES*, 1942). Scholars cannot accept the theory that this mood is primarily Germanic or Celtic, pagan or Christian, or anything else; it results, rather, from the collision of several of these elements. Two other studies of the topic call for attention. H. Galinsky, "Sprachlicher Ausdruck und Künstlerische Gestalt germanischer Schicksalsauffassung in der angelsächsischen Dichtung" (*Englische Studien*, 1941), is a tantalizing performance. It has a strong bias in favor of the heathen concept of fate and is therefore anti-Christian, but it is forcefully expressed and is something of a rarity in these days of Christian interpretation. R. E. Woolf, "The Devil in Old English Poetry" (*RES*, 1953), is a thoughtful study that makes Satan analogous to the wicked counselors of Norse myth, Bikki and Loki, and therefore even more credible as an agent of Wyrd, when Wyrd is adverse.

One customarily thinks of the treatment of nature in Old English literature as rather perfunctory, nature serving only as background for action. The more important studies of this topic, however, do not support this view. The most considerable is E. Pons, *Le thème et le sentiment de la nature dans la poésie anglo-saxonne* (1925), which places Anglo-Saxon nature poetry in the tradition of later English nature poetry. Pons particularly admires its "sens religieux de la beauté des grands spectacles," its realism of detail, and its range. Another attractive study is N. E. Enkvist, *The Seasons of the Year* (1957), which traces descriptions of the seasons from *Beowulf* to *The Shepheardes Calendar*, showing how the pagan emphasized winter and the Christian spring. Finally, one should make note of Susie L. Tucker, "The Anglo-Saxon Poet Considers the Heavens" (*Neophil,* 1957), for it takes into account various astronomical allusions, noting especially the sun and moon and the fact that the Christian poet took his New Jerusalem literally and excluded these heavenly bodies from any consideration of the Holy City.

Against this backdrop of nature the Anglo-Saxon poet placed the epic and heroic tradition on the one hand and the lyric and

One aspect of Old English poetry, the kenning, has not been treated too well. H. van der Merwe Scholtz, *The Kenning in Anglo-Saxon and Old Norse Poetry* (1927), attacks the nineteenth-century theories of the kenning and lists various types of figurative phrase, some of which he calls kennings and some not. For that matter, he does not really define a kenning at all. Unsatisfactory as this may be, the study has remained for a long time a most comprehensive consideration of the Anglo-Saxon kenning. But it is possible to derive a more thorough understanding of the device through D. C. Collins, "The Kenning in Anglo-Saxon Poetry" (*E&S*, 1959), and the appropriate pages in A. G. Brodeur, *The Art of Beowulf* (1959), are just about as important.

The studies of Anglo-Saxon metrics and prosody may have been rather few in number since 1925, but these have all been important and have provoked controversy. The center of such controversy, in the main, has been how far one should either accept or reject the theories of E. Sievers, first broached in 1885 and brought to full statement in his *Altgermanische Metrik* (1893). A good outline of these theories is found in J. R. Hulbert's revised and enlarged edition of J. W. Bright's *An Anglo-Saxon Reader* (1935). Symptoms of discontent with Sievers' system are well exemplified in S. O. Andrew, *The Old English Alliterative Measure* (1931), in which it is pointed out that a thousand lines of *Beowulf* are scanned wrong according to Sievers' own theory. The question is, of course, what is meant by *wrong?*

The controversy has resulted in a swing around a circle: the latest study suggests a return to most of the patterns as Sievers originally proposed them; indeed, it comes close to an outright application of the whole system. But in the meantime, W. E. Leonard opposed Sievers as early as 1918. Although he later modified his views somewhat, he tended to approve those of A. Heusler, whose *Deutsche Versgeschichte* (3 vols., 1925–29) was published as Vol. VIII of H. Paul's *Grundriss der germanischen Philologie.* Heusler set up the rhythmical basis on a musical analogy: thus each hemistich, the unit of the verse, contains two measures in 4/4 time, with ample allowance for rests or the prolongation of preceding syllables. Each verse must therefore be regarded as an independent rhythmic unit, which can often be separated from those preceding or following by an indefinite interval, an interval that may or may not be filled up with sound. Heusler's study is followed by that of J. C. Pope, *The Rhythm of Beowulf* (1942). Pope is particularly opposed to the B and C types of Sievers, which begin with an unaccented syllable. "As soon as we postulate a musical accompaniment, that of the harp, the peculiar position of the rests is explained." In other words, the harp has now been brought into the picture as it had not been before. Heusler and Pope differ basically only in details; Pope, for example, prefers a 4/8 measure. The theories of these two have achieved wide acceptance. But A. J. Bliss, *The Metre of Beowulf* (1958), rejects what may be called the chronometric basis and insists that the verse rests in greater probability upon ordinary prose rhythms. He sees a trochaic predominance, with the possibility of shifting stresses forward or backward to a limited degree. From such shifting only five patterns are possible, and the combination adds up to Sievers' old five types.

The identification of metrical patterns with prose rhythms had been already discussed by Marjorie Daunt, "Old English Verse and English Speech Rhythms" (*TPS*, 1946). Miss Daunt suggests that all verse is a kind of conditioned prose, and so it is with the Anglo-Saxon. She does not quarrel seriously with Sievers, but insists that his five types should be called "language patterns" instead of "metrical patterns." It seems unnecessary to say more about the remaining occasional publications on this topic except to observe that W. P. Lehmann, *The Development of Germanic Verse-Form* (1956), is probably the best comparative study.

V. TEXTS

F IRST TO BE considered, before dealing with the studies of individual works in Anglo-Saxon literature, are the general collected editions of the four great codices of poetry. Here the invaluable work is *The Anglo-Saxon Poetic Records* (1931–53), begun under the editorship of G. P. Krapp and continued after his death by his collaborator E. V. K. Dobbie. The six volumes comprise: I. *The Junius Manuscript* (1931); II. *The Vercelli Book* (1932); III. *The Exeter Book* (1936); IV. *Beowulf and Judith* (1953); V. *The Paris Psalter and the Meters of Boethius* (1932); and VI. *The Anglo-Saxon Minor Poems* (1942). As a supplementary volume we must note also Dobbie's *The Manuscripts of 'Caedmon's Hymn' and Bede's 'Death-Song,' with a Critical Text of the 'Epistola Cuthberti de Obitu Bedae'*

(1937). As for the six volumes themselves, it is hard to see how the texts could be better; the bibliography is also excellent though not complete. It is primarily an edition for experts and a definitive text. *The Exeter Book*, edited from the manuscript with a translation, appeared in part 1 as early as 1895 under the supervision of I. Gollancz; part 2, containing poems IX to XXXII, was edited by W. S. Mackie (1934). The two volumes are CIV and CXCIV of EETS.

Moreover, there have also been some good facsimile reproductions of various pieces. The most important single project in this area is the series of annual productions known as *Early English Manuscripts in Facsimile*, under the general editorship of B. Colgrave. The series was inaugurated in 1951 with K. Malone, *The Thorkelin Transcripts of Beowulf*, and then followed O. Arngart, *The Leningrad Bede* (1952); A. Campbell, *The Tollemache Orosius* (1953); Dorothy Whitelock, *The Peterborough Chronicle* (1954); C. E. Wright, *Bald's Leechbook* (1955); N. Ker, *The Pastoral Care: King Alfred's Translation of St. Gregory's 'Regula Pastoralis'* (1956); P. Sawyer, *Textus Roffensis* (2 vols., 1957–62); various editors, *The Paris Psalter* (1958); P. H. Blair, *The Moore Bede: Cambridge University Ms. Kk. 5.16* (1959); R. Willard, *The Blickling Homilies* (1960); and K. Malone, *The Nowell Codex* (1963). These are all beautiful reproductions. Another fine recent facsimile is the new version of J. Zupitza's *Beowulf* (EETS, 1959). In the introduction by the editor, N. Davis, there is an account of the part that modern photography can play in the preparation of a facsimile text. Two other fine facsimile editions of earlier vintage are I. Gollancz, *The Caedmon Manuscript of Anglo-Saxon Biblical Poetry* (1927), and R. W. Chambers, M. Förster, and R. Flower, *The Exeter Book of Old English Poetry* (1933).

Separate editions of individual works will of course be mentioned in discussion of the appropriate work, but this is the place to call attention to a distinguished series published in London under the name of the Methuen Old English Library. The series began in the 1930s but was interrupted by the Second World War; and although it resumed publication, the flow has not been so steady since 1945. It happens, however, that each of these texts is virtually definitive. To be sure, the editors vary considerably in ability and achievement, but this is to be expected in any joint scholarly enterprise. The series began with three publications in 1933: A. H. Smith, *Three Northumbrian Poems: Caedmon's Hymn, Bede's Death-Song, The Leiden Riddle*; K. Malone, *Deor*; and F. Norman, *Waldere*. Until the outbreak of World War II there was an almost annual publication. Thus B. Dickins and A. S. C. Ross, *The Dream of the Rood* (1934);

A. H. Smith, *The Parker Chronicle, 832–900* (1935); K. Malone, *Widsith* (1936); E. V. Gordon, *The Battle of Maldon* (1937); Dorothy Whitelock, *Sermo Lupi ad Anglos* (1939); and G. M. Garmonsway, *Aelfric's Colloquy* (1939). Since World War II there have been only B. J. Timmer, *Judith* (1952); Rosemary Woolf, *Juliana* (1955); Pamela O. E. Gradon, *Cynewulf's 'Elene'* (1958); and Ida L. Gordon, *The Seafarer* (1960).

VI. HEROIC POETRY

THERE HAS BEEN far more interest shown in Old English poetry than in Old English prose works. This may be simply because the poetry requires more explanations and general interpretations. The important general studies of the poems in the heroic epic tradition have already been noted. We are now concerned only with the studies of *Widsith, The Fight at Finnsburg, Waldere,* and *Beowulf,* with some attention to *The Battle of Brunanburh* and *The Battle of Maldon.*

Widsith has been associated since 1925 largely with the name of K. Malone. His edition of the poem in the Methuen Library of Old English (1936) is the definitive edition and is by and large the best work done by this scholar. He published many articles on *Widsith* before and after the publication of the text, but it is not necessary to list them here, except to refer to "*Widsith:* Addenda and Corrigenda" (*MLR,* 1936). At the same time, an important interpretation of the Widsith poet's motive is put forward in W. H. French, "*Widsith* and the Scop" (*PMLA,* 1945), which concludes that "the writer was a *scop;* his learning was merely professional; his object in displaying it was not to teach or to construct a rhapsody on heroic themes. Far from being in retirement, he was striving to remain in active service; his ultimate aim in composing the poem or in reciting it subsequently was to interest a patron in supporting him."

There have been stirrings about the genesis of the Legend of Walter. The studies of this lineage may be traced from L. L. Schücking, "Waldere und Waltharius" (*Englische Studien,* 1925), to the valuable monograph by F. P. Magoun, Jr., and H. M. Smyser, *Walter of Aquitaine: Materials for the Study of His Legend*

(1950), to B. H. Carroll, Jr., "An Essay on the Walther Legend" (*FSUS*, 1953), and the same author's "On the Lineage of the Walther Legend" (*GR*, 1953). These last studies seem to agree with the earlier theory that the Anglo-Saxons derived their fragments from some Old High German source, although the date of the fragments (near 1000) and the speakers involved in them remain highly speculative. As for *The Fight at Finnsburg*, little has been done that considers the fragment by itself and not in conjunction with the Finnsburg Episode in *Beowulf;* and even this slender output has dealt primarily with textual problems, proposed emendations of the proper names, or attempts to identify the warriors in the drama. There has been no separate edition since that by Mackie in *JEGP* (1917). The fullest discussion is R. Girvan, "Finnsburuh" (*PBA*, 1941).

There has been no lack of good texts of *Beowulf*, but in spite of a critical attitude that at times seems very conservative today, F. Klaeber, *Beowulf and The Fight at Finnsburg* (1922; 3rd ed. 1936; supplements 1941, 1950), with its magnificent apparatus, still comes off best. The older edition by W. J. Sedgefield was revised in 1935. M. Heyne and L. L. Schücking, *Beowulf*, also had a new edition (3 vols., 1947–49). The two most recent, both admirable, are F. Genzmer, *Beowulf und das Finnsburg-Bruchstück* (1953), and C. L. Wrenn, *Beowulf, with the Finnsburg Fragment* (1953, rev. and enlarged ed. 1958). Three general studies of the poem in works of book length stand out head and shoulders above the others. W. W. Lawrence, *Beowulf and the Epic Tradition* (1928), still serves as the best introduction to the work as a whole, explaining particularly well how in the action of the poem, the historical, political, and social backgrounds are worked into the structure. R. W. Chambers, *Beowulf* (1932; 3rd ed. 1959), remains an impressive requirement for any advanced study of the poem. Its most recent edition (by C. L. Wrenn) contains also a valuable chapter on the excavations at Sutton Hoo. The latest study, by A. G. Brodeur, *The Art of Beowulf* (1959), sums up admirably most of our knowledge of the style, structure, and blending of Christian and pagan elements.

Although the attempts to fit *Beowulf* into a particular historical milieu have not been successful, they are interesting and provocative. Among the more important of these is R. Girvan, *Beowulf and the Seventh Century* (1935), for although there is little likelihood that *Beowulf* could have been composed quite that early, there still is food for thought in the apparent accuracy of the historical backgrounds portrayed in the poem and in certain linguistic phenomena. By and large Girvan's findings are unconvincing even if they stimulate speculation. Further development of his ideas might produce something more solid. Much more specific is the attempt by G. Bond, "Links between *Beowulf* and Mercian History" (*SP*, 1943), to associate Beowulf with Beornwulf of Mercia and Wiglaf with Beornwulf's successor, Wiglaf. But this sets a *terminus a quo* for the poem as late as 838. Actually, little has been done to shake the traditional 725–750 date for *Beowulf*, although Dorothy White-lock, in *The Audience of Beowulf* (1951), is not averse to a date as late as 800.

The epic qualities of the hero Beowulf have been subjected to a good deal of scrutiny. K. Malone more than once, but especially in "The Old English Period" (*Literary History of England*, 1948), tends to emphasize the general Germanic ideal, which he sees not only in Beowulf but in some of the other heroes appearing in the poem. E. Wadstein, viewing the question more narrowly in "The Beowulf Poem as an English National Epos" (*APS*, 1933), considers the Beowulf poet to be ignorant of Norse geography; thus *Beowulf*, composed by an Englishman for Englishmen, is actually more English than not. All of the scholars agree on the importance of Beowulf as a heroic ideal. In fact, L. L. Schücking, "Das Königs-ideal im Beowulf" (*Englische Studien*, 1932), suggests that the poem is a kind of handbook for princes. The moot point whether Beowulf is to be a Christlike hero or only a courtly one troubles critics, most of whom tend at present to shy away from Schücking's still tenable theory. K. Brunner, "Why was *Beowulf* Preserved?" (*EA*, 1954), believes that the poetry in Cotton Vitellius A.xv was retained because it presented a hero (Beowulf) and a heroine (Judith) who were both symbolic of Christian virtues and at the same time "historical." The latter epithet is certainly debatable. B. J. Timmer, "*Beowulf*: The Poem and the Poet" (*Neophil*, 1948), is not satisfied that the poem is a *speculum principum;* nor is he persuaded that it is a pure epic, but rather a mixture of epic, homily, chronicle, lyric— obviously composed in a period of transition between the old heroic poetry and the monastic literature, and therefore not much after 700. A general outline of these problems is afforded in the brief but sharp commentary by A. Bonjour, "*Beowulf* et l'épopée anglo-saxonne" (*TR*, 1958). For the rest, Beowulf, when viewed against the background of the epic tradition described by Chadwick, Bowra, Raglan, and Routh in their above-mentioned studies, certainly possesses all the accepted qualities of an epic hero. Lawrence brought this into focus in 1928, so that there is little excuse for the scanty and belittling treatment *Beowulf* receives in E. M. W. Tillyard, *The English Epic and Its Backgrounds* (1954).

The source of *Beowulf* is still subject to inquiry. In two salient studies by J. R. Hulbert, "The Genesis of *Beowulf: A Caveat*" (*PMLA*, 1951) and "Surmises Concerning the 'Beowulf' Poet's Source" (*JEGP*, 1951), the issues are made clear. In the first, Hulbert summarizes the various theories and warns all concerned that it still has not been proved that the Beowulf Poet was a Christian of the eighth century. In the second, he argues for Scandinavian origins of a story, perhaps a composite of older lays, which were not particularly well known, since Beowulf is not known outside the poem to which his name has been given. In a few instances studies have been made of parallels between *Beowulf* and other Old English works. L. J. Peters, "The Relationship of the Old English *Andreas* to *Beowulf*" (*PMLA*, 1951), is skeptical of any influence of *Beowulf* on the Christian epic, and this doubt seems particularly justified if we give any credence to the oral-formulaic theory of poetic composition. However, C. Brown, "*Beowulf* and the *Blickling Homilies* and Some Textual Notes" (*PMLA*, 1938), thinks there is evidence that the author of the *Homilies* knew *Beowulf*, and of course there is no good way to prove that he did not. Conversely, as we shall see, the influence of homiletic and exegetic writings upon all Anglo-Saxon literature is probably stronger than was supposed in the 1930s. The same comments may be made about C. O. Chapman, "*Beowulf* and *Apollonius of Tyre*" (*MLN*, 1931), where enough parallels are found between the two works to suggest that the Beowulf poet might have known the Latin text of the *Apollonius*.

Preceding Brodeur's *Art of Beowulf* are many valuable studies, among them his own "Design for Terror in the Purging of Heorot" (*JEGP*, 1954). G. J. Engelhardt, "*Beowulf*: A Study in Dilatation" (*PMLA*, 1955), examines the methods by which the Beowulf poet expanded simple epic material into epic dimensions, presumably on the models of classical rhetoric. A. Bonjour, "The Use of Anticipation in *Beowulf*" (*RES*, 1940), has made a brilliant justification of the "forward pointings." Another device has been explored by Bonjour in "The Technique of Parallel Descriptions in *Beowulf*" (*RES*, 1951), especially to show how the repetition of a particular incident helps in the characterization of Beowulf himself. Devices of characterization are discussed by H. B. Woolf in two studies, "On the Characterization of *Beowulf*" (*ELH*, 1948) and "Unferth" (*MLQ*, 1949), in the latter of which he maintains that the Unferth episode, damaging to the dignity of the rest of the poem, nevertheless enhances Beowulf's courage and nobility of character. According to C. C. Batchelor, "The Style of the *Beowulf*" (*Speculum*, 1937), the Beowulf poet is much more wordy in the first part than in the second; and if we assume that one poet wrote the whole poem, then he learned how to write as he went along. A study by J. A. Nist, "The Structure of *Beowulf*" (*PMASAL*, 1958), elaborated in *The Structure and Texture of Beowulf* (1959), shows that the repetitions in the poem make the structure cyclic rather than linear and should be judged accordingly.

The studies discussing the unity of the poem make a striking group. There is, for example, the allegorical interpretation in A. E. DuBois, "The Unity of *Beowulf*" (*PMLA*, 1934), which sees the basic unity in "an elaborate symphony of variations." Creatures like Grendel and his dam are punishing the Danes for their moral crimes; the firedrake represents the Geats' internal quarrels, controlled by Wyrd, or God. Much more important is the vigorous essay by J. R. R. Tolkien, *Beowulf: The Monsters and the Critics* (1937; rptd. 1959), originally a Gollancz Memorial Lecture, which accuses previous writers about *Beowulf* of placing the unimportant things in the center and the important things at the edges. *Beowulf* is to Tolkien a poem, not a historical document. The hero is a man, in itself tragedy enough, more than a mere hero. Grendel and the dragon are foes of God, adversaries of the soul. These facts are central, not the wars of the Swedes and the Geats. This essay is vital, readable, and sensible; it has had its detractors, but few can deny that Beowulf the hero and man is himself the unifying principle. A. Bonjour, "Monsters Crouching and Critics Rampant: Or the Beowulf Dragon Debated" (*PMLA*, 1953), is a brilliant defense. In Tolkien's view, the unity is symbolic in the contrast between the first part, which celebrates Beowulf's youth and strength, and the second part, which portrays his old age and defeat. Others have seen the unity as lying in the style itself: the very repetition and accretion of "synonyms" build up to a cumulative creation with ultimate coherence and significance. This view is well expressed in Joan Blomfield, "The Style and Structure of *Beowulf*" (*RES*, 1938). K. Malone, "Beowulf" (*ES*, 1948), sees a unity in the spiritual quality of the hero, which is all very well, and also in the love of Germania, which may not be all very well. It is doubtful how much love of race one would find in Anglo-Saxon England of the eighth century, when men of your own race might be your enemies and even a national consciousness was pretty dim. Rather paradoxically, A. Bonjour, *The Digressions in 'Beowulf'* (1950), argues that the unity lies in the very fact that the digressions assist in the creation of a living background: "behind all the episodes is found a definite design, clear enough to allow us to say that each one plays a useful part in the composition of the poem." While not so cogent in the effect of his argument, J. L. N. O'Loughlin, *"Beowulf*—Its Unity and Purpose" (*MAE*, 1952), finds an integrating plan in the ambivalence of the evil of Grendel, who rejects the Germanic system of feud settlement and at the same time is unable to live according to Christian law. Thus the poem represents a balance between the pagan and the Christian triumphs over evil.

The importance of parallelism looms large in much of the more recent criticism of *Beowulf*. This point is made particularly well in A. Bonjour, *"Beowulf* and the Snares of Literary Criticism" (*EA*, 1957), where he puts on armor again in defense of Tolkien, in sincere vindication of the criterion of such parallelism as a valid indication of artistry. But by inference, for he does not admit it, he shows also the fallacy of oversubjective and overenthusiastic criticism. To continue along this road a bit farther: H. G. Wright, "Good and Evil; Light and Darkness; Joy and Sorrow in *Beowulf"* (*RES*, 1957), by emphasizing these antitheses, discovers an interrelated kind of unity; P. F. Fisher, "The Trials of the Epic Hero in *Beowulf"* (*PMLA*, 1958), tends to echo O'Loughlin's conclusions that the blend of heathen Germanic and Christian concepts are sufficient to establish the integrated structure of the poem. R. E. Kaske, *"Sapientia et Fortitudo* as the Controlling Theme of *Beowulf"* (*SP*, 1958), takes these two knightly qualities of the courtly tradition and concludes that the mixture of the Germanic warrior-hero and the Christian saint tends to produce a satisfactory unity of intent.

A few scholars have dissented from the idea that *Beowulf* is without flaw. T. M. Gang, "Approaches to *Beowulf"* (*RES*, 1952), frankly considers some of the attempts to find unity in the poem either sophistical or wishful. "Unless we start with a preconceived idea we may feel that we cannot contact the mind behind the poetry, and this is the prime difficulty of any literary criticism of Old English poetry, and a good reason why it should be as rare as it is." Gang has been attacked by several scholars, but he has his allies. J. C. van Meurs, *"Beowulf* and Literary Criticism" (*Neophil*, 1955), believes that present-day criticism does not take sufficient account of historical evidence and charges that critics see only what they want to see. Although opposed by A. Bonjour in *"Beowulf* and the Snares of Literary Criticism," Van Meurs has written a valuable corrective that has been badly needed in recent years. Again, H. L. Rogers, "Beowulf's Three Great Fights" (*RES*, 1955), points out that the poem's unity suffers from the fact that only in the fight with Grendel does it succeed in establishing a moral idea compatible with its source.

Some scholars have found an interest in the question of the influence of classical literature on *Beowulf*. One of the most searching of these studies in our period, I. Schröbler, *"Beowulf* und Homer" (*BGDSL*, 1939), is an admirable summation of that problem. Admitting the parallels, which are bound to take place in ethopoeia, Schröbler considers four possibilities: (1) the Beowulf poet knew Homeric poems; (2) there was a "vermittelndes Zwischenglied," or several; (3) the Germanic epic tradition was influenced by the Greek *in nascendi;* and (4) there was simply a coincidental parallel development. For (1) we should have to go back to Theodore of Tarsus and Abbot Hadrian in the seventh century; after a long and fruitful discussion, Schröbler decides that this is most improbable though not impossible. Similarly, (2) and (3) are difficult to establish. The fourth, an independent tradition developing out of similar cultural stages, seems the most likely. With Virgil the problem is less complicated. T. B. Haber, *A Comparative Study of the Beowulf and the Aeneid* (1931), agrees with Klaeber that the Beowulf poet was at least acquainted with Virgil. He is ably supported by A. Brandl, "Beowulf-Epos und Aeneis in systematischer Vergleichung" (*Archiv*, 1937), but Brandl's view that *Beowulf* is partly a political allegory of Northumbrians and Mercians and that Hrothgar's homily is directed against either King Edwin of Northumbria or King Penda of Mercia is certainly erroneous.

The tendency toward the Christian interpretation of *Beowulf* is unremitting. D. Fanger, "Three Aspects of Beowulf and His God" (*NM*, 1958), does not consider the deity in *Beowulf* to be either definitely Christian or definitely pagan, but simply the ruling force. M. B. McNamee, *"Beowulf*—An Allegory of Salvation?" (*JEGP*, 1960), having proposed the question in the title, answers rather obviously in the affirmative. D. W. Robertson, Jr., "The Doctrine of Charity in Medieval Literary Gardens: A Topical Approach Through Symbolism and Allegory" (*Speculum*, 1951), sees in Grendel's mere the scriptural garden of evil. Here the hart would rather give up his life on the shore than "hide his head in the grove surrounding the pool; this signifies the faithful Christian who seeks his Lord in the Living Waters." Since the only waters in question are those of the forbidding pool, and the hart chooses to give up his life elsewhere, such an interpretation seems not only to be far-fetched but also to do violence to the text.

That the Beowulf poet knew contemporary Latin Christian poetry is most likely, as M. Bloomfield indicates in *"Beowulf* and Christian Allegory, An Interpretation" (*Traditio*, 1951). He probably drew concepts from it, as in the case of Unferth. But again, the

net impression left by many of these strongly pro-Christian interpretations is that the scholar sees what he wants to see. Thus A.
Cabanis, *"Beowulf* and the Liturgy" (*JEGP*, 1955), sees a strong
basic resemblance between the fight with Grendel's mother and the
Harrowing of Hell; and the central part of the poem appears to be
loaded with a "complex of ideas" that assume familiarity with the
baptismal liturgy. Less freakish is the point of view in Marie P.
Hamilton, "The Religious Principle in *Beowulf*" (*PMLA*, 1946),
which calls attention to the fact that analysts of the poem interested
in the Christian elements have often overlooked the importance of the
doctrines of election and grace. A good example of this nebulous
kind of criticism is Margaret E. Goldsmith, "The Christian Theme
of *Beowulf*" (*MAE*, 1960).

The Christian interpretation of *Beowulf* has tended to defeat
the older regard for folk origins of the poem. The leading spokesman
for the heathens has been G. Hübener. Hübener's best exposition
comes in *"Beowulf* and Germanic Exorcism" (*RES*, 1935), a
restatement of earlier articles arguing that the fight with Grendel
represents the expulsion of "obsessions." Back of obsession is fear.
The building of Heorot is a source of worry or fear of misfortune.
Still another folkloristic interpretation is that of S. J. Herben,
"Beowulf, Hrothgar, and Grendel" (*Archiv*, 1938), which begins by
pointing out certain inconsistencies—the dubious sex of Grendel's
dam, the rugged scenery of Grendel's mere compared to the flat
landscape of the Danish peninsula. Grendel is, then, "a powerful,
jealous, and enraged priestcraft resident in the immediate vicinity of
Heorot, worshippers of Nerthus, a bisexual deity mentioned by
Tacitus . . . There is something bogus about Beowulf; his name is
certainly a disguise." That is to say, Beowulf equals Bee-Wolf
equals Bear equals a Christian equals a highly synthetic hero. All in
all, Herben's is a challenging study and one that seems to have been
most undeservedly forgotten among *Beowulf* scholars. The complaint against a completely Christian interpretation, however, need
not swing to such an extreme. A. Pirkhofer, *Figurengestaltung im
Beowulf-Epos* (1940), concentrates on Wiglaf (the young warrior),
Hrothgar (the old and wise ruler and counselor), and Beowulf (who
in his younger and older aspects exemplifies both), and stresses the
fact that Beowulf is courtly or knightly rather than Christian. For
if Beowulf is a Christ figure, how can Hrothgar dare to warn him
against pride? G. Storms, "The Figure of Beowulf in the Old
English Epic" (*ES*, 1959), argues that we see too much of the
legendary in Beowulf and too little of the historical for us to
consider him as having a historical prototype. The inference is that

if he is the product of legendry, almost any interpretation is acceptable as long as it binds him to the heroic and mythological tradition that created him.

Finally, we may note four important discussions of those who were to listen to *Beowulf*, or read it, as the case might be. The most striking of the four is Dorothy Whitelock, *The Audience of Beowulf* (1951). The author takes the position that the poem was meant for Christian laymen who would probably have knowledge of events and persons of Christian importance. The poem must therefore have been written some time after the conversion of Anglo-Saxon England, perhaps as late as 800. A knowledge of the story on the part of the audience is stressed by K. Sisam, "Beowulf's Fight with the Dragon" (*RES*, 1958), which emphasizes the love of the audience for the battle narrative, and by R. M. Lumiansky, "The Dramatic Audience in *Beowulf*" (*JEGP*, 1952), which finds another audience—that within the poem itself, the "functional onlookers," such as the Danes and Geats waiting in suspense beside Grendel's mere, or the Geats standing by until they hear the issue of battle with the firedrake. The inference here is that those listening to the poem or reading it might identify themselves with the "inner" audience. Although these three scholars suggest a courtly audience, at most a mixture of secular and clerical, R. Girvan, "The Medieval Poet and His Audience" (*English Studies Today*, ed. C. L. Wrenn, 1951), assumes that the poem was intended for the edification and entertainment of clerics alone.

The two famous late specimens of Anglo-Saxon epic poetry, *The Battle of Brunanburh* and *The Battle of Maldon*, have drawn little critical attention, although there have been good editions of each. The text of *Brunanburh* is that edited by A. Campbell in the Methuen Library (1938). Most of the research on the poem has gone into the identification of the battlefield; the results have been most inconclusive. Thus W. E. Varah, "The Battlefield of Brunan-burh" (*N&Q*, 1937), would place it near Burnham Hill, Lincolnshire; on the other hand, A. H. Smith, "The Site of the Battle of Brunan-burh" (*London Mediaeval Studies*, 1937), would place it at Brombor-ough in the Wirral. Since these two locations are almost on a line due east and west of each other on opposite sides of England, the divergence is symbolic. In the absence of more definite evidence no satisfactory site has as yet been determined. Of more immediate value is such a study as J. McN. Dodgson, "The Background of Brunanburh" (*Saga-Book*, 1956–57). *The Battle of Maldon* has been edited by E. D. Laborde, *Byrhtnoth and Maldon* (1936), but the Methuen Library edition by E. V. Gordon, *The Battle of Maldon* (1937), is better, especially in the revised version (1957).

VII. CAEDMONIAN AND CYNEWULFIAN POETRY

THE CAEDMONIAN POEMS have had the benefit of a few good editions of individual poems. It is not necessary to repeat mention of the facsimile editions or the Anglo-Saxon Poetic Records text. Two outstanding studies, with text, of *Genesis B* are F. Klaeber, *The Later Genesis and Other Old English and Old Saxon Texts Relating to the Fall of Man* (1913; rev. ed. 1931), and B. J. Timmer, *The Later Genesis* (1948; rev. ed. 1954). M. D. Clubb edited *Christ and Satan* (1925), and E. B. Irving, Jr., *The Old English 'Exodus'* (1953). *Caedmon's Hymn* has received special attention: its text and dialect have been closely studied by M. G. Frampton (*MP*, 1924) and it is edited as one of the poems in A. H. Smith, *Three Northumbrian Poems* (1933). The definitive text, however, is that in E. V. K. Dobbie, *The Manuscripts of Caedmon's Hymn and Bede's Death-Song* (1937). The story of the legend of Caedmon is discussed most effectively in F. P. Magoun, Jr., "Bede's Story of Caedmon: The Case-History of an Anglo-Saxon Singer" (*Speculum*, 1955). The most perceptive single study of Caedmon is C. L. Wrenn, *The Poetry of Caedmon* (1948), which is a review of Caedmonian scholarship and a discussion of the only poem generally accepted as being by Caedmon—"Caedmon's Hymn." The miracle of Caedmon's legend seems to be that he learned overnight the complex and rigid art of the Anglo-Saxon poet. One other study should be noted: J. W. Lever, "*Paradise Lost* and the Anglo-Saxon Tradition" (*RES*, 1947), which tends to confirm that Milton and Junius were close acquaintances and must have discussed Anglo-Saxon literature, and that there is in consequence an "overwhelming probability" that Milton knew and was influenced by the Caedmonian *Genesis*, presumably mostly by *Genesis B*.

The Cynewulfian poems likewise have had their students, although perhaps not so many as might be expected, considering their worth as poetry. The most notable introduction is K. Sisam, "Cynewulf and His Poetry" (*PBA*, 1933), reprinted in his *Studies in the History of Old English Literature* (1953). To Sisam, Cynewulf is an Anglian poet, later than Caedmon and the Beowulf poet, therefore in the later ninth century, as other scholars have believed. He ascribes to the poet only *Juliana, Elene*, the *Ascension (Christ II)*, and *The Fates of the Apostles*—in short, the signed poems—and gives almost half of his study to the runic signatures. In two articles by R. W. V. Elliott, "Cynewulf's Runes in *Christ II* and *Elene*" (*ES*, 1953) and "Cynewulf's Runes in *Juliana* and *The Fates of the Apostles*" (*ES*, 1953), it is shown that Cynewulf not only used the runes to spell out his name but also used the names to describe or indicate Judgment Day.

Once again, there have been excellent editions of single poems, such as Rosemary Woolf, *Juliana* (1955), and Pamela O. E. Gradon, *Cynewulf's Elene* (1958), both in the Methuen Library. The latter, however, hardly supersedes F. Holthausen, *Cynewulfs Elene* (4th ed. 1937), except for what little research has been done on the poem since Holthausen's last edition. J. J. Campbell, *The Advent Lyrics of the Exeter Book* (1959), is an unusually good edition of *Christ I*, but there has been no single edition of the three parts since A. S. Cook's *The Christ of Cynewulf* (1900). Most of the study of the signed poems has had to do with the most doubtful of the four—the *Christ*. A. Philip, "The Exeter Scribe and the Unity of the *Christ*" (*PMLA*, 1940), considers the three recognized parts to be three separate poems. On the other hand, K. Mildenberger, "The Unity of Cynewulf's *Christ* in the Light of Iconography" (*Speculum*, 1948), argues that since the three themes of the poem—Advent, Ascension, and Judgment Day—are commonly associated in Christian iconography, then the poem, despite the fact that the runic signature is in part 2 only, has a unity. Presumably this would be the kind of unity achieved in a triptych. In considering *Christ I* only, J. J. Campbell, "Structural Patterns in the Old English Advent Lyrics" (*ELH*, 1956), finds no less than twelve separate lyrics, which in his opinion come nearer to pure lyric, with musical association, than anything else in Anglo-Saxon literature. S. B. Greenfield in "The Theme of Spiritual Exile in *Christ I*" (*PQ*, 1953) argues that the major concept of the poem lies in the Incarnation.

Probably the most important work on the Cynewulfian poems as a whole is C. Schaar, *Critical Studies in the Cynewulf Group* (1949). He stresses the debt of all of the poems to Latin hagiographic and homiletic writings and emphasizes the influence of the epic poems on the four signed poems, as well as *Guthlac B* and *Andreas*. He finds *The Dream of the Rood* and *Guthlac B* closest in style to the signed poems, and *Christ III* and *The Phoenix* the most remote. Similar conclusions will be found in S. K. Das, *Cynewulf and the Cynewulf Canon* (1942), which gives a most sympathetic kind of appreciation of the poems, but the expository machinery of this book is rather too cumbersome. Both Schaar and Das, however, illustrate how far we have traveled since A. S. Cook, "Cynewulf's Part in Our *Beowulf*" (*Transactions of the Connecticut Academy of Arts and Sciences*, 1925).

Most of the studies of the unsigned Cynewulfian poems have concerned themselves with *The Dream of the Rood*. The most usable edition is now that of B. Dickins and A. S. C. Ross, *The Dream of the Rood* (1934; 4th ed. 1954), in the Methuen Library; but in spite of a rather weak introduction, H. Bütow, *Das altenglische Traumgesicht vom Kreuz* (1935), is nearer to the definitive. It is easy to select the three best special studies. Margaret Schlauch, "*The Dream of the Rood* as Prosopopoeia" (*Essays and Studies in Honor of Carleton Brown*, 1940), discusses thoroughly the elements of classical rhetoric in the poem. Rosemary Woolf, "Doctrinal Influences on *The Dream of the Rood* (*MAE*, 1958), points out that the heroic triumph over suffering, and the tensions resulting therefrom, are both portrayed and resolved in the concept of the warrior-Christ on the Cross, which in turn shares His suffering. J. A. Burrow, "An Approach to *The Dream of the Rood*" (*Neophil*, 1959), compares the poem to other Crucifixion poems and notes a certain emotional, almost romantic, concept that is not found in the later medieval treatments. This emotional "sequence" produces the unity of the poem.

VIII. ELEGIAC VERSE

THE SMALL but interesting and effective group of so-called elegiac poems, to which may be added some personal lyrics, if such a term can be admitted, has excited criticism of the most varied kind. This is especially true of *The Wanderer* and *The Seafarer*. Here the most notable efforts have attempted to explain the poems as Christian all the way through. At the same time, *Deor* and the "personal" lyrics—*The Husband's Message*, *The Wife's Lament*, and *Wulf and Eadwacer*—have occupied scholars to a lesser extent. We may consider these last-named poems first.

Deor has been edited by K. Malone (1933) for the Methuen Library. Around it are gathered some pre- and postpublication studies by the same scholar. W. W. Lawrence had already refused to see autobiographical significance in the poem (*MP*, 1911), but L. Forster, "Die Assoziation in Deors Klage" (*Anglia*, 1937), showing the rather surprising influence of T. S. Eliot, considers each of the personages and events referred to as "objects correlative" of the poet's own troubles. Only one important study has been made of *The Husband's Message*. R. W. V. Elliott, "The Runes in *The Husband's Message*" (*JEGP*, 1955), tackles the difficult runes and discovers in the names of the runes the essential message to the wife: that she should go south over the sea to join her husband. *The Wife's Lament* has had more varied and at the same time more vague interpretation. The best summary of the earlier theories about the poem is S. B. Greenfield, "*The Wife's Lament* Reconsidered" (*PMLA*, 1953), which comments on the apparent ambivalence of the wife's feelings toward her husband. An important connection between this poem and *Deor*, or perhaps merely the Weland Legend, is A. C. Bouman, "'Leodum is minum': Beadohild's Complaint" (*Neophil*, 1949), to which not enough attention has been paid. J. A. Ward, "*The Wife's Lament*: An Interpretation" (*JEGP*, 1960), believes that the distress of the wife comes from her separation from her husband rather than from any hostility toward him, so that there is perhaps a closer relationship between this poem and *The Husband's Message* than had previously been granted. The only notable study of *Wulf and Eadwacer* since 1925 is J. F. Adams, "*Wulf and Eadwacer*: An Interpretation" (*MLN*, 1958), which denies the presence of any third party by translating Eadwacer into "property-watcher." The poem therefore is the plea of a woman to her lover, Wulf, to settle down.

Only a handful of studies have considered *The Ruin*. The most striking is Cecilia A. Hotchner, *Wessex and Old English Poetry, with Special Consideration of The Ruin* (1939). This proposes that the elegiac poems in general originated in Wessex rather than Northumbria. *The Ruin*, then, refers to the Roman ruins in Bath. This theory is attacked in two articles by S. J. Herben, "*The Ruin*" (*MLN*, 1939) and "*The Ruin* Again" (*MLN*, 1944). Herben complains of inaccuracies in Miss Hotchner's study and prefers the Roman Wall for the ruin in question. G. W. Dunleavy, "A 'De Excidio' Tradition in the Old English *Ruin*?" (*PQ*, 1959), points to the possibility of a Romano-Celtic influence at work and thinks of Chester rather than Bath.

There has been much discussion of *The Seafarer* and *The Wanderer*, especially in recent years, with the general conclusions drifting away from the old idea that they are non-Christian poems with Christian touching-up toward the theory that they are unified Christian poems capable of allegorical interpretation. The tendency also has been to study them together.

The Seafarer has a good edition by Ida L. Gordon (1960) in the Methuen Library. O. S. Anderson Arngart, The Seafarer: An Interpretation (1937), unifies the poem by insisting that the sea voyage is an allegory of man's life on earth. The medieval concept of man as a pilgrim, at least as it is applicable in this poem, is stated brilliantly by Dorothy Whitelock, "The Interpretation of The Seafarer" (H. M. Chadwick Memorial Studies, 1950). The speaker is a peregrinus, and Miss Whitelock sees an analogy in the numbers of Anglo-Saxons going to the schools in Ireland, the mission fields of Germany, and the shrines of saints in distant lands. S. B. Greenfield, "Attitudes and Values in The Seafarer" (SP, 1954), explains that the poet may be more unhappy about the foregoing of earthly joys than Miss Whitelock will allow, but he tends to strain at double meanings (secular and Christian) in what he considers certain key words and phrases. In approaching the poem by way of the oral-formulaic theory. J. J. Campbell, "Oral Poetry in The Seafarer" (Speculum, 1960), detects what he believes to be an older and later layer in the structure of the poem, which sounds suspiciously like the older theory of its composition, but he approves the recent allegorical interpretations.

Studies of The Wanderer received a stimulus with the appearance of B. F. Huppé, "The Wanderer: Theme and Structure" (JEGP, 1943), which defends a unity in the poem not previously accepted. According to Huppé there are easily discernible structural elements in the poem: an introduction, a monologue by a wanderer, a brief transitional passage, a monologue by a wise man, and a conclusion. The fact that such an insistence on unity reflects upon the artistic achievement of the poet (for it is artistically a most uneven work) is no bar to this theory. The thematic structure is likewise unified by the contrast between the eternal nature of God's mercy and the transient quality of human happiness and well-being. S. B. Greenfield, "The Wanderer: A Reconsideration of Theme and Structure" (JEGP, 1951), sets the Christian tone of the introduction and conclusion against the Stoic progress of the wanderer in his growing awareness of the vanity of human wishes. On the other hand, R. W. V. Elliott, "The Wanderer's Conscience" (ES, 1958), takes the view that the wanderer is suffering from a guilty conscience because he has somehow failed his lord. The result is that he seeks consolation in Christian teaching, but the poem itself does little more than bring an ethical compromise. E. G. Stanley, "Old English

Poetic Diction and the Interpretation of *The Wanderer, The Seafarer,* and *The Penitent's Prayer*" (*Anglia,* 1956), links all three of these poems of *The Exeter Book* to penitential discipline. The possibilities of a purely allegorical approach to the poem are evident enough, though not compelling, as presented in D. W. Robertson, Jr., "Historical Criticism" (*EIE,* 1950) —not compelling because it is always possible even in a society dominated by the church, as the society of the Middle Ages certainly was, to find a poet with his secular moments. Yet Robertson's essay is a good defence of allegorical approaches. In reference to allegorical interpretations, we should note the stimulating discussions pro and con of the patristic and exegetical method in Dorothy Bethurum, ed., *Critical Approaches to Medieval Literature* (1960). Nearly all scholars now will concede the Christian quality of the poem, as it is summed up in Susie L. Tucker, "Return to *The Wanderer*" (*EIC,* 1958). The work is a unified monologue on a Christian theme, according to T. C. Rumble, "From *Eardstapa* to *Snottor on Mode:* The Structural Principle of *The Wanderer*" (*MLQ,* 1958).

Taken together, the two poems impress Ida L. Gordon, "Traditional Themes in *The Wanderer* and *The Seafarer*" (*RES,* 1954), as indebted to a tradition for their form, tone, and mood. "It is the world of elegiac thought, not the real Christian world, that supplies the poetic inspiration, and it is the stylized elegiac *genre* that gives poetic shape to these poems." This is not to deny an essential Christian unity to both works. Similarly, Vivian Salmon, "*The Wanderer* and *The Seafarer,* and the Old English Conception of the Soul" (*MLR,* 1960), while conceding the Christianity of the poems, observes also a residual non-Christian element from an older tradition. G. V. Smithers in "The Meaning of *The Seafarer* and *The Wanderer*" (*MAE,* 1957, 1959) makes much of the undoubted influence of eschatological passages from the homilies and other religious writings of the period upon the two poems. But he probably goes too far or labors a too obvious point in his inference that all Old English poetry is implicitly allegorical. In studying the two works, one must be impressed by what R. M. Lumiansky says of *The Wanderer* in "The Dramatic Structure of the Old English *Wanderer*" (*Neophil,* 1950) —that the speaker is expressing a consolation of philosophy which finds comfort in a virtuous conduct leading to God instead of a reliance upon this transitory world.

IX. ANGLO-SAXON PROSE

A DISCUSSION of the study of the Anglo-Latin writers of the Old
English period serves well as a bridge to the consideration of
the study of Anglo-Saxon prose. Of course a figure like Aldhelm
should be classified as a poet, while Bede, on the other hand, is primarily a prose writer. Eleanor S. Duckett's *Anglo-Saxon Saints and
Scholars* (1947), *Alcuin, Friend of Charlemagne* (1951), *St. Dunstan of Canterbury* (1955), and *Alfred the Great* (1956) have
already been mentioned. A few scattered studies of pre-Galfridian
Arthuriana have appeared. A notable example is K. Jackson,
"Nennius and the Twenty-Eight Cities of Britain" (*Antiquity*,
1938). C. E. Stevens, "Gildas Sapiens" (*EHR*, 1941), is a complete
job of destruction on Gildas as a historian.

Since Bede is the chief Anglo-Latin writer of the Anglo-Saxon
period, he has of course received most attention. There were many
pieces of writing about him on the occasion of the twelve-hundredth
anniversary of his death in 1935, of which the most notable were the
Hartz Lecture by R. W. Chambers, *Bede* (*PBA*, 1936), and the
collection of studies edited by A. H. Thompson, *Bede: His Life,
Times, and Writings* (1935). The latter comprises C. E. Whiting,
"The Life of the Venerable Bede," E. W. Watson, "The Age of
Bede," A. H. Thompson, "Northumbrian Monasteries," C. Peers,
"Monkwearmouth and Jarrow," W. Levison, "Bede as Historian,"
C. Jenkins, "Bede as Exegete and Theologian," B. Colgrave, "Bede's
Miracle Stories," M. James, "The Manuscripts of Bede," and M. L.
W. Laistner, "The Library of the Venerable Bede." Very useful also
is C. W. Jones, "Bede as Early Medieval Historian" (*M&H*, 1946).
M. L. W. Laistner, "Bede as a Classical and a Patristic Scholar"
(*Transactions of the Royal Historical Society*, 1933), like Jones's
study, emphasizes Bede's industry and knowledge of Latin, and
defines him as a traditionalist and a recorder of tradition. A
confirmation of the importance of such a definition is implicit in P.
H. Blair, *Bede's Ecclesiastical History of the English Nation and
Its Importance Today* (1959). The *Ecclesiastical History* has a
concordance, edited by P. F. Jones (1929). A text that has added

much to Bede scholarship is M. L. W. Laistner, *Bedae Venerabilis Expositio Actuum Apostolorum et Retractatio* (1939); its importance is attested by J. D. A. Ogilvy, "A Noteworthy Contribution to the Study of Bede" (*University of Colorado Studies: Series B, Studies in the Humanities*, 1941). There has also been a considerable interest in the Leningrad MS. of Bede's described by Olga Dobiache-Rojdestvensky, "Un manuscrit de Bède à Leningrad" (*Speculum*, 1928), and reproduced as the second volume in *Early English Manuscripts in Facsimile.*

A general survey of the writings available to the Anglo-Latin writers is J. D. A. Ogilvy, *Books Known to Anglo-Latin Writers from Aldhelm to Alcuin* (1936).

Most of the shorter studies of the Alfredian writings are restricted to details of the voyages of Ohthere and Wulfstan. In reference to these, S. Potter, "A Commentary on King Alfred's *Orosius*" (*Anglia*, 1953), is most useful. Two works on Boethius should be noted—the appropriate chapter in E. K. Rand, *Founders of the Middle Ages* (1928), and particularly Helen M. Barrett, *Boethius: Some Aspects of His Times and Work* (1940). L. Borinski, *Der Stil Königs Alfreds* (1931; 2 ed. 1934), takes much space to say less than R. W. Chambers in his *On the Continuity of English Prose.*

Much important work has been done on *The Anglo-Saxon Chronicle.* A. H. Smith edited *The Parker Chronicle, 832 to 900* (1935) for the Methuen Library; H. A. Rositzke edited *The C-Text of the Old English Chronicles* (1940); and G. N. Garmonsway, *The Anglo-Saxon Chronicle* (1953). Two other editions are of importance: E. Classen and F. E. Harmer, *An Anglo-Saxon Chronicle from British Museum Cotton MS. Tiberius B. IV* (1926); and Cecily Clark, *The Peterborough Chronicle* (EETS, 1958). A useful supplementary study is B. Dickins, *The Genealogical Preface to the Anglo-Saxon Chronicle* (1952). The editorial work in all of these is of a high order of excellence. The more important discussions of the *Chronicle* are contained in the major histories of the period. Of the many minor studies the most striking is C. L. Wrenn, "A Saga of the Anglo-Saxons" (*History*, 1940), which explores the relationship of the Cynewulf-Cyneheard episode to kindred Norse story material.

Two editions of works by Aelfric or ascribable to the tradition of Aelfric are H. Henel, *Aelfric's De Temporibus Anni* (EETS, 1942), and G. N. Garmonsway, *Aelfric's Colloquy* (1939; 2nd ed. 1947), in the Methuen Library. No less than thirty articles have appeared, treating Aelfric's language, sources, and doctrinal terminology. The difficult problem of the canon of his works is undertaken in P. A. M. Clemoes, "The Chronology of Aelfric's Works" (*The Anglo-Saxons*, 1959). A brilliant example of the possibilities of textual study is K. Sisam, "MSS. Bodley 340 and 342: Aelfric's *Catholic Homilies* (*RES*, 1931; rptd. in *Studies in the History of Old English Literature*, 1953). The potentialities of linguistic evidence for the dating of Aelfric's manuscripts are illustrated in G. K. Anderson, "Notes on the Language of Aelfric's English *Pastoral Letters* in CCCC 190 and Bodleian Junius 21" (*JEGP*, 1941). The peculiarities of Aelfric's alliterative style, which some had seen as alliterative verse in prose form, have been pretty well settled. G. H. Gerould, "Abbot Aelfric's Rhythmic Prose" (*MP*, 1925), maintains that Aelfric was not trying to compose verse, but to achieve rhetorical effects in the tradition of Latin prose. Dorothy Bethurum, "The Form of Aelfric's *Lives of the Saints*" (*SP*, 1932), concedes a certain tendency on the part of Aelfric toward verse. He wrote under the aura of Anglo-Saxon poetic tradition, but that is as far as one can go in setting him up as a poet.

The most ambitious general work on Wulfstan is K. Jost, *Wulfstanstudien* (1950), which considers at length the canon of Wulfstan's writings and the problem of other writings in Wulfstan's manner. But Dorothy Bethurum, *The Homilies of Wulfstan* (1957), is an excellent edition with an excellent introduction.

X. OTHER WORKS

AFTER CITING the studies of Wulfstan, one comes to the inevitable miscellanea in prose and poetry. The anonymous homiletic writings have received careful attention from R. Willard, notably in "Two Apocrypha in Old English Homilies" (*BEP*, 1935), which discusses, giving the text, "The Apocryphon of the Seven Heavens" and "The Three Utterances of the Soul." The relation of the latter to the Dialogues of Body and Soul is implicit in Willard's "The Address of the Soul to the Body" (*PMLA*, 1935). The homilies lead one naturally to the saints' lives. The perpetual problem of how to distinguish the historical from the legendary has been very well treated in two studies by C. G. Loomis, "The Growth of the St. Edmund Legend" and "St. Edmund and the Lodbrok (Lothbroc)

Legend" (*Harvard Studies and Notes in Philology and Literature,*
1932 and 1933). A good exposition of this particular genre of Old
English literature is C. W. Jones, *Saints' Lives and Chronicles in
Early England* (1947). The relation of these hagiographical writings to historiography, as exemplified by Bede, is a salient point in
the fine Gollancz Memorial Lecture by B. Colgrave, "The Earliest
Saints' Lives Written in England" (*PBA*, 1958). As for scriptural
commentary, it has usually been considered under the appropriate
commentator, such as Bede or Aelfric. Concerning Biblical translation, the most striking single study of *The West Saxon Gospels*, H.
Glunz's "Die lateinische Vorlage der westsächsischen Evangelienver-
sion" (*BEP*, 1928), has been absorbed in his more comprehensive
*Britannien und Bibeltext: Der Vulgatatext der Evangelien in seinem
Verhältnis zur irisch-angelsächsischen Kultur des Frühmittelalters*
(1930).

Studies of the Old English runes and glosses have advanced
considerably since 1925. Two excellent handbooks have appeared: H.
Arntz, *Handbuch der Runenkunde* (1935; 2nd ed. 1944), and R. W.
V. Elliott, *Runes* (1959). Arntz has also published a separate
Bibliographie der Runenkunde (1937). Of the two, Elliott is more
narrowly descriptive of the English runes; Arntz ranges wider and
considers more fully the importance of these runes in the interpretation of the life of the Germanic peoples. The Old English *Runic
Poem* is studied proficiently by W. Keller, "Zum altenglischen
Runengedicht" (*Anglia*, 1936), where there is a comparative discussion of Old Norse, Icelandic, and Old English runes. The most
important single publication on the glosses is H. D. Meritt, *Old
English Glosses* (1945).

Blanche C. Williams, *Gnomic Poetry in Anglo-Saxon* (1937),
remains the only edition of these relics of folk aphorism and ritual.
The riddles of *The Exeter Book* have interested many, notably Erika
von Erhardt-Siebold, who has written over a dozen solid, perceptive,
and ingenious articles on individual riddles, as well as a definitive
study of the Anglo-Latin riddles, "Die lateinische Rätsel der Angelsachsen" (*AF*, 1925). The over-all survey of such riddles, virtually
all of which should be considered belletristic compositions, is supplied most effectively in A. Taylor, *The Literary Riddle before 1600*
(1948). Many single studies of the various charms or spells have
been made, but the standard edition is still F. Grendon, *The Anglo-
Saxon Charms* (*JAF*, 1909; rptd. separately 1930).

Three editions of minor Anglo-Saxonica remain to be noted. R.
J. Menner, *The Poetical Dialogues of Solomon and Saturn* (1941),
is definitive and supplies an important introduction and analysis of

the text. Then there are two editions of *Apollonius of Tyre*. The first and more extensive is J. Raith, *Die alt- und mittelenglischen Apollonius-Bruchstücke, mit dem Text der 'Historia Apollonii' nach der englischen Handschriftengruppe* (1956) ; the second and handier one is P. Goolden, *The Old English Apollonius of Tyre* (1958).

Byrhtferth's *Manual* has not attracted attention for many years ; such neglect, however, many be due simply to the fact that S. J. Crawford edited it so well for EETS (1929) that a new edition would be superfluous. H. Henel has done much significant study of this type of medieval scholarly writing, notably "Studien zum altenglischen Computus" (*BEP*, 1934), which is a complete discussion not only of the *Handboc* but also of the *Menologium*. Finally, we must give praise to Agnes J. Robertson's masterly editions and translations of *The Laws of the Kings of England from Edmund to Henry I* (1925) and *Anglo-Saxon Charters* (1939).

The roll of distingished scholars who have been working in the field of Old English literature since about 1925, or during the past generation, is apparent from the foregoing. It is not, however, merely a question of prolific publication. The scholar who in sheer numbers of published studies outscores any other by more than two to one is too often garrulous, contemptuous of the point of view of others, prosaic, and gifted with a talent for leaving a subject rather less clear than it was before. On the other hand, many a single study, written by someone who seldom broke into print again, may be a gem of its kind. No single scholar is bigger than his subject, of course, but great respect inevitably accrues to one who chooses a particular field of study, settles down in it, and keeps alive in it. There leap to mind the names of Erika von Erhardt-Siebold and A. E. H. Swaen in connection with the Riddles, in The Exeter Book and elsewhere; of Rudolph Willard, with homiletic writings; of Philip W. Souers, with The Franks Casket; of Herbert Meritt, with the glosses; of Felix Liebermann, with Anglo-Saxon laws; of A. S. C. Ross, with the Lindisfarne and Rushworth Gospels; of Albert S. Cook with Aldhelm; of George P. Krapp and E. V. K. Dobbie, with the preparation of texts. The list could be greatly extended, particularly if one were to include some of the noted linguists of the generation, but space does not permit. Great praise is due the brilliant constellation of women scholars whose names have appeared from time to time in this report. The cultivation of the garden goes on apace, but the trend of the studies to come during the next generation, which at the moment appears to be more critical than historical, cannot as yet be determined. Only the bibliographer of the year 2000 will be able to say.

3

Middle English Literature to 1400

By *Robert W. Ackerman*
STANFORD UNIVERSITY

I. BIBLIOGRAPHIES

S PECIALISTS in the Middle English field are fortunate in the posses-
sion of J. E. Wells's monumental *Manual of the Writings in Middle English, 1050–1400* (1916), to which nine supplements have been
added, bringing the bibliographies down to the beginning of 1946. In
addition to exhaustive lists of scholarly treatises and reviews, the
Manual includes summaries of virtually all Middle English literary
works up to 1400 and brief descriptive comments on the scholarship.
The reworking of this indispensable book, now in hand, will carry the
coverage through the fifteenth century. Next in importance is the
Middle English section of *The Cambridge Bibliography of English
Literature*, Vol. I (1941), together with the supplement, Vol. v
(1957).

S. Thompson's *Motif-Index of Folk Literature* (6 vols., 1932–
36; new and enlarged ed. 1955–58) is of primary importance for the
study of literary origins. Together with additional volumes in the
same series, such as T. P. Cross's *Motif Index of Early Irish
Literature* (1952), this work is essentially a bibliography of folk-
tale motifs. Thompson's general discussion entitled *The Folktale*
(1946; rptd. 1951) provides a good introduction to the whole field,
and F. L. Utley's "Folklore, Myth, and Ritual," in *Critical Approaches to Medieval Literature*, ed. Dorothy Bethurum (1960), is
a helpful analysis of "mythic" approaches to the literature of the
Middle Ages. Another comprehensive aid, C. F. Brown and R. H.
Robbins' *The Index of Middle English Verse* (1943), aims to present
a catalog of all English poems, whether printed or still in manuscript, written between 1100 and 1500. A supplement is now in
preparation.

Earlier treatments of all aspects of the English language,
including Middle English, are listed in A. G. Kennedy's *A Bibliography of Writings on the English Language from the Beginning of
Printing to the End of 1922* (1927; rptd. 1961). Post-1922
publications on such subjects may be found in the appropriate
sections of *The Cambridge Bibliography* and the annual *PMLA*

bibliographies. More specialized bibliographical guides, such as those devoted to comparative literature, Chaucer, and medieval drama, are discussed below in conjunction with surveys of these genres or writers.

II. GENERAL TREATMENTS OF MIDDLE ENGLISH LITERATURE

O F THE TREATMENTS of the whole or of sizable areas of Middle English literature, A. C. Baugh's two-hundred page contribution, "The Middle English Period (1100–1500)," to *A Literary History of England* (1948) is easily the most reliable for ready reference. Virtually all significant works receive brief comment, although little space is allocated to critical appraisals. The three parts of Margaret Schlauch's *English Medieval Literature and its Social Foundations* (1956) dealing with the post-Conquest period also aim at a comprehensive coverage, though the fullness of the discussion of Chaucer stands in contrast to the brief yet perceptive treatment of much other literature. A good many Middle English works are analyzed here in terms of Marxist doctrine.

Dwelling as it does on the period 1066 to 1300, R. M. Wilson's *Early Middle English Literature* (1939; 2nd ed. 1951) is mainly concerned with *The Ancrene Riwle, The Owl and the Nightingale, Ormulum,* certain romances, tales, lyric poetry, and early vernacular drama. Wilson's study of the Anglo-French background of thirteenth-century English literature is especially enlightening. In his later book, *The Lost Literature of Medieval England* (1952), the same author develops the view that much early lyric poetry and some plays have been lost to us.

G. Kane's *Middle English Literature: A Critical Study of the Romances, the Religious Lyrics, Piers Plowman* (1951) is an essay in literary evaluation and thus differs markedly from the essentially historical studies listed above. In general, Kane seeks to appraise each work he discusses in terms of what he takes to be universal norms of fictional or poetic excellence. J. Speirs, who attacked Kane's book vigorously (*Scrutiny*, 1951), attempts on his part an appreciative survey in his *Medieval English Poetry: The Non-*

Chaucerian Tradition (1957). In keeping with the creed of the "new criticism," he urges that for a critic to attempt to retreat into the Middle Ages and reconstruct what a poem may have meant to its first audience or what were the intentions of the poet is irrelevant to proper appreciation of the poem today.

J. P. Oakden's two volumes, *Alliterative Poetry in Middle English,* are subtitled respectively *The Dialectal and Metrical Survey* (1930) and *A Survey of the Traditions* (1935). The earlier volume provides a painstaking classification of poems written before 1300 and during the so-called alliterative revival according to their use of alliterative lines alone or with the addition of rhyme and various stanzaic patterns. The other volume is devoted primarily to a literary appraisal of a large number of works employing alliteration, among them certain hymns, Layamon's *Brut, The Wars of Alexander, Sir Gawain and the Green Knight, Wynnere and Wastoure, Piers Plowman, Patience, Purity, Pearl,* and Scottish alliterative poems. In addition, the volume contains discussions of vocabulary, alliterative phrases, and style.

Several works are only in part concerned with vernacular literature or specifically with the Middle English period. J. W. H. Atkins, in his *English Literary Criticism: The Medieval Phase* (1943; rptd. 1952), first discusses Latin literary studies by such Englishmen as John of Salisbury, Geoffrey of Vinsauf, and Richard of Bury, and then points out attitudes toward composition that are expressed in or may be deduced from various works of the period. J. Peter, in his *Complaint and Satire in Early English Literature* (1956), is concerned with the medieval period chiefly as a background for his discussion of Renaissance literature. He argues that the spread of Christianity in Europe brought about the transmutation of satire into complaint. In this context, Peter discusses briefly *Handlyng Synne,* Orm's *Ormulum, Piers Plowman,* and certain of Chaucer's *Canterbury Tales.*

Three books with self-explanatory titles by H. R. Patch—*The Goddess Fortuna in Mediaeval Literature* (1927), *The Tradition of Boethius* (1935), and *The Other World According to Descriptions in Medieval Literature* (1950)—include considerable discussion of Middle English literature, especially of the works of Chaucer. The treatment of Boethius is of the first importance for a grasp of the fundamental orientation of the medieval mind. M. W. Bloomfield's *The Seven Deadly Sins* (1952) traces the concept of the cardinal sins from the beginnings through the Middle Ages, with particular reference to English literature.

A number of attacks on the problem of reading medieval

allegorical poetry have made their appearance. Important background discussions bearing on the development of the allegorical interpretation of Scripture are to be found in C. Spicq, *Esquisse d'une histoire de l'exégèse latine au moyen âge* (1944), Beryl Smalley, *The Study of the Bible in the Middle Ages* (1941; 2nd ed. 1952), and H. Caplan, "The Four Senses of Scriptural Interpretation and the Mediaeval Theory of Preaching" (*Speculum*, 1929). Treatments of the fundamental nature of profane allegory, and especially of the relevance of the fourfold Biblical exegesis to an understanding of allegory in profane literature, are not lacking, even though a definitive work on this topic is needed. Various related works center on Dante, such as Helen Dunbar's *Symbolism in Medieval Thought and Its Consummation in the Divine Comedy* (1929), R. H. Green's "Dante's 'Allegory of Poets' and the Medieval Theory of Poetic Fiction" (*CL*, 1957), and C. S. Singleton's "The Irreducible Dove" (*CL*, 1957). The two last-named articles dispute the question whether Dante could have intended his poem to be explicated on multiple levels corresponding to those of the Biblical exegete. On his part, M. W. Bloomfield, in "Symbolism in Medieval Literature" (*MP*, 1958), attacks as unsound the rigid application of the methods of exegesis to the interpretation of secular literature. Among the more illuminating of such investigations are three papers delivered by E. T. Donaldson, R. E. Kaske, and C. Donahue before the English Institute, published in *Critical Approaches to Medieval Literature*, ed. Dorothy Bethurum (1960). Other studies of this sort that are primarily concerned with the interpretation of individual Middle English poems—especially *Piers Plowman* and *Pearl*—are treated below.

III. BACKGROUND STUDIES

A. AUTHORSHIP, PATRONAGE, AND MANUSCRIPT PRODUCTION

THE STATUS of the profession of letters, to the extent that it existed in the Middle Ages, is obviously of primary interest to the student of literature, yet much remains to be done on the subject. Recent discussions of the problem are provided by R. C. Girvan in "The Medieval Poet and his Public" (*English Studies Today*, ed. C. L. Wrenn and G. Bullough, 1951) and in a chapter of W. T. H. Jackson, *The Literature of the Middle Ages* (1960). Popular literature, at least, would seem to have reached its audiences through oral presentation, including minstrel performances, as Ruth Crosby observes in "Oral Delivery in the Middle Ages" (*Speculum*, 1936) and "Chaucer and the Custom of Oral Delivery" (*Speculum*, 1938). In this connection, C. C. Olson's "The Minstrels at the Court of Edward III" (*PMLA*, 1941) is also interesting. H. J. Chaytor's *From Script to Print* (1945) is another pertinent work in this field. Also relevant here is the belief of R. H. Robbins to the effect that many early lyrics and carols may well have been the work of the friars. (See Sec. VII below.)

Improved facilities for manuscript production in the form of lay *scriptoria* seem to have come into existence in London in the late Middle Ages. Possibly this development is related to the evolution of a larger, more literate middle class. According to Laura Loomis in "The Auchinleck Manuscript and a Possible London Bookshop of 1330–1340" (*PMLA*, 1942), early stationers, in carrying out commissions for their patrons, employed not only ordinary scribes but also translator-versifiers, whose task it was to turn French prose into English verse. Further evidence is developed by R. N. Walpole in "The Source MS of *Charlemagne and Roland* and the Auchinleck Bookshop" (*MLN*, 1945) and by H. M. Smyser (*Speculum*, 1946). Many of the manuscripts of Chaucer's *Canterbury Tales* are said by J. M. Manly and Edith Rickert to bear the marks of being shop-made (*The Text of the Canterbury Tales*, 1, 1940). In the fifteenth century, even before the full impact of the printing presses was felt, the further expansion of the reading public would appear to have made authorship more attractive, at least as a part-time profession, to judge from the examples of Hoccleve, Henry Lovelich, John Shirley, and Malory. H. S. Bennett has explored this matter in "The Author and His Public in the Fourteenth and Fifteenth Centuries" (*E&S*, 1937), *Chaucer and the Fifteenth Century* (1947), and *English Books and Readers, 1475–1557* (1952). Henry Lovelich as a part-time poet is discussed by R. W. Ackerman (*PMLA*, 1952).

B. PAROCHIAL CULTURE AND LITERACY

Fundamental to a grasp of conditions governing the production and reception of vernacular literature are facts about the social distribution and the literacy of the medieval population. J. C. Russell's *British Medieval Population* (1948) and "Clerical Population of Medieval England" (*Traditio*, 1944) provide firmer data on this topic than G. G. Coulton's various books. Here one learns that after the visitations of the plague during the fourteenth century, the population of England probably did not exceed 2,200,000; that London, by far the largest city, numbered perhaps 35,000; and that few of the 9,000 or so parishes could count more than 80 souls. Computations of the numbers of beneficed priests, of regular clergy (monks, nuns, and friars), and of clerks—normally men in minor orders who had accepted worldly employment or were university students—are also revealing. The rapid growth of a class of craftsmen and merchants, a large proportion of whom must have acquired literacy, is still another significant factor. This body of historical fact, when combined with the close view of everyday existence afforded by such works as H. S. Bennett's *Life on the English Manor: A Study of Peasant Conditions, 1150–1400* (1937; rptd. 1948, 1960), G. C. Homans' *English Villagers of the Thirteenth Century* (1941; rptd. 1960), and Sylvia Thrupp, *The Merchant Class of Medieval London, 1300–1500* (1948; rptd. 1962), enables one to appreciate the activities and opportunities of the Englishmen of the period.

The church provided almost the sole educational opportunities, yet contemporary sources indicate that many of the humble parish clergy remained appallingly ignorant. It is likely that most clerks—not only the secular priesthood but the regulars and all others who, although not in the service of religion, had at one time inaugurated such a career by acquiring some education and entering minor orders—may be regarded as literate at least in the vernacular. The education available to the laity is treated in R. B. Hepple's *Mediaeval Education in England* (1932) and L. Thorndike's "Elementary and Secondary Education in the Middle Ages" (*Speculum*, 1940). J. W. Thompson's *The Literacy of the Laity in the Middle Ages* (1939) is concerned mainly with the Latin literacy of the aristocracy. Clara P. McMahon's *Education in Fifteenth-Century England* (1947) is especially valuable for its close account of the universities. On the whole, such evidence as is available reinforces the impression that the masses lived isolated, parish-bound lives, with scant opportunity or incentive to acquire literacy. In all likelihood the reading public was mainly concentrated in the boroughs and cities.

IV. WORKS OF RELIGIOUS INSTRUCTION

*A. MANUALS OF RELIGIOUS INSTRUCTION AND GENERAL
WORKS ON THE MEDIEVAL CHURCH*

BEGINNING in the thirteenth century, the Western church made
strong efforts to improve moral and spiritual life by prescribing
more exactly both the qualifications and the duties of parish priests.
In England, the response to this movement, in particular to the
terms of the Fourth Lateran Council (1215), took the form of
episcopal degrees, "constitutions," and other directives, some of
which came to be turned from Latin into English for the benefit of
the priest who was "not grete clerk." In this category fall such
works as Archbishop Thoresby's *Lay Folk's Catechism* (EETS,
1901), the *Speculum Christiani* (EETS, 1933), and *Instructions
for Parish Priests by John Myrc* (EETS, 1868). Other English
treatises—notably *The Prymer or Lay Folks' Prayer Book* (2 vols.,
EETS, 1895–97) and *The Lay Folk's Mass Book* (EETS, 1879)—
were obviously intended as devotional aids and penitential guides to
such of the laity as could read. This codification of the faith in these
guides included simple explications of the Creed, the Ten Commandments, the cardinal sins, the five joys of the Virgin, and the like.
Such statements of Christian tenets, along with the liturgy of the
church, formed the heart of parochial Christianity in the Middle
Ages. It is not surprising, then, to find reflections of popular
doctrine in the vernacular literature of all genres and of all levels of
sophistication.

Many of the Middle English didactic writings discussed below
bear a very close relationship to the manuals of instruction. Perhaps
the most satisfactory survey of this material is to be found in W. A.
Pantin's *The English Church in the Fourteenth Century* (1955;
rptd. 1963). More specifically, Pantin finds that such writings
perpetuate several different traditions, namely, those established by
Saint Edmund's *Speculum Ecclesiae*, William of Waddington's
Manuel des Pechiez, Friar Lorens' *Le somme le roi*, and Bishop
Grosseteste's *Templum Domini*. For an understanding of the ways in

81

which the church affected the daily life of the medieval Englishman, Pantin's book may profitably be supplemented by J. R. H. Moorman's *Church Life in England in the Thirteenth Century* (1945; rptd. 1955), F. M. Powicke's *The Christian Life in the Middle Ages* (1935), C. Dawson's *Medieval Religion and Other Essays* (1934), and G. H. Cook's *The English Mediaeval Parish Church* (1954), to mention only the more outstanding of such general works. Accounts of liturgical practices and of liturgical books—by no means irrelevant to the literature of the times—are given in S. Morison's *English Prayer Books: An Introduction to the Literature of Christian Public Worship* (1943; 3rd ed. 1949) and Dom G. Dix's *The Shape of the Liturgy* (1945; 2nd ed., rptd., 1954). Dom D. Knowles's *The Monastic Order in England* (1940; 2nd ed. 1963) and *The Religious Orders in England* (3 vols., 1948–59) are standard histories of a closely related subject. Reflections of the Mass in Middle English literature are treated in Sister Loretta McGarry's *The Holy Eucharist in Middle English Homiletic and Devotional Verse* (1936). Still other recent studies in this general field are M. Hussey's "The Petitions of the Paternoster in Mediaeval English Literature" (*MAE*, 1958) and H. Hargreave's "The Middle English Primers and the Wycliffite Bible" (*MLR*, 1956). Specialized treatments of the sacrament of penance appear in J. T. McNeill and Helena Gamer's *Medieval Handbooks of Penance* (1938) and M. W. Bloomfield's *The Seven Deadly Sins* (1952). Studies of the influence of penitential doctrine on individual literary works are noted in the appropriate sections below.

B. SERMONS, LEGENDARIES, AND PASSIONS

Recently published collections of medieval sermons include *Middle English Sermons*, ed. W. O. Ross (EETS, 1940; rptd. 1960), and a series of pulpit discourses resembling Mirk's *Festial* (EETS, 1905), the *Speculum Sacerdotale*, ed. E. H. Weatherly (EETS, 1936). The remarkable versified sermon of the first half of the twelfth century, *Poema Morale*, or *Moral Ode*, is edited with a full account of textual and linguistic matters and also of the place of this poem in English sermon literature by H. Marcus (*Palaestra*, No. 194, 1934). Sister Mary Devlin's *The Sermons of Thomas Brinton, Bishop of Rochester, 1373–1389* (1954) is also an important contribution to the subject.

Medieval sermons and literary reflections are most authoritatively discussed in G. R. Owst's two books, *Preaching in Medieval England* (1926) and *Literature and Pulpit in Medieval England*

(1933; rptd. 1961), the latter of which should be read in conjunc-
tion with G. R. Coffman's review (*SP*, 1934). Other significant
discussions are H. G. Pfander's *The Popular Sermon of the Medieval
Friar in England* (1937), the same author's "Some Medieval
Manuals of Religious Instruction in England and Observations on
Chaucer's 'Parson's Tale' " (*JEGP*, 1936), and D. W. Robertson,
Jr.'s "Frequency of Preaching in Thirteenth Century England"
(*Speculum*, 1949).

Orm's *Ormulum*, a series of gospel paraphrases and homilies
thereon, has been competently studied by H. Matthes in *Die
Einheitlichkeit des Orrmulum* (1933), which focuses upon Orm's
harmonizing of sources. In "The Language and Orthography of the
Ormulum MS." (*TPS*, 1956), R. W. Burchfield announces his
intention of providing a new transcription of the *Ormulum* manuscript and offers many important observations about Orm's language and spellings.

On the English legendaries, collections of elaborated saints'
lives, some fairly recent scholarship is worthy of note. *The South
English Legendary*, for example, comprising brief *lectiones* setting
forth the *vitae* and miracles of some ninety saints, is edited in three
volumes by Charlotte D'Evelyn and Anna Mill (EETS, 1956–59). A
more extended treatment of female saints appears in Osbern Boken-
ham's *Legendys of Hooly Wummen*, ed. Mary Serjeantson (EETS,
1938). Minnie Wells discusses the structure of the *South English
Legendary* and its relations to the *Legenda Aurea* in two different
articles (*PMLA*, 1936, and *JEGP*, 1942). A short metrical life
composed for the cult of Saint Robert of Knaresborough, founder of
the Trinitarian Order in England, has been made available by Joyce
Bazire (EETS, 1953). A recent general account of saints' legends,
including some notice of their use by certain Middle English writers,
is R. Kapp's *Heilige und Heiligenlegenden in England: Studien zum
16. and 17. Jahrhundert*, Vol. 1 (1934). *The Southern Passion*, a
metrical account of Christ's passion for the instruction of the laity,
which appears in conjunction with *The South English Legendary*, is
edited by Beatrice Brown (EETS, 1927). The similar *Northern
Passion* in two Middle English texts is published by F. Foster
(EETS, 1930), the editor of an earlier volume setting forth other
texts of the same work.

C. EXPANDED DISCOURSES ON RELIGION

One of the more encyclopedic of English doctrinal treatises,
Cursor Mundi, figures in a few relatively recent source studies. In

"Herman's *Bible* and the *Cursor Mundi*" (*SP*, 1933), Lois Borland demonstrates parallelisms in narrative structure and phraseology between the English poem and *Li livres de la Bible*, a twelfth-century Biblical paraphrase by Herman de Valenciennes. Again, P. Beichner, in "*Cursor Mundi* and Petrus Riga" (*Speculum*, 1949), notes that the English writer seems to have made considerable use of Petrus' work on the Gospels in the latter part of his poem.

A somewhat broader interest has been evinced in Robert Mannyng of Brunne's *Handlyng Synne*. C. G. Laird's "The Manuscripts of the *Manuel des Pechiez*" (*SSLL*, 1941) is, of course, a source investigation. D. W. Robertson, Jr., offers a discussion of the backgrounds of Mannyng's presentation of *The Commandments* (*MLN*, 1946), and in a more recent article argues that *Handlyng Synne* properly belongs in the tradition of confessional treatises (*Speculum*, 1947). Mannyng's life receives attention in Ruth Crosby's "Robert Mannyng of Brunne: A New Biography" (*PMLA*, 1942) and Ethel Seaton's "Robert Mannyng of Brunne in Lincoln" (*MAE*, 1943). A careful study of Mannyng's principal source, the *Manuel des Pechiez*, has been provided by E. J. Arnould (1940).

The most significant work on the various English versions of the *Somme le roi*, of which Dan Michel's *Aȝenbite of Inwyt* is the best known, is W. N. Francis' edition of the fourteenth-century prose version, *The Book of Vices and Virtues* (EETS, 1942). In his introduction, Francis notes that the work treats nearly the whole of the standard doctrinal program and that it may well have been prepared as an aid to priests unlettered in Latin. In a separate article, "The Original of the *Ayenbite of Inwyt*" (*PMLA*, 1937), Francis endorses the view that the copy of Lorens' work in MS. B.M. Cotton Cleopatra A.v. is the actual original used by Dan Michel.

D. MISCELLANEOUS RELIGIOUS WORKS

Various other works of religious didacticism, some of them allegorical in nature, have been noticed by scholars. A 976-line exhortation to dying sinners to hope for mercy, the *Speculum Misericordie*, is printed for the first time by R. H. Robbins (*PMLA*, 1939). A brief English text of the popular allegory, *The Four Daughters of God*, or the dispute and reconciliation of Mercy, Truth, Justice, and Peace, is presented by R. A. Klinefelter (*JEGP*, 1953). Recent discussions of this traditional allegory appear in S. Chew's *The Virtues Reconciled: An Iconographic Study* (1947) and Sister Mary Immaculate's "The Four Daughters of God in the *Gesta Romanorum* and the *Court of Sapience*" (*PMLA*, 1942). A minor work, *The Quatrefoil of Love*, in which the persons of the Trinity and the Blessed Virgin are allegorically represented as the leaves of a four-leaf clover, is edited by I. Gollancz and Madeleine Weale (EETS, 1935). A Middle English work loosely related to Robert Grosseteste's *Templum Domini* (in this connection see S. H. Thomson, *The Writings of Robert Grosseteste, Bishop of Lincoln, 1235–1253* [1940], p. 138) is published as an appendix to Roberta Cornelius' *The Figurative Castle: A Study in the Mediæval Allegory of the Edifice with Especial Reference to Religious Writings* (1930).

V. MYSTICISM

THE LINE between works designed to explicate the Christian way of life, such as the miscellany of writings discussed in the preceding section, and the meditations of the mystics is not easy to draw. Discussions of the fundamental nature of mysticism include Greta Hort's *Sense and Thought: A Study in Mysticism* (1936), C. Pepler's *The English Religious Heritage* (1958), and D. Knowles's *The English Mystical Tradition* (1961).

Before the fourteenth-century mystical writers are taken up, however, it is appropriate to consider the much earlier *Ancrene Riwle*, which, as a book of ascetic advice to female recluses, bears a relationship to the mystical tradition. In this connection, T. W. Coleman's " 'The Ancrene Riwle,' the Beginnings of English Mysticism" (*London Quarterly*, 1934) is of interest. This famous work, known either as the *Ancrene Riwle* or *Ancrene Wisse* (see F. P. Magoun, Jr., *ELH*, 1937), has been subjected to much study in recent years. All of the manuscripts are being edited by EETS. Some of the texts are now available and others are in preparation.

In addition to date of composition, identity of the author, and sources and analogues, scholars have been interested in determining the original language in which *The Ancrene Riwle* was composed. A summary of earlier studies of this, as well as of other questions, appears in R. W. Chambers' "Recent Research upon the *Ancrene Riwle*" (*RES*, 1925). The question of the original language, which is discussed by H. Käsmann in "Zur Frage der ursprünglichen Fassung der *Ancrene Riwle*" (*Anglia*, 1957) and Charlotte D'Evelyn in "Notes on Some Interrelations between the Latin and English Texts of the *Ancrene Riwle*" (*PMLA*, 1949), is regarded as finally settled in favor of the English language by Clare Kirchberger (*Dominican Studies*, 1954) and J. H. Fisher (*Middle Ages, Reformation, Volkskunde: Festschrift for John Kunstmann*, 1959). Miss Kirchberger also argues for dating the composition shortly after 1200 and, partly on liturgical grounds, for assuming that the author was subject to Dominican influence. Other recent studies seek to locate the place of origin, such as D. S. Brewer's "Two Notes on the Augustinian and Possibly West Midland Origin of the *Ancrene Riwle*" (*N&Q*, 1956) ; or the approximate date of composition—C. H. Talbot, "Some Notes on the Dating of the *Ancrene Riwle*" (*Neophil*, 1956) ; or on themes and motifs represented in the work— G. Shepherd, " 'All the Wealth of Croesus': A Topic in the 'Ancren Riwle' " (*MLR*, 1956).

Variant forms or adaptations of the work have likewise received attention. In addition to J. Påhlsson's edition of a late fourteenth-century version known as *The Recluse* (*LUÅ*, 1911), J. R. R. Tolkien discusses relationships between the *Ancrene Riwle* and an early exaltation to virginity in "*Ancrene Wisse* and *Hali Meiðhad*" (*E&S*, 1928). J. H. Fisher has edited *The Tretyse of Loue* (EETS, 1951), a translation and adaptation of a section of *Ancrene Riwle* dealing with spiritual love. The same writer discusses certain aspects of this treatise in "Continental Associations for the *Ancrene Riwle*" (*PMLA*, 1949). That the work known as *The Recluse* exhibits Lollard influence is pointed out by E. Colledge (*RES*, 1939). Finally, a concise treatment of recluses, or anchorets, appears in F. D. S. Darwin's *The English Mediaeval Recluse* (1944).

Basic research on the life and writings of Richard Rolle of Hampole has been carried out by Hope Allen, *Writings Ascribed to Richard Rolle, Hermit of Hampole, and Materials for His Biography* (1927). Miss Allen is also editor of *The English Writings of Richard Rolle, Hermit of Hampole* (1931), Margaret Deanesly of *The Incendium Amoris of Richard Rolle of Hampole* (1915), and E. J. Arnould of *The Melos Amoris of Richard Rolle of Hampole* (1957). Modern English renderings of two of the works are provided in Frances Comper's *The Fire of Love and The Mending of Life* (1914). Among the numerous specialized studies of Richard's English works is Antonie Olmes's "Sprache und Stil der englischen Mystik des Mittelalters unter besonderer Berücksichtigung des Richard Rolle von Hampole" (*Studien zur englischen Philologie*, 1933).

Walter Hilton's *Scale of Perfection* has enjoyed a continuous popularity from the fifteenth century to the present day, although his *Minor Works*, edited by Dorothy Jones (1929), are less well known. Two of the recent modern English renderings of *The Scale* are by G. Sitwell (1953) and L. Sherley-Price (1957). In "The Text of *The Scale of Perfection*" (*MAE*, 1936), Helen Gardner discusses the numerous manuscripts in which the work is preserved. In another paper, "Walter Hilton and the Mystical Tradition in England" (*E&S*, 1936), Miss Gardner contrasts Hilton with the more original author of *The Cloud of Unknowing*. Hilton's *Goad of Love*, a translation and adaptation of the *Stimulus Amoris*, has been published in modernized form by Clare Kirchberger (1952), with a brief, useful summary of Hilton studies as an introduction.

The Cloud of Unknowing, like several other fourteenth-century mystical treatises, retains its appeal for modern readers, as revealed by the frequent reissue of modernized versions like those of Evelyn Underhill and J. McCann. The standard edition, however, is by Phyllis Hodgson, *The Cloud of Unknowing and The Book of Privy Counselling* (EETS, 1944). Miss Hodgson's introduction includes a bibliography. The second treatise is included in the same volume with *The Cloud* because, in the editor's opinion, the two, along with *Deonise Hid Diuinite*, also in an edition by Miss Hodgson (EETS, 1955), are by the same anonymous writer. As a version of the *De Mystica Theologica* of the Pseudo-Dionysius the Areopagite, *Deonise Hid Diuinite* may have been meant to elucidate difficulties in *The Cloud*. The same hand, in the editor's opinion, is to be seen in *A Tretyse of þe Stodye of Wysdome þat Men Clepen Beniamyn*, taken from a work by Richard of Saint Victor. The theory that Walter Hilton is the author of *The Cloud* is suggested in Helen Gardner's review of Miss Hodgson's edition (*MAE*, 1947).

Although Dame Julian's *Revelation of Divine Love* is yet another treatise that has persisted in print in modernized versions, only in recent years has it excited the interest of any appreciable number of scholars. Brief essays such as that by Sister Anna Reynolds (*Leeds Studies in English*, 1952) offer comment on the background of the work. More recently, Sister Anna has also published in modernized English the shorter version of the *Revelations* under the title of *A Shewing of God's Love* (1958). P. F. Chambers' *Juliana of Norwich: An Introductory Appreciation and an Interpretative Anthology* (1955) is interesting for its remarks about Julian's identity and her anchorhold as well as her sixteen "shewings." R. H. Thouless' *The Lady Julian: A Psychological Study* (1924) is also worthy of attention. The most thoroughgoing of the studies, however, is P. Molinari's *Julian of Norwich: The*

Teachings of a 14th Century English Mystic (1958). Molinari analyzes Julian's spiritual doctrine and evaluates her visions in the light of the traditional scheme of mystical theology. This work also contains a comprehensive bibliography.

It is difficult to regard Margery Kempe as a true mystic in the same sense as Dame Julian or Walter Hilton. Her diary, discovered only in 1934, reveals her rather to have been a "creature" given to neurotic outbursts, especially when stirred by religious thoughts or spectacles. She is normally classified as a mystic largely because, until the recent discovery of her *Book*, she was known only by devotional scraps printed by Wynkyn de Worde. The earthy confession, known as *The Book of Margery Kempe*, is edited by S. B. Meech and Hope Allen (EETS, 1940), although the projected volume of notes and commentary is yet to appear. A modernized version was published by the owner of the unique manuscript, W. Butler-Bowden, *The Book of Margery Kempe, 1436* (1936; rptd. 1944).

Two minor works, the only known Middle English versions of writings of John Ruysbroek, the fourteenth-century Flemish mystic, are now available in an edition by Joyce Bazire and E. Colledge entitled *The Chastising of God's Children and The Treatise of Perfection* (1957).

VI. TRANSLATIONS AND WORKS OF SECULAR INSTRUCTION

O NLY A VERY FEW notices of Middle English translations and didactic works of obvious importance can be included here, namely, Mandeville's *Travels*, the work of Trevisa, and certain instructional treatises. Although written originally in Norman French between 1366 and 1371, Mandeville's *Travels* was very soon thereafter turned into English. This romance of travel setting forth the incredible marvels to be seen en route to Jerusalem, and thence to various parts of Asia and Africa, has remained a perennial favorite, as its numerous reprintings, to say nothing of literary influence, attest. The work may best be read today in the modernized version of the Egerton text edited by M. Letts for the Hakluyt Society

(1953). In a second volume in the same series, a French text is published. Different English texts have been edited by P. Hamelius (EETS, 1919) and M. Seymour (EETS, 1963). Until fairly recently, informed opinion favored assigning the authorship either to a certain Jean d'Outremeuse, the compiler of a world history, or to the French physician Jean de Bourgogne. Now, however, Letts, in his *Sir John Mandeville, the Man and His Book* (1949), takes the view that the author of *The Travels* was actually an Englishman named Mandeville. In a much more intensive examination of the problem, Josephine W. Bennett, *The Rediscovery of Sir John Mandeville* (1954), arrives at the same conclusion. Mrs. Bennett's book also provides the best comprehensive review of earlier studies and an excellent bibliography.

Another literary controversy of long standing, this one concerning John of Trevisa's participation in the Wycliffite translation of the Bible, is treated by D. C. Fowler in "John Trevisa and the English Bible" (*MP*, 1960). Fowler concludes that Trevisa could very well have worked at Queen's College, Oxford, during the 1370s with Hereford and others on the earlier version of the English Bible that passes under Wyclif's name.

Minor treatises of a didactic sort that have received attention are three early fourteenth-century pieces of wisdom literature: "The Good Wife Taught her Daughter," "The Good Wife Wold a Pylgremage," and "The Thewis of Gud Women." These have been edited with a valuable introduction by T. Mustanoja (*AASF*, 1948).

VII. LYRIC AND OTHER POETRY

A. LYRICS, RELIGIOUS AND SECULAR

THE EARLIER editions of Middle English lyrics have been superseded by several more recent works. Among them are C. F. Brown's editions, *English Lyrics of the XIIIth Century* (1932), *Religious Lyrics of the XIVth Century* (1924; revised by G. Smithers 1952), and *Religious Lyrics of the XVth Century* (1939). The first of these collections provides the texts of ninety-one religious and secular lyrics, many of them in macaronic English-Latin and English-

French verse. The second book contains poems by William Herebert, William of Shoreham, and Dan Michel. Robbins' *Secular Lyrics of the XIVth and XVth Centuries* (1952; 2nd ed. 1955) gives the texts of over two hundred lyrics taken from one hundred and fourteen manuscripts. The introductory essays in all these collections offer a valuable history of and commentary on Middle English poetry, particularly that in Robbins' recent work, in which a classification of the types of verse is attempted.

Still other collections are those of Frances Comper, *Spiritual Songs from English MSS. of Fourteenth to Sixteenth Centuries* (1936); H. Person, *Cambridge Middle English Lyrics* (1953; rev. ed. 1962); and G. Brook, *The Harley Lyrics: The Middle English Lyrics of MS. Harley 2253* (1948; 2nd ed. 1956). Person's book includes some sixty poems never before printed, and Brook's work is prefaced by an excellent discussion of liturgical influence and of meters. In addition, numerous other lyrics have been made available in journal articles by R. H. Robbins, R. H. Bowers, K. G. Wilson, A. K. Moore, and others.

The not inconsiderable linguistic difficulties presented by many Middle English lyrics are pointed up in articles by K. Malone, "Notes on Middle English Lyrics" and "Further Notes on Middle English Lyrics" (*ELH*, 1935, 1956), and by H. Meroney, "Line Notes on the Early English Lyric" (*MLN*, 1947). R. Menner in "The Man in the Moon and Hedging" (*JEGP*, 1949) turns to the lore of husbandry to translate difficult passages of this comic lyric. L. Spitzer provides a close literary analysis of three lyrics—"Of a Rose, a Lovely Rose," "Blow, Northern Wind," and "I Sing of a Maiden"—in "Explication de texte Applied to Three Great Middle English Poems" (*ArL*, 1951). The historical backgrounds of vernacular lyric are explored by F. Brittain in *The Medieval Latin and Romance Lyric to A.D. 1300* (1937; 2nd ed. 1951). W. Wehrle's *The Macaronic Hymn Tradition in Medieval English Literature* (1933) is also a useful study of many poems. In "The Authors of the Middle English Religious Lyrics" (*JEGP*, 1940) and also in "The Earliest Carols and the Franciscans" (*MLN*, 1938), R. H. Robbins develops more fully a theory mentioned elsewhere in his writings to the effect that the early lyrics and the carols were composed largely by friars in the interests of forwarding the religious instruction of the laity. G. Kane's *Middle English Literature*, already mentioned, distinguishes several types of religious lyric and seeks to evaluate individual poems.

The most thoroughgoing study of one large category of English lyrics is A. K. Moore's *The Secular Lyric in Middle English*

(1951), following through the development of the lyric to Dunbar. Moore believes that the secular lyric is deserving of more serious attention than the religious, which tends to reflect the taste of a much smaller and more specialized segment of the literate public. Although he is content with a rather broad definition of what constitutes a secular lyric (see R. Schoeck's review, *Speculum*, 1952), his book is a valuable commentary.

B. PEARL *AND OTHER POEMS OF RELIGIOUS INSPIRATION*

Always accorded very high rank as literature, *Pearl* has been several times edited since Morris' pioneer edition of 1864. Further, it has been often translated and, especially in recent years, subjected to much searching criticism. The most recent satisfactory edition of *Pearl* (by E. V. Gordon, 1953) is provided with a good bibliography and an admirable introductory essay summarizing much of the more important scholarship. In the present discussion, the focus is on studies appearing too recently for inclusion in Gordon's work. For a recent translation, together with a critical discussion, see Sister Mary Vincent Hillmann's *The Pearl: Mediaeval Text with a Literal Translation and Interpretation* (1961).

Among the numerous investigations of words or passages used by the *Pearl* poet are papers by Sister Mary Hillmann (*MLN*, 1941, 1943, 1944, 1945, and 1953), Marie Hamilton (*MLN*, 1943), C. H. Holman (*MLN*, 1951), A. L. Kellogg (*Traditio*, 1956), and R. W. Ackerman (*JEGP*, 1957). Since they concern key passages, a few of the above studies have a bearing on the theme of the poem as a whole. Others relate to the problem of single or multiple authorship of the four poems in the *Pearl* manuscript (MS. Cotton Nero A.x). The latter topic, mentioned only in passing in Gordon's introduction, is explored especially by J. W. Clark (*PQ*, 1949; *JEGP*, 1950; *MLN*, 1950; *MLQ*, 1951) who opposes, on the basis of vocabulary differences, the theory of the single authorship of the four poems. Among efforts to identify the *Pearl* poet by name, or at least by calling or interests, are O. Cargill and Margaret Schlauch, "*Pearl* and Its Jeweler" (*PMLA*, 1928); J. P. Oakden, *Alliterative Poetry in Middle English* (1930, 1935); C. O. Chapman, "The Musical Training of the *Pearl* Poet" (*PMLA*, 1931); the same author's "The Authorship of the *Pearl*" (*PMLA*, 1932); and E. Wintermute, "The *Pearl's* Author as Herbalist" (*MLN*, 1949).

The study of literary backgrounds is aided by C. O. Chapman's *An Index of Names in Pearl, Purity, Patience, and Gawain* (1951). Other studies in the same category are G. Bone's "A Note on *Pearl* and *The Buke of the Howlat"* (*MAE*, 1937), G. H. Gerould's "The Gawain Poet and Dante: A Conjecture" (*PMLA*, 1936), and K. Hammerle's *"The Castel of Perseverance* und *Pearl"* (*Anglia*, 1936).

The interpretations published during the last several decades embrace a wide range of possibilities. Whereas Gollancz and Osgood read the poem as the poet's lament on the death of a real daughter at the age of two, Schofield and others, as Gordon observes in his introduction, regard it as an allegory of the way to salvation or of "clene maidenhood." W. K. Greene, *"The Pearl*—A New Interpretation" (*PMLA*, 1925), finds that it illustrates the doctrine of divine grace; and Sister Mary Madeleva, *Pearl: A Study in Spiritual Dryness* (1925), views the poet as a religious of mystical inclinations. R. Wellek, in his excellent *The Pearl: An Interpretation of the Middle English Poem* (*Prague Studies*, 1933), investigates supposed traces of the Jovinian heresy and makes some progress in reconciling the elegiac and the allegorical interpretations of his predecessors. Sister Mary Hillmann's view, in "Some Debatable Words in *Pearl* and Its Theme" (*MLN*, 1945), is that the gem maiden is the dream image of an actual pearl, and that the theme is essentially a commentary on the poet's one-time absorption in worldly goods.

During the 1950s several attempts were made to demonstrate that the poet intended his work to be read on four different levels of meaning in accordance with medieval Biblical exegesis. In this vein, D. W. Robertson, Jr.'s "The Heresy of *The Pearl*" (*MLN*, 1950) and *"The Pearl* as a Symbol" (*MLN*, 1950) are followed by W. S. Johnson's "The Imagery and Diction of *The Pearl*" (*ELH*, 1953) and M. R. Stern's "An Approach to *The Pearl*" (*JEGP*, 1955). A far more elaborate effort to apply exegetical methods to the reading of the poem is B. Farragher's unpublished dissertation, *"Pearl* and Scriptural Tradition" (Boston University, 1956). This reveals more sharply, perhaps, than the other studies the difficulties inherent in the exegetical approach to the understanding of secular poetry.

Temperate and balanced contributions to our understanding of the message of the poem have been made by J. Conley in *"Pearl* and a Lost Tradition" (*JEGP*, 1955), in which the work is viewed in the light of the tradition of Boethius' *Consolation of Philosophy*, and especially by Marie Hamilton in several articles, including "The Orthodoxy of *Pearl*, 603–4" (*MLN*, 1943), "The Meaning of the Middle English *Pearl*" (*PMLA*, 1955), and "Notes on *Pearl*" (*JEGP*, 1958). The dialogue between the poet and Pearl, Mrs. Hamilton suggests, may represent one part of the soul in communion with the other on the subject of redemption in Christ. Finally, returning more directly to the elegiac theory, C. W. Moorman, in "The Role of the Narrator in *Pearl*" (*MP*, 1955), argues that to get at the heart of the poem, one should waive all questions of allegory and symbolism and concentrate on the function of the poet as narrator. In so doing, he believes, one may see that the poem follows the general theme of an elegy—that is, the poet brings himself to an acceptance of death as part of the universal plan.

C. MISCELLANEOUS POEMS

The Owl and the Nightingale, termed by W. P. Ker "the most miraculous piece of writing among mediaeval English books," has been the subject of much study. Modern renderings of the poem are provided both in J. W. H. Atkins' edition (1922) and by G. Eggers (1955). The most scholarly presentation of the two surviving texts of the poem is the diplomatic edition of J. H. G. Grattan and G. F. H. Sykes (EETS, 1935; rptd. 1959), but a more recent edition of the Cotton MS. copy alone has been published by E. G. Stanley (1960).

F. L. Utley, in *The Crooked Rib: An Analytical Index to the Argument about Women in English and Scots Literature to the End of the Year 1568* (1944), associates *The Owl and the Nightingale* with such English poems as *Cuckoo* and Dunbar's *Merle and the Nychtingaill*. These poems, he believes, form a true English genre concerned with lawyers and with debates on love and the merits of women. C. L. Wrenn comments on one of the manuscripts in "Curiosities in a Medieval Manuscript" (*E&S*, 1939). A series of discussions deals with sources and the slender evidence bearing on the date of composition. Among these are Kathryn Huganir, *The Owl and the Nightingale: Sources, Date, Author* (1931); and J. W. H. Atkins, "A Note on 'The Owl and the Nightingale'" (*MLR*, 1940). By far the most complete investigation of the language of the poem is B. Sundby's *The Dialect and Provenance of the Middle English Poem The Owl and the Nightingale* (*LSE*, 1950). Here it is decided that the poet's dialect is more nearly that of West Surrey of the early thirteenth century than of Dorset, the supposed home of Nicholas of Guildford, who names himself as the poet. This work contains an excellent bibliography as well. In H. Hässler's *"The Owl and the Nightingale" und die literarischen Bestrebungen des 12. und 13. Jahrhunderts* (1942), the genre, imagery, and rhetorical character of the poem are thoroughly examined.

The several competing interpretations of the poem that have been advanced by earlier editors, Miss Huganir, and others are reviewed in R. M. Lumiansky's "Concerning *The Owl and the Nightingale*" (*PQ*, 1953) and D. L. Peterson's "*The Owl and the Nightingale* and Christian Dialectic" (*JEGP*, 1956). Lumiansky supports the theory that the poem is to be read as a plea to a bishop for the granting of additional livings to the poet, on the grounds of his worthy accomplishments and the sanity of his judgment in the flyting of the two birds. Peterson, concerning himself with the substance of the debate rather than with the occasion of the writing, believes the poem to be an exercise in dialectic, the owl representing the triumphant viewpoint of the traditional Christian logician and the nightingale that of a sensuous, heretical rhetorician. On the other hand, M. J. Donovan, in "The Owl as Religious Altruist in *The Owl and the Nightingale*" (*MS*, 1956), holds that neither bird may claim the victory in the debate, a view also supported by Stanley in the introduction to his edition.

VIII. THE ROMANCE

A. GENERAL WORKS ON THE MIDDLE ENGLISH ROMANCES

DURING RECENT decades, several scholars have explored the concept of romance in keeping with the tradition established by W. P. Ker's famous *Epic and Romance* (1896; 2nd ed. 1908; rptd. 1958), although with more particular reference to Middle English examples. Chief among these are Dorothy Everett, in "A Characterization of the English Medieval Romances" (*E&S*, 1929) and R. Hoops, in *Der Begriff 'Romance' in der mittelenglischen und frühneuenglischen Literatur* (1929). A work of general importance to the student is *Middle English Metrical Romances* (1930), by W. H. French and C. B. Hale, a well-edited collection of twenty-seven of the best-known poems, which is provided with a sound introductory essay. Some of the poems are given only in selections, however, and others, such as *The Tournament of Tottenham*, scarcely fit the definition of romance. Also valuable for basic understanding of romance literature is A. C. Baugh's "The Authorship of the Middle English Romances" (*MHRA Bulletin*, 1950), in which evidence of clerical and minstrel authorship is pointed out in a number of romances. Baugh's essay supplements very helpfully the more general discussions of the medieval profession of letters described in Section II above.

In a later paper, "Improvisation in the Middle English Romances" (*PAPS*, 1959), Baugh discusses the appearance in some six matter of England romances of set formulas and stock themes, thus making a new application of recent studies concerning oral literature, especially Jugoslavian oral poems, Greek epics, and Old English narrative verse. (See, for example, F. P. Magoun, Jr., *Speculum*, 1953.) He believes that such romances as *Beves of Hamtoun, Guy of Warwick*, and *Richard Coeur de Lion*, although not originally the result of oral composition, bear the marks of reworking by minstrels in their not infrequent resort to stereotyped expressions. Twenty-three romances—including *Horn Childe, Guy of Warwick*, and *Athelston*—are effectively analyzed by A. McI. Trounce in a series of articles entitled "The English Tail-Rhyme Romances" (*MAE*, 1932, 1933, 1934). In J. P. Oakden's two-volume *Alliterative Poetry in Middle English* (1930, 1935) much is said about the romances in alliterative verse, but the emphasis is heavily on technicalities of meter and phraseology. The first section of G. Kane's *Middle English Literature* (1951) represents an earnest effort to evaluate as literature some sixty verse romances, the criterion of success being the romance composer's capacity to relate a tale that is at once credible and moving. Almost alone among those who have written on this subject, Kane seeks to present English romance as a genre in its own right rather than as a set of more or less crude versions of Old French romances.

Two distinguished works dealing with folk-tale elements in medieval romances are J. R. Reinhard's *The Survival of Geis in Mediaeval Romance* (1933) and H. R. Patch's "The Adaptation of Other-world Motifs to Medieval Romance," *Philologica: The Malone Anniversary Studies* (1949). The folk-tale backgrounds of a number of individual romances have been investigated as well.

Of late, fewer studies than formerly are concerned with realism in the romances, yet occasional articles and dissertations dealing with reflections of contemporaneous life are still to be found. Examples are Margaret Gist's *Love and War in the Middle English Romances* (1947), M. A. Owings' *The Arts in the Middle English Romances* (1952), P. Heather's "Precious Stones in the Middle English Verse of the Fourteenth Century" (*Folk-Lore*, 1931), and K. Lippmann's *Das ritterliche Persönlichkeitsideal in der mittelenglischen Literatur des 13. und 14. Jahrhunderts* (1933). In general, the authors of such studies agree that the romances are "realistic" in the sense of portraying with some fidelity the external details and trappings and even the mores and prejudices of their times. In their reworkings of old stories, the romance writers seem to have striven for "idealized modernity," to borrow R. M. Wilson's phrase.

B. THE NON-ARTHURIAN ROMANCES

Significant new work has appeared on approximately fifteen of those romances that are normally classified as matter of England, matter of France, or matter of Rome.

The brief fourteenth-century metrical tale *Athelston* has been edited afresh by A. McI. Trounce (EETS, 1951). The introduction to this work includes an unusually full and satisfying treatment of literary backgrounds. With respect to *Guy of Warwick*, immensely popular in medieval times, A. Ewert's edition of the Old French *Gui de Warewic* (2 vols., CFMA, 1932–33) affords material aid in understanding the various English versions. Not only has the Old French *Romance of Horn* by Thomas (Vol. I, critical ed. and notes, *ANTS*, 1955) been recently published by Mildred Pope, but W. H. French has produced a definitive discussion of the legend, to which is appended an edition of the English version known as *King Horn* (*Essays on King Horn*, 1940). In *"The Romance of Horn* and *King Horn"* (*MAE*, 1956), Miss Pope argues that the French poet, Thomas, worked from an English version of the tale. A critique of *King Horn*, in which the story is interpreted as a conflict between Horn the fighter and Horn the lover, is set forth by D. M. Hill (*Anglia*, 1957).

To turn to another matter of England romance, Cecile O'Rahilly's edition, *Eachtra Uilliam: An Irish Version of William of Palerne* (1949), is prefaced by a brief, lucid discussion in which it is concluded that the Irish romance was taken from the Middle English form of *William of Palerne*.

Of the Charlemagne romances, or the matter of France, the heretofore unprinted Fillingham texts of *Firumbras* and *Otuel and Roland* have been edited by Mary O'Sullivan (EETS, 1935).

It would be difficult to overestimate the widespread appeal of the Alexander legends (matter of Rome) in the many forms, including the romances, that they assumed during the Middle Ages. Supplementing F. P. Magoun, Jr.'s, *The Gests of King Alexander of Macedon* (1929), which provides a review of the entire medieval legend, is the ambitious work of the late G. Cary, *The Medieval Alexander* (1956), the central aim of which is to determine how Alexander the Great was regarded by various segments of the population during the Middle Ages. All the Middle English forms of the story figure in Cary's work. Still another book in this vein is F. Pfister's *Alexander der Grosse in den Offenbarungen der Griechen, Juden, Mohammedaner und Christen* (1956). A monumental multi-volume edition of the Old French *Roman d'Alexandre*, by E. C. Armstrong, A. Foulet, and others, is being currently issued, the first volume having appeared in 1937 and the seventh in 1955.

The most intensive work on the Middle English Alexander romance is the two-volume edition by G. V. Smithers (EETS, 1952, 1957). In addition to a classified bibliography, Smithers incorporates in his introduction an essay on the rhetorical aspects of *Kyng Alisaunder*, which he regards as among the very best of the Middle English romances. He also conjectures that this lengthy poem was designed for episodic delivery by minstrels.

On *The King of Tars*, rewarding articles have been written by Lillian Hornstein, "The Historical Background of the *King of Tars*" (*Speculum*, 1941), and R. J. Geist, "On the Genesis of *The King of Tars*" (*JEGP*, 1943) and "Notes on *The King of Tars*" (*JEGP*, 1948). *Sire Degarre*, edited by G. Schleich (*Englische Textbibliothek*, 1929), has been discussed by C. H. Slover, in "*Sire Degarre*: A Study of a Mediaeval Hack Writer's Methods" (*Texas Studies in English*, 1931). M. J. Donovan, in "*Sire Degare*: lines 992–997" (*MS*, 1953), argues that this romance is an imitation of Breton lais and that it may reflect historical incidents. Efforts to vindicate the romance as a work of literature have been made by G. P. Faust, in *Sire Degarre: A Study of the Texts and Narrative Structure* (1935), and W. C. Stokoe, Jr., "The Double Problem of *Sir Degaré*" (*PMLA*, 1955). The last-mentioned article contains a good review of *Sire Degarre* scholarship.

A three-text edition of the lai, *Sir Orfeo*, has been published by A. J. Bliss (1954), with a full introductory treatment of textual matters and literary associations. G. V. Smithers' "Story Patterns in Some Breton Lays" (*MAE*, 1953) offers an important commentary on this and other French and English romances, such as *Lanval*, *Yvain*, and *Sir Gowther*. R. S. Loomis, in "*Sir Orfeo* and Walter Map's *De Nugis*" (*MLN*, 1936), brings forth evidence bearing on the Celtic backgrounds of *Sir Orfeo*.

Numerous other studies of the romances are necessarily omitted from this survey, but it is worth noting that *Eger and Grime* has been edited by J. R. Caldwell (1933), and that Mabel Day completed the edition of *The Siege of Jerusalem* (EETS, 1932) initiated long before by E. Kölbing. Finally, B. J. Whiting, in "A Fifteenth-Century English Chaucerian: The Translator of *Partonope of Blois*" (*MS*, 1945), points out numerous passages in the English

Partonope that reveal not only indebtedness to various of Chaucer's poems but also the poet's skillful and effective treatment of his French source.

C. THE ARTHURIANA

The general quickening of activity in the Arthurian field during recent years is reflected in numerous studies dealing directly and indirectly with the Arthurian romances and chronicles preserved to us in Middle English. Our control of this body of commentary is greatly strengthened by several bibliographical aids and a recently published comprehensive history of the Arthurian legend. For the earlier material, the full bibliography in J. D. Bruce's *The Evolution of Arthurian Romance from the Beginnings down to the Year 1300* (1923; 2nd ed. 1928; rptd. 1958) is supplemented by two pamphlets issued by the Modern Language Association: Vol. I, *Arthurian Bibliography, 1922–1929* (1931) by J. J. Parry, and Vol. II, carrying the coverage through 1935 (1936), by Parry and Margaret Schlauch. The late J. J. Parry continued his bibliography on an annual basis in the journal *Modern Language Quarterly* from 1940 to 1955, and P. A. Brown from 1956 to 1963. In 1949 appeared the first of the annual bibliographical bulletins of the *Société internationale arthurienne*. In each of these bulletins, seven or more bibliographers assume responsibility for listing Arthurian contributions published in book form and journals in the various European countries, the United States, and Canada. Unlike the bibliography in *Modern Language Quarterly*, these are restricted to medieval Arthuriana; moreover, most of the scholarly items are concisely summarized. Another kind of aid to the student is R. W. Ackerman's *Index of the Arthurian Names in Middle English* (1952). In addition to identifying and commenting on the more than two thousand personal and place names occuring in some twenty-eight Arthurian pieces in verse and prose, this work contains a bibliography.

The Arthurian works in Middle English from Layamon's *Brut* (c. 1205) through the fifteenth-century romances of Lovelich and Malory form only one segment of the great international corpus of medieval Arthuriana. Numerous though they are, the English works do not themselves give us the whole of the complex legend as it exists in Old French literature. Moreover, as is true of the non-Arthurian romances, a great number of the English pieces were derived more or less directly from French antecedents. It follows, then, that an adequate understanding of this body of English literature entails considerable attention to the whole of the medieval legend of Arthur.

Two works of the first importance for acquiring such a perspective are J. D. Bruce's *Evolution of Arthurian Romance*, mentioned above, and *Arthurian Literature in the Middle Ages: A Collaborative History*, edited by R. S. Loomis (1959). Bruce's work perpetuates a few outmoded views, especially as to Arthurian origins; moreover, since his *terminus ad quem* is 1300, he has slight opportunity to discuss the English Arthuriana apart from Layamon's *Brut*. Nevertheless his summaries and analyses of the earlier material in Old French and the other vernaculars remain most useful. The Loomis volume, made up of contributions by thirty scholars, deals primarily with the literature composed after 1300 and also emends some of the opinions expressed by Bruce on earlier phases of the subject.

Five chapters in the Loomis book are directly concerned with the Arthurian works in Middle English: R. S. Loomis, "Layamon's *Brut*," R. W. Ackerman, "The English Rimed and Prose Romances," J. L. N. O'Loughlin, "The English Alliterative Romances," Laura H. Loomis, "*Gawain and the Green Knight*," and E. Vinaver, "Sir Thomas Malory." In the present discussion, the modest aim is to supplement some portions of these chapters by reference to a few publications not cited or not stressed by their authors. Emphasis is placed on Layamon's poem, the alliterative *Morte Arthure, Gawain and the Green Knight*, and Malory's *Morte Darthur*, since it is with these works that most of the very recent scholarship deals.

Loomis' chapter on the *Brut* of Layamon should be read in conjunction with the two preceding chapters, which treat Geoffrey of Monmouth's *Historia Regum Britanniae* and Wace's *Brut*. The most important recent publication in the field of the Arthurian chronicles is J. S. P. Tatlock's *The Legendary History of Britain: Geoffrey of Monmouth's Historia Regum Britanniae and Its Early Vernacular Versions* (1950), the concluding section of which concerns Layamon. R. Blenner-Hassett's *A Study of the Place-Names in Lawman's Brut* (1950) is also helpful.

The alliterative *Morte Arthure* is competently treated in O'Loughlin's chapter on the alliterative romances, although additional studies might well be noted—for example, R. H. Wilson's discussion of certain minor characters in the poem (*MLN*, 1956) and the first section of Dorothy Everett's "The Alliterative Revival" in *Essays on Middle English Literature* (1955). Much the most comprehensive investigation, however, is W. Matthews' *The Tragedy of Arthur: A Study of the Alliterative 'Morte Arthure'* (1960). Here it is convincingly argued that the English poet, although reworking a traditional story under the influence of *The Romance of Alexander*, nevertheless produced a poem of distinction and originality that holds a position of central importance in the so-called alliterative revival of the fourteenth century.

To Mrs. Loomis' excellent essay on *Gawain and the Green Knight*, several efforts to analyze the structure or formulate the theme of the poem may be appended. In "Myth and Mediaeval Literature: *Sir Gawain and the Green Knight*" (*MS*, 1956), C. W. Moorman rejects the notion that an identification of the myth pattern underlying *Sir Gawain*, or any other poem, is by itself a sufficient basis for a critical understanding, even though it may serve as a valuable tool. He then suggests that the main purpose of the Gawain poet is to present a semiallegorical account of the decline of the Round Table. S. Barnet (*MLN*, 1956) comments on the poet's seeming preoccupation with developing a three-part structure throughout his poem. In "The Meaning of *Sir Gawain and the Green Knight*" (*PMLA*, 1957), A. M. Markman urges that, in part at least, the literary appeal of the poem lies in the humanity of a hero who earns and proves his moral superiority before our eyes. A. B. Friedman, in "Morgan le Fay in *Sir Gawain and the Green Knight*" (*Speculum*, 1960), rejects vigorously D. E. Baughan's earlier defense of Morgan's role as the instigator of the plot (*ELH*, 1950). Friedman holds that the poet introduced Morgan le Fay, not with complete success, as a device for uniting the beheading and temptation motifs. J. Burrow, in "The Two Confession Scenes in *Sir Gawain and the Green Knight*" (*MP*, 1959), observes that the three acts of contrition, confession, and satisfaction are reflected in the poem. In some measure he repeats the argument in R. W. Ackerman's "Gawain's Shield: Penitential Doctrine in *Gawain and the Green Knight*" (*Anglia*, 1958). A careful analysis of recent scholarship devoted to the poem is provided by M. W. Bloomfield (*PMLA*, 1961).

Like the other chapters in the Loomis compilation, E. Vinaver's "Sir Thomas Malory" provides a survey of scholarship and thus performs a very large part of the task of the present review. Clearly the leading authority in this field, Vinaver has written a biography of Malory (1929) and is further the editor, in *The Works of Sir Thomas Malory* (3 vols., 1947), of the fifteenth-century Winchester Manuscript of *Le Morte Darthur* discovered in 1934. As revealed in his edition, Vinaver's position is that *Le Morte Darthur* consists actually of eight separate romances, a thesis that he supports by reference to Malory's use of his sources and to the colophons appearing only in the Winchester Manuscript. That for centuries the work has been accepted as a single romance is to be ascribed to

the editing of William Caxton. Vinaver acknowledges that there are
those who, unreconciled to this theory, continue to argue strongly
for the "unity" of *Le Morte Darthur*. Among the scholars belonging
to this camp are R. M. Lumiansky, C. Moorman, and T. C. Rumble,
some of whose contributions are listed in the final footnote in
Vinaver's chapter. More recent articles to this same effect, two by
Moorman and one by Rumble, appear in *ELH* (1960), *MS* (1960),
and *JEGP* (1960).

IX. DRAMA

A. BIBLIOGRAPHIES

LIKE ARTHURIAN literature, the field of medieval drama is well supplied with bibliographies, digests of scholarship, and over-all histories of recent date. C. J. Stratman's *Bibliography of Medieval
Drama* (1954) includes a coverage of general histories and background studies as well as of works dealing directly with Middle
English, Byzantine, French, German, Italian, and Latin dramatic
literature. The chapter "Medieval English Drama," comprising not
much less than half the entire book, is devoted to liturgical
expansions, the various mystery cycles, folk plays, and moralities.

A valuable supplement to Stratman's *Bibliography*, which is
not annotated, is M. Henshaw's "A Survey of Studies in Medieval
Drama: 1933–1950" (*Progress of Medieval and Renaissance Studies
in the United States and Canada*, 1951). Here, works bearing on the
historical development of drama are rather fully analyzed, as are
treatments of mystery cycles and individual plays in various languages, including Middle English. Still another useful work, A.
Harbage's *Annals of English Drama, 975–1700* (1940; rev. 1964),
presents a chronological table of Latin, French, and English plays
of all sorts about which records of performances in England have
been found.

B. HISTORICAL AND BACKGROUND STUDIES

The basic work on backgrounds, E. K. Chambers' *The Mediaeval Stage* (2 vols., 1903), may not be said to have been superseded,
although the same writer's essay on drama in his *English Literature*

at the Close of the Middle Ages (1945; 1947, with corrections) provides an enlightening supplement, with close attention to metrical matters. Next in importance on backgrounds and origins is K. Young's *The Drama of the Medieval Church* (2 vols., 1933). This work offers the definitive treatment of the liturgical origins of religious drama, including Easter plays, nativity plays, and other representations of Biblical material. The several efforts to discredit or seriously to modify the now well-established doctrine of liturgical origins, as well as the replies to these attempts—in particular, Maria de Vito's *L'Origine del dramma liturgico* (1938), R. Stumpfl's *Kultspiele der Germanen als Ursprung der mitteralterlichen Dramas* (1936), O. Cargill's *Drama and Liturgy* (1930), and Mary Marshall's "The Dramatic Tradition Established by the Liturgical Plays" (*PMLA*, 1941)—are reviewed in Henshaw's survey. Other works treating the backgrounds of Middle English drama include the work of G. R. Owst, already cited, *Literature and the Pulpit in Medieval England* (1933), in which one finds many convincing parallels suggesting the influence of sermons on drama. C. F. Brown, in "Sermons and Miracle Plays: Merton College MS. 248" (*MLN*, 1934), adds a note on this subject. Again, Grace Frank's *The Medieval French Drama* (1954) provides a study of Anglo-Norman plays and in other ways sheds light on early dramatic performances in England. Still a third study of use to the student of Middle English drama is W. Farnham's *The Medieval Heritage of Elizabethan Tragedy* (1936; rptd. 1956).

English Religious Drama of the Middle Ages (1955), by the veteran scholar, H. Craig, is intended to complement the work of Chambers and Young in the respect that it accounts for the development of the vernacular cyclical plays. In a review of this important book, F. M. Salter (*JEGP*, 1957) argues that Craig tends to rely too much on Continental evidence. The initial lecture in Salter's own recent work, *Mediaeval Drama in Chester* (1955), also offers a historical account in brief with some emphasis on the influence of folk elements, such as the mummers' plays. In *Early English Stages: 1300 to 1660*, Vol. I (1959), G. Wickham objects to the traditional reconstruction of medieval drama, as represented especially in Craig's recent book, on the grounds that it is derived almost altogether from extant texts of the plays and fails to take account of our present knowledge about conditions of stage performance. In his own book Wickham surveys the contributions of minstrelsy, mummings, tournaments, and other dramatic manifestations to the evolution of the theater.

Two discussions dwell on the decline of mystery plays. In

Mysteries' End: An Investigation of the Last Days of the Medieval Religious Stage (1946), H. C. Gardiner ascribes the vanishing of cyclical plays to the later distaste for the religious culture of the past and, more specifically, to episcopal opposition in England. Henshaw's "The Attitude of the Church toward the Stage to the End of the Middle Ages" (*M&H*, 1952) is a compendium of opinion about mysteries, miracle plays, and other spectacles expressed by medieval church authorities. L. G. Craddock studies "Franciscan Influence on Early English Drama" (*FranS*, 1950), and in *The Role of the Virgin Mary in the Coventry, York, Chester, and Towneley Cycles* (1933), L. Cornelius traces recurrent religious motifs. Rosemary Woolf considers the elements that several cyclical and noncyclical Abraham and Isaac plays have in common in "The Effect of Typology on the English Mediaeval Plays of Abraham and Isaac" (*Speculum*, 1957).

One of the more restricted topics of discussion in this general field is the question of the existence of actual theaters in the twelfth and thirteenth centuries. An affirmative answer is given by R. S. Loomis and G. Cohen (*Speculum*, 1945) and also by Mary Marshall (*Symposium*, 1950), although some of their evidence has been questioned by D. Bigongiari (*RR*, 1946). For a comprehensive discussion of pageants, stages, theatrical properties, and medieval dramatic theory and practice, Wickham's book, mentioned above, and such articles as G. R. Kernodle's "The Medieval Pageant Wagons of Louvain" (*TA*, 1943) are very useful.

C. THE MYSTERY CYCLES AND OTHER RELIGIOUS DRAMA

All the more important cyclical plays, not the least the Chester Cycle, have been studied from different points of view in recent decades, as indicated in Henshaw's survey. W. W. Greg's *The Play of Antichrist, from the Chester Cycle* (1935) is an edition based on a thoroughgoing study of the manuscripts; and the same writer's essays on other aspects of the cycle, including the banns, are collected in *The Trial and Flagellation with Other Studies in the Chester Cycle* (1936). To the last-named volume, F. M. Salter contributes an edition of a new manuscript of *The Trial and Flagellation*, which he himself discovered. Salter further has extended our knowledge of the banns of the Chester plays in separate publications (*RES*, 1939, 1940). The articles throw much light not only on problems of mystery play production but also on the role of English prelates in suppressing mystery plays in the late sixteenth century.

By far the most important publication on the cycle since 1950 is the collection of Alexander Lectures by Salter (*Mediaeval Drama in Chester*, 1955). Reference has already been made to the initial lecture, on the origins of religious drama. Subsequent lectures deal with the founding of the cycle, the actual production of the plays, and a critical evaluation of the plays as literature. Specific problems are discussed by A. Brown in "A Tradition of the Chester Plays" (*London Medieval Studies*, 1951), strengthening somewhat the tradition that Ranulph Higden may have been the Chester poet, and by J. A. Bryant, Jr., in "Chester's Sermon for Catechumens" (*JEGP*, 1954). In "The Corpus Christi Passion Plays as Dramatic Art" (*SP*, 1951), W. F. McNeir treats specifically the several plays in each of the four cycles—Chester, York, Wakefield, and *Ludus Coventriae* (now associated with the city of Lincoln by Craig)—that set forth the events of Christ's last days on earth. He argues that the Passion is the core of each cycle and that these plays embody new and deeper significance and a more conscious control of literary effects. Eleanor Prosser's *Drama and Religion* (1961) likewise seeks to rescue medieval drama from a too-heavy burden of historical scholarship and to treat the plays as literature.

A number of other studies are also significant. Effie MacKinnon, in "Notes on the Dramatic Structure of the York Cycle" (*SP*, 1931), observes that the entire cycle must be considered as the dramatic unit. Anna Mill, in "The York Bakers' Play of The Last Supper" (*MLR*, 1935), comments on the active role of the York bakers in presenting their portion of the Corpus Christi cycle and particularly on *The Last Supper*, a play that escaped the censor's ban in the mid-sixteenth century. In "The York Plays of the Dying, Assumption, and Coronation of Our Lady" (*PMLA*, 1950), Miss Mill points out that, although there is a paucity of evidence concerning the performance of English (as opposed to French) saints' miracles, a number of Mary plays are embedded in such cycles as the York and *Ludus Coventriae*. Further, we have for York "both the texts of and municipal records regarding the regulations and production of Mary plays." In "The Stations of the York Corpus Christi Play" (*Transactions of the Yorkshire Dialect Society*, 1948–51), Miss Mill publishes records attesting not only to the location of stations but also the the leasing of scaffold seats and the allocation of free places to dignitaries. C. F. Hoffman, Jr., (*MLN*, 1950), finds in the *Legenda Aurea* close parallels to the words of songs celebrating the virtues of the Blessed Virgin in *The Appearance of Our Lady to Thomas*. In "Alliterative Verse in the

York Cycle" (*SP*, 1951), J. B. Reese provides a metrical analysis of the plays, noting a mixture, which he considers purposeful, of syllabic and alliterative verse. Finally, in J. S. Purvis' *The York Cycle of Mystery Plays: A Shorter Version of the Ancient Cycle* (1951), and in his more complete translation published in 1957, we have modern English renderings of the cycle.

Perhaps the most important work on the Towneley Cycle in recent years is A. C. Cawley's *The Wakefield Pageants in the Towneley Cycle* (1958), a new edition of six of the thirty-one plays of the cycle from a Huntington Library manuscript. The six plays, including *Abel, Noah,* and both shepherd plays, were selected because they embody the Wakefield Master's vivid realism and illustrate his stanzaic form. This edition is provided with an excellent introduction and glossary. Also of interest are Cawley's "The 'Grotesque' Feast in the *Prima Pastorum*" (*Speculum,* 1955) and "The Wakefield First Shepherds' Play" (*PLPLS-LHS,* 1953). In the latter the author argues that *The First Shepherds' Play* is "probably more impressive as a dramatic poem than as a play." A. Williams, in *The Characterization of Pilate in the Towneley Plays* (1950), argues that, almost alone among the stock characters of cyclical drama, Pilate escapes the simplistic dichotomy between good and evil, appearing rather as a convincing human being, a tyrant of a well-defined sort, whose presence serves as an effective unifying device.

The several articles on the *Secunda Pastorum* mentioned by Henshaw include C. Chidamian's "Mak and the Tossing in the Blanket" (*Speculum,* 1947), in which it is suggested that, since blanket-tossing was a known method of expediting childbirth, this piece of business would have struck the original audiences as an appropriately hilarious part of the burlesque on the Nativity. Other writers—H. A. Watt (*Essays and Studies in Honor of Carleton Brown,* 1940) and F. J. Thompson (*MLN,* 1949)—discuss the unity of *Secunda Pastorum.* The backgrounds of the Mak story have been investigated by H. M. Smyser and T. B. Stroup in "Analogues to the Mak Story" (*JAF,* 1934) and by R. C. Cosbey, "The Mak Story and its Folklore Analogues" (*Speculum,* 1945).

On the *Ludus Coventriae,* T. B. Clark has held that the Old Testament plays of the cycle were not added until the seventeenth century (*PQ,* 1933), a theory at once rejected by Salter and Baugh (both articles in *PQ,* 1933). More recently, T. B. Fry, in "The Unity of the *Ludus Coventriae*" (*SP,* 1951), argues persuasively that this cycle is unified in terms of the patristic principle of the "abuse of power"—that is, that Satan abused his position in bringing about Christ's death. J. A. Bryant, Jr., suggests that the play known as *The Trial of Joseph and Mary* was originally composed for a group of transient players or by friars, "The Function of *Ludus Coventriae* 14" (*JEGP*, 1953).

X. PIERS PLOWMAN

FOLLOWING, or perhaps pacing, the general trend already observed in other areas of medieval literary study, the numerous works of the past twenty years or so dealing with *Piers Plowman* are rather heavily weighted in favor of interpretive studies. A strong continuing interest in textual and linguistic problems is still apparent, yet the emphasis no longer falls so completely on the vexed question of single or multiple authorship first brought to the fore by J. M. Manly early in the century.

In a thoughtful review of *Piers Plowman* scholarship up to 1939 (*Speculum*, 1939), M. W. Bloomfield discusses several treatments of literary influences, but the larger part of his essay is necessarily concerned with speculations published in the 1930s as to the author or authors of the poem and on related matters. Very likely the conclusion drawn by Bloomfield from these studies—namely, that "it is reasonable to assume today that one author (probably William Langland) wrote *Piers Plowman*"—is not an entirely just reflection of more recent work in this field. Bloomfield's review is supplemented by the classified bibliography in T. A. Knott and D. C. Fowler's *Piers the Plowman: A Critical Edition of the A-Version* (1952).

The Knott-Fowler book just cited represents the first published effort to improve on W. W. Skeat's three-text edition of 1867–84, although other editing projects are now in progress. Volume I, George Kane's edition of the A-Text (1960) is available, and the B- and C-Text volumes are to follow.

Of the numerous works treating the technicalities of the manuscripts, the following are representative: R. W. Chambers and J. H. G. Grattan, "The Text of *Piers Plowman*" (*MLR*, 1931); Chambers, *The Manuscripts of Piers Plowman in the Huntington Library and their Value in Fixing the Text of the Poem* (1935); D. C. Fowler, "The Relationship of the Three Texts of *Piers the Plowman*" (*MP*, 1952); and A. G. Mitchell and G. H. Russell, "The

Three Texts of 'Piers the Plowman'" (*JEGP*, 1953). Certain closely related studies bear on evidence as to the dates of composition, such as J. A. W. Bennett's "The Date of the B-Text of *Piers Plowman*" (*MAE*, 1943), A. Gwynne's paper with an identical title (*RES*, 1943), and B. F. Huppé's "*Piers Plowman:* The Date of the B-Text Reconsidered" (*SP*, 1949). Other scholars have interested themselves in aspects of language, such as Sister Carmeline Sullivan, *The Latin Insertions and Macaronic Verse in Piers Plowman* (1932), and H. Kittner, *Studien zum Wortschatz William Langlands* (1937).

Many of the above-mentioned discussions include some reflections as to the authorship of the poem. Manly himself, as T. A. Stroud observes (*MLN*, 1949), seems never to have abandoned his theory of multiple authorship. Again, J. R. Hulbert, in "*Piers the Plowman* After Forty Years" (*MP*, 1947), reviews several of Manly's arguments on this score that he feels still hold good in the face of many attacks, chiefly those of R. W. Chambers. A. H. Bright's *New Light on Langland* (1928; rptd. 1950) represents an enthusiastic attempt to identify the scene of the poem with Ledbury in the Malvern Hills and to demonstrate that the poet was connected with Eustace de Rokayle. F. Krog (*Anglia*, 1934) criticizes adversely Bright's *Lebensbild* of the poet, but in a later essay (*MLQ*, 1943), M. W. Bloomfield returns cautiously to some of Bright's suggestions and inquires further whether Langland could have been a Benedictine monk. H. Maisack seeks to associate the religious ideas in the poem with the Cistercian Order in *William Langlands Verhältnis zum Zisterziensischen Mönchtum: Eine Untersuchung der Vita im Piers Plowman* (1953). In "The Life and Death of Longe Wille," (*ELH*, 1950), H. Meroney impugns the use of certain pieces of internal evidence, especially the passage in B-Text referring to "Longe Wille," in speculating about the poet's name. He also considers B-Text to represent the original form of the poem.

E. T. Donaldson, in his thoroughgoing *Piers Plowman: The C-Text and its Poet* (1949), bases his acceptance of the unity of authorship on a careful scrutiny of the C-Text. He further endorses the view that Langland was a married clerk, no higher in rank than an acolyte, who made his living by offering prayers for both the living and the dead. Further, Donaldson's chapter, "The Art of the C-Revision," sets forth interesting observations about the over-all meaning of the poem.

A number of scholars seek to explain various passages in terms of social history, literary associations, theological themes, or medieval religious life. Far too numerous to list here, these contributions include M. W. Bloomfield, "The Pardons of Pamplona and the

Pardoner of Rounceval: *Piers Plowman*, B XVII 252 (C XX 218)"
(*PQ*, 1956), W. Gaffney, "The Allegory of the Christ Knight in
Piers Plowman" (*PMLA*, 1931), B. Huppé, "*Petrus id est Christus*:
Word Play in *Piers Plowman*, the B-Text" (*ELH*, 1950), G.
Sanderlin, "The Character 'Liberum Arbitrium' in the C-Text of
Piers Plowman" (*MLN*, 1941), and R. E. Kaske, "The Use of
Simple Figures of Speech in *Piers Plowman* B: A Study in the
Figurative Expression of Ideas and Opinions" (*SP*, 1951).

Some of the studies beginning with the explication of single
passages or themes develop into an effort to account for the central
intentions and the literary appeal of the poem. Of these, N. Coghill's
"The Pardon of Piers Plowman" (*PBA*, 1944) is a good example.
Here it is argued that the pardon, which in A-Text has reference
merely to the worldly morality of the denizens of the Field of Folk,
becomes in B-Text an introduction to the complex allegory of the
three ways to salvation. Sister Rose Donna, in *Despair and Hope: A
Study in Langland and Augustine* (1948), holds that Augustinian
influence is apparent in the treatment of sin, a major theme of the
poem. In "The Philosophy of Piers Plowman" (*PMLA*, 1938), H.
W. Wells suggests that the three "lives" illustrated in the poem are
mental states rather than vocational callings. H. W. Troyer, in his
influential article "Who is Piers Plowman?" (*PMLA*, 1932), traces
the growing significance of Piers as a "multifold symbol," at times
merely an individual, again a representative of all mankind, and
finally God-man or Christ. Elizabeth Suddaby makes an appeal
for reading *Piers Plowman* as a poem rather than as a social
document, a puzzling allegory, or a vehicle of great theological
truths (*JEGP*, 1955). In something of the same tone, A. G.
Mitchell's *Lady Meed and the Art of Piers Plowman* (1956)
supports the view that the central figure of Lady Meed is not merely
a personification of gain or of cupidity but rather a dramatic
personage whose total meaning emerges in her changing fortunes. In
"*Piers Plowman* and the Pilgrimage to Truth" (*E&S*, 1958),
Elizabeth Zeeman (Salter) draws fruitful comparisons between the
quest in *Piers Plowman* and the thought of certain fourteenth-
century mystics.

A more general interpretation in terms of the turmoil and aspirations of fourteenth-century religion is developed by C. Dawson, in
Mediaeval Religion and Other Essays (1935). And in *Man's Uncon-
querable Mind* (1939; rptd. 1955), R. W. Chambers sets out with
broad strokes his own conclusions as to the argument and message of
Piers Plowman. He gives particular emphasis to the passus in which
the character Imaginative (i.e., memory) reconciles the Dreamer to

Reason, thus preparing him to resume the search for Do-wel, Do-bet, and Do-best and ultimately to understand the nature of salvation.

Since the appearance of Chambers' essay, several full-scale treatments of the meaning of one or another of the three versions have been published. Despite the importance of certain of these more or less recent works, there is space here for only the most general comments. In *Piers Plowman: An Interpretation of the A-Text* (1937), T. P. Dunning rejects vigorously the notion that the poem is merely a loosely related series of vignettes satirizing social ills, a view which is reflected in the classification of the poem in Wells's *Manual* as a work of social protest. Dunning argues that the theme is the right use of temporal and spiritual goods, and also believes that his findings indicate divided authorship of *Piers Plowman* as a whole, although he later modifies this view in "Langland and the Salvation of the Heathen" (*MAE*, 1943). In a short essay, "An Interpretation of the A-Text of *Piers Plowman*" (*PMLA*, 1938), G. W. Stone, Jr., expresses general agreement with Dunning, although he stresses his feeling that the poet of the A-Text wishes to show the failure of both church and state. Greta Hort, in *Piers Plowman and Contemporary Religious Thought* (1938), believes that the root question in the poem is the eternal "What shall a man do to be saved?" The method chosen by the poet for answering this question, as revealed in the B version, is to bring into harmony two great Biblical texts: Matt. xxv.46 and Matt. xvi.19, which pertain respectively to the salvation that the righteous earn by meritorious works and to the power of the keys, or the authority of the church, through Peter, to remit the sins of man. Miss Hort also argues that Langland knew his missal better than his Bible.

D. W. Robertson, Jr., and B. Huppé, in *Piers Plowman and Scriptural Tradition* (1951), seek to show a heavy dependence in the B-Text on medieval Biblical exegesis, especially of the sort available in the so-called *Glossa Ordinaria* (*Patrologia Latina*, CXIII, CXIV). Although this book goes perhaps too far in applying to a secular poem the fourfold interpretation usually considered proper only to the Bible (see Bloomfield's review, *Speculum*, 1952), it opens up a means of arriving at a better explanation of many allusions in the poem. In "The Art of Reading Medieval Personification-Allegory" (*ELH*, 1953), R. W. Frank, Jr., draws a sharp distinction between personification, or the use of an abstraction in the function of a person, place, or thing, and symbol allegory, or allegory employing traditional symbols. It is held that personification allegory conveys a literal meaning only, whereas symbol allegory embodies in addition a figurative significance. In a later book, *Piers Plowman and the*

Scheme of Salvation (1957), Frank analyzes the two-thirds of the poem devoted to Do-wel, Do-bet, and Do-best (B, passus VIII–XX), observing that *Piers Plowman* consists mainly of personification allegory, and that its primary meaning, therefore, lies on the literal level. The key to the work, he believes, is not to be sought in scholastic philosophy, Biblical commentary, or the poet's autobiography. On this basis, he rejects the "three lives" theory and supports the view that the Trinity, each member of which assists man in his quest for salvation, provides the organizing principle. Robertson's review (*Speculum*, 1958) formulates clearly the opposition between Frank's and his own approach to the poem.

Finally, W. Erzgräber, in *William Langlands Piers Plowman, eine Interpretation des C-Textes* (1957), more nearly in line with earlier treatments, studies the poem against the background of medieval theology and presents Piers Plowman himself as the prototype of man in the state of grace. Do-wel is seen as teaching patient resignation; Do-bet, the love of God and man; and Do-best, responsibility for the state and continuance of Christendom. The contrast between Erzgräber's and Frank's books is pointed up in a review by D. C. Fowler (*MLQ*, 1959).

XI. CHAUCER

A. BIBLIOGRAPHIES, EDITIONS, AND THE CHAUCER CANON

THE LATE D. D. Griffith's *Bibliography of Chaucer, 1908–1953* (1955), the successor to Griffith's earlier work (1926) and to the pioneer bibliographies of Eleanor Hammond (1908) and others, is an indispensable guide. A series of more or less systematic surveys of Chaucer studies is also available, including R. A. Pratt's "Chaucer: The Works" (*Progress of Medieval and Renaissance Studies*, 1940), A. C. Baugh's "Fifty Years of Chaucer Scholarship" (*Speculum*, 1951), and R. R. Purdy's "Chaucer Scholarship in England and America: A Review of Recent Trends" (*Anglia*, 1951). The last-named essay, covering the period from 1930 to 1951, is the most detailed and helpful of such summaries. A convenient reprinting of many of the Chaucer articles referred to below is to be found in three recently published anthologies: *Chaucer: Modern Essays in Criticism*, ed. E. Wagenknecht (1959); *Discussions of The Canterbury Tales*, ed. C. A. Owen, Jr. (1961); and *Chaucer Criticism, The Canterbury Tales: An Anthology*, ed. R. J. Schoeck and J. Taylor (1960).

Of the modern editions of the complete works, that of F. N. Robinson (1933; 2nd ed. 1957) must be considered the best for general use. On the other hand, W. W. Skeat's great seven-volume edition (1894–97) has never been superseded. Numerous editions of single poems, such as *Troilus and Criseyde*, and also of selections from the works have appeared. Of those designed expressly for school use, perhaps E. T. Donaldson's *Chaucer's Poetry: An Anthology for the Modern Reader* (1958) and A. C. Baugh's *Chaucer's Major Poetry* (1963) are the best.

The monumental *Concordance to the Complete Works of Geoffrey Chaucer and to the Romaunt of the Rose*, by J. S. P. Tatlock and A. G. Kennedy (1927) is, of course, of first importance to the student despite the fact that it is based on the outdated Globe edition of A. W. Pollard (1898, 1913). Again, R. D. French's *A Chaucer Handbook* (1927; 2nd ed. 1947) retains its usefulness as an introduction to Chaucer. As a brief account of the life and works, with primary attention to *The Canterbury Tales*, N. Coghill's *The Poet Chaucer* (1949) fulfills much the same purpose.

Modern poetic renderings of parts, at least, of the works include T. Morrison's *The Portable Chaucer* (1949) and N. Coghill's *Geoffrey Chaucer: The Canterbury Tales* (1952). Of the two, Morrison's may be considered the more accurate and felicitous. Additional translations are G. P. Krapp's *Troilus and Criseyde* (1932). Also, the prose rendering by J. S. P. Tatlock and P. Mackaye of the complete poetical works, first published in 1914, has been reprinted as recently as 1951.

On the establishment of Chaucer's canon, F. W. Bonner's "The Genesis of the Chaucer Apocrypha" (*SP*, 1951) is interesting. In this field the most notable development has been the discovery and editing of the manuscript tract, *The Equatorie of the Planetis*, by D. J. Price (1955). Neither Price nor his linguistic collaborator, R. M. Wilson, makes a positive ascription to Chaucer of this treatise on the instrument called the *equatorium planetarum*, and most of the reviewers are inclined to reserve judgment as to Chaucer's authorship. G. Herdan (*Lang*, 1956), on the basis of a study of the Romance vocabulary of the treatise and that of Chaucer's known works, strengthens the case for ascription to Chaucer.

B. CHAUCER'S LIFE AND TIMES

In "Chaucer: The Life" (*Progress of Medieval and Renaissance Studies*, 1940), H. L. Savage comments succinctly on contributions made during the 1930s to our knowledge about the poet's life and family connections, and particularly on the researches of A. C. Baugh, H. Braddy, J. M. Manly, R. A. Pratt, and Edith Rickert. Further analyses of these and of similar works are to be found in Purdy's "Chaucer Scholarship in England and America," cited above.

Marchette Chute's *Geoffrey Chaucer of England* (1946; paperback 1958) is a generously proportioned development of the known biographical data, although one must not expect penetrating literary criticism here. Specialized studies bear on supposed kinsmen, such as two articles by A. C. Baugh (*PMLA*, 1932, 1933), or on minor events of the life, such as Margaret Galway's "Chaucer's Journeys in 1368" (*TLS*, 4 April 1958). A progress report on the work still going forward on the life records originally compiled by J. M. Manly and Edith Rickert is provided by M. M. Crow in "Materials for a New Edition of the Chaucer Life-Records" (*Texas Studies in English*, 1952). Crow's collaborator in the processing of these voluminous records, C. C. Olson, is the author of a critical sketch of Chaucer's life entitled "The Emerging Biography of a Poet" (*Third Annual College of the Pacific Lecture*, 1953). Recent information is to the effect that the Crow-Olson edition of the life records will soon be in print.

H. S. Bennett's *Chaucer and the Fifteenth Century* (1947) offers in the first three chapters an excellent brief account of the social surroundings, and especially of religious customs and attitudes of the day. Bennett further includes a sketch of Chaucer's development as a poet in terms of the influences, temporal, spiritual, and literary, that shaped his mind and his work. Later chapters on the fifteenth century and on "The Author and His Public" are likewise valuable.

Other books designed to acquaint the reader with Chaucer's fourteenth-century milieu include Sister Mary Whitmore's *Medieval English Domestic Life and Amusements in the Works of Chaucer* (1937). G. G. Coulton's well-known *Chaucer and His England* (1908; 7th ed. 1957) and perhaps Sister Mary Madeleva's *Chaucer's Nuns, and Other Essays* (1925) are still useful. Of particular value is *Chaucer's World* (1948), a compilation by Edith Rickert, C. C. Olson, and M. M. Crow of documentary materials having to do with "London Life," "Training and Education," "War," "Religion," and the like.

C. CHAUCER'S ENGLISH

A high proportion of the annual output of linguistic researches relating to Chaucer treats individual words and phrases. D. D. Griffith, in "On World Studies in Chaucer" (*Philologica: Malone Anniversary Studies*, 1949), observes that many of these notes on Chaucer's usages may and do lead to a significant clarification of his thought and poetic imagery. Numerous other investigations touch on Romance and other foreign influences on the language—for example, J. R. Hulbert's "Chaucer's Romance Vocabulary" (*PQ*, 1947) and H. T. Price's "Foreign Influences on Middle English" (*UMCMP*, 1947)—and on double consonants (K. Malone, *MS*, 1956); on the old stalking horse of the proper treatment of final -*e* and its metrical implications, E. T. Donaldson (*PMLA*, 1948) sets forth the traditional view as opposed to that espoused by J. G. Southworth (*PMLA*, 1947, 1949, and *Verses and Cadences*, 1954). Somewhat more directly concerned with literary ramifications are H. Kökeritz' "Rhetorical Word-Play in Chaucer" (*PMLA*, 1954) and P. F. Baum's "Chaucer's Puns: A Supplementary List" (*PMLA*, 1958). J. R. R. Tolkien's paper, "Chaucer as a Philologist: *The Reeve's Tale*" (*TPS*, 1934), is an interesting demonstration of Chaucer's ear for varieties of speech. Probably the best technical analysis of Chaucer's phonology, morphology, and pronunciation appears in S. Moore's *Historical Outlines of English Sounds and Inflections* (rev. A. H. Marckwardt, 1951).

D. GENERAL CRITICAL WORKS

Of the many discussions of Chaucer's works as a whole, a number must be mentioned here. G. L. Kittredge's brilliant *Chaucer and His Poetry* (1915; rptd. 1946) and R. K. Root's equally perceptive *The Poetry of Chaucer: A Guide to Its Study and Appreciation* (1922; rptd. 1957) were followed by J. L. Lowes' *Geoffrey Chaucer and the Development of His Genius* (1934; rptd. 1958). Somewhat more restricted than its predecessors, Lowes' book dwells on backgrounds and on the poems leading up to the composition of *The Canterbury Tales*. H. R. Patch's *On Rereading Chaucer* (1939) analyzes Chaucer's humor and gives considerable attention to *Troilus and Criseyde*. More specialized, and yet of importance to the student, is W. C. Curry's *Chaucer and the Mediaeval Sciences*

(1926; 2nd ed., enlarged, 1960), which provides a digest of medieval astrological and medical lore. Curry seeks here to interpret the external appearance and personality traits of the Canterbury pilgrims in fourteenth-century terms. Again, W. Héraucourt's *Die Wertwelt Chaucers: die Wertwelt einer Zeitwende* (1939) is an acute, if perhaps overprecise, anatomy of the medieval "terminology of values." The discussion of knightly ideals and of gentilesse is especially enlightening.

Critical works that have appeared since 1940 include several of distinction. P. V. D. Shelly, in *The Living Chaucer* (1940), explicates a number of the poems in tracing the evolution of Chaucer's art. His comments about *The Legend of Good Women* and *The House of Fame* are noteworthy. J. S. P. Tatlock, in his incomplete and posthumously published *The Mind and Art of Chaucer* (1950), emphasizes the poet's broad human sympathies and his refusal to adopt a reformer's frame of mind. *Troilus and Criseyde* he characterizes as a tale of romantic love. Unfortunately, Tatlock's remarks about *The Canterbury Tales* remain a mere fragment. K. Malone, in *Chapters on Chaucer* (1951), offers critical observations about most of the poems, his analysis of the style of *The General Prologue* containing, perhaps, the freshest and most helpful portion of his discussion. Malone's treatment of Chaucer as an innovator is also valuable. J. Speirs, in *Chaucer the Maker* (1951), seeks to express the values to be found in a medieval poet by a present-day reader. At times, as in his argument that *The Nun's Priest's Tale* is to be read as a burlesque of the fall of man and also in his analysis of the quality and effects of Chaucer's imagery, Speirs's insights are arresting. Yet his frequent failure to convince results, it would seem, from his conscientious avoidance of a heavy burden of historical scholarship and, more particularly, of knowledge about medieval religious life.

Chaucerian Essays (1952), by G. H. Gerould, is mainly concerned with several of the Canterbury pilgrims, notably the Pardoner, but it also dwells on Chaucer's preoccupation with pity, as revealed in *Troilus and Criseyde* and in other works. R. Preston's *Chaucer* (1952) is a remarkably stimulating, albeit unsystematic, appreciation of Chaucer's achievements, especially in the matter of verse form. C. Schaar's *Some Types of Narrative in Chaucer's Poetry* (*LSE*, 1954) deals with the various ways in which Chaucer treated his sources, and in his far more elaborate *The Golden Mirror: Studies in Chaucer's Descriptive Technique and Its Literary Background* (1955), he extends his investigation to Chaucer's depiction of human emotions. Dorothy Everett's book *Essays on*

Middle English Literature (1955) contains papers on Chaucer's "art poetical," on *The Parlement of Foules* as a type of love vision, and on *Troilus and Criseyde,* in which Miss Everett concentrates on Chaucer's departures from Boccaccio.

In *Geoffrey Chaucer* (1956), N. Coghill treats mainly Chaucer's reactions to literary influences. Somewhat in the manner of Héraucourt's book, mentioned above, J. W. Kleinstück, in *Chaucers Stellung in der mittelalterlichen Literatur* (1956), discusses the reflections of the doctrines of *courtoisie,* pity, and fortune, Mary Giffin's *Studies on Chaucer and His Audience* (1956) draws on two of the Canterbury tales and certain of the other works for evidence as to Chaucer's more or less personal relationships to his presumed listeners or readers. More recently, C. Muscatine, in *Chaucer and the French Tradition* (1957; paperback 1964), develops the thesis that Chaucer's "meaning" in his poems is a complex whole, not to be grasped apart from an understanding of the shaping effects of form and style. Muscatine then proceeds to analyze Chaucer's style in terms of the courtly and the naturalistic, or bourgeois, traditions, both of French origin, and to trace Chaucer's "feeling for the adjustment between style and meaning." The critical judgments of various of Chaucer's poems set forth in terms of these concepts are often very stimulating. Yet as various reviewers have observed, the author is occasionally led into underrating certain critics, such as Lowes, whom he stigmatizes as "post-Victorians." It is also relevant to suggest that the native stylistic tradition established by the composers of the Middle English romances could well have been explored as a more immediate source for Chaucer's practices than the French sources proposed by Muscatine.

E. E. Slaughter's *Virtue According to Love, in Chaucer* (1957) attempts an analysis of certain works on the theory that two contradictory conceptions of love were present in Chaucer's mind. More recently, P. F. Baum, in *Chaucer, A Critical Appreciation* (1958), enters a crisp protest against critics who blind themselves to any faults in Chaucer as a writer—the fallacy of "gratuitous supplementation"—or who labor to discover "profound latent philosophical meanings." Baum presents a poet who wrote from "his own fulness" and high spirits, who, when bored, became indifferent to the consistency and form of his work, and who was broadly tolerant of his contemporaries and interested in practical morality rather than in discipline.

Criticism based on a more specialized approach is represented by studies of irony, of Chaucer's supposed familiarity with formal rhetoric, and of his knowledge of patristic teachings. Two of the more important treatments of irony are Germaine Dempster's "Dramatic Irony in Chaucer" (*SSLL*, 1932; rptd. 1959) and C. M. Stavrou's "Some Implications of Chaucer's Irony" (*SAQ*, 1957). Of the numerous published efforts to demonstrate that Chaucer employed rhetorical principles, which began with J. M. Manly's famous *Chaucer and the Rhetoricians* (1926), only a few may be mentioned here: T. Naunin's *Der Einfluss der mittelalterlichen Rhetorick auf Chaucers Dichtung* (1930) and Marie Hamilton's "Notes on Chaucer and the Rhetoricians" (*PMLA*, 1932). In an unpublished dissertation, "Chaucer, Gower and the English Rhetorical Tradition" (Stanford University, 1956), J. J. Murphy rejects the largely unquestioned assumption that a strong tradition of rhetorical teaching did in fact exist in Chaucer's England. Finally, in *The Patristic Influence on Chaucer* (1953), Sister Mary Makarewicz shows how Chaucer makes use of certain concepts of patristic origin in his views on marriage, on divine and profane love, and on the vices and virtues.

E. THE CANTERBURY TALES

Including fragments, *The Canterbury Tales* is preserved to us in approximately ninety manuscripts, the discrepancies among which are directly responsible for a vast amount of scholarly activity. The culmination of one phase of this activity is the eight-volume work of J. M. Manly and Edith Rickert, *The Text of the Canterbury Tales* (1940). Here, a critical text of the *Tales* is supplemented by a full corpus of all manuscript variants. Moreover, the careful observations about manuscripts and their scribes, based on years of laborious collation, are of the greatest value to all medieval scholars. An example of more recent work in this field is R. A. Pratt's "The Order of *The Canterbury Tales*" (*PMLA*, 1951), in which the so-called "Bradshaw Shift" in the order of the tales is supported. Still other studies falling in this category are J. B. Severs' "Author's Revision in Block C of the *Canterbury Tales*" (*Speculum*, 1954); C. A. Owen, Jr.'s "*The Canterbury Tales:* Early Manuscripts and Relative Popularity" (*JEGP*, 1955); and the same writer's "The Plan of the Canterbury Pilgrimage" (*PMLA*, 1951), "The Earliest Plan of the *Canterbury Tales*" (*MS*, 1959), and "The Development of the *Canterbury Tales*" (JEGP, 1958).

Two other works should not be overlooked by the student. The first, a collaborative project edited by W. F. Bryan and Germaine Dempster, is *Sources and Analogues of Chaucer's Canterbury Tales* (1941; rptd. 1958). For the *General Prologue* and each of the tales, a critical commentary is followed by a printing of the sources and the more immediate analogues. Marginal translations are supplied for those sources and analogues in languages other than English. The second aid to students is Muriel Bowden's *A Commentary on the General Prologue to the Canterbury Tales* (1948; rptd. 1954). For each of the more important pilgrims, Miss Bowden sets forth in a discriminating manner a review of a very large body of scholarship. In *Chaucer and the Canterbury Tales* (1950), W. W. Lawrence likewise condenses much valuable information, and, in addition, he comments on the influence of the French *fabliaux* on Chaucer's tales.

Several studies in which an effort is made to formulate the motivating theme of *The Canterbury Tales* are based on two more or less opposed schools of critical thought. On the one hand are those critics who, explicitly or tacitly, conceive of Chaucer's main purpose in terms of drama, and on the other are those who find the unifying element to be moral allegory. The clearest example of the first group is R. M. Lumiansky, who, in *Of Sondry Folk: The Dramatic Principle in the Canterbury Tales* (1955), argues that the essence of the poet's art lies in the complex interrelationships between the characters of the pilgrims and the tales they tell. Whereas in some of the "performances," such as those of the Knight and the Cook, there is a simple suiting of the tale to the teller, in others, notably those of the Pardoner and the Wife of Bath, the tales embody subliminal self-revelations that greatly extend the earlier, more direct characterizations of the pilgrims. Chaucer's central aim may be described, then, as dramatic. In J. R. Hulbert's "Chaucer's Pilgrims" (*PMLA*, 1949) and in W. H. Clawson's "The Framework of *The Canterbury Tales*" (*UTQ*, 1951), the dramatic elements seem to be regarded as basic to Chaucer's purposes.

In the second category, those who favor a more allegorical interpretation, R. Baldwin, in "The Unity of the *Canterbury Tales*" (*Anglistica*, 1955), is probably the most extreme, asserting that the pilgrimage to Canterbury is the anagogical figure for the pilgrimage to the city of God and that the pilgrims, whose tales are expressions of their degrees of worldliness, are to be understood as wayfarers to eternity. The Parson was placed last by Chaucer because, as a priest, he must replace the Host as the docent and lead the way to beatitude. J. V. Cunningham's suggestion (*MP*, 1952) to the effect that Chaucer's inspiration for the notion of painting the portraits of the pilgrims at the outset of his work came not from any dramatic impulses but rather from a convention often met in dream vision allegory, is cited in support of Baldwin's thesis. P. G. Ruggiers, in

"The Form of *The Canterbury Tales: Respice Fines*" (*CE*, 1956), also considers that Chaucer wished his audiences to find a penitential journey in *The Canterbury Tales*. A. W. Hoffman's "Chaucer's Prologue to Pilgrimage: The Two Voices" (*ELH*, 1954) suggests that the pilgrims reflect simultaneously the failings of humanity and aspirations to perfection.

C. A. Owen, Jr.'s "The Crucial Passages in Five of the *Canterbury Tales:* A Study in Irony and Symbol" (*JEGP*, 1953) offers clues to the possible meaning of the tales of the Franklin, the Wife, the Merchant, the Pardoner, and the Nun's Priest. In "Chaucer the Pilgrim" (*PMLA*, 1954), E. T. Donaldson points out the need for distinguishing Chaucer the pilgrim from Chaucer the man and Chaucer the poet. Further, A. Williams' essays on the friars (*Speculum*, 1953, and *MP*, 1956) are useful for an understanding of relationships among a number of the ecclesiastics.

Many Chaucer papers are devoted to the explication of individual tales in the Canterbury group. Some notion of the general character of these investigations may be afforded by a review of those concerned with two or three of the twenty-odd tales and their narrators.

The Knight's Tale remains a favorite of commentators, probably because for many readers today it is marked by a baffling ambivalence. A. H. Marckwardt, in "Characterization in Chaucer's *Knight's Tale*" (*UMCMP*, 1947), attempts to define the differences between the characters of Palamon and Arcite, deciding, contrary to earlier opinion, that Arcite is the active man and Palamon the contemplative. W. H. French, in "The Lovers in the *Knight's Tale*" (*JEGP*, 1949), conjectures that, in accordance with traditional patterns of courtly literature, the two knights were intended by Chaucer to be of equal virtue and worth. C. Muscatine, in "Form, Texture, and Meaning in Chaucer's *Knight's Tale*" (*PMLA*, 1950), views this work as a "poetic pageant," in which decorum, or "the patterned edifice of the noble life" is re-established after a collision with disorder. Still other illuminating comments on the poem are developed by R. A. Pratt, " 'Joy after Wo,' in *The Knight's Tale*" (*JEGP*, 1958).

The Wife of Bath and her tale have been fruitfully studied from several points of view. With respect to the background of certain elements in the story, Margaret Schlauch (*PMLA*, 1946) suggests that the form of choice offered the Knight by the Loathly Lady in Chaucer's version may have been influenced by patristic commentaries on marriage. Again, B. Huppé (*MLN*, 1948) observes that Chaucer may himself have invented the rape episode that figures in the first few lines. F. M. Salter points out the tragic overtones of the character in the Wife of Bath as developed in her self-revealing tale of the forest hag who longed for love (*PTRSC*, 1954). Sister Ritamary Bradley (*JEGP*, 1956) notes the antithesis between the Wife's shallow vanity and the wisdom ironically imputed to her by Chaucer the narrator, suggesting the influence of the mirror convention, in which things as they are contrast sharply with what they ought to be. The question of whether the Wife of Bath could have been the original teller of what is now *The Shipman's Tale*, long since treated by R. F. Jones (*JEGP*, 1925), is reopened and discussed pro and con by R. L. Chapman (*MLN*, 1956), W. W. Lawrence (*Speculum*, 1958), and Pratt in "The Order of *The Canterbury Tales*" (see above).

The most elaborate study of this tale, however, is S. Eisner's *A Tale of Wonder: A Source Study of the Wife of Bath's Tale* (1957). Going beyond the early work of H. Maynadier on the subject, Eisner traces the folk theme of the Loathly Lady to legends about the sovereignty of Ireland. The rape incident, he believes, may well have been suggested by a passage in an English *Life of Saint Cuthbert*.

Speculation as to the true character of the Pardoner seems to have been touched off by Kittredge's dictum that this pilgrim is a thoroughpaced scoundrel but that his tale is "perhaps the best short narrative poem in the language" (*Atlantic Monthly*, 1893). Among the many special treatments of the Pardoner are a number worthy of attention. G. G. Sedgewick, in "The Progress of Chaucer's Pardoner 1880–1940" (*MLQ*, 1940), as his title suggests, provides a review of earlier opinion. Especially valuable is his discussion of W. C. Curry's well-known diagnosis of the Pardoner as *eunuchus ex nativitate*. Marie Hamilton (*JEGP*, 1941) argues that we should accept the Pardoner at his word, associating him with the Austin canons of Saint Mary Roncevall in London, a view later supported by A. L. Kellogg (*Speculum*, 1951) on the grounds of suggestions in the tale of Augustinian doctrines on the punishment of sin. Another paper by A. L. Kellogg and L. A. Haselmayer (*PMLA*, 1951) offers a detailed review of the abuses ascribed to medieval *quaestores* and of Chaucer's satirical representation of these abuses in the person of his pilgrim. R. P. Miller's "Chaucer's Pardoner, the Scriptural Eunuch, and the *Pardoner's Tale*" (*Speculum*, 1955) seeks to apply to the interpretation of the Pardoner's character and of his tale the resources of scriptural commentary in the spirit of Robertson and Huppé's *Piers Plowman and Scriptural Tradition*, already discussed in another connection. The eunuchhood of the Pardoner is said to be

Chaucer's means of indicating that this pilgrim is spiritually sterile, that he is *vetus homo* as opposed to the *novus homo*. At the root of his tale lies "the Christian thesis that all men should be *quaestores*," but in the true sense of the expression. It is perhaps not inappropriate to recall at this point the remarks about the occasional oversubtlety of "the critics' Pardoner" voiced by P. F. Baum in his *Chaucer: A Critical Appreciation.*

A. C. Friend (*MLQ*, 1957) has observed that the Pardoner's sermon touched on a dangerous theme, to judge from the experience of an actual secular clerk of the late fourteenth century. And finally, G. Ethel, in "Chaucer's Worste Shrewe: The Pardoner" (*MLQ*, 1959), concludes, after comparing the Pardoner with the Monk and the Friar, that he is most completely compromised by giving vent to the sin of wrath against the divine.

That others of the pilgrims and their tales have been individually studied goes without saying. Of particular interest to modern scholars are the tales of the Clerk, the Merchant, the Prioress, and the Nun's Priest, although occasional articles dealing with the remaining pilgrims and their performances are not lacking. In general, these discussions follow the pattern of the treatments of the Knight, the Wife of Bath, and the Pardoner, reviewed above. That is, the trend is toward interpretation, often in terms of medieval religion, rather than toward source studies.

F. TROILUS AND CRISEYDE *AND THE MINOR WORKS*

Discussions of *Troilus and Criseyde*, often extensive ones, are to be found in most of the general works of Chaucer criticism treated in Section IV above. Nevertheless the bibliography of commentary devoted exclusively to Chaucer's greatest poem is large and varied. The most recently published book, S. B. Meech's *Design in Chaucer's Troilus* (1959), provides a good coverage of the bulk of this scholarship.

Reappraisals of *Troilus and Criseyde* pointing toward modern interpretations began to appear in the 1930s. For example, K. Young (*PMLA*, 1938), objecting to the traditional characterization of the poem as a "modern psychological novel," holds that Chaucer retells Boccaccio's story in the tradition of medieval romance. Again, A. Mizener, in "Character and Action in the Case of Criseyde" (*PMLA*, 1939), argues that Chaucer endows his character with unchanging fundamental qualities rather than permitting her to develop under the impact of experience. This judgment does not imply any limitation of Chaucer's subtlety, inasmuch as Criseyde "reasserts with apparently inexhaustible variety of detail" all the qualities earlier ascribed to her. Further, Chaucer's Criseyde is a far more complex person than Boccaccio's. In *Chaucer's Troilus: A Study in Courtly Love* (1940; rptd. 1958), T. A. Kirby interprets Chaucer's departures from *Filostrato* largely in terms of his interest in writing a courtly love tale. This careful comparative study is of great importance. Further investigations into the influence on Chaucer of Boccaccio, Benoît de Ste. Maure, Guido delle Colonne, and the Old French *Roman de Troyle*, have been published by R. M. Lumiansky (*Speculum*, 1954), R. A. Pratt (*SP*, 1956), and C. S. Lewis (*E&S*, 1931). Close studies of individual characters, on the order of Mizener's paper, include J. S. P. Tatlock, "The People in Chaucer's *Troilus*" (*PMLA*, 1941), E. E. Slaughter, "Chaucer's Pandarus: Virtuous Uncle and Friend" (*JEGP*, 1949), and Constance Saintonge, "In Defense of Criseyde" (*MLQ*, 1954).

In "Destiny in Chaucer's *Troilus*" (*PMLA*, 1930), W. C. Curry clarifies the meaning of the terms "providence," "destiny," and "fortune," emphasizing the centrality of the teachings of fortune in the whole movement of the story. The apparent renunciation of love that figures in the epilogue of Troilus is discussed by K. Young (*MLN*, 1925) and by a series of later scholars. For example, J. L. Shanley (*ELH*, 1939) believes that the epilogue is intended to contrast Christian hope with Troilus' despair and therefore is not incompatible with the story that precedes. In coping with the same problem, A. J. Denomy, in "The Two Moralities of Chaucer's *Troilus and Criseyde*" (*PTRSC*, 1950), considers that the poem falls into the courtly love tradition, which, with its acceptance of adultery, represents a perversion of Christianity. But, by the inclusion of the epilogue setting forth a flat repudiation of "feyned loves," Chaucer seems to have been influenced by the doctrine of double truth. A helpful commentary on the Boethian material in the poem is contributed by T. A. Stroud (*MP*, 1951), and a further discussion of the operation in the tragedy of the Christian doctrines of charity and cupidity is developed by D. W. Robertson, Jr. (*ELH*, 1952). Robertson speaks, in fact, of the adversity of Troilus as the tropological fall of Adam in the garden.

In a more recent essay, M. W. Bloomfield (*PMLA*, 1957) pursues a somewhat different path to the reconciliation of the epilogue and poem and to the formulation of the theme of the whole. By maintaining a sense of distance—temporal, spatial, and esthetic —Chaucer is able to present Troilus as an ancient living before the Christian dispensation who is therefore justified in viewing his own life in completely deterministic terms. It is only in the epilogue that

Chaucer, leaving Troilus behind him in the eighth sphere, muses on the consolation that Christian faith can bring to man. The thesis expounded by S. B. Meech, in his *Design in Chaucer's Troilus* (1959), has much in common with Bloomfield's. That is, Meech argues that we are to accept Troilus as pagan and that nothing in the story encourages us to condemn the hero on Christian grounds. Chaucer, in fact, treats Troilus with a sort of philosophical detachment. This view is supported in Meech's book by a full and painstaking examination of the known sources and influences.

Much of the published commentary on the poems of Chaucer is to be found under the heading, "General Critical Works," already reviewed. Limitations of space prohibit even the mention here of those minor poems on which separate publications have appeared, but some notion of the character of this scholarship may be afforded by a brief discussion of studies concerned with *The Parlement of Foules*.

A good point of departure for a study of this poem is C. O. McDonald's "An Interpretation of Chaucer's *Parlement of Foules*" (*Speculum*, 1955), inasmuch as this article gives some attention to earlier views and provides a well-selected bibliography. Observing that the principal elements of the poem have been traced out and that interpretations differ largely as a result of the weight assigned to details, McDonald considers the central preoccupation of the poem to lie in the unequal conflict between natural love, as represented by Dame Nature, and the artificialities of courtly love, epitomized by the first tercel. R. W. Frank, Jr., in "Structure and Meaning in *The Parlement of Foules*" (*PMLA*, 1956), points out that each of the three parts of the poem—the prelude, the dream vision of the garden, and the parliament of the birds—sets forth a particular attitude toward love. The purpose of Nature's intervention in the parliament is to teach that no one view of love is complete and satisfying in itself.

The most extensive investigation of the poem, however, is J. A. W. Bennett's book, *The Parlement of Foules: An Interpretation* (1957). Denying the relevance of associating the occasion for the poem with an actual courtship, such as that of Richard II and Anne of Bohemia, Bennett comments, with a great wealth of detail, on the *Somnium Scipionis* and on the backgrounds of the paradisal garden, the Temple of Venus, and the bird parliament itself. His analysis of the significance of Nature is especially helpful. This figure, drawn from Alain of Lille, is not to be identified with blind passion or irrationality, but rather with true reason, the divinely established law of kind.

XII. GOWER

J. H. FISHER'S current study of the vexed problems of John Gower's biography has borne fruit in his "A Calendar of Documents Relating to the Life of John Gower the Poet" (*JEGP*, 1959). Also biographical are G. R. Coffman's "John Gower in His Most Significant Role" (*Elizabethan Studies and Other Essays in Honor of George F. Reynolds*, 1945), the same writer's "John Gower, Mentor for Royalty: Richard II" (*PMLA*, 1954), and G. Stillwell's "John Gower and the Last Years of Edward III" (*SP*, 1948).

Interest in the English poems of Gower has centered on *Confessio Amantis* almost exclusively. Dorothy Dilts, for example (*MLN*, 1942), strengthens the case made by Gower's editor, G. C. Macaulay, that Boccaccio's *De Genealogia Deorum* is an important source for the *Confessio*. J. B. Dwyer shows in an unpublished thesis that *Confessio Amantis* is an artistic synthesis of materials taken from manuals of religious instruction (*University of North Carolina Record*, 1951). The same writer also examines the sources of Gower's French poem, *Miroir de l'omme* (*SP*, 1951). In another vein, P. Fison ("The Poet in Gower," *EIC*, 1958) strongly defends the literary value of the *Confessio* on the grounds of Gower's sympathetic treatment of individuals of all sorts, his architectonic sense and structural skill, and his outstanding command of language.

4

French Medieval Literature

By Charles A. Knudson
UNIVERSITY OF ILLINOIS

AND

Jean Misrahi
FORDHAM UNIVERSITY

To ATTEMPT, within the limits of a single chapter, an assessment of significant research on Old French literature that has appeared in the last thirty-five years is a rash undertaking. It has required rigorous selection and the exclusion of whole genres. We omit saints' lives, with one exception, and most other religious and moral writings, scientific literature, and material that is essentially translation from other languages without significant novelty. We have, moreover, left aside or given only briefest attention to authors and categories for the understanding of which nothing of great importance has been published since 1925. The existence of good recent critical bibliographies in the field has encouraged us in this course, as has the fact that the scholarship and the controversies concerning the major works and categories of Old French literature are of sufficient interest to warrant the place and the treatment (all too succinct) that we have given them.

Jean Misrahi has contributed the sections on romance, Charles Knudson the remainder of the chapter.

I. BACKGROUND AND BIBLIOGRAPHY

ALTHOUGH the delimitation of a certain period of time for inclusion in a survey of research is necessarily arbitrary, the choice of an initial date of approximately 1925 gives good perspective in the case of Old French literature. In 1923 had appeared the Bédier and Hazard *Histoire de la littérature française illustrée* (2 vols., 1923–24; 2nd ed., rev., 1948–49), which not only contains in its first volume what is perhaps the most agreeably written history of Old and Middle French literature to be found, but which also put before a generation of scholars and students the views of the authors, J. Bédier, E. Faral, and L. Foulet, on the epic, the courtly romance, the *Roman de Renart*, and the lyric. These views may be characterized summarily as maintaining that these genres are of late, French, nonpopular origin, and have their roots not in long oral tradition (or, for Arthurian romance, in Celtic lore), but in classical sources and in the inventiveness of French poets. Persuasively argued, these views for a time captured a large public, and to an extent still hold sway, although today, forty years later, even the most faithful disciples of these masters would not defend in absolute form the theses they maintained for the origins of epic, Breton romance, and lyric.

In the Bédier-Hazard *Histoire*, the *chansons de geste* were not treated by Bédier himself; so we must turn to another work for a brief presentation of his "pilgrimage route" theory of epic origins. In the section on Old French literature in Volume XII (1921) of Hanotaux's *Histoire de la nation française* (*Histoire des lettres*, I), Bédier wrote the chapter on the *chansons de geste*, A. Jeanroy all the others. In 1925 appeared the third edition of K. Voretzsch, *Einführung in das Studium der altfranzösischen Literatur*, upholding earlier views on questions of origins and notable for the most satisfactory bibliography to appear up to its time. An English version was published in 1931, with some corrections and bibliographical additions, but with unfortunate inaccuracies in translation. *A History of Old French Literature, from the Origins to 1300*, by U. T. Holmes, Jr. (1937), is a convenient and lively survey well filled with information and with bibliographical indications supplementing those of Voretzsch. P. Zumthor's *Histoire littéraire de la France médiévale, VIe–XIVe siècles* (1954) has the interest of treating both Latin and vernacular literature. Three volumes of the *Histoire littéraire de la France* have appeared in the period under survey, with articles on fourteenth-century authors: XXXVI (1927), XXXVII (1938), and XXXVIII (1949).

Although "background" books and studies of the general medieval tradition are in principle excluded from this chapter, an exception may be made for R. R. Bezzola's still unfinished *Les origines et la formation de la littérature courtoise en Occident, 500–1200. I^e partie: La tradition impériale de la fin de l'antiquité au XIe siècle* (1944); IIe partie (en 2 tomes): *La société féodale et la transformation de la littérature de cour* (1960); and for E. Auerbach's *Mimesis: The Representation of Reality in Western Literature* (1953; German ed. 1946), which contains stylistic studies of passages from the *Roland*, *Yvain*, the *Mystère d'Adam*, and the Madame du Chastel episode in Antoine de La Sale's *Reconfort à Madame de Fresne,* "highly sophisticated versions of the *explication de texte*" (Muscatine). Medieval texts in *langue d'oïl* often serve as subjects for stylistic and esthetic criticism, to which the guide is H. Hatzfeld, *A Critical Bibliography of the New Stylistics Applied to the Romance Literatures,* 1900–52 (1953), with its Spanish translation carrying down the covering date to 1954 (1955), and completed by a supplement, *Essai de bibliographie critique de stylistique française et romane,* 1955–60, with Y. Le Hir (1961). Some of the principal elements of the "new stylistics" are briefly presented in Hatzfeld's "Esthetic Criticism Applied to Medieval Romance Literature" (*RPh,* 1948).

A tentative general chronology, according to the findings of research in our time, has been compiled by R. Levy, *Chronologie approximative de la littérature française du moyen âge* (1957), criticized and supplemented by H. Tiemann, "Die Datierungen der altfranzösischen Literatur" (*RJ,* 1957), F. Lecoy (*Romania,* 1957), and Levy and Tiemann again (*RJ,* 1959).

Old French literature has the benefit of two recent general bibliographies. The shorter (about 3000 items) is a collaborative work by American scholars: *A Critical Bibliography of French Literature* (D. C. Cabeen, gen. ed.): I, *The Medieval Period* (ed. U. T. Holmes, Jr., 1947; 2nd ed. 1952). The strong points of this work are that each part is the work of a specialist and that each item is followed by a very brief critical resumé. On the other hand, the delimitation of fields is often puzzling. While some topics were allotted enough space to permit the inclusion of items of secondary interest, some of the major fields were forced into excessive concision. More satisfactory in length is R. Bossuat, *Manuel bibliographique de la littérature française du moyen âge* (1951), which lists over 6000 items and adds 2000 more in two supplements (1955 for 1949–53; 1961 for 1954–60). Regrettable are the scarcity of critical annotation and the exclusion of Provençal.

The isolation of France from the free world and the difficulties of publishing there between 1940 and 1944 were the reasons for the appearance of such bibliographical essays as F. Lecoy, R. Lebègue, and P. van Tieghem, "Les études sur la langue et la littérature française de 1940 à 1943," (*MLR,* 1946), continued in *BAGB* (1947); J. Monfrin, "Travaux relatifs à l'ancien français et à l'ancien provençal parus en France de 1940 à 1945," (*MA,* 1948); and R. Levy, "Recent European Progress in Old French Studies," (*RPh,* 1947).

For more recent years, we may mention the listing of bibliographies by H. Tiemann (*RJ,* 1952) and O. Klapp (*ZRP,* 1957 for

1940–54), and the *ZRP*'s bibliographical *Supplementheften* (1957 for 1940–50; 1961 for 1951–55), O. Klapp, *Bibliographie der französischen Literaturwissenschaft, Bd* I, *1956–58* (1960), and on a more limited topic, Cola Minis, "Französisch-deutsche Literatur-berürungen im Mittelalter" (*RJ*, 1951 and 1955–56). For current bibliography, the annual bibliographical number of *PMLA* and the book reviews and *chroniques* of *Romania*, the *Zeitschrift für romanische Philologie*, and *Studi francesi* give full and fairly prompt coverage.

II. SAINTS' LIVES

THE OLD FRENCH *Vie de saint Alexis* must be an exception to our exclusion of saints' lives from the present survey. Although deriving directly from a Latin text, and being only one of many medieval vernacular versions of the celebrated legend, it is by far the earliest and most interesting. Recent editions abandon G. Paris' practice of turning the Anglo-Norman of the Hildesheim manuscript into Central French. That of J.-M. Meunier (1933) is less satisfying than that of C. Storey (1934), published also in an abridged class text (1946). G. Lausberg's studies in *Archiv* (1954–55, 1955–56, and 1957–58) announce another edition. E. R. Curtius, "Zur Interpretation des Alexiusliedes" (*ZRP*, 1936), and H. Sckommo-dau, "Alexius in Liturgie, Malerei und Dichtung" (*ZRP*, 1956), present valuable commentary.

III. CHANSONS DE GESTE

FOR A GENERAL study of the Old French epic in the compass of a single work, one must go back to L. Gautier's *Les épopées françaises* (4 vols., 2nd ed. 1878–92), and to K. Nyrop's *Storia dell' epopea francese nel medio evo*, trans. E. Gorra (1886; Danish ed.

1883). For the most part, the subject has grown too vast to be encompassed in a single work, even of several volumes, and special studies continue to appear at such rate as to condemn any general manual to being outdated before it can appear in print. Such was the case with M. de Riquer's excellent *Los Cantares de gesta franceses* (1952; rev. ed., French trans., 1957). This has the merits of an up-to-date general account while containing many personal views of the author on controversial questions; see the review of the first edition by D. McMillan (*Romania*, 1954). Jessie Crosland's *The Old French Epic* (1951) is a literary study of the genre, informal and personal.

General studies of the epic tend to be concerned principally with the question of origins, where the reader will find himself on the battleground between Bédierists and anti-Bédierists, or, in the terms now made popular by Don Ramón Menéndez Pidal, individualists and traditionalists. It was in *Les légendes épiques* (4 vols., 1908–13; 3rd ed. 1926–29) that Bédier published the series of studies from which emerged his celebrated thesis that the Old French epics were not the last stage of a long oral tradition beginning in early Carolingian times and constantly changing through the centuries, but that they were first born of the crusading spirit of the eleventh century and drew their historical elements from data available to poets and *jongleurs* in churches and monasteries along the great pilgrimage routes. As part of his criticism of traditionalist views, Bédier wrote a history of studies of Old French epic origins for the third volume of his *Légendes épiques*, and M. Wilmotte wrote another in *L'épopée française, origine et élaboration* (1939), the latter stressing the influence of Latin epic, ancient and medieval. Clear and useful are Rita Lejeune's lecture, "Les théories relatives aux origines des chansons de geste" (*Revue des cours et conférences*, 1937), Grace Frank's "Historical Elements in the *Chansons de Geste*" (*Speculum*, 1940), and U. T. Holmes, "The Post-Bédier Theories on the Origins of the *Chansons de Geste*" (*Speculum*, 1955). Most searching is the brilliant *Le Origini delle canzoni di gesta, teorie e discussioni* of I. Siciliano (1939; 2nd ed., French trans., 1951), summarized in *RPh*, 1953. Siciliano makes it clear that there are two fundamental but separable points in Bédier's system: the contention that the *chansons de geste* arose in the eleventh century, and the belief that the historical elements they contain had been preserved not in popular tradition or lost early epics but in monkish chronicles and the traditions of sanctuaries on the pilgrimage routes. Siciliano points out that time has not been kind to the second part of the Bédier argument, which has been whittled down not only by traditionalists like F. Lot, "Études sur les légendes épiques françaises: 4. Le cycle de Guillaume d'Orange" (*Romania*, 1927), but by otherwise good Bédierists, such as Pauphilet and, it might be added, Siciliano himself. Traditions preserved at identifiable places on the pilgrimage routes must still be taken into consideration, but no longer are they looked upon as the sole or even the principal source of epic legends.

The individualist theory has strong defenders among scholars still living or recently deceased. P. A. Becker believed to the end that for the most part the Old French epic arises and develops before our eyes, as he again affirmed in his "Ogier von Dänemark" (*ZFSL*, 1940), and E. R. Curtius studied in the Old French epics the formation and the literary ideas of individual poets, to be considered against the background of their own time: "Ueber die alt-französische Epik" (*ZRP*, 1944; rptd. in his *Gesammelte Aufsätze zur romanischen Philologie*, 1960); a fine appreciation of Curtius' epic studies is by A. Adler in *Symposium*, 1959. Recently it has been A. Viscardi who has spoken most vigorously for modern Bédierism, notably in "*Credo quia absurdum*" (*FiR*, 1956), a tilt against the theorists of the *cantilène* and the "peuple-poète," from Michelet to Fawtier and R. Louis, emphasizing the warrior aristocracy as the public for which the epics were written. Viscardi gives a general account of the Old French epic, with a strong individualist slant, in the appropriate chapters of his *Letterature d'oc e d'oïl* (1952). To be read with interest are his earlier *Posizioni vecchie e nuove della storia letteraria romanza* (1944) and "Le canzoni di gesta, i temi tradizionali, le fonti letterarie e diplomatiche" (*ASNSP*, 1937), together with the reviews of the same by A. Monteverdi in *SMed*, 1938, and *CN*, 1946. Monteverdi's judicious middle-of-the-road views on the whole epic question will be found in his *L'Epopea francese* (1947).

The question of hagiographical influences on the development of the epic has been considered in general by C. Segre, "Il *Boeci*, i poemetti agiografici e le origini della forma epica" (*Atti dell'Acad. delle Scienze di Torino*, 1955), who puts forth a moderate claim for such influence: the *chanson de geste* had its first great success in an ecclesiastical ambiance; epic poems in many cases celebrated warriors whom local legends had transported into a "sacred dimension."

The case for the traditionalists, stated frequently by Menéndez Pidal, is summarized succinctly in his lecture *Problemas de la poesía épica* (1951; also printed in the volume *Los Godos y la epopeya española*, 1956), in which he states his conviction that epic is born in heroic ages, preceding the development of written history. He chides the Bédierists for their unwillingness to take into consideration any evidence except that of surviving written texts, and joins G. Cirot and T. Frings in urging the students of Old French epic to learn the lesson taught by the history of the Spanish *cantares de gesta*. Most recently he has argued the traditionalist case for all Romance literatures in part 4 of his *Poesía juglaresca y orígenes de las literaturas románicas*, to be read in the sixth edition (1957). The traditionalist theory is also maintained by R. Louis in an extensive study "L'épopée française est carolingienne" (*Coloquios de Roncesvalles*, Facultad de Filosofía y Letras de Zaragoza, 1956), with the thesis that the *chansons de geste*, whose subjects concern themselves precisely with the great crises of the Carolingian monarchy, clearly originated in one form or another at the very time of those crises.

J. Rychner's *La chanson de geste: essai sur l'art épique des jongleurs* (1955) is more than the structural and stylistic study the title would indicate. From the observation that epic formulas are extensively used, it proceeds to the theory that not only were the *chansons de geste* transmitted orally but that improvisation entered into this process of transmission, an idea stemming from studies of M. Parry and others on the Homeric epics and modern Jugoslav heroic poetry. This hypothesis buttresses the views of Menéndez Pidal on early Romance epic, and has been taken up by M. de Riquer and R. Louis. The latter edited a number of *La Table ronde* devoted to essays on "L'épopée vivante" (Dec. 1958 and part of the issue for Jan. 1959). In the article he contributed on the *chanson de geste*, Rychner is less prudent than in his book, where he admits that the *Chanson de Roland*, at least, has a carefully composed plan that does not point to composition by improvisation. A favorable view of Rychner's book is taken by A. Bonjour in "Poésie héroïque du moyen âge et critique littéraire" (*Romania*, 1957), but his conclusions are subjected to scrutiny and refutation in a substantial article by M. Delbouille, "Les chansons de geste et le livre," in the symposium volume *La technique littéraire des chansons de geste* (1959).

There have been attempts to conciliate the traditionalist and the Bédierist positions. Siciliano maintains that their apparent conflict can be resolved. P. Le Gentil, in "La notion d'état latent et les derniers travaux de M. Menéndez Pidal" (*BH*, 1953), concludes that both Bédier and Menéndez Pidal are too absolute ("we need both their optics"), and he has spoken in the same vein in his "À propos de l'origine des chansons de geste: le problème de l'auteur" (*Coloquios de Roncesvalles*, 1956), as has J. Frappier in "Réflexions sur les rapports des chansons de geste et de l'histoire" (*ZRP*,

1957). Yet there remains a deep dichotomy between Bédierism and traditionalism. The traditionalist believes in a long and unbroken chain of popular tradition carrying the subject of an epic from its original time, most often Carolingian, to the time of the surviving texts. He is willing to postulate forms of an epic earlier than the extant texts and to use the hypotheses of earlier states and even multiple traditions to explain real or apparent inconsistencies in the surviving texts. The Bédierist (or individualist), on the other hand, endeavors to explain existing poems in the setting of the time in which they saw the light, to see the poet—or the last poet—as a creator, not simply a "dernier remanieur," and to admit a very short prehistory, if any, for the surviving epics. He may or he may not admit that the centuries before the eleventh had heroic poetry and popular traditions about Carolingian events and personages; if he does admit their existence he will not see them as making other than a general and modest contribution to the content and structure of the existing poems. The Bédierist will not willingly be a *dépeceur*, seeing in existing epics a patching together of earlier and shorter, perhaps originally separate pieces. He will resist the temptation to explain all weaknesses in structure by "earlier states," juxtaposition, and interpolations, which is a real temptation, since the twelfth- and thirteenth-century texts we have are rarely models of unity or of symmetrical and logical composition.

The music to which the epics were recited or sung is discussed by F. Gennrich, *Der musikalische Vortrag der altfranzösischen Chansons de Geste* (1923), by Jan der Veen (*Neophil*, 1957), and by J. Chailley, "Etudes musicales sur la chanson de geste et ses origines" (*Rev. de musicologie*, 1948).

A. LA CHANSON DE ROLAND

The volume of *Roland* studies has increased prodigiously in the last thirty years, and no single bibliography has been compiled to encompass them, although one can be produced by systematic *dépouillement* of a small number of articles and books. Most complete for recent studies is A. Junker's *Stand der Forschung zum Rolandslied* (*GRM*, 1956, also separate), praiseworthy for its concision and wide coverage. However, it presupposes a good knowledge of the previous research on the *Roland*, and in a brief fifty pages it cannot hope to expound the arguments of the works cited. The divisions of Junker's bibliographical essay indicate the principal subjects of continuing study of the *Roland:* the primacy of the Oxford MS., its date, the date of the poem it contains, authenticity of the Baligant episode, the meaning of line 4002, earlier stages of the text, occurrence and significance of the name Oliver, the geography of the poem, legends preceding the poem, style and artistry, and miscellaneous unsolved problems.

An excellent introduction to *Roland* studies is P. Le Gentil, *La Chanson de Roland* (1955), which summarizes briefly and clearly the facts and questions concerning text and prehistory and offers a masterful analysis of the artistry of the poem. Other good analyses are E. Faral, *La Chanson de Roland* (1934; 2nd ed. 1948), and A. Pauphilet's chapter on the *Roland* in *Le legs du moyen âge* (1950). J. Horrent's *La Chanson de Roland dans les littératures française et espagnole au moyen âge* (1951) is a substantial and meticulous enquiry into the principal *Roland* problems, particularly detailed in its treatment of texts and versions and with extensive bibliography. Horrent believes in a "première" *Chanson de Roland*, without the Baligant episode, dating from the first half of the eleventh century, of which the Oxford version would be a conscious and skillful reworking. M. Delbouille's *Sur la genèse de la Chanson de Roland* (1954) is at many points a critical examination of Horrent's conclusions, but he agrees in the belief in an earlier *Roland*. This volume is useful for orientation in contemporary *Roland* scholarship, of which it is itself a notable example.

Three of the many editions of the *Roland* call for special mention. Bédier's *La Chanson de Roland, publiée d'après le manuscrit d'Oxford et traduite* first appeared in 1922. Textual retouches were introduced in the course of the many reprintings, the last revision being dated 15 December 1937, subsequent to which Bédier published a list of errata (*Romania*, 1938). The excellent glossary by L. Foulet appeared in the supplementary volume of *Commentaires* (1927). Less attached to the letter of the Oxford manuscript is G. Bertoni, whose edition introduces emendations from the Franco-Venetian assonanced version and contains an informative and judicious introduction (1935; *editio maior* 1936). *Les textes de la Chanson de Roland*, by R. Mortier, is an invaluable edition of all the French and Franco-Italian versions of the poem, as well as the German of Konrad and the Latin *Pseudo-Turpin* and *Carmen de prodicione Guenonis* (10 vols., 1940–44).

Bédier's defense of the Oxford version may be read in the *Commentaires* or in *Les légendes épiques*, Vol. III. Others have argued the desirability of emendations from the other versions, so Bertoni and C. A. Knudson for the order of *laisses* in the episode of Abisme and in that of Ganelon's anger (*Romania*, 1937). These latter scenes have since been frequently studied, by Horrent and Delbouille, by A.

Burger, in *Essais de philologie moderne* (1951), *SN* (1955), and *CCM* (1960), and by W. S. Woods, in *SP* (1951). The merits of MS. *V⁴* have been argued by M. Wilmotte (*Bulletin de l'Académie Royale de Belgique*, 1932, also separate). P. Aebischer has studied the Old Norse prose version in *Rolandiana Borealia* (1954) and attributes to it the distinction of being "le plus ancien représentant conservé de la plus ancienne version de la *Chanson de Roland*," a version earlier than Oxford, found by the translator in an Anglo-Norman manuscript of the mid- or late twelfth century. This eminence of the Old Norse saga is not admitted in the important review by F. Lecoy in *Romania* (1955), and there are further reservations on Aebischer's work in another thorough study of the Old Norse version by E. F. Halvorsen, *The Norse Version of the Chanson de Roland* (1959).

Discussion of the authorship of the *Roland*, aside from conjectures as to the poet's station in life, his experience, and his culture, start from the interpretation of the last line (4002) in the Oxford MS.: "Ci falt la geste que Turoldus declinet." Upon the none too certain interpretations of the words "geste" and "declinet" depends whether we shall see in Turoldus the author of the poem or of its source in a document of another nature. Some scholars, without holding that we have here the poet's name, nevertheless refer to him, for convenience, as Turoldus, a practice not without its disadvantages. The proposed identifications of this Turoldus (Thorold of Envermeu, Thorold of Fécamp) have not received general acceptance; see F. Torraca in *NA* (1925). For the whole question of line 4002, see Junker, I. A. Petkanof (*Archivum Romanicum*, 1936), R. S. Loomis (*Romania*, 1951), and R. de Cesare (*Convivium*, 1955).

From the viewpoint of literary history, the capital *Roland* question is that of how the poem came into being, and all answers proposed almost necessarily draw toward one or the other of the two poles of critical opinion on the origins of the *chansons de geste:* traditionalism or individualism. It would be oversimplifying to classify every view on *Roland* origins purely and simply in terms of this dichotomy, and, as we shall see, there is a certain middle ground. Nevertheless these provide the touchstones. The traditionalist not only looks for stages of the poem earlier than the prototype of the Oxford manuscript but also sees before any fixed poem a legend going back to the events themselves, independent of written historical accounts. The pure or extreme individualist viewpoint is to admit of no previous poem on the Battle of Roncevaux differing from the Oxford text except in matters of detail, and to date the poem from the middle or the end of the eleventh century. Individualists may (like Faral) or may not (like Pauphilet) agree with Bédier in attributing germinative power to local church legends; all abandon, as hopeless if not unnecessary, the work of *dépeçage* that always comes into the search for earlier stages of the text.

At the initial date of this survey the view of J. Bédier held the front of the stage, even though the volume of *Commentaires* (1927) was disappointing in its defense of the theory of sanctuary origins. The silence of his adversaries was only momentary, however, as is well shown in F. Lot's review of P. Boissonnade's *Du nouveau sur la Chanson de Roland*, "*La Chanson de Roland*—à propos d'un livre récent" (*Romania*, 1928; rptd. in his *Études sur les légendes épiques françaises*, 1958), which claims an early date (tenth century) for the original poem. In a spirited little book, *La Chanson de Roland* (1933), R. Fawtier took up again the theory of lyrico-epic poems and of traditional continuity, maintaining against Bédier that the defeat of Roncevaux was a major disaster and a crisis in Charles's reign, which the official historiographers tried to play down, but which the voice of the people kept alive in song (an idea previously expressed by L. Gautier). Among later contributions to the support of the traditionalist viewpoint, two merit special mention: L. F. Benedetto's *L'Epopea di Roncisvalle* (1941), a well-documented and impassioned *plaidoyer*, and R. Menéndez Pidal's *La Chanson de Roland y el neotradicionalismo* (1959; rev. ed. in French, *La Chanson de Roland et la tradition épique des Francs*, 1960).

The most striking discovery of our time relating to the *Chanson de Roland* is the so-called *Nota emilianense*, presented and interpreted by D. Alonso, "La primitiva épica francesa a la luz de una nota emilianense" (*RFE*, 1953, also separately, 1954, and in his *Primavera temprana de la literatura europea*, 1961). The *Nota* consists of a few lines in Latin referring to Charlemagne's retreat from Saragossa and Roland's death at the hands of Saracens in Rozaballes. Named in Charles's company are *Rodlane belligerator fortis, Olibero, episcopo domini Torpini, Oggero spata curta, Bertlane*, and *Ghigelmo alcorbitanas*. The text may be conveniently consulted in Le Gentil. Alonso's paleographical study led him to date the *Nota* as not later than 1075, and he drew from it a traditionalistic conclusion, that it shows the existence of an epic legend on Roland and Roncevaux before the *Chanson*, differing from it in including the names of William and Bertrand. R. N. Walpole criticized Alonso's dating as inconclusive (*RPh*, 1956), and F. Lecoy has stated his skepticism (*Romania*, 1955). Menéndez Pidal submits the document to additional scrutiny in *La Chanson de Roland y el neotradicionalismo* and agrees with Alonso in his traditionalistic interpretation.

One of the principal arguments put forward by the traditionalists for postulating an earlier *Chanson de Roland* is drawn from the presence in a number of eleventh-century documents of the names of Roland and Oliver given to brothers. These data, brought to light by various searchers, among them F. Lot (*Romania*, 1928), R. Fawtier (*La Chanson de Roland*, 1933), Rita Lejeune (*Mélanges H. Grégoire*, 1950), and P. Aebischer (*RBPH*, 1953), have been thoroughly discussed by Delbouille and by S. Battaglia, "Il 'compagnonaggio' di Orlando e Oliviero" (*FiR*, 1958). The derivation and provenance of the name Oliver and the relevance of these matters to the problem of *Roland* origins have been studied both by the scholars just mentioned and by L. Spitzer (*PMLA*, 1943). The role of Oliver in the poem has been the subject of luminous and suggestive comments by Pauphilet (*Romania*, 1933), E. R. Curtius (*ZRP*, 1944), and R. R. Bezzola (in *Eumusia: Festgabe für E. Howald*, 1947).

The first secession of an individualist from integral Bédierism came with A. Pauphilet's "Sur la *Chanson de Roland*" (*Romania*, 1933). Unconvinced of the existence of *attaches locales* previous to the *Chanson*, Pauphilet concluded: "Je suis très persuadé que Roland ne fut jamais l'objet de fables et de racontars, mais que ce qui fut dit de lui . . . fut d'emblée un poème." This affirmation, at first glance so peremptory, might nevertheless be accepted by scholars of wide ranges of viewpoint. The differences would appear in the date to be ascribed to this poem and its presumed contents. Pauphilet himself would place it near the middle of the eleventh century: "La date du *Roland*" (*Études romanes déd. à M. Roques*, 1946).

Another touchstone of the difference between individualists and traditionalists is to be found in the views of critics regarding the unity of the poem in the Oxford version. The belief that this version is a carefully constructed and tightly integrated work of art supports or reinforces an individualistic point of view, as illustrated by the discussions of Bédier and C. A. Knudson (*Romania*, 1937, and *RPh*, 1950).

Among those who do not see behind the *Roland* and other *chansons de geste* a tradition in popular literature are some who would derive the genre from hagiography, notably A. Burger in "La légende de Roncevaux avant la *Chanson de Roland*" (*Romania*,

1949), which gives not only metrical evidence for a Latin poem in hexameters as the immediate source for the prose of the Pseudo-Turpin chronicle and for the *Roland* passages in the *Guide du pèlerin de Saint-Jacques*, but sees it as a hagiographical poem, to which Burger gives the title *Passio Beati Rotolandi martiris*. The argument is impressive, but, as J. Rychner has pointed out (*Romania*, 1951), there are fragile links in the chain that holds up so weighty a conclusion.

The identification of place names, personal names, and historical allusions has been much used to date and localize the poem and to support hypotheses as to the circumstances of its composition. The most extensive and ambitious essays of this type in our time, however, have been found wanting by most scholars—for example, that by Boissonnade, who endeavored to tie the *Chanson* to places and events of the second and third decades of the twelfth century in northern Spain (*Du nouveau sur la Chanson de Roland*, 1923; reviewed by F. Lot, *Romania*, 1928). H. Grégoire, in a series of studies listed in Junker and in *Mélanges E. Hoepffner* (1949), argued that the poem was written in 1085, probably at Salerno, as an *excitatorium* for continuation of Robert Guiscard's "pre-crusade" against the Byzantines on the Dalmatian coast. M. Roques took exception to this claim (*Romania*, 1940) and A. Roncaglia expressed reservations (*CN*, 1946). Wholly favorable reviews are generally not by *Roland* specialists. E. Li Gotti's argument for strong Norman attachments (*La Chanson de Roland e i Normanni*, 1949) advances to meet Grégoire's hypothesis.

The geography of the *Chanson de Roland* presents bewildering problems. It has been argued both that the poet knew Spain, or some parts of it, very well (P. Boissonnade) and that he knew it badly if at all ("L'ignorance du poète sur la géographie de l'Espagne est du reste formidable," G. Cirot, *BH*, 1933). "Turold est allé à Roncevaux," is the conclusion of A. Burger in a study, illustrated with photographs and a map, in the *Coloquios de Roncesvalles;* and the same volume contains other geographic studies by Mme. Lejeune, E. Lambert, and A. Roncaglia. The latter also contributed "Sarraguce, ki est en une muntaigne" and R. Louis, "Le site des combats de Roncevaux d'après la *Chanson de Roland*" to the *Studi in onore di A. Monteverdi* (1959). Menéndez Pidal's examination of the geographical question in *La Chanson de Roland y el neotradicionalismo* and Lambert's "Roncevaux et ses monuments" (*Romania*, 1935) should also be mentioned. Relevant to this topic is the question of the routes from France into Spain followed by pilgrims to Santiago in

the eleventh and twelfth centuries, on which an abundant documentation exists, unfortunately somewhat dispersed.

The activity in *Roland* studies has led in recent years to the
foundation of the *Société Rencesvals*, following the meeting held at
Pamplona in August 1955 on the initiative of J. M. Lacarra, and to
the publication of the papers there delivered under the title *Coloquios de Roncesvalles* (1956). A. Roncaglia has given a convenient
summary of the *Coloquios* (*CN*, 1955). The papers of the 1959
congress at Poitiers were published in *CCM* (1960); those of the
1961 Venice meeting in *CN* of the same year. The society has
undertaken to publish a *Bulletin bibliographique*, of which the first
two numbers are dated 1958 and 1960.

B. LE PELERINAGE DE CHARLEMAGNE

Several studies seek to penetrate further into the meaning, date,
and setting of this, "the most obscure of French epics" (Bédier).
Not content with Bédier's suggestion that it was written by a
jongleur to entertain the crowds at Saint-Denis for the *Lendit* fair
with a frivolous if not irreverent account of a transfer of relics,
scholars see allusions to the Second Crusade and Louis VII's part in
it (T. Heinermann, *ZRP*, 1936, and R. C. Bates in *Studies by
Members of the French Department of Yale University*, 1941), or
point out the Celtic origins of certain themes (Laura H. Loomis,
MP, 1927; Margaret Schlauch, *Speculum*, 1932). R. N. Walpole
considers the *Pèlerinage* a direct parody of the clerical *Descriptio
qualiter Karolus Magnus clauum et coronam Domini a Constantino-
poli Aquisgrani detulerit qualiterque Karolus Caluus hec ad Sanc-
tum Dionysium retulerit* (*RPh*, 1955), an interpretation that can be
reconciled with Bédier's general view. U. T. Holmes argues that the
Pèlerinage need not have been written near Saint-Denis nor on
the Continent at all, that William of Malmesbury's chronicle shows the
availability in England of the necessary historical data, and that the
parody of the Franks would have more point coming from an Anglo-
Norman (*Symposium*, 1946). P. Aebischer has studied *Les versions
norroises du "Voyage de Charlemagne en Orient"* (1956) and opts
for the theory of parody, as does H. J. Neuschäfer (*RJ*, 1959). J.
Horrent considers problems of composition in an essay contributed
to *La technique littéraire des chansons de geste* (1959); in *Le
Pèlerinage de Charlemagne: essai d'explication littéraire avec des
notes de critique textuelle* (1961) he rejects all of the above interpretations for that of comedy on a subject of rivalry between nations
turning to the advantage of France.

C. ASPREMONT

R. van Waard, in *Etudes sur l'origine et la formation de la Chanson d'Aspremont* (1937), rejects the hypothesis of a precise historical source for this epic. He calls it a pure crusade poem, based on the tradition that made Charlemagne the defender of the empire, and dates it between 1177–90. P. A. Becker does not accept the existence of such a tradition and considers the poem the free invention of a poet writing for the Norman-Sicilian *Kulturkreis* at the court of William II of Sicily, d. 1189 (*RF*, 1947). E. R. Curtius drew attention to the guiding influence of public taste, and called for a sociology of the *chansons de geste* (*RF*, 1948).

D. THE CYCLE OF GUILLAUME D'ORANGE

A general study of the numerous poems in this cycle has been begun by J. Frappier under the title *Les chansons de geste du cycle de Guillaume d'Orange*, of which the first volume (1955), after a general introduction, treats of *La Chanson de Guillaume, Aliscans*, and *La Chevalerie Vivien*. While not neglecting the thorny problems of origins and prehistory, Frappier aims particularly to emphasize the poetic and human interest of the works.

The question of origins is to the fore in P. A. Becker's *Das Werden der Wilhelm- und der Aimerigeste* (1939), which resolutely proposes a late-epic thesis. The first William epic, he maintains, was a lost poem on the struggle of William against the Saracen king, Tibaut l'Esturman, dating from about 1120; the *Couronnement de Louis, Charroi de Nîmes, Prise d'Orange*, and the original *Moniage Guillaume* are the branches of a unified poem by a single poet. This hypothesis has been critically reviewed by S. Hofer in *ZRP* (1941), with a rejoinder and supplementary studies by Becker in *RF* (1942), in "Der Liederkreis um Vivien" (*SÖAW*, 1944), and "Die Kurzverslaisse" (*ZFSL*, 1943).

The text of *La Chanson de Guillaume* has at last received the editorial treatment it deserves, at the hands of D. McMillan (2 vols., *SATF*, 1949–50). A study of the poem, therein announced, has not yet appeared. A number of questions of textual interpretation have been taken up by L.-F. Flutre, with a rejoinder by McMillan (*Romania*, 1956). Contrary to the general notion that the *Guillaume* is an early poem, McMillan maintains that both the manuscript and the poem are late: he would date the Continental poem, model for the surviving Anglo-Norman text, in the last third of the twelfth century at the earliest. This agrees with the view of S. Hofer, who sees in the text influences from the part of Wace's *Rou* dating from 1160–74 (*ZRP*, 1940). If this later dating is well founded, much that has been written about the poem on the assumption of an early date must be reconsidered.

One of the principal questions concerning the *Guillaume* is that of unity; that is, was the part of the poem that brings in the giant Renouart primitive or a later addition? Contemporary opinion generally holds to the view of duality, so Frappier (*op. cit.*) and Bruna Valtorta on the basis of a close stylistic study (*SRo*, 1939).

E. GIRART DE ROUSSILLON

The text of this poem has again become available in an edition by W. Mary Hackett (3 vols. in 2, *SATF*, 1953–55), and its historical basis is the subject of an extensive study by R. Louis, *De l'histoire a la légende*. I, *Girart comte de Vienne et ses fondations monastiques*; II–III, *Girart comte de Vienne dans les chansons de geste: Girart de Vienne, Girart de Fraite, Girart de Roussillon* (3 vols., 1946–47). Louis sees the legend migrating from the Rhone Valley to the Pyrenees, thence to Burgundy, and finally to Poitou, and he considers the poem the work of three authors. Praised in some quarters, Louis's ambitious work has been criticized by F. Lot, who had arrived at quite different conclusions as to prehistory, localization, authorship, and date (*Romania*, 1949; see also Lot's earlier article in *Romania*, 1926). P. Le Gentil has studied the meaning and structure of the poem, analyzing the action and the characters in the light of the problems of feudal relationships in the twelfth century (*Romania*, 1957).

F. OGIER LE DANOIS

A group of recent studies of the *Chevalerie Ogier* take as point of departure Bédier's thesis that the legend was formed in Italy along the pilgrimage route to Rome and was later exploited by the monks of Saint-Faron de Meaux. F. Lot criticized Bédier's reasoning in "A quelle époque remonte la connaissance de la légende d'Ogier le Danois?" (*Romania*, 1940). Mme. Rita Lejeune, like Lot, favors remote popular origins in a study of Ogier in her *Recherches sur le thème: les chansons de geste et l'histoire* (1948), parts of which are reviewed unfavorably by F. Lecoy (*Romania*, 1952). A categorical affirmation of the late appearance of the epic Ogier (after 1210) was made by P. A. Becker in a short article interesting particularly for the introductory *profession de foi* on the general question of late epic origins (*ZFSL*, 1942). P. Le Gentil concentrates on the construction of the poem, the ethical questions it treats, and the character of Ogier in "Ogier le Danois, héros épique" (*Romania*, 1957), seeing in *La Chevalerie Ogier* a call to order and reason in the conflict between the primitive manners of an earlier day and the spread of royal and ecclesiastical discipline.

G. LES LORRAINS

An outstanding effort has been devoted to this group of epics in our time by Pauline Taylor's Columbia University seminar, leading to editions of the *Garin le Loheren* by Josephine Vallerie (1947), the *Gerbert de Mez* by Miss Taylor (1952), the *Anseÿs de Mes* by H. J. Green (1939), and to a number of studies, among which should be cited Ruth Parmly's *The Geographical References in the Chanson de Garin le Loherain* (1935) and R. K. Bowman's *The Connections of the Geste des Loherains with other French Epics and Mediaeval Genres* (1940). F. Lecoy has studied the linking of the *Garin* to the *Gerbert*, with the conclusion that the first twenty-eight *laisses* of the latter poem originally were a part of the former. He dates the poem as probably after the construction of the *pont d'Avignon* (completed 1185) and before the composition of the *Guillaume de Dole* in 1212 or 1213 (*Romania*, 1956). U. T. Holmes suggests a dating of 1190–91 (*Speculum*, 1954).

IV. THE TROUBADOURS

THE LITERARY history of medieval France necessarily includes the literature in *langue d'oc* as well as in *langue d'oïl*. Nevertheless they usually have their separate manuals, which is a grave inconvenience in the case of lyric poetry, southern France's great contribution to medieval and modern culture. Nor can the study of French lyric origins confine itself to France alone. Indeed, *il n'y a plus de Pyrénées* since the case for Hispano-Arabic origins has come forward so insistently in the past thirty years, and since, more recently, fragments of Old Spanish love poetry, the *kharjas*, have been found in Arabic and Hebrew *muwashshahas*. At this point we shall be fuller than in other sections of this essay, since Bossuat's bibliography leaves out Old Provençal altogether, and the Cabeen-Holmes volume is brief and now outdated on the much-debated question of origins.

A. MANUALS, ANTHOLOGIES, AND EDITIONS

The principal modern study of troubadour verse is A. Jeanroy, *La poésie lyrique des troubadours* (2 vols., 1934). Supplementing this study in several respects, and indeed providing a good introduction to the whole field, is the same author's brief *Histoire sommaire de la poésie occitane, des origines à la fin du XVIIIᵉ siècle* (1945). Other agreeable short manuals are E. Hoepffner, *Les troubadour dans leur vie et dans leurs oeuvres* (1955), in which some depth of characterization is achieved by limiting to fifteen the number of poets treated; P. Remy, *La littérature provençale au moyen âge* (1944); and H. Davenson (H. Marrou), *Les troubadours* (1961).

Among the anthologies taking their place beside old favorites should be mentioned the first American one, R. T. Hill and T. Bergin's *Anthology of the Provençal Troubadours* (1941), and the highly praised *La Lírica de los trovadores* of M. de Riquer, Vol. I (1948). The *Vidas* of the troubadours have been re-edited by J. Boutière and A. H. Schutz, *Biographies des troubadours* (1950), and studied by B. Panvini in *Le Biografie provenzali, valore e attendibilità* (1952). The twenty-five surviving *albas* have been published by M. de Riquer, *Las Albas provenzales* (1944). Essential reference works are H. Pillet and H. Carstens, *Bibliographie der Troubadours* (1933), and I. Frank, *Répertoire métrique de la poésie des troubadours* (2 vols., 1953–57).

Recent editions of individual troubadours are too numerous to list, yet some outstanding ones should be mentioned. W. T. Pattison's *The Life and Works of the Troubadour Raimbaut d'Orange* (1952) fills a long-felt need for a critical edition and a thorough study of this important and difficult poet. Others are listed here in order of publication: *Giraldo (Guiraut) de Bornelh*, ed. B. Panvini (1949); *Jaufré Rudel e Bernardo di Ventadorn, Canzoni*, ed. S. Battaglia (1949); *The Poems of Aimeric de Peguilhan*, ed. W. P. Shepard and F. M. Chambers (1950); *Peirol, a Troubadour of Auvergne*, ed. S. C. Aston (1953); Sordello, *Le Poesie*, ed. M. Boni

(1954) (in this connection may be mentioned the essay of rehabili-
tation of Sordello by Luciana Cocito, *LI*, 1952) ; Lanfranco Cigala,
Canzoniere, ed. F. Branciforti (1954) ; *Poésies complètes du troubadour Peire Cardenal*, ed. R. Lavaud (1957) ; and for the rules of
troubadour art, Jofre de Foixà, *Vers e regles de trobar*, ed. E. Li
Gotti (1952). Of interest, finally, since the five poems it publishes
were the last remaining Occitanian inedita, is I. Frank's "Ce qui
reste d'inédit de l'ancienne poésie lyrique provençale," in *Boletín de
la Real Academia de Buenas Letras de Barcelona* (1950).

B. ORIGINS

Until the recent discovery of the short Old Spanish verses
serving as endings (*kharjas*) to Arabic or Hebrew *muwashshahas*,
some of which would appear to date from the first half of the
eleventh century, the earliest known lyrics in any Romance tongue
were those of William IX of Aquitaine, "the first troubadour" (d.
1127), followed by those of Marcabru, Cercamon, Raimbaut
d'Orange, Bernart Marti, Guiraut de Bornelh, and Jaufré Rudel, to
name the principal members of the "first generation" of troubadours. When poetical texts appear later in French, in Italian, in the
languages of the Hispanic peninsula, they bear, for the most part,
strong evidence of Provençal influence, as is clearly demonstrated in
K. Vossler's famous essay, "Die Dichtung der Trobadors und ihre
europäische Wirkung," originally a lecture delivered in French in
Nice in 1937, then published in *RF* (1937), reprinted in *Aus der
romanischen Welt* (1940–42, also 1948), in *Südliche Romania* (new
edition 1950), and in Spanish in *Romania y Germania* (1956) ; see
also I. Frank, "Du rôle des troubadours dans la formation de la
poésie lyrique moderne," in *Mélanges Roques*, Vol. I (1950). It is
natural, therefore, that the study of troubadour origins should have
a large place in the study of lyric origins for any part of the
Romance territory. And it is equally fitting that the study of lyric
origins in *langue d'oc* should be carried on with a mind open to
evidence that may be unearthed in exploring other parts of the
Romance lyric domain.

The study of troubadour origins must seek to account for the
highly novel code governing the relations of poet and his lady, to
which Gaston Paris gave the rather unsatisfactory name of *l'amour
courtois;* at the same time it must suggest a derivation for the
difficult and highly polished metrical patterns of the *cansos* and their
musical forms. A useful survey of the subject is to be found in Käte

Axhausen's 1937 Marburg dissertation, *Die Theorien über den Ursprung der provenzalischen Lyrik*. More extensive are A. Pillet, *Zum Ursprung der altprovenzalischen Lyrik* (1928), and D. Scheludko, "Beiträge zur Entstehungsgeschichte der altprovenzalischen Lyrik: I, Klassisch-lateinische Theorie; II, Die arabische Theorie" (*Archivum Romanicum*, 1927–28). Short summaries may be found in Jeanroy and in the articles by Bezzola and Spoerri mentioned below.

The theories on the origins of troubadour poetry may be classified into three groups: popular origins, Latin and liturgical origins, and Arabic origins. These are not mutually exclusive: perhaps all three influenced the development of Provençal song. This is the more likely, since no single theory is so cogent an explanation of the phenomena that it warrants excluding the others.

C. THE THEORY OF POPULAR ORIGINS

The simplest explanation of any literary phenomenon is that it developed from the life and traditions of the people among whom it first appears. This is known as the theory of popular origins, and it may be said to begin for modern scholarship with Gaston Paris's celebrated review of A. Jeanroy's *Les origines de la poésie lyrique en France au moyen âge*, published in the *Journal des savants* for 1891 and 1892, and separately in *Mélanges de littérature française du moyen âge*, II (1912). I mention the essay of G. Paris rather than Jeanroy's work itself because the former addresses itself in part to troubadour origins, with which Jeanroy was not in his book directly concerned. Before this a more naïve concept of *Volkspoesie* had prevailed, introduced by Herder and still maintained by some contemporary scholars, notably T. Frings (*Minnesinger und Troubadours*, 1949).

The strongest supporter of the theory of popular origins for lyric and epic Romance poetry has long been R. Menéndez Pidal, whose most recent treatment of the subject is "La primitiva lírica europea: estado actual del problema" (*RFE*, 1960). His views have been elaborated principally with regard to Spanish literature, but with French very much in mind: "A culture as precocious and as inventive as French cannot have waited until the eleventh or twelfth century to create (*constituir*) the popular form of its epic or lyric songs" ("Cantos románicos andalucíes: continuadores de una lírica latina vulgar," *BRAE*, 1951). In this article he points out how the discovery of the *cancioncillas* or *cantarcillos* (more usually referred

to as *kharjas*) in Hebrew and Arabic *muwashshahas* demonstrates
the soundness of his claim that the Romance lyric and epic long
existed in an *estado latente* previous to their appearance in written
documents that have been preserved. That the discovery of the
kharjas supported Frings' ideas on popular poetry was perceived by
L. Spitzer, "The Mozarabic Lyric and Theodor Frings' Theories"
(*CL*, 1952).

The difficulties of applying the theory of popular origins to
troubadour poetry are several. The literary tradition of the people
among whom it arose, as of all Romance peoples, was double. One
was the tradition of Latin literature, consisting of the known body
of classical Latin literature plus the new forms developed in
Medieval Latin. How much of this was known outside clerical circles
is not clear. The other was the popular literary tradition, about
which little is known except that the people sang songs, that some of
these were sung by women in their dances, and that the church
disapproved of some of them as licentious. Beyond this, to account
for the rise of poetry in the Midi, one can but allege the *douceur de
vivre* in those provinces, the peace and prosperity of its small courts
—and one is still only at the threshold of the question of troubadour
origins.

D. THE THEORY OF LATIN AND LITURGICAL ORIGINS

Under this heading may be grouped a number of studies that do
not form a compact group but that, in common, see the troubadour
lyric emerging from a tradition having Latin as its medium. Beside a
few scholars who saw this tradition stretching back to classic Latin
poetry is the larger number who would see the origins in Medieval
Latin compositions either of a secular or a liturgical nature. The
liturgical theory is most characteristically represented by H.
Spanke, *Untersuchungen über die Ursprünge des romanischen Minnesangs* (1940), T. Spoerri (see below), and G. Errante, *Sulla
Lirica romanza delle origini* (1943). With the liturgists are to be
found the musicologists who have studied the troubadour melodies:
J. B. Beck, *Les chansonniers des troubadours et des trouvères
publiés en fac-similé* (2 vols., 1927 and 1938), and F. Gennrich, *Der
musikalische Nachlass der Troubadours: Kritische Ausgabe der
Melodien* (1960). An older volume by Gennrich, *Musikwissenschaft
und romanische Philologie* (1918), consists of studies most of which
had previously appeared in *ZRP*; more recently he has published
Troubadours, Trouvères, Minne- und Meistergesang (1951). J.

Chailley published "Les premiers troubadours et les *versus* de l'École d'Aquitaine" (*Romania*, 1955), and in his *Précis de musicologie* (1958) provides a critical bibliography.

E. THE THEORY OF ARABIC ORIGINS

This theory alleges Arabic influence for both the form of troubadour poetry and for the troubadour ideology of love. Following early beginnings, it was argued in our time by J. Ribera in his study, *El Cancionero de Aben Guzmán* (1912), and taken up cautiously by Menéndez Pidal in the first edition of his *Poesía juglaresca y juglares* (1924). Later Menéndez Pidal became convinced of a definite connection between Arabic poetry of the ninth–eleventh centuries and Romance forms of the lyric, including the Provençal. His reasons are set forth in "Poesía árabe y poesía europea," of which an abridged form served as a semipopular lecture, delivered in Havana and published in the *Revista Cubana* (1937, also separate), and of which the scholarly and much longer text appeared in the *BH* (1918) and as the first study in a volume bearing its name (1941).

The Arabic verse form seen as a formative influence on the Romance lyric was a popular form, the *muwashshaha*, invented in the ninth century, we are told, by the blind singer, Mucáddam of Cabra (region of Cordova). Using a line half the length of the classical Arab forms, colloquial language, and admitting foreign words, the *muwashshaha* was at least seven strophes long, the strophe based on a refrain (*markaz*, Span. *estribillo*). In time, two varieties of the form may be distinguished, the *muwashshaha* proper, with a tendency toward greater correction of language, and the *zekhel* (or *zaǧal*, Fr. *zadjal*, Span. *zéjel*), more colloquial, with omission of flectional endings. One complete collection has survived in the eleventh- or twelfth-century *Diwân* of Ibn Quzmán (Aben Guzmán), studied by J. Ribera (1912) and published by A. R. Nykl, *El Cancionero del sheikh . . . Aben Guzman* (1933; rev. E. García Gomez in *Al-Andalus*, 1933).

Nykl has been the most active and enthusiastic proponent of the hypothesis of Arabic influence on the poetry of the troubadours. In 1931 he published his translation of the early eleventh-century *Tauq* of Ibn Hazm (Aben Házam) under the title, *A Book Containing the Risāla Known as The Dove's Neck-Ring*, which furnishes the material for demonstrating Arabic refinement and delicacy in the sentiment of love. (E. García Gómez translated the *Tauq* into Spanish, *El Collar de la paloma*, 1952.) Chapter iv of the Introduction, "Poetry on the Two Sides of the Pyrenees," is particularly to be noted (and appears in Spanish translation in *Al-Andalus*, 1933). In 1946 appeared his *Hispano-Arabic Poetry and Its Relations with the Old Provençal Troubadours*. In these volumes, as in a number of articles, among which we shall cite only one (*BH*, 1939), Nykl not only contributed enthusiasm and pages of interesting personal reminiscence but made available essential Arabic material, painstakingly prepared. It is regrettable that he marred the discussion with scornful comments on the competence of scholars holding opinions different from his own.

Interesting to note are the attitudes toward the Arabic thesis of two veteran *provençalisants* of the last generation. A. Jeanroy in *La poésie lyrique des troubadours* (1934) is reserved; C. Appel is more receptive in his long review of Nykl's *Dove's Neck Ring* (*ZRP*, 1932). A. J. Denomy's study, "Concerning the Accessibility of Arabic Influences to the Earliest Provençal Troubadours" (*MS*, 1953), is favorable to Nykl's views. An enquiry into possible filiation as to metrical form between the Arabic *zekhel* and Romance verse forms was carried out in great detail by P. Le Gentil in *Le virelai et le villancico: le problème des origines arabes* (1954); his conclusion, stopping short of Menéndez Pidal's confident affirmations, is a cautious *non liquet*. The volume is an excellent guide to the literature on this question.

F. THE KHARJAS: ROMANCE LINES IN HISPANO-ARABIC, ARABIC, AND HISPANO-HEBRAIC POPULAR POETRY

The question of possible Arabic influence on the Romance lyric and the broader question of the cultural relations between Arabs, Jews, and Mozarabic Spaniards in Al-Andalus took a new turn with the recent discovery of lines in a dialect of Spanish used as endings to Hebrew and Arabic *muwashshahas* of the eleventh and twelfth centuries. In 1894 Menéndez y Pelayo had noted in the poems of Judá Leví, who lived in Al-Andalus in the late eleventh and early twelfth centuries, lines of uncertain interpretation, but certainly in an Ibero-Romance dialect. No further notice was given to this subject until J. M. Millás Vallicrosa, in "Sobre los más antiguos versos en lengua castellana" (*Sefarad*, 1946), published the lines:

Responde[d]¡ Mio Cidello! venid   con bona albixara,
como rayo de sol exid   en Guadalajara.

These were taken from a *muwashshaha* in Hebrew, addressed by the poet Yĕhudá ha-Leví to the royal counselor, R. Yosef, doubtless in the last decade of the eleventh century. Soon after, S. M. Stern published a number of *kharjas* in Mozarabic dialect, "Les vers finaux en espagnol dans les muwaššahs hispano-hébraïques" (*Al-Andalus*, 1948), and "Un muwaššah arabe avec terminaison espagnole" (*Al-Andalus*, 1949). Others soon came to light, as in "Venticuatro jarŷas romances en muwaššahas árabes" by E. García Gómez (*Al-Andalus*, 1952), and about fifty were known by the time Stern published *Les chansons mozarabes, éditées avec introduction, sommaire et glossaire* (1953) and A. Roncaglia offered a selection in his *Poesie d'amore spagnole d'ispirazione melica popolaresca, dalle 'kharge' mozarabiche a Lope de Vega* (1953).

The *kharjas* offer difficulties of decipherment from nonromanic characters and difficulties of transliteration: two Arabists or two Hebraists may read the same *kharja* quite differently. Thus F. Cantera offers extensive revisions to Stern's conclusions in "Versos españoles en las muwaššahas hispano-hebreas" (*Sefarad*, 1949; see also two articles by E. García Gómez in *Al-Andalus*, 1949 and 1950).

What support does the discovery of the Romance *kharjas* give to the "Arabic thesis" of the influence of the *muwashshahas* on troubadour poetry and other early lyrics, in French, Spanish, and Portuguese? Directly none, of course, and the phenomenon may be interpreted in a fashion to embarrass that thesis. At least, as I. Frank emphasized in "Les débuts de la poésie courtoise en Catalogne et le problème des origines lyriques" (*Actas y Memorias del VII Congreso Internacional de Lingüística Románica*, II, 1955), it reorients the question, making it one of Romance popular origins rather than one of Arabic influence.

G. COURTLY LOVE

It is not always possible to keep separate the search for the origins of the poetic forms and the music of the troubadours, on one hand, and their concept of love, on the other. Most studies of origins treat of both. But courtly love, "fin amors," has been treated separately in a number of studies to be mentioned in this section.

The figure of William IX is close to the center of any enquiry into the origins of courtly love. R. R. Bezzola would give him principal credit for the innovation ("Guillaume IX et les origines de l'amour courtois," *Romania*, 1940). He essays the difficult task of explaining how a man like the whimsical Duke, "uns . . . dels majors trichadors de dompnas," could have come to write those of his poems that speak of the delicacy of his love and his submission to his lady. Bezzola formulates the suggestion that it was in competition, on the earthly plane, with the influence of the saintly Robert d'Arbrissel, who drew to his abbey of Fontevrault so many ladies of high station, including two of William's own wives and his mistress, the Vicomtesse de Chatellerault. T. Spoerri, in "Wilhelm von Poitiers und die Anfänge der abendländischen Poesie" (*Trivium*, 1944), suggests that the language of human love borrowed from that in which Bernard of Clairvaux spoke of Christian charity. In any case, troubadour poetry represents a sincere desire to raise the plane and enrich the ethical content of man's sentiments for woman.

Among recent studies of the nature and origins of courtly love are D. Scheludko's "Ueber die Theorien der Liebe bei den Trobadors" (*ZRP*, 1940), in which he sees the distinction between *fin amors* and *amors* as parallel to that between love of God and human concupiscence, and S. Pellegrini's "Intorno al vassallaggio d'amore nei primi trovatori" (*CN*, 1944). Father A. J. Denomy contributed usefully to this discussion in *The Heresy of Courtly Love* (1947) and in a series of articles: "An Inquiry into the Origins of Courtly Love" (*MS*, 1944); "Fin' Amors: The Pure Love of the Troubadours, Its Amorality and Possible Source" (*MS*, 1945); "*Jois* among the Early Troubadours: Its Meaning and Possible Source" (*MS*, 1951); and "Courtly Love and Courtliness" (*Speculum*, 1953). The ideas of Denomy and others are discussed by T. Silverstein, "Andreas, Plato, and the Arabs" (*MP*, 1949). Treatments of this theme by nonprofessionals are *L'amour et l'Occident* by Denis de Rougemont (1939; English trans., *Love in the Western World*, 1940) and R. Briffault, *Les troubadours et le sentiment romanesque* (1945).

The "amor de lonh" of Jaufré Rudel has aroused particular interest. Grace Frank interprets this as a reference to the Holy Land, from which a human love has turned the poet away ("The Distant Love of Jaufré Rudel," *MLN*, 1942). L. Spitzer has objected to this interpretation, asserting the rights of poetic imagination not comprehended by "biographists" (*Univ. of North Carolina Studies*, 1944). Mrs. Frank replied (*MLN*, 1944); the discussion was reviewed by A. R. Nykl (*Speculum*, 1945) and Jeanne Lods (*Romania*, 1950); further contributions were made by D. Zorzi (*Aevum*, 1955), Spitzer (*Romania*, 1956), and I. Cluzel (*Romania*, 1957). A new critical edition of the *canso*, with extensive annotation, was published in *Studi in onore di A. Monteverdi*, Vol. I (1959) by Rita Lejeune, who takes the view that the poem is both a crusade song and a love song.

Studies of nonlyric Occitanian texts may be listed briefly here.

The oldest monument has been re-edited by R. Lavaud and G. Machicot, *Le poème sur Boèce* (1950). *La Chanson de Sainte Foy*, ed. E. Hoepffner and P. Alfaric (1926), was translated (1940) and studied by A. Fabre in *Du nouveau sur la Chanson de sainte Foy: Aux sources de la Chanson de sainte Foy* (1943) and *Du nouveau sur la Chanson de sainte Foy: La Chanson de Roland dans la Chanson de sainte Foy* (2 vols., 1944). The romance of *Jaufré* has been edited by C. Brunel (2 vols., *SATF*, 1943) and studied by Rita Lejeune in "La date du roman de *Jaufré*" (*MA*, 1948) and M. de Riquer in "Los problemas del roman provenzal de *Jaufré*" (*Recueil de travaux offerts à M. Clovis Brunel*, Vol. II, 1955). *Le Roman d'Arles* was studied by M. Roques (*Histoire littéraire de la France*, 1949); Ingrid Arthur has published *La Vida del glorios Sant Frances* (1955); Suzanne Kravtchencko-Dobelmann, *L'Esposalizi de Nostra Dona* (*Romania*, 1944); and M. Roques, the epic poem *Roland à Saragosse* (1956). A new edition of *Flamenca* is announced (text established by M. E. Porter, English trans. M. J. Hubert).

V. LYRIC POETRY IN NORTHERN FRANCE

THE LYRIC POETRY in *langue d'oïl*, in spite of its variety and the enormous amount that has survived, has been somewhat put in the shade by the brilliance of the Provençal courtly lyric. A good part of it, indeed, derives wholly and directly from troubadour poetry, carried to the courts of northern France in the entourage of Eleanor of Aquitaine. It is not clear what part of extant French medieval verse represents earlier indigenous developments. An earlier generation (Jeanroy and Gaston Paris) pointed to the *chansons de danse* and the *refrains* included in courtly lyrics, as well as to the handful of *romances*, or *chansons de toile*, as characteristic of French lyricism before the period when imitation of the troubadours became the fashion. This view was challenged in one respect by E. Faral, who viewed the *romances* as deliberate archaizing (in Bédier-Hazard, I).

The number of genres and the number of poets do not permit a systematic bibliographical review, but only mention of outstanding contributions since the mid-twenties. H. Spanke (d. 1944) undertook

a revision of G. Raynaud's repertory of collective manuscripts:
Bibliographie des altfranzösischen Liedes, Vol. I (1955). Notable
photographic reproductions of such manuscripts are A. Jeanroy, *Le
Chansonnier d'Arras* (1925), J. B. Beck, *Les Chansonniers des
troubadours et des trouvères* (2 vols., 1927). Edith Brayer, "Une
filmothèque de la poésie lyrique médiévale" (*Mélanges I. Frank*,
1957), gives a list of *chansonniers* so far put on film. H. Petersen
Dyggve carried out a searching survey of *trouvère* onomastics,
the titles of which are to be found in his edition of the poems of
Gace Brulé (1951) and in M. Spaziani, "Gli studi di H. Petersen
Dyggve sull' antica lirica francese" (*CN*, 1953). Other notable
modern editions of considerable numbers of *trouvère* lyrics are A.
Langfors, *Recueil général des jeux-partis français* (2 vols., 1926),
A. Wallensköld, *Les chansons de Thibaut de Champagne* (1925),
H. Spanke, *Eine altfranzösische Liedersammlung* (1925), F. Genn-
rich, *Rondeaux, virelais und balladen* (2 vols., 1921–27), and H.
Petersen Dyggve, *Chansons françaises du XIIIe siècle* (*NM*, 1929–
30). F. Gennrich's *Altfranzösische Lieder* (2 vols., 1953, 1956) is
a collection of texts, accompanied by an important introduction to
the subject. Among recent anthologies should also be mentioned
Carla Cremonesi's *La Lirica francese del medio evo* (1955) and
G. Saba's *Le "Chansons de toile" o "chansons d'histoire"* (1955).

A brief but suggestive essay toward an understanding of the
formal interest of the *chanson courtoise* is R. Guiette, "D'une poésie
formelle en France au moyen âge" (*RSH*, 1949; *Romanica Gandensia*, 1960). R. Dragonetti, in *La technique poétique des trouvères
dans la chanson courtoise* (1960), presents a substantial study of
the rhetoric embodied in the thousand surviving specimens of the
genre. On versification and music, there are the substantial studies of
P. Verrier, *Le vers français* (3 vols., 1931–32), F. Gennrich,
*Grundriss einer Formenlehre des mittelalterlichen Liedes als Grund-
lage einer musikalischen Formenlehre des Liedes* (1932), W. Süchier,
Französische Verslehre auf historischer Grundlage (1952), and M.
Burger, *Recherches sur la structure et l'origine des vers romans*
(1957). For introductory treatments of medieval music in the lyrics,
see A. Machabey in *CCM* (1959), T. Gérold, *La musique au moyen
âge* (1932: an introductory manual), and two articles in *Romania*
by F. Lesure (1953) and J. Chailley (1957).

Theorizing about the origins of the medieval French lyric shows
a tendency to divide again into popular and antipopular schools,
Naturpoesie and *Kunstpoesie*, to use the Herderian terms. Leaving
aside the massive influence of troubadour poetry, the origins of
which have been discussed above, Jeanroy saw the origins in

chansons de danse (of which only one survives) and in the *refrains* that survive incorporated into later compositions. This view is parallel to seeing evidences of early romance songs sung by women in the *kharjas*, and in the *Frauenlieder* referred to by T. Frings, but Jeanroy was far from being such a primitivist as to join Frings in exclaiming, "Zurück zu Herder!" For the dance songs, essential references are P. Verrier, "La plus vieille citation de carole" (*Romania*, 1932, 1935), and M. Sahlin, *Etude sur la carole médiévale* (1940). F. Gennrich (*ZRP*, 1955) has combated the idea of Gröber and Jeanroy that the *refrains* were parts of lost, longer compositions.

The proponents of the theory of Latin origins emphasize either the classical tradition (Faral) or, leaning heavily on metrical and musical forms, liturgy and medieval Latin verse (Gennrich, Errante). Studies on the *pastourelle* show these polarizations of thought, W. P. Jones seeing in the *pastourelle* a form of folk drama, E. Faral and M. Delbouille deriving it from Latin poetry: the former from the ancient bucolic and the latter from clerical poetry of the twelfth century. An orientation in the subject is provided by S. Singer, "Die Grundlagen der Pastourelle" (*Miscellany Kastner*, 1932); other important studies are articles by E. Faral (*Romania*, 1923), insisting on the *pastourelle's* aristocratic nature, and M. Delbouille (*Memoires de l'Académie Royale de Belgique*, 1927), and books by E. Piquet (1927) and W. P. Jones (1931). Over two hundred *pastourelles* survive in Old French.

Something of a curiosity is H. Schossig, *Der Ursprung der altfranzösischen Lyrik* (1957), dedicated to the thesis that the Old French and Old Provençal songs are for the most part relics of ancient classic and Celtic fertility dances and the songs that accompanied them.

VI. ROMANCE

THE MODERN ERA in studies of the medieval French romance began with E. Faral's *Recherches sur les sources latines des contes et romans courtois du moyen âge* (1913), to which one must still return constantly, particularly when dealing with the *romans d'antiquité*. Despite the title, which might lead one to expect a study of the sources of medieval romances in general, the book makes relatively little mention of Chrétien de Troyes, Gautier d'Arras, or of later authors and those of lesser importance. Some of the chapters of the book are reworkings of earlier articles on various subjects concerning the *matière de Rome* and on the all-pervading influence of Ovid during the early stages of the development of the romance. This influence is so clearly established that it can no longer be questioned, although F. M. Warren (*MLN*, 1914) made some additions to Faral's demonstrations and also some corrections that show that in several instances texts other than those of Ovid may with equal or greater probability be sources of Old French passages cited by Faral.

Only the last chapter of the book, "Les commencements du roman courtois français," deals with the general problem of how the French romance began. Faral shows clearly the relations between the revival of classical studies in the schools of the twelfth century and the subjects, sources, rhetorical devices, and general cultural background of the earliest French romances. Their authors, he claims, were formed in the traditional study of the trivium and the quadrivium in the schools, with special emphasis on the great *auctores*, as they were called without further qualification—Virgil, Ovid, Lucan, Horace, Seneca, Juvenal, and Cicero in particular. Having seen the success with which Carolingian and other national legends were presented to a wide public in the *chansons de geste*, some clerics decided to popularize their classical literary learning in the form of vernacular romances intended for the more restricted audience of the royal and baronial courts.

Like most other scholars, Faral considered the *romans d'antiquité*, and the *Roman de Thèbes* in particular, to be the oldest romances extant, earlier than the first Arthurian romances. He specifically rejected a suggestion by Jeanroy (*Romania*, 1904) that the introduction of a strongly developed sentimental, romantic love interest into the Old French adaptation of ancient epic texts might have been due to the vogue of such passages in no longer extant *romans bretons* anterior to Chrétien de Troyes. Formed in the school of positivistic literary history of the time, Faral tended to claim that what is no longer extant never existed, or at least to minimize its extent and importance. He categorically affirms that the *Roman de Thèbes* and the shorter, approximately contemporary tale, *Piramus et Tisbé*, are not only the oldest extant *romans*, but that they had no forerunners, and were composed about 1150 under the direct inspiration of Statius and Ovid. F. M. Warren (*MLN*, 1914), however, calls attention to a curious passage in Ordericus Vitalis' *Historia Ecclesiastica*, XI: 26, in which a Moslem sultana encourages besieged Christians to stand firm and urges them to remember the ten-year siege of Troy and the heroic deeds that their *histriones* daily declaim. This was written a quarter of a century before the *Roman de Troie*, and no doubt before the *Thèbes* as well.

The question of the relations between the *romans bretons* and the *romans d'antiquité* is simply indicated by Faral's statement that the former "doivent à ces derniers d'être ce qu'ils sont." Ten years previously, in his *L'évolution du roman français aux environs de 1150* (1903), M. Wilmotte had also arrived at the conclusion that the *romans d'antiquité* were anterior to the *romans bretons* and derived essentially from ancient Latin and Christian literary sources. He returned to the subject in several articles and reviews, as well as in his *De l'origine du roman en France* (1923), and in a more developed form in his *Origines du roman en France: l'evolution du sentiment romanesque jusqu'en 1240* (1941). The general tendency of Wilmotte's studies and his chief interest are indicated by the subtitle of the 1923 *mémoire:* "La tradition antique et les éléments chrétiens du roman."

Since all the romances, whether dealing with ancient, *breton*, or Byzantine subjects, were animated by the same spirit of aristocratic elegance, display great interest in the refinements of romantic love, and show a considerable degree of resemblance in style, verse form, and literary mannerisms, Faral rightly considered that they form a single genre, the *roman courtois*. These and other, more controversial, views Faral succinctly restated in Bédier and Hazard, *Histoire de la littérature française* (1923).

Starting with this idea of the essentially "courtly" character of medieval French romance, R. Bezzola undertook to make a systematic survey of the literature of the courts of the Germanic barbarians, Visigoths, Ostrogoths, Franks, and Lombards, as well as of the Merovingian, Carolingian, and Anglo-Saxon courts, in his *Les origines et la formation de la littérature courtoise en Occident (500–1200)*. Première partie: *La tradition impériale de la fin de l'antiquité au Xe siècle* (1944). This was followed many years later by a "deuxième partie" in two volumes: *La société féodale et la transformation de la littérature de cour* (1960), which surveys systematically the development of secular letters (in both Latin and the vernaculars) first in episcopal and monastic circles, then in Celtic and Scandinavian countries, Moslem Spain and Sicily, the Byzantine Empire, and finally in the feudal courts of Italy, Germany, France, and England. A final section is devoted to the transition between the feudal epic and the courtly romance. In these volumes Bezzola just reaches the early part of the twelfth century, and consequently there is as yet no formal treatment of the vernacular French romances, although there are a number of passing references to them. In his treatment of literary activity in Celtic courts, Bezzola does indicate an openness to the evidence for considerable Celtic influence in medieval French literature. Yet, so far as the legend of Arthur himself is concerned, Bezzola agrees with Faral that Geoffrey of Monmouth was the real creator of the romantic figure of King Arthur. It is significant that in the discussion of the evidence for a pre-Galfridian Arthurian tradition, Bezzola follows Faral (*La légende arthurienne. Etudes et documents*, 3 vols., 1929) step by step, and for the Celtic hypothesis gives only one recent reference, J. Marx, *La légende arthurienne et le Graal* (1952). R. S. Loomis is not even mentioned, and, in general, American scholarship is poorly represented throughout the work.

After the pioneering studies of Wilmotte, Faral, and others of their time, there have been an enormous number of studies on various aspects of medieval romance, but no general survey of the field. For a full enumeration and analysis of medieval French romances, one must still turn to H. L. D. Ward's antiquated but still extremely useful *Catalogue of Romances in the Department of Manuscripts in the British Museum* (3 vols., 1883–1910), particularly the first volume, which alone is concerned with the courtly romances and goes far beyond a mere description of material contained in manuscripts of the British Museum. Also extremely useful is G. Paris's listing and individual analyses of all known Arthurian verse romances in the *Histoire littéraire de la France*, Vol. XXX (1888).

From the very beginnings of research in the medieval romance until the present day, scholars have necessarily been preoccupied with the fundamental question of attributions (e.g., of *Thèbes, Eneas, Philomena, Guillaume d'Angleterre*, certain *lais*, the various *Continuations* of Chrétien de Troyes' *Perceval*, and so on), identification (Chrétien de Troyes, Marie de France, Jean Renart, and others), and, above all, chronology. Studies on these points are so numerous that they cannot be even summarily listed here, but they are fortunately easily located in the bibliographies of Bossuat and of Cabeen-Holmes.

We have seen that since the work of Wilmotte and Faral it is generally admitted that the *romans d'antiquité* are earlier than the *romans bretons*. This has been seriously contested only by F. E. Guyer in a series of articles and books, particularly in "The

Chronology of the Earliest French Romances" (*MP*, 1928–29), and in *Romance in the Making: Chrétien de Troyes and the Earliest French Romances* (1954). For Guyer, all of Chrétien's works other than the *Perceval* would be earlier than 1167, and the *romans d'antiquité* would all be later, the *Roman de Troie* after 1184. F. A. G. Cowper showed the unsoundness of this last dating in "Date and Dedication of the *Roman de Troie*" (*MP*, 1929–30); Guyer's other datings have met with similar skepticism.

P. A. Becker, in "Der gepaarte Achtsilber in der französischen Dichtung" (*ASAW*, 1934), and again in "Von den Erzähleren neben und nach Chrestien de Troyes" (*ZRP*, 1935), places the *Thèbes*, *Eneas*, *Troie* trilogy in approximately the same period as the works of Chrétien, and thinks there was a sort of reciprocal inspiration and emulation between the anonymous author of *Eneas* and Chrétien when the latter was composing his *Erec et Enide*. Most scholars today, however, agree with Wilmotte and Faral that the "classical" romances are earlier than those of Chrétien. Within the classical trilogy, too, it is universally agreed that the *Roman de Thèbes* is the earliest, but opinion is sharply divided on the question of the priority of *Eneas* or *Troie*. In his *Recherches*, Faral listed the conflicting scholarly opinions on this point up to 1913, and then proceeded to give twenty-eight reasons for believing in the priority of the *Eneas*. F. M. Warren (*MLN*, 1914) agreed with Faral on this point and found his argument No. 22 particularly convincing, while Wilmotte (*Romania*, 1914) inclined to the contrary opinion. As Faral's listing shows, some critics, like L. Constans, the editor of *Thèbes* and of *Troie*, have held different opinions at different times.

This uncertainty as to chronology is due to the fact that even where we are given the name of the author in a text, little or nothing is known of his life, and the texts themselves offer little internal evidence for a precise dating. We have, at most, an occasional reference to a historical personage. In *Thèbes* and *Eneas* none at all have been found, and in *Troie* only a hyperbolic lauding of a noble lady, who is identified simply as "riche dame de riche rei" and has been taken to be Eleanor of Aquitaine (lines 13457–70, *Roman de Troie*, ed. Constans, *SATF*, VI, 1912). Even allowing for a courtier's supine flattery, in view of Eleanor's unsavory reputation it is difficult to imagine anyone imputing to her "honesté e sen e honor" and "bien e mesure e sainteé." The identification with Eleanor is not certain in any case, and although Benoît seems to have been a Norman, the queen in question may have been the wife of Philip Augustus.

Because of the paucity of identifiable allusions in the romances, scholars have attempted to establish a chronology on purely literary grounds, chiefly by comparing the romances with one another and drawing conclusions from similarities in themes, style, and especially in verbal usage, that may indicate influence of one romance upon another. Although these studies are numerous, they are rarely so cogent as to obtain general assent to their conclusions. Even when verbal similarities are granted and lead to the likelihood of one work's being influenced by another, it is virtually impossible to be certain of the direction in which the influence operated. Hoepffner, for example, traced the influence of Wace on the *Eneas* ("*L'Enéas* et Wace," *Archivum Romanicum*, 1931 and 1932), whereas Edna Frederick claimed that if there was an influence, it went the other way (*PMLA*, 1935). S. Hofer asserted that the *Thèbes* borrowed from the *Brut* ("Zur Datierung des Thebenromans," *ZRP*, 1942). Similar claims have been advanced for supposed borrowings of Thomas of Britain from Marie de France, or the reverse, of the *Yvain* from the *Roman de Rou*, or the reverse, of *Cligés* from *Eracle*, of *Thèbes* from *Lanval*, and so on indefinitely. (See I. Arnold, ed., *Le Roman de Brut*, *SATF*, I, 1938, xcii.) References to the most important of these studies will be readily found in the bibliographies, but it must be admitted that they have resulted in very few definitive and generally accepted conclusions. Only for the *Brut* do we have a precise, incontrovertible date, 1155, given by Wace himself at the end of the text.

Despite the uncertainty as to the sources and chronology of the early romances, these questions were the chief concern of the great majority of studies until quite recently. Questions of interpretation and of literary criticism received much less attention. The most important source of information on the literary and rhetorical doctrines current in the schools is E. Faral, *Les arts poétiques du XII° et du XIII° siècle: recherches et documents sur la technique littéraire du moyen âge* (1924; rptd. 1958), which includes the publication of the most important texts and a study of their doctrine. Its immediate usefulness is somewhat diminished by the lack of an index. Another work covering somewhat the same ground, although without the texts, but with a useful index, is C. S. Baldwin, *Medieval Rhetoric and Poetic* (1928). The texts and doctrines studied by Faral and Baldwin are related exclusively to medieval Latin, but they have their application to the vernacular romances composed by men trained in them. Edgar de Bruyne's *Etudes d'esthétique médiévale* (3 vols., 1946), though primarily concerned with philosophical esthetics, throws much light on medieval literary theory and practice. In regard to French texts specifically, mention should be made of F. M. Warren, "Some Features of Style in Early French Narrative Poetry" (*MP*, 1905–06, 1906–07), which is still very useful.

An interesting study of the "style" of the medieval French romance in a much broader sense of the word is F. Schürr's *Das Altfranzösische Epos; zur Stilgeschichte und innern Form der Gotik* (1926). As usual in German writing, the term *Epos* includes both epic and romance. Schürr studies the romances as an expression of the Gothic spirit among other manifestations of the civilization of the twelfth and thirteenth centuries, and particularly of the transformation of the so-called Gothic spirit in the direction of secularism.

A. ROMANS D'ANTIQUITE

For the study of the *Roman d'Alexandre* and the development of the Alexander legend, Paul Meyer's *Alexandre le Grand dans la littérature française* (2 vols., 1886) has not been replaced and must still be consulted, although it suffered from the lack of satisfactory editions of the most important texts at the time it was written. There is a good general survey of the development of the legend from ancient times in the introduction to F. P. Magoun, Jr.'s edition of *The Gests of King Alexander of Macedon: Two Middle English Alliterative Fragments, Alexander A and Alexander B* (1929), which also includes parallel passages from Orosius and the *Historia de Preliis*, whose importance for the French *Alexandre* was not recognized by Meyer. The most important work for the medieval Alexander legend is now G. Cary, *The Medieval Alexander* (1956). The introduction on the premedieval sources leans heavily on Magoun's *Gests*, but Cary develops the study of the figure of Alexander in the Middle Ages to a much greater depth and extent than any previous scholar. He studies the writings of the philosophers, moralists, theologians, preachers, and compilers of *exempla*, as well as of the romancers, and he shows that only the latter are full of unstinted praise of their hero.

The seminar at Princeton University directed by the late E. C. Armstrong initiated the monumental publication of the medieval French *Roman d'Alexandre* and its continuations; the work is still in progress under the direction of A. Foulet. From 1937 on, five volumes have appeared at irregular intervals and by different editors, and a sixth has been announced. The seminar has also inspired editions of Gui de Cambrai's *Le Vengement Alixandre* by B.

Edwards (1928), of Jean le Nevelon's (or le Venelais's) *La Venjance Alixandre* by E. B. Ham (1931), of *Five Versions of the
Venjance Alixandre* by E. B. Ham (1935), and of *La Prise de Defur
and Le Voyage d'Alexandre au paradis terrestre* by L. P. G.
Peckham and M. S. LaDu (1935). Several shorter texts, fragments,
and studies on points of detail have also come from the studies at
Princeton.

There has been very little interest in the *Roman de Thèbes* in
recent times. The only edition is still that of L. Constans (2 vols.,
SATF, 1890), although it was severely criticized by P. Meyer
(*Romania*, 1892). The most important special study is probably E.
Hoepffner's "La chanson de geste et les débuts du roman courtois" in
the *Mélanges Jeanroy* (1928), in which he develops previous ideas of
J. J. Salverda de Grave and F. Schürr on the influence of the
chansons de geste, and of the *Roland* in particular, on the *Roman de
Thèbes*.

There has been no edition of the *Roman d'Eneas* either, since
the quite satisfactory one of J. J. Salverda de Grave (2 vols.,
CFMA, 1925, 1931), which contains a good introductory study and
bibliography. There have been several specialized studies devoted
chiefly to the problem of influences between the *Eneas* and other
works. E. Levi suggested in "Marie de France e il romanzo d'Eneas"
(*AIV*, 1921–22) that Marie was the author of the *Eneas*. This was
refuted by E. Hoepffner's more plausible article, "Marie de France
et l'*Eneas*" (*SMed*, 1932). A. Pauphilet examined the episode of the
Trojans in Carthage in "Enéas et Enée" (*Romania*, 1929) and
showed how the medieval mind misunderstood and transformed the
Virgilian episode. In "*Eneas et Cligès*" (*Mélanges Hoepffner*, 1949),
A. Micha attempted to trace the direct influence of the *Eneas* on
Chrétien's romance, and Salverda de Grave less convincingly did the
same for its influence on Jean de Tuim's *Histoire de Jules Cesar* in
"Un imitateur du *Roman d'Enéas* au XIIIe siècle en France"
(*SMed*, 1932).

The latest edition of the *Roman de Troie* is still that of L.
Constans (6 vols., *SATF*, 1904–12). On the basis of a comparison of
the language and style of the *Troie*, whose author identifies himself
as "Beneeit de Sainte More" (line 132), with those of the *Chronique
des ducs de Normandie*, written by a certain "Beneeit" not otherwise
identified, Constans concludes that they could not have been written
by the same person despite the identity of the names. P. A. Becker, in
Der gepaarte Achtsilber (1934), and Carin Fahlin, the recent editor
of the *Chronique* (1951–   ), in her *Etude sur le manuscrit de Tours
de la chronique des ducs de Normandie par Benoît* (1937), reached

the contrary conclusion that the two Benoîts were one and the same.

Faral and Wilmotte rightly considered that the modern distinction between the courtly romances and the shorter narrative poems known as *contes* and *lais* is artificial and corresponds to no essential differences in theme or style. The *conte* of *Narcisus*, for example, is preceded in MS. B.N. f.fr. 19152 by the rubric *Ci commence de Narciso le roumanz*. Gautier d'Arras refers to his romance of *Ille et Galeron* as a *lai* (ed. F. A. G. Cowper, *SATF*, 1956). Chrétien refers to his *Cligés* as a *conte* (ed. Micha, *CFMA*, 1957). Our modern distinction between these terms and genres is obviously not founded on medieval usage.

The prologue of *Cligés* lists among Chrétien's previous works several translations or adaptations of works of Ovid: the *Comandemanz Ovide*, the *Art d'amors*, the *Mors de l'Espaule*, and *De la hupe et de l'aronde et del rossignol la muance*. All but the last of these works are lost; the last has been identified with the section on Philomena in the fourteenth-century *Ovide moralisé*, whose author is designated as "Crestiiens li Gois" (*Philomena*, ed. C. De Boer, 1909). This identification and the meaning of *li Gois* have been the object of much controversy, De Boer and many other scholars believing that the *Philomena* section of the *Ovide moralisé* is substantially the same as the *De la hupe et de l'aronde et del rossignol la muance* of Chrétien de Troyes, while other scholars, such as R. Levy, oppose this identification. Levy has summarized the controversy up to 1951 in his "Etat présent des études sur l'attribution de Philomena" (*LR*, 1951). Since then H. F. Williams has proposed to understand *li gois* as *le gai*, an epithet that might well have been applied to Chrétien de Troyes, whom he takes to be the author of the *Philomena* (*BBSIA*, 1958).

Two anonymous adaptations of episodes from Ovid's *Metamorphoses* are available in satisfactory modern editions: the *Piramus et Tisbé*, ed. C. De Boer (*CFMA*, 1921), and the *Narcisus*, ed. A. Hilka (*ZRP*, 1929). Both can also be read in the invaluable complete phototype reproductions of MS. B.N. f.fr. 837, published by H. Omont (1932), and of MS. B.N. f.fr. 19152, published by E. Faral (1934). The most important study of the *Piramus* still remains the chapter devoted to it in Faral's *Recherches*. The *Narcisus* has attracted only the briefest of mentions. On the whole, romances celebrating the *matière de Rome* have occupied the attention of scholars very little since 1941, when Wilmotte published his *Origines du roman en France*. Quite understandably, the great preponderance of studies has been devoted to the much more numerous and far more brilliant, entertaining, and more intriguing romances, *contes*, and *lais* devoted to the *matière de Bretagne*.

B. ROMANS BRETONS

We are very fortunate to have available many excellent bibliographical tools and general studies as guides to the enormous mass of scholarly work in the field of Arthurian romance. Chapter x, on the *matière de Bretagne*, of the Cabeen-Holmes bibliography is particularly helpful, since it provides sound, short, critical analyses and judgments of each entry, contributed by three of our foremost Arthurian specialists, the late J. J. Parry, Helaine Newstead, and W. Roach. Parry had previously published two bibliographies of critical Arthurian literature (1931, covering the period 1922–29, and 1936, with Margaret Schlauch, covering the period 1930–35). In *MLQ* (1940) Parry and Margaret Schlauch published the bibliography for 1936–39, and thereafter annually in the June issue Parry listed the publications of the preceding year. Until 1964 the work was continued by P. A. Brown. It lists without critical comment all the books and articles in alphabetical order by their authors' names, indicating by whom and where they were reviewed, and appends an index of the subjects and texts discussed.

Since the publication in 1949 of the first annual number of the *Bulletin bibliographique de la Société Internationale Arthurienne*, we have also each year another, differently organized, bibliography of studies on the *matière de Bretagne*. The works are listed under their respective national or regional headings, and are subdivided into I: texts, translations, and adaptations; II: critical and historical studies; III: critical reviews. Within each subdivision the alphabetical order is observed, and there are frequent short descriptions, without critical comment, of the more important items. The *Bulletin* also publishes news of interest to Arthurian scholars and, under the heading *Recherche et critique*, a number of articles by members of the Society.

In addition to these excellent bibliographical tools, there are two very useful general studies of the whole field of medieval Arthurian romance. The first is J. D. Bruce, *The Evolution of Arthurian Romance from the Beginnings Down to the Year 1300* (1923). The second edition (1928) is merely a reprint of the first with the addition of a bibliographical supplement by A. Hilka. This second edition was printed again in 1958.

The second general work on the whole field was published under the general editorship of R. S. Loomis, *Arthurian Literature in the*

Middle Ages (1959). Both the Bruce and the Loomis volumes transcend the national limits of French Arthurian romance and treat of the international ramifications of the legend. Since the most eminent scholars in their respective specialties have contributed the forty-one chapters of *ALMA*, this work is the indispensable starting point for future studies in the field. It does not, however, entirely replace Bruce, since the analyses of individual texts in that work are still helpful, as is its bibliography of studies up to 1928. Sixteen chapters are devoted to studies of medieval French texts, with full accounts of the present state of scholarship in important areas (Wace, the *lais*, Tristan, Chrétien de Troyes, the *Continuations* of his *Perceval*, Robert de Boron and the *Didot Perceval*, the *Perlesvaus*, the Grail legends, the Vulgate Cycle, and so on) which need not therefore be reviewed in detail here.

The bibliography of Bruce is also brought up to date in H. F. Williams, "French Arthurian Scholarship since Bruce" (*Symposium*, 1956). It provides a succinct review of research (limited not to French scholarship but to scholarship on French Arthurian texts), with brief critical comments, bibliographical indications, and occasional suggestions of desiderata in the field.

Within the field of Arthurian romance, Chrétien de Troyes is no doubt the most important single figure, as well as the author of the earliest extant Arthurian romances. Here again we have available a recent excellent general study, with selected bibliography, in J. Frappier, *Chrétien de Troyes: l'homme et l'œuvre* (1957), a particularly fine introduction to Arthurian literature and an outstanding contribution to the understanding and appreciation of Chrétien's works. Since the publication of this work and of other recent books and articles on Chrétien, earlier reviews of research and bibliographies are useful chiefly for finding discussions of minor questions not treated in more recent times. Still useful, because cumulative, unlike the Parry and *BBSIA* bibliographies, is J. R. Reinhard's *Chrétien de Troyes: A Bibliographical Essay* (1932). Mention should be made also of W. Kellerman's now twenty-five-year-old *état présent* of studies on Chrétien de Troyes, "Wege und Ziele der neueren Chrestien de Troyes-Forschung" (*GRM*, 1935).

Because of Chrétien's crucial importance for the development of the romance, the chronology of his works has preoccupied scholars from the time of G. Paris until the present day. H. F. Williams (*Symposium*, 1956) conveniently grouped references to attempts at dating Chrétien's works from the time of Bruce until 1950, when A. Fourrier, in the *BBSIA* (1950), building on previous studies of S. Hofer, proposed a new series of dates (*Erec* 1170; *Cligés* 1176;

Yvain and *Lancelot* concurrently, 1177–81; *Perceval* 1181–90), which have been widely but perhaps too hastily and uncritically accepted. (See J. Misrahi, "More Light on the Chronology of Chrétien de Troyes," *BBSIA*, 1959.)

Speculation continues as to the identity of Marie de France (U. T. Holmes, *SP*, 1932 and 1942, and *Symposium*, 1949, and R. D. Whichard in *Romance Studies Presented to W. M. Dey*, 1950). Attempts to identify Chrétien de Troyes have also been made by L. A. Vigneras in "Chrétien de Troyes Rediscovered" (*MP*, 1934–35) and U. T. Holmes and Sister M. A. Klenke in *Chrétien, Troyes, and the Grail* (1959).

Mention has been made above of studies on the attribution of the *Philomena* to Chrétien. Opinion is still divided, too, on the attribution to him of the *Guillaume d'Angleterre*. The two editors of the text, Foerster (1911) and Wilmotte (*CFMA*, 1927), are firm supporters of this attribution (see Wilmotte, "Chrétien de Troyes et le conte de *Guillaume d'Angleterre*," *Romania*, 1920), as is Franca Danelon in "Sull' ispirazione e sull' autore del *Guillaume d'Angleterre*" (*CN*, 1951). Opposed to the identification of the Chrétien who names himself as the author of the text with Chrétien de Troyes are F. J. Tanquerey ("Chrétien de Troyes est-il l'auteur de *Guillaume d'Angleterre?*" *Romania*, 1931), P. A. Becker (*ZRP*, 1935), and J. Frappier (*Chrétien de Troyes*, 1957), who thinks that the *Guillaume d'Angleterre* is the work of a gifted, but still inferior imitator of Chrétien de Troyes.

C. ORIGINS OF THE MATIERE DE BRETAGNE

The problem that has dominated Arthurian studies more than any other has to do with the origin and earliest development of the entire *matière de Bretagne*. The earliest generation of scholars, such as G. Paris and G. L. Kittredge, accepted at face value the medieval writers' numerous acknowledgments of indebtedness to traditional material learned from Breton *conteurs* and singers of *lais*. Kittredge drew attention to Irish antecedents of *Gawain and the Green Knight* (which has many French analogues) in *A Study of Gawain and the Green Knight* (1916). The following generation of scholars in France and Germany included many who claimed that there is very little traditional Celtic material in the *romans bretons*, and that they are a purely literary creation of the twelfth century, whose sources are to be found chiefly in Latin literature, ancient and medieval, in the *romans d'antiquité*, and in Geoffrey of Monmouth's *Historia regum Britanniae* (c. 1137). W. Foerster and Bruce thus minimized the Celtic contribution to Arthurian romance, although the latter was less dogmatic on the point than is sometimes asserted. J. J. Parry, for instance (in Cabeen-Holmes, No. 1054), cites a passage of Bruce as evidence of the latter's anti-Celtic bias. The passage cited, however, is not concerned with Celtic origins as such, but with the existence of Arthurian romances in French verse before the time of Chrétien. One might cite other passages as examples of Bruce's readiness to admit Continental *breton* sources; it is chiefly the insular Celtic sources that he rejects.

The most extreme adversary of the Celtic origins is no doubt E. Faral, who wrote of the "romans dits bretons" that "dans la mesure où ceux-ci doivent quelque chose à une autre source que la seule imagination de leurs auteurs, ce n'est pas à des poèms celtiques qu'ils se rattachent: c'est à une œuvre de clerc, à une sorte de mystification littéraire, par laquelle Gaufrei [Geoffrey of Monmouth] a 'lancé' la poésie bretonne." Despite Geoffrey's statements to the contrary, Faral asserts that his work is totally lacking in any popular or national character and that it was "forgé de toutes pièces" (Bédier-Hazard, I, 19). Faral defended this thesis in *La légende arthurienne; première partie: les plus anciens textes* (1929). He stated his method in the preface: "J'ai accepté de propos délibéré les risques d'une critique résolument positiviste"—which meant in practice that he would limit his study to an analysis of the earliest surviving Latin texts mentioning Arthur up to the time of Geoffrey, with the implication that these few now extant texts are sufficient to explain the genesis of the entire Arthurian corpus and that it is quite unnecessary to suppose that any other texts or traditions about Arthur and the other figures of later Arthurian romance ever existed or to search for their sources elsewhere. It is significant that this work of Faral remained uncompleted; nothing beyond the "première partie" and Geoffrey of Monmouth was ever published.

Replies to Faral's thesis may be read in the critiques of professional Celtic scholars like J. Loth (*MA*, 1931) and J. Vendryès (*Revue celtique*, 1931), and in the review by R. S. Loomis, with Faral's reply and a rebuttal by Loomis, all in *MLN* (1931).

Faral's skepticism about any developed Arthurian tradition prior to Geoffrey is shared and further argued by J. S. P. Tatlock in *The Legendary History of Britain: Geoffrey of Monmouth's "Historia Regum Britanniae" and Its Early Vernacular Versions* (1950). Tatlock's arguments are countered by Helaine Newstead in "About Geoffrey of Monmouth" (*Latomus*, 1951). The place of Geoffrey in the development of Arthurian tradition is judiciously discussed by P. Rickard in *Britain in Medieval French Literature*

1100–1500 (1956), although Rickard is overconfident when he states that "today no one doubts that the 'Matter of Britain' comes from Celtic Britain and Ireland."

H. F. Williams, also, notes that "the Celticists have been steadily gaining ground," but that "the school of Foerster, Bruce, and others is still fighting a rear-guard action" (*Symposium*, 1956). S. Hofer, in various articles and in his *Chrétien de Troyes: Leben und Werke des altfranzösischen Epikers* (1954), denies the importance of any traditional Celtic element in Chrétien's romances. He is, accordingly, commended by M. Roques for having "de son mieux dégagé son texte des hantises celtiques," yet reproached in the next breath because "il leur a fait, dans ses notes, une place que l'on peut trouver excessive" (*Romania*, 1955).

The evidence for the Celtic origin of the Arthurian legend is clearly presented by R. S. Loomis, "The Arthurian Legend before 1139" (*RR*, 1941). This article is reprinted, with many other previously published articles and one new one ("Brân the Blessed and *Sone de Nausay*"), in R. S. Loomis, *Wales and the Arthurian Legend* (1956). It sums up conveniently the arguments on both sides of the controversy with full references to the pertinent critical studies.

H. R. Patch suggested that if the controversy between the Celticists and the anti-Celticists is still going on, it is less for lack of evidence for the Celticists' case than "because—where absolute proof must be lacking—some magic spell requires that the tournament continue forever" (*RPh*, 1957). For those who don't believe in magic spells, another cause for the continuing controversy may be detected in the phrase "where absolute proof must be lacking." There are those who, like Faral, are so attached to a strict and narrow understanding of "la critique positiviste" that they prefer to attribute to the free invention of Geoffrey and the romance writers everything that cannot be directly traced to the now-extant texts and to underestimate the value of the evidence for a pre-Galfridian Arthurian legend and a pre-Chrétien Arthurian romantic tradition, even though that evidence includes the positive statements of Chrétien, Thomas, Marie de France, and many other medieval writers themselves. For Faral these are willful deceptions. The "so-called" *romans bretons* "ne sont bretons que par le lieu de la scène et par le nom des personnages, bretons par l'effet d'une couleur artificiellement obtenue, comme les *Natchez* sont un roman des Florides, comme le *Roman de la momie* est un roman d'Egypte" (Bédier-Hazard, I, 19). G. Cohen, in *Un grand romancier d'amour et d'aventure au XIIᵉ siècle* (1931; 2nd ed. 1948), adapts Faral's dictum somewhat, claiming that Chrétien's works are Celtic in the same way that Montesquieu's *Lettres persanes* are Persian, or certain eighteenth-century French romances are Chinese or Peruvian. J. Vendryès prefers another and probably more valid analogy: "il serait plus exact de dire: comme le *Cid* de Corneille est espagnol" (*Revue celtique,* 1931).

R. S. Loomis' first general survey of the question, *Celtic Myth and Arthurian Romance* (1927), was the object of several adversely critical reviews. Loomis refuted some of the arguments of his critics (*Romania,* 1928, and *SMed,* 1930), yet himself retracted some of the theses of this early work in his *Arthurian Tradition and Chrétien de Troyes* (1949).

A. C. L. Brown's *The Origin of the Grail Legend* (1943) met with a poor reception even from other scholars favorable to the Celtic origin of the Grail legend. An attempt to derive Arthurian romance from Greek sources, C. B. Lewis' *Classical Mythology and Arthurian Romance* (1932), has also been very severely criticized by scholars of all shades of opinion. (See Cabeen-Holmes, No. 1058.)

Curiously enough, one of the most intransigent attacks on the Celtic hypothesis has come recently from an outstanding Celtic scholar, K. H. Jackson, in his article, "Les sources celtiques du *Roman du Graal*," in *Les Romans du Graal aux XIIe et XIIIe siècles* (1956), although he does admit the existence of certain Arthurian legends (Merlin, Kulhwch and Olwen) prior to Geoffrey. His chief complaint is that scholars who are not professional Celticists make "fâcheuses bévues" when they speak of Celtic matters. As R. W. Ackerman has noted, this criticism would carry more weight if Jackson had specified what these blunders are (*RPh,* 1957). Jackson's objections, and some others, are discussed by R. S. Loomis in "Objections to the Celtic Origins of the 'Matière de Bretagne'" (*Romania,* 1958).

One particularly crucial aspect of the problem of Celtic origins is the question of the relation of three of Chrétien's romances, *Erec et Enide, Yvain,* and *Perceval,* to three tales, *Gereint son of Erbin, The Lady of the Fountain,* and *Peredur son of Efrawg,* in the Welsh *Mabinogion.* The Welsh versions are admittedly of later date than their French counterparts, and they show evident traces of influence from French sources. No one today, then, maintains that they are the source, direct or indirect, of Chrétien's romances; some scholars hold, on the contrary, that they are simply derivatives of Chrétien's works. Bruce summarized this so-called "Mabinogion Controversy" in his *Evolution* and concluded that the Welsh tales are simply adaptations of French models. R. Zenker answered him in "Bruce und die Mabinogionfrage" (*ZFSL, Supplementheft*, 1929). Although Parry stated in 1947 that "nothing that has been published since [Bruce] has brought [the] problem any nearer a solution" (Cabeen-Holmes, No. 1054), Loomis two years later found important new evidence for the independence of the Welsh *Gereint* from Chrétien's *Erec* and for the likelihood of their both stemming from a common source ("Two Cruces in the Text of Chrétien de Troyes," in *Mélanges de philologie romane et de littérature médiévale offerts à Ernest Hoepffner*, 1949).

The controversy on the question of Celtic origins goes on endlessly. As J. Frappier says, "La 'celtomanie' possible de telle critique n'a d'égale que la 'celtophobie' d'un autre" (*Chrétien de Troyes*, 1957). J. J. Parry, no blind partisan of R. S. Loomis, wrote nonetheless of his "The Arthurian Legend before 1139," that "some points may be assailed, but an impartial reader can hardly reject [his] thesis as a whole" (Cabeen-Holmes, No. 1061). H. R. Patch, an equally independent critic, even goes so far as to suggest that "one may ask whether a degree of irresponsibility is not involved today in the notions of any scholar who evades the conclusions Mr. Loomis has so often brought before us in these and other studies" (*RPh*, 1957). The anti-Celticists are in fact less numerous and less influential today than a generation ago, and they are obliged to make a number of concessions, but their opposition to the thesis of a massive influx of traditional Celtic legend into French romances in the twelfth century is still determined and vigorous.

Although this controversy is still very much with us, other and newer problems are coming to the forefront. The general question of the symbolic interpretation of medieval vernacular literature is the subject of lively discussion at the present time.

D. SYMBOLISM AND ALLEGORY IN THE ROMANS BRETONS

The various modes of symbolism and allegory in medieval Latin and some vernacular writings have long been known and studied. What is new in more recent scholarship is the idea that these modes of thinking and writing were much the same in vernacular romances as in theological and exegetical didactic writings, and that the romances were conceived and are to be understood by using the same approach and methods as were used by medieval commentators on Holy Scripture.

Perhaps the earliest of the clear and influential statements of this point of view is found in L. Spitzer, "The Prologue to the *Lais* of Marie de France and Medieval Poetics": "Even such 'this-worldly' poets as Marie de France and Juan Ruiz could not but see their secular works in the same light as that of the sacred books, the Bible." Marie, he concludes, is a "poeta philosophus et theologus" (*MP*, 1943). In more recent years, D. W. Robertson, Jr., has been the most persuasive exponent of this approach, particularly in two articles, "Some Medieval Literary Terminology with Special Reference to Chrétien de Troyes" (*SP*, 1951), and "The Doctrine of Charity in Mediaeval Literary Gardens: A Topical Approach Through Symbolism and Allegory" (*Speculum*, 1951). In the first he categorically asserts that all "serious poetry written by medieval Christians, whether their work is now classified as 'religious' or 'secular'. . . [must] conduce to charity." If it does not do so on the surface, "then the poem is allegorical and it is necessary to determine the *sententia* . . . The *sententia* in Christian poetry is always an aspect of Charity." Although this way of considering medieval "secular" poetry has been accepted by some scholars, there have been energetic criticisms of its doctrine and practice. A particularly sound and cogent one is M. W. Bloomfield's "Symbolism in Medieval Literature" (*MP*, 1958). In *Critical Approaches to Medieval Literature: Selected Papers from the English Institute, 1958–1959* (1960), the first three papers, under the general heading "Patristic Exegesis in the Criticism of Medieval Literature," provide excellent treatments of this general problem of method from the two opposing points of view: E. T. Donaldson, "The Opposition," R. E. Kaske, "The Defense," and a "Summation" by C. Donahue.

R. R. Bezzola's *Le sens de l'aventure et de l'amour (Chrétien de Troyes)* (1947) is less concerned with the general theory of medieval symbolism than with its application to Chrétien's *Erec* and his *Perceval* in particular. It is rich in perceptive and sensitive literary analyses, but many of its specific symbolic interpretations are based on demonstrably mistaken assumptions about the text, and some of the esthetic appreciations are forced (see J. Misrahi, *RPh*, 1951). Bezzola's teaching and example have inspired a number of studies in the same vein. His pupil Ingeborg Dubs applied his method in her *Galeran de Bretagne: die Krise im französischen hofischen Roman* (1949). The virtues and defects of the method and its application in this book have been pointed out by Helaine Newstead (*RPh*, 1950). A more substantial study, applying much the same method to Chrétien's works, is E. Köhler's *Ideal und Wirklichkeit in der höfischen Epik: Studien zur Form der frühen Artus- und Graldichtung* (*ZRP, Beihefte*, 1956).

In 1947 U. T. Holmes published the first version of "A New Interpretation of Chrétien's *Conte del Graal*" (*SP*, 1947). The following year it was republished in a revised and enlarged form in *UNCSRLL*. Its thesis is that Chrétien's *Perceval* is concerned with the conversion of the Jews, and it suggests that Chrétien was himself a converted Jew, although the demonstration of the thesis is emphatically stated to be independent of this suggestion. This thesis drew a strong criticism from R. Levy in "The Quest for Biographical Evidence in *Perceval*" (*M&H*, 1950). Sister M. Amelia Klenke, in "Liturgy and Allegory in Chrétien's *Perceval*" (*UNCSRLL*, 1951) and in "Christian Symbolism and Cathedral Art" (*PMLA*, 1955), further developed the thesis that the *Perceval* is a profoundly theological and symbolical work concerned with the triumph of *Ecclesia* over *Synagoga*. The maiden who carries the Grail is said to be *Ecclesia*. In the same year, 1955, M. Roques, in "Le Graal de Chrétien et la demoiselle du Graal" (*Romania*, separately published also in the series of the *Société de publications romanes et françaises*, 1955), independently reached the same conclusion. Sister Amelia's method and conclusions were trenchantly criticized by R. S. Loomis in "The Grail Story of Chrétien de Troyes as Ritual and Symbolism" (*PMLA*, 1956). The theses of Holmes and Sister Amelia were further developed in their jointly published *Chrétien, Troyes, and the Grail* (1959). In it Holmes provides a great deal of interesting material about the history and topography of Troyes in Chrétien's time, although this is of uncertain relevance to the interpretation of his works, since we know nothing of Chrétien's origins, education, and career, nor of the nature and duration of his association with Troyes. J. F. Benton has shown how little is known of literary activities there in "The Court of Champagne as a Literary Center" (*Speculum*, 1961).

The second half of the book, by Sister Amelia, carries the allegorical interpretation to extremes, and as one critic has noted, her "gallant, spirited, enthusiastic flights" are not easy to follow (Helen Adolf, *Speculum*, 1960). According to Sister Amelia, Perceval is to be identified with Saint Paul, his mother is true religion, Gornemant is Gamaliel, Blancheflor is chastity, the hermit of the Good Friday episode is Saint John the Evangelist, and so on. The allegory is to be interpreted on both the Old Testament and New Testament levels; an appendix provides an "Alphabetical Key to the Symbolism of Chrétien's *Perceval*" for the understandably perplexed reader.

In 1959, too, appeared D. C. Fowler's *Prowess and Charity in the Perceval of Chrétien de Troyes*, which interprets the *Perceval* as a conflict between the ideals of prowess and charity in the soul of the hero, with the final triumph of charity after the Good Friday episode. There is little apparent basis in the text for considering the

Grail and the lance as symbols of charity and prowess respectively, and for positing a conflict between those two virtues. This small volume is nonetheless interesting for its many moderate and intuitive suggestions for the interpretation of the poetry and symbolism of the *Perceval*.

Yet another interpretation is offered in Helen Adolf's *Visio pacis: Holy City and Grail* (1960), which sees the whole development of the Grail legend in the Middle Ages as essentially concerned with the Holy City and the Crusades. Miss Adolf claims that in the light of Pope Alexander III's widely circulated letter, *Cor nostrum*, of 1181, readers of the *Perceval* would have understood it as a warning of the danger to Jerusalem and a call to the Crusade. Reservations about this interpretation, but also appreciation of other aspects of the work, are expressed by Helaine Newstead (*GR*, 1962).

E. OTHER ARTHURIAN STUDIES

A good starting point for studies on Chrétien's *Lancelot* is still T. P. Cross and W. A. Nitze's monograph, *Lancelot and Guenevere: A Study on the Origins of Courtly Love* (1930), although it makes no allowance for possible humor and irony in Chrétien's treatment of the theme, as some scholars are inclined to do today. There are interesting suggestions, too, in M. Roques, "Pour l'interprétation du *Chevalier de la Charrete* de Chrétien de Troyes" (*CCM*, 1958).

W. Kellerman's *Aufbaustil und Weltbild Chrestiens von Troyes im Percevalroman* (1936) is a thoroughgoing analysis of the composition, style, and significance of the romance, although it is to a great extent superseded by J. Frappier, *Le roman breton: Chrétien de Troyes; Perceval ou le Conte du Graal* (1959). W. A. Nitze's *Perceval and the Holy Grail* (*UCPMP*, 1949) is an eclectic and sober study of the sources of the *Perceval*. J. Marx's *La légende arthurienne et le Graal* (1952) is a more detailed and more speculative work, which should be read in conjunction with the important comments of R. S. Loomis (*Speculum*, 1952) and W. A. Nitze (*RPh*, 1953).

A more specialized though fundamental book for the problems of Grail origins is Helaine Newstead's *Bran the Blessed in Arthurian Romance* (1939), which investigates the Welsh antecedents of the Grail and Grail King, as well as of other features of various Arthurian romances. The importance of Welsh traditions for Arthurian romance had already been demonstrated by R. S. Loomis.

The collection of articles published under the title of *Lumière du Graal* (1951), under the general editorship of R. Nelli, includes a number of valuable articles: J. Vendryès, "Le Graal dans le cycle breton"; J. Marx, "Le héros du Graal"; A. Micha, "Les romans du Graal," "Le Perceval de Chrétien de Troyes," and "Première visite de Perceval"; E. Hoepffner, *Estoire dou Graal* de Robert de Boron"; and J. Frappier, "Le cortège du Graal." The volume unfortunately also includes several other articles of an entirely different and unscientific character concerned with the "ésotérisme" of the Grail legends, some of them related to the current attempted revival of catharism in southern France.

In 1954 an international colloquium was held in Strasbourg under the auspices of the Centre National de la Recherche Scientifique; the papers read there by eminent Arthurian scholars were published in 1956 under the title of *Les romans du Graal aux XIIe et XIIIe siècles*. The value of these articles on various aspects of the Grail legend is further enhanced by the transcription of the discussion that followed the reading of each paper.

Of the so-called Vulgate Cycle of Arthurian Lancelot-Grail romances, the only complete edition is still that of H. O. Sommer (8 vols., 1908–1916). The first systematic study of this cycle (sometimes called the Prose Lancelot, after its central section) was F. Lot's *Etude sur le Lancelot en prose* (1918), which is still of value although it is superseded on many points by later studies, particularly those of A. Pauphilet, *Etudes sur la Queste del Saint Graal* (1921) and of E. Gilson, "La mystique de la grâce dans la *Queste del Saint Graal*" (*Romania*, 1925; rptd. in E. Gilson, *Les idées et les lettres*, 1932). The last branch of the cycle, *La Mort le roi Artu*, is available in an excellent critical edition by J. Frappier (1936), who also published in the same year a superb philological and literary study of the text in his *Etude sur la Mort le roi Artu*.

Among the more important studies that appeared too late to be mentioned in *ALMA* is P. Jonin's *Les personnages féminins dans les romans français de Tristan au XIIe siècle* (1958), whose subtitle, *Etude des influences contemporaines*, indicates that the subject matter of the book includes far more than an analysis of the female personages of the various Tristan texts; it attempts to situate the works of Béroul and Thomas and the two *Folie Tristan* texts against the background of the juridical, literary, and religious trends of the time. Jonin's ideas are further discussed by Bartina H. Wind in "Les éléments courtois dans Béroul et dans Thomas" (*RPh*, 1960) and by Helaine Newstead (*RPh*, 1962). Bartina H. Wind's second, revised edition of *Les fragments du Roman de Tristan* (1960) takes account of the numerous reviews of her first edition (Leiden, 1950), but because of the format of the series in which it appeared (*Textes littéraires français*), it omits or briefly summarizes most of the material in the fuller introductory study of the earlier edition. J. Marx, "Recherches sur le conte d'aventure canevas du Conte du Graal de Chrétien de Troyes" (*MA*, 1961), offers a highly plausible hypothesis as to the form of the Grail story as it reached Chrétien.

Jeanne Lods's edition of *Les lais de Marie de France* (*CFMA*, 1959) presents a very helpful and up-to-date bibliography and a concise introduction that reviews critically the research on the identity of Marie, the chronology of her works, the question of the anonymous *lais*, and of the Breton *lais* in general. The good edition of Marie's *Lais* by A. Ewert (1944) covers much the same ground up to its date of publication, and it has the advantage of a fuller glossary than the Lods edition.

A. Fourrier's *Le courant réaliste dans le roman courtois en France au moyen âge*, Vol. I, *Les débuts: XII⁰ siècle* (1960) is a thoroughgoing analysis of the beginnings of the realistic style that was to flourish in succeeding centuries in selected Arthurian and non-Arthurian texts (Thomas's *Tristan, Cligés, Eracle, Ille et Galeron, Partonopeus de Blois,* and *Florimont*). Fourrier examines the elements of the "roman-miroir" to be found in these texts, which still belong essentially to the "roman-évasion" period of narrative literature. The reality they mirror is in his view chiefly that of particular historical events rather than of social, ideological, and spiritual currents (see the substantial review by J. Frappier, *Romania,* 1961) studied in Jonin's work on the Tristan texts. Published in 1960, Fourrier's book could not take into account the above-mentioned articles of J. Benton and of J. Misrahi in regard to the "event" of 1164 (the long-accepted date for the marriage of Marie de Champagne to Henri le Libéral) and the chronology of Chrétien's works in general. However, in a book devoted to the representation of reality in narrative fiction, it is surprising to find no reference at all to so important a work on that subject as E. Auerbach's *Mimesis,* which includes an entire chapter on Chrétien's *Yvain.* Although Fourrier's conception of "reality" is rather circumscribed and his book must be read with caution because of its overeagerness to find allusions to specific historical events in the romances, the perceptive analyses of the chosen texts and the command of the large body of scholarly literature make it a valuable contribution to the study of the interplay between the mimetic and the imaginative aspects of medieval romance.

F. NON-ARTHURIAN ROMANCES

In comparison with the vast amount of writing on the Arthurian romances, relatively little attention has been given to the other romances and their authors. Chrétien de Troyes's contemporary, Gautier d'Arras, is the subject of articles by E. S. Sheldon, "Gautier d'Arras and Provins" (*RR*, 1931), and F. A. G. Cowper, "More Data on Gautier d'Arras" (*PMLA*, 1949), in which they attempt to identify Gautier with a certain Walterus de Atrebato, *minister et officialis Philippi comitis Flandriae as Viromanduorum*, a considerable personage who possessed a number of important fiefs. Cowper has also edited Gautier's *Ille et Galeron* (*SATF*, 1956) and further developed his ideas on the identity and chronology of Gautier in the introduction. Fourrier, in his chapter on Gautier in *Le courant réaliste*, rejects Cowper's identification of the apparently impecunious author, who gives evidence of some clerical formation, with the wealthy and important worldly figure, Walterus de Atrebato. There could well have been many Gautiers in a city as large as Arras.

In *Le courant réaliste* Fourrier provides a complete listing of the otherwise slender bibliography on Gautier d'Arras, on the *Partonopeus de Blois*, and on Aimon de Varennes, the author of *Florimont*. The last-named romance is available in the satisfactory but difficult to obtain edition by A. Hilka (1932); but for *Eracle* and *Partonopeus* we must still rely on the thoroughly antiquated editions by E. Löseth (1890) and G.-A. Crapelet (1834) respectively, although several scholars have promised editions of the *Partonopeus* and it can also be read in the phototype reproduction of MS. B.N. F.fr. 19152, published by E. Faral (1934).

Among the later authors of romance the most important is probably Jean Renart, and he has accordingly attracted more attention than the others. The first important study of his work is found in Ch.-V. Langlois, *La vie en France au moyen âge de la fin du XII⁰ au milieu du XIV⁰ siècle d'après les romans mondains du temps* (1924; 2nd ed. 1926), a work that may serve as a good first introduction to the medieval French romance. The most recent substantial studies on Jean Renart and his works as a whole are Rita Lejeune-Dehousse, *L'œuvre de Jean Renart* (1935), and Carla Cremonesi, *Jean Renart, romanziere del XIII secolo* (1950), although the pioneering article of F. M. Warren, "The Works of Jean Renart, Poet, and Their Relation to *Galeran de Bretagne*" (*MLN*, 1908), is still of value, like much of Warren's other work. Both Mme.

Lejeune and Warren, as well as E. Hoepffner (*Romania*, 1930 and 1936) and V. F. Koenig (*MLN*, 1934), deny the attribution of *Galeran de Bretagne* to Jean Renart, although its editor, L. Foulet (*CFMA*, 1925), and Carla Cremonesi, among others, defend it. The study of *Galeran* by Ingeborg Dubs has already been mentioned.

The number of new editions and re-editions of verse romances is far too great to permit their being listed here, but they are readily located in the bibliographies. The same may be said for periodical articles on particular aspects of individual texts. There have been very few studies of wide import on the miscellaneous *romans d'aventure*, which have not so far been mentioned here. G. Paris's well-known article, "Le cycle de la gageure" (*Romania*, 1903), despite its age, is perhaps the most important such study. It analyzes some forty versions of tales embodying the wager motif, including the *Guillaume de Dole* of Jean Renart and the *Roman de la Violette* of Gerbert de Montreuil.

Because of its unique character and literary value, special mention should perhaps be made of *Aucassin et Nicolette*, although there has been little research on it since the edition by M. Roques (*CFMA*, 1925) and his successive revised editions in the same series. In a long article in two sections, "Etude descriptive de la chantefable *Aucassin et Nicolette*" (ZRP, 1951, 1954), K. Rogger divides the text into two parts, the second of which, including the fantastic voyages and adventures of the heroes, is in his opinion of markedly inferior style and was presumably written by a different author. This thesis is no more convincing than Rogger's attempt to interpret many of the features of the text by reference to traditional symbolism and folklore. M. Roques has discussed the points raised by Rogger at some length (*Romania*, 1955). The best treatments of *Aucassin* are the chapter devoted to it in Grace Frank's *The Medieval French Drama* (1954) and the introduction to Roques's third revised edition (*CFMA*, 1955). The final essay in A. Pauphilet, *Le legs du moyen âge* (1950) also devoted to a study of *Aucassin* and, like the other chapters on the book (including those on the *Eneas, Tristan*, Chrétien de Troyes, and the *Perceval*), is interesting and valuable chiefly for Pauphilet's personal reflections and sensitive literary appreciations.

G. PROSE ROMANCES

Mention has already been made above of the great thirteenth-century prose romances of Lancelot, the Grail, and Tristan. For the later period as well, when the use of prose becomes increasingly frequent, research is greatly facilitated by B. Woledge's *Bibliographie des romans et nouvelles en prose française antérieurs à 1500* (1954). It lists 190 different romances, with an indication of the manuscripts and editions, early and modern, for each, as well as the most important critical studies. The forty-five pages of separate tables at the end of the volume provide a quick, informative view of all the manuscripts mentioned in the work, their locations, the printers of the early editions, the authors, titles of the works, literary themes, place names, and the names of "protecteurs" mentioned in the works.

Among the more important publications that appeared too late to be listed by Woledge is L. Thorpe's edition of *Le Roman de Laurin* (1958). The introduction provides a concise study of the entire "cycle" of the *Sept Sages de Rome*, to which the *Laurin* belongs. The great number of manuscripts and early editions of the various versions of the *Sept Sages* and its five sequels attest its great popularity in the later Middle Ages.

The most important prose romance of the fourteenth century, the enormously long and composite *Perceforest*, which combines the Arthurian legend with that of Alexander the Great and also draws on a great many other romances, as well as on ancient and medieval Latin writings, still awaits an editor. It has been studied by L. F. Flutre (*Romania*, 1949, 1950, and 1953) and is the subject of an excellent thesis by Jeanne Lods, *Le Roman de Perceforest, origines, composition, caractères, valeur et influence* (1951). Mlle. Lods has also published separately the lyric poems that are found interspersed in the prose romance in *Les pièces lyriques du Roman de Perceforest* (1953).

A final example of the Arthurian romance in prose, the voluminous compilation composed chiefly of the *Prose Lancelot and the Prose Tristan*, is analyzed for its content, narrative technique, and bearings on late medieval customs by C. E. Pickford in *L'évolution du roman arthurien en prose vers la fin du moyen âge d'après le manuscrit 112 du fonds français de la Bibliothèque Nationale* (1960). Just as the epic legends after the twelfth century drew closer to the romance until the two forms becomes almost indistinguishable, so, Pickford points out, the romance itself in the fifteenth century shows the influence of the new esthetic that characterized the development of the *nouvelle*.

VII. LE ROMAN DE RENART

A NEW EDITION of the *Roman de Renart* has been in course of publication in the *CFMA* since 1948, the first five volumes edited by
M. Roques (d. 1961). A concise general study and summary of
scholarship on the question of origins is R. Bossuat's *Roman de
Renard* in the collection *Connaissance des lettres* (1957). For the
understanding of the text, the studies of G. Tilander are invaluable:
Remarques sur le Roman de Renart (1923), *Lexique du Roman de
Renart* (1924), "Notes sur le texte du *Roman de Renart*" (*ZRP*,
1924). An interesting sidelight is provided by J. Graven, *Le procès
criminel du Roman de Renart* (1950).

VIII. FABLIAUX

T HE ONLY GENERAL study of the genre in our generation is P.
Nykrog's *Les fabliaux: étude d'histoire littéraire et de stylistique médiévale* (1957). Disagreeing with the view of Bédier that the
fabliaux were composed for the bourgeoisie, Nykrog defines his aim
as "démontrer que les textes ainsi déterminés, non seulement étaient
lus et goûtés dans les milieux courtois, mais qu'ils sont si pro-
fondément pénétrés de la façon de penser de ces milieux que pour les
bien comprendre il faut les considérer comme une sorte de genre
courtois." This study may be read not only for the thesis thus
formulated and ably argued but as a general introduction and an
état présent on the subject. J. Rychner has studied the textual
tradition in *Contributions à l'étude des fabliaux: variantes, remanie-
ments, dégradations* (2 vols., 1960).

Among the many editions, mostly of single *fabliaux*, or tales, a
few may be mentioned. C. H. Livingston has edited and studied the

fabliaux to be attributed to the sardonic Gautier le Leu in *Le jongleur Gautier le Leu: étude sur les fabliaux* (1951). Critical editions have been devoted to *Constant du Hamel* by C. Rostaing (1953), *Du Segretain moine* by V. Väänänen (1949), *Les Trois Aveugles de Compiegne* by G. Gougenheim (1932), *Le Chevalier au barisel*, by F. Lecoy (1955). S. Hofer has contributed further to research on the *Lai du mantel* (*ZRP*, 1957). *Le Lai d'Aristote* of Henri d'Andeli has been given an excellent critical edition and study by M. Delbouille (1951); J. Storost (*ZFSL*, 1956) has treated the iconography. In *L'œuvre de Jean Bodel* (1958) C. Foulon upholds the attribution to Jean Bodel of the nine *fabliaux* conventionally ascribed to one Jean Bedel. P. Nardin has edited *Les fabliaux de Jean Bodel* (1959; see the corrections by L.-F. Flutre in *Romania*, 1960).

IX. DRAMA

IN GRACE FRANK'S *The Medieval French Drama* (1954) a vast subject is admirably and concisely presented by the leading authority of our time. Her own erudition and the advances of scholarship since the general treatments of two generations ago are neatly and adequately incorporated. A briefer exposition, for the general public, is G. Cohen's *Le théâtre en France au moyen âge* (2 vols., 1928–31; in I vol., 1948). C. J. Stratman's *Bibliography of Medieval Drama* (1954) is useful but uneven and sometimes inaccurate. The celebrated Fleury manuscript is the subject of a study by Solange Corbin (*Romania*, 1953), and Edith A. Wright has published *The Dissemination of the Liturgical Drama in France* (1936).

Important texts of religious drama in French have been edited or re-edited in our period: *La résurrection du Sauveur* (1931), by Jean Wright; *La Seinte Résurrection* (1943), by T. A. Jenkins, J. M. Manly, M. K. Pope, and J. G. Wright; and the *Sponsus* (1951), by L. P. Thomas. Miss Wright is also the author of *A Study of the Themes of the Resurrection in the Mediaeval French Drama* (1935).

The publications of G. Cohen, both books and articles, which have ranged over the entire field of dramatic production in medieval France, are too numerous to list here. Twenty-four of his articles were republished in *Etudes d'histoire du théâtre en France au moyen âge et à la Renaissance* (1956), and numerous scholars contributed studies on the theater to a volume of *Mélanges G. Cohen* (1950).

Comedy in the twelfth and thirteenth centuries is represented by a small and miscellaneous group of texts. The earliest is Jean Bodel's *Jeu de saint Nicolas,* a dramatic miracle in its fundamental action, but in part comedy by virtue of its tavern and street scenes. It has been edited by A. Jeanroy (1925) and by F. J. Warne (1951), the latter edition containing a good bibliography of studies of this interesting and sometimes difficult text. Another edition has been announced by A. Henry, who has published a part of its introduction, "Introduction stylistique au *Jeu de saint Nicolas*" (*Romania,* 1961). The play is studied by C. Foulon in *L'œuvre de Jean Bodel* (1958), by P. R. Vincent, *The Jeu de saint Nicolas of Jean Bodel of Arras, A Literary Analysis* (1954), and in a large number of articles on particular topics. Of the two plays of Adam de la Halle, *Le Jeu de Robin et Marion* has received no significant new study in our period, while the occult meaning of *Le Jeu de la Feuillée* has been studied by A. Adler in *Sens et composition du Jeu de la Feuillée* (1956). The question of comic origins is treated in Grace Frank's "Beginnings of Comedy in France" (*MLR,* 1936).

Gautier de Coinci's narrative miracles have received considerable attention. Editions of one or two miracles have been published by E. von Kraemer (1953) and E. Rankka (1955), and A. Langfors has published a substantial body of texts from the Hermitage MS. (1937). Of a five-volume edition projected by V. F. Koenig, two volumes have appeared (1955, 1961).

X. LE ROMAN DE LA ROSE

THE WORK of Guillaume de Lorris and Jean de Meung has been the subject of vigorous and searching re-evaluations. In a chapter of *The Allegory of Love: A Study in Mediaeval Tradition* (1936), C. S. Lewis places Guillaume de Lorris's allegory in the tradition of the *roman courtois,* which after Chrétien splits into two currents, one concerned merely with outward adventure, the other turned to the inner psychological realities of courtly love, for the portrayal of which Guillaume found personification and allegory most fruitful. Lewis had a poor opinion of Jean de Meung as an allegorist, and sees him as an inferior literary artist, for all his merits as a satirist, a purveyor of instruction, and occasionally a vigorous thinker. The question of the originality of Jean de Meung's thought was taken up by E. Faral in "*Le Roman de la Rose* et la pensée française au XIIIᵉ siècle" (*RDM*, 1926). Drawing upon the too-little-used indications of E. Langlois, *Origines et sources du Roman de la Rose* (1891), Faral sees in the apparent chaos of ideas of the second part of the *Rose* an integral naturalism, not, however, fundamentally unorthodox. This naturalism is the product of twelfth-century humanism, which Jean de Meung absorbed principally from Alain de Lille's *De Planctu Naturae* and Jean de Hanville's *Architrenius;* Jean de Meung is not a precursor, but a talented expositor of a wide current of thought. His debt to the Aristotelian renaissance at the University of Paris, 1250–70, is the subject of two works by G. Paré: *Le Roman de la Rose et la scolastique courtoise* (1941) and *Les idées et les lettres au XIIIᵉ siècle. Le Roman de la Rose* (1947). Paré finds Jean a practiced scholastic, orthodox and even Thomist in his speculative theology, but heterodox in his philosophy of love as expressed in the discourses of Genius. Reviews to note are those of Julia Bastin (*RBPH*, 1944), A. M. F. Gunn (*RR*, 1949), and Andrée Bruel (*Speculum*, 1952).

In *The Mirror of Love: A Reinterpretation of the Romance of the Rose* (1952), A. M. F. Gunn undertakes to demonstrate the unity of the entire poem, with Jean de Meung completing and transforming Guillaume de Lorris's idea of love as an art into the view that it is a duty to God and nature. The author attempts to relate Jean de Meung's idea of love to the Platonic philosophy of plenitude, in spite of the poet's emphasis upon physical love, so un-Platonic in spirit. Gunn also defends Jean de Meung's method, in essence a *disputatio*, against the customary charges of digression, by explaining the relevance of all parts to the author's didactic and philosophical purpose. Despite reservations on certain points, critical opinion has been generally appreciative of the unusual interest and originality of this book (L. P. G. Peckham, *RR*, 1953; K. Sneyders de Vogel, *Neophil*, 1953; A. Micha, *RPh*, 1955; F. Whitehead, *MLR*, 1954).

XI. RUTEBEUF

O UR PERIOD has seen a reawakening of interest in the varied work
and the literary personality of Rutebeuf. A number of partial
editions have appeared: H. Lucas, *Les poésies personnelles de Rutebeuf* (1938) and *Poèmes concernant l'Université de Paris* (1952);
Julia Bastin and E. Faral, *Onze poèmes de Rutebeuf concernant la
Croisade* (1946); E. B. Ham, *Renart le Bestorné* (1947); and Grace
Frank's second edition of the *Miracle de Théophile* (*CFMA*, 1949)
are particularly to be mentioned. The two volumes of the *Œuvres
complètes de Rutebeuf*, by E. Faral and J. Bastin, have recently
appeared (1959–60), with voluminous critical apparatus.

The problems of Rutebeuf scholarship are principally those of
attribution, of throwing light on the circumstances and allusions in
his numerous *pièces de circonstance*, and of disengaging the poet's
literary personality. It is customary to ascribe to him some fifty-six
poems. The hypothesis of Ham, in his edition of *Renart le Bestorné*,
that these are the work of three different poets, has been rejected by
Faral (*Romania*, 1948). Since a large part of Rutebeuf's work was
what we would today call pamphleteering, the poems lend themselves
to searching historical investigation, to which Faral particularly
devoted himself. Rutebeuf's work bears most notably on the Crusade
of 1270 and on the difficulties between the university and the
mendicant orders, in which he was sharply critical of the latter, after
having written, earlier in his career, a poem in praise of the
Franciscans; see Faral, *"Le dit des Cordeliers"* (*Romania*, 1948).
Ham sees in *Renart le Bestorné* a criticism of the impending Crusade
of 1270 and its promoters (*op. cit.*, and *RPh*, 1955, where Ham
modifies this view). On the other hand Faral (*Romania*, 1948)
maintains that it refers to a royal assembly of 1261 that dealt with
the Tartar peril and decided upon a regime of austerity. Mrs. Frank
has suggested that Rutebeuf's interest in the sorry lot of Théophile
is to be explained in part by a view of himself as a fellow sufferer, as
he portrays himself in his personal poems (*RR*, 1952). Faral notes
the occurrence in Rutebeuf's work of both the Theophilus legend and
the life of Saint Mary the Egyptian (ed. Bernadine Bujila, 1949),

generally associated in men's minds, as in Villon's *Ballade pour prier Notre Dame*, with the cult of the Virgin Mary (*Romania*, 1951).

XII. MARCO POLO

B ETWEEN the six-hundredth anniversary of his death (1924) and the seven-hundredth anniversary of his birth (1954), each marked by commemorative ceremonies, a rich harvest of Marco Polo studies appeared. The most notable of these are new editions of his book, incorporating new discoveries in the matter of the perhaps insolubly complicated manuscript tradition, and continuations of the debate on the true text. L. F. Benedetto's sumptuous edition, *Il Milione* (1928), is based on MS. B.N. fr. 1116, in Italianized French, but adds the passages from the Ambrosiana copy of the Zelada MS. paralleling the passages of Ramusio's edition of 1559 which had hitherto passed as suspect. Shortly thereafter the Zelada manuscript was rediscovered in Toledo almost simultaneously by J. G. Herriot (*Speculum*, 1937) and by P. David, who furnished the text for publication by A. C. Moule and P. Pelliot in the second volume of their *Description of the World* (1938), the first volume of which contains an English translation based on MS. 1116. Benedetto's faith in the authenticity of the Ramusio-Zelada text has been sharply challenged by L. Dieu in *Revue d'histoire ecclèsiastique* (1947), the author preferring MS. 1116 and the shorter French text published by Pauthier (1865) and utilized by Yule (1871; 4th ed. 1921). A useful summary of Polo scholarship is given by M. Roques (*Romania*, 1955), and brief general accounts will be found in R. Almagía, *La Figura et l'opera di Marco Polo secondo recenti studi* (1938), and Gabriella Bosano, "La Questione Poliana" (*Italica*, 1943). L. Olschki's *L'Asia di Marco Polo* (1957; in English, 1960) is a systematic study of *Il Milione*, proposing to compile a new and up-to-date commentary. The first volume (A–C) of the alphabetized notes on Marco Polo left by P. Pelliot has appeared (1959). In "L'art de Marco Polo" (*Mélanges E. Hoepffner*, 1949), L. F. Benedetto turns from questions of text to the larger one of the merits of the book and its author's personality. He sees in Marco

Polo the soul of an explorer drawn to the unknown beyond the horizon, capable of great admiration and enthusiasm, and he calls for a recognition of the book as a luminous and objective synthesis and a great human document.

XIII. FOURTEENTH AND FIFTEENTH CENTURIES

A. GENERAL

I T IS CUSTOMARY to treat these two centuries as a unit, and because they produced no significant novelties, few great talents, and only one great poet, Villon, to depreciate them sharply in contrast to the twelfth and thirteenth centuries before and the sixteenth century coming after. An exception is made in the history of the drama, which flourished in this period. It is true that French literature does not stand out among the literatures of Europe as it did in the twelfth and thirteenth centuries. Yet Chaucer found fellow spirits among the poets of France—Machaut, Froissart, and Deschamps; and Petrarch had disciples in France who merited better than his oft-quoted dictum that outside of Italy no poets or orators were to be found. Still, this section will be relatively brief because its literary production does not raise the great questions of origins inseparable from the study of the early French epic, romance, and lyric poetry. Not included in some histories of medieval French literature, the fourteenth and fifteenth centuries are given good treatment by L. Foulet in the Bédier-Hazard. S. Hofer's rejuvenation of the material of Gröber's *Grundriss,* under the title *Geschichte der mittelfranzösischen Literatur* (2 vols., 1933–37), provides another survey and useful bibliography.

B. LYRIC POETRY

Among fourteenth-century poets, Guillaume de Machaut has received considerable attention, although primarily as a composer. Two noteworthy publications are A. Machabey, *Guillaume de Machaut: la vie et l'œuvre musical* (2 vols., 1955), and F. Ludwig, *Guillaume de Machaut: Musikalische Werke* (4 vols., 1926–43).

Christine de Pisan continues to draw the attention of numerous scholars, mostly of her own sex. In addition to a biographical study by Marie-Josèphe Pinet (1927), there have been editions of *Lavision Christine* (sic, read *L'Avision*) by Sister Mary L. Towner (1932), *Le Livre des fais et bonnes meurs du sage roy Charles V* by Suzanne Solente (2 vols., 1936–40), *Le Livre de la Paix*, by Charity C. Willard (1958), and *Le Livre de la mutacion de Fortune*, by Suzanne Solente (2 vols., 1959). Early translations of her works into English have likewise received attention. Martial d'Auvergne's *Arrêts d'Amour* have been edited by J. Rychner (1951) and Alain Chartier's *Belle Dame sans mercy et poésies lyriques* re-edited by A. Piaget (1945). E. J. Hoffman's *Alain Chartier, His Work and Reputation* (1942) is a general study. A much-needed edition of the poems of Charles d'Orléans has been provided by P. Champion (2 vols., 1923–27) and a substantial study by S. Cigada, *L'Opera poetica di Charles d'Orléans* (1960). The so-called *grands rhétoriqueurs* have been subjects of substantial publications: Chastellain in L. Hommel's *Georges Chastellain, 1415–1474* (1945), a brief study of that chronicler and poet; K. Urwin's *Georges Chastellain: la vie, les œuvres* (a Paris dissertation, 1937); and K. Hemmer's *Georges Chastellain* (a Münster dissertation, 1937). N. Dupire has published *Les faictz et dictz* of Jean Molinet (3 vols., 1936–39), *Jean Molinet: la vie, les œuvres* (1932), and an *Etude critique des manuscrits et éditions des poèmes de Jean Molinet* (1932). Kathleen Chesney has edited the *Œuvres poétiques* of Guillaume Crétin (1932) and a brief *florilège* from several poets under the title *Fleurs de rhètorique* (1950). Jean Lemaire de Belges is the subject of a study by P. Spaak (1926) and another by G. Doutrepont, *Jean Lemaire de Belges et la Renaissance* (1934). Editions of particular works include *La concorde des deux langages* (1947) and *Les épîtres de l'amant vert* (1948), both by J. Frappier, and *Le temple d'honneur et de vertus* (1957), by H. Hornik. W. F. Patterson's *Three Centuries of French Poetic Theory, 1328–1630* (2 vols., 1935) is an extensive survey of the critical writings.

C. VILLON

The most careful critical text of Villon is that of A. Longnon and L. Foulet (4th ed. 1932), but the problems of establishing such a text may not yet have been completely resolved, as F. Lecoy points out in an article critical of Longnon's excessive reliance on the Levet edition of 1489 (*Romania*, 1959). Other recent editions to be noted are those of F. Neri (1923; 2nd ed. 1944), distinguished for the judicious explicative commentary; L. Thuasne (3 vols., 1923), with lavish but not always pertinent annotation; G. Atkinson (1930); A. Jeanroy (1934); E. F. Chaney (1941); and A. Mary (1951; 2nd ed. 1957). The *poésies diverses* have been republished as the starting point for a highly subjective portrait of the poet by G. Brunelli, *Le Rime di Villon* (1953), and one of these has been studied with finesse, penetration, and erudition by L. F. Benedetto, *Il Dialogo di Villon col suo cuore* (*Atti della R. Accademia delle Scienze di Torino,* 1953). A valuable aid to textual study and comprehension is A. Burger's *Lexique de la langue de Villon* (1957).

Two useful guides are G. Moldenhauer, "Stand und Aufgaben der Villon-Philologie" (*GRM,* 1934), and L. Cons, *Etat présent des études sur Villon* (1936). The essence of his poetic genius is sought for in I. Siciliano's *François Villon et les thèmes poétiques du moyen âge* (1934). No new bibliographical information has come to light since the researches of Longnon, but specific questions are still discussed, particularly those concerning his years of wandering, 1457–61: for example, by L. Foulet in the *Mélanges A. Thomas* (1927) and the *Studies in Memory of Gertrude Schoepperle Loomis* (1927), and by Grace Frank (*MLN,* 1932, two articles). Concise and useful is L. and F. Saisset's *Le grand testament* (1938), and the history of one of his types is traced in W. H. Rice's *European Ancestry of Villon's Satirical Testaments* (1941). The character and personality of Villon have been the subject of much fanciful treatment at the hands of *littérateurs,* and the student needs to be brought back to the fundamental works on Villon's biography, especially the short monograph of G. Paris (1901) and the vast fresco of P. Champion, *François Villon, sa vie et son temps* (2 vols., 1913; 2nd ed. 1933). A lively portrait, which is at the same time a running commentary on the texts, is contained in F. Desonay's *Villon* (1933; 2nd ed. 1947), and E. F. Chaney presents *François Villon in His Environment* (1946). The excesses of sentimental appraisals of Villon's character are deflated by Grace Frank, "The Impenitence of François Villon" (*RR,* 1946), and L. F. Benedetto, "A la ricerca di Villon," in his volume *Uomini e tempi* (1953), to which may be added C. Guerrieri Crocetti, "Con Villon e i suoi moderni interpreti" (*GIF,* 1954).

D. DRAMA

The medieval drama in France reaches its flowering in the Middle French period with the great Passion plays, miracles, and an abundant production of *soties, moralités,* and farces. Notable edi-

tions are those of *La Passion d'Autun* by Grace Frank (1934) and
Jean Michel's *Mystère de la Passion* by O. Jodogne (1959). An
important text is studied in R. Lebègue, *Le Mystère des Actes des
Apôtres, contribution à l'étude de l'humanisme et du protestantisme
français au XVI° siècle* (1929), and considerable light is thrown on
the staging of the *mystères* by G. Cohen's edition of the *Livre de
conduite du régisseur . . . pour le Mystère de la Passion joué à
Mons en 1501* (1925). Miracles, particularly miracles of the Virgin,
which earlier appeared in Latin and in the vernacular in prose or
verse narrative form, appear in several notable collections, for which
see R. Glutz, *Miracles de Nostre Dame par personnages* (1954), and
Dorothy Penn, *The Staging of the Miracles de Nostre Dame par
personnages of the MS. Cangé* (1933). The story of the patient
Griselda enters French dramatic literature in the 1395 *Estoire de
Griseldis*, edited by Barbara Craig (1954) and by M. Roques
(1957). It is studied, together with the French prose versions, in E.
Golenistcheff-Koutouzoff, *L'histoire de Griseldis en France au XIV°
et au XV° siècle* (1933). Grace Frank, in "The Authorship of the
Mystère de Griseldis" (*MLN*, 1936), finds it probable that it was
written by Philippe de Mézières, to whom has been ascribed a French
prose translation, evidently the one followed by the play, from
Petrarch's Latin version of Boccaccio's tale. G. Raynaud de Lage
contests the attribution of the play to Philippe himself, but agrees
that he may have encouraged or commissioned it (*Romania*, 1958).

New editions in the field of comedy are numerous, particularly
noteworthy being those of the elusive *Recueil Trepperel* by E. Droz:
I, *Les soties* (1935) ; II, *Les farces* (with H. Lewicka, 1961) ; and G.
Cohen, *Recueil de farces françaises inédites du XV° siècle* (1949). H.
G. Harvey's *The Theatre of the Basoche* (1941) illuminates the role
of the law societies in the production of comic plays. Prominent in
Pathelin studies is the attempt to identify Guillaume Alecis as its
author by L. Cons, *L'auteur de la farce de Pathelin* (1926), and by
R. T. Holbrook, *Guillaume Alecis and Pathelin* (1928). A useful
guide to the study of this text is supplied by M. Roques, *Références
aux plus récents commentaires de Maistre Pierre Pathelin* (Pro-
gramme de l'Agrégation, 1942).

E. PROSE FICTION

The outstanding productions of fifteenth-century prose fiction
are Antoine de La Sale's book-length *Saintré* and the two collections
of shorter tales formerly attributed to him, *Les Quinze Joyes de
mariage* and *Les Cent Nouvelles nouvelles*. *Le Petit Jehan de Saintré*

was given its first critical edition by F. Desonay and P. Champion in 1927, with important studies of the author's life and of the manuscript tradition. F. Desonay has also edited other works by La Sale, *Le Paradis de la reine sibylle* (1930), *La Salade* (1935), and *La Sale* (1941). He has examined the biographical data anew in *Antoine de La Sale, aventureux et pédagogue* (1940) and studied the *Saintré* in the *Revue du 16ᵉ siècle* (1927), as has A. Coville in *Le Petit Jehan de Saintré, recherches complémentaires* (1937). M. Lecourt has discussed in detail La Sale's considerable indebtedness to Simon de Hesdin for the contents of the compilation known as *La Sale* (*Romania*, 1955). Special points of biography are examined by C. A. Knudson in *Romania* (1927) and in *RPh* (1948 and 1958). The *Quinze Joyes* have been re-edited by F. Fleuret (1936). The enigma in which the author concealed his name has been studied again and again. J. Misrahi reviews the several solutions proposed and suggests a new way of reading Antoine de La Sale; he proposes further stylistic studies to test the soundness of the attribution (*RPh*, 1955). M. Cressot has contributed a valuable *Vocabulaire des Quinze Joyes de mariage* (1939). P. Champion has published a fine edition of the *Cent Nouvelles nouvelles* (3 vols., 1928).

J. Rasmussen, in *La prose narrative française du XVᵉ siècle* (1958), attempts to derive the *nouvelle* from the older *fabliau*. His analysis of the style of late medieval prose writing, chiefly the *nouvelles*, is a rather ambitious and not always convincing psychological and esthetic interpretation of the texts under study in the light of contemporary social and cultural history. A less ambitious but more acute and successful analysis of this new literary esthetic is found in Janet Ferrier's *Forerunners of the French Novel* (1954). In the introduction and first chapter Miss Ferrier traces the origin of the style of the early novel to the episodic narrative units frequently found in late medieval prose romances rather than to the *fabliaux*, despite the similarities of themes and motifs in *fabliaux* and *nouvelles*. Her study, which continues on into Renaissance writing, provides a valuable complement and sequel to the long standard works of W. Söderhjelm on late medieval French narrative prose.

F. CHRONICLERS

Among new publications on the numerous chroniclers of the age, we shall mention only that the *Société de l'Histoire de France* edition of Froissart, begun by S. Luce and G. Raynaud, has after long interruption been resumed by L. Mirot, with Volumes XII (1931) and XIII (1957).

G. MANDEVILLE

New studies on the *Voyages* of Sir John Mandeville have concerned themselves with the question of texts and with the riddle of authorship. In M. Letts, *Mandeville's Travels* (2 vols., 1953), is published for the first time the earliest French text (1371). In 1949 the same author published *Sir John Mandeville: The Man and His Book*. Texts and authorship are extensively studied by Josephine W. Bennett in *The Rediscovery of Sir John Mandeville* (1954). Mrs. Bennett provides a useful introduction to Mandeville studies, and a defense of the value and interest of the *Voyages*, which she considers at least carefully arranged from good sources, if at times imaginary, and in any case an admirable literary creation. She rejects the traditional identification of the author as the Liège physician Jean de Bourgogne, or Jean à la Barbe, and the idea put forward by P. Hamelius, editor of the *Travels* for the EETS (1923), that the real author was Jean de Bourgogne's friend and biographer, Jean d'Outremeuse. The author was English, she believes, but not the Mandeville who killed the Earl of Ulster in 1333 and thereafter fled the kingdom to dwell on the Continent (I. Jackson, *MLR*, 1928). G. de Poerck, "La tradition manuscrite des 'Voyages' de Jean de Mandeville" (*Romanica Gandensia*, 1955), examines and suggests some changes to Mrs. Bennett's classification of the French MSS and announces a critical edition of the Ogier-Liège version.

H. HUMANISM

A century after Michelet and Burckhardt popularized their oversimplified contrast between the periods known as Middle Ages and Renaissance, historical science is still at work repairing the harm they did and re-establishing a true sense of historical continuity. This problem is not vital to the study of vernacular literature in France, which mostly follows beaten paths in the fourteenth and fifteenth centuries, but some knowledge of the results of recent scholarship is essential to a true total picture of the period. The best general account, with extensive bibliography, is F. Simone, "Per una nuova valutazione del Quattrocento francese" (*SFr*, 1957), to which add the first chapters of his *Il Rinascimento francese* (1961). A penetrating view of the question is given in E. Gilson's "Humanisme médiéval et Renaissance" in the volume *Les idées et les lettres* (1932) and in the second appendix, "Philosophie médiévale et humanisme," to his *Héloïse et Abelard* (1938). Pertinent observations are contained in E. Faral's article, "L'humanisme et la pensée médiévale," in the volume edited by H. Bédarida, *Pensée humaniste et tradition chrétienne aux XVe et XVIe siècles* (1950), and in articles by A. Chastel and A. Renaudet (*BHR*, 1945). A convenient introductory survey of the question may be found in two papers by E. F. Jacob and A. S. Tuberville, "Changing Views of the Renaissance" (*History*, 1931 and 1932).

The French humanists of the late fourteenth and early fifteenth centuries have been treated by A. Coville in *Gontier et Pierre Col et l'humanisme en France au temps de Charles VI* (1934) and *Recherches sur quelques écrivains du XIVe et du XVe siècle* (1935: Jean de Montreuil, Nicolas de Clamanges, Jacques de Nouvion). A. Combes rectifies a persistent error, originating in A. Thomas' thesis on Jean de Montreuil and repeated by Lanson and Coville, which presented Gerson as an antihumanist, in "Gerson et la naissance de l'humanisme" (*Revue du moyen âge latin*, 1945), and more fully in *Jean de Montreuil et le Chancelier Gerson, contribution à l'histoire des rapports de l'humanisme et de la théologie en France au début du XVe siècle* (1942). Gerson has been the subject of numerous publications that will not be mentioned here as they treat of him primarily as theologian and preacher; an exception may be made for M. Lieberman's extensive series of articles, "Chronologie gersonienne" (*Romania*, since 1948). The work of the translators in the time of Charles V has been the subject of a number of studies and some editions, such as those of Oresme's translations of Aristotle's *Ethics* (1940) and *Economics* (1957) by A. D. Menut; R. Levy has published a survey, "Recent Studies of Nicole Oresme" (*Symposium*, 1959). A later group of humanists is presented in F. Simone's study, "Robert Gaguin ed il suo cenacolo umanistico: 1473–1485" (*Aevum*, 1939).

5

Medieval German Literature

By *W. T. H. Jackson*
COLUMBIA UNIVERSITY

I. BIBLIOGRAPHY

THE TRADITIONAL bibliographical aids, such as Goedeke's *Grund-riss*, have been supplemented and to some extent superseded by more recent works. Ehrismann's literary history (see below) has virtually complete bibliographical information up to the time of its publication. For works before and after Ehrismann, there is J. Hansel, *Bücherkunde für Germanisten* (1959), with a shorter version for students, *Studienausgabe* (1961). R. F. Arnold, *Allgemeine Bücherkunde zur neueren deutschen Literaturgeschichte* (3rd ed. 1931), though less up to date, is still valuable, particularly for the relations between Germanics and the other disciplines. *Jahresberichte über die Erscheinungen auf dem Gebiete der germanischen Philologie* is the fullest and best of the serial aids to bibliographical knowledge. The volume that appeared in 1939 carried listings to the year 1935. The years 1936–39 were covered by Vols. XVI–XIX (New Series). In 1960 appeared Vol. I of *Jahresberichte für deutsche Sprache und Literatur* (covering 1940–45), which replaces both the *Jahresberichte für germanische Philologie* and the *Jahresberichte über die wissenschaftlichen Erscheinungen auf dem Gebiete der neueren deutschen Literatur*. The new work is not so detailed as the earlier *Jahresberichte*. The years not reported by the *Jahresberichte* have been largely covered by J. Körner, *Bibliographisches Handbuch des deutschen Schrifttums* (3rd ed. 1949), a select bibliography of all German literature, which gives a useful start on any subject; H. Widmann, *Bibliographien zum deutschen Schrifttum der Jahre 1939–50* (1951); F. Maurer, "Bibliographie zum deutschen Philologie" 1945–49 (*Archiv*, 1950–60); H. W. Eppelsheimer, *Bibliographie der deutschen Literaturwissenschaft*, Vol. I: 1945–1953 (1957), continued by J. Köttelwesch (Vols. II–V, to 1962). This is a well-arranged bibliography with listing by periods and types. Numerous articles during the period 1939–45 are listed by H. Fromm, *Germanistische Bibliographie seit 1945* (1960), which gives detailed and constructive criticism of existing works and fills in many gaps. It appeared originally in *DVLG* (1952 and 1959).

For current bibliography, the listings in the May number of *PMLA* are most useful because they appear so quickly after the close of the year under review. *YWMLS*, which appears about a year after the period reviewed, contains useful short evaluations of the works it lists (it does not pretend to completeness), although it is by no means always the most important works that are summarized, and the summaries are occasionally so brief as to be misleading. *Germanistik, Internationales Referatenorgan mit bibliographischen Hinweisen* (1960–   ) appears several times a year listing new works on Germanics, with brief critiques of the longer and more important ones. All medievalists should be grateful for the *Quarterly Checklist of Medievalia*, which lists all books and separates, and for the *International Guide to Medieval Studies*, which lists articles. Most of the literary histories and reference works listed below contain more or less complete bibliographical information. The works by Ehrismann, De Boor, and Stammler are particularly important in this respect.

II. GENERAL AND REFERENCE WORKS

B Y FAR the most important reference work for the literature of the Middle Ages is W. Stammler and K. Langosch, *Die deutsche Literatur des Mittelalters. Verfasserlexikon* (1933–55, supplement 1955). This excellent work is in four volumes, plus one of indices, with articles by specialists on all medieval writers and anonymous works. Each article has a brief bibliography. The revised edition of Merker-Stammler, the *Reallexikon der deutschen Literaturgeschichte*, by W. Kohlschmidt and W. Mohr (1955–   ), contains valuable articles on medieval technical terms and literary types. The same may be said of W. Stammler, ed. *Deutsche Philologie im Aufriss*, of which the first edition was completed in 1957 in three volumes. The second is now appearing. The range is naturally wider than that of Merker-Stammler. W. Kosch, *Deutsches Literatur-Lexikon* (2nd ed., 4 vols., 1949–58), is of limited use for the Middle Ages. J. Hoops, ed., *Reallexikon der germanischen Altertumskunde* (4 vols., 1911–19), is indispensable for the study of the prehistorical period. H. Schneider, *Germanische Altertumskunde* (2nd ed. 1951) is a useful supplement.

III. HISTORIES OF LITERATURE

G. EHRISMANN, *Geschichte der deutschen Literatur bis zum Ausgang des Mittelalters* (2 vols., 1918–35), remains the most detailed history. Although it is indispensable for coverage, summaries of minor productions, and bibliographical information, its critical judgments are often old-fashioned. A far more useful history is R. Newald and H. de Boor, *Geschichte der deutschen Literatur*. The volumes that deal with our period are the work of De Boor : I and II (1949 and 1953, with later editions) and III, part 1 (1962), which carry the history to 1350. Part 2 will presumably cover the literature of the years 1350–1450. This is an objective work, which takes full cognizance of differing viewpoints, but contrives to make a lucid case for its own. Its weakness lies in not stating the origin of these viewpoints, so that it is impossible to form any idea of the progress of scholarship from reading De Boor. There is a good selected bibliography for each topic. For the later period, the best work is W. Stammler, *Von der Mystik zum Barock, 1400–1600* (2nd ed., rev., 1950), although its sound judgments and impressive scholarship could be better organized. Its bibliographical notes are superb. *Annalen der deutschen Literatur*, ed. H. O. Burger (1952), presents a sequential and factual account of medieval literature in Vol. I, with a bibliography in a separate volume. J. Schwietering, *Die deutsche Dichtung des Mittelalters* (1932–41 ; rptd. 1957), is just the reverse —a sensitive study of literary trends and individual works, interpreted with close attention to contemporary art and religious and philosophical thought. The book is full of valuable insights, but the reader must be fairly well versed in the literature to appreciate them. The later versions of the literary history of F. Vogt and M. Koch, *Geschichte der deutschen Literatur von den ältesten Zeiten bis zur Gegenwart* (1897), should be viewed with suspicion, since they are often chauvinistic. F. Schmitt, *Deutsche Literaturgeschichte in Tabellen*, Vol. I (1949, and frequently revised) is a useful work for quick reference.

There is no lack of works on the earlier period of medieval literature, although they tend to be summaries of achievement rather than original works. G. Baesecke, *Vor- und Frühgeschichte des deutschen Schrifttums* (Vol. I, 1941; Vol. II, by Ingeborg Schröbler, 1953), presents the author's well-known views of literary influence by particular tribes. J. K. Bostock's *Handbook on Old High German Literature* (1955) is a solid and detailed history, with full reference to previous research but few opinions of its own. K. K. Klein in *Die Anfänge der deutschen Literatur. Vorkarlisches Schrifttum im deutschen Südostraum* (1954) stresses the importance for German literature of the developments in southeast Europe, especially in the period before Charlemagne, a view that has received an increasing amount of attention in recent years. The transition to the Middle High German period is well treated by L. Wolff, *Das deutsche Schrifttum bis zum Augang des Mittelalters. Von der germanischen Welt zum christlich-deutschen Mittelalter*, Vol. I, to 1158 2nd ed. 1951), and H. Schneider in the section of his literary history called *Heldendichtung, Geistlichendichtung, Ritterdichtung* (2nd ed. 1943). One work in French on the early period should be mentioned, A. Fuchs, *Les Débuts de la littérature allemande du VIIIᵉ au XIIᵉ siècle* (1952).

There are fewer general works on the High Middle Ages, but numerous special studies of various aspects of courtly culture and ethics (see below). For the later Middle Ages, the ideas expressed by G. Müller in *Deutsches Dichten und Denken vom Mittelalter zur Neuzeit* (2nd ed. 1949) are very illuminating to a well-informed reader. P. Wapnewski, *Deutsche Literatur des Mittelalters. Ein Abriss* (1960), provides an accurate brief survey of literary history. The only work in English, M. O'C. Walshe, *Medieval German Literature* (1962), is a disappointingly superficial and old-fashioned treatment.

IV. LITERATURE AND CULTURE

THE WORKS on this subject are numerous and only the most important will be mentioned. K. Vossler, *Dante and Medieval Culture* (2 vols., 1958), is a translation of his *Die göttliche Komödie* (2nd ed. 1925) and remains a source of valuable information about the relation of philosophy to literature and about medieval esthetics in gen-

eral. The important interrelation of social change and organization
are explored in two works by F. Altheim, *Literatur und Gesellschaft
im ausgehenden Mittelalter* (1949), and *Literatur und Gesellschaft
im ausgehenden Altertum* (1950). H. Kuhn's article, "Zum neuen Bild
vom Mittelalter" (*DVLG*, 1950), deals with the better appreciation
of the sophistication of medieval society evident in recent critical
writing. In relating literature to culture, there has been more
interest in the courtly period than in the later, bourgeois society. H.
Naumann's *Deutsche Kultur im Zeitalter des Rittertums* (1938) is
a monumental work, beautifully illustrated, which draws largely on
literary sources for its judgments and is hence rather old-fashioned.
W. von den Steinen's *Der Kosmos des Mittelalters von Karl dem
Grossen zu Bernhard von Clairvaux* (1959) is more concerned with
the relation between society and Christianity and sees a distinct
break between the static Carolingian and Ottonian societies and
those of the twelfth century. F. Ranke's *Gott, Welt und Humanität
in der deutschen Dichtung des Mittelalters* (1953) is an admirable
study of the relations between the secular and the religious aspects
of literature. M. Bindschedler in "Der Bildungsgedanke im Mittelalter" (*DVLG*, 1955) stresses the importance of religious teachers
and the application of their ideas to literature. J. Koch, ed.
Humanismus, Mystik und Kunst in der Welt des Mittelalters
(1953), extends the comparison to wider areas. F. Maurer in *Leid:
Studien zur Bedeutungs- und Problemgeschichte, besonders in den
grossen Epen der staufischen Zeit* (1951) examines several important literary works in the light of sorrow, which he considers to be a
dominant characteristic. He finds differing manifestations of sorrow
or suffering in all the great works of the Middle Ages. H. Kuhn's
Dichtung und Welt im Mittelalter (1959) is a collection of the
author's articles devoted to the reflection of social attitudes in
literary works. There are many useful insights and indications of
subjects for further study.

One of the most fundamental books of the last twenty years is
E. R. Curtius, *Europäische Literatur und lateinisches Mittelalter*
(1948), which by its amply demonstrated proofs of the extensive use
of formal rhetoric, particularly rhetorical "topoi," has greatly
changed our views of medieval style.

Numerous books have been written to show the influence of
particular aspects of culture on the formation of "courtly" literature. W. Stammler, "Deutsche Scholastik" (*ZDP*, 1953), is concerned with the influence of the scholastic method of proof on both
the style and thought of literature, while W. Wentzlaff-Eggebert in
"Ritterliche Lebenslehre und antike Ethik" (*DVLG*, 1949) is more

concerned with the appearance of Aristotelian and Ciceronian concepts in the education and behavior of the heroes of the romances. There is no lack of writers who wish to stress those aspects of the German knight that distinguish him from his French contemporaries: for example, H. Brinkmann, "Erbe und Abendland: Die deutsche Ritterdichtung in der geschichtlichen Welt" (*Euphorion*, 1943), and H. Naumann, *Der staufische Ritter* (1936). J. Fourquet in "Littérature courtoise et théologique" (*EG*, 1957) argues against the opinions of those who ascribe excessive influence to theological writings, and the same view is reflected in the works of W. Schröder, which re-examine the well-established idea that the literary productions of the tenth and eleventh centuries derive their distinctive character from the Cluniac monastic reforms (*PBB*, 1950). Some light is thrown on an important question of "intellectual climate" by H. J. de Vleeschauwer's article, "Bibliotheken und geistige Einheit des Mittelalters" (*DVLG*, 1953). H. Kuhn makes an attempt to distinguish between historical facts and their use in literature in his article, "Soziale Realität und dichterische Fiktion am Beispiel der höfischen Ritterdichtung Deutschlands" (*Soziologie und Leben*, 1952). Probably the most important manifestation of this relationship, the crusades, is inadequately treated by W. Wentzlaff-Eggebert in *Die Kreuzzugsdichtung des Mittelalters* (1960). The author lays far too much stress on the importance of a few documents and comes close to ignoring Romance literature and its influences on German. The very different social-literary relationships of the later Middle Ages are discussed by H. Rosenfeld, "Die Literatur des ausgehenden Mittelalters in soziologischer Sicht" (*WW*, 1955). The same subject is treated in probably its most important literary aspect in Rosenfeld's "Die Entwicklung der Standessatire im Mittelalter" (*ZDP*, 1951).

H. Kuhn offers a statement of the principles of the interpretation of medieval literature in "Zur Deutung der künstlerischen Form des Mittelalters" (*SG*, 1949), while W. Fechter, "Galle und Honig. Eine Kontrastformel in der mittelhochdeutschen Literatur" (*PBB*, 1958), studies one *topos* to illustrate literary method. Another method of treating such commonplaces is exemplified by W. Stammler, *Frau Welt. Eine mittelalterliche Allegorie* (1959). Here the author is concerned less with literary method than with tracing the classical origins of the idea. The connection between literature and other arts is treated by K. G. Just, "Musik und Dichtung" (*Deutsche Philologie im Aufriss*), and W. Stammler, *Wort und Bild. Studien zu den Wechselbeziehungen zwischen Schrifttum und Bildkunst im Mittelalter* (1962). Some problems that still await attention are presented competently by H. Fischer, "Probleme und Aufgaben deutscher Literaturforschung zum deutschen Spätmittelalter" (*GRM*, 1959). The same author presents a review of what is being done in the later period in "Neue Forschungen zur Dichtung des Spätmittelalters, 1250–1500" (*DVLG*, 1957).

Some more strictly literary studies are very important. E. Auerbach in *Typologische Motive in der mittelalterlichen Literatur* (1953) examines the problem of defining typology and shows how the interpretive technique may be effectively used in literary criticism. The same author's *Literatursprache und Publikum in der lateinischen Spätantike und im Mittelalter* (1958; English trans., 1965) attempts to establish a relation between the *sermo humilis* of the classical rhetoricians and the development of a purely Christian style. While the attempt is not entirely convincing, the evidence adduced is most useful. H. Schwietering in "The Origins of the Medieval Humility Formula" (*PMLA*, 1954) reinforces the opinion expressed in his earlier works that the prefaces to many medieval poems are under Christian rather than classical influence. In this he specifically opposes Curtius. A major work on medieval esthetics, H. H. Glunz's *Die Literarästhetik des Mittelalters* (1937), is particularly useful for *Parzival*. H. Moser's "Dichtung und Wirklichkeit im Hochmittelalter" (*WW*, 1955) provides a salutary warning that literature is, after all, literature and should not be read as theology or philosophy.

V. THE COURTLY CODE

SINCE there has been a great deal written about the existence or nonexistence of a code of courtly behavior, it will be convenient to mention here some of the most significant contributions. The first important work on the subject was G. Ehrismann, "Die Grundlage des ritterlichen Tugendsystems" (*ZDA*, 1919), in which the view was advanced that a philosophical basis for a code of courtly behavior was to be found in Bruder Wernher's reworking of the *Dogma moralium philosophorum*, attributed to Guillaume de Conches. The proposal was violently attacked by E. R. Curtius in "Das ritterliche Tugendsystem" (*DVLG*, 1943) and in *Europäische*

Literatur und lateinisches Mittelalter on the grounds that the distinctions made by Ehrismann between philosophy and conduct did not exist in his sources and that the treatise was, in any case, very unlikely to have been known to the writers of literature. H. Neumann in "Der Streit um das ritterliche Tugendsystem," *Festschrift für Karl Helm* (1951), presents a balanced view of the controversy. Although Ehrismann's view of a system derived from Aristotle via Cicero is untenable, attempts to show that a system existed still persist. It would probably be better to speak of a "feeling" rather than a system. In the same context fall the numerous attempts at an evaluation of "courtly love." There is considerable confusion between attempts to establish origins and attempts to determine a philosophical and theoretical background; good summaries of this type of scholarship are to be found in H. Kolb, *Der Begriff der Minne und das Entstehen der höfischen Lyrik* (1958), a thorough and detailed work that ascribes the origins of courtly love to the "humanism" of the twelfth century and rejects Arab influence. This is indispensable for any study of the subject, whether or not one agrees with its conclusions. A. Moret, *Les débuts du lyrisme en Allemagne des origines à 1350* (1951), offers the best available summary of scholarship on the origins of *Minnesang* and is lucid and objective in its presentation. Its weakness is the lack of positive ideas of its own and a tendency to cliché. Moret makes a special study of the problem of the nature of love in "Qu'est-ce que la Minne?" (*EG*, 1949). Studies of special aspects of the problem of terminology in medieval literature and the interpretation of words have been made by K. Korn, *Studien über Fröude and Truren bei mittelhochdeutschen Dichtern* (1932), and M. E. Fickel, "Die Bedeutung von sel, lip und herze in der frühmittelhochdeutschen Dichtung und in den Texten der mittelhochdeutschen Klassik" (diss., Tübingen, 1949).

For historical background, the major source remains W. Wattenbach, *Deutschlands Geschichtsquellen*, of which a revised edition is appearing, ed. W. Levison and others (*Deutsche Kaiserzeit*, pts. 1–4, 1938–48; *Vorzeit und Karolinger*, pts. 1–4, 1952–63). A useful work in English is by G. Barraclough, ed. *Mediaeval Germany, 911–1250* (2 vols., 1938; rptd. 1948). The most stimulating recent book, but one that must be read with caution, is F. Heer, *Mittelalter von 1100 bis 1350* (1961).

VI. TEXTS

W HEN AN IMPORTANT text of an author has appeared in the period under review, it will be mentioned under the author's name. Revised editions of standard texts are too numerous to be mentioned. The important series of texts of medieval authors remain: *Deutsche Texte des Mittelalters, Altdeutsche Textbibliothek, Quellen und Forschungen, Deutsche Klassiker des Mittelalters, Bibliothek des litterarischen Vereins in Stuttgart, Germanistische Handbibliothek,* the appropriate volumes of the *Deutsche National-Literatur, Deutsche Literatur in Entwicklungsreien,* and *Texte des späten Mittelalters.*

VII. VERSIFICATION

T HE PRINCIPLES set forth by A. Heusler in his *Deutsche Versgeschichte* (3 vols., 1925–29; 2nd ed. 1956) have remained the basis of most studies of verse form, particularly in the field of Germanic epic and in lyric poetry. Several works have appeared giving simpler versions of Heusler's rather complicated theories. Heusler's own *Deutsche Verskunst* (1925) has been reprinted several times, and O. Paul, *Deutsche Metrik* (4th ed. 1961), and S. Beyschlag, *Die Metrik der mittelhochdeutschen Blütezeit* (1950; 5th ed. 1963), provide useful introductions to the subject.

W. Kayser's *Kleine deutsche Versschule* (4th ed. 1954) is a book of a different kind, simple in approach, but presenting the author's own feelings within the formal framework. "Deutsche Verskunst" by U. Pretzel and H. Thomas in *Deutsche Philologie im Aufriss* is a useful introduction with an excellent review of research. The most recent study of versification is E. Arndt's *Deutsche*

Verslehre (1959), which is largely dependent on Heusler and goes much further than the Middle Ages.

The most original approach to the problem of early Germanic versification, that is, of the *Stabreimdichtung* and the forms associated with it, is W. Lehmann's *The Development of Germanic Verse Form* (1956), which adduces linguistic principles to explain the developments of the Germanic types of versification.

VIII. OLD HIGH GERMAN

SINCE 1930 there has been a marked decline in interest in Old High German literature, partly because the linguistic problems have been so thoroughly treated that little remains to be done, partly because the excessive stress on early German culture that characterized nineteenth-century criticism has been corrected. The most important reason is probably recognition of the fact that very little of the extant material in Old High German merits the name of literature. Interest in the *Hildebrandslied* is as high as ever, and the Biblical epics have attracted more attention than formerly. Three background works may be cited: W. Baetke, "Die Aufnahme des Christentums durch die Germanen" (*Die Welt als Geschichte*, 1943); W. von den Steinen, *Notker der Dichter und seine geistige Welt* (1948); and P. E. Hübinger, "Spätantike und frühes Mittelalter" (*DVLG*, 1952). The best works on language are still W. Braune, *Althochdeutsches Lesebuch* (1875), and the same author's *Althochdeutsche Grammatik* (1886), both of which have been frequently revised. The latter contains long selections of Old High German literature with commentary and excellent bibliographical notes. The *Althochdeutsches Wörterbuch*, ed. K. Karg-Gasterstädt and T. Frings, began to appear in 1952 and had reached *bitten* by 1963.

The best collections of texts are still K. Müllenhoff and W. Scherer, *Denkmäler deutscher Poesie und Prosa aus dem VIII.–XIII. Jahrhundert* (3rd ed. 1892), and E. von Steinmayer, *Die kleineren althochdeutschen Sprachdenkmäler* (1916). The appropriate literary histories have already been mentioned. The whole question of a literary history of Old High German is discussed by W. Schröder, *Grenzen und Möglichkeiten einer althochdeutschen Literaturgeschichte* (1959). He believes that, with the evidence we have, only the ninth century can seriously be said to have a literary history. G. Baesecke in "Die karlische Renaissance und das deutsche Schrifttum" (*DVLG*, 1949) examines the vexed question of the existence of a Renaissance, particularly as it affects vernacular writing. An important, if controversial, work on the relation between language and culture is L. Mittner's *Wurd, das Sakrale in der altgermanischen Epik* (1955).

A. HILDEBRANDSLIED

The great controversy about dialect and origins, which may be most easily followed in Braune's notes, has now died down. G. Baesecke's theory, propounded in his edition, *Das Hildebrandslied, Eine geschichtliche Einleitung für Laien* (1945), that the work was originally written in Langobardic, has had some degree of acceptance. W. Krogmann has attempted a reconstruction along these lines in *Das Hildebrandslied in der langobardischen Urfassung hergestellt* (1959) but has not received much agreement. There have been several works on the motif of father-son conflict; K. K. T. Wais's *Das Vater-Sohn-motiv in der Dichtung bis 1880* (1931) is the most far-ranging. H. Rosenfeld's "Das Hildebrandslied, die indogermanischen Vater-Sohn-Kampf-Dichtungen und das Problem ihrer Verwandtschaft" (*DVLG*, 1952) is an attempt to collate the details of the various appearances of the theme. J. de Vries sees the *Hildebrandslied* as a mixture of myth and history in "Das Motiv des Vater-Sohn-Kampfes im Hildebrandslied" (*GRM*, 1953). Most other articles are on textual and dialect problems.

B. ZAUBERSPRÜCHE

A. Schirokauer in "Form und Formel einiger altdeutscher Zaubersprüche" (*ZDP*, 1954) ascribes the survival of "medicine" formulae to their acceptance by Christians. F. Genzmer, "Die Götter des zweiten Merseburger Zauberspruchs" (*ANF*, 1948), and F. R. Schröder, "Balder und der zweite Merseburger Spruch" (*GRM*, 1953), are typical of many inconclusive articles on the identity and function of the gods in these poems.

C. MUSPILLI

Of the (often wild) attempts to explain the poem, the one really original effort is H. W. Sommer, "The Muspilli-Apocalypse" (*GR*, 1960), which demonstrates connections between the poem and Hebrew apocalyptic material and also shows that the title could be explained by Hebrew forms. Other explanations are mentioned in the text and notes to this article.

D. HELIAND

There is a new prose translation by W. Stapel (1953). Attention has been devoted to the area in which the work was composed. G. Baesecke, "Fulda und die altsächsichen Bibelepen" (*NdM*, 1948), thinks there was a strongly developed school around the Fulda monastery, while R. Drögereit, *Werden und der Heliand* (1951), uses details of dialect to attempt to show a connection between the work and the Werden area. Anneliese Bretschneider in "Heliandwortschatz and Heliandheimat" (*ZMF*, 1938) uses the same methods but applies them less dogmatically. W. Stapel studies the personality of the poet in "Der altsächsische Helianddichter" (*WW*, 1952). More critics are coming to believe that the Germanic elements in the poem have been exaggerated. Elisabeth Grosch, "Das Gottes- und Menschenbild im Heliand" (*PBB*, 1950), shows the work to be essentially Christian, and H. Rupp, "Leid und Sünde im Heliand und in Otfrieds Evangelienbuch" (*PBB* [Halle], 1956), by a detailed linguistic analysis shows that there were few concessions to the heathen view in either poem. *Heliand* uses more German words and its aims were different from Otfried's.

E. OTFRIED

Hulda Gössler, "Das Christusbild in Otfrieds Evangelienbuch und im Heliand" (*ZDP*, 1935), shows that Christ was a king in the poems, but not a worldly king. Only details are Germanized. W. Foerster's "Otfrieds literarisches Verhältnis zum Heliand" (*NJ*, 1948–50) is another comparison of the two poems. D. A. Mackenzie in *Otfried von Weissenburg, Narrator or Commentator? A Comparative Study* (1946) argues that the allegorizing commentary is inserted by Otfried to make the reading easier, while H. Rupp, "Otfried von Weissenburg und die spätantike Bibeldichtung" (*WW*, 1957), thinks Otfried regarded the earlier poems as a justification for his own treatment of the Bible story. F. Neumann in "Otfrieds Auffassung vom Versbau" (*PBB* [Halle], 1957) examines the evidence and rejects the theory that Otfried's verse forms could be based on the hexameter.

F. GEORGSLIED

F. Tschirch in "Wisolf, eine mittelalterliche Schreiberpersönlichkeit" (*PBB*, 1951) studies in detail the orthographical peculiarities of the author. J. K. Bostock writes on the same subject in *MAE* (1936).

G. LUDWIGSLIED

There are two works on the sources and connections of this interesting poem, H. Naumann, *Das Ludwigslied und die verwandten lateinischen Gedichte* (diss., Halle, 1932), which puts it in the context of Latin panegyric and hymn poetry, and R. Harvey, "The Provenance of the OHG Ludwigslied" (*MAE*, 1945).

H. NOTKER LABEO

The new edition of Notker's works by T. Stark and E. H. Sehrt is now up to Vol. III (1955). Almost all the studies are more or less directly connected with the question of translation. E. Luginbühl, *Studien zu Notkers Übersetzungskunst* (diss., Zurich, 1933), is a comparison with the Latin sources, but Ingeborg Schröbler in *Notker III von St Gallen als Übersetzer und Kommentator von Boethius' De consolatione philosophiae* (1953) and "Interpretatio Christiana in Notkers Bearbeitung von Boethius' Trost der Philosophie" (*ZDA*, 1951) seeks to establish the originality of Notker's language, style, and method. F. Leimbach's *Die Sprache Notkers und Willirams* (diss., Göttingen, 1934) is of interest in showing the development of language at the end of the Old High German period.

I. WILLIRAM

The most interesting work is that of M. L. Dittrich, "Willirams von Ebersberg Bearbeitung der Cantica Cantorum" (*ZDA*, 1948–50) and "Die literarische Form von Willirams Expositio in Cantica Cantorum" (*ZDA*, 1952–53), which examines the form of the work, shows it to be tripartite like a three-aisled church, and concludes that the author was more interested in form than content.

J. GENERAL

D. Ruprecht's *Tristitia. Wortschatz und Vorstellung in den althochdeutschen Sprachdenkmälern* (1959) is a most important study of the development of linguistic concepts in a period of transition.

IX. MIDDLE HIGH GERMAN LITERATURE

THE GENERAL tendency in the study of Middle High German litera- ture has been to concentrate on the major works, both in the edit- ing of texts and in critical studies. Several long-promised editions are still outstanding, of which perhaps the most important is that of the fragments of Eilhart's *Tristan*. Criticism in general has tended to move away from the positivistic attitudes summed up in Ehrismann's literary history. Source studies no longer dominate the field. There has been more interest in the application of findings from other areas of knowledge, particularly theology, to the interpretation of literary works. Most critics have given more weight to the Latin tradition than to individual classical works, more weight to written cultural monuments than to vague "popular influences." A great deal of attention has been paid to structural and stylistic questions, partic- ularly in the romance and the lyric. Research on the popular epics has remained conservative, and, in spite of the large number of studies, there is still little really satisfactory stylistic analysis of this genre. This is even more true of allegory, beast epic, and drama, concerning which little of real significance has recently appeared.

A. RELIGIOUS WORKS

Because of its supposed influence on secular poetry, there has been considerable interest in the religious poetry of the early Middle High German period, in spite of its admittedly limited literary value. M. Ittenbach's *Deutsche Dichtungen der salischen Kaiserzeit und verwandte Denkmäler* (1937) is a summary of the extant works with remarks on the general character of the period, while S. Singer's

"Dogma und Dichtung des Mittelalters" (*PMLA*, 1947) traces the effects of theological beliefs on poetry. W. Schröder in "Der Geist von Cluny und die Anfänge des mittelhochdeutschen Schrifttums" (*PBB*, 1950) observes that the influence of the Cluniac reforms on the development of secular literature has been exaggerated. H. Kuhn in "Gestalten und Lebenskräfte der frühmittelhochdeutschen Dichtung" (*DVLG*, 1953) regards the minor Middle High German works of the period as expressing a new, intellectual attitude, symbolized by their structure. F. Ohly in "Geist und Formen der Hoheliedauslegung im 12. Jahrhundert" (*ZDA*, 1954) and *Hoheliedstudien. Grundzüge einer Geschichte der Hoheliedauslegung des Abendlandes bis um 1200* (1958) provides excellent studies of the exegetical techniques of the period and the effect of the works on the development of the cult of the Virgin. W. Stammler in "Deutsche Scholastik" (*ZDP*, 1953) reminds scholars that scholasticism was an important mode of thought during the early Middle Ages and warns against overstressing mysticism. H. Rupp's *Deutsche religiöse Dichtung des 11. und 12. Jahrhunderts* (1958) discusses a very important problem of literary history and textual transmission. He thinks that there was much more religious poetry than that which has survived, because much oral poetry was not written down. He deals with the same problem in "Über das Verhältnis von deutscher und lateinischer Dichtung im 9. bis 12. Jahrhundert" (*GRM*, 1958), while G. Eis in "Von der verlorenen altdeutschen Dichtung. Erwägungen und Schätzungen" (*GRM*, 1956) takes quite the opposite view—that little of importance has failed to survive. M. Ittenbach in "Zur Form frühmittelhochdeutscher Gedichte" (*ZDP*, 1938) discusses the development of strophic patterns. U. Pretzel traces the gradual regularization of rhyme in *Frühgeschichte des deutschen Reims*, Vol. I (1941).

B. INDIVIDUAL WORKS

None of these is of sufficient importance to need a separate section. The content of two works on the *St. Trutperter Hohes Lied* are sufficiently explained by their titles: Margot Landgraf, *Das St. Trutperter Hohe Lied. Sein theologischer Gedankeninhalt und die geschichtliche Stellung* (1935), and W. Geppert, "Die mystische Sprache des St. Trutperter Hohen Liedes" (diss., Freie Univ., Berlin, 1952). E. F. Ohly's "Der Prolog des *St. Trutperter Hohen liedes*" (*ZDA*, 1953) is a significant piece of research because of its ingenious method. By examining the number symbolism and formal elements he determines the genuineness of the various parts. The poems of Frau Ava have been the subject of detailed studies by R. Kienast in *ZDA*, 1937 and 1940, which have established the text and showed a close connection between her work and the *St. Trutperter Hohes Lied*. H. Rupp, "[Notker's] Memento mori" (*PBB*, 1952), stresses the influence of the Cluniac reforms on the work. There is a thorough treatment of all aspects of the Wiener Genesis in S. Beyschlag's *Wiener Genesis, Idee, Stoff, und Form* (1942), which is supplemented by the structural study of E. Möser, "Der kompositorische Aufbau der Wiener Genesis" (diss., Tübingen, 1947). R. Gruenter, "Der Paradisus der Wiener Genesis" (*Euphorion*, 1955), is a contribution to the author's continuing study of the ideal landscape. There is a revised edition of Heinzel's text of Heinrich von Melk by R. Kienast, *Der sogenannte Heinrich von Melk* (2nd ed. 1960), and the review of the first edition (1946) by G. Eis (*ZDP*, 1951) offers valuable evidence for a later date than is usually assumed. There are minor stylistic studies of religious poetry by Erika Kimmrich, "Das Verhältnis des sogenannten Heinrich von Melk zur mittellateinischen Dichtung" (diss., Tübingen, 1952), and A. Schwinkowski, *Priester Wernhers Maria. Eine Stiluntersuchung* (diss., Kiel, 1932). For other works in this genre and the appropriate secondary literature, see C. Soeteman, *Deutsche geistliche Dichtung des 11. und 12. Jahrhunderts* (1963), which gives a general introduction to the subject and sections on each of the works.

C. NARRATIVE POETRY

Much of the critical work on narrative poetry has been devoted to details. The most significant general work is by P. Waremann, *Spielmannsdichtung, Versuch einer Begriffsbestimmung* (1951), which does not settle the question of what is meant by the term *Spielmannsdichtung*. (The author thinks it has little worth as the name of a literary genre but does present evidence clearly.) The question of the presentation of the narrative genres to their audience is discussed by K. H. Bertan and R. Stephan, "Zum sänglichen Vortrag mittelhochdeutscher strophischer Epen" (*ZDA*, 1957), in which the authors argue that the strophic form was suitable for singing. There have been several articles on dating problems. P. Wapnewski, "Der Epilog und die Datierung des deutschen Rolandsliedes" (*Euphorion*, 1955), uses the date of the death of Henry the Proud to date the "genuine" parts of the epilogue as 1145. L. Wolff, " 'Ze gerichte er im nu stat.' Zur Datierung des Rolandliedes" (*PBB*, 1956), dates the work around

1170. The important question of the relation between religion and secular authority in the empire is discussed by E. F. Ohly in "Zum Reichsgedanken des deutschen Rolandsliedes" (*ZDA*, 1940), and the corresponding problem with regard to knighthood is investigated by G. Fliegner, "Geistliches und weltliches Rittertum im Rolandslied des Pfaffen Konrad" (diss., Breslau, 1937). Another contribution to the dating of early works is E. Sitte, *Die Datierung von Lamprechts Alexander* (1940). D. Teusink takes up the development of courtly characteristics in *Das Verhältnis zwischen Veldekes Eneide und dem Alexanderlied* (1946).

D. KÖNIG ROTHER

The name of the hero has always been an important factor in discussing the origins of the Rother story, and T. Frings, "Rothari —Roger—Rothere" (*PBB*, 1945), carries the controversy one stage further by bringing in the personality of Roger II of Sicily. Dialect criteria are the means by which G. Kramer attempts to establish a date for the poem in "Die textkristische Bedeutung der Reime in der Heidelberger Handschrift des König Rother" (*PBB* [Halle], 1957) ; he arrives at an early twelfth-century date. K. Siegmund, on the other hand, prefers the dubious procedure of regarding the hero as a representation of the Emperor Henry VI, and thus dates the work about 1196 (*Zeitgeschichte und Dichtung im König Rother. Versuch einer Neudatierung*, 1959). W. J. Schröder, "König Rother, Gehalt und Struktur" (*DVLG*, 1955), stresses the fundamental unity of the poem; and the author's narrative techniques are examined by H. Fromm in "Die Erzählkunst des Rother-Epikers" (*Euphorion*, 1960).

E. HERZOG ERNST

There is a new text of the later version of the poem, taken from fifteenth- and sixteenth-century prints, by K. C. King, *Das Lied von Herzog Ernst* (1959), and a comparison of the various manuscript versions in Esther Ringhandt, "Das Herzog-Ernst-Epos. Vergleich der deutschen Fassungen A, B, D, F" (diss., Freie Univ., Berlin, 1955). The well-known amalgam of historical events and folk motifs that characterizes this work is explored by C. Heselhaus, "Die Herzog-Ernst-Dichtung. Zur Begriffsbestimmung von Märe und Historie" (*DVLG*, 1942), and H. Naumann, "Die deutsche Kernfabel des Herzog-Ernst-Epos" (*Euphorion*, 1950).

X. EARLY COURTLY LITERATURE

B Y FAR the greatest efforts in research and interpretation of early courtly literature have been devoted to the work of Heinrich von Veldeke and to the early history of the Tristan story. The other courtly works have been largely ignored. Several significant studies may be mentioned here, even though their scope extends to the classical Middle High German period. The most important is R. S. Loomis, ed. *Arthurian Literature in the Middle Ages* (1959), which contains articles on all the Arthurian romances and which, in spite of the inevitably uneven treatment of a large number of scholars, is the most important contribution to Arthurian studies to appear in our period. It is better in its discussion of sources, analogues, and origins than in its treatment of the esthetic value of the works. Probably the most important general work on poetic techniques in the romances is H. Emmel, *Formprobleme des Artusromans und der Graldichtung* (1951), one of the most influential of all compositional studies. A more summary work is W. F. Schirmer, *Die frühen Darstellungen des Arthurstoffes* (1958), which treats many non-German productions. A general analysis of the type appears in M. Bindschedler, *"Die Dichtung um König Artus und seine Ritter"* (*DVLG*, 1957). The following works are treatments of the special subjects stated in their titles: K. G. T. Webster, *Guinevere: A Study of Her Abductions* (1951); L. Wolff, "Die mythologischen Motive in den Liebesdarstellungen des höfischen Romans" (*ZDA*, 1947); and H. Bodensohn, *Die Festschilderungen in der mittelhochdeutschen Dichtung* (1936).

The importance of Heinrich von Veldeke as an innovator and a link between the old and the new in the courtly epic was recognized by his contemporaries, and studies of his work have been prosecuted with enthusiasm by modern scholars, particularly by T. Frings and his school. A good deal of effort has been devoted to the study and reconstitution of the dialect in which Heinrich von Veldeke wrote, but literary problems have not been neglected. Frings's own works include *Drei Veldeke Studien: Das Veldekeproblem, Der Eneideepilog, Die beiden Stauferpartien* (with G. Schieb, 1949). His *Heinrich von Veld-*

eke. Vol. I, *Die Servatiusbruchstücke und die Lieder. Grundlegung einer Veldekekritik* (with G. Schieb, 1947) is again a largely linguistic study of dialect features. Works written on the subject before Frings's are largely obsolete.

There have been the inevitable comparisons between Veldeke's *Eneide* and the French *Roman d'Enée:* for example, C. Minis in *Heinrich von Veldekes Eneide und der Roman d'Enéas: Textkritik* (*LB*, 1948). The same author compares specific passages in *Neophil,* 1949. R. Zitzmann in "Die Didohandlung in der frühhöfischen Eneasdichtung" (*Euphorion,* 1952) tries to show that the French version is romanesque and the German Gothic, a dubious distinction. J. Quint's "Der *Roman d'Enéas* und Veldekes *Eneit*" (*ZDA,* 1954) is concerned with the way in which classical episodes are medievalized. He is not impressed by the success of the adaptation, but this is less important than his analysis of the method. The love problem in Heinrich's work transcends the work itself, for there is a real question as to how conscious the author was of the distinction between sacred and profane love. F. Maurer in " 'Rechte' Minne bei Heinrich von Veldeke" (*Archiv,* 1950) argues that his author presents Dido as an example of profane love and Lavinia as a higher and more spiritual type. W. Schröder in *ZDA,* 1958, sees the difference not in two types of love but in the fates of two individuals. There is a study of the structure of the poem in an unpublished dissertation by Ernestine Comhaire, "Der Aufbau von Veldekes Eneit" (Hamburg, 1947). A fairly recent summary of Veldeke scholarship is J. Notermans, "Een kwart eeuw Veldekestudie" (*LT,* 1954). Little has appeared on the works of Herbort von Fritzlar, Albrecht von Halberstadt, and the other minor courtly poets. There is, however, an extremely useful translation into English of the *Lanzelet* of Ulrich von Zazikhoven by K. G. T. Webster, with excellent notes by R. S. Loomis (1957). Since the original text is almost impossible to obtain, this translation is of particular value. The only detailed study of the poem is W. Richter, *Der Lanzelet des Ulrich von Zazikhoven* (Deutsche Forschungen, 1934).

XI. TRISTAN

A BIBLIOGRAPHY of all Tristan material, reasonably complete up to 1939, is H. Küpper's *Bibliographie zur Tristansage* (1941). There has been less study of sources in the last two decades, and the standard work on this aspect of Tristan scholarship remains Gertrude Schoepperle, *Tristan and Isolt: A Study of the Sources of the Romance* (2 vols., 1913), which has been reprinted with additional bibliographical material by R. S. Loomis (2 vols., 1960–63). In addition to the well-known works by F. Ranke (1925) and W. Golther (1929), we should mention B. Mergell, *Tristan und Isolde: Ursprung und Entwicklung der Tristansage im Mittelalter* (1949), which, though guilty of some extravagances, presents interesting ideas on the Christian symbolism of the poems. There is still no reliable text of the Eilhart fragments, but Gertrude Schlegel in *Eilharts Tristant Handschriften* (1933) discusses the problem of establishing a text. A. Witte in "Der Aufbau der ältesten Tristandichtung" (*ZDA*, 1933) attempts a study of the structure of the poem from the extant material. H. Stolte's *Eilhart und Gottfried. Studie über Motivreim und Aufbaustil, Sprache, Volkstum, Stil* (1941) is an excellent and detailed stylistic study that makes a good case for the influence of Eilhart on Gottfried, even though the utter difference of their methods is fully appreciated. G. Cordes' *Zur Sprache Eilharts von Oberge* (1939) is a more conventional study of language. H. Eggers in "Der Liebesmonolog in Eilharts *Tristant*" (*Euphorion*, 1950) discusses the structural use of the monologue for making clear the author's as well as the chief characters' views on love. The same author also wrote "Literarische Beziehungen des Parzival zum Tristant Eilharts von Oberge" (*PBB*, 1950).

XII. CLASSICAL COURTLY EPIC

M ORE MATERIAL has been written about works in this genre than about any other during the period under review. Even the popular epic, once the subject of greatest interest to critics, has had to yield. The aims of the research have also changed. Although the questions of origins and analogues have by no means been neglected, the emphasis has shifted to the relation between the courtly ideal and religion, to the study of theological and mystical concepts in their effects on the courtly love ideal, and to the structure of the various romances, particularly the emergence of common patterns in the arrangement of incidents. There have been several rather superficial studies of style. Wolfram von Eschenbach and Gottfried von Strassburg have naturally received most attention, and while Wolfram's work has received just as much critical acclaim as ever, this acclaim has begun to be based on sound evaluation rather than on the assumption that Wolfram was a "German" poet. Gottfried's reputation now rests on the awareness that he was both a master of the technicalities of writing and a highly original thinker. No longer is he regarded as merely a rather charming but "Frenchified" court poet.

A. HARTMANN VON AUE

There has been some distinguished work by H. Sparnaay, whose most important contributions include: *Hartmann von Aue, Studien zu einer Biographie* (2 vols., 1933, 1938), which is as close to a standard work on Hartmann's life and work as we are likely to obtain; "Nachträge zu Hartmann von Aue" (*Neophil*, 1944), a supplement to his biography; and a summary article in *Arthurian Literature in the Middle Ages* (1959). H. Kuhn, "Hartmann von Aue als Dichter" (*DU*, 1952), is a perceptive, if brief, evaluation. Questions of chronology are discussed, but by no means settled, in E. Sievers, "Zur inneren und äusseren Chronologie der Werke Hartmanns von Aue" (*Festschrift P. Strauch*, 1932), and in F. Neumann, "Wann dichtete Hartmann von Aue?" (*Festschrift Panzer*,

1950). The dispute is about the chronology of the "religious" poems. No one doubts that *Erek* is the first and *Iwein* the last work. The question of the relation of Hartmann to his sources, particularly to the works of Chrétien de Troyes, has never been so important as it is with Wolfram. The following works and earlier ones, written before the period under review, have established that Hartmann shows considerable independence of Chrétien in the *Erek*, using material drawn from other, largely unknown sources, and almost complete dependence in the *Iwein*, although some critics see much originality of treatment: A. Witte, "Hartmann von Aue und Kristian de Troyes" (*PBB*, 1929), and H. Drube, *Hartmann und Chrétien* (1931). No one has yet discovered a source for *Der arme Heinrich*. H. Eggers, *Symmetrie und Proportion epischen Erzählens. Studien zur Kunstform Hartmanns von Aue* (1956), is a sound examination of the importance of arithmetical concepts in the structure of medieval poetry. It is the arithmetical proportion rather than the number symbolism that is important. W. Ohly, *Die heilsgeschicht-liche Struktur der Epen Hartmanns von Aue* (diss., Freie Univ., Berlin, 1958), sees the formal elements of the history of salvation reflected in the composition of Hartmann's works.

There is one detailed and significant study of the *Büchlein* by H. Grosse, *Hartmanns Büchlein dargestellt in seiner psycho-logischen ethischen und theologischen Bezogenheit auf das Gesamt-werk des Dichters* (1936). The Arthurian epics have not been so popular with critics as the two "Christian" works, largely because of the feeling that they are less original and that there is little left to add. There are two studies of the text of *Erek*, K. Vancsa, "Wiener *Erec*-Bruchstück" (*Jahrbuch für Landeskunde von Niederöster-reich*, 1948), and H. Stolte, "Der Erec Hartmanns von Aue" (*Zeitschrift für deutsche Bildung*, 1941). A. van der Lee, *Der Stil von Hartmanns Erec verglichen mit dem der älteren Epik* (diss., Utrecht, 1950), demonstrates how Hartmann was responsible for the modernization of the earlier epic style. H. B. Willson, "Sin and Redemption in Hartmann's Erec" (*GR*, 1958), applies the author's religious view of the courtly epics to the *Erec*, emphasizing the aspects of death and resurrection of the hero.

Of the essays on *Iwein*, one merits attention because of its unusual (and well-presented) thesis. H. Sacker, "An Interpretation of Hartmann's *Iwein*" (*GR*, 1961), sees the Arthurian court as motivated entirely by notions of glory, and Kei as its typical representative. The hero is thus in a sense bound to show himself un-Arthurian.

In view of the current popularity of theological interpretations,

it is not surprising to find numerous studies analyzing the behavior
of *Gregorius* and *Der arme Heinrich* in terms of contemporary
theology. G. Schieb, "Schuld und Sühne in Hartmanns *Gregorius*"
(*PBB*, 1950), and H. Nobel, "Schuld und Sühne in Hartmanns
Gregorius und in der frühscholastischen Theologie" (*ZDP*, 1957),
both find that the sins and virtues of the hero are depicted in
accordance with theological ideas that the audience could be assumed
to know. They find that Augustinian ideas are in general still
dominant. There are two interesting studies of the legal aspects of
the poem in matter and style, a subject, that needs still more
attention, since many speeches in the epic reflect legal training and
practice: R. Gruenter, "Über den Einfluss des genus iudicale auf den
höfischen Redestil" (*DVLG*, 1952), and F. Beyerle, *Der arme
Heinrich. Hartmanns von Aue als Zeugnis mittelalterlichen Ständes-
rechts (Festgabe für H. Fehr*, 1948). There is a good new edition of
the *Gregorius* by F. Neumann (1958). P. Wapnewski's *Hartmann
von Aue* (1962) is an excellent summary of research and a guide to
further study.

B. WOLFRAM VON ESCHENBACH

Wolfram has attracted the attention of scholars ranging from
those who wish to see in him the German poet par excellence (whose
work may be safely ignored) to those who have made a serious effort
to determine his religious, moral, and social ideas. It would be
surprising if there were not violent differences of opinion. Many
ascribe to him a systematic religiosity, which is inconsistent with his
character. There is too little allowance for the fact that he acquired
his learning orally and that it is therefore often inaccurate and
badly organized. His poem is used as a mine by those who wish to
advance strongly held theories of their own about the Grail legend.
In particular, Wolfram's sense of humor is underestimated. In spite
of these reservations, it can safely be said that more progress has
been made toward the understanding of *Parzival* in the last thirty
years than in the whole of the preceding century. It should be added
that almost all studies of Wolfram are concerned with *Parzival*.
Very little has been written on the other works.

There is a useful study of Wolfram scholarship in its earliest
period by J. Götz, *Die Entwicklung des Wolframbildes von Bodmer
bis zum Tode Lachmanns in der germanistischen und schönen
Literatur* (diss., Freiburg, 1936). Later developments are taken up
by W. J. Schröder, "Grundzüge eines neuen Wolframbildes" (*FuF*,
1950), and, under a more fashionable title, by H. Eggers, "Wol-

framforschung in der Krise?" (*WW*, 1954). R. Lowet's *Wolframs von Eschenbach Parzival im Wandel der Zeiten* (1955) is a summary of critical opinion from Lachmann to 1955. M. F. Richey's *Studies of Wolfram von Eschenbach with Translations into English Verse of Passages from His Poetry* (1957) is a useful introduction to the poet for English-speaking readers. O. Springer's chapter on Wolfram in R. S. Loomis, ed. *Arthurian Literature in the Middle Ages* (1959), is the best scholarly introduction, since it has a sound review of scholarship and a good bibliography.

By far the most important treatment of Wolfram's relations to his sources in writing the *Parzival* is by J. Fourquet, *Wolfram d'Eschenbach et le Conte del Graal* (1938), which demonstrates that Wolfram's main source was indeed the poem of Chrétien de Troyes, but probably not the version found in the extant manuscripts. There has been little serious dissent from these views, although M. F. Richey (*MLR*, 1952) stresses Wolfram's independence. F. Panzer in *Gahmuret: Quellenstudien zu Wolframs Parzival* (1940) goes over the sources and Singer's theories and concludes that Gahmuret is modeled on King Richard I of England. Helen Adolf in "New Light on Oriental Sources for Wolfram's *Parzival* and Other Grail Romances" (*PMLA*, 1947), as in many of her other works, seeks to show connections between the Grail and early Christianity and the Moslem world. Her views are summed up in *Visio pacis* (1960), which seeks to connect the various Grail poems of the late twelfth and early thirteenth centuries with specific historical events, particularly the Crusades and the fate of the Latin kingdoms in the East.

The majority of critics have abandoned "Kyot" as a true source, but there has been some attempt to argue that the name was used as a cover for sources, some of them Catharist. T. C. van Stockum in "Wolframs *Parzival* und das Problem der Quelle" (*Neophil*, 1941) advanced the somewhat complicated theory that Wolfram depended entirely on Chrétien for his first draft, then discovered a "Grail book" by Kyot and rewrote Books III–IX of *Parzival* in the light of his new knowledge. J. H. Scholte in "Kyot von Katelangen" (*Neophil*, 1949) sees Kyot as a source of orally transmitted knowledge about the House of Anjou, while E. Zeydel in articles in *Neophil* in 1950, 1952, and 1953 examines the possibility that Kyot is a cover name to explain Catharist influences or "authorities." H. and R. Kahane's "Wolframs Gral und Wolframs Kyot" (*ZDA*, 1959) assumes that Kyot existed and argues that the Grail originated in Eastern rites. W. J. Schröder's "Kyot" (*GRM*, 1959) represents the view (held by most critics, including the present author) that Kyot is fiction, a mock authority to "explain"

Wolfram's own changes in the story. In this connection we may mention the interesting article by B. Horacek, "Ichne kan deheinen buochstap" (*Festschrift Kralik*, 1954), which finds Wolfram not illiterate but also not a "bookman." His style is that of speech.

The most interesting Wolfram criticism has concentrated on the kind of world Wolfram was trying to portray: its relation to formal religion, contemporary theology, the courtly ideal, and the mysticism connected with the Grail. If there is any consensus of criticism, it is that Wolfram evolved an informal "lay piety" showing influences from several sources, and that he made it the guiding system for his hero, who ruled over a company organized on courtly lines but motivated by the desire to serve God in this world. It should be noted, however, that several critics have stressed Eastern influences and others the importance of the House of Anjou. All agree on the significance of the crusading motif for the development of Wolfram's ideal society.

There have been numerous attempts to determine the nature of the ideal world of *Parzival* and the influences that shaped it. H. Schneider in *Parzival-Studien* (1947) deals especially with the influence of Hartmann's *Iwein* and *Gregorius* and the Grail sources. A very detailed study is that of W. J. Schröder, *Der Ritter zwischen Welt und Gott* (1952), which lays stress on the importance of the House of Anjou, the Templars, and mysticism. L. Wolff in "Die höfisch-ritterliche Welt und der Gral in Wolframs *Parzival*" (*PBB*, 1955) differs from many other critics in believing that Wolfram wished to show that the courtly world was capable of achieving a synthesis between God and the world. H. Kuhn in "*Parzival*. Ein Versuch über Mythos, Glaube und Dichtung im Mittelalter" (*DVLG*, 1956) similarly stresses the resemblances rather than the differences between *Parzival* and the other courtly epics. F. Maurer in "Das Grundanliegen Wolframs von Eschenbach" (*DU*, 1956) sees the Grail as a symbol of release from original sin by God's grace, and the unity of the secular and religious worlds in Condwiramurs. The formal, patristic background, especially the Augustinian influence, is covered in some detail in P. Wapnewski, *Wolframs Parzival. Studien zur Religiosität und Form* (1955). W. T. H. Jackson in "The Progress of Parzival and the Trees of Virtue and Vice" (*GR*, 1958) shows that Parzival's sins succeed one another in the order often shown in medieval theological works and that his repentance follows the same pattern.

The various viewpoints on the question of Wolfram's religion are well summarized in H-J. Koppitz, *Wolframs Religiosität* (1959). His own conclusion is that Wolfram was not an abstract thinker but did desire to make clear his own layman's religion. Works on the Grail problem naturally go far beyond Wolfram's work. J. Marx, *La légende arthurienne et le Graal* (1952), surveys the whole field from a historical point of view, whereas L-I. Ringbom in *Graltempel und Paradies. Beziehungen zwischen Iran und Europa im Mittelalter* (1951) makes an attempt to show that the Grail ceremonies originated in Iran and produces evidence to show that the Grail may be recognized in a cult object—a pearl hanging in a temple at the "earth's center." The Grail is thus a kind of microcosm. The work is perhaps a little too ingenious. The influence of the East also figures prominently in Helen Adolf's "Christendom and Islam in the Middle Ages: New Light on the Grail Stone and Hidden Host" (*Speculum*, 1957) and in P. Ponsoye's *L'Islam et le Graal: Etude sur l'ésotérisme du Parzival de Wolfram von Eschenbach* (1957). Perhaps the most extreme example of overinterpretation of Wolfram's text is by B. Mergell, *Der Gral in Wolfram's Parzival* (1952), in which every resource is employed to give significance to any trivial remark, and the most amazing knowledge —and obscurity—is attributed to Wolfram. The widely accepted belief that Wolfram's Grail stone is connected with the "stone of humility" that Alexander the Great brought back from the earthly paradise is reinforced in the arguments advanced by W. Krogmann in "Wunsch von Pardîs" (*ZDA*, 1954). R. Wisniewski in "Wolframs Gralstein und eine Legende von Lucifer und den Edelsteinen" (*PBB*, 1957) is concerned with materials that are mostly later than Wolfram. F. Ranke in "Zur Symbolik des Grals bei Wolfram von Eschenbach" (*Trivium*, 1946) regards the use of the term "lapis exilis" as a conscious double symbol—of glory and humility of the knight and the Christian. A. T. Hatto, "On Wolfram's Conception of the Grail" (*MLR*, 1948), thinks that the figure of Kyot was invented as an "authority" in reply to critics of early versions of the work. W. Wolf in "Der Vogel Phönix und der Gral" (*Festschrift Panzer*, 1950) seeks connection between the dove that brings the wafer and the roc and phoenix of Eastern legend. He stresses particularly the renewal of youth in the later stories and thinks Wolfram's version of the Grail not only independent of French sources but older.

Of the many special features of conduct and religion in *Parzival*, two have received an unusual amount of attention, the nature of his sin and the meaning of the term *zwivel*. Usually the studies have attempted to show analogies in contemporary theology, but it should not be forgotten that *Parzival* is at all times more concerned with the object of his pursuit, whether it is the Grail or the Round Table, than he is with the salvation of his immortal soul. A relatively early study of this kind is G. Keferstein's *Parzivals ethischer Weg* (1937), which recognizes the religious background of Parzival's fault. H. Heckel, *Das ethische Wortfeld in Wolframs Parzival* (1939), approaches the problem by isolating the important "ethical" words and studying their use. J. Schwietering in "Parzivals Schuld" (*ZDA*, 1944) reviews the variety of past interpretations and the importance of the context within which the guilty acts are committed. F. Maurer in "Parzivals Sünden" (*DVLG*, 1950) attempts to distinguish between human frailty and "active" sins, such as the killing of Ither, while W. Mohr in "Parzivals ritterliche Schuld" (*WW*, 1951) concentrates on those actions of the hero that contravene knightly as distinct from theological rules. The nature of *zwivel* and particularly its relation to the sin of despair is the subject of two articles, Helen Adolf's "The Theological and Feudal Background of Wolfram's *zwîvel*" (*JEGP*, 1950) and H. Hempel's "Der *zwîvel* bei Wolfram und anderweit" (*Festschrift Helm*, 1951). Two works by G. Weber, *Der Gottesbegriff des Parzival* (1935) and *Parzival. Ringen und Vollendung* (1948), are largely concerned with religious ideas and stress the tension between the established Augustinian views and the new approaches that found their eventual expressions in Thomism. B. Mockenhaupt, *Die Frömmigkeit im Parzival Wolframs von Eschenbach* (1942), is concerned less with the theological than with the informal religious attitudes. O. Katann, "Einflüsse des Katharertums auf Wolframs *Parzival?*" (*WW*, 1957–58), denies that there was any such influence.

Much of the argument about the structure of *Parzival* has concentrated on questions of chronology of the various parts and in particular on whether the prologue was written after the work had already been partially completed. The question is discussed by M. F. Richey, "Zu der Einleitung von Wolframs *Parzival*" (*ZDP*, 1938), and by H. Hempel, "Der Eingang von Wolframs *Parzival*" (*ZDA*, 1951), who believes that the prologue is best understood as part of the dispute with Gottfried. E. Cucuel in *Die Eingangsbücher des Parzival und das Gesamtwerk* (1937) asserts that the early books were written before Book VI, not after, as some critics think. Few would deny that the ninth book is the core of *Parzival*, and W. Henzen's "Das IX. Buch des *Parzival*. Überlegungen zum Aufbau" (*Festschrift Helm*, 1951) is a careful attempt to justify its (at first sight) confusing composition. The importance of number symbolism as a structural element is stressed by H. Eggers, "Strukturprobleme mittelalterlicher Epik, dargestellt am *Parzival* Wolframs von Eschenbach" (*Euphorion*, 1953). Other types of symbolism that have been introduced into the interpretation of the poem are the heraldic, by G. F. Timpson in *GL&L* (1960), and the mystic, by H. B. Willson in *ZDP* (1960) and *GL&L* (1960).

Probably the most interesting of all the special "problems" concerns the personal and literary relationship between Wolfram and Gottfried von Strassburg. It is recognized that the two differed mainly on questions of style and the function of literature. The relation between them is discussed in great detail by K. K. Klein in "Wolframs Selbstverteidigung" (*ZDA*, 1954), which argues that Wolfram bases his criticism on a feeling of his own superior manliness and that the distinction he makes is important for all contemporary society. W. J. Schröder in "Vindaere wilder maere. Zum Literaturstreit zwischen Gottfried und Wolfram" (*PBB*, 1958) holds that style is the only subject of disagreement.

All the general works on *Parzival* treat the Gawan episodes in their relation to the main themes of the work, but the only important special treatments are G. Keferstein's "Die Gawanhandlung in Wolframs *Parzival*" (*GRM*, 1937) and a study of the structure of Book XIII by S. Johnson in "Gawain's Surprise in Wolfram's *Parzival*" (*GR*, 1958). By far the best of the few treatments of Wolfram's humor is by M. Wehrli in *Festschrift Spoerri* (1950), which rightly emphasizes that the humor is to be found not only in the individual scenes but in the treatment of the whole, and that the humor constitutes a bridge between the laity and formal religion. The important question of epic time is studied by H. Weigand in "Die epischen Zeitverhältnisse in den Graldichtungen Chrestiens und Wolframs" (*PMLA*, 1938). Rather surprisingly, in view of its importance and the frequency with which it enters into general discussions of the poem, there is only one article devoted specifically to Wolfram's conception of love, by G. Keferstein in *Festschrift Leitzmann* (1937). There is a word index to *Parzival* by A. Senn and W. Lehmann (1938).

It has already been observed that there is little critical writing on Wolfram's other works. Nevertheless J. Bumke's *Wolframs Willehalm: Studien zur Epenstruktur und zum Heiligkeitsbegriff der ausgehenden Blütezeit* (1959), a general study of the sources and purpose of the poem, deserves to be ranked among the best of Wolfram criticism. R. Kienast's "Zur Tektonik von Wolframs Willehalm" (*Festschrift Panzer*, 1950) is an ingenious attempt to show the dipartite structure and hence complete symmetry of the poem. Some critics see the *Titurel* (or *Sigune und Schionatulander*) fragments as Wolfram's most mature work. There is a general analysis by L. Wolff in *Festschrift Panzer* (1950) that deals with the development of spiritual values and the concept of love, as well as with the use of the strophic form. B. Rahn's *Wolframs Sigunendichtung* (1958) is a detailed interpretation that stresses the resemblances between Sigune and the female heroines of legend. Since she is not merely a mistress who is served, like a heroine in a courtly romance, but a heroine in her own right, Rahn argues, Wolfram's final literary goal was the glorification of true love. D. Labusch, *Studien zu Wolframs Sigune* (1959), is more concerned with her role as a penitent, because her conduct shows that by penitence she continues to love after death and thus provides a link between the natural and the supernatural worlds.

C. GOTTFRIED VON STRASSBURG

The stature of Gottfried has increased notably since 1930. It is now realized that he was far more than a polished stylist: he was a man of great culture, a profound thinker, whose study of love is one of the greatest of medieval literary achievements. Several general studies have appeared, of which the longest and most detailed is by G. Weber, *Gottfrieds von Strassburg Tristan und die Krise des hochmittelalterlichen Weltbildes um 1200* (2 vols., 1953). This is a profound book with an excellent review of research, but the author's preoccupation with theological problems renders it far too abstract and one-sided, and clarity of style is not one of its merits. Although its treatment of the theological aspects of the poem is thorough and very well informed, especially the treatment of the conflict between the Augustinian concept of the wickedness of earthly love and the courtly search for a love ideal, other equally important features of the poem are almost ignored. Basic studies that attempt a more objective evaluation are those of H. de Boor, "Die Grundauffassung von Gottfrieds *Tristan*" (*DVLG*, 1940), which stresses the resemblance between Gottfried and Reinmar and the function of the lovers as "legend" figures; M. Wehrli in *Trivium* (1946); M. Bindschedler in *PBB* (1954); W. T. H. Jackson in *Arthurian Literature in the Middle Ages* (1959). There are reviews of research by M. Bindschedler in *DU* (1953) and H. Fromm in *DVLG* (1954). The volume dealing with Gottfried von Strassburg in the *Sammlung Metzler Realienbücher für Germanisten* by G. Weber and W. Hoffman (1962) is an admirable introduction, not in the least biased towards Weber's own views.

The work that may be regarded as having prompted later studies of the connection between "Tristan love" and mysticism is J. Schwietering, *Der Tristan Gottfrieds von Strassburg und die Bern-*

hardische Mystik (1943), which establishes the influence of mysticism, particularly the resemblances in terminology. Closely connected with the role of religion in determining the conduct of the principal characters is the question of the degree of influence of standards of chivalric conduct. M. Bindschedler's article, "Gottfried von Strassburg und die höfische Ethik" (*PBB*, 1954), mentioned above, stresses the importance of these considerations and plays down the theological influences; but G. Keferstein, "Die Entwertung der höfischen Gesellschaft im Tristan Gottfrieds von Strassburg" (*GRM*, 1936), believes that the apparent compliance with the rules of courtly society is mere mockery. These disagreements are reflected also in the varying views of the meaning of the words "edelez herze." Some critics, including the present author, believe that the "edele herzen" are a special group who can understand "Tristan love," a view advanced by Maria Meyer, *Der Begriff 'edelez herze' in Gottfrieds von Strassburg Tristan und Isolde* (diss., Bonn, 1946). O. Sayce in "Der Begriff *edelez herze* im *Tristan* Gottfrieds von Strassburg" (*DVLG*, 1959) takes quite the opposite view. She thinks that both "edel" and "herze" are to be taken in the senses that can be demonstrated in other contemporary Middle High German works but does not, apparently, think that the phrase may mean more than the two separate words. P. W. Tax, *Wort, Sinnbild, Zahl im Tristanroman* (1961), discusses the development of love and believes that the "edele herzen" are a special group. Although occasionally overdogmatic, Tax advances some interesting opinions on Gottfried's attitudes. His evaluation of stylistic features is less convincing.

There has been some evidence recently that the importance of what may be called the artistic-intellectual element in the poem is being recognized. W. Mohr, "*Tristan und Isold* als Künstlerroman" (*Euphorion*, 1959) stresses that the hero shows many of the characteristics of the professional Spielmann, but W. T. H. Jackson in "Tristan the Artist in Gottfried's Poem" (*PMLA*, 1962) goes further in showing that the arts, particularly music, are essential contributors to the harmony between the lovers and that *moraliteit* is a term employed by Gottfried to describe this moral and intellectual situation.

In spite of the universal recognition of the stylistic excellence of Gottfried's poem, there are still no satisfactory studies of the subject. G. Sawicki's *Gottfried von Strassburg und die Poetik des Mittelalters* (1932) is little more than a routine application of elementary rhetorical knowledge to the poem. H. Scharschuch, *Gottfried von Strassburg. Stilmittel-Stilästhetik* (*GS*, 1938), does attempt to show the very important connection between method and poetic mood. A. Dijksterhuis, *Thomas und Gottfried. Ihre konstruktiven Sprachformen* (1935), by careful statistical analysis shows that the two authors favor different stylistic patterns, with Gottfried favoring progression and Thomas parallelism. Recently there has been a spate of studies of the nature description in *Tristan*, of which the only one of real significance is R. Gruenter, "Das Wunnecliche Tal" (*Euphorion*, 1962), which analyzes the scenes in great detail and studies the sources. This may be regarded as a definitive study. The same author's "Bauformen der Waldleben-Episode in Gottfrieds *Tristan und Isold*" (*Festschrift Müller*, 1957) is concerned with the symmetrical structure of the episode. There have been similarly detailed treatments of the prologue. H. de Boor, "Der strophische Prolog zum Tristan Gottfrieds von Strassburg" (*PBB*, 1959), demonstrates a deliberate division into two parts, one on the relation *guot/lop*, the other identifying the poem's audience. J. H. Scholte, "Gottfrieds Tristan-Einleitung" (*ZDP*, 1932) and "Gottfrieds von Strassburg Initialenspiel" (*PBB*, 1942), both produce evidence of deliberate seeking for symmetry in character-drawing and style. A. Schöne, "Zu Gottfrieds Tristan-Prolog" (*DVLG*, 1955), is also concerned with the questions of symmetry and the audience to which the poem is addressed.

There has been one full-length study of the role of Isolde of the White Hands, G. Meissburger, *Tristan und Isolde mit den weissen Händen. Die Auffassung der Minne, der Liebe und der Ehe bei Gottfried von Strassburg und Ulrich von Türheim* (1954), which treats the role as symbol of the move of Tristan toward unfaithfulness and death.

M. E. Valk has prepared a *Word-Index to Gottfried's Tristan* (1958). Gottfried's vocabulary is discussed by F. Mosselman, *Der Wortschatz Gottfrieds von Strassburg* (1953).

XIII. OTHER COURTLY ROMANCES

THERE HAS BEEN remarkably little written on these works, which in bulk far exceed the works of the great classical writers already discussed. Although no one would claim any great literary merit for most of them, they do have some interesting features that would repay investigation. Criticism up to now has been mostly concerned with sources and relations with other works.

A. MORIZ VON CRAÛN

This enigmatic romance, which may be a parody or a serious study of the *minne/lohn* relationship, has been recently edited by U. Pretzel (*AdTb*, 1962). His first edition (1956), which contained a large number of emendations of the readings of the one extant manuscript, was severely criticized. The revised edition has restored many manuscript readings. All the scholarship, as well as the numerous problems, including the uncertain date of composition, are dealt with by R. Harvey, *Moriz von Craûn and the Chivalric World* (1961), which discusses in detail not only the work itself but such associated questions as the forms of the tournament. Only the esthetic questions are somewhat sketchily treated. The edition of Pretzel and Miss Harvey's book together provide a complete bibliography.

B. RUDOLF VON EMS

No general study of the works of Rudolf has appeared in our period. There are text studies by E. Kopp, *Untersuchungen zu den Werken Rudolfs von Ems* (diss., Freie Univ., Berlin, 1957), and by C. von Kraus, *Text und Entstehung von Rudolfs Alexander* (1940). The difference in morality and religious feeling between Rudolf and the authors of the classical period is well brought out in two works on the cultural background, A. Elsberger, *Das Weltbild Rudolfs von Ems in seiner Alexanderdichtung* (diss., Erlangen, 1939), and F. Sengle, "Die Patrizierdichtung. *Der gute Gerhard.* Soziologische und dichtungsgeschichtliche Studien zur Frühzeit Rudolfs von Ems" (*DVLG*, 1950). J. A. Asher, the most active scholar in this field, has produced a good new edition of *Der guote Gêrhart* (*AdTb*, 1962) as well as a study of the influence of Hartmann on Rudolf (diss., Basel, 1948). There is a general study of *Barlaam and Josaphat* by H. Rupp in *Festgabe Bender* (1959), and on the same poem, one of the few esthetic studies of the author, R. Wisbey, "Zum *Barlaam und Josaphat* Rudolfs von Ems" (*ZDA*, 1956), which points out that the poem shows evidence of extensive use of number symbolism but relies on typology less than might have been expected in a poem on such a subject.

C. ULRICH VON TÜRHEIM

H. F. Rosenfeld has contributed two studies on the textual tradition of *Rennewart* in *ZDA* (1944) and *PBB* (1951). The only other work is a study of the proverbial elements in the poem, A. Leitzmann, "Sprichwörter und Sprichwörtliches bei Ulrich von Türheim" (*PBB*, 1942).

D. KONRAD FLECK

E. Schall, *Konrad Flecks Floire und Blanscheflur, Ein Vergleich mit den Zeitgenossen und mit dem mittelniederdeutschen Gedicht Flos und Blankeflos* (diss., Marburg, 1941), is interesting only because it is one of the few editions in which High and Low German material has been compared directly.

E. KONRAD VON WÜRZBURG

There have been a few attempts to rescue the reputation of Konrad, of which the most straightforward is that by A. Moret, *Un Artiste méconnu, Conrad de Wurzebourg* (1932); but to most readers he remains little more than a name, particularly since several of his works are available only in antiquated editions (*Partonopier*, 1871; *Trojanerkrieg*, 1858). A great deal of the literature consists, typically enough, of unpublished dissertations on routine topics.

Of the works on the poet's general achievement, the most important are the stylistic study by E. Rast, *Vergleich, Gleichnis, Metapher und Allegorie bei Konrad von Wurzburg* (diss., Heidelberg, 1936), which classifies these figures of speech, and Irmgard Riechert, *Studien zur Auffassung der "ere" bei Konrad von Wurzburg und Rudolf von Ems* (diss., Freiburg, 1952), a topic which might be studied in connection with other writers so that the whole question of *ere* could be clarified. The most significant work on an individual poem is again by A. Moret, *L'originalité de Conrad de Wurzbourg dans son poème "Partonopier und Meliur"* (1933). It is a detailed verbal, stylistic, and rhetorical comparison of the poem with its French source. D. H. Green adduces some of the features of Konrad's style to contribute evidence for his belief in the existence of a "Gothic" style in literature as well as art. The problem of the conception of classical antiquity by medieval German writers and its reconciliation with Christian ideas is the subject of two dissertations, one by S. Schell, *Mittelhochdeutsche Trojanerkriege. Studien zur Rezeption der Antike bei Herbort von Fritzlar und Konrad von Würzburg* (Freiburg i.B., 1953), the other by G. Schade, *Christentum und Antike in den deutschen Trojaepen des Mittelalters* (Freie Univ., Berlin, 1955).

F. JÜNGERER TITUREL

W. Wolf has begun a new edition of the text, of which the first volume appeared in 1955 (*DTM*, No. 45). He has also written several articles on text and authorship (*ZDA*, 1939, 1942, 1952). He believes the poem was written by Albrecht von Scharfenberg. Wolf has a study of the metrics of the poem in *Festschrift F. R. Schröder* (1959). There is an important chapter on the poem in Helen Adolf, *Visio Pacis* (1961).

G. HEINRICH VON NEUSTADT

There are two studies of his vocabulary, one by E. Öhrmann, "Italienisches bei Heinrich von Neustadt" (*NM*, 1954), the other by H. Fromm, "Ungarisches Wortgut bei Heinrich von Neustadt" (*Ural-altaische Jahrbücher*, 1959).

There is little point in dwelling on the later Arthurian romances. Almost all of the critical work consists of dissertations, largely in typescript, on minor points. A long series of dissertations from Vienna on the rhymes of these authors is typical. The third volume of H. de Boor's history gives an up-to-date survey and bibliographical information.

XIV. POPULAR EPICS

THE TERM is used for those narrative poems whose subject matter is Germanic, as opposed to the "courtly" epics whose themes are French or classical. Interest in the popular epic has declined considerably. Since few critics try to maintain the theory of strictly German origins, attention has been concentrated on the demonstrable relations between the German epics and Norse, Romance, and

Slavic works. Study of the *Nibelungenlied* naturally predominates. The "origins" theory of A. Heusler, first promulgated in his *Nibelungensage und Nibelungenlied* (1921), has been widely accepted and indeed has caused a decline in speculation on the subject. A serious challenge has come from F. Panzer in his articles (see below) and especially in his book *Das Nibelungenlied* (1955), and he has attracted a considerable critical following. He postulates much more non-Germanic influence than does Heusler. Critics are not so sure as they used to be of the qualities of the typical Germanic hero, but there is still a curious reluctance to examine characterization in the works, and stylistic studies in this genre lag far behind those in the lyric and romance.

Material on the early history of "heroic" poetry may be found in the chapter on Anglo-Saxon literature (*Beowulf*) and the sections of this book on Norse and Old High German. To these may be added the general survey of the topic by H. Schneider, "Germanische Heldensage, I" in *Grundriss der germanischen Philologie* (1928), and F. Panzer, "Die nationale Epik Deutschlands und Frankreichs und ihr geschichtlicher Zusammenhang" (*Zeitschrift für deutsche Bildung*, 1937), which stresses the features common to all national epics. Similarly K. Wais, *Frühe Epik Westeuropas und die Vorgeschichte des Nibelungenliedes*, Vol. I. (1953), sees Nibelungen material in all western European epic writings.

The disputes on the priority of the various texts no longer have any validity. The easiest approach to the problem is in the discussion by H. Brackert, *Beiträge zur Handschriftenkritik des Nibelungenliedes* (1963), in which the author separates special material from the main textual tradition but finds it impossible to establish an "original" form of the poem. The editions of the A-Text by K. Lachmann (1926), of the B-Text by K. Bartsch (1860), and of the C-Text by F. Zarncke (1899) have been frequently reprinted but not changed in any important particular. De Boor combines his reworking of Bartsch with a good facing translation.

A. NIBELUNGENLIED

Reviews of Research. By far the most important review of research for English-speaking readers is M. Thorp, *The Study of the Nibelungenlied* (1940). This traces the various attitudes toward the poem from 1795 to 1937 and offers a detailed and well-written review of scholarship. It is particularly useful for the history of the textual criticism of the poem. Two reviews that are more concerned with current criticism are H. Schneider, "Der heutige Stand der

Nibelungenforschung" (*FuF*, 1942), and J. F. Röttger, *Das Nibelungenlied im Lichte der neuesten Forschung* (1949). The most recent review is M. Fleet, "The Recent Study of the Nibelungenlied" (*JEGP*, 1953).

General Studies. The most important general work of the last two decades is F. Panzer, *Das Nibelungenlied* (1955). It is strong and original on such questions as the origins of the work and its relation to other literatures, weak in its study of form and style. It may be regarded as the culmination of the older type of popular epic criticism. W. J. Schröder's "Das *Nibelungenlied*. Versuch einer Deutung" (*PBB*, 1954) is a light-against-darkness study, showing the courtly pitted against the primitive. This view is rejected by B. Nagel in "Probleme der Nibelungenlieddeutung" (*ZDP*, 1956) as a too abstract and forced reading of the poem. His own interpretation, in "Zur Interpretation und Wertung des Nibelungenliedes" (*Neue Heidelberger Jahrbücher*, 1954), sees the work as composed by one author with a strict plan in which all details conform. D. von Kralik, "Das Nibelungenlied," in *Von deutscher Art in Sprache und Dichtung*, Vol. II (1941), also argues for individual authorship, but of finished songs that were then joined together. Although they are technically too late for this survey, mention should be made of two recent works. W. Krogmann, *Der Dichter des Nibelungenliedes* (1962), makes out a good but not completely convincing case for Der von Kürenberg as author. G. Weber, *Das Nibelungenlied* (1963), is criticism of a new sort in this field. It has little to say about the traditional source and origin controversies, but devotes itself to the cultural and, if the term may be used, philosophical backgrounds and their realization in the poem. The characters, in particular Hagen, are studied from this point of view, with interesting results. The work is at times as abstract and obscure as the author's *Tristan* study, but it is challenging and new. Weber also has an account of the poem in the Sammlung Metzler Series (1961).

H. M. Fleet, "Recent Approaches to the Problem of the Authorship of the *Nibelungenlied*" (*London Mediaeval Studies*, 1951), is a summary of views on the subject and an attempt to assess the author's originality. O. Höfler, "Die Anonymität des Nibelungenliedes" (*DVLG*, 1955), presents a more traditional view when he says that anonymity was normal in heroic poetry, as distinct from romance. Many critics have seen in the poem an attempt by an author to make a romance out of older Germanic material—for example, Nelly Dürrenmatt in her dissertation, *Das Nibelungenlied im Kreis der höfischen Dichtung* (Bern, 1945). Other critics have stressed the importance of the courtly element and questioned the author's real purpose—for example, H. Naumann in *Euphorion* (1942) and B. Mergell in *Euphorion* (1950).

Sources. We have already pointed out the continuing importance of Heusler's theory. Most of the studies here discussed are of specific questions. H. de Boor in *Das Attilabild in Geschichte, Legende und heroischer Dichtung* (1932) points out the conflict between the south-eastern, favorable view of Attila and the north-western, hostile view. This accounts for many of the discrepancies between the *Edda* and *Nibelungenlied* versions of the downfall of the Burgundians. The possibility of confusion of names, so often ignored by critics, is well brought out by G. Baesecke in "Gudrun-Kriemhilt, Grimhild-Uote, Gutthorm-Gernot" (*PBB*, 1936). D. von Kralik, *Die Sigfridtrilogie im Nibelungenlied und in der Thidrekssaga*, Vol. I (1941), expands the views noted in his general articles above. H. de Boor, "Hat Siegfried gelebt?" (*PBB*, 1939), discusses the belief that Siegfried may be connected with a historical Merovingian king. H. Schneider, particularly in *Die deutschen Lieder von Siegfrieds Tod* (1947), argues for the individuality of separate Kriemhilde and Brunhilde songs. Mary Thorp seeks to establish a definite archetype of the Nibelungen legend in *JEGP* (1938), and H. Hempel sees influence from Saxon sources, "Sächsische Nibelungendichtung und sächsischer Ursprung der Thidrikssaga" (*Festschrift Genzmer*, 1952). J. Bumke in *Euphorion* (1960) and *GRM* (1960) stresses the multiplicity of the sources. J. de Vries, *Heldenlied en Heldensage* (1961), a study of the rise of epic poetry, has a chapter on the *Nibelungenlied* that does little but repeat well-known material. The whole book is old-fashioned in its concern for "origins" rather than esthetic evaluation. The same author has a comparison between the *Nibelungenlied* and the work of Homer in *AKG* (1956) that sees both as deliberate artistic creations. As a final contribution to the sources, we may mention K. E. Wädekin, "*Nibelungenlied* und deutsch-russische Beziehungen im Mittelalter" (*PBB*, 1951), which supports the view of Slavic influence mooted by Panzer.

In sum it may be said that the numerous studies succeed in showing only that there are almost infinite possibilities of source material for the poem and in pointing up the danger of seeking exact knowledge from such fragmentary evidence.

Form and Structure. This subject is naturally connected closely with the sources. If we assume with Heusler that the poem as we know it was not put together until the late twelfth or early thirteenth century, its structure must depend largely on the form of the earlier works from which it is derived. J. Fourquet, "Zum Aufbau des Nibelungenliedes und des Kudrunleides" (*ZDA*, 1954), stresses that evidence of earlier independence is clear in the extant versions of the two works, and that the *Nibelungenlied* is held together by the motif of Kriemhild's revenge. Two discussions lay special stress on the importance of the predictions of events in the poem as structural features that help to preserve its unity by knitting events together: S. Beyschlag, "Die Funktion der epischen Vorausdeutung im Aufbau des Nibelungenliedes" (*PBB*, 1954), and B. Wachinger, *Studien zum Nibelungenlied. Vorausdeutung, Aufbau, Motivierung* (1960). Mary Thorp has two articles on the unity and style in *JEGP* (1937 and 1938).

Special Subjects. The most interesting of these deal with the characters and motivating forces in the poem. W. Schröder, "Die Tragödie Kreimhilts im Nibelungenlied" (*ZDA*, 1960), points out that her conduct is consistent and entirely motivated by love for Siegfried. He thus disagrees with H. Kuhn, who, in "Kriemhilds Hort und Rache" (*Festschrift P. Kluckhohn und H. Schneider*, 1948), regards the demand for the treasure at the end of the poem as artistically inappropriate. The character of Rüdeger has attracted some attention. The dilemma of conflicting loyalties that he faces is examined by G. F. Jones in *SP* (1960), and he is shown to be essentially a figure of *feudal* loyalty by P. Wapnewski in "Rüdegers Schild. Zur 37. Aventiure des Nibelungenliedes" (*Euphorion*, 1960). The larger question of the moral and philosophical influences that shaped the behavior of the characters, especially Rüdeger, is taken up by W. Fechter in *Siegfrieds Schuld und das Weltbild des Nibelungenliedes* (1948) and by B. Nagel, "Heidnisches und Christliches im *Nibelungenlied*" (*RC*, 1958). W. Mohr, "Giselher" (*ZDA*, 1941), is interesting in its assertion that the author used the character to show that heroic qualities need to develop. The latest study of Dietrich is by B. Nagel in *ZDP* (1959 and 1960).

There have been numerous studies of place names and their connection with the sources of the works—by T. Frings in *PBB* (1937), by F. P. Magoun, Jr., in *ZDA* (1949) and in *MS* (1945). Most interesting is K. F. Stroheker, "Studien zu den historisch-geographischen Grundlagen der Nibelungenlieddichtung" (*DVLG*, 1958), which attempts to explain the present form of the story by postulating a mixture of Burgundians, Franks, and others in North Burgundy in the sixth and seventh centuries. It was therefore in this region that the Siegfried and Burgundian stories joined. F. Panzer, "Der Weg der Nibelunge" (*Festschrift Helm*, 1951), compares the poet's description with historical fact and shows that the author knew the southern route in detail but modified fact sometimes to suit his poem.

E. Ploss, "Die Datierung des Nibelungenliedes" (*PBB*, 1958), argues that the words "Azagouc" and "Zazamanc" were taken by Wolfram from the *Nibelungenlied* and not vice-versa and hence that *Parzival* is the later work. The rather obscure question of the connection between the deaths of Brunhild and Kriemhilde is examined by Hans Kuhn in *ZDA* (1948). P. A. Becker, "Zur Jagd im Odenwald" (*PBB*, 1948), takes up and rejects the possibility of influence of the *chansons de geste* and other French works. G. Nordmeyer examines the sources of Kriemhilde's falcon dream in *GR* (1940).

B. KUDRUN

The relation between the poem and the numerous works whose principal theme is the winning or stealing of a bride is traced by H. Marquardt in *ZDA* (1933). Various theories have been advanced to account for the obvious mixture of subject matter and morality in the poem. I. Schröbler, *Wikingische und spielmännische Elemente im zweiten Teil des Gudrunliedes* (1934), thinks that the Hilde and Gudrun parts are clearly differentiated and that they grew independently. W. Jungandeas in *ZDP* (1943) and in *Die Gudrunsage in den Ober- und Niederlanden. Eine Vorgeschichte des Epos* (1948) argues that the Hilde material is Germanic but the Gudrun part is too unheroic and must be taken from thirteenth-century ballad material. B. Boesch's "Kudrunepos und der Ursprung der deutschen Ballade" (*GRM*, 1940) makes the same point. H. W. J. Kroes, "Gudrunprobleme" (*Neophil*, 1954), evolves a theory not unlike that of Schröbler, in which he postulates the existence of an eleventh-century Norse poem in which Gudrun is the victim of a raid. The conflict between the "heroic" constancy of Gudrun in the face of trials and the fact that the poem ends with reconciliation has exercised several critics, particularly L. Wolff in *WW* (1954), and brought them to the conclusion that the author did not understand heroic poetry and merely added a sentimental ending. A. Beck, "Die Rache als Motiv und Problem in der Kudrum" (*GRM*, 1956), similarly is concerned with the modifications of the revenge idea. Text criticism is somewhat limited by the existence of only one manuscript, but there are some observations by M. H. Jellinek in *ZDA* (1935). There is one style study during this period, F. W. de Wall, *Studien zum Stil der Kudrun* (diss., Königsberg, 1939). Beck remarks in the article cited above that there is much evidence in the poem of failure to develop some of the motivations that had been introduced. There is a useful introduction to the poem by Roswitha Wisniewski, *Heldendichtung III. Kudrun* (1963), in the Sammlung Metzler Realienbücher. The oldest document of Yiddish literature, an adaptation of *Kudrun* and other heroic material (c. 1382), has been edited by L. Fuks (1957). Ingeborg Schröbler comments on the work in *ZDA* (1958).

C. DIETRICH EPICS

The most comprehensive treatment is that of G. Zink, *Les légendes héroiques de Dietrich et d'Ermrich dans les littératures allemandes* (1950), a very detailed study of the sources and of the stories that antedate the written versions. The same author also has a good selection of texts, *Le cycle de Dietrich, Morceaux choisis* (1953). The main interest of T. Steche, *Das Rabenschlachtgedicht, das Buch von Bern und die Entwicklung der Dietrichsage* (1939), is similarly in ultimate and hence lost sources, but he has also a rather superficial examination of the style of the individual poems. There is a general study of the figure of Dietrich von Bern by W. Mohr, *ZDA* (1944), and H. de Boor examines heroic names in historical context, *ZDA* (1942). E. Benedikt, "Die Überlieferung vom Ende Dietrichs von Bern" (*Festschrift Kralik*, 1954), collects all the versions of Dietrich's death and concludes that the common feature they present, that is, his disappearance, suggests that the historical Theodoric's body was actually removed.

Two dissertations on *Alpharts Tod* are surveys of research rather than original contributions—H. Vogelsang, "Studien zur Entwicklungsgeschichte von *Alpharts Tod*" (Bern, 1949), and E. Maurer, "Vollständiges Glossar zu Alpharts Tod mit einer Einleitung über die bisherige Behandlung des Gedichtes in der wissenschaftlichen Literatur" (Vienna, 1952). G. Eis, "Zu Dietrichs Slawenkämpfen. I. Dietrich und Wenezlan" (*ZDA*, 1952), uses heraldry to date the poem, which he believes to be a genuine heroic poem, not a later fabrication. Caroline Brady's *The Legends of Ermanaric* (1943) is a useful work that traces the connection between the poems and their historical background, and from this information attempts to explain the contradictions in the treatment of the character. K. Ranke, *Rosengarten, Recht und Totenkult* (1951), attempts to fit the figure of Dietrich into his research on the legends of the living dead, and similarly J. Nadler, "Goldhort, Rosengarten, Gral" (*Festschrift Kralik*, 1954), sees the influence of Catharism in all three symbols. H. Becker, *Spottlied, Märchen und Heldenlied vom Rosengarten* (1955), takes the texts of three works on the same subject and shows how they underwent different treatment to produce the three types mentioned in his title.

T. Dahlberg, *Zum dänischen Lavrin und zum niederdeutschen Lorin* (1950), offers the text of the latter work and detailed textual and linguistic material, as well as the comparison mentioned in the title.

D. HÜRNEN SIEGFRIED

There is a new edition by K. C. King (1958) that has an extensive introduction dealing with problems of text and history of the story. These remarks are supplemented by his articles, "Siegfried's Fight with the Dragon in the *Edda* and in the *Hürnen Seyfrid*" (*London Mediaeval Studies*, 1937–39) and "Das Lied vom Hürnen Siegfried. The Printers and Orthography of a Sixteenth-Century German Text" (*BJRL*, 1952). S. Gutenbrunner, "Sigfrids Tod im Hürnen Seyfried. Ein Rekonstruktionsversuch" (*ZDP*, 1960), attempts to restore the strophes to the original Middle High German.

XV. LYRIC POETRY

THERE HAVE BEEN many new studies and formulations about lyric poetry during the period under review. Interest in terminology and philosophical and theological background has been greater than that in origins, and in the areas of style and metrics important new works have appeared. C. von Kraus, *Untersuchungen zum Minnesangs Frühling* (1939), sums up the author's outstanding contributions to lyric poetry in the fields of textual criticism, metrics, and interpretation of individual poems. The two most useful books on the lyric in general are of very different types. A. Moret, *Les débuts du lyrisme en Allemagne des origines à 1350* (1951), is a superbly lucid and objective account both of the rise of lyric poetry and of earlier scholarship. It has such valuable aids as lists of *Minnesänger* with all known biographical facts. Its weakness consists in its lack of any personal attitudes and its tendency to take refuge from difficult problems by the use of pleasant-sounding clichés. H. Kolb's *Der Begriff der Minne und das Entstehen der höfischen Lyrik* (1958) is a highly complex study of backgrounds, of the conception of love, and of the terminology of love poetry that goes far beyond German literature. It is particularly useful for its citation and even quotation of passages from German and the Romance languages, which support the author's views of word usage. Kolb regards the courtly lyric as a reflection of European thought of the late twelfth century ("twelfth-century humanism"); he rejects Arab influence. The literature cited in the notes to these two works amounts to a critical bibliography of medieval lyric.

Of the other works on the lyric in general that have appeared in our period, S. Singer, *Die religiöse Lyrik des Mittelalters* (1933), emphasizes the importance of the Psalms and the crusading spirit for its development, while M. Ittenbach, *Der frühe deutsche Minnesang* (1939), puts forward some original ideas on the structure of the earliest German lyric poetry. The character of the works of those poets who followed Walther von der Vogelweide is carefully studied by H. Kuhn in *Minnesangs Wende* (1952), who makes clear what their innovations were as well as their dependence on tradition.

Much of the discussion of the *Minnesang* is centered on the meaning of certain terms, including the word "Minne" itself, and the importance of such definition can be seen from the fact that H. Furstner's *Studien zur Wesensbestimmung der höfischen Minne* (1956) centers on the contrast between *hohe minne*, that is, the type of idealized love found in such poets as Reinmar, and *echte liebe*, the genuine love that occurs in some of the poems of Walther von der Vogelweide. Many discussions, such as that of P. Schmid, "Die Entwicklung der Begriffe 'Minne' und 'Liebe' im deutschen Minnesang bis Walther" (*ZDP*, 1941), concentrate on attempts to make fine distinctions between the two terms, which cannot be justified by their use in the poetry. Other studies of terminology are X. von Ertzdorff, "Studien zum Begriff des Herzens und seiner Verwendung als Aussagemotiv in der höfischen Liebeslyrik des 12. Jahrhunderts" (diss., Freiburg im Breisgau, 1958), and H. Götz, *Leitwörter des Minnesangs* (*ASAW*, 1951).

The Arabic theory of the origins of the love lyric has been accepted, at least in part, by many critics, but it is of more importance for Romance than for German poetry, since there is no question about the immediate origins of German poetry. The relation of the *Minnesang* to the Provençal, both in words and music, has been explored by T. Frings, *Minnesinger und Troubadours*

(1949). Both here and in "Altspanische Mädchenlieder aus *des Minnesangs Frühling*" (*PBB*, 1951) he presents a thesis that is gaining ground, namely, that "popular" poetry, not folk song in the nineteenth-century sense, provided the impulse for medieval love poetry. This theory does not show how its characteristic sophistication can be explained. L. Spitzer in "The Mozarabic Lyric and Theodor Frings' Theories" (*CL*, 1952) commented on these views with his usual learning and brilliance. I. Frank, *Trouvères et Minnesänger*, Vol. I (1952), performs the useful service of showing what few direct connections can be found between German poems and apparent Romance models. The second volume of the work (1956), by H. Müller-Blattau, does the same for the music.

There are two dissertations that take note of the presence of formal, didactic, and even educational elements in the lyrics, K. J. Heinisch, *Antike Bildungselemente im frühen deutschen Minnesang* (diss., Bonn, 1934), and A. Hahn, *Bildhafte Elemente im deutschen Minnesang* (diss., Bonn, 1949). The study of the landscape descriptions received new impetus with the advent of the *topos* theories of Curtius, as may be seen in A. Moret, "La nature dans le Minnesang" (*EG*, 1948) and in his book mentioned above. However, longer—though less useful—treatments of the natural description antedate Curtius: L. Schneider, *Die Naturdichtung des deutschen Minnesangs* (*Neue deutsche Forschungen*, 1938), and, for the later *Minnesang*, P. B. Wessels, *Die Landschaft im jüngeren Minnesang* (1947). A. T. Hatto's "The Lime Tree and Early German, Goliard, and English Lyric Poetry" (*MLR*, 1954) is a collection of the passages in which the lime tree is clearly a symbol of love and fertility.

It is notorious that women normally have very little to say in the *Minnesang*. The relation between their rare speeches and the preservation of the ideal of womanhood is examined by Erika Mergell, *Die Frauenrede im deutschen Minnesang* (diss., Frankfurt, 1940), and T. Frings, "Frauenstrophe und Frauenlied in der frühen deutschen Lyrik" (*Festschrift Korff*, 1957). Typical of the new approach to the criticism of the *Minnesang* is an article on the important, but hitherto unnoticed, question of how far one is justified in identifying the "I" of the poems with the author and how far it represents a "persona"—X. von Ertzdorff, "Das 'ich' in der höfischen Liebeslyrik des 12. Jahrunderts" (*Archiv*, 1960).

A. FORM AND STRUCTURE

The outstanding work of F. Gennrich on form and structure has emphasized the close association between words and music. His *Grundriss einer Formenlehre des mittelalterlichen Liedes* (1932), articles in *DVLG* (1931), and *Troubadours, Trouvères, Minne- und Meistergesang* (1951) are the standard treatments. H. de Boor, "Langzeilen und lange Zeilen in Minnesangs Frühling" (*ZDP*, 1933), shows the development of the characteristic short lines of the best period from the long lines of the earlier lyric. The relation of words and melodies is taken up by F. Ackermann in *WW* (1959) and, more formally, by A. T. Hatto and R. J. Taylor in "Recent Work on the Arithmetical Principle in Medieval Poetry" (*MLR*, 1951), which shows how the melodic pattern can be reflected in the stress- and/or syllable- count of the metrical units. The arrangement of themes and the difficult question of continuity of sense in the later lyric poetry is discussed by K. H. Bertau in his article, "Über Themenanordnung und Bildung inhaltlicher Zusammenhänge in der religiösen Leichdichtung des XIII. Jahrhunderts" (*ZDP*, 1957). There has been considerable discussion about the widespread use of the *contrafactura*, that is, the use of a melody from one song in another of a different type—for example, a hymm tune in secular poetry. There is no doubt that such *contrafacturae* existed, and the evidence produced by F. Gennrich in "Liedkontrafaktur in mittelhochdeutscher und althochdeutscher Zeit" (*ZDA*, 1948–50) seems sound. A useful recent survey of the music/text relation is R. J. Taylor, *Die Melodien der weltlichen Lieder des Mittelalters* (2 vols., 1964).

B. TEXTS

The latest editions of *des Minnesangs Frühling* have been revised by C. von Kraus (1950, 1953), and the work remains the standard edition for all lyric poets before Walther von der Vogelweide. C. von Kraus and H. Kuhn, *Deutsche Liederdichter des 13. Jahrhunderts* (2 vols., 1952–54), provides texts for the thirteenth-century writers. There is a selection from these texts in H. Kuhn, *Minnesang des 13. Jahrhunderts, mit Übertragung der Melodien von G. Reichert* (1953).

There are several excellent anthologies, such as A. Moret's *Anthologie du Minnesang* (1949) and H. Brinkmann's *Liebeslyrik der deutschen Frühe in zeitlicher Folge* (1952). M. Wehrli, *Deutsche Lyrik des Mittelalters* (1955), provides literal versions in modern German facing the Middle High German text, with notes and reproductions of the "Manesse" miniatures.

XVI. INDIVIDUAL LYRICISTS

A. EARLY POETS

THERE HAVE BEEN two useful discussions of the *Falkenlied* of Der von Kürenberg: G. Nordmeyer, "Zur Auffassung des Kürenbergfalken" (*GR*, 1943), and P. Wapnewski, "Des Kurenbergers Falkenlied" (*Euphorion*, 1959). The latter is particularly interesting for its use of the technical vocabulary of falconry in elucidating the poem. K. Rathke in *Dietmar von Aist: Form und Geist* (1932) sees Dietmar as a poet of transition who knew the French lyricists but used remodeled German forms for his own poetry. There are two general evaluations of the development and achievement of Heinrich von Veldeke as a lyric poet, by T. Frings in *Festschrift für P. Kluckhohn und H. Schneider* (1948), and by H. Thomas in *PBB* (Halle, 1956). Friedrich von Hausen's most famous poem, "Mîn herze und mîn lîp diu wellent scheiden," is analyzed by G. Jungbluth in *Euphorion* (1953).

B. HARTMANN VON AUE

There has been little written on Hartmann's lyric poetry. H. Stolte (*DVLG*, 1951) argues that the famous "widow's lament" is not, in fact, spoken by a woman but is a lament by Hartmann for his master before going on the Crusade of 1189.

C. REINMAR DER ALTE

There is a great deal about Reinmar in such general works as C. von Kraus's *Untersuchungen* and H. Kolb, *Begriff der Minne*. Special articles have dealt largely with his relations with Walther von der Vogelweide, which are discussed in the next section. There is a dictionary of his poetry by W. Bulst, *Wörterbuch zu den Liedern Reinmars des Alten* (diss., Heidelberg, 1934).

D. WALTHER VON DER VOGELWEIDE

After a period in which Walther was admired chiefly as a "German" poet, criticism has concentrated mainly on the form, meter, and religion of his poems. There has been curiously little effort to discuss the political and social aspects of his poetry. In particular, the fundamental question of what effects he hoped to produce by writing it and what kind of audience he could expect have gone unanswered. The question of patronage is, of course, fundamental, but surely he hoped that his poetry would be heard by others, particularly the uncommitted.

For factual information about the life and times of the poet, W. Wilmann's edition and notes (1924) remain standard. Lachmann's edition, of which the latest printing is edited by C. von Kraus (1959), is supplemented by F. Maurer, ed. *Die Lieder Walthers von der Vogelweide* (2 vols., 1955–56). The first volume is devoted to the moral and political songs and the second to the love poetry. The poems are arranged in each volume in (Maurer's) chronological order, and the melodies, when available, are transcribed into modern notation. There is a very useful selection with modern German facing versions and good notes by P. Wapnewski (1962).

The principal aims of Walther research were set out by C. von Kraus in *FuF* (1935). His own *Untersuchungen zu Walther von der Vogelweide* (1935) takes up many of the fundamental questions, particularly those concerned with textual problems and the interpretation of individual works.

An interesting contribution to the vexed question of Walther's place of origin is made by K. K. Klein in *Zur Spruchdichtung und Heimatfrage Walthers von der Vogelweide (Beiträge zur Waltherforschung*, 1952). He examines in particular Walther's accounts of such purely personal experiences as those described in the visit to the Tegernsee monastery and the quarrel with Gerhard Atze. He comes to the conclusion that his original home probably was the Tyrol. Criticism of the political *Sprüche* has consisted largely in comparing their ideas with those of the medieval theorists on the relation between empire and papacy; see, for example, K. Burdach in *DVLG* (1935), and J. Müller in *Neue Jahrbücher für Wissenschaft und Jugendbildung* (1936). H. Böhm's *Walther von der Vogelweide, Minne, Reich, Gott* (2nd ed. 1949) is a popular work stressing that Walther was a German-Christian poet—hardly an original conclusion. R. Zitzmann, "Der Ordo-Gedanke des mittelalterlichen Weltbildes und Walthers Sprüche im ersten Reichston" (*DVLG*, 1951), shows that the poet was fully aware of the formal world order of the church and sought to apply that concept of order to the secular world and its government. The poem in which this concept appears most clearly, "ich horte ein wazzer diezen," was discussed by R. Kienast in *Gymnasium* (1950). A. T. Hatto discussed the Ottonian poems in *Speculum* (1949).

The most important—and the most controversial—contribution to the study of the *Sprüche* is F. Maurer's *Die politischen Lieder Walthers von der Vogelweide* (1954), which argues that the brief political and social poems usually called *Sprüche* were in fact conceived as strophes of songs and were therefore written in the same melody (*Ton*). We would thus have to recognize as one song, series of strophes that must have been written at intervals of several years. This view has been sharply criticized. H. Moser in "*Sprüche* oder *politische Lieder* Walthers?" (*Euphorion*, 1958) agrees only partly with Maurer. Except for the *Sprüche*, the most detailed attention has been given to Walther's long elegy written in later life. There is a detailed study of its structure by D. Kralik, *Die Elegie Walthers von der Vogelweide* (1952), and briefer, more general accounts by M. Wehrli (*Trivium*, 1943) and H. Brinkmann (*WW*, 1954).

Although no critic denies that Walther was a deeply religious man, there have been the usual attempts to find out what kind of religious man he was. F. Wagemann, *Die Religiosität Walthers von der Vogelweide* (diss., Heidelberg, 1938), attempts to prove by a detailed examination of his utterances on ethics, God, and so forth, that he was a true member of the church. This is probably true enough, provided that one interprets "church" sufficiently generously. K. Burdach (*ZDP*, 1935) suggests that Walther created his "guter Klausner" as a type of unpolitical piety, in contrast to the church under Innocent III; H. Brinkmann states (*WW*, 1950) that he "has found a poem" that sums up Walther's views on knighthood.

Walther's relations with Wolfram von Eschenbach are discussed by T. A. Rompelmann in *Neophil* (1942), and with the bishop of Passau's entourage, by R. Newald in *Archiv für Literatur und Volksdichtung* (1949). L. Mackensen, "Zu Walthers Spiessbratenspruch" (*Festschrift Panzer*, 1950), sees the poem as evidence of a real rift with Philip II. There is an admirable study of the connections between the songs of Walther and those of Neidhart von Reuental by E. Wiessner in *ZDA* (1953), in which it is shown that the direct influence of one poem on another was slight but that Neidhart was generally influenced by Walther's poetry and ideas.

The principal contribution to the discussion of the feud between

Reinmar and Walther, by C. von Kraus in his *Untersuchungen*, consists of careful analysis of the parodistic elements both verbal and musical. D. Kralik's significant contribution to the interpretation of the poems of the feud, "Walther gegen Reinmar" (*SÖAW*, 1955), emphasizes the differences in the personalities of the poets while reviewing the language and style of the poems in detail.

There have been some significant additions to the literature on Walther's metrics. J. A. Huisman's *Neue Wege zur dichterischen und musikalischen Technik Walthers von der Vogelweide* (1950) and K. H. Schirmer's *Die Strophik Walthers von der Vogelweide* (1956) are both important studies largely concerned with number patterns in Walther's metrics. The evidence these studies produce of the significance of these patterns is striking. It should be noted that there is no doubt that Walther did make use of number symbolism. R. Ruck's *Walther von der Vogelweide, der künstlerische Gedankenaufbau im ersten Philippston und im ersten Ottoton* (1954) is a not very successful attempt to show that each *Ton* had its own rules and sequence of thought.

E. HEINRICH VON MORUNGEN

Except for Walther, more useful material has appeared about Heinrich than about any other *Minnesänger*. Most important is the realization that his poems can be shown to fit into a definite cycle that follows the various stages of the poet's "love-history." The original impetus to these studies was given by J. Schwietering in "Der Liederzyklus Heinrichs von Morungen" (*ZDA*, 1948–50), and it has been continued by several scholars. Among these are C. von Kraus in his studies of the *Minnesang* and in the notes to his edition of Heinrich's poetry (2nd ed. 1950), and J. Kibelka in his Tübingen dissertation, *Heinrich von Morungen, Lied und Liedfolge als Ausdruck mittelalterlichen Kunstwollens* (1949). F. Maurer in *Festschrift Trier* (1955) compares the rhythmic organization and the sequence of thought in the poems and shows that the relation between these two often causes the rhythmic divisions to differ from the musical. C. Grünanger, *Heinrich von Morungen e il problema del Minnesang* (1948), concentrates on the more conventional problem of the poet's conception of love within the framework of the *Minnesang*. In view of the acknowledged brilliance of his style, there has been surprisingly little about Heinrich's language. F. R. Schröder discusses it briefly in *GRM* (1950), and there is an unsatisfactory discussion of his light imagery by E. J. Morrall in *London Mediaeval Studies* (1951).

F. WOLFRAM VON ESCHENBACH

There have been a few general evaluations of Wolfram's lyric by J. H. Scholte in *PBB* (1947) and W. Mohr (on the dawn songs) in *Festschrift für P. Kluckhohn and H. Schneider* (1948). A. T. Hatto applies the arithmetical principle in his article, "On Beauty of Numbers in Wolfram's Dawn Songs" (*MLR*, 1950).

G. NEIDHART VON REUENTAL

Although the attempts at localization of Neidhart's work and demonstration of his naturalism have not altogether ceased, far more attention has recently been paid to his efforts at parody and to his metrical and linguistic techniques. Two works by E. Wiessner, *Vollständiges Wörterbuch zu Neidharts Liedern* (1954) and *Kommentar zu Neidharts Liedern* (1954), are indispensable for the study of the poet's language and allusions. Even with their aid, much remains obscure. The most convenient text of the poems is *Die Lieder Neidharts von Reuental*, ed. E. Wiessner (*AdTb*, 1955). K. Winkler's *Neidhart von Reuental. Leben, Lieben, Lieder* (1956) is an extremely detailed (and in my opinion, misguided) attempt to associate the author with specific localities and events in his assumed place of residence in the Upper Palatinate. F. R. Schröder, "Die tanzlustige Alte" (*GRM*, 1951), examines the antecedents and literary significance of the most famous of Neidhart's characters. The most useful contribution to the study of the poet's metrics is A. T. Hatto and R. J. Taylor, *The Songs of Neidhart von Reuental* (1958), which offers transcriptions of the melodies and shows how they can be used to determine the rhythmic principles of the poems and their strict observance of arithmetical proportions.

XVII. MINOR LYRIC POETS

A. GENERAL

THE MOST significant work is H. Kuhn, *Minnesangs Wende*, mentioned above, which analyzes the characteristics of the later poets. A. Schlageter's *Untersuchungen über die liedhaften Zusam-*

menhänge in der nachwaltherischen Spruchlyrik (diss., Freiburg im Breisgau, 1953) attempts to show, as Maurer does for Walther, that there was a continuity of sense and form in the *Sprüche* that made them into songs. The connection is further discussed in two articles by H. Moser in *Euphorion* (1956) and *WW* (1961).

B. INDIVIDUAL POETS

There are two general evaluations of Ulrich von Lichtenstein, H. Arens, "Ulrichs von Lichtenstein Frauendienst" (*Palaestra*, 1939) and O. Höfler, "Ulrichs von Lichtenstein Venusfahrt und Artusfahrt" (*Festschrift Panzer*, 1950). The latter is a careful study of the poet's use as literary symbols of the Arthurian system of values, which for him and his contemporaries no longer had any validity for real life. Although it is fairly old, the best account of the poet Tannhäuser and the relation between the person and the fictional character who appears in the ballad of Tannhäuser is J. Siebert's *Der Dichter Tannhäuser. Leben, Gedicht, Sage* (1934). R. Haller, *Der wilde Alexander. Beiträge zur Dichtungsgeschichte des XIII. Jahrhunderts* (diss., Bonn, 1935), uses the poet's work to show the characteristics of the lyric poetry of the fourteenth century. The only detailed study of *Der wilde Alexander* is that of H. de Boor in *PBB* (1960).

C. FRAUENLOB

H. Kretschmann's *Der Stil Frauenlobs* (1933) and I. Kern's *Das höfische Gut in den Dichtungen Heinrich Frauenlobs* (1934) are both assessments of the traditional *Minnesang* stylistic features in the poet's work. There is some valuable technical information in J. Siebert's "Die Astronomie in den Gedichten des Kanzlers und Frauenlobs" (*ZDA*, 1938) and the same author's "Meistergesänge astronomischen Inhalts" (*ZDA*, 1951). The most important study of the poet's style to appear recently is R. Krayer's *Frauenlob und die Natur-Allegorese* (1960), which isolates specific allegorical motifs, traces them to Latin sources, and shows how Frauenlob developed their use. Krayer traces a specific motif, "Der Smit von Oberlande," in *AION-SG* (1959). Frauenlob's tendency to introduce religious feeling and concepts into his poetry has led to several attempts to define his religious and philosophical attitudes, for example, K. H. Bertrau, *Untersuchungen zur geistlichen Dichtung Frauenlobs* (diss., Göttingen, 1954), and B. Peter, *Die theologisch-philosophische Gedankenwelt des Heinrich Frauenlob* (diss., Mainz,

1955). There is a brief general appreciation of the poet by M. O-C. Walshe in *GL&L* (1951).

Criticism of the numerous minor poets of the period has not advanced much beyond the stage of generalized comment. The literature in the subject may be found without difficulty in the recently published third volume of H. de Boor, *Geschichte der deutschen Literatur*, which also gives by far the best account of the later lyric.

XVIII. MINOR NARRATIVE POETRY

WORKS IN THIS genre belong to the period after the *Blütezeit* of the great romances. Only one or two works have received much critical attention.

A. MEIER HELMBRECHT

The available texts are those by F. Panzer (6th ed. 1960) and C. E. Gough (1942; 2nd ed. 1947). The attempts to determine the homeland of the author are of some importance because of the opinion of several critics that Wernher der Gartenaere actually saw the events he describes. The subject is discussed by K. Schiffmann (*PBB*, 1940), C. E. Gough (*PLPLS-LHS*, 1953), and E. Lachmann (*Der Schlern*, 1954). This problem is closely connected with the so-called realism of the poem. It has been widely assumed that the poet was describing, if not events he had seen, at least events that were typical of the actual state of society in his times. This has led to a variety of studies showing how the poem reflects contemporary customs; for example, L. Schmidt in "Zur Erdkommunion im *Meier Helmbrecht*" (*GRM*, 1954) produces evidence to show how the "emergency" communion could be given by the laity, while L. Forster, "Gotelint and the Constables" (*MLR*, 1948), and G. Nordmeyer, "The Judge in the *Meier Helmbrecht*" (*MLN*, 1948), are concerned with legal aspects of the events of the story. The best-informed study of the social background is F. Martini, "Der *Meier Helmbrecht* des Wernher der Gartenaere und das mittelalterliche Bauerntum" (*Zeitschrift für Deutschkunde*, 1937). Evaluations of the literary type and purpose of the poem differ sharply. G. Nordmeyer, "Structure and Design in Wernher's *Meier Helmbrecht*" (*PMLA*, 1952), emphasizes the comic aspects of the poem, while W. T. H. Jackson, "The Composition of *Meier Helmbrecht*" (*MLQ*, 1957), regards the work as essentially a sermon using the technique of an *exemplum* and considerable illustrative detail. The connection with the parable of the prodigal son is mentioned, among others, by H. Fischer (*PBB*, 1957). The technique and symbolism of one of the illustrative passages, the long description of the cap made for the young Helmbrecht, is discussed by E. Wirtz (*MLR*, 1954). The style of the poem is discussed by H. Seidler (*ZDP*, 1944–45), and its place in the stylistic tradition of the epic by F. Tschirch, "Wernhers *Helmbrecht* in der Nachfolge von Gottfrieds *Tristan*. Zu Stil und Komposition der Novelle" (*PBB*, 1958). Vienna dissertations of 1947 provide a *Wörterbuch* to the poem (by Leopoldine Steininger) and a *Reimwörterbuch und Reimwortverzeichnis* (by Marianne Wallnstorfer).

B. DER STRICKER

There has been great activity in the publication of texts of this author: G. Rosenhagen, ed. *Mären von dem Stricker* (*AdTb*, 1934); U. Schwab, *Die bisher unveröffentlichten geistlichen Bispelreden des Strickers* (1959); H. Mettke, ed. *Fabeln und Mären von dem Stricker* (*AdTb*, 1959); H. Fischer, ed. *Der Stricker. Fünfzehn kleine Verserzählungen* (*AdTb*, 1960); U. Schwab, ed. *Der Stricker. Tierbispel* (*AdTb*, 1960). One of these editors, U. Schwab, discusses the problems of editing in *PBB* (1959).

The role of the peasant, an increasingly important feature of this kind of poetry, is discussed by Clair Baier, *Der Bauer in der Dichtung des Strickers* (1938). E. Agricola, "Die Prudentia als Anliegen der Stricker'schen Schwänke" (*PBB* [Halle], 1955), takes up the relation between the didactic and the comic in his works.

C. PFAFFE AMIS

Only H. Fischer's attempt to determine the literary genre of the work need be mentioned (*ZDA*, 1957).

D. COMIC EPICS

There are two new texts, *Von dem übeln Wibe*, ed. K. Helm (*AdTb*, 1955) and *Der Bauernhochzeitschwank. Meier Betz und Metzen hochzeit*, ed. E. Wiessner (*AdTb*, 1957). Heinrich Wittenweiler's *Ring* has occasioned a good deal of commentary, most of it

on the subject of realism and the roots of Heinrich's humor. There is
a new text edition by E. Wiessner (2 vols., 1931–36), with a very
fine commentary. The same author has an article dealing with the life
and personality of Heinrich (*ZDA*, 1952). In *Monatshefte für den
Deutschen Unterricht* (1953), G. F. Jones argues that he was a
burgher. The same author, in his dissertation, *Realism and Social
Satire in Wittenweiler's Ring* (Columbia Univ., 1950), examines in
considerable detail the objects of Heinrich's satire and his satirical
method. In *PMLA* (1953) he makes a good case for the existence of
the "peasant brawl" as a stock literary *topos*. Others see the poem
differently. B. Sowinski, *Der Sinn des Realismus in Heinrich Wittenwilers Ring* (diss., Cologne, 1960), thinks that Heinrich portrayed
the peasants as fools operating in their own type of world. For him
the poem is strictly didactic in showing readers what to avoid. P. B.
Wessels (*WW*, 1960) examines the grotesque aspects of the poem.
Martha Keller, *Beiträge zu Wittenwilers Ring* (1935), is concerned
with such special aspects as manners and parody.

XIX. DIDACTIC POETRY

U NDER THIS heading are included short moral verses, often in
the same forms as the lyrics; longer verse works whose primary purpose is moral instruction, even though there may be a
frame story; and the beginnings of *Meistergesang*.

A. GENERAL

A. Weber in *Studien zur Abwandlung der höfischen Ethik in der
Spruchdichtung des 13. Jahrhunderts* (diss., Bonn, 1936) examines
the changing attitudes toward courtly poetry in the twelfth century, while Herta Gent's *Die mittelhochdeutsche politische Lyrik*
(diss., Breslau, 1938) attempts to determine the nature and purpose
of the political lyric, but fails, because it does not achieve a
sufficiently sharp definition of the type. The relation between poetry
and society is traced by A. Schmidt-Schukall, *Die politische Spruchdichtung, eine soziale Erscheinung des 13. Jahrhunderts* (diss.,
Munich, 1948). The theory of the Holy Roman Empire underwent
many changes in the thirteenth and fourteenth centuries as its actual

power declined. The reflection of these changes in poetry is traced by M. Scholz, *Der Wandel der Reichsidee in der nachwaltherischen Spruchdichtung* (diss., Freie Univ. Berlin, 1952).

B. WERNHER VON ELMENDORF

Articles by E. Schröder (*ZDA*, 1935) and A. Leitzmann (*ZDA*, 1948) on the date of Wernher's work are of significance only because of Ehrismann's view that Wernher's work provided the basis for a code of courtly behavior, and hence must antedate the major romances.

C. THOMASIN VON ZERKLAERE

Additional fragments of text have been published by E. Schröder (*ZDA*, 1940) and K. Helm (*PBB*, 1948). The only general work is H. Teske's *Thomasin von Zerklaere, Der Mann und sein Werk* (1933), which summarizes scholarship and adds a few new details about Thomasin that the author has discovered. The ethical and metaphysical ideas of the poet are discussed by J. Müller, *Königsberger deutsche Forschungen* (1935). C. T. Rapp's *Burgher and Peasant in the Works of Thomasin von Zirclaria, Freidank, and Hugo von Trimberg* (1936) does little more than point out where these characters occur and how the authors express their standard attitudes and morality.

D. FREIDANK

Most of the recent work has been done by F. Neumann, who made an evaluation for the "general reader" (*WW*, 1950), provided biographical details and an attempt at dating (*ZDA*, 1959), and a more specialized study, "Freidanks Auffassung der Sakramente" (*NAWG*, 1930). The importance of Freidank as a collector of proverbial wisdom and as a source for later authors is emphasized by H. Gumbel, "Brants *Narrenschiff* und Freidanks Bescheidenheit" (*Festschrift Schultz*, 1938), and "Freidanks Bescheidenheit" in S. Singer, *Sprichwörter des Mittelalters*, Vol. II (1946) and Vol. III (1947).

E. HUGO VON TRIMBERG

There is one excellent general study of the poet, F. Götting, *Der Renner Hugos von Trimberg. Studien zur mittelalterlichen Ethik in nachhöfischer Zeit* (1932), which gives special attention to the relation between the literary treatment of ethics and the actual standards of the period, and stresses in particular the Christian aspects of late medieval literature. F. Vomhof, *Der Renner Hugos von Trimberg. Beiträge zum Verständnis der nachhöfischen deutschen Didaktik* (diss., Cologne, 1959), follows the same lines. Previously unpublished fragments by the poet are to be found in *Friedberger Geschichtsblätter* (1938), *ZDA* (1933 and 1938), and *ZDP* (1958).

F. DISTICHA CATONIS

The work is not as widespread in German as in some other languages. Apart from new fragments the only important publication is L. Zatočil, *Der Neusohler Cato. Ein kritischer Beitrag zur Entwicklungsgeschichte der deutschen Catobearbeitungen* (1935).

G. MINOR WORKS

R-H. Blaser's *Ulrich Boner, un fabuliste suisse du 14ᵉ siècle* (diss., Paris, 1949) is an excellent comparative study of the content and sources of the principal European fable collections deriving from Aesop, with tables that list the presence or absence of a particular fable in each collection. The study of Boner's work is subordinated to this comparative study. A. Schirokauer has a general evaluation of the influence of Aesop in medieval German literature in *Festschrift Stammler* (1953). The standard study of the *Totentanz* is H. Rosenfeld, *Der mittelalterliche Totentanz. Entstehung, Entwicklung, Bedeutung* (1954). There are several new texts of minor didactic works: *Die Heidin,* ed. E. Henschel and U. Pretzel (1957); Johann von Konstanz, *Minnelehre,* ed. F. E. Sweet (1935); Johannes Rothe, *Ritterspiegel,* ed. F. Neumann (1936); *Das Lob der Keuschheit,* ed. F. Neumann (1934); and E. E. Hese, ed. *Die Jagd Hadamars von Laber* (1936).

H. MEISTERGESANG

Most of the works of the Meistergesang fall outside our period, but there are several excellent works from which basic information and bibliography may be obtained. The most recent of these, by an expert in the field, is B. Nagel, *Meistersang* (1962). It concentrates on factual information about the *Singschulen* and their members, and pays much attention to the musical aspects. Earlier scholarship is set forth in full. A. Taylor, *The Literary History of Meisterge-*

sang (1937), is a still indispensable account of the movement. It is supplemented by B. Nagel, *Der deutsche Meistersang. Poetische Technik, musikalische Form und Sprachgestaltung der Meistersinger* (1952). A. Taylor and F. H. Ellis, *A Bibliography of Meistergesang* (1936), is still useful.

I. BEAST EPIC

Several texts have appeared: J. W. Muller's critical edition of *Van den Vos Reinaerde* came out in a second edition in 1939; *Reinaerts Historie* (Brussels Fragments), ed. P. de Keyser (1938); G. Baesecke, *Das Gedicht vom Fuchs Reinhart (Reineke Fuchs). Nach den Casseler Bruchstücken und der Heidelberger Handschrift Cod. pal. Germ. 341* (2nd ed., by I. Schröbler, 1952). The most important of the few secondary works that have appeared are J. van Mierlo, *Het vroegste dierenepos in de letterkunde der Nederlanden: Ysengrimus van Magister Nivardus* (1943), which is a study of the Latin *Ysengrimus* but has important general information on the genre, and H. R. Jauss, *Untersuchungen zur mittelalterlichen Tierdichtung* (1959), a wide-ranging work that selects a particular theme for each of the major beast epics and shows how it is worked out. The results are interesting, if often unconvincing. There is a summary of the development of the beast epic in W. T. H. Jackson's *The Literature of the Middle Ages* (1960). J. Flinn, *Le Roman de Renart dans la littérature française et dans les littératures étrangères au moyen âge* (1963), is largely an attempt to find contemporary and topical references in the poem.

XX. DRAMA

THERE IS a detailed and accurate review of research in the field of drama between 1919 and 1956 by W. F. Michael, "Das deutsche Drama und Theater vor der Reformation. Ein Forschungsbericht" (*DVLG*, 1957). In view of the excellence of this report, its relatively recent date, and availability, it will not be necessary in this section to do more than note the principal works illustrating the trends noted by Michael and add the most significant publications that have appeared since 1956.

By far the most important of the new works is H. Kindermann,

Theatergeschichte Europas (Vol. I, 1957; Vol. II, 1959), which sets medieval German drama in its European context. It should be noted that the work is a history of the theater and that the literary aspects receive less attention than the stage. J. Stratman, *Bibliography of Medieval Drama* (1954), is utterly inadequate for German drama.

A. GENERAL WORKS

The most important work published in the period under review is K. Young, *The Drama of the Medieval Church* (2 vols., 1933), which gathers together all available texts of church drama written in Latin and from them derives the history of the type. A large number of the texts are from German-speaking areas, and Young's book is often the only place in which they can be found. Significant in a different way is R. Stumpfl's *Kultspiele der Germanen als Ursprung des mittelalterlichen Dramas* (1936), a desperate attempt to deny the role of the church in the development of the medieval drama and to trace all its characteristics to Germanic seasonal and fertility plays. Amidst a great deal of rubbish there are a few useful observations. The importance of popular elements is more realistically treated by B. Hunningher in *The Origin of the Theater* (1955). There are, of course, detailed accounts of the German drama in the literary histories of Ehrismann and Stammler. That by H. de Boor has not yet reached the appropriate period. There is a useful introduction, although inaccurate in some details, in E. Hartl, *Das Drama des Mittelalters* (Vol. I of the section of the same name in *Deutsche Literatur in Entwicklungsreihen*, 4 vols., 1937–42). Finally, E. Prosser's *Drama and Religion in the English Mystery Plays* (1961) should be carefully studied. Although the work is concerned with English drama, its (rather polemically presented) views on the overriding importance of the religious-didactic elements in medieval drama are of great importance. There is another useful general treatment by H. Brinkmann (*WW*, 1959). H. Ott, *Personengestaltung im geistlichen Drama des Mittelalters* (diss., Bonn, 1939), treats the subject rather naïvely, and H. P. Goodman, *Original Elements in the French and German Passion Plays* (1951), does little more than list incidents not in the Bible or Apocrypha.

B. LITURGICAL DRAMA

The texts, almost all in Latin, are in Young. A reply to Stumpfl's book, sharp and well founded, is R. Pascal's "On the Origins of the Liturgical Drama of the Middle Ages" (*MLR*, 1941). M. H. Marshall, "Aesthetic Values of the Liturgical Drama" (*EIE*,

1950), offers a much-needed appreciation of an aspect of the drama
that rarely is discussed.

C. VERNACULAR DRAMA

The most useful collections of texts are still those of R.
Froning, ed. *Das Drama des Mittelalters* (3 vols., 1891–92) and *Das
Drama der Reformationszeit* (1895). See also the selection by Hartl
mentioned above. There are a large number of articles listed by W.
Michael which deal with the form and origin of local processional
plays. Michael himself provides an excellent survey of the subject in
Die geistlichen Prozessionsspiele in Deutschland (1947).

The *Redentiner Osterspiel* has been edited by W. Krogmann
(1937), and there is an English translation (a rarity in this field)
by A. E. Zucker, with a useful introduction (1941). H. Rosenfeld's
"Das Redentiner Osterspiel—ein Lübecker Osterspiel" (*PBB*, 1952)
is a convincing demonstration that the play is misnamed. Two other
texts are *Das Osterspiel von Muri*, ed. F. Ranke (1944), and "The
Melk Salbenkrämerspiel: An Unpublished Middle High German
Mercator Play" by C. Bühler and C. Selmer (*PMLA*, 1948).

M. B. Evans has a detailed study of the Passion Play of
Lucerne in *PMLA* Monograph XIV (1943), the only general work on
Passion plays in our period. There are many studies of the individual
characters, for example, Renata von Stoephasius, *Die Gestalt des
Pilatus in den mittelalterlichen Passionsspielen* (diss., Berlin, 1938) ;
J. R. Breitenbucher, *Die Judasgestalt in den Passionsspielen* (diss.,
Ohio State, 1935) ; and T. Meier, *Die Gestalt Marias im geistlichen
Schauspiel des deutschen Mittelalters* (1959). However, almost all
of them suffer from being attempts at "character study," such as
would be made of a modern drama. They take far too little cognizance
of the religious and symbolic values of the figures they discuss. The
problem is recognized and discussed by W. Michael in "Die Bedeutung des Wortes *Figur* im geistlichen Drama Deutschlands" (*GR*,
1946), who shows how the word shifted in meaning from "character"
to "play" and "allegory." W. T. H. Jackson in an article on the
boasting soldier (*GR*, 1955) attempts to show how a stock figure in
the repertoire of professional actors could affect characterization.
T. Tashiro (*GR*, 1962) shows convincingly that the understanding
of the Donaueschinger Passion Play rests on the recognition of the
symbolic representation of faith, and that the central motif is
spiritual blindness, a motif that dominates both plot and structure.

There has been considerably more interest in the staging of the

plays than in their literary aspects. It will be enough merely to
call attention to the more important, since their content is in all
cases clearly indicated by the titles. H. H. Borcherdt's *Das europäische Theater im Mittelalter und in der Renaissance* (1935) is a
general work on the subject by the best-known scholar in the field at
the time. More specialized are "An Interpretation of the Stage Plan
of the Donaueschingen Passion Play" by J. W. Kurtz (*GR*, 1935);
A. M. Nagler, "Der Villinger Bühnenplan" (*JEGP*, 1955); R.
Nordsieck, "Der Bühnenplan des Virgil Raber: ein Beitrag zur
Bühnengeschichte des Mittelalters" (*Monatshefte*, 1945); and W.
Michael, "The Staging of the Bozen Passion Play" (*GR*, 1950). We
may also note two studies of particular aspects of the stage: W.
Fleming, "Das Raumproblem des Theaters" (*SG*, 1952), which
discusses the illusion of space on the stage, and Hildegard Emmel,
Masken in volkstümlichen deutschen Spielen (1936), which regards
the use of masks as a connecting link between the popular and the
religious drama.

Most of the *Fastnachtspiele*, in their extant form, belong to the
postmedieval period, and most of the material written about them
tends to be parochial in treatment. One notable exception is E.
Catholy, *Das Fastnachtspiel des Spätmittelalters. Gestalt und
Funktion* (1961), which analyzes in detail the play *Salomon und
Markolf* and on the basis of this examination draws some important
conclusions about the *Fastnachtspiel* in general—that it was primarily entertainment and that the notorious obscenity of the type was
largely ritualistic. This is a very important study.

XXI. PROSE

A. GENERAL

IN GERMANY, as elsewhere, there is very little prose in the High
Middle Ages, and even when prose writing becomes more extensive, very little of it can be called literary. In this survey we shall
confine our attention to the writings of the mystics, because of their
great influence on thought and style; to the *Ackermann aus Böhmen*,
because of its literary excellence and the large amount of critical

attention it has received in the last two decades; and to the *Volks-bücher.*

B. MYSTICS

A general treatment of mysticism as a phenomenon is R. F. Merkel's *Die Mystik im Kulturleben der Völker* (1940), while F. W. Wentzlaff-Eggebert provides a historical treatment in *Deutsche Mystik zwischen Mittelalter und Neuzeit* (1944). A review of research on the subject by A. Spamer appeared in the *O. Behagel Festschrift* (1934). The effects of mystical ideas on the thought and vocabulary of the lyric are explored by F. Hederer in *Mystik und Lyrik* (1941).

The work of J. Quint has been outstanding both in the editing of the texts of Meister Eckhart (*Die deutschen und lateinischen Werke,* ed. J. Quint and J. Koch, in progress since 1936) and in critical commentary. Eckhart's innovations in terminology and religious vocabulary are examined by T. Schneider in *Der intellektuelle Wortschatz Meister Eckharts* (1935), while his thought, and particularly his conception of the deity, are the subjects of works by B. Peters, *Der Gottesbegriff Meister Eckharts* (diss., Hamburg, 1936), and H. Ebeling, *Meister Eckharts Mystik (Studien zu den Geisteskämpfen um die Wende des 13. Jahrhunderts,* 1943). Beside his work on the texts, J. Koch also has a biographical study of Meister Eckhart, "Kritische Studien zum Leben Meister Eckharts" (*AFP,* 1959). Eckhart's legacy to the language is treated by O. Wilhelm, *Meister Eckehart und sein deutsches Erbe* (1943).

Less has been written about the other two German mystics, Suso and Tauler. C. Gröber, *Der Mystiker Heinrich Seuse* (1941), is the only general study, but there is an important examination of his place in the history of theology: J. A. Bizet's *Henri Suso et le déclin de la scholastique* (1946). His position in Christology is discussed by J. Bühlmann, *Christuslehre und Christusmystik des Suso* (1942). P. P. Wyser has a careful study of Tauler's doctrine of the "Seelengrund" in its historical aspects in *Festschrift Stammler* (1958). A sound general evaluation of the place of the mystics in literature is J. M. Clark's *The Great German Mystics: Eckhart, Tauler, and Suso* (1949). For their ethical teachings, the best general work is T. Steinbüchel, *Mensch und Gott in Frömmigheit und Ethos der deutschen Mystik* (1953). M. de Grandillac in "De Johan Tauler à Heinrich Seuse" (*EG,* 1950) is concerned, as few critics of the mystics are, with developments in prose style from Tauler to Suso. A useful collection of texts for the study of the mystics is J. Quint, *Textbuch zur Mystik des deutschen Mittelalters* (1952).

C. ACKERMANN AUS BÖHMEN

Few medieval German texts have received such attention as *Ackermann aus Böhmen*. There have been no less than six new editions in our period, even though several were already available. The new ones are by E. Gierach and E. G. Kolbenheyer (with trans., 1943), L. L. Hammerich and G. Jungbluth (1951), F. Genzmer (1951), W. Krogmann (1954, with special attention to the Czech adaptation), K. Spalding (1950), and M. O'C. Walshe (1951). There have also been numerous translations and adaptations into modern German (A. Hübscher, 1952; E. G. Kolbenheyer, 1950; F. Lorenz, 1950), and English (E. M. Kirrmann, 1958). Two critical matters have loomed large. One is the old problem that aroused the interest of Burdach: How far is the work a reflection of new "Renaissance" ideas and how far is it still medieval? Examples of articles on this and related subjects are F. H. Bäuml, "*Der Ackermann aus Böhmen* and the Destiny of Man" (*GR*, 1958), which goes over the various arguments again; A Hübner, "Deutsches Mittelalter und italienische Renaissance im *Ackermann aus Böhmen*" (*Zeitschrift für Deutschkunde*, 1937); and A. Schirokauer, "Der Ackermann aus Böhmen und das Renaissanceproblem" (*Monatshefte für den deutschen Unterricht*, 1949). Interest has recently concentrated on the formal aspects of the work. A. Hübner in *Das Deutsche im Ackermann aus Böhmen* (*SDAWB*, 1935) recognized that it was primarily a stylistic tour de force, but he was bent on proving affiliations to the *Meistersang* and so vitiated some of his own evidence. What did emerge was that the style was not necessarily that of the Renaissance. Others have followed the same line of inquiry, notably Johanna M. Reitzer in *Monatshefte für den deutschen Unterricht* (1952) and in her Colorado dissertation, *Zum Sprachlich-stilistischen im Ackermann aus Böhmen* (1954); H. Swinburne in *MLR* (1953 and 1957); and most recently, F. H. Bäuml, *Rhetorical Devices and Structure in the Ackermann aus Böhmen* (1960), which is a chapter-by-chapter examination of the rhetoric and other stylistic features of the work and a discussion of previous interpretations. It contains an excellent bibliography. The social aspects of the ploughman figure and his identification with the humble man are presented by F. Martini (*ZDP*, 1941). Besides Bäuml's book already mentioned, there are reviews of research by I. Bacon (*SP*, 1956) and E. A. Philippson (*MLQ*, 1941).

D. VOLKSBÜCHER

There has been little activity in the production of texts. The means by which the romances of chivalry were turned into popular prose narratives are explored by G. Doutrepont, *Les mises-en-prose des épopées et des romans chevaleresques du XIVe au XVIe siècle* (1939), and the relation of the *Volksbücher* to the general cultural climate of the time by W. E. Peuckert, "Der Ausgang des Mittelalters und die Volksbücher" (*Zeitschrift für den deutschen Unterricht,* 1950).

6
_____

Old Norse Literature

By Paul Schach
UNIVERSITY OF NEBRASKA

I. BIBLIOGRAPHIES AND BIBLIOGRAPHICAL AIDS

KEY BIBLIOGRAPHIES are J. S. Hannesson, *A Bibliography of the Eddas* (1955), a supplement to that of H. Hermannsson of 1920; L. M. Hollander, *A Bibliography of Skaldic Studies* (1958); J. S. Hannesson, *The Sagas of Icelanders* (1957), which brings up to date Hermannsson's bibliographies of 1908 and 1935; and H. Hermannsson, *The Sagas of the Kings and the Mythical-heroic Sagas* (1937), which supplements those of 1910 and 1912. Excellent bibliographical references are found in the *Kulturhistorisk leksikon for nordisk middelalder* (1956– ; henceforth *KHL*) and in most of the general works, editions, and translations discussed below. Most promptly published of the periodic bibliographies is the quarterly *Germanistik* (since 1960), which includes short reviews of major works. The yearly annotated American-Scandinavian bibliography in *SS* (since 1947) lists books, articles, and reviews published in the United States and Canada, scholarly works by Americans published abroad, and American translations. Most nearly complete of the annual bibliographies are those in *ANF, APS, PMLA*, and *YWMLS*, and the *Bibliography of Old Norse-Icelandic Studies* (since 1964), published in Copenhagen. Good sources for book reviews in English are *Saga-Book, SS*, and *Scan* (since 1962), which includes a current list of books and shorter contributions. The first volume contains an informative article, "Scandinavian Bibliography," by P. M. Mitchell.

The following digests are indispensable. Hermannsson delineates the principal features of earlier editions and translations and suggests plans for future work in *Old Icelandic Literature. A Bibliographical Essay* (1933). B. Sigfússon stresses the contribution of B. M. Ólsen and the beginning of the "Icelandic school" in "Islandsk Litteraturforskning 1914–1939" (*Edda*, 1940). This report is continued by H. Hamre, with emphasis on the work of Nordal and Sveinsson, in "Islandsk Litteraturforskning 1939–47" (*Edda*, 1948) and "Moderne islandsk sagagransking" (*SoS*, 1944).

The implications of Nordal's work (especially 1933–41) are evaluated by R. G. Thomas in "Studia Islandica" (*MLQ*, 1950). S. Einarsson reviews "Publications in Old Icelandic Literature and Language" from 1936 to 1940 in three papers of that title (*SS*, 1938–42). His "Old Icelandic Literature. Editions in Iceland after 1940" (*SS*, 1952) is especially valuable, since the apparatus in these editions is in Icelandic. The most incisive digest of recent saga scholarship is that of P. Hallberg, "Nyare studier i den isländska sagan" (*Edda*, 1953). Recent scholarship on the translated romances is treated by P. M. Mitchell in "Scandinavian Literature" (in *Arthurian Literature in the Middle Ages*, ed. R. S. Loomis, 1959). The most important contributions and theories in the field of Eddic poetry are evaluated by L. M. Hollander in "Recent Work and Views on the Poetic Edda" (*SS*, 1963). For the study of *rímur*, the starting point is S. Einarsson's "Report on *Rímur*" (*JEGP*, 1955). A valuable bibliographical instrument for students of the Scandinavian ballad is E. Dal's detailed history of ballad research, *Nordisk folkeviseforskning siden 1800* (1956). His "Scandinavian Ballad Research Today" (*Scan*, 1962) is the first of a series of *Forschungsberichte* in that journal.

II. GENERAL TREATMENTS OF OLD NORSE LITERATURE

THE MOST up-to-date history of the ancient and medieval literatures of Scandinavia is afforded by *Nordisk kultur VIII* (A and B), edited by S. Nordal (1943 and 1953). The first part (A) contains H. Brix's concise *Oldtidens og middelalderens litteratur i Danmark* and R. Pipping's *Den fornsvenska litteraturen*. The second part (B) consists of *Norges og Islands digtning*, by J. Helgason, a meticulous, esthetically discriminating treatment of Norwegian and Icelandic poetry free of romantic speculation, and *Sagalitteraturen*, by Nordal, a succinct account of the development of prose writing in Norway and Iceland. J. de Vries' *Altnordische Literaturgeschichte* (2 vols., 1941–42) must be used with due regard for the author's bias. The preliterary historical and legendary traditions of pagan Scandinavia are discussed by G. Turville-Petre in his stimulating study *The Heroic Age of Scandinavia* (1951). P. Lehmann, "Skandinaviens Anteil an der lateinischen Literatur und Wissenschaft des Mittelalters I–II" (*BAWS*, 1936–37) is a valuable, although uneven, survey.

The most representative anthology in English translation is *A Pageant of Old Scandinavia* (1946), edited, with selected references to significant publications in English and a stimulating introduction, by H. G. Leach. Less comprehensive is *Survivals in Old Norwegian of Medieval English, French and German Literature*, translated by H. M. Smyser and F. P. Magoun, Jr., (1941). The most extensive anthology of Old Norse literature in translation is the twenty-four volume *Sammlung Thule*, ed. S. Niedner (1911–30; rptd. 1962). A good selection of texts, including several in East Scandinavian and a number of runic inscriptions, with notes and an excellent introduction, is found in the second edition of E. V. Gordon's *Introduction to Old Norse* (1927; revised by A. R. Taylor, 1957). The *Nordisk filologi* text series, under the editorship of J. Helgason, is also representative, containing in addition to Icelandic prose and verse the *Äldre Västgötalagen* (1954) and *Fornsvenska texter* (1955), both edited by E. Wessén.

The most comprehensive work on all aspects of Scandinavian culture in ancient and medieval times is the monumental *Nordisk kultur*, edited by J. Brøndum-Nielsen, S. Erixon, O. von Friesen and M. Olsen (30 vols., 1931–53). Equally authoritative is the *Kulturhistorisk leksikon for nordisk middelalder fra vikingetid til reformationstid*, (1956–   ), of which ten volumes have appeared to date. L. Musset's concise *Les peuples scandinaves au moyen âge* (1951) is a well-balanced history, with references to specialized studies and major controversies.

A. DANISH LITERATURE

A concise discussion of the earliest periods of Danish literature is found in the initial chapters (the first of these by M. Haugsted) of P. M. Mitchell, *A History of Danish Literature* (1957). The first volume of O. Friis, *Den danske Litteraturs Historie* (1945), comprises a detailed and thorough study of Danish literature from the earliest times through the Reformation.

B. SWEDISH LITERATURE

Students of the early literature of Sweden will welcome A. Gustafson's *History of Swedish Literature* (1961). For decades the starting point for the study of this period was the first volume of H. Schück and K. Warburg, *Illustrerad svensk litteraturhistoria* (3rd ed., by Schück alone, 1926), which seeks to recreate the beginnings of Swedish literature on the basis of an assumed common Scandinavian-Germanic cultural tradition. This work was superseded by the first volume of *Ny illustrerad svensk litteraturhistoria* (1955), which contains authoritative studies by four specialists: *Forntidens litteratur*, by S. B. F. Jansson; *Medeltidens profana litteratur*, by G. I. Ståhle; *Medeltidens religiösa litteratur*, by T. Lundén; and *Ballad och Vislyrik*, by K.-I. Hildeman. Jansson limits himself largely to a discussion of runic and pictorial inscriptions and their implications for skaldic poetry, heroic legend, and Norse mythology. The annotated bibliographies in this volume and in Gustafson's *History* are exceptionally good.

C. NORWEGIAN AND ICELANDIC LITERATURE

Because of the close cultural ties between Norway and Iceland it has long been customary to treat the literatures of the two countries together. The most convenient concise introduction is E. Haugen's excellent American edition and translation of H. Beyer's *A History of Norwegian Literature* (1956), which contains many valuable references to works in English on Scandinavian culture and literature. A somewhat fuller treatment is afforded by T. Jorgenson, *Norwegian Literature in Mediaeval and Early Modern Times* (1952). The value of F. Paasche's *Norges og Islands litteratur inntil utgangen av middelalderen* (1924) has been greatly enhanced in the new edition (1957) through the substantial chapter supplements of Anne Holtsmark, which provide critical digests of recent literature. Of fundamental importance, too, is Paasche's *Über Rom und das Nachleben der Antike im norwegischen und isländischen Schrifttum des Hochmittelalters* (1934). Equally important is W. Lange, *Studien zur christlichen Dichtung der Nordgermanen* (1958), the most complete treatment of Christian influence on Old Norse poetry in the period 1000–1200. Dame Bertha S. Philpotts' comprehensive *Edda and Saga* (1931) is both readable and informative. While adhering to the "free-prose" doctrine of the origin of the sagas, she interprets these works in a perceptive manner, and her views on the Eddic poems are often quite original. The most noteworthy of these is her theory of the mimetic origin of the chant-meter lays, which she had developed in *The Elder Edda and Ancient Scandinavian Drama* (1920).

The most recent survey in English of the literature of Iceland alone is found in S. Einarsson's *A History of Icelandic Literature* (1957). Although his treatment of the prose is in large part a "popularization" of the findings of the Icelandic school, Einarsson deals objectively with the most divergent views regarding the genesis, transmission, and interpretation of the various literary genres. The enlarged Icelandic version of the book, *Íslenzk bókmenntasaga 874–1960* (1961), is better documented. To date only the first volume of E. Ó. Sveinsson's *Íslenzkar bókmenntir í fornöld* (1962), which deals primarily with Eddic poetry, has been published. A major contribution is G. Turville-Petre's *Origins of Icelandic Literature* (1953). Although the chief emphasis is on the influence of vernacular hagiographic and historical writings on the style and structure of the sagas, this book also affords an excellent introduction to Eddic and skaldic poetry and to the classical sagas of Norwegian kings and of native heroes.

The best general history of medieval Iceland is J. Jóhannesson's *Íslendinga saga I. Þjóðveldisöld* (1956), which concludes with the fall of the commonwealth (1262). Especially valuable for an understanding of the culture and poetry of the pagan period is S. Nordal's brilliantly written *Íslenzk menning*, Vol. I (1942; English trans. V. Bjarnar forthcoming). Illuminating insights into Icelandic life during the "saga age" are afforded by K. Eldjárn's richly illustrated archeological study *Kuml og haugfé úr heiðnum sið á Íslandi* (1956). Important for students of Icelandic literature is E. Ó. Sveinsson's perceptive interpretation of the *Sturlungaöld* (1940; *The Age of the Sturlungs*, trans. by J. S. Hannesson, 1953; incisively reviewed by Haugen [*JEGP*, 1957]).

III. POETRY

THE BEST brief survey of Old Norse poetry is P. Hallberg's *Den fornisländska poesien* (1962; English ed. forthcoming). Although primarily concerned with an esthetic interpretation of the poems in their present Icelandic form, Hallberg does not hesitate to advance stimulating new hypotheses regarding their origin and composition.

A. EDDIC POETRY

The *Poetic Edda* can be read in two excellent alliterative English translations, H. Bellows (1923; rptd. 1936) and L. M. Hollander (2nd rev. ed. 1962). The German translation by F. Genzmer, with an introduction by A. Heusler (4th ed., 1934), closely approximates the original in form and spirit. The lays of the *Eddica minora* are included in L. M. Hollander's *Old Norse Poems* (1936).

For the American student the selection of *Eddic Lays* (1940) edited with notes and glossary by F. Wood is the most convenient introduction to Eddic poetry in the original. This can be supplemented by *Eddische Heldenlieder* (1947), edited with a German glossary by F. Genzmer. Helgason's four-volume *Eddadigte* (1951– ; Vol. IV forthcoming) has excellent apparatus but no glossary. G. Jónsson has published editions of *Sæmundar Edda* (2 vols., 1949) and *Snorra Edda* (1949) with a valuable commentary, *Eddulyklar* (1949). H. Gering's *Glossar zu den Liedern der Edda* (1931) is indispensable for an understanding of the texts. Facsimile editions of the *Codex Regius of the Elder Edda* and of the *Fragments of the Elder and the Younger Edda* have been published as Vols. X (1937) and XVII (1945) of the *Corpus Codicorum Islandicorum Medii Aevi* (henceforth *CCI*), with important introductions by A. Heusler and E. Wessén. The standard edition of almost the entire corpus of Eddic poetry is that of G. Neckel, *Edda: Die Lieder des Codex Regius nebst verwandten Denkmälern* (2 vols.; 3rd ed. of text and 2nd ed. of glossary, 1936). H. Kuhn's thorough revision of this edition (text 1962; glossary forthcoming) has benefited from G. Lindblad's meticulous linguistic and paleographic *Studiar i Codex Regius av Äldre Eddan* (1954). (See A. Janzén's review in *SS*, 1956.)

A concise survey of the major problems and scholarship on the Eddic poems is provided by Anne Holtsmark in "Eddadiktning," "Gudediktning," and "Heltediktning" (*KHL* 3, 5, 6). A reliable guide to essential background materials is afforded by E. F. Halvorsen, "Guder og gudeætter" (*KHL* 5), and N. Lukman, "Heltesagn" (*KHL* 6). P. A. Münch and M. Olsen, *Norse Mythology* (trans. S. Hustvedt, 1926; 3rd printing 1954), is helpful in interpreting the mythological poems. The complex relationship of the gods is clarified by E. Philippson, *Die Genealogie der Götter in germanischer Religion, Mythologie und Theologie* (1953). An extremely useful survey of all previous literature on the subject of names of gods and of persons in general in the Eddic poems, with critical evaluations, is Mary Gray Porter's "A Dictionary of the Personal Names in the Eddic Poems (*Elder Edda* and *Eddica Minora*)," (unpub. diss., 1960). G. Dumézil emphasizes parallels between the mythological Eddic poems and Indic heroic poetry in *Les dieux des Germains. Essai sur la formation de la religion scandinave* (1959). The best survey of the religion of pre-Christian Scandinavia is F. Ström, *Nordisk hedendom. Tro och sed i förkristen tid* (1961). The most recent comprehensive study in English is Turville-Petre's *Myth and Religion of the North* (1964).

The discussion of the corpus of Eddic poetry as a whole is complicated by the fact that the individual lays differ greatly in theme, form, purpose, and spirit. A deeper appreciation of the subtlety of Eddic verse is promised by the semantic approach employed by W. P. Lehmann in "Lín and laukr in the *Edda*" (*GR*, 1955). Studies on metrics, style, and syntax are often illuminating. A characteristic feature of Eddic poetry (and of other forms of Icelandic literature) is elucidated by L. M. Hollander in "Verbal Periphrasis and Litotes in Old Norse" (*Monatshefte*, 1938) and "Litotes in Old Norse" (*PMLA*, 1938). Hollander has also contributed two substantial studies on the chant-meter in *JEGP* (1931) and *APS* (1932). *The Alliterations of the Edda*, by W. P. Lehmann and J. L. Dillard (1954), provides a useful instrument of research. More penetrating is R. Hollmérus, *Studier över alliterationen i Eddan* (1937), a painstaking analysis of vocalic alliteration. Even more important for a stylistic appreciation of Eddic and skaldic verse is W. Vogt's investigation, "Binnenreime in der Edda" (*APS*, 1937–38). H. Heinrichs, *Stilbedeutung des Adjektivs im eddischen Heldenlied* (1938), is a careful statistical compilation. Of the many contributions by A. M. Sturtevant, the discussion of the use of colors (*GR*, 1938) and the analysis of the verb-adverb locution (*SS*, 1940–41) should be noted here.

The interpretation of the Eddic lays cannot be divorced from the controversial question of their age and provenience. The widely divergent views on the lays included in Wood's edition are evaluated by B. Ulvestad in "How Old Are the Mythological Poems?" (*SS*, 1954). B. Nerman in *The Poetic Edda in the Light of Archaeology* (1931) infers that some of the lays stem from the Migration Period; K. Malone's "Agelmund and Lamicho" (*American Journal of Philology*, 1926; rptd. in *Studies in Heroic Legend and in Current*

Speech, by K. Malone, ed. S. Einarsson and N. E. Eliason, 1959)
traces the Helgi poems back to premigration Langobardian legends;
N. von Hofsten's *Eddadikternas djur och växter* (1957) seems to
support the theory of Norwegian origin of a large portion of the
Poetic Edda. In a series of studies culminating in *Om et norsk
skriftlig grunnlag for Eddadiktningen eller deler av den* (1958), D.
A. Seip adduces paleographic and linguistic evidence that the *Codex
regius* is based on Norwegian antecedents. A brief English summary
of the evidence is given by Seip in *Studies in Honor of Albert Morley
Sturtevant* (1952).

Contrary to the prevailing view that the mythological lays are
exclusively Scandinavian and relatively late, F. R. Schröder in
"Ursprung und Ende der germanischen Heldendichtung" (*GRM,*
1939) argues that Germanic heroic verse developed from Gothic
mythological poetry, which was strongly influenced by Eastern and
Mediterranean currents. In "Mythos und Heldensage" (*GRM,*
1955) he concludes that the Wieland legend is "ganz eindeutiger
Göttermythos." H. Rosenfeld (*PBB,* 1955, and *Verfasserlexikon,* ed.
Stammler, 1955) sees the hero of the "Wielandlied" as the symbol of
the artist in man's struggle against tyranny and traces the legend to
historical events and documents. For J. de Vries, "Bemerkungen zur
Wielandsage" (*Festschrift F. Genzmer,* 1952), the master smith is
the epitome of Gothic ornamental art, and *Völundarkviða* itself the
concrete expression of that art. Similarly, F. Wood (*GR,* 1959 and
1961) interprets the vision poem *Völuspá* as a tenth-century recast-
ing of a fourth-century Gothic lay reflecting the culture of the
Augustan period. The definitive edition of *Völuspá* is that of S.
Nordal (1923; 2nd ed. 1952).

Unlike *Völuspá, Hávamál* is not a homogeneous poem but a
composite of six or eight poems or fragments of poems reflecting
conflicting pagan attitudes. I. Lindquist's attempt in *Die Urgestalt
der Hávamál* (1956) to explain the present poem as a deliberate
reinterpretation of three earlier lays has not found general acceptance. A recent discussion of the stanzas on Odin's hanging in a tree is
"Odin am Galgen," by K. Reichardt (*H. J. Weigand Festschrift,*
1957), who adduces additional evidence in support of the Christian
interpretation as advocated by F. Ohrt in "Odin paa Træet" (*APS,*
1929–30); while Einarsson regards the passage as "probably a
reflection of widespread initiation rites" connected with shamanistic
practices—a view that seems to be rather generally held in Scandinavia.

Vafþrúðnismál is assigned by de Vries to the tenth century because of its pagan tone, but Hollander suspects it to be a later, possibly skaldic, creation. Dame Philpotts includes it among the poems containing vestiges of ritualistic drama. *Norrøne Studier* (1938) includes two important papers by M. Olsen on *Grímnismál*. In "Grímnismál og den høiere tekstkritikk" he tries to demonstrate the artistic unity of this poem, which he interprets as a pagan mystical vision, and in "Valhall med de mange dører" he attributes the large number of gates and *einherjar* to the impression made by the Colosseum on Norse vikings. According to Dame Philpotts, *Skírnismál* reflects the dramatization of a Freyr cult. The burlesque humor of *Hárbarðsljóð* and *þrymskviða* is discussed by Dame Philpotts, Hallberg, and H. M. and N. C. Chadwick, and by Paasche, who cites a similar coarse humor in the *Veda* and in medieval poetry about saints. *Hymiskviða*, which seems to be a conglomeration of four different Thór myths, has been subjected to a thorough analysis by Reichardt (*PBB*, 1933), who regards the poem as quite late (c. 1250).

A. Heusler regarded the oldest heroic lays of the Edda as the linear descendants of Gothic and German poems from the Migration Period. Recently, however, his identification of *Heldensage* and *Heldendichtung* has been challenged by F. Genzmer (*Festschrift P. Kluckholn and H. Schneider*, 1948) and by H. Kuhn (*Festschrift F. Genzmer*, 1952) with specific reference to *Hamðismál*. In *Norden och kontinenten i gammal tid* (1944), F. Askeberg suggests that the Gothic legends underlying the oldest heroic poems came directly to the North along the trade routes of the Don and the Vistula. In his detailed study of the style and meter of *Atlamál* (1934), D. Zetterholm concludes that the analytical composition and psychological penetration of this poem are the creation of a reflective scholar and not, as tradition has it, of an unlettered Greenland settler. Heusler regarded the younger heroic lays as Icelandic reshapings of traditional materials. On the basis of lexical, motival, and syntactic evidence, however, W. Mohr (*ZDA*, 1938–39) suggests that they are Icelandic translations of Danish balladlike adaptations of older Low Saxon poems. An ingenious paper by O. Springer (*JEGP*, 1951) derives the *idea* of the kenning *kumblasmiðr* "helmet smith" from German and the first element from Old English, and proposes a broader approach to the problem of the origin and growth of Eddic poetry. But many scholars today share the view of Helgason and Sveinsson that the *Poetic Edda* is Icelandic and that the burden of proof rests with those who seek to derive the various poems from distant times and places.

B. THE SNORRA EDDA

The perceptive analysis of Snorri Sturluson's remarkable *ars poetica* with which Hallberg appropriately begins his book on Old Norse poetry, and Anne Holtsmark's concise survey *Edda, den yngre* (*KHL* 3) provide a good starting point for the study of the *Prose* or *Younger Edda*. The standard critical edition is that of F. Jónsson, *Edda Snorra Sturlusonar* (1931). More convenient is the popular one of G. Jónsson (see above). For all but the specialist, *Snorri Sturluson: Edda. Gylfaginning og prosafortellingene av Skáld skaparmál*, ed. Anne Holtsmark and J. Helgason (1950), is adequate. This edition is the basis of the English translation by Jean Young, *The Prose Edda of Snorri Sturluson* (1954), with an introduction by S. Nordal. The older American translation by A. Brodeur (4th printing 1946) is also excellent. More comprehensive is the German translation by G. Neckel and F. Niedner, *Die jüngere Edda mit dem sogenannten ersten grammatischen Traktat* (1925; rptd. 1962). The facsimile editions of the *Codex Wormianus* (*CCI*, 1931) and the *Codex Regius of the Younger Edda* (*CCI*, 1940) contain important introductions by Nordal and Wessén respectively. Nordal holds that Snorri wrote this manual for poets to renew the ancient esoteric skaldic art and to help reinforce it against attacks from the church and against the growing popularity of the simpler ballads. According to Wessén, Snorri wrote the *Háttatal* ("List of Meters"), an encomium on King Hákon and Skúli jarl consisting of 102 stanzas in 100 verse forms, after his return from Norway in 1222–23. To this he first added a commentary, *Skáldskaparmál* ("Poetic Diction"), and then a delightful, euhemeristic depiction of Norse mythology, *Gylfaginning* ("The Beguiling of Gylfi"), which has been popular reading to this very day. Finally he wrote the *Prologus*, which defines his position toward the pagan myths as that of a sophisticated tolerant Christian. The present arrangement of the book is the reverse of the order of its composition.

This view of Snorri's attitude toward Norse mythology, generally held by scholars today, is vigorously advocated by W. Baetke in *Die Götterlehre der Snorra Edda* (1950) and opposed by S. Beyschlag in "Die Betörung Gylfis" (*ZDA*, 1954–55). E. Mogk in *Zur Bewertung der Snorra-Edda als religionsgeschichtliche und mythologische Quelle des nordgermanischen Heidentums* (1932) urges discretion in the use of Snorri's tales as sources of mythology and suggests that Snorri might have been the head of a "school" of mythographers. M. Kristensen's painstaking analysis, "Skjaldens

Mytologi" (*APS*, 1930–31), shows that Snorri's retelling of myths was very subjective.

C. SKALDIC POETRY

The best account of skaldic poetry in English is L. M. Hollander's *The Skalds: A Selection of their Poems* (1945). W. A. Craigie's concise *The Art of Poetry in Iceland* (1937) is helpful. Informative general treatments are F. Wagner, "Les scaldes et la poésie scaldique" (*RBPH*, 1938), and Anne Holtsmark, "Islandske skalder. Liv og diktning" (*NT*, 1937). Practically the entire body of skaldic verse can be read in the Swedish translations of Å. Ohlmarks, *Islands hedna skaldediktning* (1957) and *Tors skalder och Vite-Krists* (1958), and in his translations of the royal sagas (1961). The standard edition of the entire corpus is that of F. Jónsson, in four volumes, *Den norsk-islandske Skjaldedigtning* (1908–15), on which E. A. Kock's widely divergent *Den norsk-isländska skalde-diktningen* (2 vols., 1946–49) is based.

The mosaic technique and the stylistic subtlety of kenning usage are elucidated by G. Finnbogason, "Nogle bemaerkninger om skjaldedigtningens 'kenningar'" (*APS*, 1934–35), and C. Wood, "Concerning the Interpretation of Skaldic Verse" (*GR*, 1958). The incredible complexity of skaldic punning is demonstrated by J. Helgason in "Ek bar sauð" (*APS*, 1955). The most penetrating and comprehensive analysis of skaldic style to date is afforded by H. Lie's "Skaldestil-Studier" (*MM*, 1952) and *'Natur' og 'Unatur' i Skaldekunsten* (1957), in which he compares the anaturalistic style of Norse wood carvings and the conventionalized style of skaldic verse. The characteristic meter of skaldic poetry is discussed briefly by Lie in "Dróttkvætt" (*KHL* 3) and more fully by E. O. Sveinsson in "Dróttkvæða þáttr" (*Skírnir*, 1947). On the kenning, see Lie's concise "Kenningar" (*KHL* 8).

Probably most scholars agree with F. Jónsson, "Brage skjald" (*APS*, 1930–31), that skaldic poetry gradually evolved in Norway from simpler forms of verse. O. Moberg, "Den fornnordiska skalde-diktningens uppkomst" (*APS*, 1942–43), emphasizes the social and economic background and the magical nature of skaldic language. Å. Ohlmarks, "Till frågan om den fornnordiska skaldediktningens ursprung" (*ANF*, 1944), derives skaldic diction from the magically conditioned noa-words of the *erfidrápa* or funeral poem. T. G. Jones, "Alliteration: Welsh and Scandinavian" (*Aberystwyth Studies*, 1934), contends for Welsh origin. F. Mossé, "Skothending" (*Festschrift E. A. Kock*, 1934), thinks the Norwegians borrowed

"Irish rhyme" in Great Britain in the ninth century. The tenuous evidence of Celtic influence is summarized by G. Turville-Petre, "Um Dróttkvæði og Írskan Kveðskap" (*Skírnir*, 1954).

The three heraldic poems, which are found in Hollander's *The Skalds*, are treated by H. Lie in "Billedbeskrivende dikt" (*KHL* 1). Parallels from classical and from late medieval German literature are discussed by H. Rosenfeld in "Nordische Schilddichtung und mittelalterliche Wappendichtung" (*ZDP*, 1936). The three skaldic praise poems in Eddic meters can be read in Hollander's *Old Norse Poems*; the most important poems of the major skalds are included in *The Skalds*. Articles on the major skaldic poets and poems are found in *KHL*.

Egill-Skallagrímsson (c. 910–990), the central figure in Snorri Sturluson's *Egils saga*, was the most versatile and original of the skalds. In *Höfuðlausn*, Egill employs the end-rhyming *runhent* meter, created, according to S. Einarsson (*Scandinavica et Finno-Ugrica*, 1954), in imitation of medieval Latin hymns. On this poem see also K. Reichardt, "Die Entstehungsgeschichte von Egils Hǫfuðlausn" (*ZDA*, 1929), and O. Nordland, *Hǫfuðlausn i Egils saga* (1956).

The best account of the court skalds is that of Nordal in *Íslenzk menning*. He plausibly attributes the Icelandic monopoly in this office to the fact that for over a century (954–1066) all Norwegian kings had to regard the retinues of their predecessors (to which the court skalds belonged) as potential enemies. Being foreigners, the Icelandic poets could perform their function as relatively uninvolved, neutral historians. The transition from paganism to Christianity is reflected in the verse of Hallfreðr Vandræðaskáld, the foremost poet at the court of the missionary king Óláfr Tryggvason. His dilemma is depicted in C. Wood's paper "The Reluctant Christian and the King of Norway" (*SS*, 1959). The classicist among the skalds was Sighvatr Þórðarson, faithful counselor of kings, whose *Bersöglisvísur*, a stern admonition to Magnús Óláfsson, had a salutary influence on this king. The last of the Icelandic skalds to sing the praise of Norwegian kings were Snorri's nephews Óláfr Þórðarson and Sturla Þórðarson and his great-nephew Jón Egilsson, with whose name (1299) *Skáldatal* ends.

But the skaldic art also flourished on the farms and estates of Iceland. Second only to Egill in originality is Kormákr Ögmundarson, the most outstanding of the writers of erotic poetry. Recently B. Einarsson in *Skáldasögur* (1961) advanced the thesis that much of the erotic verse attributed to Kormákr, Gunnlaugr, and others is the product of the thirteenth century, influenced by Continental romances and troubadour poetry. Celtic parallels to the magic force of weaving are pointed out by Anne Holtsmark (*MM*, 1939, and *KHL* 2) in the macabre vision poem *Darraðarljóð*, preserved in *Njáls saga*. The verse of minor skaldic poets can be read in editions and translations of the sagas of Icelandic heroes.

The best account in English of the Christian influence on skaldic poetry is that of Turville-Petre in *Origins;* the most exhaustive treatment is that of W. Lange in his *Studien zur christlichen Dichtung der Nordgermanen 1000–1200* (1958). Lange has also published translations of some of this verse in *Christliche Skaldendichtung* (1958). *Harmsól*, regarded by Turville-Petre and others as the finest poem of the age, is discussed in *KHL* 6 by B. Einarsson, who emphasizes its similarity in tone and content to the Icelandic homilies. *Sólarljóð*, the greatest Christian vision poem in Eddic style, is included in Hollander's *Old Norse Poems*. O. Bø's excellent interpretive article "Draumkvædet" (*KHL* 3) lists the most important editions, translations, and studies of this unique piece. *Lilja*, most famous of the Icelandic Catholic poems, is discussed in the editions by G. Jónsson (1933; 2nd ed. 1951), and by C. Pilcher in *Icelandic Christian Classics* (1950).

The best treatments of *rímur* in English are found in four contributions by Sir William Craigie: *The Art of Poetry in Iceland* (1937), *The Romantic Poetry of Iceland* (1950), *Early Icelandic Rímur* (*CCI*, 1938), and *Sýnisbók íslenzkra rímna* (3 vols., 1952). Craigie stresses the similarity of the *rímur* to the French *chansons de geste* and the Middle English metrical romances and ballads, as well as their importance in preserving the Old Icelandic poetic tradition. A thorough handbook is B. Þórólfsson's *Rímur fyrir 1600* (1934.) Helgason endorses Þórólfsson's view that the *mansöngr*, the erotic lyric introduction to a *rímur* cycle, derives from the German Minnesang. Ballad research is difficult because of the late date at which ballads began to be recorded. A brief survey of the chief problems, editions, and studies is B. R. Jonsson's "Balladdiktning" (*KHL* 1); a more detailed treatment, with full bibliography, is K.-I. Hildeman's "Ballad och Vislyrik" (*Ny illustrerad svensk litteraturhistoria*, Vol. I, 1955). The standard edition of Icelandic ballads is *Íslenzk fornkvæði (Islandske folkeviser)*, by J. Helgason (6 vols., 1962 ff.).

IV. PROSE

A. FREE-PROSE VS. BOOK-PROSE

AT THE OUTSET it is necessary to touch on the "free-prose" controversy that has hampered Old Norse research for decades. The proponents of this doctrine (Heusler, Schneider, Jónsson, Liestøl, and their disciples), with individual variations, subscribe to most or all of the following postulates: (1) the sagas of native heroes were independent of the general literary development of Iceland and of Europe (1100–1400); (2) their artistic excellence precludes the possibility of individual authorship; (3) these stories arose and assumed fixed form contemporaneously with the events they relate; (4) they must therefore contain much historical truth; (5) the articulated sagas were memorized and orally transmitted for centuries, with a gradual refinement in style and diction; (6) "das Pergament fängt die gehörte Sprache des Geschichtenmannes mit der Treue des Phonographen auf" (Heusler); (7) motival and verbal similarities between sagas stem from a common tradition; (8) textual variants result from a cleavage in the tradition before its solidification. In addition, Jónsson distinguished between good old sagas recorded before 1200 and corrupt ones recorded after 1300; and Heusler, whose views can be read conveniently in his *Die Altgermanische Dichtung* (2nd ed. 1941), divided these works into genuine oral sagas and book sagas. The only systematic attempt to prove this doctrine was made by K. Liestøl in his stimulating study *Upphavet til den islendske ættesaga* (1929; *The Origin of the Icelandic Family Sagas*, 1930). Although this book is valuable for its wealth of folkloristic information, the author does not succeed in his major purpose, for, as Hallberg has shown, Liestøl assumes *a priori* the correctness of the theory he is trying to argue.

Diametrically opposed to this doctrine are the views set forth by P. Rubow in a paper in *Tilskueren* (1929; included in *Two Essays*, 1949). Rubow regards the sagas of native heroes as sophisticated fiction written in honor of prominent Icelanders and inspired by the translated romance *Tristrams saga* (1226). B.

Einarsson in *Skáldasögur* (1961) argues that some adaptation of the Tristan legend served as the model for the sagas dealing with the love theme. W. Baetke in *Über die Entstehung der Isländersagas* (1956) also rejects oral tradition as a figment; he regards the sagas as reflections of the turbulent Sturlung Age. For B. Guðmundsson the *Islendinga sögur* were *romans à clefs* based on contemporary events; his views can be best read in *Höfundur Njálu* (1958).

Between these extreme views of the sagas as recorded tradition or as pure fiction is the realistic "Icelandic school" of saga research (B. M. Ólsen, Nordal, E. Ó. Sveinsson, Turville-Petre, Hallberg). The aims and methods of this school are succinctly stated by E. Ó. Sveinsson, *Dating the Icelandic Sagas* (1958), in which he evaluates the criteria for determining the relative chronology and the literary relationship of the sagas. The Icelanders insist that research must begin with the individual works as they actually exist. Based primarily on meticulous textual investigation, their findings indicate that most sagas are artistic unities created by individual authors, who made use of a variety of sources including skaldic verse, written records, and oral traditions. Sveinsson emphasizes that conclusions must be regarded as tentative since many MSS remain to be studied and several major works, notably *Grettis saga*, have not yet appeared in critical editions. In *Sagalitteraturen*, Nordal demonstrates the emergence of the royal and ecclesiastical sagas from earlier chronicles and hagiographic writings, and the development of the first sagas of native heroes under the influence of the oldest biographies of Norwegian kings composed at the monastery of þingeyrar. An exhaustive survey of the conflicting views on the genesis of the *Íslendinga sögur* is provided by T. M. Andersson, *The Problem of Saga Origins* (1964).

B. RELIGIOUS, SCIENTIFIC, AND HISTORICAL WRITINGS

A good condensed account of homiletic literature, with full bibliography, is "Homiliebøker" (*KHL* 6), by T. Knudsen. Recent editions with informative introductions are *An Old Norwegian Book of Homilies*, ed. G. Flom (1929); *Gamal norsk homiliebók*, ed. G. Indrebø (1931); *Gammelnorsk Homiliebók etter AM 619 qv.*, ed. T. Knudsen (*Corpus Codicum Norvegicorum Medii Aevi*, 1952); *Homiliu-Bók*, ed. F. Paasche (*CCI*, 1935); *Alkuin: De virtutibus et vitiis i norsk-islandsk overlevering og Udvidelser til Jonsbogens kapitel om domme*, ed. O. Widding (1960); and "A Debate of the Body and the Soul in Old Norse Literature," ed. O. Widding and H. Bekker-

Nielsen (*MS*, 1959). Two important papers in English are Joan Turville-Petre, "Sources of the Vernacular Homily in England, Norway and Iceland" (*ANF*, 1959), and O. Widding, "Alcuin and the Icelandic Law-Books" (*Saga-Book*, 1953–57).

Turville-Petre notes that the author of *Maríu saga* used the same method of constructing his well-proportioned story as Snorri Sturluson did in compiling *Óláfs saga*. The author of the Icelandic homily on the feast of all saints had a predilection for alliterative and rhythmical prose that sometimes approaches the verse-form *fornyrðislag*, while the adaptor of the *Elucidarius*, who shunned loan words and skillfully turned the Latin philosophical terms of his source into Icelandic, wrote a highly personal style. Further information and bibliography on this work will be found in A. Salvesen, "Elucidarius" (*KHL* 3). An important contribution is the facsimile edition of *Stjórn* (*CCI*, 1956), with an introduction by D. A. Seip. Early Swedish legends are treated by V. Jansson, "Fornsvenska legendariet" (*KHL* 4).

In *Saemund Sigfússon and the Oddaverjar* (1932), H. Hermannsson evaluates the cultural contribution of Iceland's earliest historian (1056–1133), whose lost Latin chronicle of the Norwegian kings and of significant events in Iceland is referred to by later writers. Of fundamental importance for the study of the sagas is the question of the extent and influence of the writings of Ari þorgilsson, whose *Íslendingabók*, or *Libellus Islandorum* (c. 1130), is the oldest surviving example of Scandinavian narrative prose. Preserved in two late transcripts, this work has been edited by Hermannsson, with introductory essay and English translation, under the title *The Book of the Icelanders* (1930), by Anne Holtsmark, with good critical apparatus (1952), and in facsimile (both MSS), with English introduction, by J. Jóhannesson (1956). The question of Ari's authorship of *Landnámabók* has been thoroughly discussed by Hermannson (with critical review of the voluminous earlier scholarship) and by Turville-Petre. *Landnámabók* itself has been subjected to a minute textual investigation by J. Jóhannesson, whose *Gerðir Landnámabókar* (1941) is a major contribution to saga research. Hermannsson suggests that Ari had collected material on *schedulae* in connection with the organization of the Icelandic parishes (1096), but that he did not actually write the book himself. Turville-Petre argues cogently that Ari must have begun to compile *Landnámabók* not later than 1100 and that the two versions of *Íslendingabók* were merely offshoots of the more comprehensive work. A convenient edition based on the *Sturlubók* recension is included in *Íslendingabók og Landnáma*, by G. Jónsson (1946).

C. THE SAGAS

The most comprehensive study of the royal sagas, and especially the biographies of Óláfr Tryggvason, is B. Aðalbjarnarson's *Om de norske kongers sagaer* (1937), which was influenced methodologically by Nordal's pioneering *Om Olav den helliges saga* (1914). A supplement to Aðalbjarnarson's monograph is provided by the introduction to his critical edition of Snorri Sturluson's *Heimskringla* (3 vols., 1941–51). Both the method and some of the conclusions of this scholar have been challenged by S. Beyschlag in his detailed investigation, *Konungasögur. Untersuchungen zur Königssaga bis Snorri. Die älteren Übersichtswerke samt Ynglingasaga* (1950). Despite the thoroughness of the author, his conclusions seem to be predicated on the assumption of a rich, fixed oral prose tradition about the historical and legendary kings of Scandinavia. A broad but concise critical review of Scandinavian historiography is afforded by "Historieskrivning" (*KHL* 6), written by four specialists: G. Carlsson (Sweden and Finland), H. Nielsen (Denmark), Anne Holtsmark (Norway), and B. Þorsteinsson (Iceland).

An important recent edition is *Konungasögur* (3 vols., 1957), by G. Jónsson, containing early and late royal sagas. *Flateyjarbók*, a major repository for kings' sagas, was published in facsimile, with an introduction by F. Jónsson (*CCI*, 1930), and edited in four volumes by V. Bjarnar and F. Guðmundsson, with an introduction by Nordal (1944–45). A description of this codex and further bibliography are found in an article by J. Benediktsson in *KHL* 4. The most lucid account in English of the genesis and development of royal sagas before Snorri is that of Turville-Petre in his *Origins;* his discussion in *The Heroic Age* is more comprehensive but lacks bibliographical references.

E. Ó. Sveinsson in *Sagnaritun Oddaverja* (1937) has adduced weighty evidence for supposing that both *Orkneyinga saga* and *Skjöldunga saga* were written circa 1200 under the auspices of the people of Oddi in southern Iceland. Nordal suggests the possibility of influence from the *Breta sögur* on *Skjöldunga saga*. There is a discussion of the legendary background of this saga and its relationship to *Beowulf* and *Widsith* in Turville-Petre's *Heroic Age*. The best discussion in English of the history of the earls of Orkney is the introduction to Taylor's translation, *The Orkneyinga Saga* (1938), which is based on Nordal's critical edition (1913–16). Ó. Halldórsson in *KHL* 5 summarizes the most important findings on *Færeyinga saga* including its influence on later sagas, *rímur*, and ballads.

Jómsvíkinga saga has recently been edited, with English translation, by N. F. Blake (1962). The introduction includes a survey of the historical background, a discussion of the various redactions, and a literary appreciation. It had previously been translated by Hollander (1955). Hollander favors Icelandic authorship against de Vries' belief that the saga arose in Denmark, developed in Norway, and found its final form in Iceland.

Scandinavian historiography culminates in Snorri Sturluson's monumental *Heimskringla*, a grandly conceived and artistically executed, fully integrated history of Norway to the time of King Sverrir. S. Nordal's penetrating, sensitive interpretation of the man and his work, *Snorri Sturluson* (1920), is still the standard biography; a recent perceptive study is G. Benediktsson, *Snorri skáld í Reykholti* (1957). The best critical edition is that of B. Aðalbjarnarson; the introductions and footnotes (together with his monograph) comprise a detailed and comprehensive investigation of the major problems with bibliographical references. The finest translation is that of Hollander (1964).

A comprehensive survey of the classical sagas or sagas of Icelanders, with selected bibliography, is provided by E. O. Sveinsson's concise "Islendinga-sögur" (*KHL* 7). The best introduction to the genre is P. Hallberg, *Den isländska sagan* (1959; *The Icelandic Saga*, 1962). In this stimulating study Hallberg first sketches the historical, social, and literary background of the sagas. Then, after disposing of the "free-prose" doctrine, he presents a perceptive analysis of the style, structure, ideals, and character portrayal of the sagas. He is intrigued with the relationship between contemporary events and the ethos and action of the works themselves. Despite their brevity, his comments on the dissolution of saga writing and on the impact of the sagas on modern Scandinavian literature are illuminating.

Byskupa sögur (3 vols.) and *Sturlunga saga* (3 vols.) were edited by G. Jónsson with a common index in a seventh volume, *Annáler og nafnaskrá* (1948; 2nd ed. 1953). *Byskupa sögur*, Vol. I (1938), is the first volume of a critical edition being prepared by J. Helgason, who has also written the introduction to the facsimile edition *Byskupa sögur* (*CCI*, 1950). A critical edition of *Sturlunga saga* (1946) was made by J. Jóhannesson, M. Finnbogason, and K. Eldjárn. *Sturlunga saga* can be read in an abridged German translation by Baetke (1930). For a full discussion of textual problems see the essay by Jóhannesson, "Um Sturlunga sögu," in the second volume of the critical edition.

The remarkable *þorgils saga ok Hafliða*, incorporated as the second saga in the *Sturlunga* compilation, has been edited by H. Hermannsson (1945) and by Ursula Brown (1952). Hermannsson's bibliographical references are very helpful. Miss Brown shows the author to be a sophisticated narrator of unusual virtuosity and wit. In *Guðmundar saga dýra* (1940), M. Jónsson tries to account for the episodic structure of that work on the basis of multiple authorship. Rejecting this explanation, Jacqueline Simpson in "Advocacy and Art in *Guðmundar Saga Dýra*" (*Saga-Book*, 1961) convincingly demonstrates both the persuasive force and the artistic merit of the author's peripheral approach. B. Sigfússon (*KHL* 5) favors the view that this vindication of Guðmundr for his burning of the chieftain Önundr was occasioned by the admonition of Pope Innocent III (1198) to the bishops of Iceland to punish arson and manslaughter. *Hrafns saga Sveinbjarnarsonar*, which has been praised by Ker (*Collected Essays*, 1925) for its unified composition and its many incidental beauties, can be read in an English translation with an informative introduction by Anne Tjomsland, *The Saga of Hrafn Sveinbjarnarson* (1951). The purpose and the subjectivity of this biography of medieval Iceland's most famous physician are treated in an article by B. Sigfússon (*KHL* 7) and in Einarsson's *History*.

The only complete edition of the sagas and *þættir* of Icelandic heroes is *Íslendinga sögur* (12 vols., 1946–47; 2nd ed. 1953), prepared by G. Jónsson, with a valuable supplementary volume, *Nafnaskrá* (1949), containing a complete index of names, peoples, families, and the sagas concerned. The best critical editions are those in the *Íslenzk fornrit* series (1935–), under the editorship of S. Nordal, of which sixteen volumes have appeared to date. A parallel series of monographs constitute the *Studia Islandica* (*Íslenzk fræði*), likewise edited by S. Nordal (1937–). W. Baetke has founded a *Neue Folge* of the *Altnordische Textbibliothek* (1952–) and a monograph series called *Saga. Untersuchungen zur nordischen Literatur- und Sprachgeschichte* (1956–). The *Altnordische Saga-Bibliothek* is still almost indispensable for students because of its full textual notes, especially on the skaldic verses. Most of the sagas and *þættir* can be read in German translation in the *Sammlung Thule*. Collections of translations in English include *Four Icelandic Sagas* (1935) and *Eirik the Red and Other Icelandic Sagas* (1961), by G. Jones; *Three Icelandic Sagas* (1950), by M. Scargill and Margaret Schlauch; and *The Sagas of Kormák and the Sworn Brothers* (1949), by L. M. Hollander. Of especial interest to American readers is E. Haugen's *Voyages to Vinland* (1942), in which the translator has harmonized the divergent versions of the story and supplemented them from other sources.

Linguistic investigations of the texts have shed welcome light on problems of literary relations. S. B. F. Jansson in his *Sagorna om Vinland*, Vol. I (1944), demonstrates that the text of *Eiríks saga* in *Hauksbók* has been abridged in accordance with definite editorial principles. He also corroborates Nordal's contention that the more discursive version of *Fóstbræðra saga* represents the original more faithfully than the shorter one. Similarly, H. Magerøy in his exhaustive linguistic and literary analysis, *Studier i Bandamanna saga* (1957), establishes the primacy and artistic superiority of the fuller M-text of this delightful satire.

Students who are interested in the style of the sagas should begin with O. Springer's "The Style of the Icelandic Family Sagas" (*JEGP*, 1939), which provides a comprehensive survey of the field, a critical discussion of previous studies with ample documentation, and concrete suggestions regarding methods to be employed in a systematic analysis of individual sagas and of the genre as a whole. New insights into the psychological significance of the subdued, restrained language of the sagas are afforded by Maria Müller's excellent *Verhüllende Metaphorik in der Saga* (1939). The restraint and objectivity of saga style often contrast sharply with the seething emotions of the characters. In *Die Darstellung der Gemütsbewegungen in der isländischen Familiensaga* (1933) A. Gödecke outlines the ways in which feelings and mental states are depicted. H. Graf concentrates his attention on one of these in *Untersuchungen zur Gebärde in der Islendinga saga* (1939). A recent study of the women characters is R. Heller, *Die literarische Darstellung der Frau in den Isländersagas* (1958). *Dreams in Old Norse Literature and Their Affinities in Folklore* (1935), by Georgia Kelchner, is useful because it lists all the texts with English translation. G. Turville-Petre goes into the matter more deeply in "Dreams in Icelandic Tradition" (*Folk Lore*, 1958). Margarete Haeckel emphasizes the psychological, esthetic, and stylistic functions of the prophetic dreams in *Die Darstellung und Funktion des Traumes in der isländischen Familiensaga* (1934).

The aspect of saga style and structure that has been most thoroughly analyzed is dialogue. Three monographs on this problem are Irmgard Netter, *Die direkte Rede in den Isländersagas* (1935); Margaret Jeffrey, *The Discourse in Seven Icelandic Sagas* (1934); and W. Ludwig, *Untersuchungen über den Entwicklungsgang und die Funktion des Dialogs in der isländischen Saga* (1934). Miss Jeffrey demonstrates that the stylistic differences among the seven sagas are so striking that these works must be the creations of individual artists. Ludwig distinguishes between an objective form and a more modern form of dialogue used for purposes of reflection and the expression of subjective attitudes. In his analysis, "Pattern in *Njáls saga*" (*Saga-Book*, 1957–59), I. R. Maxwell develops the "principle of the integrity of episodes," a significant contribution to an understanding of the structural principle of that saga and to a deeper appreciation of the genre as a whole.

The style of the sagas is so appropriate to their content that investigation of their form leads to a consideration of their substance. Thus Hallberg proceeds logically from an analysis of style and character delineation to a discussion of dreams as an artistic vehicle for the saga writers' concept of destiny and to an explication of their values and ideals. In a perceptive paper, "The Value of the Icelandic Sagas" (*Saga-Book*, 1957–59), E. O. Sveinsson goes to the very core of the problem by showing the intrinsic merit of the sagas and their significance for the cultural development of Iceland. He characterizes this body of literature as an "essay on man," created by writers endowed with a deep understanding of human nature and an abiding faith in the dignity and freedom of the individual in his heroic struggle against adversity.

Um Njálu, Vol. I (1933), was the first of four major contributions of E. Ó. Sveinsson to our understanding of the greatest of the sagas of Icelanders. This was followed by *Á. Njálsbúð. Bók um mikið listaverk* (1943), *Studies in the Manuscript Tradition of Njáls saga* (1953), and the critical edition *Brennu-Njáls saga* (1954), in which the major findings of the first three studies are summarized. Against the earlier view of *Njála* as an aggregate of independent oral sagas about Gunnar and Njáll, Sveinsson in his first book shows this saga to be an artistic entity written about 1280 by an author who used a variety of sources and a method similar to that of Snorri in his composition of *Óláfs saga helga*. The second treatise presents a penetrating explication of the saga as a work of narrative art, with emphasis on the author's galaxy of well-delineated characters and his *Weltanschauung*, a blend of noble pagan and Christian elements that reveals the tragic impotence of human wisdom in the heroic struggle of men against destiny. A summary of Sveinsson's views can be read most conveniently in his paper "Njáls saga" (*Scripta Islandica*, 1950), which is written in Swedish. The saga is available in two good English translations: by C. Bayerschmidt and L. M. Hollander (1955) and by M. Magnússon and H. Pálsson (1960).

Of fundamental importance are several additional studies of individual sagas. In *Hrafnkatla* (1940; English trans. R. G.

Thomas, 1959) S. Nordal shows that this novella is not codified historical tradition but the artistic creation of a man of vivid and bold poetic imagination. In *Sturla Þórðarson og Grettis saga* (1938) he argues that a lost biography by Sturla Þórðarson was the chief source of *Grettis saga*. The best edition is that of G. Jónsson (1936), who demonstrates the unity of the entire saga. In his edition of *Egils saga* (1933) S. Nordal marshals the evidence in support of Snorri Sturluson's authorship of this work. Further support for this theory is provided by Ó. Larusson's genealogical study, *Aett Egils Halldórssonar og Egils saga* (1937), and by Hallberg's stylistic analysis, *Snorri Sturluson och Egilssaga Skallagrímssonar* (1962).

Sveinsson edited *Laxdœla saga* in 1934 and *Eyrbyggja saga* in 1935. His analysis of the blending of heroic-native and romantic-foreign elements in *Laxdœla* is especially valuable. An English translation by A. Margaret Arent has now been published (1964). *Eyrbyggja saga* can be read in an English translation by Schach and Hollander (1959). Critical digests of the voluminous literature on *Eiríks saga rauða* and *Grœnlendinga saga* will be found in Haugen's translation (see above), in H. Hermannsson's monograph, *The Problem of Wineland* (1936), and his critical edition of *The Vinland Sagas* (1944), and in W. Lendin's survey, "Vinlands-problemet. En översikt över nyare litteratur rörande källorna" (*Historisk Tidskrift* [Svensk], 1951). The latest views of scholars as to the date and historicity of these two tales are summarized in the introduction to the translation of the *Vinland Sagas* by M. Magnus-son and H. Pálsson (1964).

A comprehensive history of the welter of postclassical prose (much of it still unedited) remains to be written. The best introduction to that branch known as "mythical-heroic" sagas is E. O. Sveinsson's "Fornaldarsögur Norðrlanda" (*KHL* 4). The most comprehensive work on the translated romances and their Icelandic derivatives is H. G. Leach's *Angevin Britain and Scandinavia* (1921). A more recent survey is E. F. Halvorsen's "Høvisk litteratur" (*KHL* 7), with additions by H. Ronge (Sweden) and H. Toldberg (Denmark). Margaret Schlauch's brilliantly written *Romance in Iceland* (1934) contains an amazing wealth of information about Oriental, classical, chivalric and native influences and analogues in the *lygisögur*. An excellent introduction to the genre is afforded by Å. Lagerholm's exemplary edition of *Drei Lygisögur* (1927).

The popular six-volume *Riddarasögur*, ed. B. Vilhjálmsson (1954), includes Icelandic derivatives as well as translated sagas. A useful anthology of English translations is *Survivals in Old Norwe-*

gian of Mediaeval English, French, and German Literature (1941),
by H. Smyser and F. P. Magoun, Jr. In recent years several important studies of the Scandinavian adaptations of the *Chanson de Roland* have been published. The two most comprehensive treatises are
D. Kornhall's *Den fornsvenska sagan om Karl Magnus: Handskrifter
och texthistoria* (1958) and E. F. Halvorsen's *The Norse Version
of the Chanson de Roland* (1959).

Closely related to the *riddarasögur* in spirit and style is
Konungs skuggsjá (*Speculum regale*), the only original monumental
work from the Norwegian Middle Ages. The consensus of scholars is
that this book was written by Archbishop Einarr Gunnarsson for
King Hákon the Young or his brother Magnús. There is a critical
edition (1945) by L. Holm-Olsen, who has also made a study of the
MSS, *Håndskriftene av Konungsskuggsjá* (1952). It was also
published in facsimile in 1947 with an excellent introduction by Seip.
Fortunately this work, which vividly and faithfully reflects Norwegian culture around the middle of the thirteenth century, can be read
in a good translation by L. M. Larson, *The King's Mirror* (1917).

The *Fornaldarsögur Norðurlanda* have been edited in three
volumes by G. Jónsson and B. Vilhjálmsson (1943–44), and again in
six volumes by Jónsson alone (1949). Most of the studies cited as
background material for the Eddic heroic lays are also pertinent for
the heroic sagas. The relationship of these stories to folk tales and to
Celtic legends is discussed in E. O. Sveinsson's *Verzeichnis islän-
discher Märchenvarianten* (1929) and "Celtic Elements in Icelandic
Tradition" (*Béaloides*, 1959 [for 1957]); the origin of the genre in
Sveinsson's *Sagnaritun Oddaverja*. *Völsunga saga*, a prose paraphrase of the heroic lays of the *Poetic Edda* and the inspiration of
Wagner's *Ring*, can be read in an English translation by Miss
Schlauch (1930), which also contains the continuation *Ragnars
saga loðbrókar* and Ragnar's death poem, *Krákumál*. A new bilin-
gual edition of *Völsunga saga* by R. Finch is in preparation.
Hervarar saga ok Heiðreks, which preserves some of the earliest
Germanic heroic verse, was edited with full glossary by C. Tolkien
and G. Turville-Petre (1956), and with an English translation by
Tolkien (1960).

Most wildly speculated about of the *fornaldarsögur* is the ugly
duckling *þiðreks saga*, of interest primarily because of its relationship to the Middle High German *Nibelungenlied* and the Icelandic
Völsunga saga. The most convenient edition is that of G. Jónsson; a
good translation is *Die Geschichte Thidreks von Bern*, by F.
Erichsen (1924; rptd. 1962). In *Die Überlieferung und Entstehung
der Thidreksaga* (1931) D. von Kralik clarified the relationship of

the MSS and thus laid the groundwork for scientific study of this unique work. Another approach to the problem is that of W. J. Paff in his investigation, *The Geographical and Ethnic Names in the þiðreks saga* (1959). The general view is that *þiðreks saga* was composed in Norway on the basis of German sources. The best brief survey of the work and the literature on it is E. F. Halvorsen's "Didriks saga af Bern" (*KHL* 3).

7

Medieval Italian Literature

By *Vincent Luciani*
CITY COLLEGE OF THE CITY
UNIVERSITY OF NEW YORK

I N THE PAST thirty years or so studies in medieval Italian literature have been both numerous and, on the whole, good. The bitter controversies in Italy between the historical school and the adherents of Croce subsided in the twenties. Philologists and literary historians became aware of the value of esthetic criticism, and estheticians came to realize the justice of M. Barbi's dictum: "Esthetic criticism without the basis of serious historical and philological studies cannot bear good fruit." This mutual awareness has led to a cooperation that has produced extremely beneficial results in our generation.

I. GENERAL AIDS

T HERE IS no complete bibliography of Italian literature, but there are good bibliographies that cover certain periods, genres, or authors. The most useful of these are: G. Prezzolini, *Repertorio bibliografico della storia e della critica della letteratura italiana dal 1902 al 1932* (2 vols., 1937–39), and its continuation from 1933 to 1942 (2 vols., 1946–48) ; U. Bosco, *Repertorio bibliografico della letteratura italiana:* Vol. I: *1948–1949* (1953) ; Vol. II: *1950–1953* (1960) ; N. D. Evola, *Bibliografia degli studi sulla letteratura italiana (1920–1934)* (5 parts, 1938–49) ; J. G. Fucilla, *Universal Author Repertoire of Italian Essay Literature* (1941) and *Saggistica letteraria italiana: Bibliografia per soggetti: 1938–1952* (1956). Fundamental for the relations of Italian to other literatures are F. Baldensperger and W. P. Friederich, *Bibliography of Comparative Literature* (1950; rptd. 1960), and the supplements compiled by Friederich and associates in *YCGL* (1952–). Several periodicals contain useful bibliographies: for example, *Convivium, GSLI, Italica, IS, PMLA, RLI, SMed, SP*. Especially noteworthy among these are *PMLA* (1957–), because of the relative completeness of its listings, and *RLI* (1953–), because of its thorough analyses. Indispensable for Italian linguistics is R. A. Hall, Jr., *Bibliografia della linguistica italiana* (3 vols., 2nd ed. 1958).

More than any of the preceding volumes or periodical bibliographies, we strongly recommend to the student, because of its selective and synthetic character, the splendid repertory, *Problemi ed orientamenti critici di lingua e di letteratura italiana*, ed. A. Momigliano (1948–59). Its five sections (in six volumes) are titled respectively: I. *Notizie introduttive e sussidi bibliografici;* II. *Tecnica e teoria letteraria;* III. *Questioni e correnti di storia letteraria;* IV. *Letterature comparate;* V (2 vols.). *Momenti e problemi di storia dell'estetica*. Three other recent works supplement but do not supersede these *Problemi:* (1) *I Classici italiani nella storia della critica*, ed. W. Binni (2 vols., 1954–55); (2) *Orientamenti culturali: Letteratura italiana: Le Correnti* (2 vols., 1956), *I Maggiori* (2 vols., 1956); and (3) R. Frattarolo, *Dalle origini a Dante: Bibliografia della critica* (1957). These volumes will henceforth be referred to as *POCL*, I, II, III, IV, V; *I Classici italiani* . . . , as *CISC; Orientamenti culturali*, as *OCLI*.

The best recent histories of Italian literature are those of F. Flora (2 vols., 1940–41), A. Pompeati (4 vols., 1944–48), and N. Sapegno's *Compendio di storia della letteratura italiana* . . . (3 vols., 1946–47), all of which devote a volume or more to the Middle Ages, and are available in more than one edition. There are also several one-volume histories, the best of which is probably A. Momigliano's (1936). In English, there is a recent history by E. H. Wilkins (1954).

II. ORIGINS—THE DUECENTO

THE FUNDAMENTAL general recent works for this period are A. Viscardi, *Le Origini* (3rd ed. 1956), and G. Bertoni, *Il Duecento* (3rd ed. 1954, with a bibliographical supplement by A.

Vallone). Also important are M. Apollonio, *Uomini e forme nella cultura italiana delle origini: Storia letteraria del Duecento* (1934; 2nd ed. 1943), and L. Russo, *Studi sul Due e Trecento* (1946; 2nd ed. 1951).

A. Schiaffini's *Tradizione e poesia nella prosa d'arte italiana, dalla latinità medievale a G. Boccaccio* (1934; 2nd ed. 1943) provides a penetrating analysis of the various Italian prose styles and points up their dependence on the rhythmic prose and *cursus* of medieval Latin. The problem of the genesis of Italian and Romance poetry in general is treated by G. Errante in *Sulla lirica romanza delle origini* (1943). In this illuminating essay the author rejects the romantic theory of the "popular" origins of Romance poetry and contends instead that it evolved from the Latin heritage transmitted through the church. Errante's thesis concerning vernacular poetry and the corresponding one of Schiaffini with respect to prose enjoy wide acceptance. For all the main theories regarding the origin of Romance literature one should consult the admirable *Preistoria e storia degli studi romanzi* (1955), written by A. Viscardi, M. Vitale, and others.

A. EARLY TEXTS

The oldest Italian documents, such as the *Indovinello veronese* (c. 800) and the *Carte campane* (960, 963), are solely of linguistic importance. Poetic compositions of some literary value first appear in the second half of the twelfth and the early part of the thirteenth centuries. Of these, the *Ritmo laurenziano* of 1150–71 has been studied by G. Mazzoni (*SMed*, 1928; *SFI*, 1932, 1938). The *Ritmo cassinese* has been studied by E. P. Vuolo (*CN*, 1946–47) and A. Pagliaro (*Atti della R. Accademia dei Lincei*, 1957), and edited by L. Spitzer, "The Text and Artistic Value of the *Ritmo cassinese*" (*SMed*, 1952). Spitzer has likewise discussed the *Ritmo di S. Alessio* (*GSLI*, 1956); and V. Crescini, "Il discordo plurilingue di Rambaldo di Vaqueiras" (*Románica Fragmenta*, 1932). Later Florentine texts have been most recently collected by A. Castellani in his *Nuovi testi fiorentini del Dugento* (2 vols., 1951–52).

B. THE SICILIAN SCHOOL

There is a considerable literature on the poets of Sicily and other parts of Italy who were connected with the court of Frederick II and his son Manfred. Fine collections of their texts, with introductions, notes, and glossaries, are C. Guerrieri Crocetti, *La*

Magna Curia (*La Scuola poetica siciliana*) (1947), and M. Vitale, *Poeti della prima scuola* (1951). More recently there has appeared a critical edition in three volumes by B. Panvini, *La Scuola poetica siciliana* (1955–58); the first of the three volumes, *Le Canzoni dei rimatori nativi di Sicilia*, contains a retranslation of the poems into old Sicilian, whereas the other two are devoted to *Le Canzoni dei rimatori non siciliani*. A full-length study on a major poet of the school, with the critical text of his poetry, is S. Santangelo, *Le poesie di Giacomino Pugliese: testo e studio critico* (1937).

A masterly discussion stressing the contribution of the Sicilian School to the formation of the Italian poetic tradition is by A. Schiaffini, "La prima elaborazione della forma poetica italiana," in *Momenti di storia della lingua italiana* (1953). An esthetic evaluation of the poetry is G. Bertoni's "Imitazione e originalità nei poeti siciliani del primo Duecento" (*GSLI*, 1940). Some noteworthy articles on individual poets include: V. De Bartholomaeis, "Ricerche intorno a Rinaldo e Jacopo d'Aquino" (*SMed*, 1937, 1939); F. A. Ugolini, "Rinaldo d'Aquino: *Già ma' i' non mi conforto*" (*FiR*, 1954); and G. Contini, "Le rime di Guido delle Colonne" (*Boll. del Centro di Studi filol. e ling. siciliani*, 1954).

The study of the Sicilian School poses many thorny problems, created in part by the relative dearth of biographical data available for some of the poets and also by the conflicting attributions of poems in the various MSS. (See, e.g., B. Panvini, "Studio sui manoscritti dell'antica lirica italiana," *SFI*, 1953.) A hotly disputed question has been the linguistic one: Was the original language of the poems Sicilian dialect, subsequently altered by Tuscan and Northern copyists, or was it the sort of *volgare illustre* in which the poems have been transmitted to us? Monaci and De Bartholomaeis maintained that Tuscan copyists in general faithfully transcribed the original texts, whereas Cesareo, Tallgren, and Santangelo insisted that the poems were composed in literary Sicilian but modified by copyists. Bertoni, in a protracted controversy with Cesareo and Santangelo (see, e.g., *GSLI*, 1925, 1936, 1938), contended instead that the poets wrote in two languages, the Sicilian dialect and literary Italian. Two Sicilian texts, a poem by Stefano Protonotaro and a fragment by King Enzo, have been critically edited and exhaustively studied by S. Debenedetti in "Le Canzoni di Stefano Protonotaro: Parte prima: La canzone siciliana" (*SRo*, 1932) and by A. Monteverdi in "Per una canzone di re Enzo" (*SRo*, 1947). Both of these scholars staunchly supported the Cesareo thesis, concluding that the Sicilian texts are original and not retranslations (as maintained by De Bartholomaeis, that the

Italian redactions are transcriptions made by copyists, and that the poets of the school—at least those from the island—did not compose in two languages, but only in literary Sicilian.

Another controversial question is the originality of the Sicilian School. Three theories have been advanced: that the courtly poetry of the Magna Curia evolved in the main from native popular forms; that it derived its themes from the lyrics of the *langue d'oïl;* and that it was indebted mostly to Provençal poetry. The main champion of the first thesis was G. A. Cesareo, the principal supporters of the second, A. Jeanroy, E. Monaci, and G. Bertoni. The third hypothesis, however, is the one most accepted. There are two fine essays that summarize the criticism of the Sicilian School and its problems—A. Roncaglia, "Problemi delle origini" (*POCL*, III), and particularly L. De Vendittis, "Linee d'una storia della critica della Scuola Siciliana" (*Belfagor*, 1952).

C. RELIGIOUS POETRY

Because of his great importance in the history of religion and culture, the literature of Saint Francis of Assisi is incredibly vast. For instance, P. V. Facchinetti's bibliographical guide, *S. Francesco d'Assisi* (1928), contains 2577 entries. We must limit ourselves to mentioning only recent studies. The standard lives are: P. Sabatier, *Vie de St. François d'Assise* (1894; def. ed. 1931), L. Salvatorelli, *Vita di San Francesco d'Assisi* (1926), and O. Englebert, *Vie de Saint François d'Assise* (1947; rev. ed. 1956). Also important are the special studies: P. Sabatier, *Études inédites sur St. François d'Assise* (1932), and J. R. H. Moorman, *The Sources of the Life of St. Francis of Assisi* (1940).

Linguistic and esthetic criticism of Saint Francis' famous *Cantico* was greatly stimulated by L. F. Benedetto's *Il Cantico di Frate Sole* (1941), in which he upheld the thesis that the poem is a hymn to God by his creatures and not one of gratitude for His having created them. This interpretation of *per* in the *Cantico* as a preposition of agent and not of cause was rejected by Barbi (see below), by M. Casella in "Il Cantico delle creature" (*SMed*, 1943–50), and by A. Pagliaro in "Il Cantico di Frate Sole" (in *Saggi di critica semantica*, 1953), who proposed, instead that the poem is a eulogy of God through his creatures. The critical text of the *Cantico* is given by Casella (see above) and by V. Branca in *Il Cantico di Frate Sole: Studio delle fonti e testo critico* (1950). Other notable contributions on the poem are L. Spitzer, "Nuove considerazioni sul *Cantico di Frate Sole*" (*Convivium*, 1955–57), and G. Getto, *Francesco d'Assisi e il Cantico di Frate Sole* (1956).

For the Franciscan legends the works of prime importance include L. Cellucci, *Le leggende francescane del secolo XIII nel loro aspetto artistico* (1929), U. Cosmo, *Con Madonna Povertà: Studi francescani* (1940), and "*I problemi fondamentali della letteratura francescana* di Michele Barbi" (*SD*, 1943).

The literature on Jacopone da Todi is likewise considerable. His *Laudi, Trattato e Detti* have been recently edited by Franca Ageno (1953) and F. A. Ugolini (1947). Textual problems have been investigated by Franca Ageno in several articles, among them "Per il testo delle laudi di Jacopone da Todi" (*RLI*, 1943–48; *SFI*, 1950). To earlier critical studies that in various ways seek to determine what is lyrical expression and what is mystic exaltation or moral and political satire we may add L. Russo, "Jacopone da Todi mistico-poeta" (*Studi sul Due e Trecento*), and G. Getto, "Il realismo di Jacopone da Todi" (*LI*, 1956).

Information on the other *laudi* is found in M. Catalano's *I laudari dei Disciplinati assisiati* (1932), G. P. Scardin, "Le laude non-jacoponiche dei manoscritti marciani" (*Biblio*, 1939), and I. Baldelli, "La lauda e i Disciplinati" (*RLI*, 1960). Minor studies on the *laudi* are listed in Prezzolini's *Repertorio*. The origins of the Italian theater are intimately connected with the *laudi*, many of which were composed to be recited by two or more persons on religious occasions. The best collection of these early dramatic pieces is V. De Bartholomaeis, *Laude drammatiche e rappresentazioni sacre* (3 vols., 1943). Two masterly historical and critical studies are by V. De Bartholomaeis, *Origini della poesia drammatica italiana* (2nd ed. 1952), and P. Toschi, *Le Origini del teatro italiano* (1955). The definitive work on the relations of the *laudi* to music is F. Liuzzi, *La lauda e i primordi della melodia italiana* (2 vols., 1935).

A fine critical appraisal of the religious didactic poets of the North is by L. Russo, "La letteratura religiosa del Duecento," in *Studi sul Due e Trecento* (1951), and an important analysis of their style and language is L. Malagoli's *Aspetti dell'espressione letteraria negli scrittori religiosi delle origini* (1953). In addition, there are several recent editions and many studies of the work of individual poets, such as: G. Contini's "Il testo toledano del Trattato dei Mesi di Bonvesin da la Riva" (*SRo*, 1947); Adele Manzi, "L'*exemplum* nella *Vita Scholastica* di Bonvesin da la Riva" (*Aevum*, 1949); and R. Broggini, "L'opera di Uguccione da Lodi" (*SRo*, 1956), which contains hitherto unpublished material.

D. POPULAR AND JONGLEUR POETRY

The standard work is by V. De Bartholomaeis, *Rime giulla-resche e popolari d'Italia* (1926). However, fundamental for the concept of popular poetry is B. Croce's *Poesia popolare e poesia d'arte* (1933). The important collection in the Wolfenbüttel Library is carefully described by E. Lommatzsch, *Beiträge zur älteren italienischen Volksdichtung: Untersuchungen und Texte* (5 vols., 1950–63). The *Contrasto* of Cielo d'Alcamo has been the subject of several important articles in recent years by F. A. Ugolini (*GSLI*, 1940), A. Monteverdi (*SMed*, 1943–50), and others who have examined the language and the style of the poem and conclude that it is a jongleur mime with elements of courtly poetry. A. Pagliaro (*Boll. del Centro di Studi filol. e ling. siciliani*, 1953) further contends that the dialect in which it was composed belongs to the area of northeast Sicily.

The monologue *Il Detto del Gatto lupesco* has recently been reinterpreted by C. Guerrieri Crocetti in "Su un antichissimo *Detto* italiano" (*GIF*, 1952). The *Lamento della sposa padovana* has been studied by A. Monteverdi and rebaptized "Il poema della *bona çilosia*" (*SMed*, 1931). Many popular poems that appear in the notarial registers known as *Memoriali bolognesi* were last published by Adriana Caboni, *Antiche rime italiane tratte dai Memoriali bolognesi* (1941). The best recent study on them is S. Debenedetti, "Osservazioni sulle poesie dei Memoriali bolognesi" (*GSLI*, 1948).

E. GUITTONE D'AREZZO AND OTHER TUSCAN POETS

The literature on Guittone is fairly abundant, but on the "Guittoniani" and the so-called Tuscan poets of transition it is rather scarce. The only full-length monograph on Guittone is still A. Pellizzari, *La vita e le opere di Guittone d'Arezzo* (1906), but three notable stylistic studies have recently appeared on his poetry by A. Del Monte, in *Studi sulla poesia ermetica medievale* (1953), R. Baehr (*ZRP*, 1957, 1958), and Maria T. Cattaneo (*GSLI*, 1960). His possible connection with the heretical, pro-Ghibelline sect of the "Fedeli d'Amore" was investigated by A. Ricolfi (*NRS*, 1935) and by F. Egidi (*NRS*, 1937). Egidi upheld the thesis that Guittone did at first belong to the sect, whereas Ricolfi, like L. Valli before him, contended that he never did. Guittone, *Le Rime*, has been edited by F. Egidi (1940.)

A good study on the "Guittoniani" is M. Catalano's *La lirica sicilianeggiante in Toscana* (1942), and some of their lyrics are

found in G. Salinari, *La poesia lirica del Duecento* (1951). Among
the few essays on individual poets one may mention D. Pierantozzi,
"Bonagiunta Orbicciani, campione del *trobar leu*" (*Convivium*,
1948). The *Mare amoroso*, an anonymous poem replete with Provençal echoes, has been critically edited with a long commentary and
glossary by E. Vuolo (*CN*, 1952, 1956–57), and keen observations
on it have been offered by L. Spitzer (*CN*, 1956–57).

F. LITERATURE IN PROVENÇAL, FRENCH, LATIN

The most comprehensive anthology of early literature written
by Italians in other languages is *Le Origini: Testi latini, italiani,
provenzali e franco-italiani*, edited with notes and Italian versions by
A. Viscardi and others (1956). The Italian poets who composed in
Provençal and the relations of the troubadours to Italy in general
have been discussed at length in our period by V. De Bartholomaeis
in *Poesie provenzali storiche relative all'Italia* (2 vols., 1931) and
Primordi della lirica d'arte in Italia (1943). Recent critical editions
of individual poets, supplied with ample notes and fine introductions,
are: Sordello, *Poesie*, ed. M. Boni (1954); Lanfranco Cigala, *Il
Canzoniere*, ed. F. Branciforte (1954); and Luchetto Gattilusio,
Liriche, ed. M. Boni (1957). A. Viscardi's fine anthology, *Letteratura franco-italiana* (1941), gives all pertinent information concerning the Franco-Italian romances of chivalry.

Critical editions of two important French works written by
Italians are Marco Polo, *Il Milione*, ed. L. F. Benedetto (1928), and
Brunetto Latini, *Li Livres dou Tresor*, ed. F. J. Carmody (1948). A
useful, though far from complete, bibliography of the extensive
literature on Marco Polo is G. Scognamillo's "Saggio di bibliografia
poliana" (*ICS*, 1954). Especially important among the numerous
studies of the Venetian are *Nel VII centenario della nascita di Marco
Polo* (1955) and *La civiltà veneziana del secolo di Marco Polo*
(1956), collective volumes that contain good essays on the life, the
work, the language, and the influence of the great traveler. L.
Olschki's *L'Asia di Marco Polo* (1957; Eng. trans. 1960) is a
splendid introduction to the study of his life and work. F. J.
Carmody has contributed "Latin Sources of Brunetto Latini's
World History" (*Speculum*, 1936) and other studies of Latini.

There are good modern editions of two Latin works of considerable interest for Italian letters. Guido delle Colonne's *Historia
destructionis Troiae*, ed. N. E. Griffin (1936), is a possible source
for Boccaccio's *Il Filostrato* and Chaucer's *Troilus and Criseyde*.

Salimbene de Adam's *Cronica*, ed. F. Bernini (2 vols., 1942), supplies valuable information about Italian writers of his time. F. Bernini has contributed several essays on the interesting friar, among them "La bizzarra cronaca di frate Salimbene" (*Riv. d'Italia*, 1926). Notable recent studies include A. Momigliano, "Motivi e forme della *Cronica* di Salimbene," in *Cinque saggi* (1945), and N. Scivoletto, *Fra Salimbene da Parma e la storia politica e religiosa del secolo decimoterzo* (1950).

G. ITALIAN PROSE

Much early Italian prose is translation, particularly from Latin. A valuable guide is the introductory material in C. Segre's anthology, *Volgarizzamenti del Due e Trecento* (1953). Critical or textual studies of note include F. Maggini, *I primi volgarizzamenti dei classici latini* (1952), which examines Fra Guidotto's *Fiore di Rettorica*, Brunetto's versions of three Ciceronian orations, and the first renditions of Livy and Sallust. Examples of Guido Faba's prose are found in A. Monteverdi's "Le formule epistolari volgari di Guido Fava" (in *Saggi neolatini*, 1945) and in A. Castellani's "Le formule volgari di Guido Faba" (*SFI*, 1956). A superb stylistic analysis is A. Schiaffini's "La tecnica della prosa rimata nel Medio Evo latino, in Guido Faba, Guittone e Dante" (*SRo*, 1931; republished, revised, in *Tradizione e Poesia*).

The romance of chivalry known as *Tristano riccardiano* has been re-edited by L. di Benedetto, *La Leggenda di Tristano* (1942). The later *Tristano veneto*, however, has yet to be published in its entirety. These and later epic romances were exhaustively examined by E. G. Gardner for their use of Breton matter in his authoritative *The Arthurian Legend in Italian Literature* (1930). A fine esthetic evaluation is L. Russo's "La letteratura cavalleresca dal *Tristano* ai *Reali di Francia*" (*Belfagor*, 1951).

There is no critical edition of *Il Novellino* (or *Le cento novelle antiche*), but some good texts are available, one profusely annotated by L. Di Francia (1930) and another prepared by C. Alvaro (1940). The sources of the tales have been recently investigated by R. Besthorn, *Ursprung und Eigenart der älteren italienischen Novelle* (1935). Problems of text, chronology, and authorship are discussed in detail by A. Monteverdi in *Studi e saggi sulla letteratura italiana dei primi secoli* (1954). An important esthetic appraisal is M. Sansone's *Il "Novellino"* (1948), and an acute stylistic analysis is made by S. Battaglia (*FiR*, 1955).

H. DOLCE STIL NOVO

The best collections of poems by the *stilnovisti* are *Rimatori del dolce stil novo* (1939), ed. L. di Benedetto; C. Cordié, *Rimatori del Dolce stil novo* (1942) ; G. Salinari, *La poesia lirica del Duecento* (1951) ; and G. Contini, *Poeti del Duecento*, Vol. II (1960). At the beginning of the century various hypotheses were advanced concerning the nature and the originality of the *stil novo* and its conception of love. More recent critics have insisted that the novelty of the *stil novo* resides mainly in its more profound and refined psychological insight and depends upon the artistic sensibility of individual poets ; see for example, N. Sapegno (*Cultura*, 1930) ; F. Figurelli, *Il dolce stil novo* (1933) ; L. Russo, "Lo Stilnovo" (*Belfagor*, 1954) and "Guinizelli, Cavalcanti e altri minori" (*Belfagor*, 1956). A fine survey of the history of the concept is by E. Bigi, "Genesi di un concetto storiografico: *Dolce stil novo*" (*GSLI*, 1955), and a penetrating study on its theory of love has been made by B. Nardi, "Filosofia dell'amore nei rimatori italiani del Duecento e in Dante," in *Dante e la cultura medievale* (2nd ed. 1949).

Important special studies on Guido Guinizelli include R. Garzia's "Il Guinizelli e la sua poesia cortese" (*Archivum Romanicum*, 1933) ; M. Casella, "Al cor gentil repara sempre amore" (*SRo*, 1943), which gives the critical text of the poem, with interpretation and a history of its manuscript tradition ; and S. D'Arco Avalle, "La tradizione manoscritta di Guido Guinizzelli" (*SFI*, 1953).

On the *Rime* of Guido Cavalcanti there is now available a splendid critical edition by G. Favati (1957), with a fine introduction. Esthetic and stylistic studies on the poet have been particularly abundant in the last few years. Among the best are G. Favati, "Tecnica ed arte nella poesia cavalcantiana" (*SPetr*, 1950) ; Maria Corti, "La fisionomia stilistica di Guido Cavalcanti" (*Atti della R. Accademia dei Lincei*, 1950) ; W. T. Ewert, "Die Balladen Guido Cavalcantis" (*RF*, 1951) ; and P. Bigongiari, "Guido Cavalcanti" (*Paragone*, 1957). The abstruse theory of love expounded by Guido in his *Donna me prega* has inspired various conflicting interpretations by B. Nardi, "L'averroismo del'primo amico di Dante" (*SD*, 1940) ; M. Casella, "La canzone d'amore di Guido Cavalcanti" (*SFI*, 1944), which also gives the critical text of the poem and the history of its manuscript tradition ; J. E. Shaw, *Guido Cavalcanti's Theory of Love: The "Canzone d'Amore" and Other Related Problems* (1949) ; and G. Favati, "La canzone d'amore del Cavalcanti" (*LM*, 1952). It may be added that these diverse interpretations have given rise to sharp polemics.

Important esthetic and stylistic studies on Cino da Pistoia include A. Livi, "Saggio su Cino da Pistoia" (*Inventario*, 1946) ; D. De Robertis, "Cino da Pistoia e la crisi del linguaggio poetico" (*Convivium*, 1952) ; and Maria Corti, "Il linguaggio poetico di Cino da Pistoia" (*CN*, 1952). The minor *stilnovisti*, Lapo Gianni, Gianni Alfani, Dino Frescobaldi, and others, are studied in the essays of Figurelli, Russo, and Sapegno referred to above, as well as in Bertoni's *Il Duecento* and Sapegno's *Il Trecento*. An important article on Frescobaldi is D. De Robertis, "Il 'Caso' Frescobaldi : Per una storia della poesia di Cino da Pistoia" (*SUS*, 1952).

I. COMICO-REALISTIC POETRY

The compositions of the poets variously referred to as realistic, bourgeois, comic, autobiographical, burlesque or jocose are found in three fine editions : *Sonetti burleschi e realistici dei primi due secoli*, ed. A. F. Massèra (1940) ; *Rimatori comico-realistici del Due e Trecento*, ed. M. Vitale (2 vols., 1956) ; and especially *Poeti giocosi del tempo di Dante*, ed. M. Marti (1956).

Before this last decade scholars had been attracted mostly to the personality and the work of Cecco Angiolieri and had paid little attention to the many other realistic poets. One had to rely for interpretation of their works on the cursory treatments in Croce's *Poesia popolare e poesia d'arte* (1933), in N. Sapegno's *Il Trecento* (1934), and in Previtera's *La poesia giocosa e l'umorismo* (1939), among others. This lacuna has now been filled by M. Marti's masterly *Cultura e stile nei poeti giocosi del tempo di Dante* (1953), which links all this jocose verse to the realistic medieval Latin and Romance tradition in general and to Goliardic poetry in particular and regards it as a more or less conscious opposition to the *dolce stil novo* (a point also made by Sapegno).

Since D'Ancona's famous essay on Angiolieri (*NA*, 1874), the Sienese poet has inspired a host of critical studies, which in the main repudiate the old scholar's portrait of Cecco as a romantic confessor of his woes. The best of the recent works on the poet include M. Marti, *Cecco Angiolieri e i poeti autobiografici tra il 200 e il 300* (1946), which makes melancholia (in the sense of a bitter material dissatisfaction) the unifying motif of Cecco's poetry ; B. Maier, *La personalità e la poesia di Cecco Angiolieri* (1947) ; and F. Figurelli, *La musa bizzarra di Cecco Angiolieri* (1950), which insists upon the poet's comic realism, characterized by a penchant for the theatrical, the popular, and the external. The question of the genuineness of the poems ascribed to Cecco was first seriously posed by Adele Todaro,

Sull'autenticità dei sonetti attribuiti a Cecco Angiolieri (1934), and later by M. Marti (*GSLI*, 1950). The former contended that only seventy of the one hundred fifty sonnets assigned to Cecco by Massèra were really his, whereas the latter concluded that one hundred nine were definitely authentic, nineteen were the work of Mei dei Tolomei, and the others were of doubtful attribution.

J. ALLEGORICAL AND DIDACTIC POETRY

Modern critical editions are available for the major allegorical poems of the end of the Duecento. Many appear in L. di Benedetto's *Poemetti allegorico-didattici del secolo XIII* (1941), which also includes Brunetto Latini's *Il Tesoretto* and *Il Favolello* and some minor compositions. A more recent edition, based on the texts of Parodi, Mistruzzi, and di Benedetto and supplied with a good introduction and copious notes, is G. Petronio, *Poemetti del Duecento: Il Tesoretto, Il Fiore, L'Intelligenza* (1951).

A hotly disputed question has been that of the authorship of *Il Fiore*. In 1881 F. Castets attributed the poem to Dante, and his thesis found favor with some, although by no means all. More recently, two important studies have accumulated significant evidence against this attribution, Sister Mary D. Ramacciotti, *The Syntax of "Il Fiore" and of Dante's "Inferno" as Evidence in the Question of the Authorship of "Il Fiore"* (1936), and B. Langheinrich, "Sprachliche Untersuchung zur Frage der Verfasserschaft Dantes am Fiore" (*DDJ*, 1937). Both studies contain a detailed history of the controversy concerning the poem.

Cecco d'Ascoli's *L'Acerba* may be consulted in a good text with a detailed introduction and copious notes by A. Crespi (1927). Francesco da Barberino's *Reggimento e costumi di donna* has been edited by G. E. Sansone (1957), a text severely criticized by Franca Ageno (*RPh*, 1959). Recent studies on Cecco d'Ascoli (Francesco Stabili) include L. Thorndike, "More Light on Cecco d'Ascoli" (*RR*, 1946), and M. Alessandrini, *Cecco d'Ascoli* (1955). A notable monograph on Barberino is R. Ortiz, *Francesco da Barberino e la letteratura didattica neolatina* (1948).

K. PRE-HUMANISM

In recent years several good studies have appeared on the Paduan and other precursors of Petrarch: for example, G. Vinay, "Studi sul Mussato: I. Il Mussato e l'estetica medievale" (*GSLI*, 1949); R. Weiss, *Il primo secolo dell'Umanesimo* (1949), which includes chapters on Geremia da Montagnone and Geri d'Arezzo, and "Lovato Lovati (1241–1309)" (*IS*, 1951); and Guido Billano-vich, "*Veterum vestigia vatum* nei carmi dei preumanisti padovani" (*IMU*, 1958), a study of echoes of Roman poets in the lyrics of Lovati, Mussato, and Zambono di Andrea. A particularly important contribution is K. M. Setton, "The Byzantine Background of the Italian Renaissance" (*PAPS*, 1956), a masterly survey of Byzan-tine influence in Italy from the early Middle Ages to the Quattro-cento.

III. DANTE ALIGHIERI

A. GENERAL AIDS

THE LITERATURE on Dante is incredibly extensive, but fortu-nately the student can find his way through the maze with the help of some good bibliographies, handbooks, and special periodicals devoted to the poet. For the period before 1920 one can rely on the Cornell University *Catalogue of the Dante Collection Presented by Willard Fiske*, compiled by T. W. Koch (2 vols., 1898–1900), and the *Additions 1898–1920*, compiled by Mary Fowler (1921). For studies from 1920 to 1949 there are available N. D. Evola, *Bibliografia dantesca (1920–1930)* (1932); Helene Wieruszowski, "Bibliografia dantesca degli anni 1931–1937" (*GD*, 1938; and *GD*, 1940 for 1938–39); and A. Vallone, *Gli studi danteschi dal 1940 al 1949* (1950).

Greater profit can be drawn, however, from special surveys and guides on the one hand and from the Dante journals on the other, because of their critical and selective character. Among the first are four works that complement one another extremely well: U. Cosmo, *Guida a Dante* (1947; Eng. trans. 1950); A. Vallone, *La critica dantesca contemporanea* (1953); D. Mattalìa, "Dante Alighieri" (*CISC*, I); S. A. Chimenz, "Dante Alighieri" (*OCLI–I Maggiori*, I). Four Dante journals are currently being published: *Deutsches Dante-Jahrbuch* (1867, 1869, 1871, 1877, 1920–); *Annual Re-ports of the Dante Society of America* (1822–); *Studi danteschi* (1920–); *L'Alighieri* (1960–). The last two contain the best analytical surveys of Dante literature.

Of the many introductions of the life and work of Dante, three stand out above the rest: M. Barbi, *Dante: Vita, opere e fortuna*, in *Enciclopedia italiana* (1931; also pub. separately 1933, 1952; Eng. trans. 1954); F. Maggini, *Introduzione allo studio di Dante* (1936; 3rd ed. 1948); S. A. Chimenz, *Dante* (1954) and in *OCLI—I Maggiori*, I (1956). Also noteworthy is F. Schneider, *Dante: Eine Einführung in sein Leben und sein Werk* (1935). A good biography is U. Cosmo, *Vita di Dante* (1930; 2nd ed. 1949). The most exhaustive full-length treatments of Dante's life and work are N. Zingarelli, *La vita, i tempi e le opere di Dante* (2 vols., 1931; 2nd ed. 1948), and M. Apollonio, *Dante: Storia della "Commedia"* (2 vols., 1951). Apollonio's critical synthesis presupposes a great preparation on the part of the reader and hence should not be consulted until one is well versed in the life and works of Dante and in the manifold problems of Dante criticism. Biographical studies are not so abundant as they were before 1930. However, of fundamental importance is the *Codice diplomatico dantesco*, edited by R. Piattoli (1940), which contains all the public documents from 1189 to 1371 relating to the Alighieri family and to Dante's life. Finally, the most authoritative editions of Dante's complete works are *Tutte le opere di Dante Alighieri*, ed. E. Moore (1894; 4th ed., by P. Toynbee, 1924), and *Opere di Dante, testo critico della Società Dantesca Italiana* (1921). Special critical texts of individual works will be referred to below.

B. VITA NUOVA

The best text is that of M. Barbi (1932), an improvement on the one prepared by him for the *Testo critico* of 1921. Good recent editions of this work are those of N. Sapegno (1932; 2nd ed. 1943) and D. Mattalìa (1936).

The interpretation of the *Vita Nuova* plays a prominent role in the important Pietrobono-Barbi controversy. Ever since *Il Poema sacro* (1915), L. Pietrobono had consistently maintained: (1) that the *Vita Nuova* is a mystical work; (2) that it was retouched after the composition of the *Convivio* so that Beatrice could be extolled instead of the *donna gentile*, for whom the first version was presumably written; (3) that the *Convivio* is an exaltation of human speculation; and (4) that the *Commedia* constitutes a return to mysticism, but of a sort corresponding to that of Saint Bonaventura. M. Barbi rejected all four hypotheses in his famous "Razionalismo e misticismo in Dante" (*SD*, 1933, 1937; now also in *Problemi di critica dantesca*, Vol. II, 1941). Both here and in his life of Dante he contends that the three works do not form a trilogy, the first part of which is mystic, the second rationalistic, and the third a return to faith. At most, one might speak of three periods in Dante's life: the first dedicated to love poetry, the second to philosophy, and the third to politico-religious reform. Pietrobono replied to Barbi, without changing his position, in "Il rifacimento della *Vita Nuova* e le due fasi del pensiero dantesco" (*GD*, 1934) and "Filosofia e teologia nel Convivio e nella Commedia" (*GD*, 1940). B. Nardi agreed with Pietrobono's *rifacimento* thesis in "Dalla prima alla seconda *Vita Nuova*" (*Nel mondo di Dante*, 1944) and in other studies; whereas A. Pézard took exception to it in "Avatars de la *donna gentile*" (*Annales du Centre Univ. Médit.*, 1947–48).

General essays that insist on the mystical character of the *Vita Nuova* include F. Biondolillo's *Il problema critico della Vita Nuova* (1932) and *Poetica e poesia di Dante* (1949). The relations of the booklet to the *dolce stil novo* are discussed by F. Biondolillo, *Dante creatore del dolce stil nuovo* (1937), by Figurelli (*Belfagor*, 1948), and by L. Russo (*Belfagor*, 1954), among others. Also significant for its criticism of the *Vita Nuova* is E. Gilson, *Dante et la philosophie* (1939), a large section of which is devoted to demolishing the various allegorical metamorphoses that the Beatrice of Dante's piece is made to undergo by P. Mandonnet in *Dante le théologien* (1935). A noteworthy original interpretation is C. S. Singleton, *An Essay on the "Vita Nuova"* (1949), which conceives of Beatrice's death as analogous to that of Christ.

C. RIME

Dante's lyrics, edited by M. Barbi for the *Testo critico* of 1921, are now available in part in a better text, the *Rime della "Vita Nuova" e della giovinezza*, Vol. I (1956), ed. F. Maggini with the aid of the notes left by Barbi. Still fundamental for its study of the manuscript tradition of the poems is M. Barbi, *Studi sul Canzoniere di Dante* (1915). Noteworthy recent essays on the *Rime* and the problems they present include N. Sapegno, *"Dolce stil nove:* Le rime di Dante" (*Cultura*, 1930); K. McKenzie, "Observations on Dante's Lyrical Poems" (*ARDS*, 1934); and F. Biondolillo, *Le rime amorose di Dante* (1960). The extreme difficulty of classifying and dating Dante's lyrics and of identifying the various ladies mentioned in them is clearly demonstrated by D. Mattalìa, "Ordine e disordine nelle *Rime* di Dante" and "La *Quaestio de mulieribus*," in *La critica dantesca: questioni e correnti* (1950), which also includes a good bibliographical appendix.

Contributions on specific poems or groups of poems may be classified as follows: (1) the early lyrics up to the end of the *Vita Nuova* period; (2) the sonnet controversy with Forese Donati; (3) the compositions for "la montanina" and for Madonna Pietra; (4) the allegorical canzoni, particularly *Tre donne*. The first group have been studied by M. Barbi, "Per chi o quando sia composta la canzone *E' m'incresce di me*" (*SD*, 1935), L. Pietrobono (*GD*, 1936), and F. Montanari, "L'esperienza poetica di Dante fino alla *Vita Nuova*" (*LI*, 1955). Barbi maintains against Pietrobono that *E' m'incresce* was composed for Beatrice. For decades Pietrobono expressed the conviction that Dante loved two women, Beatrice and the *donna gentile*, and consistently identified Lisetta, the "pargoletta," Pietra, and even Matelda with the latter. He contends that *E' m'incresce* was written for the *donna gentile* and not Beatrice.

The definitive work on Dante's controversy with Forese is M. Barbi, "La tenzone di Dante con Forese" (*SD*, 1924, 1932–33). The poems written for Pietra have been studied in our period by A. Ricolfi (*Giorn. di politica e letteratura*, 1933), J. B. Fletcher (*PMLA*, 1938), and A. Vezin, "Dantes Casentino-Erlebnis" (*DDJ*, 1943). Vezin speaks for those scholars who identified Pietra with the "montanina," whereas Ricolfi and Fletcher insisted that she symbolized the corrupt church. Be that as it may, most scholars have believed that Pietra is a real woman and not a symbol. The influence of Arnaut Daniel on the *rime pietrose* has been recently investigated by E. Melli (*FiR*, 1959). In the fine "L'esperienza della *petrose* e il linguaggio della *Divina Commedia*" (*Belfagor*, 1957), L. Blasucci acutely points out how the stylistic traits of these lyrics foreshadow those of the masterpiece.

The famous canzone of Dante's exile, *Tre donne intorno al cor*, has been most recently interpreted by M. Casella (*SD*, 1951) and by K. Foster (*IS*, 1954). The other allegorical canzoni are usually discussed in connection with the *Convivio*.

C. CONVIVIO

The critical edition superseding that of the *Testo critico* of 1921 was prepared by G. Busnelli and G. Vandelli, with an introduction by M. Barbi (2 vols., 1934–37). Its commentary, however, was severely criticized by B. Nardi in *Nel mondo di Dante* (1944) for its excessive parallels with Thomism. Nardi had earlier given his conception of an ideal commentary for the treatise in "Alla illustrazione del *Convivio* dantesco" (*GSLI*, 1930). The textual problems of the work have been recently discussed in three illuminating essays:

M. Casella (*SFI*, 1944), V. Pernicone (*SD*, 1949), and Maria S. Simonelli (*SD*, 1951, 1953–54), the last being most exhaustive.

Important critical studies of a general or special nature include J. E. Shaw, *The Lady "Philosophy" in the "Convivio"* (1938) ; A. Pézard, "Le *Convivio* de Dante, sa lettre, son esprit" (*Annales de l'Univ. de Lyon*, 1940) ; B. Nardi, "Le figurazioni allegoriche e l'allegoria della *donna gentile*," in *Nel mondo di Dante* (1944) ; and G. Ledig, "Vom Bankett des Geistes" (*DDJ*, 1948–49). Before consulting these essays and others, however, the student is advised to read B. Nardi, "Le rime filosofiche e il Convivio nello sviluppo dell'arte e del pensiero di Dante" (*LI*, 1956), which is a fine introduction not only to the treatise but also to some of Nardi's main ideas. The prose style and language of the *Convivio* are keenly analyzed by Schiaffini and others.

D. DE VULGARI ELOQUENTIA

The critical edition that has replaced the one prepared by P. Rajna for the *Testo critico* of 1921 is A. Marigo's (1938; 3rd ed., rev. by P. G. Ricci, 1957), with an Italian translation and commentary. Recent notable essays on the linguistic theories expounded in the treatise and on Dante's use therein of rhythmic prose (the *cursus*) include F. Di Capua, *Insegnamenti retorici medievali e dottrine estetiche moderne nel "De vulgari eloquentia" di Dante* (1945) ; A. Pagliaro, "La dottrina linguistica di Dante" (*Quaderni di Roma*, 1947) ; and G. Vinay, "Ricerche sul *De vulgari eloquentia*" (*GSLI*, 1959).

E. MONARCHIA

The edition prepared by E. Rostagno for the *Testo critico* of 1921 has been largely superseded by those of A. C. Volpe (1946) and G. Vinay (1950), which include Italian versions of the treatise and excellent commentaries. The *Monarchia* is at the center of most studies concerned with Dante's political thought, although some give attention also to the ideas in the *Convivio*, the political *Epistolae*, and the *Commedia*. More recent discussions of Dante's political doctrines are: T. Silverstein, "On the Genesis of *De Monarchia* II, v" (*Speculum*, 1938) ; M. Barbi, "Nuovi problemi della critica dantesca" (*SD*, 1938, 1939, 1942) —the sections entitled "L'ideale politico-religioso di Dante," "L'Italia nell'ideale politico di Dante," and "Impero e Chiesa"; F. Battaglia, *Impero, Chiesa e stati particolari nel pensiero di Dante* (1944) ; A. P. d'Entrèves, *Dante as a Political Thinker* (1952); C. T. Davis, *Dante and the Idea of Rome* (1957); E. H. Kantorowicz, "Man-Centered Kingship: Dante," in *The King's Two Bodies: A Study in Mediaeval Political Theology* (1957). The theories that have been most disputed are those of Ercole, above all his thesis of the three phases of Dante's political thought and that of Dante's belief in *regnum italicum*. Nardi rejects the theory of the three phases, maintaining instead that the poet's political ideas were already formed when he composed the *Convivio*. Barbi and Battaglia take exception to Ercole's hypothesis that in Dante's mind all Italy constituted one kingdom. They insist that the poet could not possibly conceive of Italian political unity in the modern sense. These scholars, however, all agree that Dante's empire, although an ideal state, was not a fantastic utopia, for it had its roots firmly planted in historical reality. Two studies that seek to explain the genesis of Dante's political thought through the juridical works of his time are A. Solmi, "Dante e il diritto" (*Dante e l'Italia*, 1921), and F. Ruffini, "Dante e il protervo decretalista innominato," in *Scritti giuridici minori* (1936).

F. OTHER WORKS

The best studies on the text and prose style of the *Epistolae* are by E. G. Parodi in *Lingua e letteratura*, ed. G. Folena, Vol. II (1957), and F. Di Capua, *Fonti ed esempi per lo studio dello "Stilus Curiae Romanae" medioevale* (1941), which includes rhythmical analyses of four of Dante's epistles.

There are many contributions on single letters, particularly the one addressed to Cangrande della Scala, the authenticity of which has been hotly disputed. At the turn of the century Torraca and Moore considered it genuine, whereas D'Ovidio and Luiso asserted the contrary. The best recent discussions of the problem are: H. Pflaum (*GD*, 1938), E. R. Curtius (*RF*, 1943), and F. Mazzoni (*Atti della R. Accademia dei Lincei*, 1955) – all convinced of the genuineness of the letter; M. Porena (*Atti della R. Accademia dei Lincei*, 1933), L. Pietrobono (*GD*, 1939), F. Schneider (*DDJ*, 1957), and C. G. Hardie (*DDJ*, 1960) – all of whom argue against its authenticity; and A. Mancini (*Atti della R. Accademia dei Lincei*, 1942–43), who contends that only part of the letter is genuine.

The most notable studies on the *Eclogae* since 1930 include A. Belloni, "Genesi e caratteri della Bucolica dantesca" (*La Rassegna*, 1930); G. Mazzoni, "Dante e il Polifemo bolognese" (*ASI*, 1938);

and C. Battisti (*SD*, 1956). As for the *Quaestio*, the only important recent article to add to those published at the turn of the century is F. Mazzoni, "La *Quaestio de aqua et terra*" (*SD*, 1957).

IV. DIVINA COMMEDIA

A. EDITIONS

THE BEST critical texts are those of E. Moore in *Tutte le opere di Dante Alighieri* (1894; 4th ed. 1924), G. Vandelli in the *Testo critico* of 1921, and M. Casella (1923). Useful for their variants are the editions of D. Guerri (1933) and N. Zingarelli (1934). There are many editions with fine commentaries. The two authoritative ones of more than half a century ago, by G. A. Scartazzini and T. Casini, should now be consulted in the revisions of G. Vandelli (10th ed. 1938) and S. A. Barbi (6th ed. 1938) respectively. Other important commentaries are those of C. H. Grandgent (rev. ed. 1933) and M. Porena (3 vols., 1946–47). Fine commentaries that are esthetic in emphasis are those of C. Grabher (3 vols., 1934–36) and A. Momigliano (3 vols., 1945–47). Special mention must be reserved for two others: the edition of N. Sapegno (3 vols., 1955–57), with excellent esthetic and historical materials, and H. Gmelin's scholarly *Kommentar* (3 vols., 1954–57) to his German translation. The vast documentation of this last work makes it indispensable for the student of the *Commedia*.

The entire question of what constitutes a proper commentary on the *Commedia* was discussed, with his usual acumen and erudition, by M. Barbi, "Per una più precisa interpretazione della *Divina Commedia*" in *Problemi di critica dantesca* (Series I, 1934) and "Per un nuovo commento della *Divina Commedia*" (*SD*, 1935, 1937). These two studies point out the virtues and defects of many earlier commentaries.

B. DATE

There are two major theories concerning the date of composition of the *Commedia*—Barbi, Rossi, and one group contending that it was begun in 1306 or 1307, and Vossler, Pietrobono, and another group maintaining that it was not initiated until after Henry VII's death in 1313. Among the essays that uphold one or the other of these views one should consult L. Pietrobono, "L'argomento barberiniano e la data della *Divina Commedia"* (*GD*, 1931), which opposes the arguments of the Barbi School. A third thesis, which suggests that the first seven cantos of the *Inferno* were composed in 1301–2, just before Dante's exile, has been staunchly defended by G. Ferretti, *I due tempi della composizione della Divina Commedia* (1935), and "La data dei primi sette canti dell' Inferno" in *Saggi danteschi* (1950). Ferretti's theory has not found favor with most scholars, yet his work has been justly praised for its erudition and its profound knowledge of Dante's poem.

Most scholars consider the date of Dante's imaginary journey to be 1300. In the recent *Anno del viaggio e giorno iniziale della Commedia* (1956), Walter and Teresa Parri give a history of the question and then conclude with F. Angelitti (see *AAPont*, 1897) that the chronological and astronomical data in the poem confirm 1301 and not 1300 as the year of the trip.

C. LITERARY SOURCES

The general work that should still be first consulted is K. Vossler, *Die Göttliche Komödie* (2 vols., 1907–10; 2nd ed. 1925; Eng. trans., *Medieval Culture*, 1929), which provides a superb synthesis of the religious, philosophical, ethico-political, and literary heritage bequeathed to Dante. A detailed investigation of literary sources is A. Rüegg, *Die Jenseitsvorstellungen vor Dante und die übrigen literarischen Voraussetzungen der "Divina Commedia"* (2 vols., 1945), which explores Dante's possible debt to the portrayals of the other world by Homer, Plato, Cicero, Vergil, Saint Paul, authors of the Irish visions (especially Adamnan, Tundal, Alberic), and Moslem legends. Dante's debt to classical and Biblical antiquity is the subject of many fine studies: for example, J. Oeschger, "Antikes und Mittelalterliches bei Dante" (*ZRP*, 1944); A. Franz, "Dante zitiert" (*DDJ*, 1949, 1951); H. Gmelin, "Dante und die römischen Dichter" (*DDJ*, 1953); and P. Renucci, *Dante disciple et juge du monde gréco-latin* (1954). Especially noteworthy is A. Renaudet, *Dante humaniste* (1952), a study of the religious and heroic myths and other elements of classical antiquity that combined with medieval culture to form Dante's Christian Humanism. Still useful for the influence of Virgil is D. Comparetti's classic *Virgilio nel Medio Evo* (new ed., by G. Pasquali, 2 vols., 1937–41).

Dante's possible acquaintance with the *Visio Sancti Pauli* has been examined by G. Ricciotti, *L'Apocalisse di Paolo Siriaca* (2 vols., 1932), and by T. Silverstein (*Harvard Studies and Notes in Philology and Literature*, 1937). A. Mirra discounts the influence of the *Visio Alberici* on Dante (*Misc. Cassinese*, 1932). Other medieval sources have been diligently investigated by various scholars. The question of Dante's debt to the Moslem visions was first seriously posed by M. Asín Palacios, *La escatología musulmana en la Divina Comedia* (1919), which created a sensation on its first appearance. Italian scholars on the whole saw no valid bases for accepting Palacios' conclusions, but they paid tribute to him for having demonstrated the deep affinity between Islamic and Christian representations of the other world. The history of the polemic aroused by the book was published, with a bibliography, by Asín Palacios himself in articles and finally in the second edition of *La escatología musulmana en la Divina Comedia* (1943). The problem has been reopened by E. Cerulli, *Il "Libro della Scala" e la questione delle fonti arabo-spagnole della Divina Commedia* (1949), and J. Muñoz Sendino, *La Escala de Mahoma* (1949). Their discovery of Latin, Castilian, and French versions of a major Islamic legend did not, however, appreciably modify the skepticism of other scholars. Notable essays inspired by Cerulli are those of U. Bosco (*SD*, 1950), M. Porena (*Atti della R. Accademia dei Lincei*, 1950), L. Olschki (*CL*, 1951), and T. Silverstein (*JNES*, 1952).

D. DANTE AND MEDIEVAL THOUGHT

Dante's debt to medieval philosophy has been the subject of many important studies since 1930. Scholars have investigated the sources of his thought from Aristotle to Saint Thomas and Averroes, from Saint Augustine to Saint Bonaventure and Joachim of Flora. Many still contend that the poet was influenced mainly by Thomas Aquinas. A major exponent of Dante's Thomism was G. Busnelli, whose thesis is upheld in many writings, most recently in the commentary to the Busnelli-Vandelli edition of the *Convivio* (2 vols., 1934–37). The major opponent of those who insist on Dante's Thomism is B. Nardi, whose position was made clear in essays as early as 1911. He called attention to the importance and the originality of Dante's philosophic system, evolved from the study of many sources and not from Saint Thomas alone, and he neatly divided Dante's philosophic development into three stages corresponding respectively to the *Convivio*, the *Monarchia*, and the

Commedia. Nardi's best studies are collected in *Saggi di filosofia dantesca* (1930), *Dante e la cultura medievale* (1942; 2nd ed., enlarged, 1949), and *Nel mondo di Dante* (1944). Among his major contentions therein are that Dante was more indebted to Albertus Magnus than to Thomas Aquinas, that he was greatly influenced by Neoplatonic theories, and that he derived a great deal from Arabic and Averroistic doctrines. Most of Nardi's views are supported by E. Gilson in his excellent *Dante et la philosophie* (1939; Eng. trans. 1948).

Studies that investigate the influence of Plato and the Neoplatonists on Dante include R. Resta, *Dante e la filosofia dell'amore* (1935); G. Ledig, "Dante als Platoniker" (*DDJ*, 1944–45); and the many essays of J. A. Mazzeo, now collected in his *Structure and Thought in the "Paradiso"* (1958) and *Medieval Cultural Tradition in Dante's "Comedy"* (1960).

The standard work on Dante's knowledge of Boethius is still R. Murari, *Dante e Boezio* (1905), although one may also consult L. Alfonsi, *Dante e la "Consolatio philosophiae" di Boezio* (1944). Studies on Dante and the mystics include L. Cicchitto, *Postille bonaventuriane-dantesche* (1940); C. Calcaterra, "Sant' Agostino nelle opere di Dante e del Petrarca," in *Nella selva del Petrarca* (1942); P. P. Chioccioni, *L'Agostinismo nella Divina Commedia* (1952); and A. Masseron, *Dante et Saint Bernard* (1953). Dante's debt to John of Salisbury and to Alain de Lille is explored respectively by A. Pézard, "Du Policraticus à la Divine Comédie" (*Romania*, 1948), and by A. Ciotti, "Alano e Dante" (*Convivium*, 1960). The vast influence of Albertus Magnus on the poet is pointed out by A. Bassermann, "Auslese aus einem Dante-Kommentar" (*DDJ*, 1932). Traces of Neo-Pelagianism, Stoicism, and Platonism are found and stressed by Nancy Lenkeith, *Dante and the Legend of Rome* (1952). General studies of note on Dante's philosophy include G. Gentile, *La profezia di Dante* (1933), K. Mosler, *Dante: Eine Einführung in seine Ideenwelt* (1938), and H. Gmelin, *Dantes Weltbild* (1940). A fine essay on one aspect of his thought is V. Cioffari, *The Conception of Fortune and Fate in the Works of Dante* (1940). A good summary of Flora and the Joachites is to be found in L. Tondelli, *Il Libro delle Figure dell'abate Gioachino da Fiore* (1940; 2nd ed. 1953). Finally, Dante's knowledge of medieval science has also been much studied. Among the more recent contributions we may mention G. Boffito, "Saggio d'un commento scientifico alla *Divina Commedia*" (*GD*, 1936), E. Crivelli, "Dante e gli alchimisti," and P. Caligaris, "Nota di astronomia dantesca" (*LI*, 1952).

E. CRITICISM

Modern esthetic criticism of the *Commedia* may be said to originate with F. De Sanctis' *Storia della letteratura italiana* (1870) and his *Saggi critici* (1865–72). He pointed to what constituted poetry and what non-poetry in the work, evinced a strong predilection for the pulsating humanity of the *Inferno* and tended to devaluate the other two canticles. In *Die Göttliche Komödie* (1907–10), K. Vossler echoed De Sanctis' sentiments, particularly with respect to the *Paradiso*, but modified his opinion in the second edition of his opus (1925). It was B. Croce's *La poesia di Dante* (1921), however, that was destined to inspire a thorough reappraisal of the *Commedia*. Croce defined the poem as a theological romance, complicated by a political and ethical utopia. This romance, the structure of the poem, is didactic and practical in intent, and should be distinguished from the poetry, which resides in detached lyrical episodes. Croce's fundamental distinction, already implicit in De Sanctis, led to many discussions on the unity of the *Commedia*. The studies that best clarify the problem of structure and poetry include S. Breglia, *Poesia e struttura nella Divina Commedia* (1934); W. Vetterli, *Die ästhetische Deutung und das Problem der Einheit der Göttlichen Komödie in der neueren Literaturgeschichte* (1935); M. Rossi, *Gusto filologico e gusto poetico: Questioni di critica dantesca* (1942); and M. Sansone, "Natura e limiti del rapporto di struttura e poesia nella critica dantesca" (*Studi di storia letteraria*, 1950). Other critics, however, have sought the dominant, unifying motif of the poem without concerning themselves directly with the tensions between exposition and poetry. A. Momigliano has stressed the "landscape" (*ASNSP*, 1932), which his disciple, G. di Pino, later narrowed down to gradations of "light" (*La figurazione della luce nella "Divina Commedia,"* 1952). In *Dante e la poesia dell'ineffabile* (1934), L. Tonelli suggested the dominant motif of the poem to be the expression of the ineffable; whereas G. Getto (*Aspetti della poesia di Dante*, 1947) declared it to be the respect for intellectual endeavor. F. Flora has insisted upon the unity of the poem although indicating a different tonality for each canticle (*LM*, 1956). Whatever their limitations, all these efforts have greatly enriched Dante criticism with penetrating insights into the nature of the poem. In particular, they have pointed out the subtle beauties of the *Paradiso*, which has received much attention from Italian critics since the 1920s. It may be noted parenthetically that in the United States it is the *Purgatorio* that has received the most attention recently. In less than a decade five serious works have appeared on this canticle: H. Hatzfeld's fine analysis, "The Art of Dante's *Purgatorio*" (*SP*, 1952) ; F. Fergusson, *Dante's Drama of the Mind: A Modern Reading of the "Purgatorio"* (1953) ; B. Stambler, *Dante's Other World: The 'Purgatorio' as Guide to the 'Divine Comedy'* (1957) ; E. de' Negri's perceptive "Tema e iconografia del *Purgatorio*" (*RR*, 1958) ; and C. S. Singleton's noteworthy *Dante Studies 2: Journey to Beatrice* (1958). Modern trends in Dante criticism are summarized by A. Vallone, *La critica dantesca contemporanea* (1953).

F. ALLEGORY AND SYMBOLISM

Many Dante scholars, whether nurtured on Croce's esthetics or on Barbi's historico-philological method, tend for different reasons to minimize the importance of allegory in the *Commedia*. Others, however, make it their primary concern and often strain their imaginations to unearth mystic hidden meanings and correspondences. The writer exerting most influence on modern allegorical interpretations was G. Pascoli, who, in *Minerva oscura* (1898) and elsewhere, contended that the theme of the *Commedia* was the abandonment of the active for the contemplative life. In our period, B. Nardi, like Pietrobono, has accepted the view that the allegory of the *Commedia* consists of the necessity for liberating mankind from the renewal of original sin caused by the donation of Constantine (*SD*, 1942, and *Dante e la cultura medievale*, 1942; 2nd ed. 1949). This interpretation has been challenged by M. Barbi (*SD*, 1937), who also took exception to attempts to reduce the structure of the poem to too rigorous a unity by any system of correspondences and cross references. Great interest in Dante's allegory and his use of symbols has been evinced by American scholars, some possibly under the influence of T. S. Eliot's *Dante* (1929). Among the earlier studies one may mention Helen F. Dunbar, *Symbolism in Medieval Thought and Its Consummation in the Divine Comedy* (1929), and J. B. Fletcher, "Dante's School of the Eagle" (*RR*, 1931) and "Dante's 'Image' in the Sun" (*RR*, 1933). The most significant contributions, however, are those made by C. S. Singleton in several essays and the volumes *Dante Studies 1: Commedia: Elements of Structure* (1954) and *Dante Studies 2: Journey to Beatrice* (1958). Singleton departs from the premise that Dante's allegory is explicit in the theology of his day and makes a clear distinction between allegory and symbolism on the one hand and between the "allegory of poets" and the "allegory of theologians" on the other. He maintains that Dante employed the latter in his poem in order to imitate God's way of writing. Hence Beatrice appears as an analogy of Christ, whose triple advent she mirrors. Singleton's interpretations are based ultimately on the studies of E. Auerbach, who contended that although Dante used the "pagan" allegorical method in his poem, he evinced an even greater preference for the Christian figural method. This thesis he set forth in "Figura" (*Archivum Romanicum*, 1938) and further exemplified in "Figurative Texts Illustrating Certain Passages of Dante's *Commedia*" (*Speculum*, 1946).

Extreme esoteric interpretations of the *Commedia* have been in the main rejected by serious Dante scholars, but they often command critical attention. This is the case with L. Valli's *Il linguaggio segreto di Dante e dei "Fedeli d'Amore"* (1928), an elaboration of theories expressed by G. Rossetti in *La Beatrice di Dante* (1842) and other works. His thesis of a secret sect with a secret language opposed to the corrupt church was worked out further by his disciple A. Ricolfi in many essays and was accepted by J. Evola, *Il mistero del Graal e la tradizione ghibellina dell'Impero* (1937). Valli and Ricolfi applied their theories to all the works of Dante and his contemporaries, whereas others concentrated only on the *Commedia*. A. Dempf considered the poem a bold attempt to propagate the secret doctrines of such Spirituals as P. Olivi in his *Sacrum Imperium: Geschichts- und Staatsphilosophie des Mittelalters und der politischen Renaissance* (1929; Ital. trans. 1933). R. E. John in *Dante* (1946) elaborated the thesis that the poet was a Knight Templar and that the allegory of the *Commedia* can be interpreted as relating to events in the history of the Order as well as to its doctrines and ritual.

There is an extensive literature on particular allegorical representations in the poem, such as the Greyhound, the DXV, Matelda, and the procession in Eden. Fundamental for the first is V. Cian's *Oltre l'enigma dantesco del Veltro* (2nd ed. 1945; originally *Sulle orme del Veltro*, 1897), whose valuable analytical bibliography lists all previous theories of note. Cian's thesis that the Veltro is an emperor and not a pope or an Italian leader like Cangrande or Uguccione della Faggiola is widely accepted. A more recent theory, that he is a great chieftain born under a favorable constellation, is developed by L. Olschki, *The Myth of Felt* (1949). The DXV prophecy and its relation to the Greyhound have been studied most recently by M. Barbi in "Per la genesi e l'ispirazione centrale della *Divina Commedia*" (*SD*, 1932, 1938; now in *Problemi fondamentali per un nuovo commento alla Divina Commedia*, 1955). According to Barbi, both DXV and the Veltro symbolize the emperor Henry VII. In a recent study by M. Porena (*AALIAM*, 1937 [for 1934–35]),

Matelda represents the active and the contemplative life; for L. Pietrobono (*GD*, 1938) she symbolizes the wisdom of the Old Testament; to C. S. Singleton (*ARDS*, 1954), original justice.

G. CHARACTERS: LECTURAE DANTIS

Dante as a character in the *Commedia* is the subject of several studies, including, recently, G. Contini, "Dante come personaggio-poeta" (*Approdo letterario*, 1958). The role of Dante's guides in the poem is naturally discussed in many of the works mentioned in our survey; but a full treatment is found in M. Casella, *Le guide di Dante nella Divina Commedia* (1944), which investigates the function and the meaning of Virgil, Matelda, Beatrice, and Saint Bernard. There are many excellent recent essays on single characters or single cantos of Dante's poem. Noteworthy among the interpretations of two or more cantos published since 1930 are M. Barbi, "Con Dante e coi suoi interpreti" (*SD*, 1931–32), on Francesca and Farinata; A. Chiari, *Letture dantesche* (1939; 2nd ed. 1946), on the so-called "comic" cantos of the *Inferno*; M. Casella, "Interpretazioni" (*SD*, 1949–56), essays on Cato and five cantos of the *Paradiso*; and M. Fubini, *Due studi danteschi* (1951), one of them on the Ulysses canto. G. Getto has included many notable *lecturae* in his indispensable *Letture dantesche*, of which two volumes have appeared, one containing critical readings of each canto of the *Inferno* (1955) and the other, of each canto of the *Purgatorio* (1958). Special note must also be made of A. Pézard's erudite *Dante sous la pluie de feu (Enfer, chant XV)* (1950), which advances the bold thesis that the sinners of the canto are being punished not for sodomy but for blasphemy, violence against the liberal arts, and Brunetto Latini specifically for his ignoring Italian in favor of French in composing the *Trésor*.

We conclude with a reference to the various *Lecturae Dantis*. The first series, initiated in 1900 and published by Sansoni (Florence), is still in part valuable, but it is being supplanted by the *Nuova Lectura Dantis* (1950–), ed. S. A. Chimenz, and by the *Lectura Dantis Siciliana* (1955–). A list of recent *Lecturae* for almost every canto may be found in R. Frattarolo, *Dalle origini a Dante: Bibliografia della critica* (1957). Many notes on Dante's use of words and figures are found in such volumes as G. Federzoni, *Studi e diporti danteschi* (1902; 3rd ed. 1935), and P. Toynbee, *Dante Studies* (1921). The most prolific author of glosses is probably H. D. Austin, whose notes are in large part collected in three long articles: "Di alcune metafore controverse nell'opera di Dante" (*GD*, 1932), "Notes to the *Divine Comedy:* A Supplement to Existing Commentaries" (*PMLA*, 1940), and "Dante and the Mineral Kingdom" (*RPh*, 1950–51). Notes on Dante's use of words are published almost regularly in *Lingua Nostra* (1939–) under the rubric "Parole di Dante."

H. STYLE

Dante's style and language, his use of similes, metaphors, and other devices have inspired many fine studies, some by exponents of the new esthetic stylistics approved by Croce. Fundamental are the penetrating essays of L. Malagoli, *Linguaggio e poesia nella Divina Commedia* (1949) and *Storia della poesia nella Divina Commedia* (1950), in which he stresses the "expressive concreteness" of Dante's language, its visual, spatial, realistic, and dramatic character in relation to the general linguistic expression of the Duecento. Less ambitious but equally brilliant is L. Spitzer's reading of one canto, "Speech and Language in *Inferno* XIII" (*Italica*, 1942). Notable essays on aspects of Dante's style and narrative devices employed by him include: A. Sacchetto, *Il gioco delle imagini in Dante* (1947); E. R. Curtius, "Neue Dante-Studien I" (*RF*, 1947), which examines the poet's use of *periphrasis* and *annominatio;* E. Auerbach, "Dante's Prayer to the Virgin (*Paradiso* XXXIII) and Earlier Eulogies" (*RPh*, 1948); Yvonne Batard, *Dante Minerve et Apollon: Les images de la Divine Comédie* (1952); L. Spitzer, "The Addresses to the Reader in the *Commedia*" (*Italica*, 1955); G. Marzot, *Il linguaggio biblico nella Divina Commedia* (1956).

I. DANTE'S FORTUNA

The best orientation for the student of Dante's *fortuna* is a recent volume that digests and organizes the vast material in the old standard works of Scartazzini, Farinelli, Toynbee, and others: W. P. Friederich, *Dante's Fame Abroad, 1350–1850: The Influence of Dante Alighieri on the Poets and Scholars of Spain, France, England, Germany, Switzerland and the United States: A Survey of the Present State of Scholarship* (1950). The prestige of Dante in Italy has inspired numerous studies. Besides the lucid surveys of F. Maggini (*POCL*, III) and D. Mattalìa (*CISC*, I), there are good individual essays, such as U. Cosmo, *Con Dante attraverso il Seicento* (1946), and A. Vallone, *La critica dantesca nell' Ottocento* (1958). Indispensable for the student of the early commentators on the *Commedia* from Jacopo Alighieri to R. Andreoli are the three superb volumes of *La Divina Commedia nella figurazione artistica e nel secolare commento*, ed. G. Biagi, G. L. Passerini, E. Rostagno,

and U. Cosmo (1924–39). There are no recent surveys of Dante's
fortuna in France and Spain comparable to that of Friederich.
Several essays, however, have been written on the influence he
may have exerted on individual French and Spanish authors.
His prestige in Portugal and Brazil has been explored by H.
de C. F. Lima, "Dante em Portugal e no Brasil" (*EIP*, 1941). A
new survey of Dante's *fortuna* in England is being made by C.
Dédéyan, "Dante en Angleterre" (*LR*, 1958–), which by March
1961 had reached the Elizabethan and Jacobean periods. Other
recent studies of note include: O. Doughty, "Dante and the English
Romantic Poets" (*EM*, 1951); Dorothy L. Sayers, "Dante and
Milton" in *Further Papers on Dante* (1957); and Barbara Seward,
The Symbolic Rose (1960), which examines Dante's influence on
James Joyce and T. S. Eliot. Surveys of Dante in Germany more
recent than Scartazzini's include: T. Ostermann, *Dante in Deutschland: Bibliographie der deutschen Dante-Literatur 1416–1927*
(1929), with additions and a continuation (1928–30) in *DDJ*,
1935; Clara C. Fuchs, "Dante in der deutschen Romantik" (diss.,
Marburg, 1932); F. Wagner, "Dante in Deutschland: Sein staat-
lichkirchliches Bild von 1417–1699" (diss., Heidelberg, 1934).

An area of Dante studies that has been well explored in the past
two decades is his *fortuna* in the United States. The standard volume
on the subject is Angelina La Piana, *Dante's American Pilgrimage:
A Historical Survey of Dante Studies in the United States 1800–
1944* (1948), which is supplemented by J. Chesley Mathews' many
essays on the influence of Dante on American writers from Irving
and Hawthorne to Melville—in particular, "Emerson's Knowledge of
Dante" (*Univ. of Texas Studies in English*, 1942), "Echoes of
Dante in Longfellow's Poetry" (*Italica*, 1949), and "James Russell
Lowell's Interest in Dante" (*Italica*, 1959).

V. THE TRECENTO

FUNDAMENTAL for the literature of the fourteenth century is N.
Sapegno, *Il Trecento* (1934; 2nd ed. 1955). Important for many
authors of the period is B. Croce, *Poesia popolare e poesia d'arte*

(1933), and for its cultural climate, the lectures by various scholars collected in *Il Trecento* (1953).

A. FRANCESCO PETRARCA: GENERAL AIDS

The most useful bibliography of the period before 1916 is the Cornell University Library *Catalogue of the Petrarch Collection Bequeathed by Willard Fiske,* compiled by Mary Fowler (1916). For studies published since then one must rely on various sources: for example, J. G. Fucilla, "Literature of the Renaissance: Italian" (*SP*, 1939–); E. Bonora, "Francesco Petrarca" (*CISC*, I); U. Bosco, "Francesco Petrarca" (*OCLI–I Maggiori*, I). Even more valuable is the superb analytical bibliography appended to C. Calcaterra, "Il Petrarca e il Petrarchismo" (*POCL*, III). Other indispensable tools for the student are the reviews *Annali della Cattedra Petrarchesca di Arezzo* (1930–40) and the current *Studi petrarcheschi* (1948–).

The best general studies on Petrarch's life and works are L. Tonelli, *Petrarca* (1930); N. Sapegno, "Il Petrarca," in *Il Trecento* (1955); E. Carrara, *Petrarca* (1937); H. de Ziegler, *Pétrarque* (1940); U. Bosco, *Petrarca* (1946) and "Francesco Petrarca" (*OCLI–I Maggiori*, I).

B. BIOGRAPHY

Great strides have been made in the study of Petrarch's eventful life, thanks in particular to the investigations of A. Foresti and E. H. Wilkins. Foresti's keen analysis of chronological and textual problems and his intimate knowledge of the poet's life and work are best evident in his masterly *Aneddoti della vita di Francesco Petrarca* (1928). Wilkins' contributions are equally significant. The most important of his numerous essays are "The Coronation of Petrarch" (*Speculum,* 1943), "Petrarch's Ecclesiastical Career" (*Speculum,* 1953), "Petrarch in Provence, 1351–1353," in *Studies in the Life and Works of Petrarch* (1955), *Petrarch's Eight Years in Milan, 1353–1361* (1958), and *Petrarch's Later Years* (1959). Notable studies by others include C. Segre, "Il Petrarca a Montpellier" (*NA*, 1929); F. Rizzi, *Francesco Petrarca e il decennio parmense (1341–1351)* (1934); and R. Weiss, "Il Petrarca e i Malatesta," in *Il primo secolo dell'Umanesimo* (1949).

Petrarch had numerous friends, and his relations with them have been carefully studied by many scholars: for example, A.

Foresti, "Giovanni da Ravenna e il Petrarca," in *Aneddoti della vita di Francesco Petrarca* (1928); *Petrarcas Briefwechsel mit deutschen Zeitgenossen*, ed. P. Piur and K. Burdach (1933), with a valuable introduction and appendix and the poet's correspondence with Charles IV and Johann von Neumarkt; E. G. Léonard, "Victimes de Pétrarque et de Boccace: Zanobi da Strada" (*Etudes Italiennes*, 1934); and N. P. Zacour, "Petrarch and Talleyrand" (*Speculum*, 1956). The poet's relations with Dionigi di Borgo S. Sepolcro, Luigi Marsili, and other Augustinians are the subject of U. Mariani, *Il Petrarca e gli Agostiniani* (1946). The fundamental study for his friendship with Boccaccio, "il primo discepolo," is G. Billanovich, *Petrarca letterato: I. Lo scrittoio del Petrarca* (1947). The poet's connection with Nelli is thoroughly explored by E. H. Wilkins, "A Survey of the Correspondence Between Petrarch and Francesco Nelli" (*IMU*, 1958).

C. LAURA

Petrarch's Laura has been identified with Laure de Sade by the Abbé de Sade, E. Sicardi, G. A. Cesareo, and more recently by N. Quarta, *Laura de Sade* (1942); with Laure de Sabran by F. Flamini; and with Laure de Chiabau by F. Brisset, *Laure de Pétrarque* (1931). Very few consider her to be a symbol. None of these hypotheses have much foundation. Laura was indeed a real person in flesh and blood and not a symbol, but who she was and of what family it is impossible to say at the present state of research. For a history of the problem and sane conclusions, one should consult, among others, H. Hauvette, "Ce que nous savons de Laure" (*Etudes Italiennes*, 1927), and E. Carrara, "La leggenda di Laura" (*Annuali dell'Istituto Superiore di Magistero del Piemonte*, 1934).

La data fatale. The fateful date in Petrarch's life was the sixth of April, the day of his enamorment (1327), of Laura's death (1348), and of Christ's crucifixion. Since Good Friday did not fall on 6 April either in 1327 or 1348, scholars were confronted with an insoluble puzzle until C. Calcaterra pointed to the solution, now accepted by leading Petrarchists (*La "data fatale" nel "Canzoniere" e nei "Trionfi" del Petrarca*, 1926; repub. as "Feria sexta aprilis" in *Nella selva del Petrarca*, 1942), that the poet followed, not the Paschal computation of the church, but the tradition according to which Christ was said to have died on 6 April, and that since there is no mention anywhere in the lyrics of 6 April as a Friday there is no inconsistency.

D. LATIN WORKS

Editions. Since 1925 many of Petrarch's Latin works have been re-edited critically or at least in acceptable fashion. The critical editions that have so far appeared in the "Edizione Nazionale" of Sansoni (Florence) are *L'Africa*, ed. N. Festa (1926) ; the monumental *Le Familiari* (*Familiarum rerum libri*), ed. V. Rossi and U. Bosco (4 vols., 1933–42) ; and *Rerum memorandarum libri*, ed. G. Billanovich (1943). The Testament has been edited by T. E. Mommsen with an English translation (1957), and the following five works, with Italian versions, are in the edition of Petrarch's *Prose*, published by Ricciardi (1955) : the *Secretum*, by E. Carrara ; the *De vita solitaria*, by G. Martellotti ; the *Posteritati*, the *De sui ipsius et multorum ignorantia*, and the *Invectiva contra eum qui maledixit Italie*, by P. G. Ricci. In addition to these there are several other recent editions, although some of Petrarch's Latin works must still be consulted in old editions.

Studies. Petrarch's Latin works have nearly all been studied at least in part. An important essay on the *Africa* is by E. Carrara, "Sulla soglia dell'*Africa*" (*SRo*, 1931), which investigates the sources of the poem's exordium. The *De viris illustribus* and Lombardo della Seta's continuation thereof have been diligently examined by G. Martellotti, who published the lives of Jacob and Joseph (*SPetr*, 1949), as well as *La vita di Scipione l'Africano* (1954). The *Secretum*, Petrarch's confession, has been discussed at length by G. A. Levi, "Pensiero classico e pensiero cristiano nel *Secretum* e nelle *Familiari* del Petrarca" (*Atene e Roma*, 1933) ; C. Calcaterra, "Sant' Agostino nelle opere di Dante e del Petrarca," in *Nella selva del Petrarca* (1942) ; and D. Phillips, "Petrarch's Doctrine of Meditation" (*VUSH*, 1951), a study of the first dialogue. The best studies on the *De otio religioso* and the *De vita solitaria* are those of G. Rotondi (e.g., *Aevum*, 1935, and *RLI*, 1936). The most notable essay on the *De remediis utriusque fortune* is K. Heitmann, *Fortuna und Virtus: Eine Studie zu Petrarcas Lebensweisheit* (1958). E. H. Wilkins has supplied us with a serviceable manual on *Epistolae metricae* (1956).

Petrarch's prose letters, widely consulted in connection with his biography, have perhaps not been considered enough for their style and their moral content. Fine studies of this sort are by E. Allodoli, "Il Petrarca narratore" (*Annali della Cattedra Petrarchesca*, 1935–36), which calls attention to the poet's narrative gifts in the letters; D. Phillips, "Petrarch's Ethical Principles" (*Italica*, 1947), based mainly on the correspondence; and A. S. Bernardo, "Dramatic Dialogue in the Prose Letters of Petrarch" (*Symposium*, 1951), followed by an essay on the use of dramatic dialogue and monologue in other works (*Symposium*, 1953). An indispensable tool of research for the letters is E. H. Wilkins, *Petrarch's Correspondence* (1960).

E. CANZONIERE

The genesis of Petrarch's *Rime* has been exhaustively studied by E. H. Wilkins in his fundamental *The Making of the "Canzoniere" and Other Petrarchan Studies* (1951), which divides the process of evolution of the work into nine stages, represented by four reference collections and nine separate forms. M. Porena's publication in 1941 of the facsimile of MS. Vat. lat. 3196—which corresponds to Wilkins' first reference collection—inspired several fine essays on Petrarch's method of composition, in particular, G. Contini, *Saggio d'un commento alle correzioni del Petrarca volgare* (1943), and A. Romanò, *Il codice degli abbozzi (Vat. lat. 3196) di Francesco Petrarca* (1955).

The partially autographed MS. Vat. lat. 3195 represents the final form of the *Rime*. It was published in facsimile by E. Modigliani (1904), and has served as the basis for all modern editions. The best of these are *Le Rime sparse e i Trionfi*, ed. E. Chiòrboli (1930); *Rerum vulgarium fragmenta*, ed. G. Contini (1949); and *Rime e Trionfi*, ed. R. Ramat (1957). The best annotated texts include *Rime*, ed. G. Carducci and S. Ferrari (1899; now available in G. Contini's presentation, 1957), and *Le Rime sparse*, ed. E. Chiòrboli (1924).

Modern esthetic criticism of the *Rime* may be said to originate with De Sanctis' *Saggio critico sul Petrarca* (1869; new ed. 1954). The great critic regarded the love for Laura as the center of Petrarch's poetic world, and his opinion was echoed by B. Croce (in *Poesia popolare e poesia d'arte*, 1933), who would not, however, concede his predecessor's contention that there were other, if minor, inspirations for the poetry. Croce's narrowness has been strongly opposed by most major critics of Petrarch: for example, A. Momigliano, *Storia della letteratura italiana* (1936); C. Calcaterra, *Nella selva del Petrarca* (1942); U. Bosco, *Petrarca* (1946); and others who stress the poet's introspection and point out that the inspirations for his lyrics are, besides the love for Laura, a profound

sense of the evanescence of life and beauty, the paradox of a desire
for and fear of death, and an incessant feeling of discontent and self-
pity. Calcaterra and Bosco, moreover, maintained that Petrarch's
full poetic personality was to be sought in all his works, Latin as well
as Italian. Fundamental for the history of Petrarch criticism is E.
Bonora, "Francesco Petrarca" (*CISC*, 1).

F. OTHER STUDIES

Problems such as the date of composition of *Italia mia*, the
identity of the *Spirito gentil*, and the division of the *Rime* "in vita"
and "in morte," which were hotly debated by scholars decades ago,
have lost some of their appeal today. Recent scholars and critics
have evinced a preference for esthetic analyses or linguistic interpretations of certain poems. Noteworthy among them are: A. Momigliano, "L'elegia politica del Petrarca" (*Annali della Cattedra
Petrarchesca*, 1937), a superb analysis of *Spirito gentil* and *Italia
mia;* B. Croce's critique of the sonnets 315–317 and the canzone
"Quell'antiquo mio dolce empio signore," in *Poesia antica e moderna*
(1940); F. Maggini, "La canzone delle visioni" (*SPetr*, 1948); and
E. Williamson, "A Consideration of *Vergine bella*" (*Italica*, 1952).
There are some good recent essays on the style and language of
Petrarch's poetry: Adelia Noferi, "Per una storia dello stile petrar-
chesco" (*Poesia*, 1946–47); G. Contini, "Preliminari sulla lingua del
Petrarca" (*Paragone*, 1951), which acutely contrasts Dante's plu-
rilingualism with Petrarch's unilingualism; D. Bianchi, "Di alcuni
caratteri della verseggiatura petrarchesca" (*SPetr*, 1956), a well-
documented study of the poet's rhymes and his use of hiatus, elision,
alliteration, repetition; D. Alonso, "La poesia del Petrarca e il
Petrarchismo" (*LI*, 1959).

G. RIME DISPERSE

The poems not included in the *Canzoniere* and known as *Rime
disperse* were first published by A. Solerti (1909). In reviewing this
edition, E. G. Parodi stressed their importance in the evolution of
the poet's technique and acutely pointed to the likelihood that some
lyrics in the collection were the work of Boccaccio or others. These
problems are now being studied by D. Bianchi, among whose many
contributions we single out "Intorno alle *Rime disperse* del Petrarca: Il Petrarca e i fratelli Beccari" (*SPetr*, 1949) and "Petrarca o Boccaccio?" (*SPetr*, 1952).

H. I TRIONFI

The point of departure for modern critical studies on the *Trionfi* is R. Serra's "Dei *Trionfi* di F. Petrarca," *Scritti,* Vol. ɪɪ (1938), an impressive and well-documented investigation of the sources, the classical erudition, and classical imitations in the poem. Serra pointed to the many echoes of Dante and rejected the arguments adduced in favor of Boccaccio's *Amorosa Visione* as a source for the work. In "Per la genesi dei *Trionfi*" (*Rinascita,* 1941), however, V. Branca added new evidence in support of Boccaccio's influence. In "La prima ispirazione dei *Trionfi* del Petrarca" (*GSLI,* 1941), C. Calcaterra contended that the *Trionfo d'Amore* was conceived as a classical reply to the medieval *Roman de la Rose,* that the poet's guide was Giovanni d'Arezzo, and that the poem was begun in 1340–42 and not in 1356, as Serra believed. The most comprehensive recent study is C. F. Goffis, *Originalità dei "Trionfi"* (1951), which rejects Calcaterra's hypotheses concerning the date of composition and the identity of the guide and his conception of the work as a "dialectic allegory of redemption and salvation." For Goffis the *Trionfi* are a lyrical vision, a re-elaboration of the poetic matter of the *Rime.*

I. PETRARCH AND HUMANISM

A good gage of the progress in research in the poet's classical knowledge since De Nolhac and Sabbadini is U. Bosco, "Il Petrarca e l'Umanesimo filologico (postille al Nolhac e al Sabbadini)" (*GSLI,* 1942). Other notable studies on the subject include A. Bobbio, "Seneca e la formazione spirituale e culturale del Petrarca" (*Biblio,* 1941), and the many contributions of G. Billanovich, among them "Petrarca e Cicerone" (*Miscellanea Giovanni Mercati,* Vol. ɪᴠ, 1946), the already mentioned *Petrarca letterato* (1947), and "Petrarch and the Textual Tradition of Livy" (*JWCI,* 1951).

Special essays that stress Petrarch's new vision of life, his opposition to Aristotelianism, his Platonism, and his ideal of human dignity include those by G. Gentile, "Il carattere della filosofia del Petrarca" (*NA,* 1934), N. Sapegno, "Il Petrarca e l'Umanesimo" (*Annali della Cattedra Petrarchesca,* 1938), and J. H. Whitfield, *Petrarch and the Renascence* (1943). This conception of Petrarch is consistent with that of E. Garin in *La Filosofia,* Vol. ɪ (1947), and G. Saitta, *Il pensiero italiano nell'Umanesimo e nel Rinascimento,* Vol. ɪ (1949), who insist, moreover, that Petrarch found a harmony between antiquity and Christianity. Studies that stress the poet's

Catholicism in order to minimize his pre-Renaissance outlook upon
life are by L. Tonelli, *Petrarca* (1930), and C. Calcaterra, *Nella
selva del Petrarca* (1942). Petrarch's Platonic Humanism fits nicely
into G. Toffanin's thesis of a Christian Renaissance, expounded in
Storia dell' umanesimo italiano dal XIV al XVI secolo (1933; 3rd
ed. 1943; Eng. trans., by E. Gianturco, 1954).

Related to Petrarch's Humanism are his political ideas, his
profound sense of *romanità*, which are more recently analyzed by G.
Gentile, "Il pensiero politico del Petrarca" (*NA*, 1942), R. De
Mattei, *Il sentimento politico del Petrarca* (1944), and L. Russo,
"Politicità del Petrarca" (*Belfagor*, 1949).

J. INFLUENCE—PETRARCHISM

Petrarch's immense influence on European culture was exerted
less by his Latin works than by his Italian poetry. The imitation of
the latter, or what is known as Petrarchism, manifested itself in
various ways. It became a first phase in the evolution of the
technique of many major poets attracted to Petrarch's introspective
analysis of the love conflict. This "intrinsic" Petrarchism characterizes some of the work of lyricists from Du Bellay, Camões,
Spenser, and Tasso down to Carducci, producing likewise a cult of
anti-Petrarchism. Countless minor poets, however, were attracted to
Petrarch's verse forms and his use of conceits, antitheses, and other
artifices. The heyday of this manner, a conventionalism baptized by
Croce a "giuoco di società," was the Cinquecento. Historians of
Petrarchism usually takes pains to distinguish between its manifold
manifestations and to differentiate the debt to Petrarch from the
debt to his Italian imitators.

The *fortuna* of Petrarch's humanistic work, for long somewhat
neglected, is now commanding more attention. A. Farinelli traced the
Spanish vogue of the *De remediis* and the *Trionfi* in *Italia e Spagna*
(Vol. I, 1929). In *Petrarca und Deutschland in der dämmernden
Renaissance* (1933), he indicated the German predilection for the
Latin works. More recent studies of note are by M. Dykmans, "Les
premiers rapports de Pétrarque avec les Pays-Bas" (*Bull. de l'Inst.
hist. belge de Rome*, 1938), G. Billanovich (*Petrarca letterato*,
1947), and F. Simone, "Note sulla fortuna del Petrarca in Francia
nella prima metà del Cinquecento" (*GSLI*, 1950–51), a detailed
survey of the *fortuna* of the Latin works and the *Trionfi*.

The influence of the *Rime* is traced generally by C. Calcaterra,
"Il Petrarca e il Petrarchismo" (*POCL*, III). Important recent
essays on Italian Petrarchism are G. Marzot, "Il tramite del

petrarchismo dal Rinascimento al Barocco" (*SPetr*, 1956), and L. Baldacci, *Il Petrarchismo italiano nel Cinquecento* (1957). The standard recent work for French and English Petrarchism is A. Meozzi, *Il Petrarchismo Europeo* (*Secolo XVI*) (1934), whose long preface acutely analyzes Petrarchism and its manifestations in Europe. Also worthy of mention is M. Praz, "Petrarch in England," in *The Flaming Heart* (1958). Fundamental for the influence of the *Canzoniere* and its Italian imitators in Spain are the numerous studies of J. G. Fucilla, now collected with revisions and additions in his definitive *Estudios sobre el Petrarquismo en España* (1960). Portuguese Petrarchism has also been investigated by Fucilla in several essays, now gathered in his *Studies and Notes* (*Literary and Historical*) (1953). Important for the *fortuna* of Petrarch in Germany is Lidia Pacini, *Petrarca in der deutschen Dichtungslehre vom Barock bis zur Romantik* (1936), and in the Netherlands, Catharina Ypes, *Petrarca in de Nederlandse letterkunde* (1934). Petrarchism in other lands has been explored by E. Várady, "Studi petrarcheschi in Ungheria" (*SPetr*, 1948), and by A. Cronia, "Il petrarchismo del Cinquecento serbo-croato" (*SPetr*, 1948) and "Saggio bibliografico sulla fortuna del Petrarca in Cecoslovacchia" (*SPetr*, 1956). Special studies on the relationship of Petrarch to individual authors are not only abundant but often excellent.

K. GIOVANNI BOCCACCIO: GENERAL AIDS

There are no periodicals devoted solely or mainly to Boccaccio, but there is continuity in the bibliographical material available on him. For editions and studies published through 1938 one can consult G. Traversari, *Bibliografia boccaccesca* (1907), and V. Branca, *Linee di una storia della critica al "Decameron" con bibliografia boccaccesca completamente aggiornata* (1939). The period from 1939 to the present is covered by J. G. Fucilla's yearly "Literature of the Renaissance: Italian" (*SP*, 1939–).

The standard studies on Boccaccio's life and works are H. Hauvette, *Boccace: Étude biographique et littéraire* (1914); G. Lipparini, *La vita e l'opera di Giovanni Boccaccio* (1927); N. Sapegno, "Il Boccaccio," in *Il Trecento;* C. Grabher, *Giovanni Boccaccio* (1945); J. Luchaire, *Boccace* (1951); V. Branca, "Giovanni Boccaccio" (*OCLI–I Maggiori*, I).

L. BIOGRAPHY

The study of Boccaccio's early years is replete with problems. Modern scholars admit that Boccaccio's minor works can illuminate his psychological experiences, but they deny that they contain clues to specific facts, names, or dates. This conclusion, first reached by S. Battaglia in "Elementi autobiografici nell'arte del Boccaccio" (*Cultura*, 1930), was largely repeated by G. Billanovich, *Restauri boccacceschi* (1945), and by V. Branca, "Schemi letterari e schemi autobiografici in Boccaccio" (*Biblio*, 1946). Billanovich, for instance, presents evidence against the hypothesis of Boccaccio's Parisian birth and that of his love for Maria d'Aquino. Studies on periods of his life include A. Foresti, "Il Boccaccio a Ravenna nell'inverno 1361–62" (*GSLI*, 1931), and E. G. Léonard, *Boccace et Naples* (1944). The standard work for his relations with Petrarch is Billanovich's *Petrarca letterato* (1947).

M. MINOR ITALIAN WORKS

All of Boccaccio's minor Italian works are now available in good texts published in the *Scrittori d'Italia* series of Laterza (1918–41). There are in addition two recent critical editions: *Teseida*, ed. S. Battaglia (1938), and *Amorosa Visione*, ed. V. Branca (1944). The latter text was deemed faulty by G. Contini (*GSLI*, 1945–46), and more so by V. Pernicone, who, in his "Gerolamo Claricio collaboratore del Boccaccio" (*Belfagor*, 1946), took Branca to task for his overreliance on the Claricio redaction of the *Amorosa Visione*. The question of Boccaccio's correction of this poem and the role of Claricio in altering the manuscript are discussed in detail by E. Raimondi, "Il Claricio: Metodo di un filologo umanista" (*Convivium*, 1948). Besides the aforesaid editions there are a few annotated texts, the most important of which is the recent *Decameron-Filocolo-Ameto-Fiammetta*, ed. E. Bianchi, C. Salinari, and N. Sapegno (1952).

Of major importance are the studies of V. Branca, who has pointed out the decisive influence of the popular *cantàri* on Boccaccio in *Il cantare trecentesco e il Boccaccio del "Filostrato" e del "Teseida"* (1936), demonstrated that the *Caccia di Diana* was composed by the poet (*ASNSP*, 1938), studied "*L'Amorosa Visione*: tradizioni, significati, fortuna" (*ASNSP*, 1942), and supplied us with a precious list of manuscripts of all Boccaccio's works and a long study on the text of the *Rime* in *Tradizione delle opere di Giovanni Boccaccio* (1958). The *Rime* have also been examined by G. R. Silber, *The Influence of Dante and Petrarch on Certain of Boccaccio's Lyrics* (1940). A masterly essay is V. Pernicone's "Il Filostrato di Giovanni Boccaccio" (*SFI*, 1929), which determines the date of composition, investigates the sources, and analyzes the characters and the poetry of the work.

The minor work that has received the most attention in recent years is the *Fiammetta*. Its sources have been studied by D. Rastelli in "Le fonti autobiografiche dell'*Elegia di Madonna Fiammetta*" (*HumB*, 1948) and "Le fonti letterarie dell'*Elegia di Madonna Fiammetta*" (*Saggi di Umanismo Cristiano*, 1949). Its manuscript tradition has been exhaustively examined in "Per il testo della *Fiammetta*" (*SFI*, 1957,) by A. E. Quaglio, to whom we are also indebted for the impressive *Le Chiose dell'Elegia di Madonna Fiammetta* (1957), which goes far to prove that these glosses, believed by Pernicone to be Boccaccio's, were in reality written by an anonymous admirer. Studies on the other works are not many. Among them we might mention D. Rastelli, "Pagine sul *Ninfale Fiesolano*" (*Saggi di Umanismo Cristiano*, 1952), and A. Limentani, "Tendenze della prosa del Boccaccio ai margini del *Teseida*" (*GSLI*, 1958).

Boccaccio's cult of Dante has been the subject of several fine essays. After editing the *Comento*, D. Guerri published *Il Commento del Boccaccio a Dante: Limiti della sua autenticità e questioni critiche che n'emergono* (1926), in which he upheld the thesis that it was only in part the work of Boccaccio. This theory was refuted in detail by G. Vandelli, "Su l'autenticità del Commento di G. Boccaccio" (*SD*, 1927). Other notable essays include L. Fontana, "Il culto del Boccaccio per Dante" (*RLI*, 1943–48), and G. Billanovich, "La leggenda Dantesca del Boccaccio: Dalla lettera di Ilaro al Trattatello in laude di Dante" (*SD*, 1949), which attributes the authorship of Fra Ilaro's letter to Boccaccio. A new critical edition of the *Comento* is being prepared by G. Padoan, who has set forth his criteria for it in his "Per una nuova edizione del *Comento* di Giovanni Boccaccio" (*SD*, 1958).

N. LATIN WORKS

The only Latin works available in good modern editions are *Opere latine minori* (*Buccolicum Carmen, Carminum et Epistolarum quae supersunt, Scripta breviora*), ed. A. F. Massèra (1928), and *Genealogie Deorum Gentilium Libri*, ed. V. Romano (2 vols., 1951).

The *Genealogia* is the only Latin work that has attracted recent attention. Its textual tradition has been studied by P. G. Ricci, "Contributi per un'edizione critica della *Genealogia Deorum Gentilium*" (*Rin*, 1951), and generally by V. Romano (*Belfagor*, 1953). Boccaccio's poetics—the defense of poetry in Books XIV–XV of the *Genealogia*—is the subject of a fine essay by F. Tateo (*FiR*, 1958). Other Latin works are studied by P. G. Ricci in "Studi sulle opere latine e volgari del Boccaccio" (*Rin*, 1959). Important for Boccaccio's Humanism in general are several articles of Cornelia G. Coulter, among them "Boccaccio and the Cassinese Manuscripts of the Laurentian Library" (*CP*, 1948).

O. DECAMERON

There is still no critical edition of the *Decameron*, but the way has been paved for it by such masterly studies on the manuscript tradition as those by M. Barbi (*SFI*, 1927), Maria S. Simonelli (*ASNSP*, 1949), and V. Branca (*SFI*, 1950, 1953). The best recent editions are those of V. Branca (2 vols., 2nd ed. 1956), C. S. Singleton (2 vols., 1955), and N. Sapegno (2 vols., 1956), who based his text mostly on Branca's. The publication of Singleton's edition led to a minor storm of controversy as to the relative merits of his text and Branca's. A well-balanced evaluation of both is by N. Sapegno (*GSLI*, 1956).

There are many penetrating critical studies of the *Decameron*. In the main they react to De Sanctis' brilliant but unilateral appraisal of the work as the antithesis of the *Divine Comedy*, as a human comedy that exalts the flesh and the senses and whose dominant tone is comic. This criticism was generally accepted until 1924, when A. Momigliano called attention in his anthology to Boccaccio's chivalric ideal and to the beauty of the serious tales, those of tragic passion, tender love, and generous sentiments. This led U. Bosco and others to seek a formula that would at once reconcile the comic and the serious in Boccaccio's opus. In *Il Decameron: Saggio* (1929), Bosco contended that this dominant, unifying motif was the author's unqualified admiration for the power of human intelligence in all its forms. In *Il Trecento*, Sapegno admitted the exaltation of human intelligence as one source of inspiration for the work but insisted that another source was the power of human passion. G. Petronio, in *Il Decamerone: Saggio critico* (1935), broke down intelligence into amorality and astuteness ("spregiudicatezza e saviezza"). Momigliano was critical of Bosco's thesis, maintaining that Boccaccio's artistic world was too complex and varied to be reduced to a single formula (*Corriere della sera*, 7 June 1930; now in *Elzeviri*, 1945). Similar sentiments were echoed by L. Russo in the critical notes to his selection of tales (1939), important essays recently republished as *Letture critiche del Decameron* (1956). N. Vitale, in *Temi certaldesi* (*Consensi e dissensi*) (1943), not only rejected Bosco's formula but returned to De Sanctis' thesis of a comic and sensual Boccaccio. Recently, in

Vita di forme e forme di vita nel "Decameron" (1958), G. Getto proposed the art of *savoir-vivre* as the dominant theme of the work. Whatever their theories, all these studies contain fine esthetic analyses of tales in the *Decameron*.

According to De Sanctis, Boccaccio's conception of man and of passion distinctly foreshadowed the Renaissance. Though some recent critics accept this view, G. Lipparini considered Boccaccio an essentially medieval spirit (*La vita e l'opera di Giovanni Boccaccio,* 1927), and more recently V. Branca advanced a similar thesis in his fundamental *Boccaccio medievale* (1956). Branca argues that the *Decameron* reflects the medieval tradition, that even its prose owes less to classical models than heretofore supposed, and that, in fine, it is pre-eminently the epic of the merchant. Boccaccio seeks to portray man in this mercantile world, at grips with three dominant forces in life — fortune, love, ingenuity. G. Leone lays stress on the economic as the major theme of the *novelle* in his *Johannes utilitatum: Saggio sul Decamerone* (1956). In "Interpretazione del Decameron" (*Convivium,* 1957), M. Marti points to the influence on Boccaccio of the medieval realistic and jocose tradition.

Another characteristic of recent Boccaccio criticism is the attention paid to the relation of the minor works to the masterpiece. In "Schemi lirici nell'arte del Boccaccio" (*Archivum Romanicum,* 1935), S. Battaglia noted the recurrence of the cornice scheme in several works. Petronio in his essay, Grabher (*Boccaccio,* 1945), Russo (*Studi sul Due e Trecento,* 1951), and G. di Pino (*La polemica del Boccaccio,* 1953), all seek the unifying themes in his entire Italian production and trace the gradual process whereby he freed himself from the shackles of rhetoric and classical erudition as well as from the autobiographical elements that abound in the minor works. The interest in the latter is further evidenced by modern Boccaccio anthologies, which are usually entitled *Dal "Decameron" e dalle Opere minori.* Such are, for example, those of V. Pernicone (1936), N. Sapegno (1937), L. Russo (1938), and C. Grabher (1942).

Histories of Boccaccio criticism are by V. Branca, *Linee di una storia della critica del "Decameron"* . . . (1939), and G. Petronio, "Giovanni Boccaccio" (*CISC,* 1). The general design, the cornice, and the introduction are discussed by F. Neri, "Il disegno ideale del Decameron" (*Mélanges H. Hauvette,* 1934).

P. INFLUENCE

Boccaccio's *fortuna* has been well explored only with respect to Italy and to England. His Italian influence has been examined by L.

Di Francia, *Novellistica*, Vol. I (1924), O. Löhmann, *Die Rahmen-erzählung des Decameron, ihre Quellen und Nachwirkungen* (1935), and A. Chiari, "La fortuna del Boccaccio" (*POCL*, III). His *fortuna* in England has been investigated by H. G. Wright in many pieces, culminating in the comprehensive *Boccaccio in England from Chaucer to Tennyson* (1957). Also useful is J. Raith, *Boccaccio in der englischen Literatur von Chaucer bis Painters Palace of Pleasure* (1936). There is an extensive literature on the relations of Boccaccio and Chaucer. Significant recent studies are to be found in *Sources and Analogues of Chaucer's Canterbury Tales* (1941), ed. W. F. Bryan and Germaine Dempster; R. A. Pratt, "Chaucer's Use of the *Teseida*" (*PMLA*, 1947); and S. B. Meech, *Design in Chaucer's Troilus* (1959), which contains a detailed comparison of the poem with the *Filostrato*. The problem of Chaucer's possible acquaintance with the *Decameron* is examined by M. Praz, "Chaucer and the Great Italian Writers of the Trecento" (*Monthly Criterion*, 1927; now in *The Flaming Heart*, 1958). For other countries one might mention A. Farinelli, "Boccaccio in Ispagna" in *Italia e Spagna*, Vol. I (1929), which points to the vogue of the Latin works, the *Corbaccio* and the *Fiammetta*, and A. Cronia, "La fortuna del Boccaccio nella letteratura céca" (*LI*, 1954).

Of special interest are the detailed studies of the vogue of single tales or their themes in European literature: for example, L. Fassò, *La prima novella del "Decameron" e la sua fortuna* (1931); E. Golenistcheff-Koutouzoff, *L'histoire de Griseldis en France au XIVe et au XVe siècle* (1933); J. Raith, *Die Historie von der vier Kaufleuten* (1936); and L. Sorieri, *Boccaccio's Story of "Tito e Gisippo" in European Literature* (1937).

Q. MINOR POETS

Many of the minor poets remain to be edited and studied. There is, however, a superb anthology, with copious selections, bibliography, and notes, by N. Sapegno, *Poeti minori del Trecento* (1952). Good recent critical studies, however, do exist with comments and texts for some of the poets: for example, Franca Ageno, *Il Bianco da Siena: Notizie e testi inediti* (1939); E. Li Gotti, *La poesia musicale italiana del secolo XIV* (1944); and the essays on Cino Rinuccini and Matteo Frescobaldi in E. Li Gotti's *Restauri trecenteschi* (1947).

R. NARRATIVE POEMS

These are the popular *cantàri* in *ottava rima* that draw their material from legends, classical history or mythology, the lives of the saints or the Carolingian and Arthurian cycles. They are in the main fairly brief (an average of 400 to 600 lines) except for a few long epics of chivalry. Of the first group E. Levi published twelve in his *Fiori di leggende: Cantari antichi:* Serie I: *Cantari leggendari* (1914). More recent publications include F. A. Ugolini, "I cantari di Piramo e Tisbe" (*SRo,* 1934), with the text of four poems of the fourteenth and fifteenth centuries; *Cantari di Tristano,* ed. G. Bertoni (1937); and U. Cianciòlo, "Contributo allo studio dei cantari di argomento sacro" (*Archivum Romanicum,* 1938), which lists these *cantàri* and gives the text of the hitherto unpublished *Leggenda di S. Torpete.* F. A. Ugolini has studied the poems based on classical themes in his important *I cantari d'argomento classico* (1933), which also includes an appendix of unedited texts. The narrative poems on religious subjects are analyzed in P. Toschi's notable *La poesia popolare religiosa in Italia* (1935).

Three of the long popular epics have been critically edited in recent years: *La Spagna,* by M. Catalano (3 vols., 1939–40), of which the first volume is a masterly study of the poem and its relation to the *Chanson de Roland* and to Italian Carolingian material and the third, the text of *La Rotta di Roncisvalle* and a briefer *cantàre;* Niccolò da Càsola, *La Guerra d'Attila,* a poem in Franco-Italian, ed. G. Stendardo (2 vols., 1941); and *Li fatti de Spagna,* a northern Italian text, ed. R. M. Ruggieri (1951; only Vol. I published so far).

Antonio Pucci's vast production is largely unavailable in good texts. Moreover, much of it is found in special collections, a list of which is published in Sapegno's *Il Trecento.* Good recent editions are *Le Noie,* ed. K. McKenzie (1931), with a fine introduction; the critical text of *Della Vecchiezza,* also by McKenzie (*Speculum,* 1940); *Il Contrasto delle donne,* by A. Pace (1944); and *Libro di varie storie,* by A. Varvaro (1957). The best critical study on Pucci is N. Sapegno, "Scrittori del Trecento: Antonio Pucci" (*Civiltà moderna,* 1931–32). There is a real need for a good complete edition of Pucci's works and a comprehensive study of his life and his literary production.

S. RELIGIOUS PROSE

The religious literature of the century is extensive and still largely unedited. An idea of its quantity and quality may be obtained from two anthologies, which contain many selections from both published and unpublished works: *Mistici del Duecento e del Trecento,* ed. A. Levasti (1935), and *Prosatori minori del Trecento:*

Vol. I, *Scrittori di religione*, ed. G. De Luca (1954), which also presents the full text of *I Fioretti di San Francesco* and Girolamo da Siena's *Il soccorso dei poveri*. A general critical appraisal of religious literature is found in G. Petrocchi, *Ascesi e mistica trecentesca* (1957). One cannot stress too strongly that the literary historian, in evaluating this religious prose, is constantly confronted with the problem of distinguishing artistic expression from eloquence, didactic or moral intent, theology or mystical exaltation.

The groundwork for a critical edition of the *Fioretti* has been laid in "Inchiesta sulla tradizione manoscritta dei *Fioretti di San Francesco*" (*FiR*, 1957), by G. Petrocchi, to whom we also owe a study on the evolution of the work, "Dagli *Acti Beati Francisci* al volgarizzamento dei *Fioretti*" (*Convivium*, 1954). The work has been critically evaluated by A. Momigliano in his *Studi di poesia* (1938) and its language analyzed by Gianna Tosi, *La lingua dei Fioretti di San Francesco* (1938). Quite recently G. Petrocchi critically edited *La vita di frate Ginepro* (1960).

There are a few recent studies on Passavanti and Cavalca: for example, Carmelina Naselli's monograph, *Domenico Cavalca* (1925); G. Getto, *Umanità e stile di Jacopo Passavanti* (1943); and A. Olga Rossi, "*Questione del Cavalca:* Further Findings" (*PMLA*, 1949), which contends that the source for the *Pungilingua* as for all Cavalca's works, is Peraldus' *Summa virtutum ac vitiorum*. The literature on Saint Catherine of Siena is so vast that we can mention only few of the more important works by her and on her of interest to the literary historian. There is a good text of her *Libro della Divina Dottrina, volgarmente detto Dialogo della Divina Provvidenza*, ed. Matilde Fiorilli, revised by S. Caramella (1928). One volume of a new critical edition of her *Epistolario*, by E. Dupré Theseider, has appeared (1940). Sigrid Undset, *Catherina of Siena* (1951; Eng. trans. 1954), and A. Grion, *Santa Caterina da Siena: Dottrina e fonti* (1953), must likewise be mentioned. Important critical studies that essay to differentiate the poetic, the oratorical, and the mystical elements in the saint's style and language include N. Festa, "La lingua e lo stile nell'epistolario di Santa Caterina" (*Studi cateriniani*, 1938), and A. Giannini, "Poesia ed oratoria di S. Caterina da Siena" (*Aevum*, 1948).

T. SECULAR PROSE

Critical texts of many of the major Trecento chronicles appeared before 1920, particularly in the collections *Rerum Italicarum Scriptores* and *Fonti per la Storia d'Italia*. The prime *desider-*

ata remain the critical editions of the *Cronica* of Giovanni Villani, its continuation by Matteo and Filippo Villani, and the *Storia fiorentina*, by Ricordano Malispini. A fine anthology with critical comments is R. Palmarocchi, *Cronisti del Trecento* (1935).

There is no complete modern edition of Ser Giovanni Fiorentino's *Il Pecorone* nor a complete text of Giovanni Sercambi's *Novelliero*. One must hence rely on S. Battaglia's fine collection from *Il Pecorone* (1944) and on the collections of Sercambi's *Novelle*, edited by A. D'Ancona (1866; 1871) and by R. Renier (1889). Good studies, however, are not lacking on the two writers: among them are E. Li Gotti, "Storia e poesia del Pecorone" (*Belfagor*, 1946); G. Petrocchi, "Il novelliere medioevale del Sercambi" (*Convivium*, 1949); and L. Russo, "Ser Giovanni Fiorentino e Giovanni Sercambi" (*Belfagor*, 1956).

Most of the romances are available only in nineteenth-century editions, but Andrea da Barberino's *I Reali di Francia* were critically edited recently by G. Vandelli and G. Gambarin (1947) and his *L'Aspramonte* by M. Boni (1951). The Venetian fragment known as the *Tristano Corsiniano* was published by M. Galasso (1937). Important essays on these romances include: G. Osella, *Il Guerrin Meschino* (1932), an analysis of the work and a history of its textual tradition; P. H. Coronedi, "*L'Aquilon de Bavière*" (*Archivum Romanicum*, 1935), an exhaustive study of this French epic of Raffaele Marmora; M. Boni, "Note sul cantare magliabechiano d'Aspramonte e sull'*Aspramonte* di Andrea da Barberino" (*GSLI*, 1950), a good source investigation; and R. Ambrosini, "Spoglio fonetico, morfologico e lessicale del *Tristano Corsiniano*" (*ID*, 1955–56).

Other prose works are by Guido da Pisa, *I Fatti d'Enea*, ed. A. Marenduzzo with notes (1906; 2nd ed. 1940); Giuliana Giannardi, "Le *Dicerie* di Filippo Ceffi" (*SFI*, 1942), with the critical text of the *Dicerie;* Paolo Certaldi, *Libro di buoni costumi*, ed. A. Schiaffini with a fine introduction (1945); Andrea Capellano, *Trattato d'amore*, Latin text with two unpublished Tuscan versions, ed. S. Battaglia (1947); and a new edition of the Tuscan translation of Marco Polo's *Il Milione* by R. Allulli (1954).

The basic studies on the biography of Franco Sacchetti are F. Pieper, *Franco Sacchetti, Bürger von Florenz und Dichter* (1939), which includes an invaluable concordance-commentary of his work, and E. Li Gotti, *Franco Sacchetti, uomo "discolo e grosso"* (1940), and some chapters in his *Restauri trecenteschi* (1947). Before the 1930s Sacchetti's works were available only in defective editions. M. Barbi bewailed this situation and offered valuable suggestions in

"Per una nuova edizione delle novelle del Sacchetti" (*SFI*, 1927). His advice was heeded, for we now have good texts of the writer's extant production: *Il libro delle Rime* (1936) and *La Battaglia delle belle donne, Le Lettere, Le Sposizioni di Vangeli* (1938), all ed. A. Chiari; and *Il Trecentonovelle*, ed. V. Pernicone (1946). These are the texts used by A. Borlenghi in his edition of Sacchetti's *Opere* (1955), which comprises the *Trecentonovelle* and selections from the other works. In the last decade or so there have been some fine critical evaluations of Sacchetti's art: V. Courir, "Nota critica al *Trecentonovelle* di Franco Sacchetti" (*ASNSP*, 1947); L. Russo, "La letteratura comico-realistica nella Toscana del Due e Trecento" (*Belfagor*, 1947); and particularly L. Caretti, *Saggio sul Sacchetti* (1951). They all agree in essence with Croce and Sapegno that Sacchetti, the moralist with a firm religious faith, cannot be separated from Sacchetti, the storyteller full of common sense, endowed with a flair for the fabulous (Courir), for the strange and the comical (Courir, Russo), and for a "daily magic" whose objective is movement (Caretti). Caretti, moreover, traces the evolution of the author's realism from the *Battaglia* and of his moralizing habit from the *Lettere* and *Sposizioni* to their fusion in the *novelle*, with the *Rime* conceived as a literary and technical interlude. For the history of Sacchetti criticism one should consult R. Ramat, "Franco Sacchetti e la critica" (*Belfagor*, 1946), and A. Borlenghi, "Posizioni della critica sacchettiana" (*LM*, 1953).

8
___

Medieval Spanish Literature

By John E. Keller
UNIVERSITY OF NORTH
CAROLINA

D URING THE PAST thirty years research in some areas of
medieval Spanish literature has been abundant, notably in
lyric poetry, concerning which startling discoveries have been made;
a great deal has been written, too, about epic poetry; the *Libro de
buen amor* has been the center of much scholarly investigation and
controversy. The present survey will treat recent scholarship on
these and other literary topics in some detail. Genres that are less
strictly literary—legal works, histories, treatises on scientific
subjects—will be treated briefly when they have a bearing on
literature.

I. GENERAL AIDS

A. BIBLIOGRAPHIES

F ORTUNATELY, Spanish literature for the medieval period has
two very complete bibliographies. J. Simón Díaz, *Bibliografía
de la literatura hispánica*, Vol. III (1953) is the best, covering all
aspects of medieval Spanish literature and writing. Its 1276 pages
listing manuscripts, editions, translations, scholarship, and reviews
make it the indispensable and basic bibliography. H. Serís, *Manual
de bibliografía española. Primera Parte* (1948) and *Segundo Fascí-
culo de la Primera Parte* (1954), present a copious, up-to-date
medieval bibliography. Both Simón Díaz and Serís offer occasional
critical annotations.

The two-volume *Manuel de l'Hispaniste* of R. Foulché Delbosc
and L. Barrau-Dihigo (2nd ed. 1959) is regarded by many scholars
as the best bibliographical guide to the field of Spanish studies. The

parts devoted to the Middle Ages are comprehensive. The Spanish section of T. R. Palfrey, J. Fucilla, and W. Holbrook, *A Bibliographical Guide to the Romance Languages and Literatures* (5th ed. 1963) is reasonably complete and helpful to its year of publication. R. Grismer's *A Bibliography of Articles and Essays on the Literatures of Spain and Spanish America* (1935), although outdated, is still useful for the Middle Ages. Maggs Brothers' *Books Printed in Spain and Spanish Books Printed in Other Countries*, compiled by S. de Laredo (1927), is a bibliography of Spanish bibliographies. Extensive and sound is G. Bleiberg and J. Marías, *Diccionario de la literatura española* (1949; 2nd ed. 1953); and the *Spanish Language and Literature in the Publications of American Universities* (1952), by J. Delk and J. Greer, though not complete, is helpful. The *Católogo de los incunables de la Biblioteca Nacional* of D. García Rojo and G. Ortiz de Montalván (1945; 2nd ed. 1958) provides valuable and necessary information on early editions, supplementing the old but very useful *Ensayo de una bibliografía española de libros raros y curiosos* (4 vols., 1863–89) of B. Gallardo, which also lists over twelve thousand manuscripts in the Biblioteca Nacional. Also useful are J. Rodríguez de Castro, *Biblioteca española* (2 vols., 1781–86); P. de Gayangos, *Catalog of Spanish Manuscripts . . . in the British Museum* (4 vols., 1875–93); and Clara Penney, *List of Books Printed before 1601 in the Library of the Hispanic Society of America* (1929). Two valuable and up-to-date continuing bibliographies may be mentioned: J. López de Toro, *Inventario de los manuscritos en la Biblioteca Nacional* (1955–), with six volumes published, and A. Palau y Dulcet, *Manual del librero español e hispanoamericano* (2nd ed. 1948–58), with fourteen volumes published. A. Millares Carlo, *Literature española hasta fines del siglo XV* (1950), contains excellent bibliographies for each chapter.

In the area of comparative literature there is W. Friederich and F. Baldensperger, *Bibliography of Comparative Literature* (1950; rptd. 1960), and its continuation in *YCGL* by K. Selig and H. Frenz. The serial bibliography in *PMLA* lists many valuable items for medieval Spanish literature, as does the serial bibliography in *RFE*.

B. PALEOGRAPHY

Three manuals of paleography have helped to clear up some of the problems of editing manuscripts in Spanish: Z. García Villada, *Paleografía española* (2 vols., 1923); A. Millares Carlo, *Tratado de paleografía española* (2nd ed. 1932) ; and A. Floriano Cumbrena, *Curso general de paleografía y diplomática española* (2 vols., 1946).

C. HISTORY

Large segments of Spanish literature in the Middle Ages were concerned with Spanish history, making necessary some knowledge of this history. The monumental three-thousand-page *Diccionario de historia de España* (1952), ed. R. Menéndez Pidal, provides the usual as well as the unusual information; Menéndez Pidal's *The Spaniards in Their History*, trans. W. Starkie (1950), also makes important contributions. Likewise valuable for the medievalist are the volumes devoted to the Middle Ages in A. Ballesteros, *Historia de España y su influencia en la historia universal* (2nd ed., 12 vols., 1943–48). More recent and general are H. Livermore, *A History of Spain* (1958) ; W. Atkinson, *A History of Spain and Portugal* (1960), which makes interesting connections between literature and history; and P. Aguado Bleye, *Manual de historia de España* (3 vols., 7th ed. 1954–56). The history of the medieval period is treated in Vols. I and II of R. Merriman's four-volume *The Rise of the Spanish Empire* (1918–34).

J. Amador de los Ríos, *Historia social, política y religiosa de los judíos de España y Portugal* (1960), in the new one-volume revised edition, is still a classic and still a standard work. A. Castro, *The Structure of Spanish History* (1954), a translation of Castro's second and revised Spanish version of *España en su historia* (1948), entitled *La realidad histórica de España* (1954), among a great number of other subjects, treats the Moors and the Jews in Spain and shows that these peoples exercised an even greater influence than scholars had formerly accorded them, especially in the areas of the history of ideas, thought, and, by extension, literature. F. Baer's *Die Juden in Christlichen Spanien* (2 vols., 1929 and 1936) is worth consulting, as is also A. Neuman's *The Jews in Spain* (2 vols., 1942), which treats their social, political, and cultural life, as well as their history. S. Katz in *The Jews in the Visigothic and Frankish Kingdoms of Spain and Gaul* (1937) traces the life of the Jews and shows the effect of persecution from the times of the Visigoths. An especially reliable treatment is that by J. Millás Villacrosa, "Historia de los judíos españoles" (*Sefarad*, 1946).

The works of A. González Palencia are authoritative in their treatment of Moorish and Arabic Spain. His *Historia de la España musulmana* (4th ed. 1945) and *Moros y cristianos en la España medieval* (1945) show the impact and steady influence of Spanish Islam on the rest of the Peninsula in the areas of politics and culture; his *Historia de la literatura arábigo-española* (2nd ed. 1945) summarizes relations between Islam and the West, especially as regards literary influences. *La España musulmana* (1946), by C. Sánchez Albornoz, gives selections from contemporary Arabic and Latin sources. E. Lévi Provençal, *Histoire de l'Espagne musulmane* (3 vols., 2nd ed., rev. and enlarged, 1950–53), drawing upon the entire corpus of Hispano-Arabic relations, is sound and comprehensive. Although F. Javier Simonet, *Historia de los mozárabes de España* (1903), is still a classic on the Christians who lived under Arabic culture, I. de las Cagigas, *Minorías étnico-religiosas de la Edad Media*, planned in eleven volumes—on the *mozárabes*, on the *mudéjares*, on the *moriscos*, and on the Jews—published in 1947 and following, is now the most complete study on the minorities both Christian and non-Christian during the Middle Ages, notably of the Jews under both Moslem and Christian domination and the Moslems in Christian Spain.

The backgrounds of Spanish religious life, so important to the literature of the Middle Ages, may be consulted in J. Pérez de Urbel, *Los monjes españoles en la Edad Media* (2 vols., 1933–34) and in *El monasterio en la vida española de la edad media* (1942). Daily living has been treated by J. Rubió y Balaguer in *Vida española en la época gótica* (1943), "gótica" indicating the medieval period from the twelfth century through the fifteenth.

D. HISTORIES OF LITERATURE

Owing to its reliability and critical excellence, save in areas where it has been rendered outdated by more recent research, the *Historia crítica de la literatura española* of J. Amador de los Ríos (7 vols., 1861–65) is still a fundamental work. The best general factual study of medieval Spanish letters, valuable for a straightforward and informative approach to both major and minor works in all genres, is A. Millares Carlo, *Literatura española hasta fines del siglo XV* (1950). Still in progress is the vast *Historia general de las literaturas hispánicas* . . . , the first volumes of which (1949 and 1951) treat matters of interest to medievalists. Edited by G. Díaz-Plaja, with contributions from specialists in the various genres, it will in time offer valuable, if uneven, studies of various aspects of medieval Spanish literature. A careful and critical treatment of selected areas of medieval Spanish literature is to be found in A. Valbuena Prat, *Historia de la literatura española* (2 vols., 1937; 3 vols., 6th ed. 1960). His *El Sentido católico en la literatura española*

(1941), one of the rare studies of ecclesiastical influences on Spanish writing, is useful for a proper understanding of these influences.

Space does not permit the listing of all of the numerous manuals of Spanish literature, many of which treat the Middle Ages. Especially useful for factual information are the manuals of G. Northup (3rd ed. 1960), J. Hurtado and A. González Palencia (6th ed. 1949), A. del Río (2nd ed. 1961), E. Mérimée and S. Morley (rev. ed. 1930), and K. Schwartz and R. Chandler (1961).

E. ANTHOLOGIES

Few anthologies devoted strictly to medieval Spanish literature exist, although D. Alonso, *Poesía de la Edad Media y poesía de tipo tradicional* (1935 and 1942), does provide an anthology of medieval Spanish poetry. The two-volume *Textos hispánicos dialectales* (1960) of M. Alvar contains materials interesting to the medievalist. Volume I of J. de Entrambasaguas, *Antología histórica de la lengua española* (1941), is broad in scope, with representative selections from medieval writers; E. Kohler, *Antología de la literatura española de la Edad Media* (1957), likewise has a broad range, but it presents too many selections from outmoded and poor editions and offers very brief introductory remarks for the selections. The first volume of A. and A. del Río, *Antología general de la literatura española* (2nd ed. 1961), contains selections from all the genres of medieval Spanish literature and from most of the individual works, although a good many are again taken from outmoded editions. It should be used only in the second edition, as the first has many typographical errors. J. Ford's *Old Spanish Readings* (1939) offers only brief selections, but scholarly and detailed notes and introductions. Tatiana Fotitch, *An Anthology of Old Spanish* (1962), is the best up-to-date anthology, good for literature and language studies.

F. MISCELLANEOUS

A few works dealing with culture, literary criticism, and esthetics should be listed: E. Peers, *Spain: A Companion to Spanish Studies* (5th ed., rev. and enlarged, 1956), is very helpful; M. Menéndez Pelayo, *Historia de las ideas estéticas en España* (1940), provides scholarly guidance difficult to find in the development of literary tastes; H. Hatzfeld, "Esthetic Criticism Applied to Medieval Romance Literature" (*RPh*, 1948), is a key article in medieval esthetics. A fundamental work is the three-volume *Etudes d'esthétique médiévale* (1946; Spanish trans. 1958–59), by E. de Bruyne. F.

López Estrada's *Introducción a la literatura medieval española* (2nd ed. 1962) is invaluable for its excellent criticism of the tools necessary for medieval studies, and as a guide to the medieval literature of Spain in all its phases.

The geography of Spain is treated by Ruth Way and Margaret Simmons, *A Geography of Spain and Portugal* (1962); early Spanish and Moorish coins may be profitably studied in F. Mateu y Llopis, *La Moneda española* (1946); heraldry is carefully treated in J. de Atienza, *Nobiliario español: Diccionario heráldico de apellidos españoles y de títulos nobiliarios* (3rd ed., rev. and augmented, 1959); medieval Latin writers in Spain are listed in M. C. Diaz y Díaz, *Index scriptorum latinorum medii aevi hispanorum* (1959); and L. Martínez Kleisner, *Refranero general, ideológico español* (1953), lists large numbers of proverbs, among them numerous examples from medieval works, although he does not give pages or lines in the text from which they are drawn.

G. PERIODICALS

Articles on medieval Spanish literature frequently appear in the usual scholarly journals. The following, devoted primarily to Spanish literature, may be listed: *Sefarad* dealing with Hispano-Jewish matters, and *Al-Andalus* with Hispano-Arabic, are of signal importance, for in these two journals have appeared some of the recent significant studies on early lyric poetry; others valuable for consultation are *Boletín de la Real Academia Española, Bulletin Hispanique, Bulletin of Hispanic Studies, Hispanic Review, Nueva Revista de Filología Hispánica, Revista de Archivos, Bibliotecas y Museos, Revista de Filología Hispánica, Romania, Filologia Romanza, Hispanófila, Studi Medievali, Romance Philology, Le moyen âge, La Ciudad de Dios* (of the Escorial), *Revue hispanique, Revista de Filología Española,* and *Speculum.*

II. LYRIC POETRY

THE RECENT discovery of primitive Spanish poems written in Arabic or Hebrew characters and called variously *kharjas, harchas,* or *jarŷas* has created an entirely new bibliography. The earlier scholarship has been treated in Chapter 4 of this volume, in connection with the origins of troubadour poetry. We can, therefore, begin here with S. M. Stern's *Les chansons mozarabes, Editées avec introduction, annotations, sommaire et glossaire* (1953), a fundamental book on the *kharjas* presenting theories that have been widely accepted. The articles of D. Alonso are likewise basic to an understanding of the *kharjas*, especially his "Cancionillas *de 'amigo'* mozárabes" (*RFE*, 1949), in which he indicates the importance of these poems and gives parallels between them and the *cantigas de amigo*. E. García Gómez, *Poesía arábigoandaluza: breve síntesis histórica* (1952), is a monument of work in early Spanish lyric verse, but his most important summary and assessment of previous studies on early Andalusian lyric is "La lírica hispano-árabe y la aparición de la lírica románica" (*Al-Andalus*, 1956). He was the first to collect Arabic *kharjas* in his "Veinticuatro jarŷas romances en muwaššahas árabes" (*Al-Andalus*, 1952), supplementing the findings of Stern, who had first published *kharjas* written in Hebrew, and he continues the work on Hebrew *kharjas* in "Las jarŷas mozárabes y los judíos de al-Andalus" (*BRAE*, 1957). In this article García Gómez answers the arguments of F. Cantera in "La canción mozárabe" (*Publicaciones de la Universidad Internacional 'Menéndez Pelayo,'* 1957). Cantera had insisted that early lyric poetry for the most part came from the Biblical tradition of the Hebrews, and García Gómez refutes this, stating that since the poems were often in Arabic, Hebraic influence, particularly Biblical influence, was unlikely. Other significant studies are J. Millás Villacrosa, *La poesía sagrada hebraica-española* (2nd ed. 1948) and "Sobre los más antiguos versos en lengua castellana" (*Sefarad*, 1946).

Two articles are particularly valuable for their comments on the relationships between *kharjas* and other early poetry. T. Frings in "Altspanische Mädchenlieder aus des Minnesangs Fruhling" (*BGDSL*, 1951) pointed up the spontaneous origin of lyric poetry in various areas of Europe. L. Spitzer continued and enlarged this theory in "The Mozarabic Lyric and Theodore Frings' Theories" (*CL*, 1952). Perhaps the best general summary of studies on the *kharjas* in English is G. Brenan's appendix to his *Literature of the Spanish People* (1957). Another excellent if somewhat general study is to be found in J. Trend's *The Language and History of Spain* (1953). Other significant studies of this genre are W. Mettmann, "Zur Diskussion über literargeschichteliche Bedeutung der mozarabischen Jarchas" (*RF*, 1958); J. Corominas, "Para la interpretación de las jarĝas recién halladas" (*Al-Andalus*, 1953); E. Alarcos Llorach, "Una nueva edición de la lírica mozárabe"

(*Archivum de Oviedo*, 1953); and R. Menéndez Pidal, "Cantos románicos andalusíes (Continuadores de una lírica latina vulgar)" (*BRAE*, 1951). Finally, E. Asenio's *Poética y realidad en el cancionero peninsular de la Edad Media* (1957) offers a stimulating reevaluation of the origins of medieval Spanish poetry and attempts to show how great a unifying force this poetry had in its themes. An exhaustive bibliography of materials on the *kharjas* appears in H. Heger, "Di bisher veroffentlichten Harǧas und ihre Bedeutungen" (*ZRP Beihefte*, 1960), supplemented by P. Le Gentil, "La strophe zadjalesque, les Khardjas et le problème des origines du lyrisme roman" (*Romania*, 1963).

Lyric poetry in Spanish, as distinct from Mozarabic, has received careful study. The works of R. Menéndez Pidal have changed the entire viewpoint on this poetry. Three of his works are fundamental: *La primitiva poesía lírica española* (1919), republished in *Austral* (1922), with additional notes on the *kharjas*, under the title *Poesía popular tradicional;* "Poesía árabe y poesía europea" (*BH*, 1938), republished in *Austral* (1938); and "De primitiva lírica española y antigua épica" (*Austral*, 1951).

For the troubadour influence in Spanish poetry the standard work is still M. Milá y Fontanals, *De los trobadores en España* (1861). A valid study also is M. Menéndez Pelayo, *Historia de la poesía castellana en la Edad Media* (4 vols., 2nd ed. 1911–16). The famous poem *Razón de amor*, one of the few lyrics surviving from medieval Castilian, may be studied in the editions of R. Menéndez Pidal (*Revue Hispanique*, 1905) and in a penetrating modern study by L. Spitzer, "*Razón de amor*" (*Romania*, 1950). Galician-Portuguese poetry, the vehicle of most of Spain's medieval lyric poetry, can be studied most thoroughly in J. Filgueira Valverde, "Lírica medieval gallega y portuguesa" (*Historia General de las literaturas hispánicas*, Vol. I, 1951). Also valuable is H. Jenner, "La glosa española, estudio histórico de su métrica y de sus temas" (*RFE*, 1943), for its sound information about the *cancioneros*. The best study of the influence of Spanish and Portuguese lyrics upon one another is to be found in the careful and scholarly *La poésie lyrique espagnole et portugaise à la fin du moyen âge:* Vol. I, *Les thèmes et les genres* (1949) and Vol. II, *Les formes* (1953), by P. Le Gentil. Valuable, too, is Le Gentil's "Discussion sur la versification espagnole médiévale—à propos d'un livre recent" (*RPh*, 1958). A survey of themes of courtly love is by E. Dermenghem, " 'Thèmes de la poésie amoureuse' en le génie d'oc" (*CS*, 1943); and there is a bibliography by A. Nykl, *Troubadour Studies. A Critical Survey of Recent Books in this Field* (1944).

Arabic poetry as such has been generally studied in connection with the origins of troubadour poetry. The publications of A. Nykl and others have been discussed in connection with Provençal poetry in the chapter on medieval French literature. In addition to Arabic, there was an indigenous Jewish poetry in medieval Spain, discussed by J. Millás Villacrosa in *La poesía sagrada hebraico-española* (2nd ed. 1948) and *Selomó ibn Gabirol como poeta y filósofo* (1945); of interest, too, is his *Yehuda ha-Levi como poeta y apologista* (1947). A good insight into Hebrew poetry in Spain can be gained from studying the beginning chapters of M. Alvar, *Endechas judeo-españolas* (1953).

J. Fitzmaurice-Kelly's anthology of Spanish verse, *The Oxford Book of Spanish Verse* (2nd ed., by J. Trend, 1942) is one of the more useful anthologies of lyric poetry with sound introductory remarks. Valuable, too, is J. Cohen's *Penguin Book of Spanish Verse* (1956).

Sacred verse may be studied in B. R. Wardropper, *Historia de la poesía lírica a lo divino en la cristianidad occidental* (1958), which traces religious verse from its earliest beginnings across the entire Spanish Middle Ages into the seventeenth century. Included under sacred verse are the *Cantigas de Santa María*, composed under the patronage of King Alfonso X, "El Sabio," and claimed by Spain through her king and by Portugal through language, since the *Cantigas*, like most medieval lyric verse in Spain, were written in Galician-Portuguese. The entire corpus of the *Cantigas* has been edited by W. Mettmann (3 vols., 1959–64). J. Trend in *Alfonso the Sage and Other Essays* (1926) gives a good general treatment of the contributions of King Alfonso. A study full of little-known facts with sound and penetrating historical interpretation is Evelyn Proctor's *Alfonso X of Castile, Patron of Literature and Learning* (1951). The best treatment of the music of the *Cantigas* is H. Anglés, *La música de las Cantigas de Santa María* (1943), which contains facsimiles and transcriptions of the music. This is a truly masterly critical study, superseding one of the same title (1922) by J. Ribera.

The articles about the many aspects of the *Cantigas* are too numerous to mention here, although some are noted in the Portuguese section of this book, and a few of the most important must be listed below. A. Solalinde, "El códice florentino de las *Cantigas* y su relación con los demás manuscritos" (*RFE*, 1918), is still necessary for an understanding of the complete corpus of the songs; Dorothy Clarke, "Versification in Alfonso el Sabio's *Cantigas*" (*HR*, 1955), and F. Hanssen, "Los versos de las *Cantigas de Santa María*"

(*AUC*, 1901), treat versification, as does the latter's article "Los endecasílabos de Alfonso X" (*BH*, 1913) ; A. Bell, "The *Cantigas de Santa María* of Alfonso X" (*MLR*, 1915), is still reliable, and S. Gili Gaya, "Una nota para las *Cantigas*" (*RFE*, 1921) is worth consulting.

G. London, "Bibliografía de estudios sobre la vida y la obra de Alfonso X el Sabio" (*Boletín de Filología Española*, 1960), listing some 260 items devoted to this king and his works, many of which treat the *Cantigas*, though not complete, is the fullest.

III. EPIC AND LONG NARRATIVE POEMS

THE ESSENTIAL work on Spanish epic poetry is R. Menéndez Pidal's *Cantar de Mío Cid. Texto, gramática y vocabulario* in *Obras Completas* (1944–45), also printed as *Poema de Mío Cid: Edición y notas* (1946). This scholarly masterpiece furnishes the most nearly complete background to be found on the *Poem of the Cid*, the most important Spanish epic poem. Other works of Menéndez Pidal should also be consulted, for he is the final authority. His old but sound *L'épopée castillane à travers la littérature espagnole* was published first in 1910 from a series of lectures given by the author at Johns Hopkins University in that year and was translated into French by H. Mérimée with an introduction by E. Mérimée. A second version, translated into Spanish by Menéndez Pidal himself and published in 1959, contains new notes and references to subsequent research. Menéndez Pidal states that he has not altered the original. His *La épica española y la francesa comparadas* (1951) is a general summary of his earlier works on the epic; *La España del Cid* (2 vols., 4th ed. 1947) is a complete study of the life of the hero of the poem and of his times, published in *Obras Completas*, Vols. VI and VII, as well as in *Austral* (1950) ; his *Poesía juglaresca y juglares. Aspectos de la historia literaria y cultura de España* (2nd ed. 1945) not only treats the works of the troubadours but also traces their poetry in the later *mester de clerecía;* his older "Relatos poéticos en las crónicas medievales" (*RFE*, 1923) and his *Reliquias de la poesía española* (1951) theorize that epics grew out of reports of events and are therefore realistic and historical rather than fictional. His most recent thinking is revealed in *Poesía juglaresca y orígenes de las literaturas románicas* (6th ed., 1957), and especially in his *La Chanson de Roland y el neotradicionalismo* (1959), where he adduces that *The Song of Roland*, and hence the *Poem of the Cid*, is the product of a succession of poets rather than the work of a single poet. A second edition of this book exists in French entitled *La chanson de Roland et la tradition épique des Francs, revue et mise à jour par l'auteur avec le concours de René Louis, traduite de l'espagnole par I. M. Cluzel* (1960). See also the long and excellent critical review of the book by F. Lecoy in *Romania* (1963). Menéndez Pidal's most recent article, "Dos poetas en el *Cantar de Mío Cid*" (*Romania*, 1961), pursues the subject of plurality of authorship in the *Poema of the Cid*.

Others who hold similar views are K. Vossler, in "Hispanischer Traditionalismus" (*Die Neue Zeitung*, 1949), and P. Le Gentil, "La notion d'état latent et les derniers travaux de Menéndez Pidal" (*BH*, 1953), the latter especially important in studies of epic poetry.

M. Milá y Fontanal's *De la poesía heroica popular castellana* (2nd ed. 1959) reproduces the older study of Milá with comments of great value by M. de Riquer, who brings the study up to date, making the book one of the fundamental treatments of Spanish epic poetry. Other investigations by de Riquer are also worth consultation: "L'épopée vivante en Espagne" (*TR*, 1959) and his important *Los cantares de gesta franceses. Sus problemas, su relación con España* (1952), which sets forth a significant eclectic theory for epic origins stressing that all theories hitherto put forward are possibly in part reliable. G. Guerrieri Crocetti, *Il Cid e i cantari di Spagna* (1957), treats the *Poema de Mío Cid* and shows its relationships to other Spanish epics.

Scholars may still profitably consult E. Lévi Provençal, "Le Cid de l'histoire" (*Revue historique*, 1937), and W. Entwistle, "Remarks Concerning the Historical Account of Spanish Epic Origins" (*Revue hispanique*, 1933), as well as Entwistle's latest ideas as stated in "Remarks Concerning the Origins of Spanish Cantares de Gesta" (*RPh*, 1947–48). E. de Chasca, *Estructura y forma en el Poema del Cid* (1956) explicates the poetic imitation of history in Castilian epics, while L. Spitzer, "Sobre el carácter histórico del *Cantar de Mío Cid*" (*NRFH*, 1948), sees historicity woven into a novelesque and fictional poem; and R. Menéndez Pidal, "Poesía e historia en el 'Mío Cid.' El problema de la épica española" (*NRFH*, 1949), likewise supports the poem's historicity.

Structure and versification of the *Poema del Cid* have been studied by A. Castro, *España en su historia* (1948) and in the translation of the second version of this book, known as *La realidad histórica de España* (1954), which bears the title *The Structure of Spanish History*, trans. E. King. In these books Castro contrasts the several aspects of *The Song of Roland* and *The Poem of the Cid* as to meter, esthetic qualities, historicity, and style, insisting that the *Poema* is not really an epic at all, but rather a novelized chronicle, or, to be more exact, a distinct and new genre with no analogy in other literatures. D. Alonso's "Estilo y creación en el 'Poema del Cid' " (*Ensayos sobre poesía española*, 1944) is perhaps the most complete stylistic study of the *Cid* after Menéndez Pidal, and in some aspects even more penetrating.

Two translations of the *Poema del Cid* into Modern Spanish are good: that of P. Salinas (1936), published with the Old Spanish as edited by Menéndez Pidal, and the translation of A. Reyes (1932), republished with the edition of Menéndez Pidal in V. Oelschläger's *Poema del Cid in Verse and Prose* (2nd ed. 1963). The best English translation is that of L. Simpson, *The Poem of the Cid* (1957); J. Markley's *The Epic of the Cid* (1961) is also good.

Versification has been studied by W. Leonard in "La métrica del *Cid*" (*RABM*, 1931) and "The Recovery of the Metre of the *Cid*" (*PMLA*, 1931); also by A. Morley, "Recent Theories about the Metre of the *Cid*" (*PMLA*, 1933); and by C. Aubrun, "La métrique de *Mio Cid* est regulière" (*BH*, 1947). B. Gicovate, "La fecha de composición del 'Poema de Mío Cid' " (*Hispania*, 1956), offers arguments for a later dating than had been suspected.

There are excellent general studies of the epic of Spain by R. Menéndez Pidal, *La leyenda de los infantes de Lara* (1896), and C. Reig, *El Cantar de Sancho II y cerco de Zamora* (1947). G. Guerrieri Crocetti's *L'epica spagnuola* (1944) is likewise general, but sound.

The best studies for the extant lines of the epic *Roncesvalles* are R. Menéndez Pidal's *Tres poetas primitivos* (1948) and J. Horrent's *Rouncesvalles. Etude sur le fragment du cantar de gesta conservé à l'Archivo de Navarra* (1951) and "Rouncesvalles, ou la tradition française remaniée en l'Espagne" in his *La Chanson de Roland* (1951). Valuable also is R. Ruggieri's "L'epopea di Roncisvalle" (*CN*, 1942) and C. Aubrun, "De la mesure des vers anisosyllabiques médiévaux 'Le Cantar de Roncesvalles' " (*BH*, 1951). The themes of the Spanish epic are discussed by E. von Richthofen, "Notas sobre temas épico-medievales" (*BFC*, 1959) with some valuable comments on general medieval themes.

Other Spanish epics, which survive only in the form of prose chronicles or accounts, have received some attention. M. Defourneaux has studied them with particular attention to the lost epic of

Bernardo del Carpio (*BH*, 1943), with sound facts as to sources and influences; the older and more detailed study of A. Franklin, "A Study of the Legend of Bernardo del Carpio" (*HR*, 1937), goes into the legendary and historical sources of the poem as found in medieval Spanish chronicles; consult also W. Entwistle's "The 'Cantar de Gesta' of Bernardo del Carpio" (*MLR*, 1928); the excellent comparative study of J. Horrent, *La Chanson de Roland dans les littératures française et espagnole* (1951), contains a good investigation of *Bernardo*.

The *Poema de Fernán González* was edited with careful critical apparatus by C. Marden (1904), an edition superseded only by that of R. Menéndez Pidal in *Reliquias de la Poesía Epica Española* (1951). R. Menéndez Pidal did a detailed review of Marden's edition for *Archiv* (1903). The edition of A. Zamora Vicente (1946) offers more recent discussion of some of the aspects of the poem and presents in footnotes the prose versions found in the *Primera Crónica General*. The same author has "Una nota al 'Poema de Fernán Gonzales'" (*Revista de Filología Hispánica*, 1945), and differs with Marden as to origins of the poem in the *Continuatio Hispana*; J. P. Keller gives a good treatment of the poem's form in "Structure of the Poema de Fernán González" (*HR*, 1957). Isabel von Dyherrn, *Stilkritische Untersuchung und Versuch einer Rekonstruktion des "Poema de Fernán González"* (1937), reconstructs whole passages of the lost epic; and E. Correa Calderón, "Reminiscencias homéricas en el 'Poema de Fernán González'" (*Estudios dedicados a Menéndez Pidal*, Vol. IV, 1953), shows parallels existing between the Spanish poems and ancient epics.

The best edition and the most concise and informative study of the *Libro de Alexandre* are by R. Willis (1934), although the strictures of the review by A. Solalinde (*HR*, 1936) should be kept in mind. Willis' *The Debt of the Spanish 'Libro de Alexandre' to the French 'Roman d'Alexandre'* (1936) is a valuable comparative study, as is his *The Relationship of the Spanish 'Libro de Alexandre' to the 'Alexandreis' of Gautier de Châtillon* (1934). The latest and most authoritative critical treatment of the *Libro* is E. Alarcos Llorach, *Investigaciones sobre 'Libro de Alexandre'* (1948). H. Arnold's "Notes on the Versification of 'El Libro de Alexandre'" (*Hispania*, 1936) is also worthy of consultation.

The best and most authoritative study of the *Libro de Apolonio* is that of C. Marden, *Part I: Text and Introduction* (1917), and *Part II: Grammar, Notes, and Vocabulary* (1922). One should read the review of these by A. Solalinde (*RFE*, 1923). The only translation into English is that of R. Grismer and Elizabeth Atkins (1936). The metrical peculiarities may be studied with confidence in

H. Arnold's "A Reconsideration of the Metrical Form of 'El Libro de Apolonio'" (*HR*, 1938), which gives evidence of creative ability and a lack of dependence on sources, pointing to something more than a mere reworking or translation of foreign originals. More on this subject can be read in M. García Blanco, "La originalidad del 'Libro de Apolonio'" (*RIE*, 1945).

For the lost epic of the Infantes de Lara (or Salas) the best study is again by R. Menéndez Pidal, *La leyenda de los Infantes de Lara* (1896). His "Historicidad de la leyenda de los Infantes de Lara" (*Libro-Homenaje Goyanes*, 1929–30) continues his treatment. Also valuable are A. Monteverdi, "Il cantare degli Infanti de Salas" (*SMed*, 1934), and E. Moreno Báez, "El Poema de los Infantes de Salas" (*Insula*, 1947).

Representing the decadence of the epic genre in Castilian is the *Cantar de Rodrigo*, or *Las mocedades de Cid* in the *cuaderna vía* of the fourteenth century, edited by F. Wolf (1847), with a good introduction in German by B. Bourland (*Revue hispanique*, 1911), and by R. Menéndez Pidal in *Poema de Mío Cid y otros monumentos de la primitiva poesía española* (1919). The last named is the best edition with the most valuable study. This edition is also found in his *Reliquias de la Poesía Epica Española* (1951).

The long narrative poem in *cuaderna vía*, *Libro de miseria de omne*, a fourteenth-century version of the *De Contemptu mundi* of Innocent III, has been carefully studied by M. Artigas with an excellent edition (2 vols., *BBMP*, 1919–20). Other good studies are those of A. Hämel, *Literaturblatt für germanische und romanische Philologie* (1924), and Artigas, "Ein unbekanntes spanisches Gedicht aus dem Mittelalter" (*Spanien*, 1920).

The 312-line *Poema*, or *Historia de Yuçuf*, the most representative example of *aljamiada* literature (Spanish words written in Arabic or Hebrew characters), should be studied in the introductory notes of I. González Llubera's edition, *Coplas de Yoçef. A Medieval Spanish Poem in Hebrew Characters* (1935). R. Menéndez Pidal, "Poema de Yuçuf": materiales para su estudio . . . (*RABM*, 1902), is indispensable; J. Saroihandy, "Remarques sur le Poème de Yúçuf" (*BH*, 1904), is important.

Three books treat the theme of the Trojan War. The thirteenth-century *Historia troyana polimétrica* has been carefully edited by R. Menéndez Pidal in collaboration with E. Varón Vallejo, with the best study of the poem, *Historia troyana en prosa y verso, texto hacia 1270* (1934). The reviews of A. Carrión (*La Ciencia Tomista*, 1936) and G. Cirot (*BH*, 1936) add perspective. Two important studies are A. Solalinde, "Las versiones españolas del

'Roman de Troie' " (*RFE*, 1916), and R. Menéndez Pidal, "Dos voces oscuras de la 'Historia Troyana' en prosa y verso" (*RFE*, 1934), together with Pidal's "Historia Troyana polimétrica" in *Tres poetas primitivos* (1948).

Two poems bear the title *Crónica Troyana*. The first, a fourteenth-century translation into Spanish from the work of Guido delle Colonne, partly in prose and partly in verse, has been examined most thoroughly by A. Rey and A. Solalinde in *Ensayo de una bibliografía de las Leyendas Troyanas en la Literatura Española* (1942). The second *Crónica Troyana*, a fourteenth-century translation of Benoît de Sainte-Maure's *Roman de Troie*, should be studied also through Solalinde's article (*RFE*, 1916).

The best edition of *Poema de Alfonso XI* is that of Yo Ten Cate (1956), which must be consulted with her *Poema de Alfonso XI. Estudio preliminar y vocabulario* (1942). In the text itself she presents a paleographic edition and a critical edition side by side. Indispensable, too, are the works of D. Catalán Menéndez Pidal, *El Poema de Alfonso XI* (1953) and *Un cronista anónimo del siglo XIV* (n.d., but after 1953), which latter relates the poem to chronicles. See also his "La oración de Alfonso XI en el Salado. El Poema, la Crónica inédita y la Historia" (*Boletín de la Real Academia de la Historia*, 1952). G. David, "The Debt of the 'Poema de Alfonso Onceno' to the 'Libro de Alexandre' " (*HR*, 1947), treats influence, as does E. Carre Aldao, "El Poema de Alfonso XI" (*Influencias de la literatura gallega en la castellana*, 1915).

The prose *Crónica de Alfonso XI* does not appear in modern editions and may best be read in the several sixteenth- and seventeenth-century editions listed by Simón Díaz in his often mentioned *Bibliografía de la literatura hispánica*, Vol. III (1953).

IV. INDIVIDUAL AUTHORS, WORKS, AND GENRES

A. GONZALO DE BERCEO

A SOLALINDE'S is the standard edition of the *Milagros de Nuestra Señora* (1922), and its introductory study is adequate; reviews are by J. Aguado (*La Ciencia Tomista*, 1923) and G. Cirot

(*BH*, 1925) ; see also the excellent edition of C. Marden, *Veintitrés milagros. Nuevo Manuscrito de la Real Academia Española* (1929), and the reviews of G. Cirot (*BH*, 1931) and B. Gaiffier (*AnBol*, 1930). More recent and containing supplementary material is V. Mengod, "Sobre los milagros mariales de Berceo" (*Atenea*, 1949). The only volume containing most of Berceo's works is by F. Janer (1864), but as this contains modernizations and arbitrary paleographical transcription, its primary use is for a readable text of the works. A. Hämel's edition, *Milagros de Nuestra Señora* (1926), contains a good introduction in German, but only seventeen of the *milagros*. Solalinde's edition of *Sacrificio de la Misa* (1913) is scholarly. The reviews of A. Castro (*Revista de Libros*, 1914) and F. de Onís (*La Lectura*, 1914) should be read in connection with it. Two editions of *Vida de Santo Domingo de Silos* are worth consulting, that of J. Fitz-Gerald (1904) and the recent and very scholarly edition of A. Andrés (1958), which latter contains a detailed introduction and notes. Important studies on Berceo are the introductory remarks to the edition of the *Milagros* by E. Matus Romo (1956) ; G. Menéndez Pidal's *Selección, estudio y notas por Gonzalo de Berceo* (1941) ; the general, but sound, *Studi sulla poesia di Gonzalo de Berceo* of G. Guerrieri Crocetti (1942) and his *Gonzalo de Berceo* (1947). Berceo's language is discussed by Crocetti in "La lingua di Berceo" (*SMed*, 1943).

Berceo's versification was examined by F. Hanssen, *Metrische Studien zu Alfonso und Berceo* (1903), and in J. Fitz-Gerald's detailed *Versification of the Cuaderna Vía as Found in Berceo's Vida de Santo Domingo* (1905). H. Arnold, "Irregular Hemistichs in the *Milagros* of Gonzalo de Berceo" (*PMLA*, 1935), is a lucid and detailed study. B. Gicovate offers a stylistic appraisal of Berceo's work in "Notas sobre el estilo y la originalidad de Gonzalo de Berceo" (*BH*, 1957), as does J. Ferer, "Berceo: aspectos de su estilo" (*Hispania*, 1950). A. del Campo studies the allegory in "La técnica alegórica en la introducción de los 'Milagros de Nuestra Señora'" (*RFE*, 1944). A brief but very helpful study of the sources of the *Milagros* and their parallels in other writing is A. Rey's "Correspondence of the Spanish Miracles of the Virgin" (*RR*, 1928).

Berceo's other works offer interesting parallels with similar works in other literatures and are often the most representative examples of their genres in Castilian. J. Pérez de Urbel in "Manuscritos de Berceo en el Archivo de Silos" (*BH*, 1930) deals particularly with the *Vida de Santo Domingo;* J. Fitz-Gerald in "Gonzalo de Berceo in Spanish Literary Criticism before 1780" (*RR*, 1910) studies some ten authors before S. de Vergara who treated Berceo's works. L. Pfandl's "Zu Gonzalo de Berceo" (*Archiv*, 1922) is a short but valuable study. And the importance of Berceo's humor is introduced by G. Cirot, "L'humour de Berceo" (*BH*, 1942).

B. *JUAN RUIZ:* EL LIBRO DE BUEN AMOR

Since nearly all lyrics written by Spaniards in the fourteenth and fifteenth centuries were in Galician-Portuguese rather than in Castilian, treatment of such poems is to be found in the Portuguese section of the present survey. A notable exception is, however, the *Libro de buen amor* of Juan Ruiz, Archpriest of Hita, considered by many to be one of the most important books in Spanish literature. The best edition is still that of J. Ducamin (1901), but the edition of J. Cejador y Frauca (2 vols., 1913) is a standard and valuable text with many notes. The reviews of the former by C. Marden (*MLN*, 1901), E. Mérimée (*BH*, 1901), and R. Foulché-Delbosc (*Revue hispanique*, 1901) contribute to a better understanding of the *Libro;* the critical reviews of Cejador y Frauca's edition by A. Castro (*Rev. de Libros*, 1913) and G. Cirot (*BH*, 1913) likewise correct, supplement, and explain matters left unexplained by the editor, Cejador. The two best linguistic studies are J. Aguado, *Glosario sobre Juan Ruiz, poeta castellano del siglo XIV* (1929), and H. Richardson, *An Etymological Vocabulary to the Libro de Buen Amor* (1930). The former has notes and lengthy explanations as well as etymologies. The only translation into English, E. Kane, *The Book of Good Love* (1933), though far from literal, catches the flavor of the original very well. H. Arnold, "The Octosyllabic 'cuaderna vía' of Juan Ruiz" (*HR*, 1940), discusses the book's *raison d'être* as well as its versification. Scholars still consult the sound study of the *Libro* in Vol. I of Menéndez Pelayo's *Antología de poetas líricos castellanos* (new ed. 1944–45) and also Menéndez Pidal's *Poesía árabe y poesía europea* (1941), which argues that the *maquamat* of the Hebrews and Arabs did not influence the structure of the *Libro*. The best study of the plan and unity of the *Libro* can be found in the classic study of F. Lecoy, *Recherches sur le 'Libro de buen amor'* (1938). Again, the critical review of this book by E. Alarcos Llorach (*RFE*, 1943) makes valuable additions. Of signal importance, too, is the chapter devoted to Juan Ruiz in A. Castro's *The Structure of Spanish History* (1954), in which the author adduces that the book is not at all didactic, as many scholars have insisted, but is based on the autobiographical plan of the Arab *maquamat*. He demonstrates convincing parallels, denied by García

Gómez, between *Libro de buen amor* and *The Dove's Neck-Ring* of Ibn Hazm. This book represents Castro's latest thinking on the subject of the *Libro de buen amor*. G. Gybbon-Moneypenny, "Autobiography in the *Libro de buen amor* in the Light of Literary Comparisons" (*BHS*, 1957), reinforces the idea of the influence of the *maquamat* on Juan Ruiz, but sees, too, a relationship with the autobiographical form used by other medieval European authors, exclusive of Arabic influence.

The studies of M. R. Lida de Malkiel on the Archpriest of Hita should all be taken into account, for her thinking on the subject is among the most significant in recent years. Her "Notas para la interpretación, influencia, fuentes y texto del *Libro de buen amor*" (*NRFH*, 1959) is valuable, but in "Una interpretación más de Juan Ruiz" (*RPh*, 1961) she revises certain of her former ideas and finds in the *Libro* a stronger didactic intent. She favors the idea of the influence of the Arabic *maquamat*, perhaps in a form peculiar to the writings of Jewish authors in Languedoc and Catalonia, rather than the form used by Ibn Hazm. Her *Libro de buen amor, Selección* (1941) begins with an informative essay in which she traces the influence of the book across the centuries. Her *Two Spanish Masterpieces: The Book of Good Love and The Celestina* (1961), based upon public lectures she delivered at the University of Illinois (1959–60), is a penetrating study. The review of this book by O. Green (*RPh*, 1962) supplements its value.

L. Spitzer likewise stressed the didactic as well as the recreational qualities of the *Libro*, "Zur Auffassung des Kunst des Arcipreste de Hita" (*ZRP*, 1934), and stated that the version that we have today is a *refundición* of an earlier version. Two scholars in particular have insisted that the recreational and entertaining aspects of the *Libro* were most important: G. Bertini, *Saggio sul libro de 'Buen Amor', dell' Arcipreste de Hita. L'unità del poema* (1927), and S. Battaglia in "Saggio sul 'Libro de Buen Amor' dell' Arcipreste di Hita" (*Nuova Cultura*, 1930). Battaglia strives to show in "Motivi d'arte nel 'Libro de buen amor'" (*Nuova Cultura*, 1931) a psychological development in the book that most scholars find not characteristic of medieval writing.

J. Gimeno Casalduero has studied the structure and background of the *Libro* in "Sobre la 'oración narrativa' medieval: estructura, origen, supervivencia" (*Anales de la Universidad de Madrid*, 1957–58). An analysis of certain of the fables in the *Libro* by E. Eizaga y Gondra, *Un proceso en el 'Libro de buen amor'* (1942), adduces that the fables are parodies of judicial decisions; J. E. Keller's *Motif-Index of Mediaeval Spanish Exempla* (1949) classifies the motifs of the *Libro* (and of a large number of medieval tales) according to the system of Stith Thompson. G. Miró Quesada has studied the background of the *Libro's* famous go-between, Trotaconventos (*Letras* [of Lima], 1943). The philosophical meaning is treated by A. Benito Durán, *Filosofía del Arcipreste de Hita* (1946). W. Kellerman (*ZRP*, 1951) treats the allegorical aspects of the seasons in the *Libro* and sees didacticism as the purpose of the book. T. Hart, *La alegoría en el Libro de buen amor* (1959), sees the *Libro* as definitely didactic and examines it in the light of medieval theories of typological interpretation; O. Green, "On Juan Ruiz' Parody of the Canonical Hours" (*HR*, 1958), compares it with other incidences of such parody and observes that the *Libro* is the first parody in Spanish. U. Leo, *Zur dichterischen Originalität des Arcipreste de Hita* (1958), makes interesting comparisons with similar works in other literatures and rejects the didactic aspects attributed to the work by Mrs. Malkiel and others. Leo's book has been carefully criticized by T. Hart (*MLN*, 1960). The influence of the *Libro* is treated by L. Moffatt, "Evidence of Early Mention of the Archpriest of Hita and His Works" (*MLN*, 1960).

C. PEDRO LOPEZ DE AYALA

The fourteenth-century *Rimado de Palacio*, one of the last poetical works in *cuaderna vía*, has been best edited by A. Kuersteiner (2 vols., 1920). This editor's "The first 'Cántica sobre el fecho de la Iglesia' in Ayala's 'Rimado' " (*Studies in Honor of A. Marshall Elliott*, 1911) provides the best material on the *Rimado*. J. de Cossío, "Una estrofa del canciller Ayala" (*BBMP*, 1923) is valuable. A complete study of López de Ayala and his works is V. Díaz de Arcaya's *El Gran Canciller D. Pedro López de Ayala: su estirpe, su cuna, vida y obras* (1900), which also discusses the famous *Crónicas* discussed in this chapter under Chronicles and Histories. The best study of the author's life, however, is by J. de Contreras, *Biografía del Canciller D. Pedro López de Ayala* (1923), supplemented by the more up-to-date *Introducción a la biografía del canciller Ayala con apéndices documentales*, containing an informative prologue by J. de Ybarra y Bergé (1950). Facts not included in these two are to be found in A. López de Meneses, "Nuevos datos sobre el Canciller Ayala" (*Cuadernos de Historia de España*, 1948). A. Castro, "El Canciller López de Ayala" (*Aspectos del vivir hispánico*, 1949), is a valuable interpretative and critical study. Dorothy Clarke discussed metrical problems in "Hiatus, Synalepha, and Line Length in López de Ayala's Octosyllables" (*RPh*, 1948), as did J. de Cossío, "Una estrofa del canciller Ayala" (*BBMP*, 1923), and F. Hanssen in his old but valuable "De los versetes de antigo rrymar de López de Ayala" in his *Miscelánea de Versificación Castellana* (1897). A more recent study is Helen Sears's "The 'Rimado de Palacio' and the 'De Regimine Principum' Tradition of the Middle Ages" (*HR*, 1952).

D. SANTA MARIÁ EGIPCÍACA

The Spanish *Vida de Santa María Egipcíaca* has interested scholars for its original handling of a standard medieval theme. The old but still standard study of A. Mussaffia, "Uber die Quelle der altspanischen 'Vida de S. Maria Egipcíaca' " (*Sitzungsberichte der Kaiserlichen Akademie der Wissenschafte*, 1863), is valuable. A. Millares Carlo gives the essential facts and criticism in his *Historia de la literatura española hasta fines del siglo XV* (1950). Anna Monti, *La leggenda di Santa Maria Egiziaca nella letteratura medioevale italiana e spagnuola* (1938), is the best study. The best edition is R. Foulché-Delbosc, *Vide de Santa María Egipcíaqua conforme al códice del Escorial* (1907), which is paleographical.

E. LIBRO DELS TRES REIS D'ORIENT

This work of Aragonese origin was edited by P. José Pidal (*Revista de Madrid*, 1840) and was published by F. Janer (1864; new ed. 1952). A facsimile edition was published by A. Huntington (1904). The edition of R. Menéndez Pidal appears in *Poema de Mío Cid y otros monumentos de la primitiva poesía española* (1919).

F. DEBATES

R. Menéndez Pidal has a general discussion of debates in his edition, *Disputa del alma y el cuerpo* (*RABM*, 1900). A comparative study is that of A. Solalinde, "La disputa del *Alma y el Cuerpo*. Comparación con su original francés" (*HR*, 1933); and P. Pidal treats the debate in *Fragmento de un poema inédito* in his *Estudios Literarios*, Vol. I (1890). The debate *Elena y María* is treated in an edition by R. Menéndez Pidal (*RFE*, 1914). *Razón de amor con los denuestos del agua y el vino*, the latter part of which is a typical medieval debate, was edited by F. Morel-Fatio ("*Textes Castillans inédits du XIIIᵉ siècle*. I. Poème d'amour," *Romania*, 1887). Especially informative is the discussion of Carolina Michaëlis de Vasconcellos, "Observações sobre alguns textos lyricos da antigua poesía peninsular" (*Revista Lusitana*, 1902).

G. DANZA DE LA MUERTE

The study of J. Amador de los Ríos, "Sobre la tradición poética de la *Danza de la Muerte* hasta principios del siglo XVI" (*Historia Crítica de la literatura española*, Vol. VII, 1865), is still a standard treatment and reliable. The notes and introductory material offered with the selections from the *Danza* in J. Ford's *Old Spanish Readings* (1939), although brief, contain a good critical study. Spanish versions have been compared with those of other countries by W. Mulerrt, "Sur les danses macabres en Castille et en Catalogne" (*Revue hispanique*, 1933). Valuable, too, is E. Segura Covarsí, "Sentido dramático y contenido litúrgico de 'Las Danzas de la Muerte'" (*CL*, 1949). An excellent study for critical appraisal, sources, influences, and interpretation of the *Danza* can be found in A. Valbuena Prat, *Historia de la literatura española*, Vol. I (1960). The best edition is that of R. Foulché-Delbosc (*Textos Castellanos Antiguos*, 1907), but the edition of C. Appel in *Beiträge zur Romanischen und Englischen Philologie* . . . (1902) should likewise be consulted.

H. DRAMA

The only remnant of truly medieval drama in Spain, the *Auto de los Reyes Magos*, can best be studied in the introduction and notes to the edition of R. Menéndez Pidal (*RABM*, 1900); the notes and introductory remarks of J. Ford in *Old Spanish Readings* (1939) are again helpful; A. Parker's "Notes on Religious Drama in Medieval Spain and the Origins of the Autos Sacramentales" (*MLR*, 1935) is still standard. G. Cirot's "Pour combler les lacunes de l'histoire du drame religieux en Espagne avant Gómez Manrique" (*BH*, 1943) and G. Contini's *Teatro religioso del Medioevo fuori d'Italia* (1949) summarize what is known of the early drama of Spain, the latter offering the text of the *Auto de los Reyes Magos* with a translation into Italian. B. Wardropper studies style in "The Dramatic Texture of the *Auto de los Reyes Magos*" (*MLN*, 1955). R. Donovan in *The Liturgical Drama of Medieval Spain* (1958) offers a study of the Latin dramas of Spain important to an understanding of peninsular literature in the vernacular. Two old and standard works are still valuable: J. Crawford, *Spanish Drama*

Before Lope de Vega (1922; rev. ed. 1937), and A. Valbuena Prat, *Literatura dramática española* (1930).

I. PROVERBIAL BOOKS

Medieval Spanish proverbs have received little attention, to judge by the paucity of publications on the subject. *Flores de filosofía* was studied in the old edition of J. Knust, *Dos obras didácticas y dos leyendas* (1878). Knust also studied the *Bonium o Bocados de oro* in *Mittheilungen aus dem Eskurial* (1879), and *Poridad de poridades* under the title "Ein Beitrage zur Kenntniss der Escorialbibliothek" (*Jahrbuch für romanische und englische Literatur*, 1869). The most recent scholarly treatment of proverbs is found in the introduction to the edition of A. Rey, *El libro de los cien capítulos* (1960), and in L. Kasten's edition, *Poridat de poridades* (1957). Worthy of mention is M. Zapata y Torres, "Breves notas sobre el *Libro de los cien capítulos* como base de las *Flores de filosofía*" (*Smith College Studies in Modern Languages*, 1929). Eleanor O'Kane's collection of proverbs, "Refranes y frases proverbiales españoles de la Edad Media" (*Anejos del Boletín de la Real Academia Española*, 1959), is a good introduction to the use of proverbs in medieval Spanish literature, with many examples. The review of her study by J. E. Keller (*Speculum*, 1961) points out works that she omitted. A University of North Carolina unpublished doctoral dissertation by J. Johnson, "The Proverb in the Medieval Spanish Exempla" (1958), treats proverbs in collections of *exempla* —*Conde Lucanor, Exenplos por a.b.c., Libro de los engaños, Calila y Dimna*, and the like.

The *Proverbios del Sabio Salomón* may best be studied in the editions of J. Alemany Bolufer (1928) and A. Paz y Melia (*Opúsculos literarios de los siglos XIV a XVI*, 1892).

The *Proverbios Morales* of the Rabbi Sem Tob have received insufficient attention since G. Ticknor studied them in his *History of Spanish Literature*, Vol. III, (1849), save for the careful investigations of I. González Llubera presented in the introduction to his edition (1947) and in his "The Text and Language of Santob de Carrión's *Proverbios Morales*" (*HR*, 1940). The older study of J. Amador de los Ríos, "Rabbi don Santo de Carrión" (*Estudios históricos, políticos y literarios sobre los judíos de España*, 1848), is still a standard reference. Sem Tob's versification has been treated more recently by A. Turi, "Las coplas del rabbi Don Sem Tob" (*Unversidad* [de Santa Fé], 1945). His language has been studied

by E. Alarcos Llorach, "La lengua de los 'Proverbios Morales' de
don Sem Tob" (*RFE*, 1951).

J. NOVEL OF CHIVALRY

Amadís de Gaula, the only novel of chivalry (except possibly *El
Caballero Zifar*) known to be of medieval origin, has been the subject
of much discussion. The first significant appraisal of *Amadís* and
European society was by E. Baret, *De l'Amadis de Gaula et son
influence sur les moeurs et la littérature au XVIᵉ siècle* (1853), a
standard work, indispensable as a reference, though superseded by
recent studies in certain details. Standard also and indispensable is
the study of M. Menéndez Pelayo in *Orígenes de la novela* (3rd ed.
1946). Old but useful for its detailed proof of the close relationship
of *Amadís* to the French Provençal prose romances is Grace
Williams, "The Amadís Question" (*Revue hispanique*, 1909). H.
Thomas, *Spanish and Portuguese Romances of Chivalry* (1920;
Spanish trans. 1952), contains important bibliographical studies of
Amadís and its continuations; N. Alonso Cortés, "Montalvo el del
Amadís" (*Revue hispanique*, 1933), also contains bibliographical
material. W. Entwistle, *A lenda arturiana nas literaturas da
península ibérica* (1942), earlier published in English without the
important appraisal found in the Portuguese, treats the Portuguese
claims to authorship and other matters concerning *Amadís*. M. R.
Lida de Malkiel, "El desenlace del *Amadís* primitivo" (*RPh*, 1953),
offers an important new theory on the early development and origin
of *Amadís*, well supported by arguments and documentation and now
generally accepted. S. Gili Gaya's *Amadís de Gaula* (1956) is the
best study in stylistics of the novel. A. Rodríguez-Moñino, A.
Millares Carlo, and R. Lapesa, *El primer manuscrito del "Amadís de
Gaula"* (1957), reprinted from *BRAE*, edits and studies recently
discovered fragments of an early fifteenth-century manuscript of
Libro III.

The studies of E. Place on *Amadís* are both authoritative and
comprehensive: "El *Amadis* de Montalvo como manual de cortesía
en Francia" (*RFE*, 1955) is a detailed investigation of the influence
of *Amadís* as a courtesy book in France; "Amadís of Gaul, Wales or
What?" (*HR*, 1955) disproves the long-standing allegations that
Gaul meant Wales; "Fictional Evolution, the Old French Romances
and the Primitive Amadís Reworked by Montalvo" (*PMLA*, 1956)
contains new interpretations of what is known concerning *Amadis;*
and Place's definitive edition, two of whose four volumes have

already appeared (1959 and 1962) will present for the first time the text of the reputed princeps edition of Saragossa (1509). Volume I contains Book I of the text and a full study of editions, translations, and adaptations of the four books. It is the best all-round appraisal of *Amadís* and *Amadís* studies yet made. Volume II reproduces Montalvo's Libro II. There is a full bibliography of *Amadís* studies in J. Simón Díaz, *Bibliografía de la literatura española*, Vol. III (1953), and the supplement, "Nuevos datos bibliográficos sobre libros de caballería" (*RL*, 1955).

El Caballero Zifar, part novel of chivalry and part Byzantine romance, has received little published notice. The reliable edition of C. Wagner (1929), which includes the variants from MSS. M, P, S, has been reissued by M. de Riquer (2 vols., 1951) with a careful introduction but without the variants found in Wagner's edition. Also important are Wagner's "The Sources of the 'Cavallero Cifar'" (*Revue hispanique*, 1903) and A. Krappe's "Le mirage celtique et les sources du 'Chevalier Cifar'" (*BH*, 1931).

K. BRIEF NARRATIVE

The best studies besides M. Menéndez Pelayo's often mentioned *Orígenes de la novela*, Vol. I (3rd ed. 1946), are to be found in the introductions to editions of the brief narrative works in prose; however, J. Amador de los Ríos, *Historia crítica de la literatura española*, Vol. IV (1863), is still valuable for some of the early works in prose, notably *Calila y Dimna* and *El Conde Lucanor*. For the former, the best studies are still the introductions to the editions of J. Alemany Bolufer (1915) and A. Solalinde (1917), supplemented by the review of Alemany's edition by Solalinde (*RFE*, 1915) and of Solalinde's edition by G. Cirot (*BH*, 1922). The edition of C. Allen (1906) offers interesting comparisons with Latin texts. It was reviewed carefully by R. Menéndez Pidal (*Cultura Española*, 1916). The comparative study of C. Brockelmann in *Encyclopedia of Islam*, Vol. II (1913), entitled "Kalila-wa dimna," is a factual and reasonably complete treatment, as is A. Hottinger, *Kalila und Dimna: Ein Versuch zur Darstellung der arabisch-altspanischen Übersetzungskunst* (1958). V. Chauvin, *Bibliographie des ouvrages arabes* . . . , Vol. III (1898), contains the most comprehensive bibliography of versions of *Calila y Dimna* and *Libro de los engaños* and is a necessary tool for comparative studies.

El libro de los engaños y asayamientos de las mujeres has been treated in the introduction to the edition of A. González Palencia,

Versiones castellanas del 'Sendebar' (1946), which reproduces the well-known edition of A. Bonilla y San Martín (1904) and presents a complete list of Spanish versions and of parallels in other literatures. The outdated study by D. Comparetti, *Researches Respecting the Book of Sindibad* (1882), is worth mentioning for its remarks on the Oriental background of the *Libro de los engaños*. J. E. Keller's edition (2nd ed. 1956) and his translation, under the title of *The Book of the Wiles of Women* (*MLA* Translation Series, No. 2, 1959), summarize recent views that the purpose of the book was recreational, as opposed to the former belief that it was didactic. In a review of Keller's edition, " 'Sindibad' in Medieval Spain: A Review Article" (*MLN*, 1956), G. Artola gives a nearly complete account of the *Book of Sindibad,* and therefore of the *Libro de los engaños,* in the medieval period.

Two old works are still the best introduction to the Spanish version of *Barlaam and Josaphat :* the introduction to the edition of F. Lauchert, *La estoria del rey Anemur e de Iosaphat e de Barlaam* (*RF,* 1893), and F. de Haan, "Barlaam and Josaphat in Spain" (*MLN,* 1895). Chauvin's bibliography lists other studies. G. Moldenhauer treats the origins of *Barlaam* in Spain in *Investigación y Progreso* (1927) and in his *Die Legende von Barlaam und Josaphat auf der Iberischen Halbinsel. Untersuchungen und Texte* (1929: see the valuable review by G. Cirot, *BH,* 1931).

Don Juan Manuel's *El Conde Lucanor* may be studied in J. Amador de los Ríos, *Historia Crítica de la literatura española,* Vol. IV (1863), and in M. Menéndez Pelayo's *Orígenes de la novela,* Vol. I (3rd ed. 1946). H. Knust and A. Birch-Hirschfeld in the introduction to their edition (1900) pointed to parallels in other literatures, not all of which, by the way, are relevant, as demonstrated in the detailed notes to the edition of A. González Palencia (1940) and discussed in the edition of F. Sainz de Robles (1945). M. R. Lida de Malkiel's "Tres notas sobre Don Juan Manuel" (*RPh,* 1950–51) gives interesting and scholarly insights into the connections between antiquity, the Latin culture of the Middle Ages, and the works of Don Juan Manuel, with special attention to the proverbs in his works. The only translation of the most commonly read and studied part of *El Conde Lucanor* is J. York's *Fifty Pleasant Tales of Patronio* (1924), preceded by a scholarly introduction by J. Trend. A. Giménez Soler's *Don Juan Manuel. Bibliografía y estudio crítico* (1932) offers an indispensable bibliography and evaluation of the *Conde Lucanor* and other works of Don Juan Manuel.

The only volume containing the greater part of Don Juan

Manuel's works is that of F. Janer (1860), which offers editions, unfortunately modernized arbitrarily, of *Libro del caballero et del escudero, Libro Infinido, De las armas, De las maneras de amor, Libro de los Estados* (parts 1 and 2), *Libro de los fraires predicadores, Libro de Patronio* (part 2), and *Tractado en que se prueba por razon que Sancta María está en cuerpo et alma en paraíso.* A much better edition of *Libro de las armas* is that of A. Giménez Soler (*Univ.* [of Zaragoza], 1931); the *Libro del cavallero et del escudero* was edited by S. Graefenberg (*RF*, 1893), and R. Menéndez Pidal's review of it should be consulted (*Revista Crítica de Historia y Literatura*, Vol. I, 1896); the *Libro de la caza*, one of medieval Spain's greatest works on falconry, by J. Castro y Calvo (1947), with excellent notes and critical study, supersedes the old editions of J. Gutiérrez de la Vega (1879) and reproduces that of G. Baist (1880); J. Blecua, *"Libro infinido" y "Tractado de la Asunción"* (*Univ. of Granada*, 1952), contains a scholarly study of the two works in the title.

The *Castigos y documentos del Rey Don Sancho*, an excellent example of the genre of the *Diall of Princes* in Spain, receives the most up-to-date and scholarly treatment in the edition of A. Rey (1952), whose introduction is excellent. It supersedes the remarks of P. Groussac, "Le livre des 'Castigos a documentos' attribué au roi D. Sanche" (*Revue hispanique*, 1906).

El Libro de los gatos can be studied in the works of Amador de los Ríos and M. Menéndez Pelayo, cited at the beginning of this section. L. Hervieux, *Les fabulistes latins: Etudes de Cheriton et ses dérivés* (1898), stresses that the *Libro* is a translation of the *Fabulae* of Odo of Cheriton, an English cleric of the thirteenth century. The introductions to two editions may be consulted for more detailed study: G. Northup's (*MP*, 1908) and J. E. Keller's (1958). The latter summarizes many articles written about the title of the book.

Spain's longest collection of brief narratives, *El Libro de los exenplos por a.b.c.*, compiled by Clemente Sánchez de Valderas, must be considered as a part of the corpus of medieval works, even though it was written in the first half of the fifteenth century. It can best be studied in the introductions to two editions: that of F. Morel-Fatio (1878), which offers only the text of the first seventy-two of the four-hundred-odd divisions, and that of J. E. Keller (1961), which contains the complete edition of all the stories found in the two extant manuscripts. On the sources of the book there is a valuable article by A. Krappe, "Les sources du *Libro de los exemplos por a.b.c.*" (*BH*, 1937).

L. HISTORIA DE LA DONCELLA TEODOR

This oriental novelesque work, filled with proverbial wisdom, probably translated into Spanish in the fourteenth century, should be studied in M. Menéndez Pelayo's "La Doncella Teodor. Un cuento de 'Las Mil y Una Noches,' un libro de cordel y una comedia de Lope de Vega" (*Homenaje a D. Francisco Codera*, 1904).

M. DEMANDA DEL SANTO GRIAL

The material in Spanish on the quest of the Holy Grail, while not copious, is substantial. K. Pietsch's *Spanish Grail Fragments* (1924) offers in Vol. I a carefully prepared text with an introduction treating the various manuscripts, but with insufficient space allotted to Arthurian material in Spain; Vol. II, however, contains valuable commentary and at least a general orientation to this material. G. Bertoni's monograph *San Gral* (1940) is more comprehensive, although one should read in connection with it the review of E. Richter (*Revista de Filología Hispánica*, 1940). P. Bohigas Balaguer, "Los textos españoles y gallegoportugueses de la demanda del Santo Grial" (*RFE*, 1925), the review of G. Cirot (*BH*, 1926), and M. Rodríguez Lapa's monograph *A Demanda do Santo Graal* (1930) are other useful studies.

N. HISTORICAL WORKS OF THE THIRTEENTH AND FOUR-TEENTH CENTURIES

Spain's great medieval histories and chronicles, especially those written under the patronage of King Alfonso X, contribute greatly to literature. Reworkings of the Bible and legends and fables of classical antiquity and from medieval folklore abound, particularly in the Alfonsine *General Estoria,* in the *Crónica General,* and in subsequent chronicles. Even prose versions of lost epic poems, extremely important to the development of Spanish letters, appear in these histories.

A. Solalinde was most active in treating the *General Estoria* of Alfonso X. His edition (1930) of the *Primera Parte* is detailed and scholarly. It is supplemented by his corrections and additions in *RFE* (1930). The critical reviews of this edition, G. Northup (*MP,* 1931) and C. Marden (*MLN,* 1932), make valuable additions. The edition of the *Segunda Parte* by A. Solalinde, L. Kasten, and V. Oelschläger (1961) continues the scholarly and careful editing of the *Primera Parte.* Interesting source studies are Solalinde's "El juicio de París en el 'Alexandre' y en la 'General Estoria' " (*RFE*, 1928) and "El 'Physiologus' en la *General Estoria* de Alfonso X" (*Mélanges offerts à F. Baldensperger*, 1930). L. Kiddle has "A Source of the 'General Estoria.' The French Prose Redaction of the 'Roman de Thèbes' " (*HR*, 1936) and "The Prose 'Thèbes' and the 'General Estoria.' An Illustration of the Alphonsine Method of Using Source Material" (*HR*, 1938); and Solalinde offers "Fuentes de 'General Estoria' de Alfonso el Sabio" (*RFE*, 1934).

The *Crónica General*, or *Crónica de España*, has been masterfully edited by R. Menéndez Pidal as *Primera Crónica General, o sea Historia de España* . . . (1955). The edition of J. Filgueira Valverde, *Crónica General de España. Selecciones de lo redactado en la Corte de Alfonso X* (1943), contains valuable notes and introductory study that offers facts not found in the edition of Menéndez Pidal. For an interesting concept of Alphonsine history among the Arabs of Spain see M. Atuña's "Una versión árabe compendiada de la 'Estoria de España' de Alfonso el Sabio" (*Al-Andalus*, 1933). Valuable material on the sources of this history are G. Cirot, "La 'Chronique Générale' et le *Poème du Cid*" (*BH*, 1938); A. Solalinde, "Una fuente de la 'Primera Crónica General': Lucano" (*HR*, 1941); and Dorothy Donald, "Suetonius in the *Primera Crónica General* through the *Speculum Historiale*" (*HR*, 1943).

The *Gran Conquista de Ultramar*, Spain's longest history of the Crusades and for the most part a translation or paraphrase of the *Historia Rerum in Partibus Transmarinis Gestarum* of William of Tyre, contains interesting elements not found in other historical books. Its novelesque treatment of the theme of the Swan Knight is unique, for example, and has called for special study by E. Mazorriage in his edition of this episode entitled *Leyenda del Caballero del Cisne* . . . Vol. I. *Texto* (1914), and by A. Bonilla y San Martín, *Las leyendas de Wagner en la literatura española* (1913), which places the Swan Knight in the over-all panorama of Spanish letters. The edition of *Gran Conquista* by P. de Gayangos (1858) is useful for general content but not for linguistic studies, as the text has been greatly modernized. For important parallels and influences see also G. Paris, "La 'Chanson d'Antioche' provençale et la 'Gran Conquista de Ultramar' " (*Romania*, 1888), and the brief but important study of A. Rey, "Las leyendas del ciclo carolingio en la 'Gran Conquista de Ultramar' " (*RPh*, 1949–50).

The *Crónicas de los Reyes de Castilla*, or *Crónicas de Alfonso X, Sancho IV y Fernando IV*, have been carefully studied by J. Puyol, "El presunto cronista Fernán Sánchez de Valladolid" (*Bol. de la Real Acad. de la Historia*, 1920). Valuable is C. M. del Rivero,

"Indice de las personas, lugares y cosas que se mencionan en las tres Crónicas de los Reyes de Castilla: Alfonso X, Sancho IV y Fernando IV" (*Hispania* [of Madrid], 1942, and separate, 1943).

The *Crónica de Alfonso Onceno*, which drew upon the *Poema de Alfonso Onceno*, has not been edited in modern times, but the doctoral dissertation of D. Catalán y Menéndez Pidal (1951) offers an excellent and scholarly treatment of its backgrounds, quality, and sources.

O. SCIENTIFIC WORKS, TREATISES ON GAMES, AND LEGAL WORKS

The famous Alphonsine scientific works brought to the realm of Spanish literature new concepts of Oriental wisdom, superstition, and belief, together with a new vocabulary. The *Libros del Saber de Astronomía* must still be consulted in the old edition of M. Rico y Sinobas (5 vols., 1863–67). Several important studies by O. Tallgren may be consulted for the backgrounds of thirteenth-century astronomy, among the most important of which are "Observations sur les manuscrits de l'astronomie d'Alphonse X" (*NM*, 1908), "Sur l'astronomie espagnole d'Alphonse X et son modèle arabe" (*Commentationes orientalicae in honorem Knut Tallquist*, I, 1925), and "Un point d'astronomie gréco-arabo-romane. A propos de l'astronomie espagnole d'Alphonse X" (*NM*, 1928).

The famous *Lapidarios*, known generally to English speakers as the *Lapidary*, have not been studied with the care they deserve, nor is there any complete edition save the facsimile edition in color (Madrid, 1881), with a prologue by J. Fernández Montaña. The best study of this manuscript is that of J. Cardosa Gonçalves, *O 'Lapidario del Rey Don Alfonso X el Sabio.' Estudo deste manuscrito iluminado do século XIII* (Lisbon, 1929), which concentrates on the actual manuscript rather than on its literary aspects. Four articles by J. Nunemaker treat alchemy in the *Lapidario*: "Noticias sobre la alquimia en el 'Lapidario' de Alfonso X" (*RFE*, 1929); "Nota adicional sobre la alquimia en los lapidarios alfonsinos" (*RFE*, 1931); "The Madrid Manuscript of the Alfonsine Lapidaries" (*MP*, 1931); and "An Additional Chapter on Magic in Mediaeval Spanish Literature" (*Speculum*, (1932), which treats several aspects of magic in the thirteenth century. Sources are studied in J. H. Nunemaker's "In Pursuit of the Sources of the Alfonsine Lapidaries" (*Speculum*, 1939).

King Alfonso's *Libro de Ajedrez, Tablas e Dados*, an interesting and detailed treatment of the games of chess, dice, and backgammon, has been reproduced in facsimile as *The Spanish Treatise on Chess Play, Written by Order of King Alphonse the Sage in the Year* 1283, with an introduction, which should be longer and more detailed, by J. White (2 vols., 1913). J. Trend's "Alfonso el Sabio and the Game of Chess" (*Revue Hispanique*, 1933), though brief, gives an excellent introduction to the *Libro*.

The edition by K. Vanderford of *Septenario* (1945) has a brief introduction, but the *Septenario* deserves more study than it has had. Vanderford also shows relationships between the *Septenario* and the *Siete Partidas* in "El 'Septenario' y su relación con las 'Siete Partidas' " (*Revista de Filología Hispánica*, 1941).

King Alfonso's vast *Siete Partidas*, a detailed and comprehensive treatment of medieval Spanish law and description of the obligations of the many social classes to one another, has been translated masterfully into English (1931) by S. Scott, with excellent and scholarly introduction and notes by S. Lobingier and bibliography by J. Vance. No Spanish edition of the full thirteenth-century text has been prepared, and the translation, is, therefore, the most complete rendition of the medieval work. A. Solalinde's "Una fuente de las 'Partidas.' La 'Disciplina Clericalis,' de Pedro Alfonso" (*HR*, 1934) is an interesting treatment of one of the literary sources of the *Partidas*, pointing to the importance of this legal codex in the field of literature. The literary backgrounds of the *Partidas* are explored by A. Batres Jáuregui in "Las *Siete Partidas* consideradas bajo el aspecto literario" in this author's *Estudios históricos y literarios* (1887), which, though old, is the most nearly complete study of these matters. C. Limón Miguel studies interesting aspects of medieval education in "Ideas pedagógicas en el libro de 'Las Siete Partidas' " (*Revista Española de Pedagogía*, 1946).

P. BIBLICAL STUDIES

Spanish Scriptural texts are an important genre in medieval Spanish literature. Sister Francis Gormly's "The Use of the Bible in Representative Works of Medieval Spanish Literature, 1250–1300" (diss., Catholic Univ. of America, 1962) is an investigation of the use of the Bible in the works of Berceo and in other devotional poetry, in the *General Estoria*, and in the *Castigos e documentos del rey don Sancho*. The studies of Margherita Morreale provide a better understanding of the part Scripture played in Spanish letters. Her "Apuntes bibliográficos para la iniciación al estudio de las Biblias medievales en castellano" (*Sefarad*, 1960) is a good orientation to Biblical studies in Spanish; her "Biblia romanceada y

Diccionario Histórico" (*Homenaje a Dámaso Alonso*, Vol. II, 1961)
is a standard and important study of the vocabulary of Spanish
Scripture as it developed from Latin, French, and other vernacular
languages. T. Montgomery's *El Evangelio de San Mateo según el
Manuscrito Escurialense I.I.6. Texto, Gramática, Vocabulario*
(1962) is a carefully edited text with very scholarly treatment of
speech, word order, syntax, and morphology of this Gospel. A.
Castro, A. Millares Carlo, and A. Battistessa, *Biblia medieval
romanceada judío-cristiana, versión del Antiguo Testamento en el
Siglo XIV sobre los textos hebreo y latino* (2 vols., 1950–55),
provides editions of other Biblical texts in Spanish. O. Hauptman,
"The 'General Estoria' of Alfonso el Sabio and Escorial Biblical
Manuscript I. j. 8" (*HR*, 1945) and "A Glossary of the Pentateuch
of Escorial Biblical Manuscript I. j. 4" (*HR*, 1942), belongs to any
listing of Hispanic Biblical investigations.

9

Medieval Catalan Literature

By Joan Ruiz i Calonja

AND

Josep Roca i Pons

INDIANA UNIVERSITY

A. BIBLIOGRAPHY

There is no comprehensive, up-to-date bibliography of Catalan literature. The most useful guides for the period under review are J. Vives and R. Aramon, "Bibliografia de llengua i literatura catalana" (*Anuari de l'Oficina Romànica de Lingüística i Literatura*, 1929–34, and separately 1929–35), the annual or biennial reviews of research in *YWMLS*, and the section "Aspectos culturales" of the *Indice Histórico Español. Bibliografía Histórica de España e Hispanoamérica, Centro de Estudios Históricos Internacionales de la Universidad de Barcelona* (1953–), of which six volumes have been published. Recent work is recorded in the annual bibliographies of *PMLA* and *RFE*. For additional assistance, particularly with respect to the political, social, and cultural backgrounds of Catalan literature, the student should consult the extensive bibliographies of M. García Silvestre, *História sumària de la literatura catalana* (1932), and J. Ruiz i Calonja, *História de la literatura catalana* (1954). Articles on Catalan literature regularly appear in *Estudis Romànics* (1913–35, 1947–) and *Anuari de l'Institut d'Estudis Catalana* (1907–).

B. LITERARY HISTORIES

The most comprehensive account of Old Catalan literature is J. Rubió i Balaguer's contribution to the *Historia general de las literaturas hispánicas*, Vols. I (1949) and III (1953). M. de Riquer's *Resumen de literatura catalana* (1947) is concise, but penetrating and informative on the medieval period. W. Giese, "Grundzüge der Entwicklung der alteren katalanischen Literatur" (*Archiv*, 1932), should be read in connection with them. The first six volumes of M. de Montoliu's monumental work, *Les grans personalitats de la literatura catalana* (1957–60), deal with medieval authors. Since they were written long before their actual publication, their scholarship is somewhat outdated, but their criticism is so stimulating as to make them worthy of attention all the same. Finally, mention should be made of a new series of introductory manuals: J. Molas, *Literatura catalana antiga, Volum I. El segle XIII* (1961); J. Romeu, *Literatura catalana antiga. Volum II. El segle XIV* (1961); and J. Molas, *Literatura catalana antiga. Volum III. El segle XV. Primera part* (1963). The work in all of them is up to date and reliable.

C. TEXTS AND ANTHOLOGIES

The best and most complete collection of old Catalan authors is *Els Nostres Clàssics, Editorial Barcino.* The texts are well edited and are provided with good introductions and notes. Other collections occasionally publishing medieval material are *Collecció Popular Barcino, Societat Catalana de Bibliòfils,* and *Institut d'Estudis Catalans.* Two general anthologies pay considerable attention to the older literature: L. Nonell, *Antologia de la prosa catalana. De Llull a Josep Pla* (2 vols., 1957–58), and R. Tasis, *Antologia de la poesia catalana. De Ramon Llull a Jacint Verdaguer* (1949). Especially interesting for English readers is the *Anthology of Catalan Lyric Poetry* (1953) by J. Triadú, with an extensive introduction.

D. POETRY

For a sound general survey of the medieval Catalan lyric, whose course is divided into three periods called Provençal, French, and Italian, the student should consult J. Fuster, *La poesia catalana fins a la renaixença* (2 vols., 1954). A more detailed treatment of the first period, extending from the eleventh to the thirteenth century, is provided by J. Massó Torrents' *Repertori de l'antiga literatura catalana, Vol. I. La poesia* (1932). Three indispensable works on the troubadour movement itself are A. Jeanroy, *La poésie lyrique des troubadours* (2 vols., 1934), E. Hoepffner, *Les troubadours dans leur vie et dans leurs oeuvres* (1955), and I. Frank, *Répertoire métrique de la poésie des troubadours* (2 vols., 1953–57). There is a brief introduction to the subject by M. de Riquer, *Resumen de literatura provenzal trovadoresca* (1948). Both Provençal and Catalan literature claim *La Chanson de Sainte Foy,* edited by E. Hoepffner and P. Alfaric (2 vols., 1926). The case for its Catalan character is set forth by M. Jampy in "Un poema català del segle XI al Conflent. *La Canço de Sante Fe*" (*La Paraula Cristiana,* 1928). A new style of lyric poetry emerged in the fourteenth century under French influence. Its variety of form together with its extraordinary dexterity and subtlety is discussed by A. Jeanroy in "La poésie provençale dans le Sud-ouest de la France et en Catalogne du début au milieu du XIVe siècle. C. Le groupe catalano-aragonais" (*Histoire Littéraire de la France*, Vol. XXXVIII, 1941) and by A. Pagès in *Les "cobles" ou poésies lyriques provenço-catalanes de Jaume, Pere et Arnau March* (1949). J. M. Casas Homs's edition, *"Torcimany" de Luis d'Averçó. Tratado rétorico gramatical y diccionario de rimas. Siglos XIV–XV* (2 vols., 1956), is also of importance for the light it throws on the origin of the "Gàia Ciència." The third and last stage in the development of the medieval Catalan lyric took place in the fifteenth century, when French influence gave way to Italian. M. de Riquer, in *Comentaris crítics sobre clàssics catalans* (1935), and P. Le Gentil, in *La poésie lyrique espagnole et portugaise à la fin du moyen âge* (2 vols., 1949–53), have demonstrated how much of the poetry of the period derived from Dante and Petrarch. It should not be thought, however, that the earlier traditions lost their holds on the Catalan lyric entirely. Provençal influence, for example, can still be found in the "cancioneros," as O. H. Green (*PMLA*, 1949) has ably shown. Auziàs March, the greatest of medieval Catalan poets, is now available in a new edition by P. Bohigas (1952), which, for all of its considerable merits, does not entirely supplant that of A. Pagès (2 vols., 1912–14), and in an excellent anthology by J. Fuster (1959). His influence on Spanish literature, particularly of the sixteenth century, is discussed by M. de Riquer, *Traducciones castellanas de Ausiás March en la Edad de Oro* (1946), and M. del Pilar Arrando, *Ausiás March y Garcilaso de la Vega, poetas del dolorido amar* (1948). We are also indebted to M. de Riquer for a new edition, with an excellent introduction and commentary, of Jordi de Sant Jordi (1955). The only modern study of any significance on Roiç de Corella is J. Carbonell, "Les paraules en l'estil de Joan Roiç de Corella," in *Homenatge a Carles Riba* (1954). Jaume Roig's satire, *Spill*, has been re-edited by R. Miguel i Planas (1952). Finally, by way of background, attention should be drawn to the works of the eminent musicologist, H. Anglès, *La música a Catalunya fins al segle XIII* (1934) and *La música en la corte de los Reyes Católicos* (3 vols., 1941–51).

E. PROSE

The origin and growth of medieval Catalan historiography may be studied in three works of outstanding merit: R. Alos-Moner, *Autors catalans antics. I. Historiografia* (1932); F. Valls i Taberner, "Els inicis de la historiografia catalana," in *Matisos d'història i de llegenda* (1932) ; and R. B. Tate, "The Influence of Italian Humanism on the Historiography of Castille and Aragon during the Fifteenth Century" (diss., Belfast, 1955). An important collection of primary sources is by A. Rubio i Lluch, *Diplomatari de l'Orient català, 1301–1409* (1947). Volume I of a new edition by M. Coll i Alentorn of the foremost Catalan chronicler, Bernat Desclot, appeared in 1949. Desclot's puzzling "prosifications" are discussed by Coll i Alentorn in his introduction and by F. Soldevilla in "Les prosificacions en el primers capítols de la Crónica de Desclot" (*Boletín de la Real Academia de Buenas Letras de Barcelona*, 1958). P. Bohigas, in the introduction to his edition of the *Llibre del Consolat de Mar* (3 vols., 1930–33) and in his *Tractats de cavalleria* (1947), gives an authoritative account of the legal literature.

Ramón Lull has attracted widespread attention in recent years. His Catalan works are now available in an excellent edition entitled *Obres essencials* (2 vols., 1957–60). There are good introductions to his thought by T. and J. Carreras i Artau, *Historia de la filosofía española: Filosofía cristiana de los siglos XIII al XV* (2 vols., 1939–43), and by R. Pring-Mill, *El microcosmos lul.lià* (1961). Lull's seventh centenary was celebrated with the publication of a collection of commemorative essays, *Miscal.lània lul.liana*, in *Estudis Franciscans* (1934–35). The most significant contributions to Lullian scholarship since 1936 are noted in R. Aramon "Publicacions lul.lianes" (*Butlletí de la Societat Catalana d'Estudis Històrics*, 1953), B. Mendía, "Bibliografía luliana contemporánea (años 1935–50)" (*Archivum Franc. Hist.* XLIV, 1951), and in the periodical *Estudios Lulianos*, founded by the Maioricensis Schola Lullistica in 1957. The great Spanish edition of Lull's *Obras literarias* (1948) is by M. Batllori and M. Caldeteny. M. Batllori edited Arnau De Vilanova's *Obres catalanes* (2 vols., 1947) and is also the author of an article, "L'antitomisme pintoresc d'Arnau de Vilanova" (*Vuit segles de cultura catalana a Europa*, 1958; 2nd ed., enlarged, 1959) ; and Carreras i Artau of an article, "Doctrina y práctica de la interpretación de los sueños en Arnau de Vilanova" (*Actes du IX Congrès International d'Histoire des Sciences*, 1960). J. Carreras i Artau, "Fray Francisco Eiximenis. Su significación religiosa, filosófico-moral, política y social" (*Anales del Instituto de Estudios Gerundenses*, 1946), is the best general statement of his over-all thought. His political philosophy is discussed in more detail by A. López Amo, "El pensamiento político de Eiximeniç en su tratado de *Regiment de Prínceps*" (*Anuario de Historia del Derecho Español*, 1946), and by F. Elías de Tejada, *Las doctrinas políticas en la Cataluña medieval* (1950). On Saint Vincent Ferrer, we have an admirable edition of the *Sermons* by J. Sanchis Sivera (1932) and an important study by J. Fuster, "Notes per a un estudi de l'oratòria vicentina" (*Revista Valenciana de Filología*, 1954). Among the humanists, Bernat Metgé's works have been edited by M. de Riquer (2 vols., 1959) and Ferran Valentí's *Traducció de les Paradoxa de Ciceró: Parlament al gran e general consell* by J. M. Morató i Thomàs (1959).

A short but perceptive article by P. Bohigas, "La matière de Bretagne en Catalogne," appeared in the *Bulletin bibliographique de la Société Internationale Arthurienne* (1961). From the same scholar has come a definitive study of the chivalric novel, "Orígenes de los libros de caballería," in the *Historia General de las Literaturas Hispánicas*, Vol. I (1949). The two most important Catalan novels of the Middle Ages, *Tirant lo Blanch* and *Curial e Güelfa*, have been re-edited, with valuable introductions, in the period under review; the former by M. de Riquer (1947) and the latter by R. Aramon (1930) and by R. Miquel i Planas (1932). *Tirant lo Blanch* has also been the subject of a number of distinguished scholarly studies: among them W. J. Entwistle, "Tirant lo Blanch and the Social Order of the End of the Fifteenth Century" (*Estudis Romànics*, 1949–50); D. Alonso, "*Tirant lo Blanch*, novela moderna" (*Revista Valenciana de Filología*, 1951), on its merits as a realistic novel; and J. Corominas, "Sobre l'estil i manera de Martí Joan de Galba i de Joanot Martorell" (*Homenatge a Carles Riba*, 1954), on the problems of authorship. The Oriental sources of the novel have been investigated by S. Bosch, "Les fonts orientals del *Tirant lo Blanch*" (*Estudis Romànics*, 1949–50), and by C. Marinesco, "Du nouveau sur *Tirant lo Blanch*" (*Estudis Romànics*, 1953–54). P. Bohigas discusses the structure of *Curial e Güelfa* in *Homenatge a Antoni Rubió i Lluch* (1936).

F. DRAMA

J. Romeu has published, with appropriate commentary, all the important texts of medieval Catalan drama in two works of exemplary editorial scholarship, *Teatre hagiogràfic* (3 vols., 1957) and *Teatre profà* (2 vols., 1962). An interesting monograph by Florence Whyte, *The Dance of Death in Spain and Catalonia* (1931), draws attention to the similarities between the Catalan translations and those in other European languages.

10

Medieval Portuguese Literature

By Thomas R. Hart
UNIVERSITY OF OREGON

M EDIEVAL PORTUGUESE LITERATURE is conventionally held to end with the publication, in 1516, of the *Cancioneiro geral* of Garcia de Resende. This survey observes this convention, and, with one or two exceptions, mentions only works published since 1930.

A. GENERAL AIDS

An indispensable guide to printed editions, not limited to literary texts, is M. A. Valle Cintra, *Bibliografia de textos medievais portugueses* (1960). A descriptive bibliography of the more important medieval manuscripts, classified according to their present location, is given by S. da Silva Neto, *Textos medievais portugueses e seus problemas* (1956). B. W. Diffey, "Bibliography of the Principal Published Guides to Portuguese Archives and Libraries" (*Proceedings of the International Colloquium of Luso-Brazilian Studies*, 1953), is primarily concerned with materials of interest to the historian rather than to the student of literature. Early printed books are described in the *Bibliografia geral portuguesa: século XV* (2 vols., 1941–44).

Continuing bibliographies are provided by several periodicals. The most nearly complete is that of *PMLA*. That of *NRFH*, while not quite so extensive, is especially useful for its listing of reviews; *RFE* also includes reviews but is far less comprehensive than either of the above. Most of the recent volumes of *YWMLS* include a section on Portuguese, highly selective but valuable for its brief analyses and appraisals of the works listed.

B. VERSIFICATION

No comprehensive work on Portuguese metrics has appeared in the period under review. A brief introduction to the versification of the early lyrics is the chapter on "métrica e língua" in M. Rodrigues Lapa's *Lições*, cited below. A number of difficult problems are discussed by C. Cunha, *Estudos de poética trovadoresca* (1961).

Important studies of the metrical practice of individual poets include D. C. Clarke, "Versification in Alfonso el Sabio's *Cantigas*" (*HR*, 1955), and the notes to C. Cunha's editions of Martim Codax and Joan Zorro, cited below. For the later period there is much useful information in P. Le Gentil, *La poésie lyrique espagnole et portugaise à la fin du moyen âge. Deuxième partie: les formes* (1953).

C. HISTORY

A readable short survey is C. Nowell, *A History of Portugal* (1952) ; H. Livermore, *A History of Portugal* (1947), is somewhat more detailed. Standard longer works in Portuguese are D. Peres et al., *História de Portugal: edição monumental commemorativa do 8º centenário da fundação da nacionalidade* (8 vols., 1928–38), and F. de Almeida, *História de Portugal* (6 vols., 1922–29). A. J. Saraiva, *História da cultura em Portugal* (3 vols., 1950–62), is, despite its title, not a narrative history but a series of provocative and often polemical essays on Portuguese social, economic, and cultural history from a liberal point of view; the first volume deals with the Middle Ages.

D. HISTORY OF LITERATURE

The best introduction is M. Rodrigues Lapa, *Lições de literatura portuguesa: época medieval* (4th ed. 1956), which maintains a good balance between literary history and literary criticism; information on authors, manuscripts, and editions is complemented by interpretive essays of real insight and often of considerable length, on the major figures. Each chapter is followed by a critical bibliography; in the text itself Rodrigues Lapa gives much space to an appraisal of recent scholarship. He is particularly good at pointing out the implications for Portuguese studies of work in the other medieval literatures.

A somewhat similar treatment is A. J. da Costa Pimpão, *História da literatura portuguesa. Idade média* (2nd ed. 1959). Like Rodrigues Lapa, Costa Pimpão takes literature to mean primarily imaginative literature, though, again like Rodrigues Lapa, he gives much attention to historians (Fernão Lopes, Zurara) and moralists (D. Pedro, D. Duarte). He adds, however, another qualification, insisting that "the first quality we must demand in the history of any country's literature [is] its national originality." Thus, Costa Pimpão makes only passing mention of the *matéria de Bretanha*

other than the *Amadís*, while Rodrigues Lapa devotes a whole
chapter to it. A number of works not discussed, or discussed only
briefly, in the two histories just mentioned, are given fuller treatment
in M. Martins, *Estudos de literatura medieval* (1956). Martins
stresses theological writing and includes works in Latin by Portuguese authors.

Less detailed treatments of the medieval period may be found in
the general histories of Portuguese literature, of which the best are
perhaps G. C. Rossi, *Storia della letteratura portoghese* (1953),
and A. J. Saraiva and O. Lopes, *História da literatura portuguesa*
(1954; 3rd ed., enlarged, 1961). Useful shorter works include G. Le
Gentil, *La littérature portugaise* (2nd ed. 1951); M. de Riquer,
Resumen de literatura portuguesa (1947), which stresses relations
with Spanish literature; and, perhaps the most readable of the three,
A. J. Saraiva's highly personal *História da literatura portuguesa* in
the *Colecção Saber* (1951).

E. ANTHOLOGIES

Two collections that cover the whole range of medieval Portuguese literature are K. S. Roberts, *An Anthology of Old Portuguese*
(c. 1956), and J. J. Nunes, *Crestomatia arcaica* (3rd ed. 1943). An
excellent small anthology for use in schools is M. Rodrigues Lapa,
Crestomatia arcaica (3rd ed. 1960).

F. VERSE

The most important genre of medieval Portuguese literature is
lyric poetry; indeed, insofar as purely imaginative literature is
concerned, there is hardly anything else. Though some sort of
theatrical representations doubtless existed in the Middle Ages, no
texts have come down to us. See I. S. Révah, "Gil Vicente a-t-il été le
fondateur du théâtre portugais?" (*Bulletin d'histoire du théâtre
portugais*, 1950) and "Manifestations théâtrales pré-vicentines: les
'momos' de 1500" (ibid., 1952); and E. Asensio, "De los momos
cortesanos a los autos caballerescos de Gil Vicente" (*Anais do
primeiro congresso brasileiro de língua falada no teatro*, 1958).
Medieval prose consists largely of works translated from other
vernaculars, notably Old French, or from Latin, and of works that
belong less to literature than to theology or historiography. The
prose works, in any case, belong to the later Middle Ages; for the
earlier period, the twelfth and thirteenth centuries, we have nothing
but lyric poetry.

The best brief introduction to the medieval lyrics is in Rodrigues Lapa's *Lições*, already cited. The second chapter is a critical survey of recent theories on the origins of romance lyric poetry. Older views are discussed at greater length, and with more exclusive acceptance of the theory of liturgical origins, in Lapa's *Das Origens da poesia lírica em Portugal na Idade-Média* (1929). Another good survey, with ample bibliography, is J. Filgueira Valverde, "Lírica medieval gallega y portuguesa," in G. Díaz-Plaja, ed. *Historia general de las literaturas hispánicas*, Vol. I (1949). A useful bibliographical aid is S. Pellegrini, *Repertorio bibliografico della prima lirica portoghese* (1939).

Two of the three great medieval *cancioneiros* have appeared in new editions. H. H. Carter has published *Cancioneiro da Ajuda: A Diplomatic Edition* (1941); the older edition of C. Michaëlis de Vasconcellos (2 vols., 1904) is, however, still useful for its valuable notes. The *Cancioneiro Colocci-Brancuti* is being published in a critical edition accompanied by a facsimile of the manuscript. Seven volumes have appeared, edited by E. P. and J. P. Machado, *Cancioneiro da Biblioteca Nacional (antigo Colocci-Brancuti): leitura, comentários e glossário* (1949–58). The *cantigas de amigo* have been published in a critical edition by J. J. Nunes, *Cantigas d'amigo dos trovadores galego-portugueses* (3 vols., 1926–28). A similar edition of the *Cantigas d'amor dos trovadores galego-portugueses* (1932) is limited to poems not included by C. Michaëlis de Vasconcellos in the text and appendices of her edition of the *Cancioneiro da Ajuda*. An extensive selection from all three *cancioneiros* is included in Roberts' *Anthology*, already cited. Smaller anthologies, primarily for school use, include H. Cidade, *Poesia medieval*, I: *cantigas de amigo* (4th ed. 1959), in the *Textos literários*, and A. J. da Costa Pimpão, *Cantigas d'el rei D. Dinis* (1942). S. Pellegrini, *Auswahl altportugiesischer Lieder* (1928), and G. Bertoni, *Antiche liriche portoghesi* (1937), both publish texts.

The works of a few of the individual troubadours have appeared in critical editions. C. Cunha's *O cancioneiro de Joan Zorro* (1939) and *O cancioneiro de Martin Codax* (1956) are especially valuable for their elaborate linguistic notes and the editor's scrupulous attention to problems of versification.

The best esthetic appraisal of the *Cantigas de amigo* is in E. Asensio, *Poética y realidad en el cancionero peninsular de la edad media* (1957). The third chapter, "La poética del paralelismo," is an excellent formal analysis of parallelistic verse, based on an extensive acquaintance with recent studies in literary theory. Asensio rejects the notion that the essence of this poetry is immobility:

there is progression, but a retarded progression, an interplay of repetition and variation, in which the former always predominates. D. M. Atkinson, "Parallelism in the Medieval Portuguese Lyric" (*MLR*, 1955), is a persuasive statement of the more traditional view. Students of comparative literature will be interested in C. M. Bowra's "Paralelo entre cantares gregos e portugueses" in A. F. G. Bell et al., *Da poesia medieval portuguesa*, trans. A. A. Dória (2nd ed., rev. and enlarged, 1947). I. Pope, "Medieval Latin Background of the Thirteenth-Century Galician Lyric" (*Speculum*, 1934), adduces musicological evidence in support of the theory of liturgical origins. There is a new edition in three volumes by W. Mettmann of Alfonso el Sabio's *Cantigas de Santa Maria* (1959–64). An important linguistic study is R. Rübecamp, "A linguagem das *Cantigas de Santa Maria* de Afonso X, o Sábio" (*BdF*, 1932–33). The versification of the *Cantigas* is discussed in the article by D. C. Clarke, already cited.

The gap between the medieval *cancioneiros* and the *Cancioneiro geral* is bridged by the Galician poems included in the predominantly Castilian *Cancionero de Baena*. The Galician texts contain many Castilianisms, some of which doubtless were introduced by copyists. R. Lapesa, "La lengua de la poesía lírica desde Macías hasta Villasandino" (*RPh*, 1953), proves, however, that many must be attributed to the poets, for most of whom Galician was an acquired language; earlier attempts to reconstruct the texts in a more purely Galician form are shown to have been often misleading.

Our survey of Old Portuguese verse ends with the *Cancioneiro geral* of Garcia de Resende, published in 1516 but containing many compositions written in the second half of the preceding century. Although still generally considered inferior in poetic value to the earlier *cancioneiros*, it has recently begun to receive more attention from scholars. J. Ruggieri, *Il Canzioniere di Resende* (1931), stresses the juxtaposition of themes already present in the medieval lyrics with newer elements drawn from the Spanish and Italian poetry of the Renaissance. A readable introduction, emphasizing the importance of the work for an understanding of contemporary Portugese society, is A. Crabbé Rocha, *Aspectos do "Cancioneiro geral"* (1949).

G. PROSE

In prose fiction, the most important contribution has been the publication of the *Demanda do Santo Graal* in two different editions, both by the Brazilian scholar A. Magne. The first edition (3 vols.,

1944) was severely criticized because of the inaccuracy of Magne's transcription and his silent suppression of portions of the text, apparently on moral grounds. He has now begun the publication of a new edition, *A demanda do Santo Graal: reprodução fac-similada e transcrição crítica do cód. 2594 da Biblioteca Nacional de Viena*, Vol. I (1955).

A number of religious texts have appeared in scholarly editions, among them the *Livro de solilóquio de Santo Agostinho*, ed. M. A. Valle Cintra (1957); the *Orto do esposo*, ed. B. Maler (2 vols., 1956); the *Miragres de Santiago*, ed. J. L. Pensado (1958); and the *Virgeu de consolação*, ed. A. de Bem Veiga (1958). A critical edition, by A. de Almeida Calado, of the *Obras* of Frei João Álvares has appeared in the Acta Universitatis Conimbrigensis (1959–60). The first volume contains the *Trautado da vida e feitos do muito vertuoso senhor ifante dom Fernando;* the second includes Frei João's translations of the rule of Saint Benedict, of several sermons of Saint Augustine, and of a portion of the *Imitation of Christ.*

In historical writing, the Portuguese version of the *Crónica geral de Espanha de 1344* is now available in a superb edition by L. F. Lindley Cintra (2 vols., 1951–54). The six-hundred-page introduction is a fundamental contribution to the study of medieval historiography in the Iberian peninsula. G. Eanes de Zurara's *Crónica da Guiné* was published in a modernized edition by J. de Bragança (1937); another edition, by A. Dias Dinis, with the title *Crónica dos feitos de Guiné*, appeared in 1949. An important study is J. de Carvalho, "Sôbre a erudição de Gomes Eanes de Zurara," in his *Estudos sôbre a cultura portuguesa do século XV*, Vol. I (1949).

But interest has naturally been centered on the great figure of Fernão Lopes. M. Lopes de Almeida and A. de Magalhães Basto have edited the *Crónica de D. João I* from an unpublished manuscript in the Public Library of Evora (1949). Fresh appraisals of Lopes' place in the history of Portuguese literature have been made by H. Cidade, in his *Liçoes de cultura e literatura portuguesas* (3rd ed. 1951), and A. E. Beau, in his *Estudos*, Vol. I (1959). Of Beau's three studies, all previously published, the most important for the student of literature is the first, "A preocupação literária de Fernão Lopes." A brief and readable introduction is A. J. Saraiva, *Fernão Lopes*, in the *Colecção Saber* (1951?), which includes a selection of modernized texts. Some of Saraiva's ideas are given more extended treatment in his *História da cultura em Portugal*, already cited.

Turning finally to the moralists, D. Duarte's *Leal conselheiro* has appeared in an annotated critical edition by J. M. Piel (1942), who has also edited the *Livro da ensinança de bem cavalgar toda sela* (1944). A good brief introduction to the philosopher king is Rodrigues Lapa's study in his *Lições*, which stresses the value of the works, especially the *Leal conselheiro*, as an exercise in self-portraiture. D. Pedro's *Livro da virtuosa bemfeitoria* has been edited by J. Costa (3rd ed. 1946). R. Ricard, "L'infant D. Pedro de Portugal et *O livro da virtuosa bemfeitoria*" (*BEPIF*, 1954), emphasizes the role of personal observation in D. Pedro's work.

11

Medieval Celtic Literature

By Charles Donahue
FORDHAM UNIVERSITY

MEDIEVAL LITERATURE has been recorded and transmitted in two groups of Celtic languages, the Goedelic group, first found in Ireland, and the Brittonic group, first found in Britain. Modern Goedelic languages are Irish (or Irish Gaelic), Scottish Gaelic, and the almost extinct Manx. Modern Brittonic languages are Welsh, Cornish (which became extinct in the eighteenth century), and Breton, spoken in northwest France. The ancestor of Breton was brought to Gaul in the fifth and sixth centuries by British refugees from the Saxon invasions. The original Celtic language of Gaul, which was apparently more closely related to Brittonic than to Goedelic, died before the beginning of the Middle Ages. Our material is divided into four sections: I. Works concerned equally with the medieval literature of both groups; II. Medieval Goedelic literature; III. Medieval Brittonic literatures; and IV. External relations of Medieval Celtic literature of both groups.

I. WORKS CONCERNED EQUALLY WITH BOTH BRITTONIC AND GOEDELIC LITERATURE

THE STANDARD history of Celtic philology up to the beginning of the present century is V. Tourneur's *Esquisse d'une histoire des études celtiques* (1905). There is no survey of the thirty years preceding the period here under review, but materials for that survey are to be found in the book reviews and the *Chronique* of *Revue celtique*, which from its foundation in 1870 until 1934 was a rallying point for the sparse and widely dispersed Celticist forces. In that year J. Vendryes, the editor, had difficulty with his publisher, who held legal title to the name *Revue celtique*. Despite great personal sacrifices, Vendryes kept this valuable institution alive under the name *Etudes celtiques*. The fourth volume of *EC* was interrupted from 1940 until 1948 by Vendryes' refusal to seek, in his words, "the *nihil obstat* of a *Feldwebel*." Since 1948 *EC* has appeared regularly, and at present is, under Vendryes' successor, E. Bachellery, a central fact in Celtic studies.

Since its foundation in 1897, *Zeitschrift für celtische Philologie* has provided a welcome counterpoint to *Revue celtique* and *EC*. The editor, J. Pokorny, was in exile during the war, and one volume of the *Zeitschrift* in which political influence was observable appeared in 1943. In 1953, normal publication was resumed under Pokorny and is continuing. One fruit of Pokorny's exile during the war years is the valuable "Keltologie" in *Wissenschaftliche Forschungsberichte* (1953), a bibliography of Celtic studies covering the years when war had interrupted communication.

Ogam, a general Celtic periodical begun at Rennes in 1949, is current. It has been strong in articles on Celtic mythology and in French translations of Irish material.

Journal of Celtic Studies, under the direction of H. Meroney, began in 1949 and concluded its first volume, dedicated to F. N. Robinson, the dean of American Celtic studies, in 1950. The two numbers of the second volume appeared in 1953 and 1958. After that, publication ceased.

K. Jackson's *A Celtic Miscellany* (1951) is the best general anthology of translations from the Celtic languages. It includes postmedieval material, but the Middle Ages are generously represented. The translations are original and painstaking, the selections varied and fresh. There is a brief but important introduction stating Jackson's conviction that the poets and philosophers of the Celtic renascence who wrote of Celtic mistiness, magic, and remoteness had misread Celtic literature and the Celtic character. The selections are chosen to illustrate Celtic sense for fact, the rough and sometimes grim humor of the material, and the extraordinary precision it reveals of both observation and statement.

Shortly before the onset of the period under review Cecile O'Rahilly in her *Ireland and Wales* (1924), followed by C. H. Slover in "Early Literary Channels between Britain and Ireland" (*University of Texas Studies in English*, 1926–27), opened a way to the comparative study of literary influences between Ireland and Wales. This way has been followed in a number of studies discussed below (Secs. III and IV). *The Growth of Literature*, Vol. I (1932), of H. M.

and Nora K. Chadwick introduced fresh points of view into comparative studies and has influenced thinking in the Celtic field. The Chadwicks' conviction that many widely dispersed people, even in cases where influence in the old sense is quite out of the question, produce similar imaginative works under similar social and historical conditions provides a new dimension of comparative studies. Even more influential in Celtic studies has been their documentation of the fact that courtly, elaborate, and schooled imaginative composition is possible without the use of writing. There can be, and often have been, "unwritten literatures." We shall have a number of occasions to recur to these views. It may be added that the Chadwicks present an excellent survey of the heroic literature of Ireland and Wales as it appeared at the beginning of the period under review.

One of the first books to show some influence from the Chadwicks is K. Jackson's *Studies in Early Celtic Nature Poetry* (1935). The volume contains several translations of Irish and Welsh nature poems with notes. The texts are followed by a discussion that considers such questions as influence between Irish and Welsh. But Jackson, in the Chadwick manner, is more concerned with the two bodies of verse as parallel testimonies to the manner of development of one widespread kind of poetry. Old English elegiac verse is also taken into consideration.

II. MEDIEVAL GOEDELIC LITERATURE

G OEDELIC SPEAKERS from the north of Ireland invaded and settled in western Scotland in the sixth century, bringing with them the language we know in its modern form as Scottish Gaelic. During the whole of the Middle Ages Gaelic Scotland shared a common language, a common culture, and a common written and unwritten literature with Ireland. Common Gaelic was the language of cultivated speakers in Scotland until the fourteenth century. K. Jackson's lecture, "Common Gaelic: The Evolution of the Goedelic Languages" (*PBA*, 1951), may be consulted. Common Gaelic and its literature were shared to an uninvestigated extent by the Manx Goedels. Strictly speaking, the matter of this section should be called "Common Gaelic Literature." We use the less accurate but familiar term "Irish," not forgetting that the Lowland Scots called the language of their Highland neighbors "Erse."

R. I. Best's *Bibliography of Irish Philology and of Printed Irish Literature* (1913) and its successor, *Bibliography of Irish Philology and of Manuscript Literature, Publications 1918–1942* (1942), give almost complete coverage. Of Irish periodicals still current the oldest is *Ériu*, which since 1904 has been appearing with articles meeting the most exacting philological standards. It contains some translations but no book reviews. *Celtica* (1946–), which despite its name carries mostly Irish material, does have book reviews; so does *Éigse* (1939–), which prints shorter articles and gives more attention to Modern Irish. *Éigse* occasionally carries an article in Irish, but despite strong opposition in some quarters, most Irish scholarship on medieval literature is in the English language. *Irish Historical Studies* (1938–) reviews publications of Irish texts and, in its surveys of Irish periodical literature, notices much of philological interest.

The corpus of raw material for the study of medieval Irish literature is large, and the number of those engaged upon it has never been great. Nevertheless, during the period under survey some important general questions have been raised concerning the character of Irish medieval literature, the forces at work in it and upon it, and the most promising lines of investigation. At the same time, what may be called "preliminary philological processing" has been pushed forward and aids for it have been improved. Finally, an increasing number of literary works and groups of works have been subjected to more detailed investigation, and the results have appeared in studies, improved editions, and sometimes improved and more accurate translations. We shall consider the three activities in the order named.

The best handling of the general course of Irish medieval literature, its movements, periods, and turning points is R. Flower's posthumous *The Irish Tradition* (1947). Flower talks in terms of manuscripts, scriptoria, schools, scribes, and authors rather than of abstract literary works. He follows the course of the Irish tradition from the monasteries of the late sixth and early seventh centuries to the death in poverty of the last of the schooled bards, David Ó Bruadair, in 1698. A professional paleographer, Flower combined great philological rigor with a sensitive response to his material and felicity in rendering Irish verse in English. *Irish Tradition* is the best introduction to medieval Irish literature. It is also an important guide to future studies.

M. Dillon helped to prepare Flower's material for the press. His

Early Irish Literature (1948) is, whether by plan or not, an admirable companion to Flower. Dillon lays before the student typical works of Irish literature. The most important form in early Irish was the saga, a prose tale of varying length (about 100 to 6000 lines) interspersed with rhythmical alliterative passages ("retorics") or syllabic and rhymed verse ("lays"). Most of the book is given over to presenting sagas in translation or summary. The works are carefully chosen and accompanied by valuable observations on character and dating. There is a chapter on poetry. The result is an accurate, unpretentious book indispensable both to the Celticist and to the beginner. The latter should take it up immediately after Flower.

Discussion about the general character of Irish literature has tended, during the period under review, to center on R. Thurneysen's monumental *Die irische Helden- und Königsage* (1921). Only a portion of the original plan was completed, the introduction and the section dealing with the sagas of the Ulster Cycle, which are, in general, the most archaic sagas. The introduction deals with manuscript materials for the study of Irish sagas and with the native *filid* and the monks who were concerned with their production and transcription. The sagas of the Ulster Cycle are then exhaustively handled in terms of previous studies, manuscripts, versions and their relations, and dates. There is a detailed summary of each saga, and, where necessary, of each version. Thurneysen's basic assumption is that he is examining a literary tradition, one expressed in writing. Nevertheless he refers to developments that may have taken place in oral tradition, even after the writing of sagas had started. He also believes that before the use of writing there was some kind of native oral tradition about heroes. This tradition may have had a historical basis. Cuchulainn, he believes, may really have existed.

G. Murphy, in an article in *Ériu* (1952) and in his brief but important *Saga and Myth in Ancient Ireland* (1955), has objected to even the moderate bookishness of Thurneysen. The Irish sagas contained in manuscripts, he insists, are not the medieval literature of Ireland. That was an unwritten literature, carried on by professional storytellers. What is in the manuscripts is only a pale reflection of their oral art, "related to living story-telling much as the museum of today is related to living material culture." The Chadwicks' *Growth of Literature* (see above) was influential in developing Murphy's views; so was the growing awareness of the living art of the native Irish or Scots Gaelic storytellers such as S. Delargy describes in his Rhŷs lecture, "The Gaelic Story Teller" (*PBA*, 1945). Murphy sees Irish storytelling as a continuous process extending from the present back into a remote common Celtic or even Indo-European past.

Factual basis for an assumption of a very ancient tradition of Irish storytelling may be afforded by the parallels between Irish and Sanskrit literature cited by M. Dillon in his Rhŷs lecture, "The Archaism of Irish Tradition" (*PBA*, 1947). Such parallels may, however, be the result of wandering popular tales rather than of a common heritage from Indo-European times. Murphy is indubitably on firmer ground in his insistence on the direct and intimate connection between contemporary storytellers and medieval Irish literature. Ireland and Gaelic Scotland are great repositories of modern oral story, and recording of the material has been active during the period under review. S. Ó Súilleabháian's *A Handbook of Irish Folklore* (1942; rev. ed. 1963) is a survey by a master of it. T. P. Cross's *Motif-Index of Early Irish Literature* (1952), a supplement to Thompson's *Motif Index*, with cross references, is a valuable tool in a field where interesting results are beginning to appear.

In *Irisches Erzählgut im Abendland* (1957), J. Szövérffy draws on both medieval and modern material. Máire MacNeill's recent and very significant study, *The Festival of Lughnasa* (1962), uses both early medieval Patrician documents and modern oral tales of Patrick to throw light on the original and pagan significance of Garland Sunday, celebrated early in August at the time of the ancient Feast of Lughnasa.

The central point of J. Carney's interesting *Studies in Irish Literature and History* (1955) seems to be a conviction that even Thurneysen conceded too much to unwritten literature. Far from being, as Murphy believed, merely monastic reports on an oral tradition, Irish sagas, he holds, are independent compositions by monks who used traditional Irish elements only sparingly and whose work is to be explained largely in terms of the Latin literature cultivated in the monasteries. Few have been willing to go along with Carney in his conviction that the native tradition is an almost negligible nucleus in existing Irish sagas. Nevertheless the earliest documents we have are the work of monks and do contain Christian elements. These elements must be understood if the sagas are to be understood. Insisting on this point, Carney has advanced the study of medieval Irish literature. He also shows a welcome awareness of possible connections between medieval Irish and other northern literatures, English and Scandinavian. Most critics would probably agree with the reserved but generally favorable view J. Marx took of Carney's study in *EC* (1956) and feel that H. Meroney's strictures in *Journal of Celtic Studies* (1958) are too severe. Nonetheless it must be admitted that Carney does sometimes satisfy himself with evidence that would seem tenuous to many philologians.

Another objection to Thurneysen's view of Irish heroic material is to be found in T. F. O'Rahilly's *Early Irish History and Mythology* (1946). O'Rahilly's book is perhaps the weightiest work on ancient and medieval Ireland to appear during the period under review. M. Dillon (*Speculum*, 1947) called it the most important book on Irish history since E. O'Curry's *Lectures on the Manuscript Materials of Ancient Irish History* (1861). In "Keltologie," however, Pokorny subjected the work, particularly the handling of comparative linguistic material, to a very severe critique, which won the approval of K. Jackson (*ZCP*, 1954) and of Bachellery (*EC*, 1955). An exquisitely balanced estimate of the work by Vendryes, doing justice to its *affirmations trop péremptoires* as well as to its stimulating insights, appeared in the "Necrology" of *EC* (1956).

The book is of interest to historians, to linguists, and only in the third place to literary students. O'Rahilly's insistence, however, that all the older sagas, not only the Mythological Cycle but also the Ulster and Finn cycles, are euhemerized myth and not, as Thurneysen believed, history, or fictional imitation of history, is obviously of importance for the interpretation of heroic saga. To take it seriously would involve a reinterpretation of much in the older sagas and a new view of the native tradition that preceded them. So far, attempts on the part of literary students to meet the challenge have been too tentative to be discussed.

If challenges of this importance are left for decades unaccepted and unrejected the reason is perhaps that Irish philology is still partly in what may be called the pioneer period. Most philological energy is being directed into efforts to edit, interpret on a purely linguistic level, and date the considerable body of material that has lain untouched or almost untouched. Among the tools of philological pioneering are catalogues, unedited manuscript material in facsimile or other form, and, on a different level, works such as grammars.

The third volume of R. Flower's *Catalogue of Irish Manuscripts in the British Museum*, containing introductions, indices, and plates for paleographical study, revised and seen through the press by M. Dillon, appeared in 1953. The second volume appeared in 1926, together with a first volume completed by S. H. O'Grady in the 1890s. Flower's work involved a careful comparative study of the material in the manuscripts and provided the basis for parts of his *Irish Tradition*. The *Catalogue of Irish Manuscripts in the Royal*

Irish Academy, begun in 1926, was complete in seven volumes in 1958. The first fascicle of a new catalogue of the Irish manuscripts in the National Library of Ireland appeared in 1961.

Five volumes have appeared in the series of collotype facsimiles of Irish manuscripts inaugurated by the Manuscripts Commission. Perhaps the most interesting of these to literary students is R. Best's *MS. 23 N 10 (formerly Betham 145) in the Library of the Royal Irish Academy* (1954). It is a later manuscript copied around 1575, but it contains texts from the *Cín Dromma Snechta,* "The Little Book of Druim Snechta," a lost manuscript cited in several extant manuscripts and known to have contained very ancient texts. G. Murphy (*Ériu,* 1952) dates the *Cín* in the early eighth century.

The Book of Leinster (c. 1161–1201), the second oldest manuscript containing extensive saga texts and other Irish literary material, is now being published in a text that follows the manuscript meticulously and without editorial change. The first volume edited by R. Best, O. Bergen, and M. O'Brien appeared in 1954, the third in 1957.

The English version of Thurneysen's basic *Handbuch* (1909), *A Grammar of Old Irish* (1946), trans. D. A. Binchy and O. Bergin, incorporates Thurneysen's revisions and is essentially a revised second edition of what K. Jackson called (*Speculum,* 1948) "this greatest work of the greatest Celtic scholar."

With better tools the period under review has seen the appearance of a considerable number of new texts, edited, interpreted, and dated. It has seen, too, a considerable number of improved editions of texts of particular interest to literary students. Many of these texts have appeared in the series published by the Dublin Institute for Advanced Studies called *Medieval and Modern Irish Series* (henceforth *MMIS*). The series contains carefully prepared texts, not necessarily definitive, but usually better than those previously available. The texts are provided with variants, notes on difficulties, and glossaries. Introductions discuss manuscripts, language, and dating. The volumes have no translations, but in some cases the new texts have been made the basis of new translations published elsewhere.

The best and fullest collection of Irish saga texts in English is T. P. Cross and C. Slover, *Ancient Irish Tales* (1936; henceforth *AIT*). It is an anthology of translations from the previous half-century, some of them retouched by the editors. The collection would have been of greater value to students if the sources of the texts had been clearly stated and an editorial opinion of the method and reliability of the translator offered. Some of the translators, such as

W. Stokes, K. Meyer, and J. Dunn, aim at careful, close renderings;
others, such as S. H. O'Grady, allow themselves much greater
license.

G. Murphy's *Early Irish Lyrics* (1956; henceforth *EIL*) is a
collection of shorter poems, most of them unattached. A number of
the poems, however, are included in sagas or associated with saga
material. Some of these will be noted below. The work is rightly
regarded as a little philological masterpiece and one of the most
useful volumes to appear during the period under review. It provides
new and carefully edited texts of the poems and meticulous and
original translations with notes.

R. Thurneysen's German translations in *Sagen aus dem alten
Irland* (1901) are still of great value. The French translations by
various hands in H. D'Arbois de Jubainville's *L'épopée celtique en
Irelande* (1892) tend to be rather free, at times almost paraphrases.
Those in G. Dottin's *L'épopée irlandaise* (1926) are more exact.
Beginning in 1957, a new series of French translations of medieval
Irish texts by C. J. Guyonvarc'h has been appearing in *Ogam*.
Guyonvarc'h aims at a careful literal rendering and makes critical
use of preceding translations. In the case of a number of recently re-
edited texts, that of Guyonvarc'h is the only translation based on the
new edition.

The central saga of the Ulster Cycle is *Táin Bó Cúailgne*, "The
Cattle Raid of Cooley." It is a tale of epic scope recounting the
singlehanded defense of Ulster by the young hero Cuchulainn against
the forces of the rest of Ireland, led by Ailill and Medb, king and
queen of Connacht. The saga exists in three recensions, and the
pages analyzing the complex material are among the most brilliant
in Thurneysen's *Heldensage*. Thurneysen dated the earliest draft of
Recension I in the early eighth century. He rejected earlier dates on
the ground that there was no written form of literary Irish prior to
the eighth century. After over a decade of work with archaic texts,
Thurneysen revised his opinion in an article on poems attributed to
the early seventh-century Colman Mac Leneni (*ZCP*, 1933). He was
now convinced that literary Irish had been written as early as the
late sixth century and suggested that legends connecting the mid-
seventh-century poet Senchan Torpeist with the "recovery" of the
Táin might mean that the original draft of Recension I was written
down in the mid-seventh century, perhaps at the dictation of
Senchan.

Recension II is a reworking and restylization of Recension I,
made in the early twelfth century and found in the late twelfth-
century *Book of Leinster*. The most important publication about

Recension II during the period under review is Cecile O'Rahilly's *The Stowe Version of Táin Bó Cúailgne* (1961). The Stowe version is a variant of Recension II produced in the fifteenth century by simplifying the elaborate language of the Leinster version. Miss O'Rahilly re-examines the relation between the manuscripts of Recension II and Recension III, and treats in detail the language of the Stowe version. There is a glossary but no translation. The material is of particular value for scholars interested in the relation between late medieval literature and the modern oral tradition.

Longes Mac N-Uislenn, "The Exile of the Sons of Uisliu," is connected with the *Táin* in that it explains how the giant Ulster warrior Fergus happened to be an exile in Connacht and hence engaged against Ulster in the raid. The saga, however, centers interest on the figure of Deirdriu, her lament for her lover Noísiu, and her suicide brought on by Conchobar, king of Ulster. The *Longes* is the outstanding older saga in the tragic mode. It has been made available to students in a distinguished edition by V. Hull (1949). The work has a new text with copious notes designed to show students how that text was arrived at from the manuscripts. A detailed discussion shows why the text should be regarded as an early eleventh-century redaction of a ninth- (or perhaps eighth-) century original. There is a full glossary and a new translation that aims only at precision but succeeds in conveying what Dillon calls the "Cistercian bareness of the early sagas." The translation supersedes that in A. H. Leahy's *Heroic Romances of Ireland* (1905), which is the basis of the *AIT* version. The later version, a fifteenth-century redaction with the title *Oided mac nUsnig,* which, in Lady Gregory's adaptation, has been influential in Anglo-Irish literature, has been neglected during the period under review except for a word by Dillon (*Early Irish Literature*) defending its "baroque" style. The last translation of the fifteenth-century original is still that of W. Stokes in *Irische Texte,* Vol. II, part 2 (1887).

Scéla Mucce Meic Dathó, "The Story of Mac Dathó's Pig," is a comic saga with a touch of the cruelty so noticeable in the material of the Ulster Cycle. Many regard it as artistically the most perfect saga of the cycle. It is Old Irish, perhaps late eighth- or early ninth-century. It is edited by Nora Chadwick from *The Book of Leinster,* with an introduction and notes intended for beginning students, and a full glossary, as the sole text in *An Early Irish Reader* (1927). The introduction deals with manuscripts and the general character of the work but oddly omits any consideration of the relation between the language and the date of the saga. The translation is the best available in English. The translation of K. Meyer in *Hibernica*

Minora (1894), followed in *AIT*, is based on a later manuscript, where the characteristic tight style of the *Leinster* version has been relaxed. R. Thurneysen edited the saga in *MMIS* (1935).

The sagas of the Ulster Cycle were regarded by the monks who wrote them down as historical material. Monastic chroniclers considered King Conchobar of Ulster a contemporary of Christ and made appropriate entries in their annals. There are also sagas of kings earlier than Conchobar and sagas of much later kings, kings who appear in the annals during the period (after the later fifth century) in which the entries are regarded as having genuine historical value. All these sagas are usually classified together as sagas of the kings. Sagas of kings who were themselves historical are in many cases clearly fictitious and associate figures who, if we may believe the annals, were certainly not contemporaries. M. Dillon's *The Cycles of the Kings* (1946) handles many of these sagas. His treatment is less exhaustive than Thurneysen's treatment of the Ulster Cycle, but similar in method, in accuracy, and in utility.

Orgain Denna Rig, "The Destruction of Dind Rig," is one of five short texts edited by D. Greene in *MMIS* (1955) in a volume entitled *Fingal Rónáin*. The text seems to have been derived from a late Old Irish (ninth-century) version. The hero of the saga, Labraid Longsech, was a king of Leinster assigned by the annalists to the fourth century B.C. He is the earliest figure handled in a saga of kings, and obviously legendary is the account of his exile, his attack—with the aid of the men of Munster—on Dind Rig, and his vengeance for his father (by roasting his guilty uncle Cobthach with seven hundred men and thirty kings in an iron house where they had been invited to a feast). J. Vendryes' "La destruction de Dind Rig" (*EC*, 1958) contains a careful French translation of Greene's text. This translation supersedes that of W. Stokes (*ZCP*, 1899). Vendryes adds an introduction and useful appendices on motifs of interest, grammar, and metrics. He discusses the general style of the saga with reference to the problems raised by G. Murphy regarding the relation between written and oral tradition.

Togail Bruidne Dá Derga, "The Destruction of Da Derga's Hostel," an eleventh-century compilation of much older material, tells how Conaire, king of Tara, brought about his destruction by the involuntary violation of his taboos (*gessa*). It has been edited by Eleanor Knott (*MMIS*, 1936). The best translation is still that of W. Stokes (*Revue celtique*, 1901–2), reproduced with minor changes in *AIT*. In general this effective but puzzling piece has received little attention. O'Rahilly, in *Early Irish History*, finds in the saga popular tradition regarding a prehistoric invasion of Leinster seen from the point of view of the conquered people. *Orgain Denna Rig* (see above), he holds, deals with the same event from the point of view of the conquerors. Such conjectures are of interest primarily to historians. If confirmed, they might have some bearing on the literary interpretation of the sagas.

The Finn Cycle contrasts with the Ulster Cycle in ethos and social structure. Cuchulainn is a champion of the king of Ulster; Finn, the leader of an independent war band, the *fian*. In her penetrating *Gods and Heroes of the Celts* (1949), translated from the French original (1940) by M. Dillon, Marie-Louise Sjoestedt-Jonval speaks of Cuchulainn as a "hero of the tribe"; of Finn, as a "hero outside the tribe." J. Weisweiler (*ZCP*, 1953) contrasts the cattle-herding culture of the Ulster Cycle with the deer-hunting culture of the Finn Cycle.

G. Murphy's *The Ossianic Lore and Romantic Tales of Medieval Ireland* (1955) is an excellent introduction to the Finn material. The largest earlier work of the cycle, *The Colloquy of the Ancients*, a collection of rhymed poems, is framed in a prose account of the meeting between Saint Patrick and the senile remnants of Finn's war band, Cáilte and Oisin (Macpherson's Ossian, Yeat's Usheen). The selections in *AIT* are from S. H. O'Grady's *Silva Gadelica* (2 vols., 1892). Several poems from the colloquy are included in *EIL*. A linguistic analysis of the verbal system of *The Colloquy*, by R. Nuner (*ZCP*, 1959), supports a conclusion that the prose sections are as late as 1200–1225.

Duanaire Finn, "The Poem-Book of Finn," found in a manuscript of the early seventeenth century, contains poems composed at various dates. Some seem to be as early as the twelfth century. The edition of the Irish Text Society consists of a first volume of thirty-five poems and translations by J. MacNeill (1908), a second volume of thirty-four additional poems and translations (1933) by G. Murphy, and a third volume with notes and an essay on the poems, also by G. Murphy (1953). The third volume is an outstanding contribution to literature about Finn. Murphy accepts and defends O'Rahilly's theory that Finn originated in myth and not in history. *EIL* has some poems from the *Duanaire*.

Preternatural beings, called *aes side*, "people of the mounds," are part of the world of Irish saga. Marie-Louise Sjoestedt-Jonval in her *Gods and Heroes* describes with great sensitivity their mode of being and their relation to human space and time. Some of them at least are partly euhemerized pagan gods. In some sagas the people of the *side* are the principal actors, and these sagas are grouped by modern scholars in what they call the Mythological Cycle. *Tochmarc*

Étaine, "The Wooing of Etain," is of the ninth century and one of the oldest sagas of the cycle. It was known only in fragmentary form until 1930, when a complete version was found in a collection of manuscripts acquired by the National Library of Ireland. This version was edited by O. Bergin and R. Best with a translation in *Ériu* (1938). The translation supersedes the one from Leahy's *Heroic Romances* (see above) in *AIT*.

Another new saga, *Altrom Tige Dá Medar*, "The Nurture of the Houses of the Two Milk Vessels," was edited from a sixteenth-century manuscript and translated into English by Margaret Dobbs (*ZCP*, 1930). There is another edition and translation by Lilian Duncan in *Ériu* (1932). The saga connects the people of the *síde* with the Patrick legend, and is considered in relation to modern folk tales by Máire MacNeill in *The Feast of Lughnasa* (see above).

In some sagas the people of the *síde* are called the *Tuatha Dé Danann*, "The Peoples of the Goddess Dana." Under that name they became a part of the fictional prehistory of Ireland, the *Book of the Taking* (see below). *Cath Maige Tuired*, "The Battle of Moytura," a saga telling of the victory of the *Tuatha Dé Danann* over another group of preternatural beings, the Fomorians, helped prepare the way for later pseudohistorical developments. The saga is in a sixteenth-century manuscript but contains old forms. V. Hull, "The Four Jewels of the *Tuatha Dé Danann*" (*ZCP*, 1930), points out that the saga is quoted by Cormac (d. 908) in his *Glossary*. At least some of it must have been in existence at that time. An accurate German version by G. Lehmacher (*Anthropos*, 1931) supersedes the English version of W. Stokes (*Revue celtique*, 1891), which is reproduced in *AIT*. A much later recension of the saga has been edited in normalized spelling by B. Ó Cuiv, *Cath Muighe Tuireadh* (1945). J. de Vries' comment in *Keltische Religion* (1961) is primarily of mythological interest.

The history of places and of place names, *dindsenchas*, is a special category closely related to the saga literature. The first volume of E. Gwynn's *The Metrical Dindsenchas* appeared in 1903. The work was completed with the fifth and last volume during the period under review (1935). The Irish text throughout is accompanied by translations. The last volume contains a general introduction, indices, and glossary of rarer words. Gwynn holds that a collection of poems on places, some of them as early as the ninth century, was in existence by the early twelfth century. The prose parts, consisting of résumés of poems and parts of poems, were composed perhaps in the first quarter of the twelfth century.

A second product of the Gaelic learning of the eleventh and

twelfth centuries is *Lebor Gabála Érenn*, "The Book of the Taking of Ireland." This imposing collection of mnemonic poems, with summaries and explanation in prose, recounts the invasions of Ireland from that of the antediluvian Cessair until the final "taking" by the sixth group of invaders, the sons of Míl, descendants of Goedel Glas and supposed ancestors of the ruling Gaelic-speaking warrior class. The work contains a great deal of what looks like euhemerized myth and a great deal of fiction and speculation by medieval *sapientes*. In general, modern scholars feel that it contains little or nothing of real historical value. For those interested in Irish myth and in Irish national sentiment in the Middle Ages the work is still of importance. Prior to the period under review it was accessible only in manuscripts and facsimiles and in a sixteenth-century version, ed. J. MacNeill and R. A. S. Macalister (1916). The appearance of Macalister's edition of the medieval version, *Lebor Gabála Érenn*, in five volumes (1938–56), with introduction and notes, has made the work accessible. Macalister's analysis of the elaborate manuscript material, although independent, does not differ in any important respect from the findings of A. G. Van Hamel (*ZCP*, 1914) and Thurneysen, *Zu irischen Handschriften und Literaturdenkmälern* (2 vols., 1912–13). There are three separate recensions of the prose; Macalister prints all three. Most of the poems are identical in all recensions, and only one text of each is necessary.

The details of Macalister's editorial work and translation have been subjected to minute and unfavorable scrutiny: those in his first three volumes by P. Walsh (*Irish Historical Studies*, 1940–41), those in his fourth volume by D. Binchy (*Celtica*, 1951). The larger issues raised by Macalister's edition, however, such as his analysis of the general structure of the work and his views on the wholly mythological character of the first five invasions, perhaps deserve more detailed discussion than they have yet received.

Macalister seems to be on firm ground in his insistence that the work as a whole is a conflation of two originally independent books. The first was a "Taking of Ireland," which developed the parallel between the history of the Goedels and the history of Israel, as in Section II of the present *LG* and, as in Section VIII, brought the Goedels to Ireland, the promised land. The second was apparently a kind of "Book of Origins," developed from euhemerized myths. From this book the interpolated invasions handled in Sections III–VII were derived.

The considerable activity with Irish religious literature during the generation preceding the period under review is well handled by J. F. Kenney, *The Sources for the Early History of Ireland*, Vol. I,

Ecclesiastical (1929), a book that in general exceeds the promise of its title. During the period under review the field has been regularly tended in a series of notes and articles by the eminent Bollandist, P. Grosjean, in *AnBol*. W. M. Heist's comparative study, *The Fifteen Signs before Doomsday* (1952), contains a translation of the particularly difficult poems treating of Doomsday in the late tenth-century *Saltair na Rann*, "The Psalter of Quatrains." Literature adapting the classics to medieval Irish taste has been kept in view by R. T. Meyer's edition of *Merugud Uilix Maic Leirtis*, "The Wanderings of Ulysses Son of Laertes" (*MMIS*, 1958), and his papers on the Middle Irish version of the *Pharsalia* of Lucan (*PMASAL*, 1959) and on the *Thebaid* of Statius (ibid., 1962).

It has been commonly held that Irish verse was originally rhythmic, alliterating, and unrhymed, and that syllabic verse and rhyme were introduced in imitation of Latin hymns. G. Murphy's posthumously published detailed survey, *Early Irish Metrics* (1961), followed the accepted doctrine. In his recent "Indo-European Metrics and Archaic Irish Verse" (*Celtica*, 1963), C. Watkins, pointing to the fact that some Old Irish unrhymed verse of great antiquity is syllabic, suggests that Irish verse derives from a very ancient Indo-European syllabic measure, descendants of which are discernible in Sanskrit, Greek, and Slavic. If Watkins' learnedly defended suggestion wins acceptance, one of the many interesting consequences will be that the Latin hymn will no longer have to be regarded as a decisive influence on the development of Irish versification.

In *Über die älteste irische Dichtung* (2 vols., 1913–14), K. Meyer edited with translation and commentary a body of alliterative verse that he believed to be in the main earlier than 700. Most of Meyer's poems are attributed to named poets. In some cases these poets are stated to have served fourth-century kings, and the language, although archaic, could not be really that early. False attributions accompanied by artificially archaic texts are very common in Irish, and Meyer's collection did not prevent Thurneysen, as we have seen, from insisting that there was no Irish literary tradition prior to the eighth century (see above). After Thurneysen's work with legal texts had convinced him that seventh-century Irish existed as a written language and was recognizable even in corrupted later copies, he turned to poetic texts and edited some fragments attributed to Colman mac Leneni, an abbot who died early in the seventh century (*ZCP*, 1933). He held these fragments to be authentic and further suggested that *Amra Choluimb Chille*, "The Eulogy of Columb Cille," is genuinely archaic and could have been composed and written down shortly after Columba's death (c. 597). V. Hull (*ZCP*, 1961) comments on Stokes's translation and accepts the late sixth-century date.

After the twelfth century a considerable body of elaborate rhymed poetry, mostly encomiastic or religious, begins to find its way into manuscripts. The authors, who are usually named, are called bards. Just how they differed from their predecessors, also authors of encomiastic (and satiric) poetry, who were called *fílid* (singular *fíli*), is not entirely clear. G. Murphy's "Bards and Filidh" (*Éigse*, 1940) may be consulted. A very considerable body of bardic verse has been made available during the period under review, most of it by L. MacKenna, who provides careful texts, notes, and translations in *Aithdioghluim Dána* (2 vols., 1939–40), a selection of religious and historical poems, *The Book of Magauran* (1947), and *The Book of O'Hara* (1951). The poems range in date from the thirteenth to the sixteenth century.

III. MEDIEVAL BRITTONIC LITERATURES

IN BRITTONIC there was no common literary language during the medieval period, such as the common Gaelic of Ireland and Scotland. Welsh, Cornish, and Breton were distinct although still mutually comprehensible varieties of Brittonic as early as the seventh century. Existing Brittonic medieval literature is mostly Welsh. Although it is certain that motifs and characters of the literature were shared by the Cornish and the Bretons, we cannot think of a common literary culture extending through the Middle Ages comparable to the Goedelic. We deal with Welsh first and then, briefly, with Cornish and Breton.

For the bibliography of Welsh literature students are dependent on *Biblioteca Celtica*, which covers "publications relating to Wales and the Celtic peoples and languages." R. G. Gruffydd's "Literature," a chapter in *Celtic Studies in Wales*, ed. E. Davies (1963), is an excellent ordered listing, with brief comments, of important recent publications and very important but more remote ones.

Important articles relevant to medieval literature appear in *Y*

Cymmrodor (1877–), *Transactions of the Honourable Society of Cymmrodorion* (1892–), *Bulletin of the Board of Celtic Studies* (1921–), and *Llên Cymru* (1950–). The first three named carry some articles in Welsh; the last is entirely in Welsh. In general there has been an increasing tendency during the period under review to use the Welsh language for scholarly discussion of medieval Welsh literature.

The corpus of Welsh medieval literature is not quite so great as that of Irish. But it is still formidable and, as in Irish, the earlier material is known only in a modified and garbled form in late manuscripts. Large selections from older manuscripts have long been available in *The Myvyrian Archaiology of Wales*, ed. O. Jones, E. Williams, and W. O. Pughe (3 vols., 1801–07). Later, W. F. Skene printed the oldest manuscripts containing heroic poetry in *The Four Ancient Books of Wales* (2 vols., 1868). The text is accompanied by a translation that is sometimes unintelligible and sometimes incorrect, but still useful, if only for giving a general idea of what the material is about.

Both works belong to prescientific philology and can hardly be regarded even as first steps toward what I have called preliminary philological processing. By good fortune or sound strategy, however, Welsh scholars devoted the years immediately before the period under review to subjecting their ancient literature to exactly such a preliminary processing. J. G. Evans was the most active scholar in this work. In 1887 he collaborated with J. Rhŷs on *The Text of the Mabinogion and Other Welsh Tales from the Red Book of Hergest*. In 1907 his *White Book Mabinogion* appeared. Meanwhile he began his series of accurate diplomatic editions with facsimiles of the Four Ancient Books: *The Black Book of Carmarthen* (1906), *The Book of Aneirin* (1908), *The Book of Taliesin* (1910), and *The Poetry in the Red Book of Hergest* (1911). The translations by Evans in some of these books are not highly regarded. In a series of *Reports* (1898–1910), published by the Historical Manuscripts Commission, Evans described individual Welsh manuscripts and collections. E. Owens' *Catalogue of the Manuscripts Relating to Wales in the British Museum* appeared in four parts between 1900 and 1922. Notes on manuscripts appear regularly in *NLWJ* (1939–), of which a *Handlist of Manuscripts* appears as a supplement (1943–).

Starting from a soundly laid base, Welsh scholarship advanced to a decisive breakthrough during the period under review. The breakthrough concerned the poems, often obscure and corrupt, attributed in the four ancient books to the *cynfeirdd*, the "early" or "first poets," among whom Aneirin and Taliesin are named. There is a good reason to believe that these two were historical figures who lived around the year 600. But much of what was attributed to them is marked as later by language and historical reference. Numerous false attributions cast doubt on all attributions, and during the period preceding the one under review skepticism was fashionable. Over the past thirty years Ifor Williams' rigorous philological scrutiny of these ancient texts has provided a firmer footing for the early history of Welsh literature.

He has been able to demonstrate that some of the material attributed to Aneirin and Taliesin was, probably, composed around the turn of the sixth century and may be correctly attributed in the manuscripts. He first attacked the problem of Aneirin, to whom only one poem, the *Gododdin*, is attributed. *Gododdin* is the name of a northern Brittonic people who lived in the vicinity of what is now Edinburgh. The poem tells how three hundred picked warriors of the Gododdin, sent by their king, Mynyddawg, against the Angles of Bernicia and Deira at Catraeth (Catterick in Yorkshire), fought bravely against odds and fell. Only the poet returned to sing of their heroism. In *Canu Aneirin* (1938), Ifor Williams showed that about four-fifths of the extant poem goes back to an original of the early seventh century and may well be the work of Aneirin. K. Jackson's review (*Antiquity*, 1939) and C. A. Gresham's English translation of parts of the introduction (ibid., 1942) may be consulted. A translation of a portion of the poem is to be found in Jackson's *Celtic Miscellany*.

Nevertheless, a linguistic objection to accepting so early a date for Welsh poems still remained. British, the ancestor of the Brittonic languages, was known to have retained the Indo-European endings. Some linguists held that these endings had not yet disappeared in the sixth century. The poems for which a sixth-century origin was now being claimed, however, make metrical sense in Old and Middle Welsh. They would not make metrical sense if the British forms, mostly one syllable longer, were restored. K. Jackson's *Language and History in Early Britain* (1953), a carefully dated study of the sound changes in the Brittonic languages until the twelfth century, supports the position already taken by J. Morris-Jones in "Taliesin" (*Y Cymmrodor*, 1918) that primitive Welsh already existed in the later sixth century and that the poems attributed to Taliesin and Aneirin would have been metrical at that time.

Morris-Jones' long article presented six poems attributed to Taliesin and addressed to Urien, known to have been king of the Britons of Rheged (north of the Solway Firth) in the late sixth

century. Ifor Williams, who had been engaged in studying the verse
falsely attributed to Taliesin (see below), published his version of
the Taliesin canon in *Canu Taliesin* (1960). He attributed twelve
poems to Taliesin, including five of those attributed by Morris-
Jones.

Ifor Williams' thinking on at least some of the false attributions was expressed publicly in his Rhŷs lecture "The Poems of
Llywarch Hen" (*PBA*, 1933) and was developed with texts and
detailed commentary in *Canu Llywarch Hen* (1935). There is some
evidence that Llywarch Hen was a historical figure, a ruler in the
North, like Urien, sometime in the sixth century. A considerable
body of poetry is attributed to him, much of it in triadic stanzas.
The style and manner is not sixth-century, and in any case a royal
poet is probably an anomaly in this context. Williams' conclusion
was that this highly emotional elegiac poetry was put into the mouth
of the old king as a fictional figure. Some of the stanzas are parts of
dialogue, some are monologue. They were intended for performance
in the course of a narrative by a professional storyteller, a
cyfarwydd, who connected the dramatic verses with a prose narrative, perhaps impromptu. Williams also discusses other clusters of
poems that may have been parts of sagas about ancient kings. One of
these poems, a lament by Heledd (daughter of Cyndrwyn, a ruler in
East Wales in the seventh century) for her brother, Cynddylan, is
translated from the Williams' text in *A Celtic Miscellany*. Ifor
Williams dates these poems in the ninth century.

In *Chwedl Taliesin* (1957), "The Saga of Taliesin," Williams
applies his theory of Welsh saga to a body of later poems attributed
to Taliesin. Here interpretation is aided by the fact that a late prose
tale, *Hanes Taliesin*, "The History of Taliesin," is actually found in
a sixteenth-century manuscript. Williams believes the poems in
question are of the early tenth century and that they formed part of
a saga of Taliesin, which had come into being sometime in the ninth
century. The *Hanes Taliesin* is the descendant of still a third version
(early fifteenth-century), which had been subjected to strong ecclesiastical influence. In his Dublin *Lectures on Early Welsh Poetry*
(1944), Ifor Williams expounded his views on Welsh sagas with
reference to parallel developments in Ireland.

With the aid of co-workers, Ifor Williams has secured a firmly
anchored beginning for Welsh literary history, and in his theory of
the origin of the Welsh saga he has provided a powerful incentive for
further investigation. T. A. Parry made early use of the anchored
beginning in his indispensable *Hanes Llenyddiaeth Gymraeg hyd
1900* (1944). The work has been translated by H. I. Bell, *A History*

of Welsh Literature (1955). The translation is admirably done, its value to non-Celticists being increased by Bell's talent for translating Welsh into English verse and by his thoughtful appendices where the elements of Welsh metrics are made clear. The large bibliography of the original, indispensable to the professional, is reduced to a useful selection of works in English.

The general increase of interest in early Wales arising from recent discoveries is reflected in two important collections of essays by scholars of what may perhaps be called the Nora K. Chadwick circle, *Studies in Early British History* (1954, henceforth *SEBH*) and *Studies in the Early British Church* (1958). Here, Rachel Bromwich's "The Character of Early Welsh Tradition" in *SEBH* deserves mention as a suggestive survey of the early tradition in the light of the discoveries of the period under review. It is full of hints for possible future investigations and is a valuable guide to present activities in Welsh studies. The collection of studies edited by R. S. Loomis, *Arthurian Literature in the Middle Ages* (1959, henceforth *ALMA*), is primarily concerned with external relationship and will be considered in the following section. It reflects the state of activity within Welsh studies, however, and some of the papers are so important from a purely internal Welsh point of view that they will be mentioned below.

Much that is perplexing still remains in the verse of the ancient books. Some will doubtless yield in the future to the powerful techniques that have been developed for dealing with it. R. S. Loomis has attacked a portion of one difficult piece from *The Book of Taliesin* in his " 'The Spoils of Annwn': An Early Welsh Poem," in *Wales and the Arthurian Legend* (1956; revised version of article in *PMLA*, 1941). The poem is probably of the tenth century. A careful text and a translation that notes variant possibilities is accompanied by a learned comparative commentary that uses Continental Arthurian material as well as Welsh and Irish parallels. The conclusion that the poem is a "mosaic of Welsh bardic lore" about the Celtic other world is solidly based.

A. O. H. Jarman's *Ymddiddan Myrddin a Thaliesin* (1951), "The Colloquy of Merlin and Taliesin," is a careful edition, with a long introduction and notes, of a brief poem in *The Black Book of Carmarthen*. The poem discusses a raid of Maelgwn of Gwynedd (northwest Wales) against Dyfed (south Wales) and a battle far off to the north at Arfderydd (Arthuret in Cumberland near Carlisle). On the basis of a careful study of the language, Jarman suggests 1050–1100 as its date. In "The Welsh Myrddin Poems" (*ALMA*) he translates fragments of other Myrddin poems and

discusses the pre-Geoffrian state of the Merlin story, Merlin's
identity with the madman Lailoken, known in Joceline's life of Saint
Kentigern and other northern hagiographical material, and the
evidence for Arfderydd as the battle where Merlin-Lailoken went
mad. The curious split between Welsh and northern interests in
Ymddiddan reflects an early movement of northern Brittonic material south into Wales. The Lailoken-Merlin story took the same route
as the poems of Taliesin and Aneirin.

The Welsh sagas that have come down to us intact are not, as
the early Irish sagas are and the hypothetical early Welsh sagas are
believed to be, in a mixture of prose and verse. They are prose tales.
Familiarity with the collection of these tales in *The Red Book of
Hergest* in the translation of Charlotte Guest has long been almost
requisite for English literacy. Even the mistaken title *Mabinogion*
has become part of the English language, and it would be pedantic to
alter it. A solid contribution of the period under review is *The
Mabinogion* of G. Jones and T. Jones, which in 1949 replaced the
Guest translation in the Everyman edition. As English prose the new
translation is not unworthy of its predecessor. Those who like a
plain style will prefer it. It is, of course, much more accurate, based
on a wholly new but unpublished Welsh text that gives primacy to
the version in *The White Book of Rhydderch*, a manuscript about a
hundred years earlier than *The Red Book* (c. 1400). A useful
introduction acquaints the reader with the more important results of
modern research.

The tales comprising the collection are not of the same
antiquity or literary character. The first four tales form a group
that was apparently regarded as a single tale, *The Mabinogi*
(singular), made up of four "branches." Ifor Williams' *Pedeir
Keinc y Mabinogi* (1930), "The Four Branches of the Mabinogi," is
the standard Welsh edition of the group. Ifor Williams gives
linguistic evidence for his conviction that the existing texts go back
to a written redaction made in the latter half of the eleventh century.

The literary interpretation of the four branches owes a great
deal to the work of W. J. Gruffydd, whose earliest works on the
subject, a general introduction to the work as a whole, with some
investigation of the first branch, *Pwyll Prince of Dyved* (*THSC*,
1913–14), and a detailed study of the fourth branch, *Math Vab
Mathonwy* (1928), antedate slightly the period under review. They
have been followed by *Rhiannon, An Inquiry into the Origins of the
First and Third Branches of the Mabinogi* (1953).

It was Gruffydd who proposed the generally accepted theory
that *Mabinogi*, related to Welsh *map*, "son," "boy," is the name of a

kind of story concerned with a child or a young man. The meaning was extended to include a story of the hero's life. *Keinc* is used, like its French equivalent *branche,* for a part or section of a story. The first four tales, then, are parts of a single hero's story. There must be a single hero—and he can be only Pryderi—whose conception and birth are the main theme of the first branch, who appears in the second and third branches, and who dies in the fourth branch.

In his detailed studies of the individual branches (all except the second) Gruffydd uses a comparative method, finding parallels particularly in Irish, and reduces the complex and often puzzling material to myths on the one hand and folktale motifs on the other. He then reconstructs the stages by which the story developed. Gruffydd's general views are widely accepted today and appear in Parry's *Hanes* and the introduction to the Jones *Mabinogion.* J. Loth's unfavorable article about *Math* (*Revue celtique,* 1929) is generally regarded as much too severe. Doubtless many details in Gruffydd's work are vulnerable, but what is sound in it affords a firm base for comparative study of *The Mabinogi.*

In handling the second branch of *The Mabinogi* in *Branwen, Daughter of Llŷr* (1958), P. Mac Cana collects parallels with Irish literature. He assembles a very suggestive and valuable body of material. Like Carney, Mac Cana tends to assume that parallels are to be accounted for by literary borrowing rather than by a common debt to a flexible and developing oral tradition.

Of the four native independent tales, *Culhwch and Olwen* is the oldest. It may have existed in some written form before *The Mabinogi.* The existing text, however, is believed to be descended from a recension of around 1100. The basic fable is the Giant's Daughter. In meeting his tests to win Olwen, Culhwch seeks and gets the assistance of Arthur and his heroes. Here we have a pre-Geoffrian Arthur and his court. Arthur is not a monarch of the high Middle Ages but a leader of warriors and hunters in the manner of Finn Mac Cumail. This is the traditional Arthur of the Welsh storytellers. The tale has Irish affinities that have not yet received detailed study. The humor is broad and the tone much more boisterous than that of *The Mabinogi.* E. L. Foster's paper on *Culhwch* in *ALMA* is the most recent and fullest treatment.

A second native tale with Arthurian material, *The Dream of Rhonabwy,* has been separately edited with introduction, glossary, and notes by M. Richards in *Breudwyt Ronabwy* (1948). *Breudwyt* is the only Welsh tale to use the common medieval device of a dream as the framework of a story. Its style is elaborate and very different from that of the other native tales. The work apparently owes little,

at least stylistically, to oral tradition. Richards dates it around
1220. Despite the late date, the Arthurian elements are independent
of Geoffrey. They are discussed by Foster in *ALMA*.

The last group of tales in *The Mabinogion*, called in the Jones
translation "The Three Romances," is *The Lady of the Fountain*,
known to modern scholars as *Owein, Peredur*, and *Gereint*. These
three tales are composed in an ornate prose similar to that of
Rhonabwy. Like *Rhonabwy*, they represent a written tradition. All
three tales are late, dating from around 1200. A common characteristic, not shared by *Rhonabwy*, is that they are all closely related
to French Arthurian poems of Chrétien de Troyes. *Gereint* corresponds to *Erec, Owein* to *Yvain*, and *Peredur* to *Percival*. Some
earlier scholars assumed that the Welsh tales derive, as translations
or adaptations, from Chrétien. The most thorough study of the
problem is that of R. S. Loomis in *Arthurian Tradition and Chrétien
de Troyes* (1949). Loomis comes to the conclusion that none of the
Welsh authors knew Chrétien. *Gereint* and *Owein* are Welsh adaptations of French romances, perhaps Breton in origin, which Chrétien
also used. The case with *Peredur* is more complicated. The author
seems not to be following a single source but drawing on a reservoir
of material known also to Chrétien's source. Foster treats the tales
in *ALMA* with particular attention to the Welsh and Cornish
material in them. In a later article, "Le cortège du Château des
Merveilles dans le roman gallois de *Peredur*" (*EC*, 1960), J. Marx
holds that the existing *Peredur* may have been influenced by the
French *conte* that was Chrétien's acknowledged source. He believes,
however, that there was an earlier Welsh version without French
influence and that the procession in which a bleeding head is carried
on the Grail belongs to this earlier version.

The tales in *The Mabinogion* range from the mid-eleventh to
beyond the beginning of the thirteenth century. The early tales
reflect the plain prose style of the professional storyteller; the later
ones are more literary. The art of the professional storyteller was
apparently declining as Wales moved into the later Middle Ages.
Somewhat as in Ireland, there was a tendency to incorporate the
material of the sagas in mnemonic literature. In Wales the favorite
form was the triad. Rachel Bromwich has edited and translated this
important body of literature, with an English introduction and
commentary, in *Trioedd Ynys Prydein* (1961). Mrs. Bromwich had
previously discussed the Arthurian material in the triads in *ALMA*.

The *Historia Brittonum* attributed to Nennius makes it clear
that early Irish efforts in pseudo history were known in Wales and
that Welsh learned circles were making a modest start of their own

in the genre. Whether Wales could have rivaled Ireland in mendacity
can never be known, however, since mendacity in Welsh history was
pre-empted by Geoffrey of Monmouth's *Historia Regum Britanniae.*
Here was a glorious enough past, and pseudo history in Wales
became a matter of translation and adaptation from Geoffrey. One
version of the Welsh *History of the Kings* was edited by H. Lewis,
with extensive grammatical notes, in *Brut Dingestow* (1942). John
J. Parry's *Brut y Brenhinedd* (1937), another and later version, has
an English translation and introduction. An English translation by
R. E. Jones of the somewhat shorter *Brut Tysilio* is printed along
with the Latin text of Geoffrey in A. Griscom's *The Historia Regum
Britanniae of Geoffrey* (1929). Both Lewis and Parry reject
Griscom's suggestion that the *Brut Tysilio* (or any other chronicle)
gives independent testimony to a Welsh tradition incorporated in a
"very old book in the British language," which Geoffrey said he was
translating. In a review of Parry's book, R. Thurneysen (*HZ*, 1938)
expresses forcefully his conviction that Geoffrey's *Historia* is
schwindelhaft and that the Welsh versions have no other source than
Geoffrey's Latin text.

A considerable body of courtly and schooled verse, mainly
encomiastic and elegiac, composed between the early twelfth and late
thirteenth centuries is the work of a group of poets traditionally
called *gogynfeirdd*, "nearly early poets" (cf. *cynfeirdd*, above) ; in
English they are called "the poets of the princes." In its difficulty
and its appeal to what must have been a schooled audience, this
poetry has obvious affinities both with Irish bardic poetry and with
the work of the Icelandic skalds. Such comparative questions have
been treated by J. Vendryes in *Poésie galloise des XIIe et XIIIe
siècles dans ses rapports avec la langue* (1930) and in his twenty-
four-page lecture in *La poésie de cour en Irlande et en Galle* (1932).
T. H. Parry-Williams includes a discussion of the *gogynfeirdd* in his
"Welsh Poetic Diction" (*PBA*, 1946). J. Lloyd-Jones in his Rhŷs
lecture, "The Court Poets of the Welsh Princes" (*PBA*, 1948),
discusses the poems with the expertise of a lexicographer. The
publication by J. Morris-Jones and T. H. Parry-Williams of the
fifteenth-century *Llawysgrif Hendregadredd* (1933) made available
one of the two most important collections of the *gogynfeirdd*. The
other collection is in *The Red Book of Hergest*. In general this body
of poetry has received relatively little editorial attention during the
period under review. A notable exception is J. Vendryes, who in
Revue celtique and *EC* (1930–48) published a series of critically
edited texts with notes and careful French translations.

English translations of three poems of the *gogynfeirdd* begin the section on bardic poetry in *A Celtic Miscellany*. The first of these poems is a lament, apocalyptic in tone, on the death of Llewelyn ap Gruffudd, the last of the Welsh princes, whose defeat in 1282 brought Welsh independence to an end. The defeat meant the end of the sovereignty of the Welsh princes. They were reduced to the state of an impoverished nobility, and the bards became *beirdd yr uchelwyr*, "the bards of the nobility." Wandering from one great house to another, they kept Welsh poetry alive until the end of the medieval period.

The fourteenth century, however, is dominated by the figure of Dafydd ap Gwilym, who is, in the opinion of many, the greatest Welsh poet. A member of the nobility, he did not lead the life of a typical bard but was nonetheless deeply versed in the technique of Welsh poetry. His technical innovations profoundly influenced the practices of professional bards. T. Parry's definitive edition, *Gwaith Dafydd ap Gwilym* (1952), is one of the great Welsh philological works of the period under review. It established Dafydd's canon, rejecting 177 of 329 attributions. This restriction of the canon means that all previous work on Dafydd requires some correction, as, for example, T. M. Chotzen's valuable *Recherches sur la poésie de Dafydd ap Gwilym* (1927). The value of the English translations of H. I. Bell and D. Bell in *Dafydd ap Gwilym* (1942) remains equally great, however, whether one is dealing with canonical poems or with apocrypha. (Seventeen of the fifty poems are noncanonical.)

Of the several editions of *beirdd yr uchelwyr* that have appeared during the period under review the most interesting to the reader without Welsh is E. Bachellery's admirable *L'oeuvre poétique de Gutun Owain* (3 vols., 1950–51). The work contains a critical text, notes, and a careful French translation. Gutun Owain is regarded as one of the greatest bards of the nobility. He lived in the latter half of the fifteenth century. The end of the Middle Ages for Welsh poetry comes with the relaxing of bardic restrictions and the introduction of a new metrical freedom.

The extant imaginative literature from the Middle Ages is small in Cornish and in Breton almost nonexistent. Brief selections from late medieval and early modern miracle plays in Cornish will be found in Jackson's *Celtic Anthology*. In Ireland, a Breton counterpart of *MMIS* has begun with R. Hemon's *Trois poèmes en Moyen-Breton* (1962). Hemon's *La langue bretonne et ses combats* (1947) has a bibliography that covers literary studies.

IV. EXTERNAL RELATION OF MEDIEVAL
CELTIC LITERATURE

THERE ARE two areas of external relationship where significant work has been carried on during the period under review. The first area is that of the literary relations between early medieval Celtic and the literature of late imperial Rome, particularly that of Gaul. Older studies are covered in J. F. Kenney's *Sources*. To these Mrs. Chadwick has added in her paper in *SEBH* a notable survey of late Gaulish Latin literature, with particular reference to possible echoes in insular Celtic.

In *The International Popular Tale and Early Welsh Tradition* (1961), K. H. Jackson applies folkloristic methods to *The Mabinogion* and other Welsh tales and makes some clarifications. His suggestion that some plots and motifs in Irish may derive from popular tales imported into Britain during the imperial periods and his protest against considering all Welsh-Irish parallels a result of Irish influence on Welsh are both worthy of careful consideration.

The second area is that of Celtic influence on medieval Arthurian material. Here, a steady accumulation of significant parallels has been going on throughout the period under review. A brief and judicious survey of this activity is contained in the chapter on French medieval literature. The publication of the group of papers assembled by R. S. Loomis in *ALMA* signals what one may call a second breakthrough in Celtic studies during the period under review. After the appearance of *ALMA* it would be difficult to maintain at once a respect for philological evidence and the so-called anti-Celtic view associated with the names of admittedly great Arthurians, such as J. D. Bruce, E. Faral, and J. S. P. Tatlock—the view that assigns a decisive role in the origin and early development of the Arthurian saga to Geoffrey of Monmouth. Besides the papers already mentioned, Helaine Newstead's on the origin of the Tristan legend and K. H. Jackson's on the Arthur of history and on Arthur in early Welsh verse are of particular interest. R. S. Loomis' paper, "The Origin of the Grail legends," may now be supplemented by his *The Grail, from Celtic Myth to Christian Symbol* (1963), where justice is done to the influence of Christianity on the development of the material, but forced readings of a hidden Christianity in texts not patently religious are avoided. In addition, the book displays again Loomis' power of making Arthurian and Celtic materials mutually illuminating.

INDEX OF PROPER NAMES

(Medieval authors are in most instances entered under the first name.)

411